Irish Business and Society

Governing, Participating and Transforming in the 21st Century

Irish Business and Society

Society

Governing, Participating and Transforming in the 21st Century

Edited by

JOHN HOGAN, PAUL F. DONNELLY AND
BRENDAN K. O'ROURKE

GILL & MACMILLAN

Gill & Macmillan
Hume Avenue
Park West
Dublin 12
with associated companies throughout the world
www.gillmacmillan.ie

978 07171 4990 2

Index compiled by Grainne Farren
Print origination in Ireland by Carole Lynch
Printed by GraphyCems, Spain

The paper used in this book is made from the wood pulp of managed forests. For every tree felled, at least one is planted, thereby renewing natural resources.

A CIP catalogue record is available for this book from the British Library.

Contents

List of Tables

List of Figures

Contributors

Frank Barry, PhD, is Professor of International Business and Economic Development at Trinity College Dublin. He holds a PhD in Economics from Queen's University, Ontario, and has previously held positions at the universities of California, Stockholm and New South Wales, and with Harvard Institute for International Development. He is a specialist in international trade, foreign direct investment and economic development, and is a resource person with the African Economic Research Consortium. Among his publications are an edited volume on *Understanding Ireland's Economic Growth* (Macmillan Press, 1999) and a co-authored book on *Multinational Firms in the World Economy* (Princeton University Press, 2004).

Niamh M. Brennan, PhD, is both a chartered accountant and a chartered director. She holds the Michael MacCormac Professorship of Management and is Academic Director of the Centre for Corporate Governance at University College Dublin. She is Chairman of the Dublin Docklands Development Authority, and is a non-executive director of the Health Services Executive. Previously, she held non-executive positions with Ulster Bank; Lifetime Assurance, Bank of Ireland's life assurance subsidiary; Coillte, the State forestry company; and Co-Operation Ireland, a voluntary body promoting north–south relations in Ireland. She served for seven years on the audit committee of the Department of Agriculture and Food. She chaired the government-appointed Commission on Financial Management and Control Systems in the Health Services, and was vice-chairman of the government-appointed Review Group on Auditing. She has published widely in the areas of financial reporting, corporate governance and forensic accounting.

Robert Briscoe recently retired as Programme Director of the Centre for Co-operative Studies at University College Cork and as Senior Lecturer in the Department of Food Business and Development. He previously worked at the Sydney campus of St Francis Xavier University, Canada, where he was Professor of Organisational Behaviour, and at the University of the South Pacific, where he was Professor and Head of the Department of Management and Administration, and Head of the School of Social and Economic Development. More recently, he worked in eight countries as a Small Business and Co-operatives Specialist with the International Labour Organisation. His teaching and research interests are in the management and development of co-operatives and he has published widely in the field, having successfully completed a wide range of national and international research assignments in co-operatives.

Helen Chen, PhD, has lectured in the University of Warwick (UK), City University of Hong Kong, University of Kent (UK) and Carleton University (Canada). She is currently lecturing in Dublin Institute of Technology. She lectures on international marketing, international business, and data collection and analysis. Her research interests include consumer behaviour, international marketing and foreign market entry modes. She has published in the *Journal of Marketing Science*, the *Journal of Organizational Computing and Electronic Commerce* and the *Journal of State Asset Management* and has had a number of book chapters published.

Marian Crowley-Henry, PhD, is an international business specialist who has taught in University College Cork, Ceram Graduate School of Management (Sophia Antipolis, France), and Dublin Institute of Technology. She is currently a lecturer in international business and organisational behaviour at the National University of Ireland, Maynooth. Marian has published in some of the top journals in the world, including the *Journal of Organizational Change Management* (2007) and *International Studies of Management and Organization* (2007), and has presented her research work at international conferences, including the International Labour Process conference, Workshop on Expatriation, the International Conference on Labour Flexibility, and the Academy of Management. Her research interests include international HRM, migration, career theory, identity and critical management.

John Cullen, PhD, lectures in leadership and organisational behaviour at the School of Business and Law, NUI Maynooth. He researches on leadership and management development and is particularly interested in how changing understandings of selfhood impact managers, employees and workplaces. Among his 100 publications are articles in peer-reviewed journals such as *Human Relations*, *Human Resource Development Review*, *Journal of Management Development* and the *Journal of Management, Spirituality and Religion*. His most recent book is *Communication and Knowledge Sharing at Work: An Introduction* (Blackhall, 2008). He has written on management and business-related topics for the *Irish Times*, *Irish Independent*, *Sunday Business Post* and *Irish Examiner*, and his research has been discussed in *MIT Sloan Management Review*. He won the LIRG/Elsevier Award in 2001 for his research on recruitment markets for information workers.

Jennifer K. DeWan received her PhD in anthropology from Columbia University, New York in May 2008. Her doctoral thesis, on which her chapter in this collection is based, was an ethnographic and historical examination of social change in Ireland through the lens of feminist political activism. She is in the process of editing her dissertation for publication. Research areas of interest include: civil society and the state; citizenship, politics and governance; human rights and health issues; and critical social theories and research methods. She has lectured in women's studies at University College Cork and Columbia University. Jennifer has been using her academic experience in an applied context, helping to set up a reproductive and sexual health advocacy organisation in Cork.

Paul F. Donnelly, PhD (UMass). Paul's research interests cover organisation studies (particularly from a processual perspective through such lenses as actor-network theory and path dependence theory), international business, globalisation and management education, and he has an affinity with a critical management studies perspective. At the University of Massachusetts at Amherst he taught in the areas of global business, behaviour in the global economy, organisational behaviour, management and human resources management. Now at the Dublin Institute of Technology, he teaches strategy at the undergraduate level, and business ethics, negotiation, organisation behaviour and theory, and global marketplace at the postgraduate level. He co-edited (with John Hogan and Paddy Dolan) the volume *Approaches to Qualitative Research* (Oak Tree Press, 2009). A Fulbrighter, he is Vice President (2009–2011) and President-elect (2011–2013) of the Irish Fulbright Alumni Association. Prior to academia, he worked in various middle management roles with Telecom Éireann (now Eircom).

Mary Faulkner, BA, HDipEd, DipLS, DipArbLaw, Barrister-at-Law is Dean of the School of Law at the Honorable Society of King's Inns, Dublin. She has taught law modules at both undergraduate and postgraduate levels in the area of torts, with particular reference to employer liability and health and safety law. She co-authored *Your Guide to Irish Law* and recently had *The Essentials of Irish Labour Law* published by Gill and Macmillan. Her research interests focus on the Irish industrial relations regulatory environment and health and safety law.

Gerard Hastings, PhD, OBE, is the first UK Professor of Social Marketing and the founder and Director of the Institute for Social Marketing and the Cancer Research UK Centre for Tobacco Control Research, based at the University of Stirling and the Open University. He researches the applicability of marketing principles, such as consumer orientation, relationship building and strategic planning, to the solution of health and social problems. He also conducts critical marketing research into the impact of marketing activities on public health. He is a member of the European Alcohol and Health Forum, and a Specialist Advisor to the UK Parliament Health Select Committee during its inquiry into alcohol. He is also a member of the Alcohol Focus Scotland Executive Committee. He is the author of numerous peer-reviewed academic papers and books. Gerard Hastings was awarded an OBE in the Queen's Birthday Honours List in 2009 for services to healthcare.

John Hogan, PhD, is a lecturer in Irish politics and international political economy at Dublin Institute of Technology. His research interests focus on developing frameworks for identifying and understanding policy change, and studying the global regulation of the lobbying industry. He has published in a wide range of journals including *Acta Politica*, *Canadian Journal of Political Science*, *The Political Quarterly*, *Irish Political Studies*, and the *Asian Journal of Latin American Studies*. He has had chapters published in various edited volumes and has presented his research at numerous conferences, including the American Political Science

Association's annual conference and the Political Studies Association's annual conference in the UK. He has also been awarded two Irish Research Council for the Humanities and Social Sciences (IRCHSS) postgraduate research scholarships, as well as an IRCHSS Strand One professional scholarship.

Patrick Kenny, MBS, is a lecturer in the School of Marketing of Dublin Institute of Technology, where he teaches undergraduate and postgraduate courses in management and marketing strategy. He is also a doctoral student at the Institute for Social Marketing in the University of Stirling in Scotland, where his research involves investigating the relationship between marketing and normative perceptions about alcohol use among university students. He is a regular media commentator on issues of alcohol marketing and ethics and has acted as an expert court witness on issues surrounding advertising regulation.

William Kingston, PhD, is a former associate professor, and continues to teach and research innovation in the School of Business, Trinity College Dublin. He has been widely published in various Irish and international journals. His books include: *The Political Economy of Innovation*; *Direct Protection of Innovation*; *Innovation, Creativity and Law*; *Interrogating Irish Policies*; and *Beyond Intellectual Property: Matching Information Protection to Innovation*.

Margaret-Anne Lawlor, PhD, is a lecturer in marketing communications at the College of Business, Dublin Institute of Technology. Her research interests include children's interaction with advertising and young people's consumption of new and emerging media. She has previously published in the *European Journal of Marketing*, *Irish Marketing Review* and the *Services Industries Journal*, and in a number of issues of the *Journal of Marketing Management*. Margaret-Anne has presented papers at a number of national and international academic conferences, such as the American Marketing Association Conference, and has also addressed a number of practitioner conferences in Ireland, including the National Marketing Conference. She has published over forty articles in Irish practitioner publications, such as *Marketing*, *Irish Marketing Journal* and *Shelflife*.

Karlin Lillington, PhD, is a journalist and columnist with the *Irish Times*, primarily covering technology. She has always been especially interested in technology and its intersection with culture, society and politics. She has also written for a wide range of other publications, including the *Guardian*, *Wired News*, *The Scientist* and *New Scientist*, and appears regularly on national radio to discuss technology issues. She has written on Donegal-born computer programmer Kate McNulty Mauchly in *Lab Coats and Lace* (Women in Technology and Science, 2009), a book on Irish women scientists and technologists. She is also on the board of Irish national broadcaster RTÉ. She holds a PhD in Anglo-Irish Literature from Trinity College Dublin.

Roderick Maguire (LLB, LLM (Lond.), MA (Lond.), BL) is a practising barrister and lecturer at Dublin Institute of Technology. His master's studies included crime control and public policy, and he has published on the topic in the *Commercial*

Law Practitioner, the *Irish Times* and the *Family Law Journal*. He is the editor of the bi-monthly Commercial Law Update in the *Commercial Law Practitioner*. He is a vice-chairman of the Employment Appeals Tribunal, a member of the Dispute Resolution Chamber panel of the Football Association of Ireland, and a director of Just Sport Ireland, an independent specialised dispute resolution service established by the Sports Federation of Ireland. He is a member of the Sales Law Review Group established by the Minister for Enterprise, Trade and Employment in 2008.

Rebecca Maughan is a lecturer in the College of Business at Dublin Institute of Technology. Her research interests are interdisciplinary and qualitative in nature, and include: corporate social responsibility (CSR) and family firms; internal organisational influences on CSR; corporate governance; qualitative research methods; and innovative approaches to accounting education. She holds an MAcc, is a member of the Institute of Chartered Accountants in Ireland and is currently pursuing a PhD at the University of Amsterdam. Ongoing research projects include a case study of the CSR process at a large private Irish company and a study of the role of non-executive directors in the governance of semi-state bodies.

Breda McCarthy, PhD, is a lecturer in marketing at the School of Business, James Cook University, Australia. She has worked in National University of Ireland Galway, Waterford Institute of Technology and University College Cork. Her research interests focus on cultural tourism, social networks, innovation and the strategy formation process in SMEs. She is particularly interested in conducting case-based research on small to medium-sized organisations, where the focus is on the nature of innovative practices across diverse industries. She has published in various edited volumes and in journals such as the *International Journal of Entrepreneurship and Innovation*, *International Journal of Tourism Policy*, *Irish Journal of Management*, *Social Enterprise Journal*, *Irish Marketing Review* and *Management Decision*. She has presented her research at various conferences, including the Advances in Tourism Marketing Conference (AIMC), the International Conference on Arts and Cultural Management (AIMAC), the Irish Academy of Management (IAM), British Academy of Management (BAM) and European Academy of Management (EURAM) conferences. Breda has been the recipient of an Irish Research Council for the Humanities and Social Sciences (IRCHSS) award, as well as a Fáilte Ireland Research Fellowship in 2006/2007.

Olive McCarthy, PhD, is a lecturer with the Department of Food Business and Development and a researcher with the Centre for Co-operative Studies, University College Cork. Research interests include organisation and management issues, stakeholder participation in co-operatives, and performance measurement. Her research has mainly been conducted on credit unions, community co-operatives and agricultural co-operatives, on which she has published widely. She is involved at local and national level in the credit union movement and currently serves on the Credit Union Advisory Committee, which advises the Minister for

Finance on credit union issues. She is the academic director of the Diploma in Credit Union Studies and the MBS in Co-operative and Social Enterprise in UCC.

Conor McGrath, PhD, is an independent scholar, and deputy editor of the *Journal of Public Affairs*. He was a lecturer in political lobbying and public affairs at the University of Ulster in Northern Ireland from 1999 to 2006. His books include *Lobbying in Washington, London and Brussels: The Persuasive Communication of Political Issues* (2005), *Challenge and Response: Essays on Public Affairs and Transparency* (2006, co-edited with Tom Spencer), *Irish Political Studies Reader: Key Contributions* (2008, co-edited with Eoin O'Malley), and *The Future of Public Trust: Public Affairs in a Time of Crisis* (2008, co-edited with Tom Spencer). He has edited a collection of three books published by Edwin Mellen Press in 2009: *Interest Groups and Lobbying in the United States and Comparative Perspectives*; *Interest Groups and Lobbying in Europe*; and *Interest Groups and Lobbying in Latin America, Africa, the Middle East, and Asia*.

John McHale, PhD, is Established Professor and Head of Economics at the J. E. Cairnes School of Business and Economics, National University of Ireland, Galway. He previously held positions as Associate Professor of Economics at Queen's University, Canada, and as Assistant and Associate Professor of Economics at Harvard University. He received his PhD in economics from Harvard in 1996. He has been a consultant to the World Bank on various migration and development projects and has published widely on topics related to international migration.

Gary Murphy, PhD, is Associate Professor of Government in the School of Law and Government at Dublin City University, where he is also the University's Dean of Graduate Studies. He has published widely on Irish politics, notably in the area of interest group behaviour, and is currently interested in the regulation of lobbying. He recently published with Raj Chari and John Hogan the first book-length study of the topic *Regulating Lobbying: A Global Comparison* (Manchester University Press, 2010). His major reinterpretation of post-war Ireland, *In Search of the Promised Land: The Politics of Post-War Ireland*, was published by Mercier Press in 2009. He is the current President of the Political Studies Association of Ireland.

Mary C. Murphy, PhD, is a lecturer in politics with the Department of Government, University College Cork. A graduate of Queen's University Belfast, she has a specific interest in Northern Ireland and the European Union and has published in this area. She was guest editor of a special issue of *Irish Political Studies* in 2009 on 'The Europeanization of Party Politics in Ireland, North and South' and her forthcoming book on Northern Ireland and the European Union is due to be published by Manchester University Press in 2010. She is also Co-Convenor of the European Studies Specialist Group of the Political Studies Association of Ireland (PSAI).

Mary P. Murphy, PhD, is a lecturer in Irish politics and society in the Department of Sociology, NUI, Maynooth. Primarily working in the field of political sociology, her research interests include globalisation and welfare states, the politics of redistribution, power and civil society, and gender. Her journal publications include *Administration* and *Community Development Journal*. In 2009, she published chapters in Ó Broin and Kirby (eds) *Power, Democracy and Dissent*; Barry (ed.) *Where Are We Now: New Feminist Perspectives on Women in Contemporary Ireland*; Cronin *et al.* (eds) *Transforming Ireland: Challenges, Resources, Opportunities;* and Adshead *et al.* (eds) *Contesting the State.* She also published Studies in Social Policy No. 23: *Reframing the Irish Activation Debate: Accommodating Care and Safeguarding Social Rights,* the Policy Institute, Trinity College Dublin. Prior to academic life, Mary worked full-time in social justice campaigning groups and represented anti-poverty interests in national policy institutions, including the National Economic and Social Council (NESC), the National Economic and Social Forum (NESF) and national policy processes. She continues to be an active advocate for social justice and equality.

Kate Nicholls, PhD, is a graduate of the University of Auckland (New Zealand) and the University of Notre Dame (Indiana). She is currently an Assistant Professor in the Department of Political Science at the National University of Singapore, where she teaches comparative and European politics. She has research interests in both comparative political economy and transitions to democracy, and enjoys engaging in cross-regional, qualitative research projects that combine these themes, with specific interests in Ireland, Southern Europe, Australasia and South America. She has previously published in *West European Politics*, *Government and Opposition*, and *Commonwealth and Comparative Politics*, and is the co-author of *Labour Politics in Small Open Democracies* (with Paul Buchanan, 2003).

Jesse Norris completed a PhD in sociology at the University of Wisconsin-Madison in 2007. His dissertation, based on a comparative study of governance mechanisms in Ireland and Portugal, is entitled 'Searching for Synergy: Governance, Welfare and Law in Two EU Member States'. He has presented papers at the American Sociological Association annual meetings and at other conferences. In addition to his focus on experimental governance, his research has analysed the global justice ('anti-globalisation') movement and the post-conviction modification of prison sentences. He next plans to undertake research on attempts to reduce the working hours of junior doctors (medical residents) in the United States and the European Union. He is currently pursuing a Juris Doctor degree at the University of Wisconsin Law School.

John O'Brennan, PhD, is a lecturer in European politics and society in the Department of Sociology at NUI Maynooth. He previously lectured at the University of Limerick and Varna Economics University, Bulgaria. His books include *The Eastern Enlargement of the European Union* (Routledge, 2006), *National Parliaments within the Enlarged European Union: From 'Victims' of Integration to Competitive Actors?* (co-edited with Tapio Raunio, Routledge, 2007) and *The EU and the Western Balkans: Stabilisation and Europeanisation through Enlargement?*

(Routledge, 2010). He has also written extensively about Ireland's relationship with the EU and his work has appeared in journals such as the *Journal of Balkan and Near East Studies*, *Cambridge Journal of International Affairs*, *European Political Science*, *Global Society*, *Journal of European Integration*, and *Parliamentary Affairs*. He has also published numerous articles in international newspapers such as *Die Welt*, *El País*, the *Guardian*, the *Irish Times*, the *International Herald Tribune*, and the *Japan Times*.

Kevin O'Leary, MPhil, is a lecturer in human resource management at Dublin Institute of Technology, where he teaches on a number of undergraduate, postgraduate and continuing personal development programmes. Kevin previously worked in a number of large Irish and multinational manufacturing organisations, where he held a range of HR positions. In his MPhil research he explored the various influences that inform the choice of private sector organisations to enter into local partnership arrangements with their trade unions.

Brendan K. O'Rourke, PhD, works at the Dublin Institute of Technology, where he focuses on learning in the area of discourses of the economy. His academic publications include articles on interview methodology, owner-managed firms and the nature of economics expertise. Brendan has supervised a range of research in issues such as volunteering organisations, industrial buying and creativity. Currently, he is particularly interested in discourses of strategy and enterprise. Brendan is also the co-founder of the Discourse Analysis Group (DAG) at DIT. DAG is a specialist group of academics who have published extensively in the area of discourse analysis.

Connie Harris Ostwald, PhD, is the primary economist in the graduate International Economic Development programme at Eastern University, St Davids, Pennsylvania. She teaches international economics, economic development and social entrepreneurship in Eastern's programme for development professionals around the world. She has taught in China, South Africa, Kenya, Romania, Italy, Thailand and Mexico. Her research interests focus on the social justice aspects of economic growth and development. She has published her work on justice and poverty in various journals, and has presented workshops on social entrepreneurship as a means of economic development at various conferences. She also consults with organisations in the private sector, as well as non-profit NGOs.

Patrick Phillips, BA, MSc., earned a degree in marketing from Dublin Business School, as well as a master's in Strategic Management from the Dublin Institute of Technology. He is currently studying for an MBS in human resource management at Dublin City University, and previously spent eighteen months working in recruitment and selection for Harvey Nash plc. He is also a member of the Chartered Institute of Personnel and Development, Ireland. His research interests include organisational learning and employee motivation.

Gillian Smith received a BA from Trinity College Dublin and an MA from Dublin Institute of Technology. Her MA thesis, entitled 'Corruption: A View from the

Oireachtas', examined the attitudes of Oireachtas members to corrupt scenarios. The research was based on surveys, interviews and observation undertaken during 2007/2008, when she worked in the Seanad. Other research interests include public sector accountability structures, interest groups and lobbying.

Nicola Timoney, PhD, is an economist lecturing at Dublin Institute of Technology. She originally qualified with a BA in political economy and national economics and an MA from University College Dublin. With the assistance of a French Government scholarship, she studied for a Diplôme des Études Approfondies at Université de Rennes, and then a Doctorat en Économie Publique at Université de Droit, d'Économie, de Sciences Sociales de Paris. She lectures on a variety of topics in economics, including introductory economics, economics of health care, international trade, labour economics and international business. She has presented seminars to trade union groups, student societies, and to returned development workers. She participated (in 2000) in an EU-funded specialist programme of training for civil servants in Laos in preparation for membership of the Association of Southeast Asian Nations. Her recent focus of study is the labour market in Ireland, and the topic of migration.

Michael Ward, PhD, is Head of the Department of Food Business and Development at University College Cork and Director of the UCC Centre for Co-operative Studies. Michael grew up on a dairy farm in Monaghan, and has researched, taught and published extensively in the fields of co-operative organisation and management. He has been the recipient of public funding, e.g. from the Royal Irish Academy, Stimulus and the EU Septimus programme, as well as numerous relevant consulting assignments, e.g. Waterford and Glanbia Co-ops and Údarás na Gaeltachta. Special care has been taken to disseminate the findings of his research. He has also been active in developing successful new postgraduate and distance education programmes in the fields of co-operative organisation, food marketing and rural development, courses that have benefited from the findings of his research and that of his colleagues in the Centre for Co-operative Studies.

Geoffrey Weller, PhD, is a postdoctoral researcher interested in how individuals engage as volunteers in civil society. His most recent work focuses on how young adults construct themselves as volunteers through discursive identity work and the use of social capital. He received his PhD from the College of Business of the Dublin Institute of Technology in 2009. Before entering academia, he worked in public relations for Leonard Cheshire Disability and the Work Foundation and was a journalist with the BBC.

Acknowledgements

First of all, we would like to thank Marion O'Brien of Gill and Macmillan. We are particularly indebted to Marion for her support of, and belief in, this project. All at Gill and Macmillan were a delight to work with, and we are grateful for the team's efficiency throughout this process.

We acknowledge the support of the College of Business, Dublin Institute of Technology, and thank Paul O'Sullivan, Dean and College Director, Kate Uí Ghallachóir, Head of the School of Marketing, and all of our DIT colleagues for their support and encouragement.

We are enormously grateful to all the contributors whose work constitutes this volume and who variously hail from the Dublin Institute of Technology, Trinity College Dublin, University College Dublin, University College Cork, NUI Maynooth, NUI Galway, Dublin City University, University of Stirling (UK), Columbia University (US), Eastern University (US), University of Wisconsin (US), National University of Singapore, James Cook University (Australia), and the *Irish Times*.

As always, we thank all of our families and friends for their unwavering support.

The editors,
Dublin,
June 2010.

Abbreviations

ACCA	Association of Chartered Certified Accountants
ALMP	active labour market programmes
CDB	County/City Development Boards
CEO	chief executive officer
CIF	Construction Industry Federation
CII	Confederation of Irish Industry
CIU	Congress of Irish Unions
CPI	Corruption Perceptions Index
CPRS	Central Policy Review Staff
CSO	Central Statistics Office
CSR	corporate social responsibility
CVP	Community and Voluntary Pillar
DETE	Department of Enterprise, Trade and Employment
DIC	Department of Industry and Commerce
DSFA	Department of Social and Family Affairs
DSW	Department of Social Welfare
DoE	Department of Education
DoF	Department of Finance
DoT	Department of the Taoiseach
EC	European Commission
ECB	European Central Bank
ECOFIN	Economic and Financial Affairs Council
ECSC	European Coal and Steel Community
EEC	European Economic Community
EFTA	European Free Trade Area
ELC	Employer-Labour Conference
EMAS	European Eco-management and Auditing Standard
EMS	European Monetary System
EPTR	Export Profits Tax Relief
ESRI	Economic and Social Research Institute
EU	European Union
FDI	foreign direct investment
FIE	Federation of Irish Employers
FUE	Federated Union of Employers
GATT	General Agreement on Tariffs and Trade

GDP	gross domestic product
GNP	gross national product
GI	Globalisation Index
GRECO	Group of States against Corruption
IBEC	Irish Business and Employers' Confederation
ICTU	Irish Congress of Trade Unions
IDA	Industrial Development Authority
IEB	Irish Export Board
IFA	Irish Farmers' Association
IFSC	Irish Financial Services Centre
ILO	International Labour Organisation
IMF	International Monetary Fund
IP	intellectual property
IPA	Institute of Public Administration
ISPA	Irish Social Policy Association
ISSA	International Social Security Association
ITUC	Irish Trades Union Congress
JLCs	Joint Labour Committees
MEP	Member of the European Parliament
NAMA	National Asset Management Agency
NAPS	National Anti-Poverty Strategy
NEAP	National Employment Action Plan
NESC	National Economic and Social Council
NESDO	National Economic and Social Development Office
NESF	National Economic and Social Forum
NGO	non-governmental organisation
NIEC	National Industrial Economic Council
NPB	National Pensions Board
NU	National Understanding
NWA	National Wage Agreement
ODCE	Office of the Director of Corporate Enforcement
OECD	Organisation for Economic Co-operation and Development
OMC	open method of co-ordination
OPW	Office of Public Works
OSI	Office for Social Inclusion
P2000	Partnership 2000
PCW	Programme for Competitiveness and Work
PESP	Programme for Economic and Social Progress
PNR	Programme for National Recovery
PPF	Programme for Prosperity and Fairness
PRCA	Public Relations Consultants Association Ireland
PRII	Public Relations Institute of Ireland
PR-STV	proportional representation through single transferable vote

PSORG	Public Services Organisation Review Group
RAPID	Revitalising Areas by Planning, Investment and Development
RTÉ	Raidió Teilifis Éireann
SEC	Securities and Exchange Commission
SFI	Science Foundation Ireland
SIPO	Standards in Public Office Commission
SIPTU	Services, Industrial, Professional and Technical Trade Union
SSIA	Special Savings Incentive Account
TD	Teachta Dála (Member of the Dáil)
TI	Transparency International
TRIPS	Trade-Related Aspects of Intellectual Property Rights

Introduction: Reflections on Issues in Irish Business and Society

John Hogan, Paul F. Donnelly and Brendan K. O'Rourke

INTRODUCTION

In this introductory chapter we will put the book and its aims in context and provide the reader with a guide to the wide-ranging, diverse and thought-provoking contributions contained between its covers. In order to do so, this chapter is structured as follows. The first section looks at the context within which this book finds itself and which makes its appearance particularly apposite. The second section deals with the aims of the book as we editors have come to conceive of them. We then provide the reader with an overview of the book's themes and structure.

CONTEXT

The first decade of the twenty-first century has witnessed a swing from the apparently triumphant thirty-year march of deregulated business to the seemingly necessary, and very expensive, rescue by a state and society of 'private' companies that are now judged to be too big to be allowed to fail. It would seem that the doctrine of free market capitalism is now suffering the same loss of faith that the doctrine of communism suffered during the 1970s, when the price of maintaining stability and the status quo was social and economic stagnation (Rutland 1994:xi). Given the failures of these ideologies of the past to deal satisfactorily with either the narrower economic problems or the wider concerns of society, trying to gain an understanding of business and society appears a daunting prospect beset with numerous difficulties, but a challenge that nevertheless must be risen to.

Over the past half century, relations between Irish business and society, how they are governed, and how participation in business and society is exercised, have been tested, challenged and transformed. Currently, Ireland, along with the wider global political economy, is struggling to deal with the consequences of the worst international economic downturn since the end of the Second World War, while Ireland itself is also trying to come to terms with the implosion of its house price bubble and its wider implications. Although this is a period of unprecedented economic flux, exogenous shocks and, to some extent, internally generated crises, are nothing new to Ireland and its small open economy. We have weathered such events in the past, and, no doubt, will have to do so again in the future. It is what we have learned from our previous experiences, and can bring to bear in our dealings with current events, that is of crucial value.

Although the business and societal structures that enabled Ireland achieve great economic success over the past two decades are still in place, a series of questions now faces the country: Are these structures still fit for the purposes they were initially designed to address?; Can they be adapted to the new reality of the changed world?; Or do they need to be revised, or even discarded, in favour of something radically different? The end of the first decade of the twenty-first century is an ideal time to take stock of the state of business and society in Ireland.

An Increasingly Integrated and Dynamic Society

Given the world in which we live today, Ireland is home not only to Irish businesses but also to foreign businesses and investments. Further, business in Ireland is answerable not only to Irish society, but also to societies beyond the country's borders, for Ireland has become one of the most open and globally integrated economies in the world following the policy decision, taken in the late 1950s, to embrace free trade.

With this in mind, it is helpful to recall that business has responsibilities to society, as determined by society itself, for business exists at the pleasure of society and its laws: notwithstanding the status of legal personhood granted to businesses over the decades, it is society that grants them a licence to operate and it is society that can withdraw such permission. As noted by Cadbury (1987:70), '[b]usiness is part of the social system and we cannot isolate the economic elements of major decisions from their social consequences'. Thus, Cadbury (1987) argues, it is society that sets the framework within which business must operate, with responsibilities running both ways: business has to take account of its responsibilities to society, while society has to accept its responsibilities for setting standards to which business must conform.

Indeed, at the 2010 World Economic Forum, questions were asked not just about the failings of bankers, but about the kind of society we wished to have, with French President Nicolas Sarkozy calling for a 'deep, profound change' in the wake of the financial crisis and saying he wished to restore a 'moral dimension' to free trade. In asking 'what kind of capitalism we want', Sarkozy asserted the need to 're-engineer capitalism to restore its moral dimension, its conscience', for '[b]y placing free trade above all else, what we have is a weakening of democracy' (BBC News 2010).

Looking back in time, we have our understandings of the 1929 crash, and the events it precipitated, culminating in the Great Depression, to help us in reflecting on what we are experiencing today. It is useful to recap the conventional learning from that period. The stock market crash was built on easy credit, exuberance and a light to non-existent regulatory regime. To all intents and purposes, when it came to regulation, 'the market' was seen to reign supreme and it was the market that would act as a self-regulating mechanism. However, the market failed, the stock market crashed, banks collapsed and a vicious cycle of business bankruptcies, unemployment and falling demand kicked in and all began their spiral downwards. In the USA, the Republican government of the time stood on the sidelines and did nothing to intervene. It was only after the election in 1932 of Democratic Party candidate Franklin Delano Roosevelt as president that the government started to act, putting in place regulations aimed at preventing the mistakes of the past happening again. Globally, the fallout saw protectionism replace free trade and helped fan the flames of anti-capitalist movements. In some countries, the unemployed masses, in their desperation, turned to nationalist movements and demigods for salvation, the most notorious of these being the Nazi movement in Germany. Thus, the Great Depression contributed to the circumstances that led to the outbreak of the Second World War. It was only in the wake of that conflict that tentative moves towards free trade were initiated with the conclusion of the first General Agreement on Tariffs and Trade (GATT) in 1948. Or so received wisdom tells us.

Today, it seems that, as in the Great Depression, governments and central banks throughout the world are intervening to contain the impact of the credit crunch. Society is once again bearing the brunt of the resultant fallout through unemployment, increased national debt, increased taxation, decreased public services, etc. And there is the uncalculated, and perhaps incalculable, human cost in terms of the knock-on effects of unemployment: the time lag in regaining employment; the impact on the person of being unemployed and seen as an unproductive and draining member of society; the cost to families in terms of children possibly not being in a position to achieve their potential through decreased levels of access to opportunities for learning; and so on.

If anything, and leaving aside the myriad lessons that are almost daily presented the world over in terms of the actions of business in society, the mistakes that precipitated both the Great Depression and today's global recession highlight the importance of understanding business and society in context, of perceiving business as part and parcel of society and of not seeing society as subservient to business. Furthermore, business cannot be seen to operate outside society, as if society does not matter; rather, business must be seen as one part of the jigsaw that constitutes society.

What is perhaps most telling of all is that the majority of business and political leaders never saw, indeed failed to see, either the Great Depression or the current global recession coming. On both occasions, the mantra 'this time it's different' rang out as it has many times before (Reinhart and Rogoff 2009). Each time, we were told that we were experiencing a new era in finance and capitalism. We can but wonder whether lessons will finally be learned this time around. In the meantime, none of us, including the so-called 'experts' on whose words we hang as we look to make our way out of the current debacle, has a crystal ball to foresee the future. Rather, we are now engaged in constructing our future, with the shock of the recession providing us with an opportunity to create the kind of society that, this time, might just see the re-engineering of capitalism with a conscience and a moral dimension.

THE CHALLENGES OF A CHANGING SOCIETY

In all of this, whither Ireland? Where does this leave us and how we see Irish business and society moving forward? Context is important and, while it is crucial not to be constrained by the past, it is just as important to build a sense of where we have come from so that we can be more informed about where we wish to go. As such, with an opportunity to reflect and an eye to the future, the chapters of the book provide us with some of the context necessary to question and inform our perspective of business, society and the intersection of the two.

We are not dealing with a static picture; rather we are confronted with an ever-changing context, one that is complex and multi-faceted. Also, we are not living or operating within a vacuum, either in terms of business in relation to society, or Ireland in relation to the world. Rather, business is an integral part of society and Ireland is an integral constituent of the global political economy. Indeed, given how open we are as an economy, we are very much influenced by events across the wider world, and what we do also has a bearing upon the world, however small that impact might be.

Ireland has very firmly pitched its tent as welcoming inward investment, so much so that it is recognised as one of the easiest countries in which to do business: it is ranked seventh of 183 countries, and third in the European Union (EU) (World Bank 2010). Meanwhile, trust in government and business in Ireland is not just at an all-time low; it is the lowest of all twenty-two countries surveyed in Edelman's 2010 Trust Barometer (Edelman 2010), with just 31 per cent of those surveyed trusting business and 28 per cent trusting government (compared to a global average of 50 per cent and 49 per cent respectively). Indeed, trust in the institutions of government and business in Ireland has been on a downward trend since the 2007 survey, underlining a potentially deep institutional scepticism. In addition, two-thirds of Irish respondents to the 2010 survey consider all stakeholders (including government, employees, customers, society at large and investors/shareholders) equally important to a chief executive officer's (CEO) business decisions, compared to half as important in the EU countries surveyed. Overall, Edelman (2010) drew a number of conclusions from the global 2010 barometer that are pertinent to where we are today and going forward. In particular, Edelman found that profit has become the least important criterion in assessing corporate reputation, being superseded by performance on a number of measures, including transparency and role in society, and there has been a swing away from a singularly shareholder view to an encompassing stakeholder view.

Given this, a greater understanding of the linkages between business and society, and how these change and evolve, will enable a better appreciation of contemporary Ireland, and how it has come to be currently constituted. Within less than a generation, Ireland has gone from being one of the countries with the lowest income in Europe to having one of the highest (Haughton 2008). This transformation has brought great prosperity in its wake. However, such prosperity is rarely shared equally across the whole of a society. As a result, problems have arisen in terms of inequality of incomes, opportunities and quality of life. As the Celtic Tiger era fades into history, what kind of society has it left behind? Debates about the problems of equity and fairness in our society, suppressed to some extent by the euphoria of new-found prosperity over the past decade, in particular, have now taken on a renewed relevance as the dole queues have once more lengthened and others leave the country in search of work abroad.

How Irish businesses are governed, and how they participate in society, has changed radically in recent years. The level of responsibility of business to society, and what society expects of its businesses, has also undergone a transformation. The relationships between business and government, in particular, have come under renewed scrutiny in light of the house price bubble collapsing and the banking sector crisis. This led to calls for increased regulation of business, particularly in the financial sector, increased enforcement of such regulations, and increased regulation of business and government relations. A rethinking of the responsibilities of Irish businesses to the wider society will be necessary if the country is to maintain its economic competitiveness, as well as its credibility as an investment option for foreign businesses into the future. The issue of cronyism in the upper echelons of our society is also something that we, as a people, have to confront. We are a small country, so the potential for the existence of cronyism should not come as too much of a surprise, but what we do to combat this, and its negative impact on society as a whole, is critical.

Society has increasingly sought to set the bar higher for businesses in terms of the standards it expects of them, and, as a result, businesses have been forced to take on board considerations that received scant attention in the past, such as protecting the environment and ethically sourcing supplies. Basic economic measures of business performance are no longer sufficient to capture the whole of the role these organisations play in our society, as their responsibilities towards society now encompass achieving more broadly shared goals.

The relationships between business and society must also be understood within the context of the wider political economy. At the start of the twenty-first century, Ireland finds itself located at the edge of an increasingly integrated European continent. Where a century ago Europe was moving inexorably towards war, today the continent seems more peaceful and contented than at any time in its long history. Being one of twenty-seven member states of the expanding EU, Irish business and Irish society are presented with a vast range of opportunities and challenges that earlier generations could not have imagined: opportunities in the form of what increasing integration within the EU represents in terms of markets for Irish businesses, and freedom of movement for citizens and capital; but also challenges in terms of the increased levels of competition confronting those same businesses. As a society, we are also having to face up to what it means to be a sovereign state when some of our autonomy is gradually being yielded to EU institutions, while economic sovereignty, in the form of policies running counter to those of our competitors, or to the expectations of the international financial markets, has also been greatly diminished. This has led to new kinds of thinking about the relationships between citizens and their society, workplace and government. For instance, what does it mean to be an Irish citizen and an EU citizen, when the EU stretches from Galway, in the west of Ireland, all the way to Narva, on the border with Russia? No longer can any one society, or its businesses, seek to exist in splendid isolation.

The Celtic Tiger era, a period of unprecedented growth, has left many questions in its wake. From seeking answers to these questions, we can draw a range of lessons that might enable us to manage our economy and society in a better and more equitable fashion, once the recession ends and economic expansion returns. Thus, the contributors to this volume examine the state of Irish business and society today and, in this light, contemplate how it might develop into the future.

AIMS AND USES OF THIS BOOK

The main aim of this book is to provide readers with a wide-ranging understanding of the debates surrounding the relationships between business and society in twenty-first-century Ireland. The decisions that businesses make all have a social impact, from production decisions to efforts to influence government policies. As such, Irish business constitutes a fundamental element within Irish society, making it a major social actor. But if business occupies such a position in society, what obligations does it have to society? And, how do these obligations square with what many see as its profit-maximising *raison d'être*?

Of course, given the contexts we have discussed, it is not surprising that we are not the first to produce a volume on such issues. Internationally, many fine minds, struggling to grapple with the problems the world now faces, have in the last few years presented their solutions in the form of best-selling books addressing global business and societal issues (e.g. Kinsley 2008; Reich 2008; Sen 2009; Stiglitz 2010; Wilkinson and Pickett 2009).

This volume addresses Irish society, with its own unique culture and institutions. Just as on the global stage, there have been a considerable number of Irish books on this topic in recent times, both from individual authors (e.g. Allen 2009; Cooper 2009; O'Toole 2009) and from particular disciplinary perspectives (e.g. O'Hagan and Newman 2008; Share *et al.* 2007). What this volume adds to the debate on business and society is the presentation of a variety of disciplinary perspectives from leading business researchers, economists, sociologists and political scientists. Within its covers are contained thirty contributions from thirty-five authors based in a wide range of institutions of higher learning from across Ireland and beyond. Thus, this collection represents a significant set of resources from which the reader can draw.

This volume seeks to break down the barriers that separate and isolate disciplines, such as sociology, economics and politics. The intention is to provide the reader with an encompassing understanding of national and international issues and events and to facilitate intellectually challenging and honest dialogue between viewpoints that often remain isolated from each other. As the issues discussed in this volume will be of interest to a broad spectrum of academic disciplines, in addition to professional and general readers, the various contributors have made their works as open and accessible as possible, while still grounding them in the rigour that such studies require. One of the primary intentions in putting together this edited volume is to disabuse readers of the often-voiced misconception that there must surely be one best discipline to provide us with a comprehensive understanding of a business or societal issue. The contributors to this book use an array of approaches from a variety of disciplines to examine and understand problems.

Therefore, readers from a range of disciplinary backgrounds should be able to use this book as a wide-ranging text on Irish business and society, something that has been sorely lacking until now. Additionally, they should find the book helpful in complementing some of their discipline-specific readings and texts on business, economics, sociology and politics in Ireland. Our hope is that readers will see that it is through questioning our society, its structures and institutions, and by holding a mirror up to them, that we can improve matters for all. Problems in society are not only issues that have to be solved and resolved, they also contain lessons – lessons that we can learn from, and in so doing, avoid having to repeat mistakes into the future.

THEMES AND STRUCTURE OF THE BOOK

As already noted, this volume presents a series of unique insights into various aspects of Irish business and society. The volume title in itself suggests a number of overarching themes, namely governing, participating and transforming. The use of the gerund here is deliberate, for it underscores that what we are dealing with is not static; rather it is dynamic, with change ever present. The use of the gerund also underscores that these over-arching themes point to and incorporate the past, present and future. Figure 1.1 represents but one way of organising the various themes of the book's chapters.

Figure 1.1 Overarching themes and allied sub-themes of this book

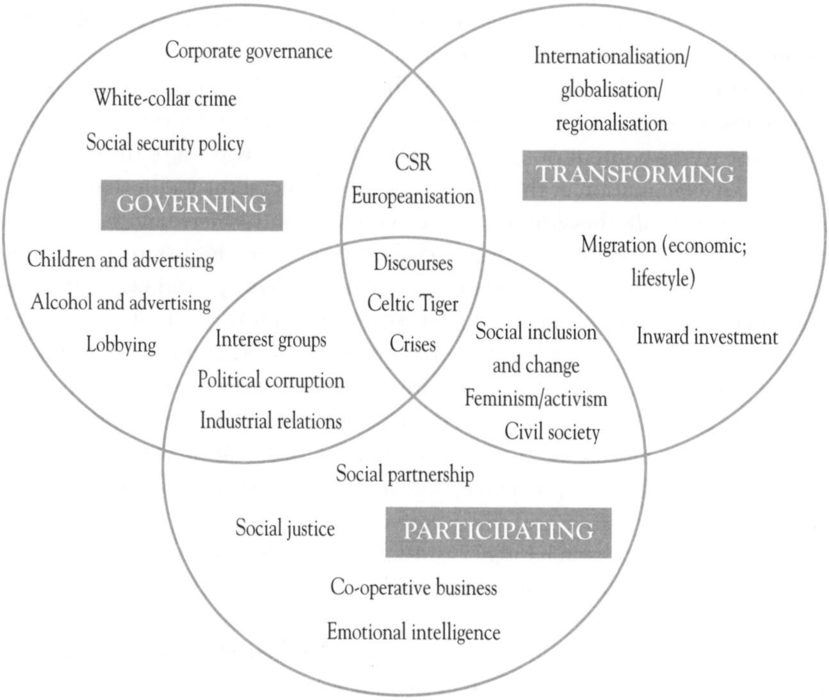

To make managing these resources somewhat easier, the book has been divided into five main sections, each containing a series of interrelated chapters. The chapters themselves are relatively short, but captured within each is the insight of a specialist's expertise, and their unique understanding of, and perspective on, a vital aspect of Irish business and society.

Each of the five sections examines an overarching theme, or set of themes, through a variety of disciplinary lenses, thus providing both a macro and a micro perspective on the chosen topic. Each chapter, as a self-contained unit critically examining a topic in Irish business and society, also constitutes an aspect of the greater whole, much as each institution within a society is also part of something bigger and, as such, must be appreciated with this contextual understanding in mind. Altogether, the approach we have adopted provides the reader with an inclusive and rounded understanding of how business and society has evolved and developed into how it is today.

An essential element of all the chapters is that they are intellectually honest. This may mean facing up to certain unpleasant truths about our businesses and our society, and, where the contributors judge it necessary, this is done unflinchingly. Thus, the reader is presented with a book that constitutes a relatively diverse presentation of aspects of Irish business and society.

All the contributors to the volume are writing from their own areas of expertise. But they also recognise that, as this is a multidisciplinary text, the presentation of their arguments must be as accessible as possible to a wide spectrum of readers. The various chapters show how there are multiple ways in which to examine issues in society. This highlights how each discipline has its own take on society, but also how these understandings can intersect.

Turning to the content of the book itself, Section I, spanning Chapters 1 to 6, contains an examination of the making and unmaking of the Celtic Tiger. This is the context in which the relations between business and society have been shaped in recent years. The chapters examine: the changes to the labour market and employment situation in the country in the period between 1988 and 2008; the role played by certain vested interests in policy decisions that have operated against the interest of the wider society; the role played by the Industrial Development Authority (IDA) in opening the Irish economy to outside investors; the specific discourse of enterprise that is particular to Ireland; the politics of Irish social security policy; and, finally, the structural problems in the underlying framework of the Irish political economy. In all, these chapters present a range of views on both the positive and the negative aspects of the Celtic Tiger era.

Section II, comprising Chapters 7 to 12, looks primarily at the issues of governance, regulation and social justice. Companies in Ireland are governed through a complex set of legal and organisational structures. It is these structures that make up the firm's system of corporate governance. Despite this, a number of large Irish corporations, in particular in the financial services sector, have recently been hit by a series of scandals that raise questions as to their governance structures. These chapters provide a review of: corporate governance in Ireland; the practice of corporate social responsibility in an Irish context; the issue of white-collar crime, and how the legal system has dealt with it; the problem of political corruption; the issue of regulating the growing lobbying industry; and, finally, an examination of the issue of social justice in Ireland. The authors of these chapters argue that much has been done to deal with problems in our business, political and societal institutions, but also that much remains to be done. They also point out that, although Ireland's recent prosperity brought great benefits to society as a whole, it has also brought other problems in its wake, including issues of corruption, a lack of accountability, and those sections of the community that were left behind during the era of prosperity.

In Section III, Chapters 13 to 18, the overall theme is partnership and participation. Since 1987, a series of tripartite agreements, usually of three years' duration, have been reached between the government and the social partners – the primary economic interest groups in Irish society. While these agreements were initially seen as a means of correcting the serious fiscal imbalances that had arisen within the economy during the late 1970s and early 1980s, they subsequently took on a broader character, encompassing social policy and addressing issues of equality in society and social justice. These chapters give an overview of: the impact of economic crises on the changing influence of trade unions in Irish society; the workings of the enterprise-level partnership model; the various forms of partnership governance in Irish social inclusion policy; the co-operative approach to business; the role that emotional intelligence plays in resolving workplace conflicts; and, finally, how the law deals with the workplace and industrial relations. The authors of the first three chapters of this section provide a macro, as well as a micro, examination of aspects of the Irish social partnership, how it has evolved, and what the future might hold for it. The latter three chapters examine how society develops its own businesses when public and private interests fail to do so, and how conflicts in the workplace can be resolved by a variety of means.

The book then moves on to considering international issues of relevance to Irish business and society in Section IV, which runs from Chapter 19 to Chapter 24. As Ireland is a small open economy, the international environment has had a huge impact on relations between Irish business and society. In light of the fact that the domestic market is so small, all major Irish companies must export in order to grow, and, in so doing, they must compete with international rivals who are usually from larger economies wherein economies of scale are more easily achieved. The development of the global corporation and the increasing integration of Europe have all impacted upon Irish society. These chapters examine: the position of Ireland in the EU in the wake of two Lisbon referendums, and an EU of twenty-seven member states; the changed relationship with Northern Ireland; the issue of how Ireland presents itself and its culture to the world; the challenges and opportunities presented by the internationalisation of careers, in the context of an increasingly multicultural workforce and society; the economics of migration in Ireland, from both a historical and current perspective; and, finally, rounding out the section, and linking with the section's opening chapter, is a discussion of the Europeanisation of Irish public policy.

The final section of the book, Section V, which comprises Chapters 25 to 31, looks at interests and concerns in contemporary Ireland. Interest groups, and their input into policy making, constitute a vibrant, vital and integral part of contemporary Irish liberal democracy. In Ireland, in the era of corporatism, interest groups have become part of the policy-making process. They provide another channel by which citizens can present their opinions to government. However, of crucial importance is the strong influence on policy decisions of concern to the whole of society by groups that do not necessarily speak for the broad populace. In particular, these chapters examine the role played by interest groups in Irish society; how civil society operates and its relationship with the state; the changing role and composition of the women's movement in Irish politics; the issue of alcohol advertising and how it is regulated; the issue of advertising aimed at children; the use of high-technology communication devices in business, and their implications for the development of a surveillance society; and, finally, the place of spirituality in the modern workplace.

In all, we feel that these sections, and their chapters, encompass a great range of issues that are of critical importance to understanding contemporary Irish business and society. That there is overlap between some of the chapters, despite the fact that their authors come from different disciplinary backgrounds, and in some cases are based outside Ireland, highlights how a modern society is a highly complex and integrated entity. Thus, issues of political concern are also of economic and social concern, and vice versa, highlighting the value of an interdisciplinary volume such as this.

CONCLUSION

In compiling this volume, our aim has been to fill a gap that has existed too long in Irish academia, drawing together, as it does, business and social science research to provide a multi-dimensional set of perspectives on our country at the start of a new century filled with opportunities and challenges. Although there are a range of business, economics, sociology and politics texts that look at Ireland, none is as broadly interdisciplinary as this. The absence of a volume such as this has meant that some third-level courses on business and society have been taught using either British or US texts. While those books are fine, and present the reader with a comprehensive understanding of contemporary issues in British or US business and society, they are not ideal for an Irish audience. Although Ireland is a western liberal democracy, like Britain and the US, the fact remains that it is also different from both of those countries for a host of reasons. Such differences can only be fully addressed through a dedicated volume. Thus, we have produced this book to provide the reader with a critical analysis of what is currently taking place at the nexus of a variety of aspects of business and society in Ireland.

The chapters in this book are grouped into related sections, but each contribution is also a self-contained unit. In this way, readers can, by examining just one chapter, gain an insight into a contemporary issue in Irish society. The general reader can dip into the book, while the student or academic is provided with the opportunity to familiarise themselves with a more comprehensive understanding of the broader issues at play.

Of course, none of these chapters are presented totally value-free, devoid of a wider impact. The nature of each chapter – its structure, arguments and point of view – is influenced by the perspective of its author or authors. Thus, certain chapters are written from a left-leaning perspective, while others come from the right of the political spectrum. This will provide for a more balanced appreciation of the issues set out, while also offering insights into how perspective influences understanding of a topic. Our hope is that readers from across a range of backgrounds, political persuasions and interests will find this a useful volume in assisting them to gain a more comprehensive understanding of Irish business and society. In summation, our intention is not to be prescriptive and, while contributors point to the implications and possible solutions to the issues raised in their chapters, there is space to re-imagine our past and present into a qualitatively different, and potentially better, future.

References

Allen, K. (2009) *Ireland's Economic Crash: A Radical Agenda for Change*. Dublin: Liffey Press.

BBC News (2010) 'Davos 2010: Sarkozy Calls for Revamp of Capitalism', 27 January [online]. Available: http://news.bbc.co.uk/2/hi/business/8483896.stm (last accessed 6 February 2010).

Cadbury, A. (1987) 'Ethical Managers Make Their Own Rules', *Harvard Business Review* September–October: 69–73.

Cooper, M. (2009) *Who Really Runs Ireland? The Story of the Elite Who Led Ireland from Bust to Boom . . . and Back Again*. Dublin: Penguin Ireland.

Edelman (2010) *Edelman Trust Barometer 2010 Irish Results* [online]. Available: http://www.edelman.ie/index.php/insights/trust-barometer/ (last accessed 6 February 2010).

Haughton, J. (2008) 'Growth in Output and Living Standards', in J.W. O'Hagan and C. Newman (eds) *The Economy of Ireland: National and Sectoral Policy Issues*, 10th edn, pp. 145–73. Dublin: Gill & Macmillan.

Kinsley, M. (ed.) (2008) *Creative Capitalism: A Conversation with Bill Gates, Warren Buffett, and Other Economic Leaders*. New York, NY: Simon and Schuster.

O'Hagan, J.W. and Newman, C. (eds) (2008) *The Economy of Ireland: National and Sectoral Policy Issues*, 10th edn. Dublin: Gill & Macmillan.

O'Toole, F. (2009) *Ship of Fools: How Stupidity and Corruption Sank the Celtic Tiger*. London: Faber and Faber.

Reich, R.B. (2008) *Supercapitalism: The Battle for Democracy in an Age of Big Business*. Thriplow: Icon Books.

Reinhart, C.M. and Rogoff, K. (2009) *This Time is Different: Eight Centuries of Financial Folly*. Princeton, NJ: Princeton University Press.

Rutland, P. (1994) *The Politics of Economic Stagnation in the Soviet Union: The Role of Local Party Organs in Economic Management*. Cambridge: Cambridge University Press.

Sen, A. (2009) *The Idea of Justice*. London: Allen Lane.

Share, P., Tovey, H. and Corcoran, M.P. (2007) *A Sociology of Ireland*, 3rd edn. Dublin: Gill and Macmillan.

Stiglitz, J. (2010) *Freefall: America, Free Markets, and the Sinking of the World Economy*. New York, NY: WW Norton.

Wilkinson, R. and Pickett, K. (2009) *The Spirit Level: Why More Equal Societies Almost Always Do Better*. London: Allen Lane.

World Bank (2010) *Doing Business 2010: Reforming Through Difficult Times*, Washington DC [online]. Available: http://www.doingbusiness.org/documents/ fullreport/2010/DB10-full-report.pdf (last accessed 6 February 2010).

Section I

The Making and Unmaking of the Celtic Tiger

The chapters comprising this section look at a number of areas of relevance to the making and unmaking of a period that has become ubiquitously known as the Celtic Tiger: changes in the labour force over the past twenty years; the power of vested interests in Irish politics and the process of economic policy making; the emergence and evolution of the Industrial Development Authority (IDA); the enterprise discourse that has dominated how we talk and think about business and its relationship with society; the politics of welfare in Ireland; and the failures of the Irish economic experiment and some possible remedies to bring about change. Chapter 1, by Nicola Timoney, looks at labour and employment in Ireland in the era of the Celtic Tiger. Seeing the outstanding feature of this era as the expansion of the labour force, the chapter provides an overview of key developments in the Irish labour market over the period 1988 to 2008. It examines the size and composition of the labour force, considers the rewards to labour by way of the minimum wage, the distribution of income, and the issue of internationalisation and competitiveness of labour costs, and explores the experience of social partnership. The chapter closes by discussing some of the major challenges facing the labour market in the near future.

Moving to Chapter 2, which deals with the political economy of policy making in Ireland, Frank Barry argues that the power of vested interests and the particular characteristics of democratic electoral systems frequently lead to policy decisions that operate against the interests of society as a whole. The chapter examines decision making in some of the now widely acknowledged policy errors of the boom period. However, this chapter also considers how 'political cover' has enabled a number of beneficial historical policy changes to be achieved. This analysis provides some suggestions as to how decision-making processes might be reformed to secure more advantageous outcomes in the future.

In Chapter 3, Paul F. Donnelly traces the evolution of the IDA through the lens of path dependence theory. The story charts the IDA's creation within protectionism in 1949 and its subsequent evolution in an environment of free trade. The chapter follows the IDA's emergence as the state's pre-eminent industrial development agency, its re-creation as a state-sponsored organisation and the growing political, institutional and monetary resources afforded it in return for delivery on objectives. However, the increasing reliance on foreign investment to meet targets, at the expense of indigenous industry, eventually surfaces as a challenge in the early 1980s and culminates in the IDA being split into separate agencies in 1994.

Another important element of process in policy making is the language a society uses for talking about business, and Chapter 4 examines how this both facilitates and constrains how business is done. Brendan K. O'Rourke describes and analyses a dominant way of talking and thinking about business, called 'enterprise discourse'. This form of business discourse relies heavily on seeing all organisations as best when following the mythology of how it is imagined that small, but fast-growing, private enterprises are run. An understanding of enterprise discourse, its features and a sense of it as a discourse dependent on the historical circumstance in which it emerged is useful.

Mary P. Murphy, in Chapter 5, looks at the politics of Irish social security policy over the period 1986 to 2006. Offering a case study of the Irish social welfare policy community, and curious about why the Irish social welfare system has developed in a different direction from that of other English-speaking countries, the chapter asks whether a relative absence of Irish social welfare reform can be explained by examining the politics of welfare. 'Policy architecture' is offered as a way of framing an examination of how the general Irish political institutional features interact with the institutions and interests of the Irish social welfare policy community.

Finally, pondering whether the Irish economic experiment is doomed to fail, in Chapter 6 Bill Kingston begins by arguing that the global banking disaster has hurt Ireland more severely than other developed countries because, from the foundation of the state, government intervention progressively became the characteristic way of running the country. Seeing the crisis as delivering proof that intervention does not work, allied with the vagaries of an electoral system that results in constrained and weak governments and a civil service that cannot be held accountable for what it does, or fails to do, the chapter makes a case for dismantling much of the state apparatus supporting, and puts forward some interesting alternatives to, intervention.

Chapter 1

Labour and Employment in Ireland in the Era of the Celtic Tiger

Nicola Timoney

INTRODUCTION

This chapter examines the changes and key developments in the labour market in Ireland over the twenty-year period from 1988 to 2008. The Celtic Tiger was first and foremost an era of strong economic growth at national and per capita levels. But the increase to unprecedented levels in the numbers at work in Ireland was probably the greatest achievement of the period. Improvement in the employment situation was the aspect of economic growth that most directly affected the lives of people in the country.

The first section of this chapter provides an outline of what happened in terms of the labour force increasing with the overall population. Participation rates – percentage of those in an age group actually seeking work – increased. Numbers actually at work increased to over two million for the first time in the history of Ireland. The sectoral pattern of this employment is then examined.

In the second section, the 'rewards' to labour are examined. First, a specific policy initiative affecting rewards to labour – a minimum wage – was introduced in 2000. The pattern of distribution of earnings is then briefly reviewed, together with available data on income distribution. A trend towards internationalisation of the labour force has been present for some time, since net migration became positive from 1995 onwards. Some evidence on the effects of this internationalisation has become available. Drawing together the developments affecting rewards to labour, the effects on competitiveness of labour for a small open economy such as Ireland are considered. The evidence suggests an initial improvement in wage competitiveness, especially in relation to manufacturing, in the 1990s.

The third section of the chapter investigates the role of social partnership in these developments before considering the current challenges. The great improvement in the labour market, as expressed in the dramatic reduction in unemployment, and the outstanding performance in terms of economic growth, coincided, at the very least, with the experience of social partnership. A new form of social partnership (from 1987) preceded the boom: another renewal in Irish neo-corporatism is required now, as a response to the current crisis.

OUTLINE OF THE LABOUR FORCE

Figure 1.1 shows how, in the twenty years from 1988 to 2008, the overall population of Ireland increased by approximately a quarter, while the labour force increased by two-thirds.

Figure 1.1 Total population and labour force (aged 15 and over), 1988–2008

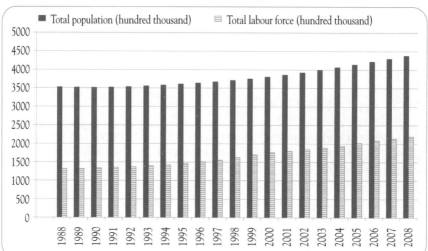

Source: derived from ILO (2009a) © data.

The labour force – defined here as persons aged 15 and over who are economically active – increased from 1.3 million persons in 1988 to 1.6 million in 1998, and to 2.2 million in 2008. Following Hastings, Sheehan and Yeates (2007:75), we may define the period 1997 to 2007 as the 'Eye of the Tiger', although precise timings may differ. We see here that the increase in the size of the labour force – those at work or seeking work – is particularly evident over those years, rising from to almost 1.6 million in 1997 to 2.1 million in 2007. The labour force increased by 38 per cent over those ten years, while the population increase was close to 17 per cent.

Changes in Labour Force Participation in Ireland: Male and Female

The overall participation rate is the percentage of the population over 15 years that is seeking a job. There had been a steady rise in the Irish participation rate from 1988, when participation of the adult population in the labour force was 52 per cent, as shown in Table 1.1. By 2008, participation had reached 62 per cent. Comparing Ireland internationally, using data from the International Labour Organisation (2009b), we see that Ireland's overall participation rate is now close to the world average. Distinguishing male participation and female participation, Ireland's rate of male participation has been, and remains, a little lower than the world average. The trend for male participation is downwards for the world average, but somewhat upwards for Ireland in recent years. For women, the participation rate in Ireland changed from being below the world average in 1998 to equalling it in 2008. There are thus noticeable differences in the pattern of male and female participation for Ireland, within the context of an overall increase in participation.

Table 1.1 Comparative labour force participation rates (age 15+) in percentage

	1988	1998	2008
World – overall participation	64	63	63
Ireland – overall participation	*52*	*55*	*62*
World – male participation	79	76	74
Ireland – male participation	*71*	*68*	*72*
World – female participation	49	49	52
Ireland – female participation	*34*	*42*	*52*

Source: derived from ILO (2009b) © data.

Figure 1.2 Participation in the labour force: rates for men and women, 1988–2008

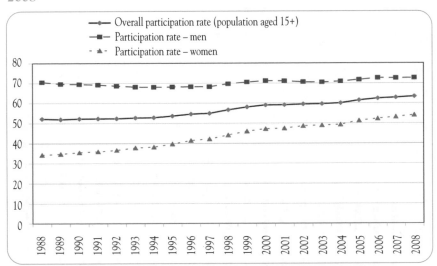

Source: derived from ILO (2009a) © data.

Figure 1.2 gives a fuller picture of the trends in participation in Ireland from 1988 to 2008. There is little variation in the participation rate of men over the twenty years, while changes in the participation of women are more marked.

The numbers at work – persons employed – is a central aspect of the country's economic progress over the past twenty years. In Ireland, the numbers at work increased more than either the total population or the population aged 15 and over.

As the height of the bars in Figure 1.3 shows, the total number at work increased from 1.1 million in 1988, to almost 1.5 million in 1998, and reached 2.1 million in 2008. This near doubling of the numbers at work is the most striking feature of the labour market experience in Ireland over the twenty-year spell: again, the increase over the years 1997 to 2007 was particularly strong.

Changes in the Sectoral Composition of the Workforce

In addition to the changes in the numbers of persons at work overall, there have been changes in the sectoral composition of the workforce, that is, in the economic sector or industry in which people work. Changes in occupations are not considered here (see O'Connell and Russell 2008); rather, consideration is given to sectoral changes that have taken place from 1988 to 2008, as illustrated in Figure 1.3.

Figure 1.3 Employment by sectoral classification, 1988–2008

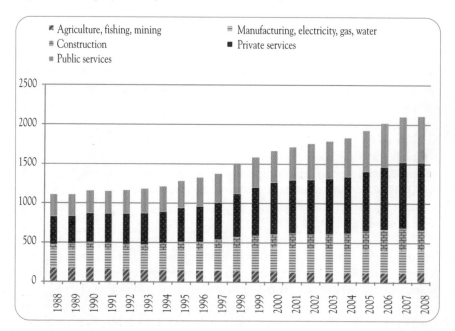

Source: derived from ILO (2009c) © data.

Figure 1.3 shows the sectoral composition of employment, classified into public services, private services, construction, manufacturing and energy, and agriculture (with fishing and mining).[1] The two sectors that stand out as having the largest increases in numbers employed are private services and construction.

In the broad category of private services, numbers employed more than doubled over the period 1988 to 2008, with the largest increases in the time since 1996. Within private services, the largest increases in employment were in the categories of *Real Estate, Renting and Business Services* and *Hotels and Restaurants*, where employment quadrupled. In *Financial Intermediation*, numbers at work more than doubled (from 41,000 to over 90,000 persons), whereas in *Transport, Storage and Communications*, and in *Wholesale and Retail, Motor Vehicles*, numbers employed just less than doubled. This last category nevertheless employs the largest number of persons in the total of private sector services, with over 300,000 persons in 2008.

In construction, employment quadrupled in the total time period from 1988 to 2007, reaching its peak number of 282,000 persons employed in 2007. The surge in numbers employed is most noticeable from 1997 onwards, but a clear decline is evident in construction employment in 2008.

Total numbers employed in public services less than doubled in the two decades from 1988. Within the public service category, larger increases in numbers employed occurred in the *Health and Social Work* area than in *Education* or in *Public Administration and Defence*. Again, the most striking rise in numbers occurred in the *Health* area since 1997. Increased employment in services is a trend common in industrialised economies (Schettkat and Yocarini 2006:128), with possible reasons being the change in the pattern of demand with higher incomes, and the lack of increases in labour productivity in many services compared with manufacturing. For Ireland, a political imperative to improve the health services was present since the late 1980s. Increased government expenditure on health became possible with the marked improvement in the public finances as a result of the Celtic Tiger.

The sector with the most notable drop in numbers employed from 1998 to 2008 is agriculture, continuing its longstanding downward trend. In the combined sector of agriculture, forestry and fishing, numbers working decreased by approximately 40,000 persons. This resulted in the share of the workforce in agriculture and related activities in the total workforce almost halving, from over 10 per cent in 1998 to near 5 per cent in 2008.

These figures show an unusual picture of sectoral composition of employment in a developed country. The decline in numbers at work in agriculture is a usual feature of economic development. An expansion in services is also normal: 'employment in the advanced economies shifts with remarkable regularity towards services as income per capita rises' (Schettkat and Yocarini 2006:144), but the rapidity of the increase in employment in marketed services seen here for Ireland is unusual. The increase in employment share in construction was exceptional:

from employing 6 per cent of the total at work in 1988, the construction sector expanded to account for 13 per cent of the total in 2006 and 2007 (ILO 2009c).

REWARDS TO LABOUR

Rewards or returns to labour could be considered from several points of view: from the monetary rewards to the distribution and equality aspect, to the issue of international comparison. This section thus begins with consideration of the minimum wage and then moves on to consider issues related to distribution and inequality, and the internationalisation of labour.

The Minimum Wage

The industrial relations framework in Ireland is described by von Prondzynski (1998) as *voluntaristic* – that is, built on the premise that it will, for the most part, be regulated by voluntary collective bargaining (to be considered in the third section of the chapter). This idea of voluntarism 'not only led trade unions to avoid the law, it also persuaded successive governments to avoid legal intervention where possible, and most employers were also willing to accept an alternative regulatory environment based on collective bargaining' (von Prondzynski 1998:56). The minimum wage – a policy explicitly based on legal enforcement – thus stands out as a major exception to this framework. The national minimum wage was introduced in Ireland in April 2000, following lively debate on its desirability by trade unions and employers' organisations.

Prior to April 2000, minimum wages were set by Joint Labour Committees (JLCs). The wages agreed in these committees were often quite low, and covered less than a quarter of the total labour force. Enforcement was also relatively weak (O'Neill 2004:3). A government-established commission recommended the introduction of a national minimum wage in its 1998 report. It also suggested that the minimum wage should be set at around two-thirds of median earnings, and that it should take into account employment, overall economic conditions and competitiveness. At the time of the report, it was noted that this fraction of median earnings would suggest a wage of £4.40 (€5.59) per hour. Following this, the government introduced legislation in April 2000 setting the national minimum wage at £4.40 per hour for all adult workers (and a lower rate for younger workers). The introduction of this minimum wage directly affected about 15 per cent of the workforce at the time. O'Neill (2004:6–8) shows that those most likely to be affected by the minimum wage, based on an examination of their position in 1997, were younger workers in the 21–24 age group, and women workers. In terms of occupational classification of the low paid, those working in sales, personal services and labourers were most likely to be affected. O'Neill (2004) also shows that three sectors were significantly more likely to have low-paid workers: the textile and apparel sector; the retail sector; and the hotel, restaurant and bar sector. Since its introduction in 2000, the minimum wage has been modified six times, the most recent rate being set in 2007 at €8.65 for adult workers.

The effects of the introduction of a minimum wage on the labour market have been the subject of investigation, and controversy, from the 1980s onwards in the United States (e.g. Brown 1988). The effects of the minimum wage on employment, on unemployment and on distribution of income are investigated, and set against the view of the minimum wage as being fundamentally an issue of justice and fairness. In line with the results for other countries, the finding from O'Neill's (2004) Irish study was that minimum wages have no adverse effect on employment when the internationally comparable survey methodology is used.

However, O'Neill (2004) also examined more closely those firms that reported that they would not have increased wages by as much were it not for the minimum wage legislation. Using this more refined measure of the impact of the legislation, a significant negative effect on employment was found. It appears that employment growth was reduced by the small numbers of firms most severely affected by minimum wage legislation. In terms of the overall labour market in Ireland in the period immediately after the introduction of the minimum wage, employment growth continued. Strong economic growth and tight labour market conditions (the strength of aggregate demand in comparison to aggregate supply in the economy) led to overheating, to pressure on productive capacity. Upward pressure on pay levels resulted from the ensuing tight labour market. From 2002 to 2007, both the labour force and the numbers employed in Ireland continued to grow, as illustrated in Figures 1.1 and 1.3 above. The unemployment rate rose very slightly from 2002 to 2003, but continued at historic low levels of close to 4 per cent for several years more, as will be seen in Figure 1.7.

The existence of legislation on a minimum wage is, nevertheless, a fundamental change in the labour market in Ireland. For future negotiations within social partnership, it sets a different basis from other consensual agreements.

Distribution and Inequality

Another important aspect of the rewards to labour is the issue of distribution. Dimensions of inequality to be considered include: first, changes in relative earnings among employees over time; second, inequality in the distribution of income; and, third, summary measures of inequality.[2]

In many industrialised societies, rising inequality in the distribution of earnings is a feature of economic growth. To examine earnings inequality, a variety of measures may be used. Survey methods, which typically focus on annual earnings of full-time employees, are used in an attempt to view trends over a longer time. Analysis of the trends in dispersion of earnings may be carried out by examining the highest and lowest deciles or quintiles (tenths or fifths) of the distribution, and by expressing the highest or lowest as a proportion of the median (or middle) income. Studies of earnings differentials are also used to consider aspects of returns to education, relative earnings in public or private sectors, and comparative earnings levels of migrant workers.

The study by O'Connell and Russell (2008) examines earnings in the period 1994 to 2000. Their study shows that rapid economic growth in the 1990s in Ireland seems to have reduced wage inequalities. Examination of the data on relative earnings by educational attainment shows a lack of change: the difference in earnings between those with upper secondary education and those with tertiary education was virtually constant. Another study, covering 1994–2001, addresses the question of whether the changing labour market had an effect on the nature of inequality in Ireland, and concludes, 'we find no evidence that the underlying nature of inequality in Ireland was greatly affected by the rapid growth over this period' (Doris et al. 2008:18).

Earnings are relevant for those in employment: income may include additional items such as transfer payments. Measurement of the distribution of income is subject to particular difficulties as to data and appropriate methods of comparison. Whether the household or the person is the unit of comparison is one issue. It is now usual to focus, when measuring income inequality, on persons rather than households, and to assume that all members of the household share a common standard of living, which is measured by making an adjustment to household income to reflect the number of people living in the household. This adjustment is done by using 'equivalence scales', which attach different weightings to adult members of the household and to children.

According to the OECD (2008) study, changes in income distribution over the period from the mid-1980s to the mid-1990s were dominated, in Ireland and elsewhere, by changes at the top of the distribution. That is, in many countries, the top quintile increased its share of income. For the time from the mid-1990s to 2000, however, the trend is less clear-cut. In Ireland, middle-income groups gained significantly at the expense of both higher- and lower-income groups, as shown by Förster and Mira d'Ercole (2005:15). This is confirmed until the mid-2000s by the OECD (2008:31).

The Gini coefficient is the most widely used summary measure of inequality.[3] In terms of OECD members, Ireland's figure for the mid-2000s, at 0.328, is above the OECD average.[4] Comparing Ireland with the European Union (EU) of twenty-seven members in 2007, the Gini coefficient for Ireland is also above average, but similar to that of eight other countries, including the UK (Nolan 2009:493). Trends in the Gini coefficient for a longer timeframe (OECD 2008:53) suggest that from the mid-1980s to the mid-1990s there was little change in inequality measured for Ireland, while from the mid-1900s to mid-2000s there is evidence of some reduction. The most recent information available (CSO 2009a:20) confirms stability since 2005 in both the Gini coefficient and the quintile shares as measures of distribution, with some move towards a more equal distribution in 2007 and 2008.

Trends in income distribution are part of the assessment of poverty. Relative poverty, as the phrase implies, is not concerned with the absolute level of goods and services an individual can afford, but with how much an individual can afford relative to others in the society. In general, the poorest households are headed by persons not employed. One measure of relative poverty considers persons with 60 per cent or less of median disposable income as poor. By this definition, there was a significant increase in the poverty rate in Ireland in the latter half of the 1990s. 'The numbers falling below relative income thresholds derived as proportions of mean or median income have certainly risen over the economic boom' (Nolan and Maître 2008:38). This trend of increased risk of poverty continued up to 2005 (Kirby and Murphy 2008:13–14).

In summary, Ireland is a country with relatively high inequality, as summarised by the Gini coefficient. This high level of income inequality has been relatively stable over time. Summary measures of inequality did not worsen between 1988 and the latest data available. How, then, is the popular perception of widening inequality in the boom to be reconciled with the statistical measures? If everyone experienced the same proportional increase in incomes, the conventional inequality measures would be unchanged, but 'absolute widening gaps in incomes could dominate popular perceptions' (Nolan 2009:496). This explanation of the difference in the statistical measures and the popular perception of widening inequality is also illustrated in the Hierarchy of Earnings, Attitudes and Privilege Analysis (TASC 2009:13).

The state's interventions through taxation and income support have an effect on inequality and on the incidence of poverty. According to Nolan and Maître (2008:36–7), the change in income distribution as a result of the state's polices in Ireland is comparable to that of the United Kingdom, less than that of Canada or Australia, but greater than that of the United States. Social transfers, such as social welfare payments and benefits in kind, play a smaller role in reducing poverty in Ireland than the EU average. 'Ireland currently ranks lowest in the EU-15 in terms of social spending as a share of GDP' (Nolan 2009:499).

THE INTERNATIONALISATION OF LABOUR

A new feature of the labour market in Ireland is the trend towards internationalisation of labour, in line with other developed economies. In this section, two aspects of this internationalisation are examined briefly in relation to Ireland. The first is the changing composition of the labour force through migration. The second issue, as addressed by the International Monetary Fund (IMF) (2007:161–92), is whether this larger pool of labour from emerging markets and developing countries is adversely affecting compensation and employment in the advanced economies, such as Ireland.

The transformation of Ireland from a country of outward migration for many decades, to one of inward migration in recent years, is remarkable (see Chapter 23 for more discussion). For more than a hundred years, from 1841 to 1961, the history of Irish population was one of decline. For all that time, net migration exceeded the natural increase resulting from an excess of births over deaths. Positive net migration was first recorded in the 1970s, but it is only from the Census data of 1996 that we begin to see a significantly positive net migration, dominated at first by returning Irish (see O'Hagan and McIndoe 2008:114–17).

Figure 1.4 Net migration to and from Ireland, 1988–2008

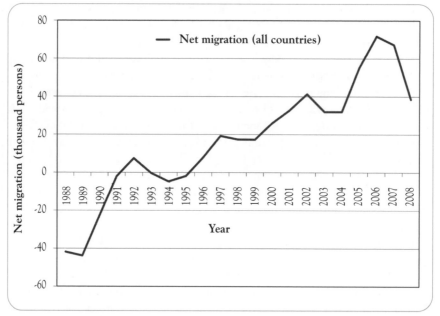

Source: CSO (2009b).

Figure 1.4 shows the net migration out of and into Ireland from 1988 to 2008. The significant out-migration occurring in the later 1980s is evident. Ireland was losing close to 40,000 persons per annum, that is, approximately one per cent of the population. From 1991 (see O'Hagan and McIndoe 2008), this trend began to reverse, with inflows and outflows close to balance. Initially, the inflows consisted of approximately half returning Irish and half immigrants from other countries. The period of definite and increasing in-migration is evident from 1997, and it continued strongly until 2006. From 2004, the acceleration in the inflow is from new member states of the EU, notably those located in Eastern Europe. Ireland was one of the three existing member states to allow full access to work to persons from the newer member states (except Romania and Bulgaria). The Census report (CSO 2007) on employed persons by nationality shows that 85 per cent of the workforce was of Irish nationality at the time of Census 2006. The remaining 15 per cent included 5 per cent from the new accession states to the EU, and 3 per cent from the United Kingdom, with persons from the older EU members and those from all other countries accounting for 2 per cent and 5 per cent respectively of the total workforce.

Figure 1.5 Mean and median hourly earnings by nationality working in Ireland

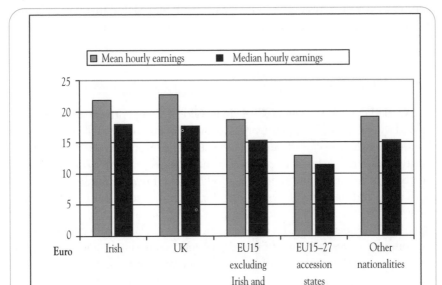

Source: CSO (2009c).

Consideration of the education level of migrants to Ireland leads Barrett and Duffy (2007:15) to state that 'with respect to educational qualifications, it should be noted that the proportion of immigrants with third-level qualifications (31.8 per cent) is identical to the proportion with third-level qualifications in the native Irish population'. Barrett and Duffy (2007:9) also state that 'it should be noted that collectively immigrants in Ireland are a remarkably educated group'. Their analysis shows that the exceptionally high level of qualification of earlier migrants has been moderated by the lower levels of qualification of more recent arrivals. In terms of occupational attainment, the evidence is that it is lower for immigrants to Ireland than for natives, even controlling for age and education.

Efforts to examine the integration of the immigrant group into the labour force suggest limited integration, without noticeable improvement to date. Barrett and Duffy (2007:13) note, 'all we can conclude is that we are not finding evidence of integration'. The impact of immigration on the compensation of employees is problematic to assess. As a first step, Figure 1.5 gives some suggestion from 2007 data.

Average hourly earnings are highest for Irish workers, both male and female. The levels for workers from the other 'older' EU members are somewhat lower; but those for persons from the newer EU member states are substantially lower. As mentioned earlier, the evidence suggests that more recent migration into Ireland from the more recent EU member states includes persons less well qualified than those of earlier migration. The limited data available suggest, therefore, that the earnings pattern of migrants mirrors their educational levels, as is the case for Irish workers.

Competitiveness

The World Economic Forum (2009:4) in its Global Competitiveness Report, puts forward a definition of competitiveness as '*the set of institutions, policies and factors that determine the level of productivity of a country*. The level of productivity, in turn, sets the sustainable level of prosperity that can be earned by an economy' [emphasis in original], and then shows indicators for over a hundred countries. With an overall ranking of twenty-fifth for Ireland, some areas of competitive advantage or disadvantage under the heading of labour market efficiency are identified. Competitive disadvantage is shown for Ireland in the categories of 'flexibility of wage determination and pay and productivity', and competitive advantage for the category of 'co-operation in labor–employee relations'. Recognising that wage costs are one component of competitiveness, information on wage costs in Ireland compared with its trading partners is provided by Central Bank Quarterly Bulletins (e.g. Central Bank 2009:44–5).

Ireland experienced very high unemployment rates in the 1980s. Despite this, in the early 1980s wages in Ireland rose relative to those of the country's trading partners. However, from 1986 to 1996, this trend was reversed (Walsh 2003:13). The interpretation given by Walsh (2003) is that the unprecedented rise in Irish unemployment during the mid-1980s gradually brought about a painful adjustment and this led to a moderation in wage inflation.

A distinction can be made between the trend in wage competitiveness for the economy as a whole, and that for the manufacturing sector in particular. For the economy as a whole, the data suggest that Ireland gained in competitiveness throughout much of the 1990s, with a decline in the cost measure in comparison with the trading partners. However, since 2000, a noticeable deterioration in competitiveness by this measure has taken place. It appears that unit labour costs increased more rapidly than in our trading partners, thanks to weak gains in productivity combined with relatively strong wage increases.

For manufacturing, the picture is different, in that the very competitive position Ireland held in the 1990s would seem to have changed far less. This picture is illustrated in Figure 1.6, where 1995 is the base year. The illustration seems to confirm the idea that wage moderation, especially in the newer technology manufacturing industry, was a major contributor to the recent strong economic growth. The Central Bank of Ireland cautions, however, that within this definition of manufacturing, there are very different experiences for the new technology, largely foreign-owned enterprises and indigenous firms. By and large, the report says, the downward trend in relative unit wage costs in manufacturing industry is dominated by the foreign-owned sector and 'the competitiveness position of many indigenous firms in more traditional sectors is much weaker' (Central Bank 2008:54).

Figure 1.6 Irish unit wage costs relative to trading partners (in common currency)

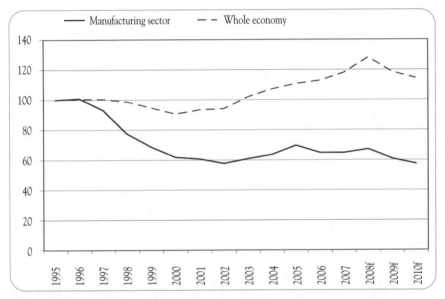

Source: Central Bank of Ireland (2009) (reprinted with permission).

In the 1990s, earnings in the Irish economy lagged behind those in north-western European countries, and compensation per employee and earnings before deductions increased faster than those of most European countries, especially around the turn of the century (O'Connell and Russell 2008:52).

ROLE OF SOCIAL PARTNERSHIP

Over the decades since the 1960s, a range of institutions emerged which facilitated the development of social partnership (see Chapters 13 and 14). One of these institutions, the National Economic and Social Council (NESC), was established in 1973. Membership of the NESC includes nominees from the Irish Congress of Trade Unions (ICTU), the Irish Business and Employers' Confederation (IBEC), and a range of farming organisations. In addition, the secretaries general of five key government departments are members, and a number of independent experts are also included. The secretary general of the Department of the Taoiseach normally chairs NESC meetings and advises the government through that department.

The function of NESC, in its own description is:

> to analyse and report to the Taoiseach (Prime Minister) on strategic issues relating to the efficient development of the economy and the achievement of social justice and the development of a strategic framework for the conduct of relations and negotiation of agreements between the government and the social partners. (NESC 2009)

The NESC had, for some time, argued the case that 'Ireland's economic and social performance could be enhanced by the development of a more sophisticated and wide-ranging system of social consensus' (O'Donnell 1999:60). A 1986 NESC report, *A Strategy for Development 1986–1990*, showed an analysis of the crisis then facing the Irish economy, and spurred the development of consensus between the main political parties as to how to deal with the situation. The result of this work evolved into an agreed understanding of economic and social problems, the implementation of a consensual approach to distributional issues, and the ability of government to adopt a strategic, as opposed to a typically short-run, perspective. Following years of 'drift', a common negotiated approach to solving problems became possible. It was agreed that, given Ireland's membership of the then European Economic Community (EEC), income levels that would maintain the competitiveness of an internationally trading open economy were necessary. It was also agreed that the process of social partnership should be capable of handling distributional conflict.

Studies and reports prepared by the NESC 'present government with the shared view of the social partners and senior civil servants' (O'Donnell 1999:56). Following the success of the 1986 report in presenting a shared understanding of the problems facing the country, and an approach to resolving them, the NESC developed its analyses of strategic policy issues. Since then, the negotiation of each partnership agreement has been preceded by an NESC strategy report.

From 1997, formal recognition was accorded to the 'social pillar', comprising a large number of community, voluntary and religious groups. Partnership activities have also extended to sectoral, local and workplace levels. Other institutions are concerned with monitoring the progress and the implementation of the agreements. The National Centre for Partnership and Performance has fulfilled this role since the Partnership 2000 agreement.

The institutional 'architecture' of the social partnership had, by the year 2007, evolved to the arrangement summarised in Roche (2007:404). In brief, the social partners comprise government, the trade unions (represented by ICTU) and the employers (represented principally by IBEC). A summary of the seven agreements negotiated to date is shown in Table 1.2.

Table 1.2 The social partnership programmes

Programme for National Recovery (PNR)	1987–1990
Programme for Economic and Social Progress (PESP)	1991–1994
Programme for Competitiveness and Work (PCW)	1994–1996
Partnership 2000 (P2000)	1997–2000
Programme for Prosperity and Fairness (PPF)	2000–2003
Sustaining Progress	2003–2005
Towards 2016	2006–2016

Source: Irish National Organisation of the Unemployed (2009).

Each social partnership agreement has included a percentage wage increase to be phased in over the life of the agreement. Other economic policy measures, notably on taxation, and social policy measures came to be included in successive agreements.

It may useful to review the agreements in the light of the headings mentioned above. Increases in the labour force and in the numbers at work were shown in Figures 1.1–1.3. Employment creation and reduction in the unemployment rates feature prominently in the earlier partnership agreements. The Programme for National Recovery (PNR) stated that 'the objective of the employment strategy will be to create viable jobs in the legitimate economy and not in the "black economy"' (DoT 1987:26). In the second agreement, 'the creation of employment and the consequent reduction of unemployment and involuntary emigration is the primary policy objective of Government' (DoT 1991:43). Measures on education, training and increased female participation are also mentioned in that agreement, with a view to addressing the long-run employment problems, together with an explicit reference to the 'crisis of long-term unemployment' (DoT 1991:43, 65, 75). Similarly, in the Programme for Competitiveness and Work (PCW), the key challenge is given as increasing 'the number of people at work within our economy and . . . [reducing] the level of unemployment' (DoT 1994:7). By the time of Partnership 2000 (P2000), and the subsequent Programme for Prosperity and Fairness (PPF), long-term unemployment is mentioned principally in the context of ensuring that Irish society becomes more inclusive, and that the benefits of growth are more equally distributed (DoT 1996, 2000:3). By the time of the Sustaining Progress agreement, the huge improvement in the unemployment picture is noted, and the elimination of long-term unemployment by 2007 is targeted. Unemployment was not mentioned in the original Towards 2016 document. Figure 1.7 shows the improvement in the unemployment rates in Ireland from 1988.

Figure 1.7 Seasonally adjusted annual average standardised unemployment rates

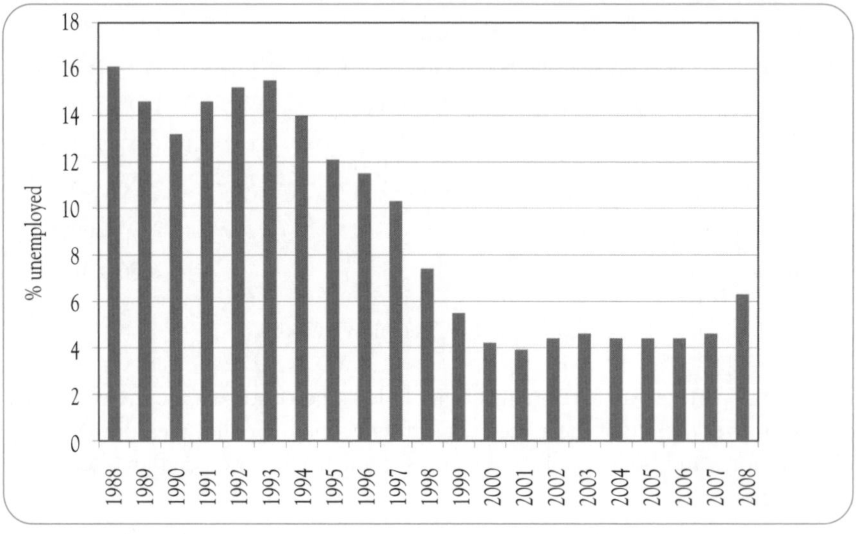

Source: CSO (2009d).

The concept of a minimum wage is first mentioned in the second of the social partnership agreements in the early 1990s. In the PCW and P2000 agreements, concern is expressed about full enforcement of the rates of pay agreed by the JLCs. It was not until the PPF that a formal commitment to introduce a minimum wage appeared: this commitment was honoured in 2000, the first year of that programme. Later partnership agreements adjusted the level of the minimum wage and suggested that those earning this minimum should be removed from the income tax net (DoT 2003:39).

The earlier agreements mentioned distribution issues only very briefly. P2000 is the first to mention the idea of sharing the benefits of growth and the need for policies to tackle poverty and to support social inclusion. As the name implies, the PPF gave a greater prominence to issues of inequality, stating, 'the core objective of the programme is to build a fair, inclusive society in Ireland' (DoT 2000:5). A range of initiatives on poverty reduction was introduced, and a substantial allocation of government expenditure promised.

On the topic of migration, the earlier social partnership agreements stressed the reduction in involuntary emigration as an objective. Immigration first appears in the PPF, some years after net migration had become positive, as shown in Figure 1.4 above. Consultation with the social partners to develop a comprehensive policy framework on migration, and the first mention of multiculturalism in the labour market, appear in Sustaining Progress, whereas the monitoring of changing trends in employment, including those of workers from overseas, features in Towards 2016 (DoT 2006:99).

Figure 1.8 Annual percentage change in gross domestic product (constant prices): Ireland and developed countries compared

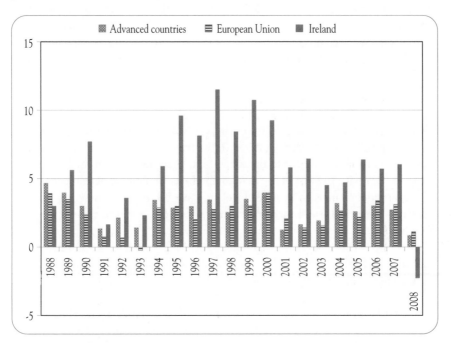

Source: IMF (2009).

The issue of competitiveness is not directly addressed in the PNR, but there is specific mention of Ireland's full participation in the international economy and in the EEC. The PCW agreement states that the government wished 'to maintain and strengthen the consensus approach of recent years, to underpin our strong economic performance . . . and, critically, to deepen the competitiveness of the Irish economy', recognising that sustainable employment expansion is dependent on increased competitiveness (DoT 1991:5, 10). The development of the indigenous sector is emphasised, as it was considered an area where improved competitiveness would yield most in terms of value-added, employment and incomes in Ireland. For P2000, a key objective is stated as 'the continued development of a modern economy operating within the constraints of international competitiveness' (DoT 2000:3). In the PPF, the vital importance of maintaining competitiveness is likewise emphasised. By Sustaining Progress, concern about rising domestic costs and profit levels and a need to renew competitiveness are expressed. In the most recent agreement, the need to enhance productivity and competitiveness is to the fore (DoT 2006:15).

To review Ireland's economic performance in the time of social partnership, Figure 1.8 shows the growth rate of the country's gross domestic product (GDP)

compared with the EU area and with Advanced Countries (as defined by the IMF). It may be seen that, in fact, over the entire span from 1989 to 2007, the rate of GDP growth in Ireland exceeded that in the other groups of countries. The unprecedented economic boom coincides at least with the experience of social partnership. We see, also, that the peak of the era of the Celtic Tiger may be put at 1997 to 2007. In 2008, Ireland's rate of economic growth turned negative.

Assessment of Social Partnership

There is a surprisingly strong degree of support from a variety of sources for social partnership in Ireland. Sweeney (1998:90), writing on Ireland's economic miracle, says that 'a crucial ingredient to the success has been the social consensus, which began in 1987 with the first of the new comprehensive national agreements'. Most political parties of any significance in Ireland have been in government in various coalitions since 1987, and the partnership process has survived this (O'Donnell 2008:88).

The start of this process is explained by Ray MacSharry, who was minister for finance from 1987 to 1988, and Padraig White, who was director of the Industrial Development Authority (IDA) until 1990:

> The NESC conclusions were . . . a highly significant achievement: the social partners had accepted the need for tough remedial measures as part of the integrated strategy, set in a medium-term context. Having looked into the economic abyss, it seemed that all those involved – employers, unions and farmers – had stepped back and had then acted in concert to check a national drift towards disaster. . . . They accepted a balanced package of measures which, in the medium term, might ensure economic redemption. . . . Yet what was most impressive was the unanimity of the social partners' support and their acceptance that tough measures were unavoidable. (MacSharry and White 2000:124–5)

Senior business representatives interviewed by Sweeney (2008:117) were also supportive of Ireland's social partnership and believed that it contributed to economic success. In addition, trade union leader David Begg said that 'the big advantage of the social partnership process was that it gave an incredible amount of stability to that whole environment . . . From a business perspective, you almost had the best of all worlds. This was the catalyst for the take-off' (Sweeney 2008:118). It seems that stability and industrial peace were and are the most valued aspect of the process, appreciated by all sides.

In addition, it is suggested that the engagement of unions, employers, and other civil society actors in wide-ranging policy deliberations requires a reflection on policy priorities. Not only do interest groups understand each others' perspectives more fully, they may also rethink their own interests and even identities

(Hardiman 2006:346). Working groups are set up in the process of social partnership, which involve regular meetings and interactions between key leaders, providing a 'powerful channel of communication between the social partnership arena and the administrative and legislative system' (Hardiman 2006:347).

A less enthusiastic endorsement is given in Clinch, Convery and Walsh (2002). Comparing partnership with the decentralised wage bargaining process common in other countries, they recognise that social partnership has benefits 'principally in terms of minimising the resources that have to be devoted to wage bargaining at the level of the firm' and that a decentralised process might imply a loss of industrial peace (Clinch et al. 2002:92).

In summary, a very important contribution of social partnership is that it has put in place processes that resolve major conflict, often long before the public is even aware it is looming. It is part of a more participative and inclusive society where social partners express their views, and, importantly, are heard (Sweeney 2008:125).

In recent years, criticism of the whole process of social partnership has emerged. For example, Allen (2000:104) suggests that ICTU's status has risen in inverse proportion to the share that workers gain from the national economy. He further suggests that union leaders negotiate and then impose the agreements on unions' rank and file membership. However, Roche (2007:411, emphasis in original) says that 'the view that union leaders can, or need, *impose* policies on members is untenable'. It is true that social partnership has not received uncritical support from union leaders, and that some have been forced to withdraw from the process either because of intra-union factionalism, or because of dissent among members.

A second line of criticism, attributed to former Taoiseach John Bruton, is that the process gives insufficient weighting to democratically elected representatives (Hastings et al. 2007:205). The agreements are negotiated by the social partners, but the legislature – the Oireachtas – has almost no influence on the actual negotiations and has typically been presented with the final agreement.

A third aspect of criticism concerns the introduction of wider social objectives in the negotiations. One statement from economists, criticising aspects of social partnership, is to the effect that this widening of objectives is a form of 'social engineering' and should not have a role in wage negotiations, although a linking of taxation policy with a pay deal is understandable, to preserve take-home pay (Clinch et al. 2002:94). Others suggest, by contrast, that the wider social justice agenda has been given inadequate attention. According to David Begg, 'Ireland's great *economic* success could have generated a great *social* success if we had done things differently' (Sweeney 2008:40, emphasis in original). He suggests that cuts in income and business taxes in the 1990s should have been more modest, and we could then have had a fairer society. It is also alleged that the community and voluntary groups have difficulty asserting their priorities, have felt government support waxing and waning, or have been sidelined (Hardiman 2006:367). There seems to be recognition that social partnership in Ireland has been neutral from a distributional aspect (Baccaro and Simoni 2007:450), and that it did not attempt to compress inter-sectoral wage differentials. The experience has been one of 'solidarity without equality' (Roche 2007:399). The value of social welfare payments was preserved, by union insistence, but the commitment to reducing inequalities was weak.

The final criticism of social partnership concerns its very core – the negotiation of a pay deal for both the public and the private sector. A percentage wage increase is a key feature of each of the agreements. It is voluntary, but compliance levels have been good, and drift has not been significant. The suggestion is that social partnership has resulted in creating and maintaining wage moderation in Ireland (Teague and Donaghey 2009:63). The earlier agreements of the recent phase of social partnership, the PNR especially, tied wage agreements to what was feasible in Irish indigenous industry. This meant that wages in the foreign-owned modern manufacturing sector were held back. As productivity increases were much greater in the modern sector, a considerable gain in competitiveness ensued.

For the more recent agreements, the agreed wage increase was more related to the demands of the public service trade unions, strongly represented in the ICTU. The result has been the loss of competitiveness, which, as explained by Peter Sutherland (chairman of BP and of Goldman Sachs International, former Attorney General of Ireland, EU Commissioner and Director General of the World Trade Organisation) is all the more serious since Ireland is part of a monetary union (quoted in Sweeney 2008:20).

CONCLUSION

The Irish labour market was transformed over the period of the Celtic Tiger, especially the 'eye of the Tiger' years from 1997 to 2007. On the supply side of the labour force, the population increased, the participation rate rose, the labour force grew, and the employment numbers increased considerably. On the demand side, the rate of economic growth contributed to the huge requirement for workers. This demand was initially met by Irish workers and, soon afterwards, by an influx of workers from other countries. The outcome of these changes was that compensation levels improved for the majority of workers. On inequality, changes at the extremes of the distribution do seem to be present, but, in general, the existing inequality levels in Ireland continued.

The principal lesson to be drawn from this experience is that changes in the labour and employment experience of the country, which would have been difficult to imagine two decades ago, did in fact occur, and in a relatively short space of time. Job creation on a scale that seemed unlikely in the past, in a country with very high unemployment rates, is possible.

There are two principal challenges facing the labour market in the near future. The first is the issue of labour costs as one element of competitiveness. It seems that a reduction in compensation to restore the competitiveness of Irish output and exports is required, and is already under way (Forfás and National Competitiveness Council 2009:17). The second major challenge is the continuance of the social partnership model, reflecting the difficulties of the economy in general. Future wage levels, conditions of employment and the social model we have had depend on a successful adaptation of social partnership. An adaptation of social partnership led into the economic boom from the unpromising situation of the 1980s. There is reason to hope it may do so again.

Notes

1 The International Standard Industrial Classification of all Economic Activities (ISIC-Rev.3) was used. Data from LABOSTA has been summarised for Figure 1.3 as follows: Categories A, B and C together as *Agriculture, Fishing and Mining*. Categories D and E together as *Manufacturing and Electricity, Gas and Water Supply*. Category F is *Construction*. Categories G (Wholesale and Retail Trade), H (Hotels and Restaurants), I (Transport, Storage and Communications), J (Financial Intermediation) and K (Real Estate) are combined as *Private Services*. Categories L (Public Administration and Defence), M (Education), N (Health and Social Work), and categories P, Q and X are all included in *Public Services*.

2 For Ireland, studies rely on the Economic and Social Research Institute's Household Survey in 1987, and the 1994 and 1997 Living in Ireland surveys. From 2003, the Central Statistics Office has compiled the Survey on Income and Living Conditions (SILC), in accordance with European Union requirements.

3 The Gini coefficient is calculated from the cumulative income distribution curve known as the Lorenz curve (the cumulative shares of the population, from the poorest to the richer, against the cumulative share of income they receive). The area between the Lorenz curve and the 45° line, as a ratio of the whole triangle, is the Gini coefficient. A smaller number indicates greater equality.

4 For the available data on Gini coefficients 2001 to 2006, see Kirby and Murphy (2008:13). For more recent years, see CSO (2009a: 20).

References

Allen, K. (2000) *The Celtic Tiger: The Myth of Social Partnership in Ireland*. Manchester: Manchester University Press.

Baccaro, L. and Simoni, M. (2007) 'Centralized Wage Bargaining and the "Celtic Tiger" Phenomenon', *Industrial Relations* 46(3): 426–55.

Barrett, A. and Duffy, D. (2007) 'Are Ireland's Immigrants Integrating into its Labour Market?', Discussion Paper No. 2838, Forschungsinstitut zur Zukunft der Arbeit (Institute for the Study of Labour), Bonn.

Brown, C. (1988) 'Minimum Wage Laws: Are they Over-rated?', *Journal of Economic Perspectives* 2(3): 133–45.

Central Bank of Ireland (2008) *Quarterly Bulletin* (1). Dublin: Central Bank and Financial Services Authority of Ireland.

— (2009) *Quarterly Bulletin* (3). Dublin: Central Bank and Financial Services Authority of Ireland.

Clinch, P., Convery, F. and Walsh, B. (2002) *After the Celtic Tiger: Challenges Ahead*. Dublin: O'Brien Press.

CSO (Central Statistics Office) (2007) *Reports of the Census 2006*, Table 29 [online]. Available: http://www.cso.ie/census/Census2006_Volume7.htm (last accessed 21 November 2009).

— (2009a) *Survey on Income and Living Conditions 2008* [online]. Available: http://www.cso.ie/releasespublications/documents/silc/Current/silc.pdf (last accessed 15 January 2010).

— (2009b) *Estimated Population Migration (Persons in April) (Thousand) by Sex, Year, Origin or Destination and Country* [online]. Available: http://www.cso.ie/px/pxeirestat/Dialog/varval.asp?ma=PEA02&ti=Estimated+Population+Migration+(Persons+in+April)+(Thousand)+by+Sex,+Year,+Origin+or+Destination+and+Country&path=../Database/Eirestat/Population%20Estimates/&lang=1 (last accessed 20 November 2009).

— (2009c) *Mean and Median Hourly Earnings by Year, Nationality, Sex, Employment* [online]. Available: http://www.cso.ie/px/pxeirestat/Dialog/varval.asp?ma=NSA31&ti=Mean+and+Median+Hourly+Earnings+by+Year,+Nationality,+Statistic,+Sex+and+Employment+Status&path=../DATABASE/Eirestat/National%20Employment%20Survey/&lang=1 (last accessed 20 November 2009).

— (2009d) *Database Direct* [online]. Available: http://www.cso.ie/px/pxeirestat/Dialog/varval.asp?ma=LRA03&ti=Seasonally%20Adjusted%20Annual%20Average%20Standardised%20Unemployment%20Rates%20%28SUR%29%20by%20State%20and%20Year&path=../Database/Eirestat/Live%20Register/&lang=1 (last accessed 20 November 2009).

DoT (Department of the Taoiseach) (1987) *Programme for National Recovery*. Dublin: Stationery Office.

— (1991) *Programme for Economic and Social Progress*. Dublin: Stationery Office.

— (1994) *Programme for Competitiveness and Work*. Dublin: Stationery Office.

— (1996) *Partnership 2000*. Dublin: Stationery Office.

— (2000) *Programme for Prosperity and Fairness*. Dublin: Stationery Office.

— (2003) *Sustaining Progress*. Dublin: Stationery Office.

— (2006) *Towards 2016*. Dublin: Stationery Office.

Doris, A., O'Neill, D. and Sweetman, O. (2008) 'Does Growth Affect the Nature of Inequality? Ireland 1994–2001', Working Paper, Department of Economics, Finance and Accounting, National University of Ireland, Maynooth [online]. Available: http://economics.nuim.ie/research/workingpapers/documents/N1930708.pdf (last accessed 15 January 2010).

Forfás and National Competitiveness Council (2009) *Benchmarking Ireland's Performance*, Annual Competitiveness Report, Vol. 1 [online]. Available: http://www.forfas.ie/media/ncc090818_acr_2009.pdf (last accessed 22 November 2009).

Förster, M. and Mira d'Ercole, M. (2005) *Income Distribution and Poverty in OECD Countries in the Second Half of the 1990s*, Working Paper No. 22, Social, Employment and Migration Working Papers. Paris: OECD.

Hardiman, N. (2006) 'Politics and Social Partnership: Flexible Network Governance', *Economic and Social Review* 37(3): 343–74.

Hastings, T., Sheehan, B. and Yeates, P. (2007) *Saving the Future: How Social Partnership Shaped Ireland's Economic Success*. Dublin: Blackhall.

ILO (International Labour Organisation) (2009a) *LABORSTA Labour Statistics Database*, Table E5 [online]. Available: http://laborsta.ilo.org/ (last accessed 25 October 2009).

— (2009b) *Key Indicators of the Labour Market (KILM)*, Table 1a [online]. Available: http://kilm.ilo.org/ (last accessed 13 November 2009).

— (2009c) *LABORSTA Labour Statistics Database*, Table 2b [online]. Available: http://laborsta.ilo.org/ (last accessed 16 October 2009).

IMF (International Monetary Fund) (2007) *World Economic Outlook: Spillovers and Cycles in the Global Economy*. Washington, DC: IMF.

— (2009) *World Economic Outlook Database* [online]. Available: http://www.imf.org/external/pubs/ft/weo/2009/02/weodata/index.aspx (last accessed 4 September 2009).

Irish National Organisation of the Unemployed (2009) [online]. Available: http://www.inou.ie/policy/partnership/historyofinouin.html (last accessed 17 November 2009).

Kirby, P. and Murphy, M. (2008) *A Better Ireland Is Possible: Towards an Alternative Vision for Ireland* [online]. Available: www.communityplatform.ie/uploads/A%20Better%20Ireland%20-%20pdf.pdf (last accessed 21 November 2009).

MacSharry, R. and White, P. (2000) *The Making of the Celtic Tiger: The Inside Story of Ireland's Boom Economy*. Cork: Mercier Press.

NESC (National Economic and Social Council) (1986) *A Strategy for Development 1986–1990: Growth, Employment and Fiscal Balance*. Dublin: NESC.

— (2009) [online]. *Welcome to the NESC* [online]. Available: http://www.nesc.ie/ (last accessed 22 November 2009).

Nolan, B. (2009) 'Income Inequality and Public Policy', *Economic and Social Review* 40(4): 489–510.

Nolan, B. and Maître, B. (2008) 'Economic Growth and Income Inequality: Setting the Context', in T. Fahey, H. Russell and C.T. Whelan (eds) *Quality of Life in Ireland: Social Impact of Economic Boom*, pp. 27–41. Dordrecht: Springer.

O'Connell, P.J. and Russell, H. (2008) 'Employment and Quality of Work', in T. Fahey, H. Russell and C.T. Whelan (eds) *Quality of Life in Ireland: Social Impact of Economic Boom*, pp. 43–66. Dordrecht: Springer.

O'Donnell, R. (1999) 'Social Partnership: Principles, Institutions and Interpretations', in P.J. O'Connell (ed.) *Astonishing Success: Economic Growth and the Labour Market in Ireland*, pp. 52–70. Geneva: International Labour Office.

— (2008) 'The Partnership State: Building the Ship at Sea', in M. Adshead, P. Kirby and M. Millar (eds) *Contesting the State: Lessons From the Irish Case*, pp. 73–99. Manchester: Manchester University Press.

OECD (Organisation for Economic Co-operation and Development) (2008) *Growing Unequal?: Income Distribution and Poverty in OECD Countries*. Paris: OECD.

O'Hagan, J. and McIndoe, T. (2008) 'Population, Migration and Employment', in J. O'Hagan and C. Newman (eds) *The Economy of Ireland: National and Sectoral Issues*, 9th edn, pp. 112–44. Dublin: Gill & Macmillan.

O'Neill, D. (2004) 'Low Pay and the Minimum Wage in Ireland', in D. Meulders, R. Plasman and F. Rycx (eds) *Minimum Wages, Low Pay and Unemployment*, pp. 3–26. Basingstoke: Palgrave Macmillan.

Roche, W.K. (2007) 'Social Partnership in Ireland and New Social Pacts', *Industrial Relations* 46(3): 395–425.

Schettkat, R. and Yocarini, L. (2006) 'The Shift to Services Employment: A Review of the Literature', *Structural Change and Economic Dynamics* 17(2): 127–47.

Sweeney, P. (1998) *The Celtic Tiger: Ireland's Economic Miracle Explained*. Dublin: Oak Tree Press.

— (2008) *Ireland's Economic Success*. Dublin: New Island.

TASC (2009) The HEAP Chart (Hierarchy of Earnings, Attitudes and Privilege Analysis) [online]. Available: http://www.tascnet.ie/upload/file/9644%20HEAP%20BOOKLET(1).pdf (last accessed 16 January 2010).

Teague, P. and Donaghey, J. (2009) 'Why has Irish Social Partnership Survived?' *British Journal of Industrial Relations* 47(1): 55–78.

von Prondzynski, F. (1998) 'Ireland: Corporatism Revived', in A. Ferner and R. Hyman (eds) *Changing Industrial Relations in Europe*, 2nd edn, pp. 55–73. Oxford: Blackwell.

Walsh, B.M. (2003) 'The Transformation of the Irish Labour Market: 1980–2003', *Journal of the Statistical and Social Inquiry Society of Ireland* 33(1): 83–115.

World Economic Forum (2009) *The Global Competitiveness Report 2009–2010*. Geneva: Global Competitiveness Network.

Chapter 2

Politics and Economic Policy Making in Ireland

Frank Barry

Democratic national governments tend to be subject to such strong pressure
from vested interests within their own territories that many of their decisions
operate against the interests of society as a whole. (FitzGerald 2000:117)

INTRODUCTION

Taoiseach Brian Cowen admitted, during a television appearance on the *Late Late
Show* in 2009, that certain policy errors that had deepened the subsequent
economic crisis could, with hindsight, be seen to have been made over the boom
period. He asserted, however, that 'all policy decisions were based on the best
advice available at the time' (RTÉ 2009).

This is a strange claim for a politician to make, in that it seems to deny a role
for *politics* in political decision making. All policy choices have distributional
consequences, no matter how much Ireland's political parties seek to sell
themselves simply as better managers of the economy. The taoiseach's assertion
can also be criticised for seeking to airbrush out of the picture the concerns that
many expressed at the time these policy decisions were made.

A thorough study of the interplay between politics and economic policy would
be more than a lifetime's work. This chapter confines itself to analysis of a number
of historical policy decisions that seem to offer illuminating insights. Some of the
policy changes studied advanced the public interest. Amongst these were the
opening up of the economy, the liberalisation of air access, deregulation of the taxi
market and resolution of the fiscal crisis of the 1980s. Analysis of these episodes
illustrates some of the processes by which policy errors can come to be rectified.
Other episodes shed light on less benign aspects of the policy-making process. The
chapter considers in this light some of the now widely acknowledged policy errors
of the boom period: the pro-cyclical stance of fiscal policy, the failure to counteract

I am grateful to Karen White for research assistance on the air access liberalisation process and to
Stephen Weir, whose 2009 paper – which forms part of his PhD research – explores the history of taxi
market deregulation. This chapter forms part of an IRCHSS-sponsored project on 'Turning
Globalisation to National Advantage: Economic Policy Lessons from Ireland's Experience'.

the property market bubble, and 'decentralisation' – the attempted dispersal across the country of a large number of government departments and state agencies. Concluding comments offer tentative suggestions on how decision-making processes might be reformed to secure more beneficial outcomes.

POLITICS AND THE SHIFT FROM PROTECTIONISM TO OUTWARD ORIENTATION

The above quote from former taoiseach Garret FitzGerald suggests that well-functioning societies must develop mechanisms that can provide political cover to help stave off detrimental interest-group pressures. The shift away from protectionism that began in the late 1950s provides several examples of where such cover can be found.

By that time it had become clear that the protectionist policies followed in Ireland since the early 1930s had run out of steam. Four hundred thousand people emigrated over the course of the 1950s – the highest level since the 1880s – while the rest of Western Europe boomed on the back of post-war reconstruction (Ó Gráda 2008). As always, however, there were vested interests with a stake in the existing policy regime.

Popular history ascribes the subsequent turnaround in policy, and in Ireland's economic fortunes, to T. K. Whitaker, the recently appointed secretary of the Department of Finance, whose galvanising report on economic development appeared in 1958, and to Seán Lemass, who implemented elements of this new thinking when he took over from de Valera as taoiseach in 1959. Garret FitzGerald (1968) notes how Lemass used the publication of Whitaker's *Economic Development* alongside that of the government's First Economic Programme to provide political cover for the policy reversal. By doing so, FitzGerald (1968:26) writes, 'the government made it clear that the Programme was not, and was not claimed to be, a policy prepared by the government party, but was a national programme, prepared by the head of the civil service'. This allowed it to be seen as transcending party politics.

Lee (1989:352) offers a complementary and amusing commentary. 'It may be surmised', he notes,

> that Lemass had little ambition to inflict on his backbenchers, or on de Valera, the enlightenment that would be willingly proffered from the opposition benches about the manner in which Fianna Fáil had at last seen the light, and was now reneging on its earlier self. Nor would any astute politician wish to sacrifice the advantage accruing to his party from a 'plan' ostensibly based on the work of a non-party civil servant. The de-politicisation of 'planning' was too useful an asset to be wantonly surrendered to the capricious vagaries of Dáil debates.

Less frequently remarked upon by historians is the Export Profits Tax Relief (EPTR) scheme introduced in November 1956 by a short-lived non-Fianna Fáil government, only the second such administration to hold power since 1932. Its importance is more obvious to economists, as EPTR marks the genesis of Ireland's low corporation tax strategy. The latter – in the words of Padraic White, former managing director of the IDA – 'remains to this day the unique and essential foundation stone of Ireland's foreign investment boom' (MacSharry and White 2000:250). Just how important this foreign investment has been to the Irish economy is worth recalling. Foreign multinationals account for one out of every two jobs in Irish manufacturing and one out of every five jobs in services – far higher proportions than recorded elsewhere in Europe or indeed in most of the world. The inflows of foreign direct investment (FDI) associated with the single European market and the global high-tech boom of the 1990s were in turn one of the driving forces behind Ireland's Celtic Tiger era.

The Dáil records of the mid-1950s reveal much discussion on both sides of the house of the need to stimulate exports, yet Fianna Fáil thinking remained sharply divided on the question of foreign capital. 'Since 1948,' as Bew and Patterson (1982:69) write, 'Lemass had been prepared to ruminate rather indecisively in public on the possible role of foreign capital in the Irish economy.' His trip to the USA in the autumn of 1953 was aimed partly at attracting American investment, yet his Dáil speeches in the summer of 1955, while in opposition, criticise the then tánaiste's efforts towards the same end. Lemass also criticised the government's acceptance of a proposal from an Anglo-American combine to erect an oil refinery in Cork harbour, which represented the largest sum ever invested in a single private enterprise in the country (e.g. Dáil Debates, vol. 152, col. 1145, 14 July 1955).

The ambiguity of Lemass's position was motivated both by political oppositionism and by a desire to paper over the cracks between his growing acceptance of the need for – and Fianna Fáil's traditional hostility towards – foreign capital. As Bew and Patterson (1982:70) point out, 'foreign capital was, for nationalist ideologues, a far more explosive issue than protection. After all, protection was only a means to an end – the building up of a native Irish industry.' While Lemass was prevaricating, de Valera is quoted as railing against handing over Irish resources to foreigners 'festooned with tax reliefs' (Bew and Patterson 1982:87).

EPTR, as first introduced 'in the bleak mid-winter' of the 1950s, allowed a 50 per cent tax remission on profits earned from increased export sales. The policy was sold in public as a stimulus to exports rather than to foreign capital. Crucially, however, from the political point of view, EPTR's introduction by a non-Fianna Fáil government helped Fianna Fáil to finally ditch its ideological objections to foreign industry, which responded rapidly to the new tax reliefs. Upon returning to power, Fianna Fáil expanded the tax remission to 100 per cent and eased the legal restrictions on foreign ownership that it had enacted in the 1930s. Fianna Fáil had also embraced, upon its return to office, the first coalition government's establishment of the Industrial Development Authority (IDA) in 1949, though it had rejected the move whilst in opposition. The senior Fianna Fáil figure Kevin Boland later wrote of his shock and bewilderment 'to find that the principle of Irish ownership of industry, which was central to the Republican policy as I had always understood it, was gone' (Boland 1977:117).

This episode serves to illustrate how occasional changes in government can facilitate the abandonment of growth-inhibiting ideologies, much as the Blair government in the UK benefited from many of the changes introduced by previous Conservative administrations – changes which it would not itself, for political reasons, have been able to make. 'Blair's generation of Labour politicians felt compelled to accept the Thatcherite settlement on the economy. He, in turn, forced the Tories to accept a new, more social democratic consensus that government had a responsibility to invest in public services and deliver social justice' (Rawnsley 2007).

While EPTR did not directly threaten established (protectionist) interests, it led to a considerable strengthening of the export lobby. This increased the pressure for further liberalisation, of the type represented by the signing of the Anglo-Irish Free Trade Area Agreement in 1965 and European Economic Community (EEC) accession in 1973. Analysts refer to this process as one of 'cascading' or 'juggernaut' reforms (e.g. Baldwin and Robert-Nicoud, 2007).

POLITICS AND THE 1966 ANNOUNCEMENT OF 'FREE EDUCATION'

The 'juggernaut' reform process behind the economic liberalisation of the late 1950s and early 1960s also led to a sea change in educational policy (Barry 2007). The UK's early industrialisation had ensured the evolution of a well-developed system to provide an intermediate layer of technicians. It was recognised that the Irish education system would need to provide this intermediate layer from scratch, if human resources were to be available to sustain the industrial expansion that liberalisation brought.

This recognition led to the commissioning of the hugely influential 1965 report *Investment in Education* (DoE 1965). The report's two central propositions were that a non-meritocratic education system was wasteful of natural talent, and that investment in the education of that talent had contributed significantly to European post-war economic growth.

Investment in Education generated newspaper headlines with its finding that over half of Irish children were leaving school at or before the age of thirteen. Garvin (2004) provides an account of the constellation of conservative forces that viewed this outcome as acceptable, and the policy reform literature (e.g. OECD 2007) identifies the creation of a sense of crisis as a way of weakening such opposition. *Investment in Education* might be seen as an example of such a strategy being employed.

The report paved the way for the introduction, shortly afterwards, of 'free' (i.e. taxpayer-funded) second-level education and access to school transport networks. Though educational participation in Ireland had been expanding in previous decades, these reforms had a substantial impact on the participation rates of those from less well-off backgrounds (Denny and Harmon 2000).

The reforms were announced by Donogh O'Malley in his first major speech as minister for education on Saturday 10 September 1966. The announcement caused consternation in government as the proposals had not been approved by cabinet. The choice of day and venue – a meeting of the National Union of Journalists – ensured that it received saturation coverage, and the enthusiasm of the public response forced the government's hand. The Department of Finance was furious, but any failure to sanction the policy, once announced, would have been politically disastrous.

Whether or not Taoiseach Seán Lemass had prior knowledge of the announcement has been the subject of heated debate among historians. Lemass denied it, and issued a written rebuke to O'Malley on 12 September (Walsh 2009:191). Five members of the cabinet later told Brian Farrell, however, of their belief that Lemass had seen the text in advance (Farrell 1991:107).

The noted journalist John Healy, who was a close friend of O'Malley's, published his recollections on the twentieth anniversary of O'Malley's death (Healy 1988a, b). He suggests that not only had Lemass seen the text in advance but had actually amended it:

> On Thursday afternoon [O'Malley] brought the script into the Taoiseach's office. . . . On page five of the script there was the crucial paragraph announcing the setting up of universal secondary education which would be subject to a means test. Lemass took his pen and drove it through the means test phrase, saying to O'Malley: 'This is 1966, the anniversary of the Proclamation: it's about time we started to treat all the children of the nation equally.' (Healy 1988a:49)

If this account is correct, it provides a further – if underhand – example of how opposition to reform processes can be overcome.

POLITICS AND AIR ACCESS LIBERALISATION

'Regulatory capture' occurs when a state agency charged with overseeing an industry in the public interest comes, over time, to view its goals as synonymous with those of the entities it regulates and begins to act in their commercial interests. The Beef Tribunal unearthed many instances of government departments supporting the commercial interests of the beef sector to the detriment of the public good (O'Toole 1994). The failure of the Department of Education to investigate the abuses associated with the industrial schools system, as revealed in the Ryan Report of 2009, represents a similar process. It typically only comes to public attention when exposed to careful probing, by tribunals of inquiry for example, or, as in the case to be explored here, when draconian legislation is deemed necessary to protect the status quo.

Had the Air Transport Bill of June 1984 passed into legislation as planned, the future of air access, and of the Irish airline and tourism industries, would have been very different. The original anti-competitive bill threatened travel agents offering airline tickets at prices below those approved by the minister with loss of their licence, a fine of up to £100,000 and a prison term of up to two years. By the time the bill was finally passed, its anti-competitive stance had been completely reversed and the Dublin–London route deregulated. Fares fell by more than 50 per cent on the first day of deregulation in 1986, passenger numbers increased by 65 per cent over the first full year, and Ryanair was on its way to becoming Europe's largest airline.

The attempt to have the draconian bill rushed through as emergency legislation followed the lifting by the Supreme Court of a temporary injunction restraining one particular company from selling unapproved fares. Without the bill, according to the Fine Gael minister of state, 'discounting and other malpractices [could emerge] on a scale that would undermine approved tariff structures and could have serious implications for airlines generally and for Aer Lingus in particular' (Dáil Debates, vol. 352, col. 855, 27 June 1984).

While strong party discipline typically ensures that government legislation is passed with little difficulty, a parliamentary revolt led by Deputy Desmond O'Malley delayed passage of the bill and led ultimately to the U-turn. A former Fianna Fáil minister and future founder of the Progressive Democrats (PDs), O'Malley had recently become an independent TD. His arguments in the Dáil succeeded in influencing both Fine Gael backbenchers and some members of the Fianna Fáil opposition.

O'Malley, in turn, was strongly influenced by the policy interventions of a group of economists led by Seán Barrett. He referred in the Dáil on 27 June 1984 to a newspaper interview published that morning in which Barrett had argued that:

> new legislation is better introduced after calm consideration of all the diverse factors which make up the national interest: in aviation, international trade, tourism, regional development and employment. These factors are so diverse and complex that they cannot be dismissed by this hasty Bill. (O'Byrnes 1984: 6)

A concurrent public statement issued by the group of ten academic and financial services economists led by Barrett argued that 'it would appear that the Government and Opposition care more about the interests of State monopolies than the public as a whole' Barrett (2009:3). Echoing this, O'Malley asked:

[Is it] in our national interest that this should be so or will we continue to make the mistake of equating Ireland's national interest with the health of Aer Lingus's balance sheet? . . . Aer Lingus take the view that it is better to sell 100 seats at $200 rather than 200 seats at $100. The revenue would be exactly the same . . . The national interest would be greatly helped by having an additional 100 people visit this country but Aer Lingus would prefer to fly the plane with 100 empty seats . . . The truth is that Aer Lingus . . . have followed policies which were ill-advised and damaging to our economy. If this Bill is passed, it copperfastens for all time those policies. That is a tragedy and a disgrace. (Dáil Debates, vol. 352, cols 871–2, 27 June 1984)

The bill was warmly welcomed by some Fianna Fáil TDs, including Ray Burke, in whose constituency many Aer Lingus workers lived. The government began to give ground, however, as its own backbenchers began to swing behind O'Malley. By February 1985, the Minister for Communications was recommending that the penalty of imprisonment be dropped and he announced his intention to amend the bill so as to provide more open competition between travel agents and airlines (Irish Times 1985; Coughlan 1985). The second stage of the bill was delayed until May 1985, eleven months after its initial introduction. This exposed how exaggerated had been the fears expressed by the minister as to the possible consequences for Irish aviation were the bill not passed immediately.

By May 1985, O'Malley was able to refer to a recent paper, by Brussels' Competition Commissioner Peter Sutherland, which identified air transport as one of the worst 'black holes' in Europe in terms of absence of competition (Dáil Debates, vol. 358, col. 1853, 22 May 1985). This triggered a shift on the part of the Fine Gael Minister for Communications, Jim Mitchell, who stated that 'I am all for a very liberal air transport regime provided it is done together. . . . Therefore the proposals of the Commission are welcome. The only way is to get progress throughout Europe together' (Dáil Debates, vol. 358, col. 1857, 22 May 1985).

The deregulation in Irish aviation came about when the Minister announced in December 1985:

I have approved in principle a new air service from Dublin to Luton, return, costing £99. I have given Ryanair the go ahead and it will be announced by my Department later today. It will be welcomed by many people and is another indication of the policies consistently pursued by me since I became Minister for Transport and subsequently Minister for Communications. (Dáil Debates, vol. 362, col. 1052, 4 December 1985)

Deputy O'Malley responded, in the Dáil, that 'it is contrary to the policies followed up to now but I congratulate the Minister' (Dáil Debates, vol. 362, col. 1054, 4 December 1985). In response to the government's claim that it had always been pro-competition, O'Malley noted that:

I have succeeded in having the Bill amended by the Minister 31 times. . . . Some of the highly objectionable features and the ridiculous penal provisions in the Bill have been removed and if that is not a fundamental change I do not know what is. (Dáil Debates, vol. 363, cols 2300 and 2307, 12 February 1986)

This episode reveals several points of interest from a political economy perspective. First is the insidious nature of regulatory capture, which only becomes apparent when the system is thrown into crisis. This is amply illustrated by the fact that the relevant government department still supports the current virtual monopoly position of Dublin Bus, which is equivalent to that enjoyed by Aer Lingus at the time the anti-competitive bill was introduced. Second is the particular difficulty that arises when a public company is involved:

One is not allowed debate the merits or demerits of a more liberal or more restrictive air transport policy here, or more liberal access or restrictive access to the country. The whole thing is immediately painted in terms of whether one is for Aer Lingus or against them. (Desmond O'Malley, Dáil Debates, vol. 357, col. 2256, 22 May 1985)

Third is the opportunity that a 'crisis' can afford for reform-minded experts (in this case the group of economists) to have their case heard. It is easier in the absence of a crisis for the political and administrative system to ignore them. And fourth, as in the case discussed earlier, is the search for political cover as long-standing policies are reversed. In the present case this took two forms. The first was by reference to European Commission proposals, which were working in the same direction as the amendments proposed by O'Malley. The second was the attempt by politicians on all sides to claim that they had never been anti-competitive:

I am delighted to hear that there were many people in the House with whom some of these matters did not find favour, because we were led to believe I was the only one with whom they did not find favour . . . I have noticed in recent times that when one is victorious one suddenly acquires many allies which one might not have had in times of difficulty. (Desmond O'Malley, Dáil Debates, vol. 363, col. 2306, 12 February 1986)

POLITICS AND DEREGULATION OF THE TAXI MARKET

The 1978 moratorium on the issuing of new taxi licences for Dublin attracted little attention during the recessionary decade of the 1980s, but excess demand for taxi services grew as economic recovery began. By 1991, existing taxi licences were changing hands for between IR£30,000 and IR£50,000 (Weir 2009). An official Interdepartmental Committee Report on the taxi industry issued in 1992 recommended a 'strategy of gradual liberalisation', but the taxi lobby launched a major campaign of disruption, including a blockade of Roscrea, the hometown of the Minister for the Environment, Michael Smith TD. It would take another eight years for any substantial liberalisation to take effect.

Dublin County Council in 1995 approved a recommendation from its Taxi and Hackney Sub-Committee that 200 new licences should be issued, but this decision was rescinded following intensive lobbying and further blockades by taxi drivers. A similar recommendation in 1997 provoked a blockade of Dublin city on the day of the presidential election in October of that year.

The PD leader, Mary Harney, who was in coalition government with Fianna Fáil at the time, promised in an interview with the *Sunday Business Post* at Christmas 1998 that this would be the 'last Christmas of taxi mayhem' (RTÉ 1998). The taoiseach's brother, Noel Ahern TD, responded that 'I must record my shock and horror at some of the headline-seeking comments of the Tánaiste!' (McNally 1999:9). Fianna Fáil support for the taxi lobby centred around the fact that many taxi drivers gave freely of their services in bringing elderly and disabled supporters to the polls on election day (much as their support of publicans can be traced back to the latter's provision of free facilities for constituency group meetings), and from the fact that one, at least, of their most vocal TDs on the issue came from a taxi-driving family.

The PDs, on the other hand, were influenced by their economically liberal ideology (as seen earlier in the case of Desmond O'Malley), by the fact that they attracted the support of different sectional interests than Fianna Fáil, and by the fact that the PD minister of state with responsibility for the taxi sector, Bobby Molloy, represented a non-Dublin constituency. The coalition's review of their Programme for Government in summer 1999 mandated Molloy to proceed with a proposal to increase the taxi fleet by 3,100, but the Fianna Fáil pro-taxi lobby was to be appeased by the allocation of 2,600 of the new licences to existing taxi plate holders.

The taxi drivers reacted once again with strikes, protests and blockades. In the midst of the protest, four hackney drivers sought a judicial review challenging the minister's power to restrict the number of taxi licences. The High Court ruled in October 2000 that the minister was acting *ultra vires* in this regard. The government considered appealing the ruling to the Supreme Court, but, on the advice of the Attorney General, Michael McDowell, that such an appeal would be likely to fail, the government proceeded to legislate for the new reality by totally revoking all numerical restrictions on the issuing of taxi licences. The High Court – which is of course more independent of interest groups – had achieved what government at all levels had failed to do, and the sector was deregulated.

POLITICS AND THE RESOLUTION OF THE FISCAL CRISIS OF THE 1980S

Organised interests are known to be most harmful when they are strong enough to cause major disruptions, but not sufficiently encompassing to bear a significant fraction of the societal costs associated with pressing their own claims (Olson 1982). This closely describes the organisation of Irish and UK industrial relations in the 1960s and 1970s. In language reminiscent of Olson, Hardiman (1994:150) notes that over this period, 'no single bargaining group believed it had to pay any attention to the impact of its activities on the overall state of economic performance. Yet the cumulative consequences of everyone's bargaining practices were proving more and more harmful to overall economic performance.'

Proponents of the model of social partnership that emerged in Ireland in the mid- to late 1980s argue that participation in the process was sufficiently encompassing that the macroeconomic consequences of the pay deals reached would be taken into account. Whether or not one subscribes to this view of partnership (see Barry 2009a for references to the debate), it was critical along one dimension at least, in that it helped to provide political cover for the fiscal consolidation that was finally implemented in 1987.

Political wrangling had prevented earlier fiscal consolidation, as trenchant opposition criticism had encouraged the defection of government coalition partners or the withdrawal of support for minority governments over the earlier part of the 1980s. The newly developed social partnership process helped secure a way out of this prisoner's dilemma, as described by Ray MacSharry, the finance minister who implemented the fiscal cutbacks of the 1987–89 period:

> The NESC [National Economic and Social Council – the social partnership secretariat] analysis of what was wrong and the prescription of what needed to be done was agreed by all the social partners – including employers, trade unions, farmers and others – without dissent. . . . It set debt stabilisation as a minimum objective of fiscal policy, while relying on public spending cuts – not taxation – to achieve that adjustment. This was the most critical part of its overall strategy. The boldness of the NESC approach, the consensus of the social partners in backing it, and Fine Gael's generous promise of political support on fiscal policy all created a new opportunity to tackle, finally, the public finances. (MacSharry and White 2000:62)

The political cover provided by the Tallaght Strategy of then Fine Gael leader Alan Dukes was of course the other main factor in facilitating what all the previous governments of the decade had failed to achieve (MacSharry and White 2000, Chapter 3). Unfortunately, this will prove difficult to replicate in the future, given that Dukes was deposed as leader of Fine Gael shortly afterwards and his stance – which many commentators have lauded as patriotic – has been ridiculed as politically disastrous by others (e.g. Finlay 1998).

POLITICS AND POLICY ERRORS OVER THE BOOM PERIOD

This section discusses some of the policy errors that are now widely acknowledged to have been committed over the boom period. These include the long-standing pro-cyclical stance of Irish fiscal policy, the failure to counteract the property price bubble, the lax regulation of the Irish financial system and the extent to which the Irish tax structure was allowed to become so vulnerable to an economic downturn.

Government stabilisation policy must *by definition* be counter-cyclical; that is, it must act to dampen, rather than accentuate, the business cycle. Lane (2003) shows, however, that Ireland stands out among Organisation for Economic Co-operation and Development (OECD) countries as exhibiting above average pro-cyclicality. Nor is this just a recent phenomenon; pro-cyclicality had also been identified in the Irish budget deficits of the 1960s and 1970s (Lane 1998). Charlie McCreevy, who was finance minister from 1997 to 2004, mocked economists' warnings of the dangers of this stance with his widely publicised dictum: 'When I have money, I spend it; when I don't, I don't' (*The Economist* 2009:52).

Minister McCreevy's populist dismissal of the Economic and Financial Affairs Council's (ECOFIN) 2001 criticism of Ireland's fiscal over-stimulation represented a tragically missed opportunity to exploit external fiscal commitments as political cover to help overcome the political pressures to act in this way. The European Commission raised further concerns about the pro-cyclicality of policy in 2007. It is not insignificant that 2002 and 2007 were both election years in Ireland. However, instead of tightening fiscal policy, Minister McCreevy introduced further income tax reductions along with the profligate Special Savings Incentive Accounts (SSIA) scheme in 2001. While such tax reductions may have helped to keep the lid on wage demands in the earlier years of social partnership, their impact increasingly registered as a stimulus to aggregate demand, as the responsiveness of labour supply decreased (Barry and FitzGerald 2001). The legacy of McCreevy's approach, which continued after his departure, was that the country found itself with no stabilising margin when the global recession struck in 2008. The country was then forced into destabilising fiscal contraction.

With monetary policy handed over to the European Central Bank (ECB) since Ireland's adoption of the euro, and with the historically low interest rates that ensued, it became even more important that fiscal policy be used to dampen the property bubble that ultimately burst in 2007. Lane (1998:14) had warned that the fact that 'fiscal policy in Ireland has in general not behaved counter-cyclically . . . imposes costs on the Irish economy that are likely to become more severe in any future European monetary union'. However, Irish fiscal policy continued to be pro-cyclical. The construction sector became even more bloated by a series of property-related tax incentives, and it had grown to about twice the average size recorded in Europe and the USA by the time the bubble burst.

Irish banks and Irish tax revenues had also been allowed to become dangerously exposed to the construction sector. When the bubble burst, revenue sources such as stamp duty, capital gains tax and capital acquisitions tax all but dried up, while the banking system, which had also become overexposed to the property sector, had to be bailed out by the taxpayer. As Honohan (2006:68–71) points out:

> [A] financial system which reacts quickly to policy deviations can be a great discipline on governments that learn to anticipate these reactions and stay on the straight and narrow path . . . In moments of dangerous fiscal excess and competitiveness pressures, the financial system did in the past act as a watchdog. If, in the past, the watchdog was prone to bark too readily . . . thereby creating unnecessary currency crises, it is muzzled today, given EMU [Economic and Monetary Union] membership.

This suggests that careful financial regulation would have been even more important under EMU than it was beforehand. Instead, lax regulation allowed huge financial imbalances to emerge in the funding of the bubble (see Honohan 2006 for details).

Is there a political economy dimension to why the property boom was allowed to spiral so far out of control? To answer this, one must first ask who gained from the explosion in property prices. The answer is of course that it was principally property developers, even though many of them may have lost their fortunes in the subsequent meltdown. While house prices skyrocketed, the proportion of the price accounted for by the cost of the site rose from around 15 per cent – a level that is apparently normal by international standards – to between 40 and 50 per cent (Casey 2003). And property developers have long been major contributors to the Fianna Fáil party, as graphically illustrated by the preponderance of property development and construction company advertisers in the anniversary publication *Republican Days: 75 Years of Fianna Fáil*. This situation can only be rectified by reform and rigorous policing of the laws governing political contributions.

Another policy error committed over the boom period – though not directly related to the subsequent economic crisis – was the so-called 'decentralisation' programme announced unexpectedly by Minister for Finance Charlie McCreevy in his budget speech of December 2003. The plan envisaged that up to eight government departments and a number of state agencies, along with roughly one-third of all Dublin-based civil servants, would be relocated from Dublin. The initial timescale for the programme was to be the end of 2006. The process attracted huge resistance from those who were supposed to relocate, however, and appears to have been effectively terminated as a result of the 2008 OECD review of Irish public management. Given that the review actually said very little about the programme, this might be taken as another example of the search for political cover to facilitate a reversal of policy.

The decentralisation programme had all the characteristics of a political 'stroke' designed to garner electoral support in the regions. There was no documentation to suggest that any research or analysis of international experience had been carried out. The locations chosen bore no relationship to the National Spatial Strategy which the government had launched a year earlier. The use of the term 'decentralisation' outraged those who had long argued for – and used the term to refer to – the transfer of responsibility to democratically elected lower levels of government. And particularly worrying to many analysts was the threat it represented to the efficiency of the policy-making system.

One of the champions of decentralisation, the then minister for state at the Department of Finance, Tom Parlon, wrote that 'the advent of broadband, the internet and e-mail, instant messaging and other advanced communication technologies now means that for many business functions, location is irrelevant' (Irish Times 2005). Research shows, however, that this assuredly does not apply to strategy and policy development functions, where physical proximity remains crucial (Bannister and Connolly 2009).

CONCLUSIONS

Even politicians who desire to act in the public interest are constrained by the need to retain the support of the electorate, which requires paying particular attention to varying combinations of sectional interests and swing voters. The interests of some of these sectional groups are aligned – occasionally and, for the most part, temporarily – with the broader public good, and social welfare is likely to be enhanced when the political voice of these groups is strengthened. The strengthening of the export lobby by the introduction of EPTR in 1956 increased the likelihood of 'cascading reforms' because their interests were aligned with further trade liberalisation, as represented by Ireland's accession to the EEC in 1973. Astute reform-minded politicians know the importance of assembling a coalition whose interests are aligned with the reforms.

Of course the main political pressures for EEC entry in the period up to 1973 came from Irish agricultural interests. These interests became protectionist, and hostile to further global trade liberalisation, once EEC membership was achieved (Barry 2009b). The process of cascading reforms has been stymied by the privileged position attained by Irish agricultural interests in the Irish–European Union policy-making nexus. Political scientists refer to such a privileged position as emerging from a 'closed policy community' in which other interests – frequently those of consumers – are excluded to yield a false appearance of consensus. Some ideas on how such closed policy communities can be cracked open are advanced below.

Garret FitzGerald was quoted earlier in the chapter to the effect that strong vested interests frequently lead to decisions being taken which are against the interests of society as a whole. This problem can be reduced when 'political cover' is available to politicians who wish to move from growth-inhibiting to growth-enhancing policies. We saw that the overturning of protectionist policies was assisted by the political cover that Whitaker's document provided in 1958, while occasional changes of government can help in overcoming growth-inhibiting ideologies, as seen in the case of the second inter-party government of the 1950s. Indeed, this is one of the economic benefits that democratic systems have to offer. More prosaically, of course, as seen in the case of the Air Transport Bill of 1984, politicians also seek to cover up policy U-turns by denying that any U-turns have been made!

McCreevy as finance minister failed to avail of the political cover that ECOFIN's criticism of Ireland's pro-cyclical fiscal stance offered, and this was one of the major policy errors of the boom period. Of course, political cover to shift from growth-inhibiting to growth-enhancing policies is useful only if politicians choose to avail of it. We have identified, in the case of the Air Transport Bill, how important was the intervention of the group of reform-minded experts who became involved in the case, and how the lack of expert consultation was one of the factors behind the 'decentralisation' debacle. The Irish policy-making system is far too closed and insulated from critical debate to be able to produce consistently good decisions, and a further detrimental consequence of its closed and cartelised nature is the extent to which it facilitates regulatory capture.

How can we move from the present cartelised 'marketplace for ideas' – where good ideas have only restricted opportunities to challenge bad ones – to a more open and competitive one? A first step would be to introduce a clearer line of demarcation between where expert policy advice ends and political decisions begin. Its absence facilitates an evasion of responsibility on all sides. There is an analogy here with one of the principles identified as characterising good practice in the remit of competition authorities in Europe. As Laudati (1998: 405, emphasis added) notes:

> some national authorities have adopted a two-step procedure, with assessment of cases on competition grounds done by the independent antitrust authority, and assessment on other grounds, such as social and industrial policy, done by a government ministry. *This has the advantage of shielding those responsible for competition assessment from political pressure and of exposing political decisions through increased transparency.*

Valid criticisms, even from within the expert community, can be ignored when policy advice and decision making take place behind firmly closed doors. The 'marketplace for public-policy ideas' must become a more open and competitive one if policies are to be adequately scrutinised and decision making improved.

References

Baldwin, R. and Robert-Nicoud, F. (2007) 'A Simple Model of the Juggernaut Effect of Trade Liberalisation', Centre for Economic Policy Research Discussion Paper No. 6607.

Bannister, F. and Connolly, R. (2009) 'Government by Wire: Distance, Discourse and the Impact of Technology', in A.J. Meijer, K. Boersma and P. Wagenaar (eds) *ICTs, Citizens and Governance: After the Hype*, pp. 198–213. Amsterdam: IOS Press.

Barrett, S. (2009) *Deregulation and the Airline Business in Europe*. London: Routledge.

Barry, F. (2007) 'Third-Level Education, Foreign Direct Investment and Economic Boom in Ireland', *International Journal of Technology Management* 38(3): 198–219.

— (2009a) 'Social Partnership, Competitiveness and Exit from Fiscal Crisis', *Economic and Social Review* 40(1): 1–14.

— (2009b) 'Agricultural Interests and Irish Trade Policy over the Last Half-Century: A Tale Told Without Recourse to Heroes', Working Paper No. 91, Institute for British–Irish Studies, University College Dublin.

Barry, F. and FitzGerald, J. (2001) 'Irish Fiscal Policy in EMU and the Brussels–Dublin Controversy' in *Fiscal Policy in EMU: Report of the Swedish Committee on Stabilization Policy in EMU*, pp. 81–101. Stockholm: Statens Offentliga Utredningar.

Bew, P. and Patterson, H. (1982) *Seán Lemass and the Making of Modern Ireland 1945–66*. Dublin: Gill & Macmillan.

Boland, K. (1977) *Up Dev!* Dublin: Boland.

Casey, J. & Co. Ltd (2003) *Building Industry Bulletin: An Analysis of Economic and Marketing Influences on the Construction Industry*. Dublin: Hansa Print.

Coughlan, D. (1985) 'Mitchell Drops Jail Penalty in Air Fare Rules', *Irish Times*, 27 February, p. 5.

Denny, K. and Harmon, C. (2000) 'Education Policy Reform and the Return to Schooling from Instrumental Variables', Working Paper No. 7, Institute For Fiscal Studies Working Paper, London.

DoE (Department of Education) (1965) *Investment in Education: Report of the Survey Team Appointed by the Minister for Education in October 1962*. Dublin: Stationery Office.

DoT (Department of the Taoiseach) (1987) *Programme For National Recovery*. Dublin: Stationery Office.

Economist, The (2009) 'Ireland's Economy: The Party is Definitely Over', 21 March: 51–52.

Farrell, B. (1991) *Seán Lemass*. Dublin: Gill & Macmillan.

Finlay, F. (1998) *Snakes and Ladders*. Dublin: New Island.

FitzGerald, G. (1968) *Planning in Ireland*. Dublin: Institute of Public Administration.

— (2000) 'Diluting Lobbies and Unleashing Growth' in R. O'Donnell (ed.) *Europe: The Irish Experience*, pp. 111–22. Dublin: Institute of European Affairs.

Garvin, T. (2004) *Preventing the Future: Why was Ireland so Poor for so Long?* Dublin: Gill & Macmillan.

Hardiman, N. (1994) 'Pay Bargaining: Confrontation and Consensus', in D. Nevin (ed.) *Trade Union Century*, pp. 147–58. Dublin: Mercier Press.

Healy, J. (1988a) 'The Wild One', *Magill* March: 41–50.

— (1988b) 'The Wild One', *Magill* April: 41–9.

Honohan, P. (2006) 'To What Extent Has Finance Been a Driver of Ireland's Economic Success?', *Quarterly Economic Commentary* Winter: 59–72.

Irish Times (1985) 'Air Transport Bill Amended', 7 February, p.5.

— (2005) 'Good for the Regions and Good for Dublin', 10 June, p.16.

Lane, P. (1998) 'On the Cyclicality of Irish Fiscal Policy', *Economic and Social Review* 29(1): 1–16.

— (2003) 'The Cyclical Behaviour of Fiscal Policy: Evidence from the OECD', *Journal of Public Economics* 87: 2661– 75.

Laudati, L. (1998) 'Impact of Community Competition Law on Member State Competition Law', in S. Martin (ed.) *Competition Policies in Europe*, pp. 381–410. Amsterdam: North-Holland.

Lee, J. (1989) *Ireland 1912–1985: Politics and Society*. Cambridge: Cambridge University Press.

MacSharry, R. and White, P. (2000) *The Making of the Celtic Tiger: The Inside Story of Ireland's Booming Economy*. Dublin: Mercier Press.

McNally, F. (1999) 'Harney Taxi Comment Criticised', *Irish Times* 4 January, p.9.

O'Byrnes, S.(1984) 'Air Fares Bill is Anti-Consumer', *Irish Independent*, 27 June, p. 6.

OECD (2007) *Economic Policy Reforms: Going for Growth*. Paris: OECD.

— (2008) *Ireland: Towards an Integrated Public Service*. Paris: OECD.

Ó Gráda, C. (2008) 'Ireland in the 1950s', in M. Miley (ed.) *Fifty Years of Research and Development in Irish Farming and Food*, pp. 1–11. Carlow: Teagasc.

Olson, M. (1982) *The Rise and Decline of Nations*. New Haven, CT: Yale University Press.

O'Toole, F. (1994) *Meanwhile Back at the Ranch: The Politics of Irish Beef*. Dublin: New Island.

Rawnsley, A. (2007) 'The Reckoning' from *The Blair Years 1997–2007* (*Observer* Newspaper Supplement), 8 April [online]. Available http://www.guardian.co.uk/politics/2007/apr/08/tonyblair.labour16 (last accessed 17 October 2009).

RTÉ (1998) 'Government Set to Deregulate Pub and Taxi Licensing laws' [online]. Available http://www.rte.ie/news/1998/1226/harney.html (last accessed 13 November 2009).

— (2009) *The Late Late Show*, Friday 4 September (interviewer: R. Tubridy). Dublin: RTÉ.

Walsh, J. (2009) *The Politics of Expansion: The Transformation of Education Policy in the Republic of Ireland, 1957–72*. Manchester: Manchester University Press.

Weir, S. (2009) 'The Irish Taxi Lobby', paper delivered to the Annual Conference of Political Studies Association of Ireland, Liverpool Hope University, 9–11 October.

Chapter 3

Forming Ireland's Industrial Development Authority

Paul F. Donnelly

INTRODUCTION

Taking path dependence as a lens (see Donnelly 2009), this chapter traces the creation and (re)production of Ireland's Industrial Development Authority (IDA). The story that unfolds takes as its starting point Ireland's turn to protectionism following the general election of 1932, and charts the increasing investment by successive governments in the machinery of protection and the creation of the IDA in 1949 as an autonomous agency within an institutional matrix focused on protection. The story then moves on to tell of the gradual shift away from protection towards free trade, a repositioning that witnessed the emergence of the IDA as the pre-eminent agency of state dealing with industrial development and its re-creation as a state-sponsored organisation. The story traces the growing commitment to the IDA in terms of political, institutional and monetary resources, with the IDA in turn reinforcing that commitment through delivery on its objectives, largely in the shape of new job creation.

Essentially, the story is illustrative of increasing returns reinforcing the chosen path of industrial development, itself reinforcing the IDA as the principal instrument through which such development occurs. However, as the story continues to unfold, the increasing reliance on foreign investment to meet targets, at the expense of indigenous industry, eventually surfaces as a challenge to the IDA in the early 1980s and culminates in the IDA being split in 1994 into separate agencies: Forfás, IDA Ireland and Forbairt (now Enterprise Ireland). (For a more detailed account, see Donnelly 2007:109–271.)

Forfás is the policy advisory and co-ordination board for enterprise, trade and science and technology in Ireland, and in it are vested the state's legal powers for industrial promotion and the development of trade and technology. Through Forfás, powers are assigned to Enterprise Ireland for the development and promotion of the indigenous industry sector and to IDA Ireland for the promotion of inward investment.

Prior to moving on to the IDA story proper, a brief insight into path dependence theory would be of benefit.

PATH DEPENDENCE AS LENS

Recognising calls for more processual and historically informed theorising, path dependence theory (Arthur 1994; David 1985, 1987, 1994; North 1990) offers a way of articulating the organisational as an ongoing dynamic over more dominant ways of thinking and knowing that are more static. Those who are not familiar with the path dependence approach think that it is no more than recognition that 'history matters', such that path dependence is equated with 'past dependence' (Antonelli 1997). However, path dependence characterises a special type of organisational process, at the heart of which is an entrapping process that, over time and (partly) dependent on prior choices and events, radically limits the scope of action (Sydow *et al.* 2009). Viewed as an idea through which 'history' is commonly made visible, the path dependence approach holds that a historical path of choices has the character of an irreversible branching process with a self-reinforcing dynamic in which positive feedback increases, while at the same time the costs of reversing previous decisions increase, and the scope for reversing them narrows sequentially, as the development proceeds. Thus, preceding steps in a particular direction induce further movement in the same direction 'because the *relative* benefits of the current activity compared with other possible options increase over time' (Pierson 2000:252, emphasis in original), thereby eventually leading into a non-reversible state of total inflexibility or lock-in (David 1985).

As Mahoney (2000:511) notes, path-dependent analyses have at least three defining characteristics: (1) they entail the study of causal processes that are very sensitive to events that occur early on in an overall historical sequence; (2) given the contingent character of these early historical events, they cannot be explained by preceding events or initial conditions; and (3) when contingent historical events occur, path-dependent sequences are reflected in essentially deterministic causal patterns. Adapting Mahoney (2001:112), these characteristics are elaborated into an analytic structure based on his view that path dependence refers to 'a specific type of explanation that unfolds through a series of sequential stages', as shown in Figure 3.1.

'Antecedent conditions' refers to historical factors that define available options and shape selection processes. These conditions characterise a wide range of actions, where decisions made cannot be predicted by past events or initial conditions. However, to a degree, antecedent conditions are also influenced by the past (Child 1997), in that they are influenced by historically framed and imprinted contingency and not by wholly unrestricted choice (Sydow *et al.* 2009). Reflecting antecedent conditions, then, at least two options are open for selection at the critical juncture, which represents the point when one option is chosen and the dynamics of self-reinforcing processes are set into motion.

The choice is consequential because it leads to the creation of an evolving and narrowing organisational path that, building into structural persistence, becomes increasingly difficult to reverse over time. It is here that positive feedback or increasing returns become active through self-reinforcing dynamics of set-up or fixed costs (the higher the costs, the greater the incentive for individuals and organisations to stay on path), learning effects (experience of an existing path leads to higher returns from its continuing use), co-ordination effects (benefits of a given path increase as others adopt the same option) and adaptive expectations (self-fulfilling character of 'picking the right horse') (Arthur 1994:112). Thus it is that, once a specific selection has been made, it becomes increasingly difficult with the passing of time to return to the initial critical juncture when at least two options were still available. As noted by Arthur (1989, 1994), increasing returns to adoption are realised not at a single point of time but rather dynamically, such that each step along a particular organisational path produces consequences that increase the relative attractiveness of that path for the next round. As effects begin to accumulate, they generate a powerful cycle of self-reinforcing activity, contributing to lock-in: flexibility becomes severely constrained and the organisational path is fixed and takes on a quasi-deterministic character. Sydow, Schreyögg and Koch (2009) suggest that organisational paths, because of their social character, require a modified conception of lock-in. Thus, instead of a fully determined lock-in, Sydow, Schreyögg and Koch (2009:695) argue for conceiving of lock-in 'as a matter of degree, accounting for variance in the actual practicing of the organizational path'.

Figure 3.1 Analytic structure of path-dependent explanation

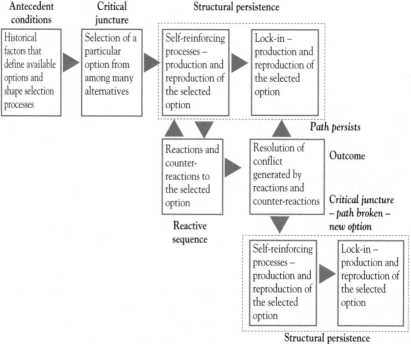

Source: adapted from Mahoney (2001:113).

The continued existence of an organisational path over time has the potential to activate a sequence of causally linked events that, when activated, materialise separately from the factors that originally produced the path. In such reactive sequences (Mahoney 2001), which comprise chains of events that are both temporally ordered and causally connected, the final event in the sequence is the outcome of interest. A reactive sequence is often set in motion by an initial challenge to the existing organisational path, with counter-reactions to this opposition then driving ensuing events in the sequence. Reactive sequences are typically marked by properties of reaction and counter-response, as patterns put in place during critical juncture periods are resisted or supported. Although such resistance may not be path-breaking, it can trigger an outcome or critical juncture that results in the development of a new organisational path.

With the above framework in mind, we now turn to the IDA's story.

EMERGING WITHIN PROTECTIONISM: CREATING THE IDA

With a sluggish economy, the Great Depression in train and economic nationalism on the rise internationally, two possible paths to economic development were on the table at the time of the 1932 Irish general election, namely free trade or protectionism. With the protectionist platform winning the day, the new government embarked on a path that continued in force for almost two and a half decades, underpinned by Fianna Fáil, the party advocating protectionism, winning five successive general elections and remaining in power for almost two decades (see Figure 3.2).

As it was, Fianna Fáil invested significant political capital in protectionism as the means to achieving economic independence, appealing to economic nationalism and engaging in an economic war with Great Britain (Kennedy et al. 1988). Additionally, the government set about building the protectionist machine through passing legislation and establishing appropriate organisations. Through layering (Thelen 2003), legislation (e.g. Control of Manufactures Act 1932; Control of Prices Act 1932; Control of Imports Act 1934) and supporting organisations (e.g. Industrial Credit Corporation, 1933; Prices Commission, 1937) were added to partially re-negotiate elements of the protectionist machinery, while strengthening it in the process. These various legislative moves also exhibit learning effects, as can be seen in the adaptations made to various pieces of legislation constituting the machine (e.g. Control of Manufactures Act 1934; Control of Prices Act 1937; Control of Imports Act 1937). The investment in these legislative and organisational assets, which were specific to protectionism, added to the resilience of the institution and deepened the equilibrium established by the turn to self-sufficiency. Further, co-ordination effects and adaptive expectations were evident in the support for this infrastructure, not just by government, but also by industrialists.

By the late 1940s, protectionism was coming under pressure because of its inefficiency, the saturated domestic market, migration from the land, increasing unemployment and emigration, and a deteriorating balance of payments (Dáil

Debates, vol. 119, cols 1584–5, 9 March 1950). While continuing with the policy of protectionism, a new Fine Gael-led inter-party government (1948–51) sought to combat its ills through engaging a more proactive industrial policy centred in a new organisation, the IDA (*Irish Independent* 1949:5; Dáil Debates, vol. 119, cols 1586–95, 9 March 1950).

Figure 3.2 The protectionist path, 1932–1958

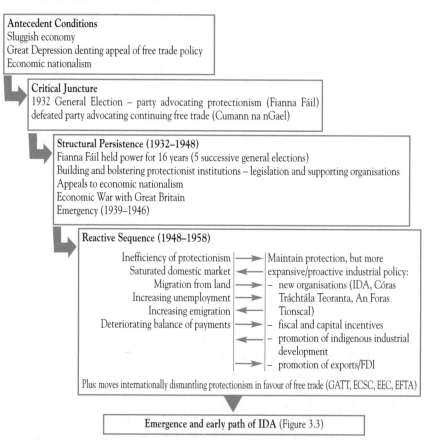

Source: Donnelly (2007:148).

In establishing the IDA in 1949, the government chose between establishing an autonomous body and the existing civil service arrangements, opting for the former and investing in a path to bring about its creation (see Figure 3.3). That path involved high set-up costs, not to mention adaptive expectations, entailing negotiating the proposal within government and the civil service and then selling the idea to the media, to industrialists, to members of the coalition parties and to the party faithful. It entailed recruiting the IDA executive (i.e. Authority) members and establishing the IDA as an administrative body in advance of any legislation passing through the Oireachtas, itself a large investment should the initiative have failed in its passage through the legislative process at any of the formal veto points. It entailed drafting legislation and steering its passage through the legislative process, with each stage dependent on the passage of preceding stages. Indeed, in proposing legislation to the Oireachtas, government had to be sure that it would have the support of its own members to ensure safe passage, whatever about the position taken by the opposition.

Figure 3.3 The IDA's early path

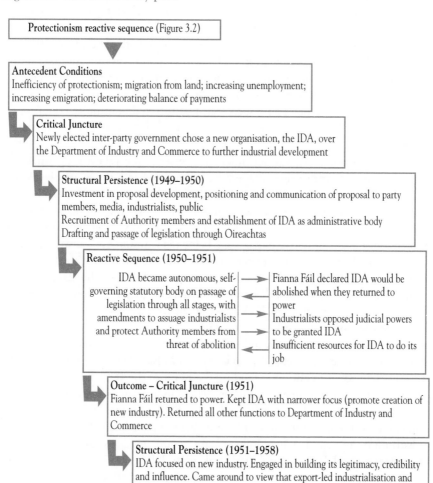

Source: Donnelly (2007:151).

Thus, even before coming to the Oireachtas, there were already significant start-up costs and expectations as to what the IDA would achieve. Such was the investment that, on once again returning to power in 1951, rather than abolish the IDA, as it had threatened to do (Dáil Debates, vol. 119, cols 1618–19, 9 March 1950), Fianna Fáil instead refocused the IDA on industrial development, taking away the administrative role that was seen as best resting with civil servants and freeing it to focus on promoting industrial development (Dáil Debates, vol. 126, cols 1514–15, 12 July 1951). Following this critical juncture, the IDA became established as part of the nascent industrial development institutional landscape.

The IDA represented layering, in the sense that the protectionist institutional matrix was left in place, and this layer, while an attempt to improve matters, represented learning effects and further investment, by way of co-ordination effects and adaptive expectations, in making protectionism work. Thus, from 1932, an interdependent institutional matrix was built in support of protectionism, resulting in quite substantial complementarities, with institutional arrangements mutually reinforcing each other. In essence, institutional arrangements constituted a stable equilibrium, its resilience being such that institutional continuity conditioned change and exhibited strong tendencies towards only incremental adjustment (Pierson 2004).

A critical feature of path-dependent processes is the relative 'openness' or 'permissiveness' of early stages in a sequence compared with the relatively 'closed' or 'coercive' nature of later stages (Abbott 1997; Mahoney 2001). This can be seen in the sequence that emerged in reaction to protectionism, where new conditions were overwhelming the specific mechanisms that previously reproduced the protectionist path. Tentative moves were being made towards an outward-looking orientation, albeit not in any concerted or co-ordinated fashion at the outset and from within the definite confines of protectionism. Initially, the IDA favoured protectionism to encourage indigenous industrial development. However, through experience on the ground, the IDA's view gradually changed to seeing export-led industrialisation as the only way to develop the Irish economy and foreign investment as a source for such industrialisation, resulting in its recommendation that the restrictions on foreign capital be eased (Walsh 1983, cited in Girvin 1989: 180–1). The government, in extending the remit of the IDA, began to actively encourage foreign investment to fill gaps where indigenous industry had failed to seize opportunities. Subsequently, further modifications were made to facilitate foreign investment, with industrial policy moving from a focus on import substitution and indigenous industry to encouraging exports and foreign investment (Dáil Debates, vol. 163, col. 453, 2 July 1957). Thus, reflecting learning effects, co-ordination effects and adaptive expectations, we see a growing shift in policy, itself requiring the investment of political capital in articulating, supporting and institutionalising that shift.

Following North (1990:98–9), therefore, the continuity of protectionism was not inevitable given that the mechanisms of reproduction were subsequently eroded over the course of the reactive sequence that paved the way for the emergence of a new equilibrium. Throughout the late 1940s and the 1950s, the decreasing returns to the protectionist path, when combined with the effects of population movement, began to erode the mechanisms of reproduction that generated its continuity. While government sought to bolster protectionism with mechanisms that included new state organisations (e.g. the IDA (1949); Córas Tráchtála Teoranta (1951); An Foras Tionscal (1952)) and incentives (e.g. capital and training grants, tax relief on exports) to promote industrial development, this was insufficient to address the decreasing returns. Of interest is that institutional responses in support of protectionism, to include the nascent IDA, proved plastic enough to fit with an outward-looking reactive sequence and institutional matrix developing in parallel, a sequence driven by the need to deal with new conditions, which included increasing moves towards free trade and mobile investment capital internationally.

CHANGING POLICY: FROM PROTECTIONISM TO FREE TRADE

As has already been seen, the rules of the game were changing through the 1950s and successive governments were becoming more frustrated with protectionism in the face of increasing inefficiencies. Despite efforts to actively encourage industrial development and the development of exports, the inefficiencies of the protectionist path were proving immune to such incremental change (DoF 1958a:2). It was only with the government's Programme for Economic Expansion (DoF 1958b) that all these efforts were pulled together into a coherent policy of outward-looking economic development, underpinned by industrial development that embraced export-oriented foreign direct investment (FDI). In marking a critical juncture, this programme represented a significant, path-shifting investment on the part of government in a highly visible policy that effectively sounded the death knell for protectionism (see Figure 3.4).

Essentially, the move towards a more outward-looking economic development policy entailed considerable start-up costs, particularly political and particularly for Fianna Fáil, which had preached protectionism for two decades. This represented a fundamental shift in policy, and government had to both divest itself of protectionism and embrace a more open policy that included accepting foreign investment as a vehicle through which to achieve both industrial and economic development. Further, it meant government investing in promoting this highly visible policy change, investing in the creation of new meaning around the new policy and investing in its implementation. It meant considerable start-up costs for the civil service in reorienting itself away from managing protectionism to putting in place new institutions to manage a more open economy. It also meant investing in engagement with ongoing moves internationally towards freer trade (i.e. General Agreement on Tariffs and Trade (GATT), European Coal and Steel Community (ECSC), European Economic Community (EEC), European Free Trade Area (EFTA)) and the changes such engagement would require, such as the development of complementary policies, the negotiation and signing of treaties, and the implementation of these treaties. Further, it meant investment in the development, promotion and implementation of successor economic development plans that built on, and so reinforced, the path established by the critical juncture (i.e. Second Programme for Economic Expansion (DoF 1963, 1964); Third Programme for Economic and Social Development (DoF 1969)). Equally, these investments were not just monetary; they were also in reorienting the collective mindset, disengaging it from the policy of the past and engaging it with the policy of the future.

Figure 3.4 Reorienting the path from protectionism to outward-looking economic development

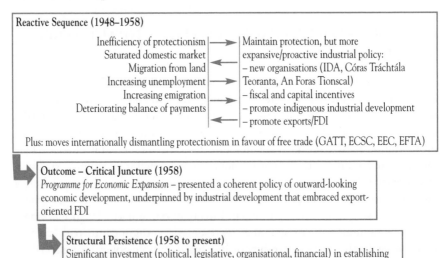

Source: Donnelly (2007:207).

From a policy learning perspective (Pierson 1993), Ireland's story of economic development is illustrative of policy constituting 'important rules of the game, influencing the allocation of economic and political resources, modifying the costs and benefits associated with alternative . . . strategies, and consequently altering ensuing' development (Pierson 1993:596). While government shaped the outward-looking economic development policy, this policy can be seen, following Pierson (1993), to have subsequently produced politics, with the policy serving to shape politics. This being so, economic development policy can be seen to have produced resources and incentives (e.g. the IDA, the need to create jobs) for government, with positive feedback (e.g. jobs created) influencing continued investment in the policy. Such policy feedback facilitated the expansion in scope and scale of economic development, with economic development policy shaping industrial development policy, which, in turn, shaped later developments and served to reinforce the path taken.

The government's main objective in terms of industrial policy was to create the conditions necessary for private enterprise to drive industrial development. Thus, in terms of adaptive expectations, we see it explicitly expressed as part of government policy that protection is increasingly untenable in a world that is sensed to be moving towards free trade and in opposition to an industrial development policy that both welcomes foreign participation and is export-oriented. This new approach to economic development established the path to be followed and it is in line with this critical juncture that moves along the path of export-led industrialisation and economic co-operation with Europe were subsequently made. It was in this context that the IDA was created.

FROM MINOR STATUTORY BODY TO MAJOR STATE-SPONSORED AGENCY: BUILDING THE IDA

The policy change favouring free trade also marked a critical juncture for the IDA (see Figure 3.5) in focusing its efforts and positioning it as the focal organisation in attracting FDI (DoF 1958b:40), effectively turning it into an investment promotion agency, with co-ordination effects and adaptive expectations seeing increases in the organisation's scope and resources through the success of its efforts. In the years immediately following this policy change, and illustrative of learning effects, co-ordination effects and adaptive expectations, the IDA invested in marketing campaigns and opened offices in the USA and Europe that garnered foreign investment for the country, such investment garnering further funding for the IDA to facilitate its work, each move reinforcing further moves along the burgeoning path of FDI as a means of achieving industrial development.

In terms of complementary institutional developments, besides the financial incentives machinery (i.e. various grant schemes), other legislative moves complemented and facilitated the IDA's work, particularly in the area of taxation (i.e. export profits tax relief). Through the 1950s and 1960s, the IDA gradually built the country's reputation as a base for manufacturing industry and its reputation and identity as the country's industrial development organisation. This period acted as the 'pilot stage' in attracting new industries to the country, albeit the pilot provided much of the manufacturing sector's diversification and growth (O'Neill 1972:44).

The IDA's success met with operational limitations, however (Little 1967a). As matters stood, the IDA operated within the tight constraints of the civil service bureaucracy, with no control over the assignment or withdrawal of its staff, nor over its structure. On the one hand, the IDA was being asked to play an increasingly demanding, key role in the country's economic development, while on the other being handicapped through not having the operational autonomy to deliver on that role. To bring about change, in the late 1960s the IDA engaged US consultants Arthur D. Little (1967a, b) to assist it in a major reappraisal of Ireland's industrial development apparatus. The review concluded that achieving full employment rested on encouraging foreign firms to establish operations in the country, requiring more than just charging the IDA with the undertaking; the IDA would also need far greater resources than were given it, in addition to the capacity and flexibility to control its own operations.

Figure 3.5 The IDA's path from minor statutory body to major state-sponsored super-agency

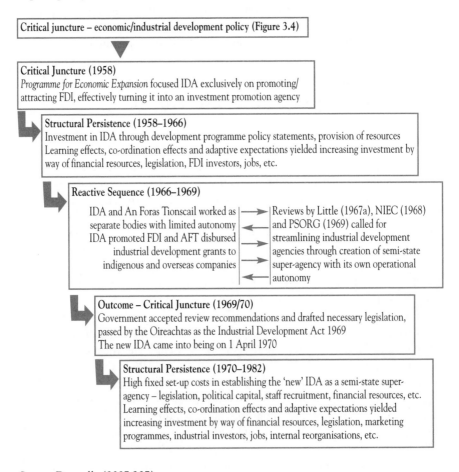

Source: Donnelly (2007:207).

All in all, Little (1967a) represented a blueprint that was subsequently followed in re-creating the IDA as an autonomous state-sponsored organisation, charged with the key task of co-ordinating and delivering on Ireland's industrial development policy. Indeed, Padraic White (White 2006) noted that it was the IDA itself that both engineered the Little review and directed its content:[1]

> Ted O'Neill and company commissioned A. D. Little to write the script. They basically wrote the script. Because they came to the limits of what you could do in the Civil Service. Ted O'Neill said, 'We couldn't hire a typist. We'd six international offices. Imagine all the expenditures involved, promotions involved, tied with the civil service. We basically commissioned A. D. Little. We basically wrote the script for them. We basically wrote the legislation. The government of the day said, "Yes, we want a super-agency that will take this thing to a new level." That was the 1960s. It was an amazing act. [. . .] I think the influence of people like Ted O'Neill and Joe Walsh as trusted public servants within the Department of Industry and Commerce, I think they had a huge influence. As I say, they were trusted and that thread of how they ended up with A.D. Little and they said basically, 'we need a new agency'.

Reviews by the National Industrial Economic Council (NIEC 1968) and the Public Services Organisation Review Group (PSORG 1969) echoed and reinforced the reorganisation recommended in Little (1967a). On foot of these reviews, and by way of critical juncture, the Industrial Development Act 1969 streamlined agencies dealing with industrial development and concentrated the expertise within an expanded IDA having full control over its own internal operations. It gave the IDA the status of a state-sponsored organisation with national responsibility for the furtherance of industrial development, in addition to consolidating decision-making power concerning industrial development within the organisation. Government maintained overall control through its power to appoint the IDA's members, its broad responsibility for setting industrial policy and its broad control over the organisation's budget. Additionally, government proactively legitimised the IDA's role and position, making it clear through the reorganisation legislation that both industrial development and the IDA's central role in it represented a vital, long-term programme for Ireland to which it was committed.

Having invested considerable set-up costs in re-creating the IDA, in terms of, for example, consultants' reports, political capital, legislation and dissolution of agencies, the new IDA came into being as a state-sponsored body on 1 April 1970. From enactment of the establishing legislation there followed considerable investment in a highly specific asset, namely an autonomous industrial development organisation, which entailed physical specificity (e.g. the IDA as an industrial development organisation, industrial development legislation, policies and programmes, party political platforms on industrial development – all of which involved design characteristics particular to industrial development); human specificity (e.g. the IDA's specialised knowledge of the industrial development environment resulting from learning by doing, and its special relationships with various actors resulting from repeated interactions with these actors); and dedicated assets, where the value of all assets derived from continuance of industrial development to which they were applied (Pierson 2004).

Now vested with the formulation and implementation of national and regional industrial policy and freed from the shackles of the civil service to manage its own affairs, the IDA put in place systems, structures and institutional arrangements that have persisted over time. Re-creating the IDA entailed introducing a new organisation structure and meeting its expanded mandate, which saw the organisation engage in a major recruitment drive. In seeing industrial development as a co-operative process, requiring the participation of a range of development organisations, the IDA from early on saw value in building contacts throughout the country and devoted significant staff resources to managing them through representations of key personnel on a range of main boards, committees and organisations (e.g. Córas Tráchtála Teoranta, Shannon Development, Institute of Public Administration, Irish Council of European Movement, Ireland–Japan Economic Association, Regional Development Organisations, County Development Teams). It also decided to carry out many of its executive functions through committees, with delegated grant-giving powers, on which other interests participated, e.g. the Confederation of Irish Industry (CII), the Irish Export Board (IEB), research institutes, universities and government departments.

The new IDA also invested in creating a Janus-faced organisation (see Figure 3.6), with one face managing the needs of and relationship with industry and the other face managing the needs of and relationship with government, very much placing the IDA itself in the position of a co-ordinating mechanism, the benefits of its activities being enhanced through co-ordinating with the activities of both government and industrial investors. Having the ear of government, the IDA was active in generating further complementarities with other policy areas, such as education and physical infrastructure. As the increasingly credible experts, the IDA was in the unique position of being able to say to government what was needed to facilitate and encourage industrial development and the delivery of new jobs, such that government listened and acted accordingly. Arguably, the IDA was able to use its position to generate increasing complementarities, thereby increasing its value and reinforcing its own position.

Building on its learning since promotional activity commenced in 1955, the new IDA adopted a more intensive and focused method of promotion, encompassing a more selective approach, direct marketing, advertising and public relations. Having identified a sector or niche area, the task was then to single out the winning companies before they became more widely known and attractive to other development agencies. Early on, the IDA recognised the importance of putting 'our eggs in the best baskets' (McLoughlin 1972:35) and saw opportunity in influencing the make-up of foreign investment through identifying priority industrial sectors and established leaders in these sectors to arrive at a portfolio of investment possibilities to which the organisation applied its marketing effort

(IDA 1970/71:15–16; O'Neill 1972). The attractiveness of industrial sectors was assessed not only according to the criterion of commercial viability, but also on indicators of national economic benefit, to include: growth potential in international markets; potential for long-term commercial stability; low probability of technological obsolescence; potential for high added value in terms of use of indigenous raw materials or manufactured products; high content of skilled male labour in total employment; and low capital-intensity, or if capital-intensity was high, good potential for linkage or spin-off benefits (IDA 1974; McLoughlin 1972; O'Neill 1972).

Figure 3.6 The IDA as a Janus-faced co-ordinating mechanism in 1970

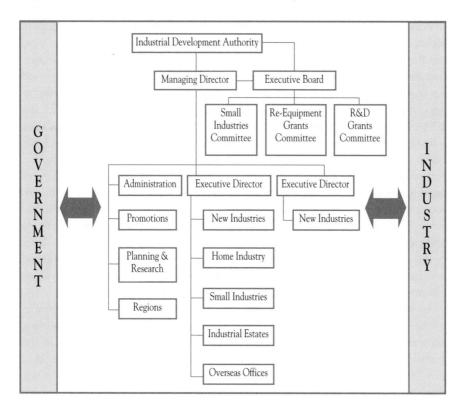

Source: Donnelly (2007:179).

Having ascertained priority sectors, the process moved on to identifying and rating established leading companies according to the criteria of commercial soundness, growth potential, ability to fund new investments, locational mobility and history of responding to advantages of new investment locations (O'Neill 1972). As noted by O'Neill (1972:46–7), in the case of just one product area, this process whittled

21,000 companies at the start down to 1,235 candidate companies based on the criteria of interest to the IDA. Projects were rejected where: the viability of the parent company was in question; the capital intensity would be too great for a small country with limited resources; there would be an undue negative effect on the environment; Irish political or social mores would reprove the product produced; and where low-cost labour would be the only consideration. Projects considered particularly worthy came from companies that were leaders in their field, were high-tech, high-skill and high-added value, offered long-term growth potential, used the country's natural resources, presented spin-off prospects to existing firms, provided jobs quickly, located in less developed parts of the country and helped sell Ireland as an FDI location (Telesis 1982: 173).

This process yielded a number of priority sectors for future industrial development, among which were electronics, pharmaceuticals and medical technologies, in effect representing the early part of a sequence that would later yield significant results. For example, the IDA's sectoral strategy for the electronics industry was itself formulated in 1974, a strategy which, over the years, proved successful in the creation of path-dependent industrial clustering due to agglomeration or co-ordination effects. As noted by Killeen (1979:7), '[i]n 1974, the IDA identified the electronics sector as one which would expand rapidly in the following years. We prepared a special development strategy for the sector which has been actively implemented.' Ireland's comparative advantage in information technology was not a given; rather, it was created through a sequence of events unfolding over time, for example the IDA's strategy to focus effort on developing this sector for inward investment, successes in attracting high-profile companies in the sector, etc., each of these events reinforcing the path-dependent industrial clustering and yielding increasing returns due to agglomeration or co-ordination effects. Prior to the selective strategy that emerged within the IDA in the early 1970s, Ireland had no electronics industry to speak of, but by 1982, some 130 of the world's leading electronics companies were manufacturing in Ireland (Haughey 1982).

In effect, and revealing learning effects and adaptive expectations in refining a strategy it had pursued since the 1960s, the IDA went about attracting leading companies in the field, a strategy that contributed to increasing returns in the spatial location of production (Arthur 1994; Krugman 1991). These companies in turn attracted suppliers, skilled labour, specialised services and appropriate infrastructure, and contributed to the development of social networks, which facilitated the exchange of information and expertise. Further, the presence of these companies and the concentration of these factors contributed to Ireland's attractiveness for other firms in the sector, in effect acting like magnets and influencing the locational decisions and investments of these other companies.

Thus, working from within the constrained choice-set presented by the chosen path to achieving industrial development, namely the active sourcing of foreign investment to create sustainable jobs, the IDA, on the back of a strong planning process and cognisant of its limited resources, prioritised industrial sectors and targeted leading companies that the organisation expected would deliver a high national economic and social benefit into the future. In essence, and building on the learning gained from its earlier promotional efforts in using leading companies to attract others, co-ordination effects and adaptive expectations came into play in adopting this selective, targeted approach, with success over time reinforcing the approach such that it became self-fulfilling. That is, the approach delivered investment and jobs, which reinforced continued investment in the approach, which delivered further investment and jobs as agglomeration effects came into play, with the winning companies attracting investment from others in the sector, this positive feedback itself reinforcing the value of the IDA as an industrial development organisation, especially when set against the poor performance of indigenous industry.

By way of delivering results for government, and also by way of focusing the organisation on its mandate, following its re-creation in 1970, the IDA instituted a highly quantified approach that was new to state agencies at the time, namely annual targets for the creation of jobs, which were made public in advance and subsequently reported on so that the organisation could be seen to be performing in delivering results (MacSharry and White 2000:194). These highly visible performance measures served to reinforce the chosen path to industrial development, with achievement of targets being evidence to government and the public that the IDA were delivering results, which encouraged continued investment in the IDA, in turn delivering on targets and so on. Such were the co-ordination effects afforded by the IDA in terms of job creation that, in tandem with learning effects and adaptive expectations, the organisation's requests for exchequer funding, for both incentives and administration, were invariably looked upon favourably.

In terms of programme development (e.g. re-equipment and modernisation, product and process development, service industries, project identification, enterprise development), the IDA's programmes are illustrative of the learning by doing that occurred over time and that served to consolidate its position as the national industrial development organisation. All are indicative of its capacity to learn and to innovate, in the process ensuring its continued relevance as the focal point in co-ordinating industrial development policy formulation and implementation. Effectively, over time, the IDA developed programmes suited to the particular industrial development challenges it faced, illustrating that a significant amount of learning by doing had occurred in the increasingly complex industrial development system.

While the 1950s and 1960s were about building and consolidating the IDA's identity, credibility and legitimacy, following the critical juncture that created the 'new' IDA super-agency, the 1970s was a period of building the organisational form and further consolidating the organisation's credibility and legitimacy. The decade was capped by a progress report (IDA 1979:3-4) citing a litany of achievements, including an expanded, autonomous organisation employing almost seven hundred highly skilled staff, client company investment of £2.7bn (compared to £130m in the 1960s) for a total grant commitment of £831m and job approvals of 192,000 (compared to 45,500 for the 1960s), with 99,000 in domestic industry. To all intents and purposes, it appeared as though the significant investment of resources in the IDA, allied with its own learning and the increased co-ordination of policies and activities to fit with its interests, was delivering according to expectations, this positive feedback reinforcing the IDA as an organisational form. However, from the relative glory of the 1970s, the IDA moved to more challenging times in the 1980s.

BACK TO THE FUTURE: FROM STATE-SPONSORED SUPER-AGENCY TO AGENCY FOCUSED ON FDI

From a path-dependence perspective, the story moves from one of structural persistence to a reactive sequence that culminates in a critical juncture leading to the reorganisation of the IDA in 1994. According to Wickham (1983), Ireland's success in attracting FDI lay in the very particular situation of the IDA. As has already been noted, the organisation was effectively the sole industrial development body in the country: it had, to Telesis (1982), remained unchallenged by any power centre either in the country or outside it; it was shielded from political interference that would have impacted both policy formulation and implementation; its 'discretionary' decision making was suited to dealing with private enterprise; and it was in a position to legitimate itself to all stakeholders as fulfilling an important national task.

Though Wickham's (1983) observation points to success with foreign investment, concerns gradually emerged throughout the 1970s about an over-reliance on such investment and its tenuous links with the economy, not to mention a dualistic industrial structure and the influence of external interests on national sovereignty (e.g. Cooper and Whelan 1973; *The Economist* 1977; Jacobsen 1978; Kennedy and Dowling 1975; Long 1976). These concerns led the National Economic and Social Council (NESC) in 1978 to commission a five-part review to ensure that government industrial policy was suited to creating an internationally competitive industrial base in Ireland.

One of the reviews, Telesis (1982), had the greatest impact of all in regard to the IDA and to industrial development policy. After a decade of relative glory through the 1970s, Telesis brought the IDA's legitimacy into question at a time when the country was experiencing the effects of a global recession, a poor foreign investment climate, mounting domestic economic problems and increasing unemployment (IDA 1980–83; MacSharry and White 2000; Telesis 1982).

In assessing Ireland's then industrial policy, Telesis was complimentary on a number of fronts. It considered that the country had a clearly articulated, very advanced, extensive and consistent industrial policy, with inventive and energetic state agencies devising programmes to deliver on policy goals. With particular reference to the IDA, the review observed that it had succeeded in developing what was arguably the most dynamic, active, efficient and effective organisation of its kind in the world, with a well-earned reputation as the leading organisation in the field.

However, the Telesis review also noted that weaknesses in industrial policy had contributed to weaknesses in the country's industrial structure, thus limiting the success of the country's industrial development. The review's main criticism was that industrial development had largely depended on FDI, while indigenous industry languished. It criticised the practice of creating and counting job approvals over the creation and counting of actual jobs delivered, commenting that, while there was value politically to government and motivationally to the IDA in touting job approval targets, the gap between approval and reality had the effect of creating expectations in the general population that were then not met. And from a governance perspective, it noted that, legally, government departments were responsible for determining strategy, with the IDA and other development agencies responsible for strategy implementation. However, the reality was that the IDA formulated strategy in line with its job creation mandate, while government departments were lacking in both staff numbers and information sufficient to formulate strategy and oversee the implementation of this strategy by the relevant agencies.

The overall impact of Telesis was to refine both the IDA and industrial development policy (DIC 1984; IDA 1981–83). Changes were bounded and incremental, with the IDA still very much the lead industrial development organisation. The outcome of Telesis and the debate it engendered was the setting of an adjusted course, building on past success and reflecting the lessons learned from experience gained to that point. In many respects, given the complexity of the problems it confronted – a worsening fiscal crisis and increasing unemployment – government relied heavily on the pre-existing industrial development policy and organisational framework, adjusting at the margins to accommodate the demands of the situation (Pierson 1993). The above tallies with Hall's (1989:11) proposition that 'prior experience with related policies' is such that 'states will be predisposed towards policies with which they already have some favourable experience'.

While the global recession of the early 1980s, and its effects, engendered an industrial policy debate, the result was on-path responses entailing layering onto the existing industrial development institution. The IDA remained the focal organisation, foreign investment remained an important source for jobs and greater attention was now to be paid to indigenous industry, with the IDA and government coalescing around this on-path response through their collective effort at articulating an industrial development policy that validated the approach taken over the preceding decades and that acknowledged the accrued learning that facilitated incremental change. It was not the case that the IDA had not been doing anything with indigenous industry; rather collective learning suggested it needed to invest more into what it was already doing.

With Telesis still very much in the background, the late 1980s witnessed a number of threats to the IDA in terms of its position as the central industrial development organisation (MacSharry and White 2000:212), while the early 1990s witnessed yet another review of industrial policy with major ramifications for the IDA (Department of Enterprise and Employment 1993; Industrial Policy Review Group 1992). Representing another critical juncture, the outcome of the review saw the Department of Enterprise and Employment (formerly Industry and Commerce) reclaim the role of determining industrial policy and of supervising its implementation from the IDA, which was split into three separate organisations.

Thus, the policy refocus recommended from Telesis onwards found subsequent expression in the formal re-creation in January 1994 of the IDA as three separate, autonomous bodies, each with its own board and its own distinct mission and goals. All three agencies operate within a framework that facilitates co-operation and mutual support, with Forfás, the umbrella agency, focusing on policy, Forbairt (now Enterprise Ireland) charged with promoting indigenous industry and IDA Ireland responsible for attracting FDI to Ireland.

From the relative success of the 1970s, the IDA entered the 1980s under a cloud created by the Telesis (1982) review, which was exacerbated by the poor economic and jobs climate throughout the decade. The structural persistence that marked the 1970s gave way to a reactive sequence that saw questioning of both the IDA and the mechanisms generating its continuity, finding subsequent expression in the critical juncture that brought about the re-creation of the IDA (see Figure 3.7).

From a path-dependence perspective, the change to the IDA as an industrial development organisation arguably remains within the bounds of the path being pursued since the critical juncture of the 1950s. What has transpired in the interim is that much policy learning and organisational learning has ensued, such that the state continued to invest in refining its industrial development policy and the institutional and organisational arrangements established in support of that policy. The IDA of 1955 has continued on through to the IDA Ireland of today, in terms of its sole focus on promoting internationally mobile investment by foreign interests in Ireland. The IDA that emerged from the late 1960s, incorporating indigenous along with foreign industry, was subsequently renegotiated in the early 1990s, so that the organisational structure that existed internally was externalised through the creation of separate agencies out of the existing divisional structure.

Figure 3.7 The IDA's path from industrial super-agency to agency focused on FDI

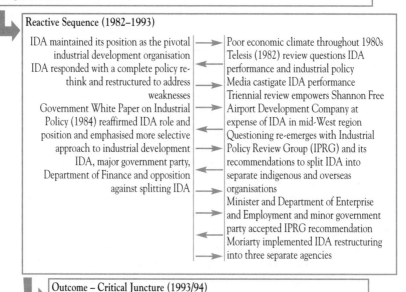

Outcome – Critical Juncture (1969/70)
Government accepted review recommendations and drafted necessary legislation, passed by the Oireachtas as the Industrial Development Act 1969
The 'new' IDA came into being on 1 April 1970

Structural Persistence (1970–1982)
High fixed set-up costs in establishing the 'new' IDA as a semi-state super-agency – legislation, political capital, staff recruitment, financial resources, etc.
Learning effects, co-ordination effects and adaptive expectations yielded increasing investment by way of financial resources, legislation, marketing programmes, industrial investors, jobs, internal reorganisations, etc.

Reactive Sequence (1982–1993)

IDA maintained its position as the pivotal industrial development organisation
IDA responded with a complete policy re-think and restructured to address weaknesses
Government White Paper on Industrial Policy (1984) reaffirmed IDA role and position and emphasised more selective approach to industrial development
IDA, major government party, Department of Finance and opposition against splitting IDA

Poor economic climate throughout 1980s
Telesis (1982) review questions IDA performance and industrial policy
Media castigate IDA performance
Triennial review empowers Shannon Free Airport Development Company at expense of IDA in mid-West region
Questioning re-emerges with Industrial Policy Review Group (IPRG) and its recommendations to split IDA into separate indigenous and overseas organisations
Minister and Department of Enterprise and Employment and minor government party accepted IPRG recommendation
Moriarty implemented IDA restructuring into three separate agencies

Outcome – Critical Juncture (1993/94)
Government drafted legislation to split the IDA into three separate organisations, passed by the Oireachtas as the Industrial Development Act 1993
Forfás, Forbairt and IDA Ireland came into being on 1 January 1994

Source: Donnelly (2007:207).

CONCLUSION

Taking all of the above together, what emerges is a path dependence picture of the IDA's creation in the context of a protectionist path, and subsequent production and reproduction in the context of a free trade path. We see the critical junctures marking the turn to protectionism and then to free trade, in addition to the critical junctures marking the IDA's establishment, then its focus on development of new industry and re-focus on FDI, followed by its re-creation as a super-agency with national responsibility for all aspects of industrial development policy and implementation, and most recently its re-focus on FDI, with its responsibility for policy development and indigenous industry centred in separate, new agencies.

Post-critical junctures, positive feedback mechanisms come into play to produce and reproduce structural persistence. We see large set-up costs and ongoing investment, initially in protectionism and subsequently in a policy geared towards free trade, for example policy statements, policy documents, legislation, new institutions and organisations, ongoing commitment of resources (financial, political, legislative), etc. We see the knowledge gained in the operation of both policy regimes contributing to positive feedback in their continued use, such feedback incurring continued investment aimed at greater efficiency and effectiveness, for example in the fine-tuning of legislation and the establishment of complementary organisations. Increased use of each policy regime encouraged investment in linked and complementary activities, in turn making each regime more attractive. And adaptive expectations drove continued investment in both policy regimes to reduce uncertainties, whereby the greater the expectation that policy would continue in force, the greater the actions that would be adapted to realise those expectations. The self-fulfilling character of expectations contributed to the policy winning broader acceptance and increased the dynamic of co-ordination effects.

We also see such large set-up costs and investment going into the IDA, producing and reproducing an increasingly specific industrial development asset. Tremendous amounts of learning by doing has occurred in what has increasingly become a complex system, with the IDA developing strategies suited to the particular institutional matrix it has confronted. We see widespread co-ordination effects, with particular courses of action encouraged, and others discouraged, given the anticipated actions of others within the industrial development sphere. We see growing complementarity between the outward-looking policy of economic development and the IDA as the increasingly focal organisation delivering on the country's industrial development. Co-evolving over an extended period of time, the interactions between the two have created densely linked institutional matrices (North 1990).

However, we also see that paths have not continued indefinitely, as was the case with protectionism and with the IDA itself. A reactive sequence emerged in response to the growing disquiet with protectionism, which culminated in the outcome or critical juncture that saw the outward-looking economic development policy take its place. The initial fortunes of the IDA played out within this reactive sequence. Its establishment attracted the threat of abolition by the opposition and it became bogged down in managing protectionism to the detriment of promoting industrial development. However, the outcome or critical juncture was favourable to the IDA in setting it on its path as an industrial development organisation through removing from it its bureaucratic burden administering the protectionist machine. The critical juncture that saw the organisation's role re-focused to attract FDI was influenced by the reactive sequence at the broader level of economic policy. The subsequent reactive sequence that resulted in the re-creation of the IDA as a semi-state super-agency was a response to the perceived and real inefficiencies of having multiple state agencies dealing with industrial investment and doing so from within the operational confines of the civil service. And the reactive sequence that began with the Telesis review in 1982 and culminated in 1994 with the re-creation of the IDA as three separate agencies reflected ongoing debate over the needs of foreign and indigenous investors, the scope of industrial policy and the division and location of policy development and policy implementation responsibility.

In the final analysis, from relatively contingent and unpredictable beginnings have co-evolved both an institution and an organisational form. In the case of the IDA, both the forces for structural persistence and those of reactive sequences have contributed to producing and reproducing an increasingly fine-tuned, specific asset, an organisational form that, *ex ante*, could not have been predicted when it was first established.

Today, supporting export-oriented, foreign multinational organisations, which employ some 136,000 people and account for some €110bn or 70 per cent of total exports, and continuing to promote and attract inward investment (IDA 2010), IDA Ireland remains an important organisation in the Irish enterprise development institutional landscape. Notwithstanding this, with the Special Group on Public Service Numbers and Expenditures (2009:79–82) report, and its recommendations to rationalise the various aspects of IDA Ireland and other development agency operations, only time will tell what will become of IDA Ireland into the future. Notwithstanding appearances, change is ever present.

Notes

1 Mr White joined the IDA in 1969 and served as head of the Home Information Division, then head of the Planning Division, and then Executive Director with responsibility for planning, regions, public relations, promotions and development co-operation. He succeeded Michael Killeen as managing director in 1981, a position in which he served until 1990.

References

Abbott, A. (1997) 'On the Concept of a Turning Point', *Comparative Social Research* 16: 85–105.

Antonelli, C. (1997) 'The Economics of Path Dependence in Industrial Organization', *International Journal of Industrial Organization* 15(6): 643–75.

Arthur, W.B. (1989) 'Competing Technologies and Lock-in by Historical Small Events', *Economic Journal* 99(394): 116–31.

— (1994) *Increasing Returns and Path Dependence in the Economy*. Ann Arbor, MI: University of Michigan Press.

Child, J. (1997) 'Strategic Choice in the Analysis of Action, Structure, Organizations and Environment: Retrospect and Prospect', *Organization Studies* 18(1): 43–76.

Cooper, C. and Whelan, N. (1973) *Science, Technology, and Industry in Ireland: Report to the National Science Council*. Dublin: Stationery Office.

Dáil Debates [online]. Available: http://historical-debates.oireachtas.ie/en.toc.dail.html.

David, P. (1985) 'Clio and the Economics of QWERTY', *American Economic Review* 75(2): 332–7.

— (1987) 'Some New Standards for the Economics of Standardization in the Information Age', in P. Dasgupta and P. Stoneman (eds) *Economic Policy and Technological Performance*, pp. 206–39. Cambridge: Cambridge University Press.

— (1994) 'Why Are Institutions the "Carriers of History"? Path Dependence and the Evolution of Conventions, Organizations, and Institutions', *Structural Change and Economic Dynamics* 5(2): 205–20.

Department of Enterprise and Employment (1993) *Employment through Enterprise: Response of the Government to the Moriarty Task Force on the Implementation of the Culliton Report*. Dublin: Stationery Office.

DoF (Department of Finance) (1958a) *Economic Development*. Dublin: Stationery Office.

— (1958b) *Programme for Economic Expansion (PEE)*. Dublin: Stationery Office.

— (1963) *Second Programme for Economic Expansion (Part 1)*. Dublin: Stationery Office.

— (1964) *Second Programme for Economic Expansion (Part 2)*. Dublin: Stationery Office.

— (1969) *Third Programme for Economic and Social Development 1969–72*. Dublin: Stationery Office.

DIC (Department of Industry and Commerce) (1984) *White Paper on Industrial Policy*. Dublin: Stationery Office.

Donnelly, P. (2007) 'Organizational Forming in (A)modern Times: Path Dependence, Actor-Network Theory and Ireland's Industrial Development Authority', unpublished PhD dissertation, University of Massachusetts at Amherst [online]. Available: http://proquest.umi.com/pqdlink?Ver=1&Exp=02-13-2015&FMT=7&DID=1694711661&RQT=309&attempt=1&cfc=1 (last accessed 14 February 2010).

— (2009) 'Focusing on Process and History: Path Dependence', in J. Hogan, P. Dolan and P. Donnelly (eds) *Approaches to Qualitative Research: Theory and its Practical Application*, pp. 125–50. Cork: Oak Tree Press.

Economist, The (1977) 'Wooing the Foreigner', 9 April, p. 13.

Girvin, B. (1989) *Between Two Worlds: Politics and Economy in Independent Ireland*. Dublin: Gill & Macmillan.

Hall, P. (ed.) (1989) *The Political Power of Economic Ideas: Keynesianism Across*

Nations. Princeton, NJ: Princeton University Press.

Haughey, C.J. (1982) 'Ireland's Corner on US Business', *Christian Science Monitor*, 24 May, p. 23.

IDA (Industrial Development Authority) (1971–1993) *Annual Reports*. Dublin: Industrial Development Authority.

— (2010) 'IDA End of Year Statement 2009' [online]. Available: http://www.idaireland.com/news-media/press-releases/ida-ireland-end-of-years-3/index.xml (last accessed 30 January 2010).

Industrial Policy Review Group (1992) *A Time for Change: Industrial Policy for the 1990s*. Dublin: Stationery Office.

Irish Independent (1949) 'New Industrial Advisory Body – Bigger Output the Aim', 14 February, p. 5.

Jacobsen, J.K. (1978) 'Changing Utterly? Irish Development and the Problem of Dependence', *Studies: An Irish Quarterly Review* 67(268): 276–91.

Kennedy, K.A. and Dowling, B.R. (1975) *Economic Growth in Ireland: The Experience Since 1947*. Dublin: Gill & Macmillan.

Kennedy, K.A., Giblin, T. and McHugh, D. (1988) *The Economic Development of Ireland in the Twentieth Century*. London: Routledge.

Killeen, M. (1979) *The Electronics Revolution and Its Impact on Ireland*. Dublin: Industrial Development Authority.

Krugman, P. (1991) 'History and Industry Location: The Case of the Manufacturing Belt', *American Economic Review* 81(2): 80–3.

Little, A.D. (1967a) *Review of the Structure of the Industrial Development Authority*. Dublin: Industrial Development Authority.

— (1967b) *Review of Incentives for Industry in Ireland*. Dublin: Industrial Development Authority.

Long, F. (1976) 'Foreign Direct Investment in an Underdeveloped European Economy: The Republic of Ireland', *World Development* 4(1): 59–84.

MacSharry, R. and White, P. (2000) *The Making of the Celtic Tiger: The Inside Story of Ireland's Boom Economy*. Cork: Mercier Press.

Mahoney, J. (2000) 'Path Dependence in Historical Sociology', *Theory and Society* 29(4): 507–48.

— (2001) 'Path-Dependent Explanations of Regime Change: Central America in Comparative Perspective', *Studies in Comparative International Development* 36(1): 111–41.

McLoughlin, R.J. (1972) 'The Industrial Development Process: An Overall View', *Administration* 20(1): 27–38.

NIEC (National Industrial Economic Council) (1968) *Report on Industrial Adaptation and Development* (NIEC Report No.23). Dublin: Stationery Office.

North, D.C. (1990) *Institutions, Institutional Change and Economic Performance*. New York, NY: Cambridge University Press.

O'Neill, T.S. (1972) 'Industrial Development in Ireland', *Administration* 20(1): 39–50.

Pierson, P. (1993) 'When Effect Becomes Cause: Policy Feedback and Political Change', *World Politics* 45(4): 595–628.

— (2000) 'Increasing Returns, Path Dependence, and the Study of Politics', *American Political Science Review* 94(2): 251–67.

— (2004) *Politics in Time: History, Institutions, and Social Analysis.* Princeton, NJ: Princeton University Press.

PSORG (Public Services Organisation Review Group) (1969) *Report of the Public Services Review Group 1966-1969 (The Devlin Report).* Dublin: Stationery Office.

Special Group on Public Service Numbers and Expenditures (2009) *Report of the Special Group on Public Service Numbers and Expenditures*, Vol.II. Dublin: Stationery Office.

Sydow, J., Schreyögg, G. and Koch, J. (2009) 'Organizational Path Dependence: Opening the Black Box', *Academy of Management Review* 34(4): 689–709.

Telesis (Telesis Consultancy Group) (1982) *A Review of Industrial Policy* (NESC Report No. 64). Dublin: Stationery Office.

Thelen, K. (2003) 'How Institutions Evolve: Insights from Comparative Historical Analysis', in J. Mahoney and D. Rueschemeyer (eds) *Comparative Historical Analysis in the Social Sciences*, pp. 208–40. New York, NY: Cambridge University Press.

White, P. (2006). Personal interview, 9 May 2006.

Wickham, J. (1983) 'Dependence and State Structure: Foreign Firms and Industrial Policy in the Republic of Ireland', in O. Höll (ed.) *Small States in Europe and Dependence*, pp. 164–83. Vienna: Braumüller.

Chapter 4

Enterprise Discourse: Its Origins and its Influence in Ireland

Brendan K. O'Rourke

INTRODUCTION

The language a society has for talking about business both facilitates and constrains how we represent business, how we build the roles involved and how we construct the relationships between business and the rest of society (Fairclough 1992:64). In Irish society, as in many societies, the resources for talking and thinking about business can be typified by what is called 'enterprise discourse' (Carr 2000a; Fairclough 1991; Jones and Spicer 2009). To be able to think critically about business and its relationship with society, an understanding of this dominant discourse, its features and a sense of it as a discourse dependent on the historical circumstance in which it emerged is useful. Such an understanding of enterprise discourse and its operation in Ireland is what this chapter aims to provide.

The chapter is structured as follows. The next section focuses on the emergence of enterprise as a discourse from the start of capitalism. It aims to provide the reader with a sense of what tasks the word 'enterprise' has been set in the past and so give an understanding of the layers of meaning that enterprise discourse can carry today. The following section deals with the particular meanings enterprise discourse has taken on in Ireland in more recent times, showing its interaction with the national context. The chapter concludes that readers can be more conscious of and, when appropriate, more liberated from, enterprise discourse.

THE EMERGENCE OF ENTERPRISE AS A DISCOURSE

Enterprise Discourse: French, English and German Beginnings

Enterprise discourse can be traced back to early writings on the entrepreneur in France, the United Kingdom and Germany. Until the twelfth century, the typical use of the word 'entrepreneur' in its native France was to describe the individual who, before the functions of planner, architect, builder, etc. became specialised, undertook the general responsibility for building. As such functions became specialised, the 'entrepreneur' came to mean the overall project leader of works (typically construction), usually under privilege granted by government and often designed for defensive or military purposes (Hébert and Link 2006:112–13). In the early 1730s, the French-Irish economist and businessman Richard Cantillon wrote of the 'entrepreneur' in his famous *Essai sur la Nature du Commerce en Général* (Cantillon 1959 [1755]:167). Cantillon used the concept of the entrepreneur to help explain the dynamic nature of the then emerging market system to those of the older view, who thought that production was determined by direction of the landowners (O'Mahony 1985:261). For Cantillon, the entrepreneur handled the uncertainty created by buying at a known price to sell at an unknown price. Cantillon's stress on economic *function*, rather than social status, was novel: 'Social standing was practically irrelevant to Cantillon's notion of entrepreneurship' (Hébert and Link 2006:18). This contribution, which asserts that background or social class is irrelevant, is clearly an attractive feature of enterprise discourse.

Cantillon was one of the few economists explicitly referred to in Adam Smith's (1982 [1776]) famous *Wealth of Nations* (von Hayek 1985 [1931]: 217–218). Smith stressed the role of entrepreneur as a prudent provider of capital. This view of the entrepreneur was taken up by the American founding father and republican Thomas Jefferson (1743–1826), who stressed the need for such property owning to be widely distributed. Mills (2002 [1951]:8–9) points out the ideological role of Smith's and Jefferson's capital-owning entrepreneur in this classical age of capitalism by quoting the great American lexicographer, Noah Webster, as asserting in 1787 that 'An equality of property, with the necessity of alienation constantly operating to destroy combinations of powerful families, is the very *soul of a Republic*' (emphasis in original).

The British economist Jeremy Bentham (1748–1832) tried to inject some glamour and creativity into the idea of entrepreneur: 'Bentham's entrepreneur is an exceptional individual, one above the common herd; a minority in society' (Hébert and Link 2006:44). Subsequently in English-speaking economics a more Smithian, mundane and less exciting view took hold for some time. The entrepreneur, and, indeed, any study of innovation in which an entrepreneur might partake, was submerged beneath the technical study of how markets attained equilibria. This technical and mathematical approach to markets was best studied without the messiness created by innovative and disturbing entrepreneurs. In the anglophone world, the enterprise discourse temporarily retreated.

While English-speaking economics, generally, had reduced the role of the entrepreneur to almost a mere supplier of capital, German-speaking economics was developing richer conceptions of the entrepreneur. Later, through the influence on American academia of German-speaking intellectuals, these richer views of the entrepreneur had a powerful influence on all English-speaking thinking on business. Johann Heinrich von Thünen (1783–1850), building on his compatriots' development of French and English sources, combined the ideas of the entrepreneur as risk-bearer and as innovator. Hébert and Link (2006:53) argue that von Thünen also 'turns the discussion from the trials of the entrepreneur into a kind of "crucible" theory of the development of entrepreneurial talent. . . . Adversity in the business world thereby becomes a training ground for the entrepreneur.' With the work of Wilhelm Roscher (1817–1894), what became known as the Historical School dominated German-speaking thinking about business, displacing less historical economics (see Grimmer-Solem and Romani (1999) for discussion of the Historical School). Gustav Schmoller (1838–1917) saw the spirit of enterprise as a central factor in the economy, with the entrepreneur possessing daring and creativity (Hébert and Link 2006:53). From disputes over methodology between Schmoller and Carl Menger (1840–1921), we can trace the subsequently very influential contribution of the Austrian School of Economics (for a sympathetic overview of this radically anti-government school of economics, see Boettke 2008). More directly, Schmoller influenced the work of the later Historical School writers, Werner Sombart (1863–1941) and Max Weber (1864–1920). Both Sombart and Weber developed the concept of the entrepreneur, although Weber was much more influential on its subsequent development. Weber's view that culture, in particular the Protestant Christian ethic, is key to the entrepreneurial spirit of capitalism continues to inspire researchers (Carr 2003; Lewis and Llewellyn 2004).

A Latency Period for Enterprise Discourse

Despite the emphasis in the late nineteenth and early twentieth centuries of German-speaking scholarship on the role of the entrepreneur, the first few decades of the twentieth century saw the entrepreneur sidelined. Even in Germany, there was considerable consensus that the small, and so presumably more entrepreneurial, firms were in a 'death-struggle' (Bögenhold 2000). For America, Berle and Means (1933) showed that the separation of ownership from control had resulted in the rise of the professionally managed firm. There had been a move from entrepreneurial capitalism to managerial capitalism.

Mainstream economics, in response to the rise of managerial capitalism, the establishment of the Soviet Union and, perhaps most important, the Great Depression of the 1930s, was initially in crisis. The dominant solution to this crisis was offered by Keynes (1973 [1936]) and those who advocated macroeconomic management of the economy by government and neglected the microeconomic role of the entrepreneur. The dominance of this view, and an associated view that planning and scientific expertise within the corporation (Galbraith 1967) is all-important, seemed to bear fruit in the long-lasting post-war boom in the developed world.

Despite the dominance of the Keynesian and corporatist view, the entrepreneur was to blossom again. While the mainstream consensus neglected entrepreneurs, the influence of the old German-speaking celebration of the entrepreneur was quietly growing almost underground. Joseph Schumpeter and Frederick von Hayek had both left continental Europe behind as the Nazis rose to power. Von Hayek with his wife, Hella, had published a German translation of the work of that French–Irish advocate of the entrepreneur, Richard Cantillon (von Hayek 1985 [1931]). The particular contribution of von Hayek was to point out the usefulness of detailed, contingent and local knowledge of circumstances, typically possessed by entrepreneurs, but generally sneered at by scientific planners:

> [T]he shipper who earns his living from using otherwise empty or half-filled journeys of tramp-streamers, or the estate agent whose whole knowledge is almost exclusively of temporary opportunities, or the *arbitrageur* who gains from local differences of commodity prices, are all performing eminently useful functions based on specialist knowledge of circumstances of the fleeting moment not known to others. (von Hayek 1945:522)

Casson (2002) refers to this contribution of the Austrian School as 'low-level' entrepreneurship, in contrast to the 'high-level' entrepreneur of Schumpeter. Schumpeter was influenced by both the Austrian tradition and the mainstream, at least in Germany, Historical School. Schumpeter's 'high-level' entrepreneur was the driver of economic progress through the entrepreneurial role of the innovator who unleashes the forces of 'creative destruction'. Those interested in these views remained an enthusiastic, and almost underground, few until the 1970s.

Renaissance and Critique

After the oil shock of the early 1970s, the collapse of the Bretton Woods system and the persistence of stagflation, the economics discipline, then dominated by the Keynesian consensus, needed to find a source of vigour. The entrepreneur came to the rescue in the form of, most famously, Milton Friedman, who, in various works, brought into the mainstream an enthusiasm for the free market and the entrepreneur (e.g. Friedman and Friedman 1980) from its confinement in the writings of von Hayek and Schumpeter. It was from this revival of the entrepreneur that we can trace the academic roots of the enterprise discourse that came to political dominance with Margaret Thatcher and Ronald Reagan.

In the UK, the enterprise culture was promoted by figures such as Sir Keith Joseph and Sir Alfred Sherman, who, through the Centre for Policy Studies, ideologically took over the Conservative Party (Keegan 1984). This was, self-consciously, a cultural campaign, with Sherman declaring his wish 'to reshape the climate of opinion . . . to fight vigorously on this front of the battle of ideas' (as quoted in Keegan 1984:47). A quote from Joseph (cited in Keegan 1984:47) is prescient of the persistence of the enterprise culture beyond the Thatcher administration:

I decided to devote myself to trying to persuade anyone interested that Western Europe countries had done better for their peoples whatever the names of the governing parties, by using the engine of a decentralized, profit-seeking competitive economic system more understandingly than we had done.

It was through a critique of Thatcherite views that much of the culture, ideology, policy and discourse (CIPD) school of studying enterprise emerged. Much of the CIPD literature on enterprise comes from a left-wing perspective (Armstrong 2005; Fairclough 1991); however, right-wingers, too, have recognised the importance of enterprise culture and discourse (Lavoie and Chamlee-Wright 2000). There have also been less explicitly politically positioned CIPD works (Carr 2000a). Nonetheless, what is evident is that enterprise as a discourse has been recognised as an important discourse of our time by a variety of scholars from a range of political opinions.

Enterprise discourse became both pervasive and persistent. Much entrepreneurship has become policy and the free spirit of enterprise is now institutionalised. As Jones and Spicer (2005:179) rather dramatically put it, 'entrepreneurship has bled out of its heartland . . . and has stained nearly every aspect of public life'. This 'staining' has been so thorough, according to some, that 'the character of the entrepreneur can no longer be represented as just one among a plurality of ethical personalities, but must be seen as assuming an ontological priority' (du Gay 1996:157). Others have argued that the success of enterprise promoters may have been exaggerated and bemoan the term 'enterprise culture' as carrying 'the unwarranted implication that they have achieved their intended aim' (Armstrong 2005:7). However, Armstrong (2005) himself documents the persistence of the enterprise discourse in the speech of Gordon Brown, who, from 2007, became the third prime minister of the UK after that first modern crusader, Margaret Thatcher, to bring the 'spirit of enterprise' to that high political office. Whereas Armstrong (2005) prefers to talk of entrepreneurialism as a policy, he not only shows the substantial financial commitment to such a policy, but also illustrates the durability and extent of 'enterprise-speak'. Du Gay and Salaman (1992:615) are correct in pointing out that enterprise discourse is so pervasive that its operation in particular organisations is better understood by seeing it within the grander 'social and political rationality of enterprise'.

Enterprise discourse is not just dominant in state (EU, UK, Ireland, USA, etc.) policy towards small business (Carr 2000b), but is even more pervasive. Enterprise, too, is advocated as the vigour needed for reforming the large organisations of the public sector (Osborne and Gaebler 1993). While warning against assuming 'that entrepreneurial behaviour is as high on the agenda of public service managers as it is for some politicians', Llewellyn *et al.* (2000: 170) go on to conclude that it 'does appear to have entered the discourse of public management'. This is borne out in the studies of particular public service organisations and sectors: Doolin (2003) looks at the introduction of enterprise into New Zealand public hospitals; Cohen, Musson and Duberley (2004) look at general medical practitioners and scientists dealing with enterprise discourse in the UK's National Health Service; and Bridgman (2007) looks at enterprise in the UK university sector.

Enterprise is also promoted as the solution to many of the problems of large private sector companies. Kanter (1983:23) argues that there is a need to re-infuse 'more American organizations with the entrepreneurial spirit responsible for America's success in the past'. Though she does not argue with the view that the entrepreneurial spirit has traditionally been found in small firms, the title of one of her books, *When Giants Learn to Dance*, encapsulates her contention that enterprise is needed in large organisations (Kanter 1989). Another advocate of enterprise in larger corporations more confidently noted that, despite its association with the new and the small, 'entrepreneurship is being practised by large and often old enterprises' (Drucker 1985:20). Peters (1993) is more evangelical in his urging of 'necessary disorganisation', as he celebrates enterprise as the antidote to what he sees as the problem of bureaucracy. Curiously, these large and complex organisations are of the very kind whose rise to prominence heralded the change from entrepreneurial to managerial capitalism.

In the last three decades, the discourse of enterprise, born with the small in-between traders at the dawn of capitalism, has been travelling, and no doubt evolving, in the lands of political rhetoric, large established public bureaucracies and large private sector corporations. Discourses are not parroted by dupes; rather, they are deployed with creativity and innovation by humans with agency, who both draw on discourses and shape their evolution. In this regard, Hendry (2004) argues, for example, that the development of enterprise discourse in large organisations seems to have involved imposing on the identity of the enterprising individual an accountability that was in previous incarnations of the entrepreneur, as a small business founder and owner, alien to the entrepreneur's autonomous nature. Du Gay (2004:37) even contends that, at least to some extent, various 'different understandings and conceptions of enterprise are non-reducible'.

ENTERPRISE DISCOURSE: IRISH DEVELOPMENTS

Strategy and enterprise in Ireland are influenced by both global and EU developments. However, it would be incorrect to assume that Irish discourse was merely a 'local adoption'. Indeed, to some extent, state policy development may have flowed the other way: for example, there are reasons to believe that Ireland has been disproportionately influential on the EU's enterprise policy. First, high Irish economic growth rates during the Celtic Tiger period have coincided with the development of the EU's enterprise policy, thus giving the impression that Ireland can serve as a model for EU economic policy. Second, Ireland, too, has to some extent been seen as an acceptable mixture of Anglo-American (light-touch regulation, low taxation, liberalised financial governance) and European (social partnership, collective bargaining) economic models. Nevertheless it is useful when focusing on the Irish situation to look at developments flowing from Europe.

The Influence of the European Union on Irish Enterprise Discourse

Since at least 1973, when Ireland became a member of the European Economic Community (EEC), European policy has had a major impact on Irish public discourse, particularly issues concerned with enterprise. Striking examples of this can be seen in the National Development Plans 1994–1999 and 2000–2006. Here was a strategic investment in Ireland that was massive – the plans involved spending of nearly €80bn (Leddin and Walsh 2003:91). The EU funded these plans, with Structural Funds injecting an average of about 1.7 per cent of GDP each year in the 1989–1999 period and the percentage getting smaller after that, due both to high growth in Ireland and to reducing transfers (Hegarty 2003:2). Perhaps even more important, the EU's involvement was associated with an increase in the strategic planning competence of the Irish public sector (Hegarty 2003:13). The European Commission (EC) laid the criteria for the development of the plans and the Irish, with their long experience of dealing with distant bureaucracies, became aficionados of the European planning process.

The significant influence of the EU on Irish strategy and enterprise makes it worthwhile to make some observations on EU discourse in this area. Perhaps because of the diversity of national industrial and enterprise policies across the EU, the EU has historically had an industrial policy that has stressed the removal of barriers to competition, rather than a more interventionist approach (Andresso and Jacobson 2005:479). At this level, EU policy can be seen as a promoter of the free-market enterprise culture. However, European social policy and labour rights practices (e.g. European Worker Director rules) have acted to create 'social market' limits to the 1980s Anglo-American model. Furthermore, while lacking the political or legal competence to be *dirigiste*, the EU has provided through reports, policy statements, inter-state study exchanges and debates a large source of discourse on these matters. To a great extent, this kind of debate reflects the theoretical views on strategy and planning discussed above. However, the use of enterprise in EU strategy and planning has a specificity in EU discourse that is worth further discussion.

The use of the word 'enterprise' in official portfolios of the EC is indicative of the rise of enterprise discourse within the EU. It can be traced as far back as 1994, when an 'Enterprise Policy, Small Business and Distributive Trades' (EC 1994:9) portfolio was introduced. At that time, this portfolio was just one of four areas of responsibility of one of the ordinary commissioners. The 'enterprise' word then disappeared from portfolio titles of the Santer Commission (1995–1999) (EC 1995), but returned with greater prominence in the Prodi Commission (1999–2004), with an entire commissioner dedicated solely to 'Enterprise and

Information Society' (EC 2004a). The first Barroso Commission (2004–2010) elevated enterprise to the portfolio of 'Enterprise and Industry', which was held by no ordinary commissioner, but by Günter Verheugen, a Commission vice-president with an expanded directorate-general (Beesley 2004). The vice-presidential status of the Enterprise and Industry portfolio has been maintained in the new Barroso Commission expected to be in office until 2014 (EC 2010). Clearly, the word 'enterprise' has been receiving greater prominence in the EU.

EU enterprise policy is more than bland, inoffensive words of enthusiasm. The words, at least, are decisive, as can be seen in statements such as the following:

A healthy 'churning' rate of company creation and destruction improves efficient resource allocation in an economy by increasing competitive pressure. To release entrepreneurial potential, the European Union must take serious steps to make Europe more attractive for business activity. It is also clear that Europeans must change their attitudes towards entrepreneurship. (EC 2004b:15)

Whether the costs of such 'healthy churning' have been fully weighed is not so clear, but what the EC is clear on is that 'Europeans must change their attitudes': European enterprise policy is about culture and individual psychology (Aligica and State 2005:250). Indeed, the EC's Enterprise and Industry Directorate General (ECEI-DG) has even ventured into the classroom with its best practice advice on helping to create an entrepreneurial culture (ECEI-DG 2004:1). The Brussels bureaucracy, in stepping up its efforts 'to increase the appreciation of entrepreneurs in society', takes quite a socially oriented responsible approach so as to 'promote greater awareness of a career as an entrepreneur, foster entrepreneurial mindsets including the promotion' of *responsible* entrepreneurship practices' (EC 2005a:5, emphasis added).

The EC has declared that '[t]he guiding principle for authorities must therefore be to "think small first" – regulations that are appropriate for smaller companies will generally also be appropriate for larger ones' (EC 2004b:15). In this statement, the EC has adopted the fondness for the small, noted as a key characteristic of enterprise discourse by writers such as Jones and Spicer (2005:179). In all of this, policy of the Council of the European Union (CEU), as agreed in the Lisbon agenda, is being followed: 'The competitiveness and dynamism of businesses are directly dependent on a regulatory climate conducive to investment, innovation and entrepreneurship' (CEU 2000: para. 14). While some have felt that EU policy on entrepreneurship 'continues to be somewhat shrouded in a veil of ambiguity' (Aligica and State 2005:250), from the foregoing discussion we can see that the promotion of 'enterprise culture' of the kind written about by Keat (1991), Carr (1998) and Gray (1998) has been adopted by the EU.

While recognising that EU enterprise culture has been essentially part of the same phenomenon exemplified in the UK since the government of Prime Minister

Thatcher, some peculiarities of the EU discourse are worth noting. The term 'competitiveness' occurs very frequently in EU documents (e.g. EC 2005b). To anglophone ears, this sounds very much in line with the enterprise culture of the UK, evoking the cut and thrust of competitive market rivalry between firms. However, a close inspection of measures of competitiveness (e.g. EC 2005b: Table 5-30) reveals that EU competitiveness refers more to what might be termed 'international comparative efficiency'. Thus, in EU terms, 'competitiveness' has no particularly entrepreneurial flavour and could be equally at home in a 'planned economy' as an 'enterprise discourse'.

Another issue in EU enterprise policy is a concern to stress the growth of particular sectors, which is clearly more statist than a pure 'let the market decide' approach characteristic of what has been described as transparent neo-liberal discourse (Phelan 2007). Within the EU institutions, there appears to be some confusion as to which sectors might be favoured. Writing in a more enthusiastic time for information technology, the CEU seemed to favour a strengthening of the services sector, noting, for example, that '[c]ontent industries create added value by exploiting and networking European cultural diversity' (CEU 2000: para. 9). On the other hand, the CEIE-DG has come to a more traditional stress on manufacturing:

> The Enterprise DG has therefore developed a new Industrial Policy (adopted by the Commission in December 2002), which will focus on the improvement of the framework-conditions for developing entrepreneurial activities. . . .
>
> . . . Industry is at the core of our policy concerns. Despite the rise of the service sector, industry continues to play a central role as an engine of growth. Continued growth of productivity in the manufacturing sector has been at the root of the sustained increase in wealth, and has led to a growing demand for services. (EC 2004b:9)

EU enterprise policy is more statist, too, in trying to integrate enterprise discourse into a broader church of ideologues than is the case in the UK. For example, the Lisbon statement argued that social welfare systems were an asset in the entrepreneurial process of economic adjustment:

> The Union possesses a generally well-educated workforce as well as social protection systems able to provide, beyond their intrinsic value, the stable framework required for managing the structural changes involved in moving towards a knowledge-based society. (CEU, 2000: para. 3)

Furthermore, the EC promises that it 'will strengthen its support for activities to reduce the burden of risk intrinsically linked to entrepreneurship' (EC 2005a:5). Such unnatural interferences with the market economy are a far cry from the ideological antipathy to the 'dependency culture' of the welfare state, characteristic of British Conservatives in the 1980s or of Reaganomics in the USA at around the same time.

At times, EU enterprise policy seems to be more open to supporting small business enterprises, even if they are not destined for fast growth:

> SMEs are very different in nature: some seek rapid growth and bigger markets; others are only active in local or regional markets. As this diversity has to be reflected in policy-making, the new approach embraces initiatives and actions to unlock the full potential of all types of enterprises ranging from start-ups and high growth 'gazelles' to traditional enterprises, including craft sector, micro-enterprises, social economy enterprises and family SMEs. (EC 2005a:4)

Such public policy support for non-'gazelle' firms is rather different from what it might be in more purely anglophone discourse, where firms can be derided for lack of growth, as can be seen in Lewis and Llewellyn's (2004:7) discussion of 'trundlers'. The justification for such support for non-gazelle firms in EU policy is partly based on:

> . . . a comprehensive view of SMEs' role in society that highlights their importance as an important factor of economic and social cohesion at local and regional level. Moreover, most SMEs are committed to corporate social responsibility, which allows them to improve their performance and competitiveness while having a positive impact on the local community and the environment. (EC 2005a:4)

This new EU view of the socially responsible entrepreneur contrasts, perhaps, with a more opportunistic view of the entrepreneur that might have been prevalent in state bureaucracies up to this point.

Despite the differences between the EU's version and other versions of enterprise discourse, the discourse itself serves to homogenise policy objectives. Indeed, some have argued that the peculiar tensions and incoherencies of EU enterprise policy powerfully achieve this homogenisation of EU and other enterprise policy objectives:

> To sum up, the comparison with the USA offers a functional device for identifying various policy areas to be targeted. Lacking a unique or coherent vision or policy model, this simple approach is a workable substitute. Its limits are set by a certain intrinsic lack of imagination and by the reactive nature of the policy design implied. However, this catch-up, 'follow-the leader' type of approach has a strong motivational element. (Aligica and State 2005:253)

Irish State Policy Developments

I divide Irish state policy developments concerning strategy and enterprise since political independence in 1921 into four policy phases. The phases, as defined and described here, are just one possible construction among many. They do not differ greatly from standard understandings of the stages of Ireland's economic development (e.g. Haughton 2008; Leddin and Walsh 2003); rather, they try to constitute these stages in a way that illustrates important developments for enterprise discourse in Ireland. The first, well recognised as the state-building phase, lasts from 1922 to 1931 and coincides with recovery from the First World War, the War of Independence and the Civil War. The second phase, which I here call 'Ourselves Alone', involves significant economic isolation and depression lasting from 1932 to 1957. The third phase, here labelled as the phase of 'Strategising for an Open Economy', began in 1958 and involved both an opening up of the economy and a confidence in strategic planning. My fourth phase, which begins less definitely in 1973 and, perhaps because we are still in it, appears to be much more complex and full of turns and reversals, I regard as the 'Globalisation of Irish Enterprise' period.

State-Building Phase

In the state-building phase from 1922 to 1931, the newly independent government adopted a very liberal attitude to economic development. It was quickly made clear that the Irish revolution was not like the Russian. Though engaging in some protection of indigenous industry, the new state concentrated in the main on providing an environment suitable for a largely agricultural economy with significant exports to the UK. This meant fiscal conservativism and a generally laissez-faire attitude. The one exception to this was in the area of what were called 'state enterprises'. In the Dáil debates of the time, one member supported a government plan for a state electricity enterprise with the following words:

> Deputy Thrift asks can we be absolutely certain that it will be a commercial success. I ask myself, is that the test that is applied by a great nation going to war? Countries have taken the great risk of declaring war without knowing that they were going to win; they had courage in themselves, in their own capacity and their own resources, and they counted upon winning through. This policy of caution that is recommended to us is very good in small commercial enterprises, but as the experts have warned us, this is not to be viewed as merely a commercial enterprise. (Dáil Debates, vol. 10, cols 2008–9, 3 April 1925)

The clear expression that the state could and should be a greater risk-taker, rather than a 'merely small commercial enterprise', is in clear contrast to later views of enterprise. Furthermore, it is clear that the model of a small enterprise is not seen as the ideal model for all organisational activity in the way it is in more recent enterprise culture.

Ourselves Alone Phase

From 1932, there was a sharp change in government policy, with a striving towards economic self-sufficiency, partly reflecting an international rise in protectionism resorted to as a result of the start of the Great Depression. To some extent, this economic policy was necessitated by a nationalist political policy that was trying to overcome restrictions to Irish political independence flowing from the 1922 settlement with the UK: the resulting trade dispute (more romantically termed the 'economic war') would have forced a move towards national economic self-sufficiency. However, it is also important to recognise that this period reflects a harking back to the policy of historic Sinn Féin, which originally had a very significant economic element to its policy. Indeed, the rugged independent self-sufficiency of the phrase 'Sinn Féin' (an Irish Gaelic expression translated as 'ourselves' or 'ourselves alone') chimes with modern enterprise culture's self-reliance, though with a less individualistic tone. As well as its protectionist theme, this phase of Irish economic policy also involved the increased development of the state enterprise sector that had begun earlier, showing again a collectivist flavour to the enterprise culture in the Ireland of that time. However, until 1958 there was a definite hostility to planning, despite the popularity of planning in other western democracies: for example, Geiger (2000) provides a discussion of this in the context of Ireland's lack of enthusiasm for the Marshall Plan, while Lee (1989:227–34) shows the hostility to economic planning, even during the 'Emergency' of the Second World War.

Strategising for an Open Economy Phase

The third phase can probably be traced to the aftermath of the Second World War, though 1958 is commonly identified as the date when Irish economic policy turned outwards. This also marked an acceptance of the benefits of strategy in the form of planning. Following mainland Europe's planned reconstruction in the post-1945 period, Ireland's delayed embrace of planning was signalled with the publication of the first Programme for Economic Expansion (DoF 1958). Such a programmatic, or planned, approach to policy continued in the Second Programme 1964–1970 (DoF 1963, 1964) and with the 1969 Third Programme for Economic and Social Development 1969–1972 (DoF 1969). From 1958, protectionist measures were dismantled, stress was placed on the need for exports to lead growth, and encouragement of multinational enterprises replaced the policy of creating state enterprises. The Industrial Development Authority (IDA) focused its efforts on, and had much success in, attracting multinational investment into Ireland. By 1973, Ireland had joined the EEC and has since become one of the most open economies in the world (Dreher 2006:1094).

Globalisation of Irish Enterprise Phase

The fourth phase of development of enterprise discourse in Ireland brings us from 1973 up to 2010. It incorporates diverse conditions of tentative and short-lived recovery from the oil crisis (1973–1976), a state spending-driven boom (1977–1979), a period of deep depression and state foreign indebtedness (1980–1986), a period of recovery and spectacular economic growth during which Ireland was referred to as the Celtic Tiger (1987–2008), followed now by a period of downturn. Despite the diversity of this fourth phase, there is a unity in it that consists of an increasing complementation of the internationalisation policy with an encouragement of what was initially referred to as 'indigenous industry' (Telesis 1982) and then increasingly 'enterprise'. Also throughout the era, Ireland, like most of the rest of the world, moved from a strong faith in a programmatic approach to policy to more 'strategic thinking' and enterprise than 'strategic planning' approaches. While Ireland's conversion to planning had been much slower than the rest of the world, disillusionment with planning was at least as rapid in Ireland as elsewhere in the face of the new world of uncertainties created by the first oil crisis. The 1975 budget speech of the minister of finance has been much quoted in this regard:

> Of all the tasks which could engage my attention, the least realistic would be the publication of a medium or long-term economic plan based upon irrelevancies in the past, hunches as to the present and clairvoyance as to the future. (Dáil Debates, vol. 277, cols 220–1, 15 January 1975)

There was what might be regarded as one more involvement with old-style government planning in the form of a very ambitious debt-finance plan for rapid development between 1977 and 1980. While initially boosting the economy, this experience of planning was generally regarded as a disaster due to the depression and debt burden that followed. From these experiences, there was a definite hostility to old-style government planning in Ireland. However, there were two counter-tendencies. One was the kind of planning promoted by Europe, which was discussed above. The other was the more native emergence of the social partnership approach (for a fuller discussion of social partnership see Chapter 14). The shift towards encouraging indigenous, rather than just multinational, firms can be traced back to 1973 (O'Farrell 1986:13) with the initial policy stress on creating linkages between multinational firms and indigenous enterprises. A report published by the National Economic and Social Council (NESC) (Telesis 1982) indicated the policy of greater support for 'indigenous' industry was a consensus one. While the Telesis report did not explicitly emphasise the term 'enterprise',

Carr (1998) traces to it the origins of a key component (selectivity) of Ireland's enterprise culture policy. Despite strategic thinking moving in the direction of more support for indigenous industry, policy implementation was still open, at least up to the early 1990s, to the charge of neglecting small firms and Irish entrepreneurs. In the late 1980s, the IDA (the principal state agency of the time), in the polite words of an official report, 'created an institutional gap regarding support for micro-enterprise' (Fitzpatrick Associates 2004:9) by closing down their Small Industry Programme, their only instrument aimed at small enterprises. It is hard to imagine Margaret Thatcher's UK government of the time allowing such an 'institutional gap'.

An even more explicit move than the landmark Telesis Report (1982) to enterprise culture was apparent in the equally significant Culliton Report (1992:52), which stated that 'the contribution of productive enterprise to our social and economic objectives should be an issue of primary importance at all educational levels to de-emphasise the bias towards the liberal arts and the professions'.

The term 'enterprise' became even more entrenched when, in 1993, a key government department changed its title from 'Industry and Commerce' to 'Enterprise and Employment'. The context of this move is worth remarking on as it reflects some of the particularities of the way the term 'enterprise' was deployed in Ireland. The change in the title was made under a Labour Party (a party aligned with the European Socialist Group in the EU parliament) minister. Furthermore, this move was seen partly as a left-wing attempt to undermine the dominant and conservative Department of Finance. Thus, whereas enterprise discourse has been seen as a project of right-wing Thatcherism, which has been adopted by a collaborating New Labour in the UK, in Ireland its appropriation by Labour can be viewed as less of a break from traditional left policy. In 1994, following a major shake-up of the government agencies helping business, the agency aimed at indigenous industry was named Forbairt (an Irish Gaelic word meaning 'development' or 'progress', distinct from the Gaelic *fiontar* that is much closer to 'enterprise'). Perhaps the choice of the word *forbairt* might have represented a less than whole-hearted adoption of the private enterprise culture at the time. Forbairt was renamed Enterprise Ireland in 1998 under the Progressive Democrat (aligned with the liberals in the European parliament, though generally perceived as Ireland's free-market party) minister, Mary Harney. Of note, too, is the fact that the state agency dealing with foreign investors has retained its well-recognised abbreviation IDA in its new title 'IDA Ireland', although the 'A' now stood for 'agency' rather than the more imperious 'authority' (for further discussion see Chapter 3). Here the word 'enterprise' was thus directed at indigenous, rather than multinational, business. Under the same right-leaning minister, Mary Harney, the Department of Enterprise and Employment was retitled in 1997 as the Department of Enterprise, Trade and Employment. The insertion of the word 'trade' reflected the stamp of a new minister in a new administration, but also a concern not to neglect the international aspects of business by concentrating too much on the more indigenous-oriented word 'enterprise'.

That enterprise discourse is now firmly established in Irish policy as evidenced by the titles of the following major reports on what used to be termed 'industrial policy':

- *Shaping Our Future – A Strategy for Enterprise in Ireland in the 21st Century* (Forfás 1996)
- *Enterprise 2010: A New Strategy for the Promotion of Enterprise in Ireland in the 21st Century'* (Forfás 2000)
- *Towards an Entrepreneurial Society: Ireland's Response to the Green Paper 'Entrepreneurship in Europe'* (DETE 2003).

Though a 2004 report (Enterprise Strategy Group 2004) did not manage to get the terms 'enterprise' or 'entrepreneurial' into its title, its pages are replete with the language of enterprise (that there are ten occurrences of the word 'enterprise' itself in the 404-word letter submitting the report to the minister is indicative, compared to one use of 'economic' and no occurrences of the word 'planning').
'Planning' lost its dominance in the early 1970s and the rise of enterprise discourse in public debate can be seen in Lee's (1989) highly influential history bestseller. This text marks the embrace in Irish policy discourse of the importance of enterprise and is worth quoting at some length:

> Telesis and the IDA fundamentally agreed that native businessmen of the necessary quality simply were not, for whatever reason, available. Sixty years after independence, fifty years after blanket protection, twenty years after the Committee of Industrial Organisation, fifteen years after the Anglo-Irish Free Trade Agreement, eight years after entering the EEC, a native entrepreneurial cadre of the requisite quality had failed to emerge. (Lee 1989:535–6)

As we have seen, there was historically a nationalistic flavour to the term 'enterprise' in Ireland and, more recently, enterprise has been used as a synonym for indigenous, as opposed to multinational, businesses, though the enterprise sector has also served as a term to cover both indigenous and foreign-owned firms. Enterprise culture in Ireland has not been without its critics (e.g. Kirby *et al.* 2002:10–13). In particular, there has long been a feeling that the Irish version of enterprise culture might be more associated with protectionism and rent-seeking than with the vigorous and creative international version of enterprise (e.g. O'Hearn 2001).

CONCLUSION

We have seen how enterprise discourse has developed over several centuries, taking on various functions over that time, adding various shades of meaning and strengthening its ability to give shape and understanding to the world. Enterprise discourse has come to be the dominant language in which we talk about business and society.

This dominance of enterprise discourse we have seen not only in the post-Thatcherite UK and post-Reagan USA, but also in EU and Irish policy. Enterprise discourse in EU policy is not an exact copy of what it is the UK or the USA. We have also seen that Ireland has added its own flavours and style to enterprise discourse. This is to be expected. People do not parrot exactly what has been said by others in every circumstance; rather they use their imaginations, their knowledge of the particular circumstances and their knowledge of the people with whom they are conversing to adapt common resources for talking to their circumstances. Enterprise discourse nevertheless forms a large part of those common resources.

Since the 1980s enterprise discourse has reconceived small businesses, large companies and institutions, such as hospitals and universities, as all best managed in a particular way. This particular way of managing is the way it is fancied that innovative, risk-taking, entrepreneurial heroes run thrusting, fast-growing, small, young firms. Enterprise discourse allows us to talk powerfully about business. It can enthuse us, help us reduce unnecessary red tape and bureaucracy, give us the confidence to take risks and live with the responsibility. Enterprise discourse can also frame our discussions in ways that may not be so helpful. Running a large organisation as if it were a small, young, fast-growing enterprise can lead to a dismissal of expertise, a lack of transparency and an absence of accountability required at such a scale and level of complexity. The story of the failure of Anglo Irish Bank (Murphy and Devlin 2009), like much of the current global economic crisis, shows an excess of enterprise discourse to be a major characteristic of our current problems.

To discuss our future we need a common language about business and society. For the last thirty years or so, enterprise discourse has been the dominant way to talk about these issues. As we try to learn the lessons from the Celtic Tiger years and rise to the challenges of the second decade of the twenty-first century, we have to rethink our society's approach to business and organisation. At such times, we need to be particularly conscious of the role of enterprise discourse and be prepared to question its assumptions and its boundaries, knowing that its present dominant form has, itself, been shaped by the circumstances of history and that we can, in turn, shape its future.

References

Aligica, P.D. and State, M. (2005) 'Ambiguity, Imitation and Innovation: Notes on the Conceptual and Operational Facets of the EU Approach to Entrepreneurship Policy', *International Journal of Entrepreneurship and Innovation* 6(4): 249–58.

Andresso, B. and Jacobson, D. (2005) *Industrial Economics and Organization: A European Perspective*, 2nd edn. Maidenhead: McGraw-Hill.

Armstrong, P. (2005) *Critique of Entrepreneurship: People and Policy*. Basingstoke: Palgrave Macmillan.

Beesley, A. (2004) 'McCreevy to Hold Key Post at Heart of European Economy', *Irish Times*, 13 August, p. 1.

Berle, A.A. and Means, G.C. (1933) *The Modern Corporation and Private Property*. New York, NY: Macmillan Co.

Boettke, P.J. (2008) 'Austrian School of Economics', in D.R. Henderson (ed.) *The Concise Encyclopedia of Economics*, 2nd edn [online]. Available: http://www.econlib.org/library/Enc/AustrianSchoolofEconomics.html (last accessed 26 February 2010).

Bögenhold, D. (2000) 'Limits to Mass Production: Entrepreneurship and Industrial Organization in View of the Historical School of Schmoller and Sombart', *International Review of Sociology* 10(1): 57–71.

Bridgman, T. (2007) 'Freedom and Autonomy in the University Enterprise', *Journal of Organizational Change Management* 20(4): 478–90.

Cantillon, R. (1959 [1755]) *Essai sur la Nature du Commerce en Général* (trans. H. Higgs). London: Royal Economic Society/Frank Cass and Co.

Carr, P. (1998) 'The Cultural Production of Enterprise: Understanding Selectivity as Cultural Policy', *Economic and Social Review* 29(2): 27–49.

— (2000a) *The Age of Enterprise: The Emergence and Evolution of Entrepreneurial Management*. Dublin: Blackhall.

— (2000b) 'Understanding Enterprise Culture: The "Fashioning" of Enterprise Activity within Small Business', *Strategic Change* 9(7): 405–14.

— (2003) 'Revisiting the Protestant Ethic and the Spirit of Capitalism: Understanding the Relationship between Ethics and Enterprise', *Journal of Business Ethics* 47(1): 7–16.

Casson, M. (2002) 'Entrepreneurship', in D.R. Henderson (ed.), *The Concise Encyclopedia of Economics*, 1st edn [online] Available: http://www.econlib.org/library/Enc1/Entrepreneurship.html (last accessed 26 February 2010).

CEU (Council of the European Union) (2000) 'Presidency Conclusions: Lisbon European Council 23 and 24 March, 2000' [online]. Available: http://ue.eu.int/ueDocs/cms_Data/docs/pressData/en/ec/00100-r1.en0.htm (last accessed 15 February 2010).

Cohen, L., Musson, G. and Duberley, J. (2004) 'Enterprising Professionals: Scientists, Doctors and their Customers', *International Journal of Entrepreneurship and Innovation* 5(1): 15–24.

Culliton, J. (1992) *Report of the Industrial Policy Review Group – A Time for Change: Industrial Policy for the 1990s*. Dublin: Stationery Office.

Dáil Debates (1919–2005) [online]. Available: http://historical-debates.oireachtas.ie/en.toc.dail.html.

DETE (Department of Enterprise, Trade and Employment) (2003) *Towards an Entrepreneurial Society: Ireland's Response to the Green Paper 'Entrepreneurship in Europe'*. Dublin: DETE.

DoF (Department of Finance) (1958) *Programme for Economic Expansion*. Dublin: Stationery Office.

— (1963) *Second Programme for Economic Expansion (Part 1)*. Dublin: Stationery Office.

— (1964) *Second Programme for Economic Expansion (Part 2)*. Dublin: Stationery Office.

— (1969) *Third Programme for Economic and Social Development 1969–72*. Dublin: Stationery Office.

Doolin, B. (2003) 'Narratives of Change: Discourse, Technology and Organization', *Organization* 10(4): 751–70.

Dreher, A. (2006) 'Does Globalization Affect Growth? Evidence from a New Index of Globalization', *Applied Economics* 38(10): 1091–110.

Drucker, P.F. (1985) *Innovation and Entrepreneurship: Practice and Principles*. London: William Heinemann.

du Gay, P. (1996) 'Organizing Identity: Entrepreneurial Governance and Public Management', in S. Hall and P. du Gay (eds) *Questions of Cultural Identity*, pp. 151–69. London: Sage.

— (2004) 'Against "Enterprise" (but not against "enterprise", for that would make no sense)', *Organization* 11(1): 37–57.

du Gay, P. and Salaman, G. (1992) 'The Cult[ure] of the Customer', *Journal of Management Studies* 29(5): 615–33.

EC (European Commission) (1994) *Directory of the Commission of the European Communities (June 16)*. Luxembourg: Commission of the European Communities.

— (1995) 'New Commission Portfolios Distributed and Working Groups Set Up' IP/95/60 [online]. Available: http://europa.eu/rapid/pressReleasesAction.do?reference=IP/95/60&format=HTML&aged=0&language=EN&guiLanguage=en (last accessed 24 February 2010)

— (2004a) 'The Prodi Commission's Term of Office Ran from 16 September 1999 until 21 November 2004' [online]. Available: http://ec.europa.eu/archives/commission_1999_2004/index_en.htm (last accessed 25 February 2010).

— (2004b) *The Directorate General for Enterprise and Industry Activities and Goals, Results and Future Directions*. Luxembourg: Office for Official Publications of the European Communities.

— (2005a) *Implementing the Community Lisbon Programme – Modern SME Policy for Growth and Employment* (COM (2005)551 final of 10 November 2005) Brussels: Commission of the European Communities.

— (2005b) *Final Report: Publishing Market Watch*. Brussels: European Commission.

— (2010) *The Members of the Barroso Commission (2010–2014)* [online]. Available: http://ec.europa.eu/commission_2010-2014/index_en.htm (last accessed 25 February 2010).

ECEI-DG (2004) *Helping to Create an Entrepreneurial Culture*. Brussels: European Commission: Directorate-General for Enterprise and Industry.

Enterprise Strategy Group (2004) *Ahead of the Curve – Ireland's Place in the Global Economy*. Dublin: Forfás.

Fairclough, N. (1991) 'What Might We Mean by "Enterprise Discourse"?' in R. Keat and N. Abercrombie (eds) *Enterprise Culture*, pp. 38–57. London: Routledge.

— (1992) *Discourse and Social Change*. Cambridge: Polity Press.

Fitzpatrick Associates (2004) *Review of the Role of County and City Enterprise Boards in the Development of Micro-Enterprises*. Dublin: Forfás.

Forfás (1996) *Shaping Our Future – A Strategy for Enterprise in Ireland in the 21st Century*. Dublin: Forfás.

— (2000) *Enterprise 2010: A New Strategy for the Promotion of Enterprise in Ireland in the 21st Century*. Dublin: Forfás.

Friedman, M. and Friedman, R. (1980) *Free to Choose: A Personal Statement*. Harmondsworth: Penguin.

Galbraith, J.K. (1967) *The New Industrial State*. Harmondsworth: Penguin.

Geiger, T. (2000) 'Why Ireland Needed the Marshall Plan But Did Not Want It: Ireland, the Sterling Area and the European Recovery Program, 1947–8', *Irish Studies in International Affairs* 11: 193–215.

Gray, C. (1998) *Enterprise and Culture*. London: Routledge.

Grimmer-Solem, E. and Romani, R. (1999) 'In Search of Full Empirical Reality: Historical Political Economy, 1870–1900', *European Journal of the History of Economic Thought*, 6(3): 333–64.

Haughton, J. (2008) 'The Historical Background', in J.W. O'Hagan and C. Newman (eds) *The Economy of Ireland*, 10th edn, pp. 2–28. Dublin: Gill & Macmillan.

Hébert, R.F. and Link, A.N. (2006) 'Historical Perspectives on the Entrepreneur', *Foundations and Trends in Entrepreneurship* 2(4): 1–152.

Hegarty, D. (2003) 'Framework for the Evaluation of the Structural Funds in Ireland', paper presented at the Fifth European Conference on the Evaluation of the Structural Funds, Budapest, 26–27 June.

Hendry, J. (2004) 'Cultural Confusions of Enterprise and the Myth of the Bureaucratized Entrepreneur', *International Journal of Entrepreneurship and Innovation* 5(1): 53–7.

Jones, C. and Spicer, A. (2005) 'Outline of a Genealogy of the Value of the
    Entrepreneur', in G. Erreygers and G. Jacobs (eds) *Language, Communication
    and the Economy*, pp. 179–98. Amsterdam: Benjamins.
— (2009) *Unmasking the Entrepreneur*. Cheltenham: Edward Elgar.
Kanter, R.M. (1983) *The Change Masters: Corporate Entrepreneurs at Work*.
    London: Routledge.
— (1989) *When Giants Learn to Dance*. New York, NY: Simon and Schuster.
Keat, R. (1991) 'Introduction: Starship Britain or Universal Enterprise', in R.
    Keat and N. Abercrombie (eds) *Enterprise Culture*, pp. 1–19. London:
    Routledge.
Keegan, W. (1984) *Mrs Thatcher's Economic Experiment*. London: Penguin.
Keynes, J. M. (1973 [1936]) *The General Theory of Employment, Interest and
    Money*. Cambridge: Cambridge University Press.
Kirby, P., Gibbons, L. and Cronin, M. (2002) 'Introduction: The Reinvention of
    Ireland: A Critical Perspective', in P. Kirby, L. Gibbons and M. Cronin (eds)
    Reinventing Ireland: Culture, Society and the Global Economy, pp. 1–18.
    London: Pluto.
Lavoie, D. and Chamlee-Wright, E. (2000) *Culture and Enterprise: The
    Development, Representation and Morality of Business*. London: Routledge/Cato
    Institute.
Leddin, A. and Walsh, B.M. (2003) *The Macroeconomy of the Eurozone: An Irish
    Perspective*. Dublin: Gill & Macmillan.
Lee, J. (1989) *Ireland, 1912–1985: Politics and Society*. Cambridge: Cambridge
    University Press.
Lewis, P. and Llewellyn, N. (2004) 'Introduction to the Special Issue: Enterprise
    and Entrepreneurial Identity', *International Journal of Entrepreneurship and
    Innovation* 5(1): 5–8.
Llewellyn, N., Lawton, A., Edwards, C. and Jones, G. (2000) 'Entrepreneurship
    and the Public Sector: Issues and Applications', *International Journal of
    Entrepreneurship and Innovation* 1(3): 163–73.
Mills, C.W. (2002 [1951]) *White Collar: The American Middle Classes* (50th
    anniversary edn). New York, NY: Oxford University Press.
Murphy, D. and Devlin, M. (2009) *Banksters: How a Powerful Elite Squandered
    Ireland's Wealth*. Dublin: Hachette Books Ireland.
O'Farrell, P. (1986) *Entrepreneurs and Industrial Change*. Dublin: Irish
    Management Institute.
O'Hearn, D. (2001) *The Atlantic Economy: Britain, the US and Ireland*.
    Manchester: Manchester University Press.
O'Mahony, D. (1985) 'Richard Cantillon: A Man of His Time: A Comment on
    Tarascio', *Journal of Libertarian Studies* 7(2): 259–67.
Osborne, D. and Gaebler, T. (1993) *Reinventing Government: How the
    Entrepreneurial Spirit is Transforming the Public Sector*. London: Plume.
Peters, T. (1993) *Liberation Management*. London: Pan Macmillan.

Phelan, S. (2007) 'The Discourses of Neoliberal Hegemony: The Case of the Irish Republic', *Critical Discourse Studies* 4(1): 29–48.

Smith, A. (1982 [1776]) *The Wealth of Nations*. Harmondsworth: Penguin.

Telesis (1982) A *Review of Industrial Policy*, NESC Report No. 64. Dublin: National Economic and Social Council.

von Hayek, F.A. (1985 [1931]) 'Richard Cantillon: Introduction and Textual Comments by Friedrich A. Hayek, Written for Hella Hayek's 1931 German Translation of Richard Cantillon's Essai' (trans. Micheál Ó Súilleabháin), *Journal of Libertarian Studies* VII(2): 217–47.

— (1945) 'The Use of Knowledge in Society', *American Economic Review* 35(4): 519–30.

Chapter 5

The Politics of Irish Social Security Policy 1986–2006

Mary P. Murphy

INTRODUCTION

Across the world, social security systems are under pressure. Given that Kearney's (2003, 2004, 2005, 2006, 2007) Globalisation Index (GI) consistently ranked Ireland as one of the world's most globalised countries, we might expect the pressures of globalisation on Irish social welfare policy to be relatively strong (McCoy 2008). However, an examination of Irish social welfare policy over the period 1986–2006 suggests limited impact on Irish social security policy from global and domestic pressures (Cousins 2005; Kirby and Murphy 2008). Irish social welfare change was qualitatively different from, and less than, that of other liberal welfare regimes and small open European economies. In particular, we see limited evidence of movement from a redistributive welfare state to a 'productivist' or work-oriented reordering of social policy to meet economic needs. The relative lack of change seems inconsistent with the reordering of the Irish economy towards greater competitiveness and the associated significant increase in demand for Irish labour. There is less focus on welfare-to-work strategies, little progress relating to women's access to employment, less upgrading of income incentives and tackling of unemployment traps, less conditionality and less extension of conditionality to groups outside the formal live register than one might expect (Cousins 2005:339; NESF 2006; Sweeney and O'Donnell 2003:33). Alber and Standing (2000) conclude there is 'arrested development' of Irish social welfare.

This chapter questions this slowness to adapt and asks whether lack of reform can be explained by examining the politics of welfare. The concept of path dependency has some explanatory potential. Simply explained, path dependency means that institutions are self-reinforcing, that policy, once developed in a particular direction, is locked into that policy choice and is difficult to change (Pierson 2001). This means that we can expect the original construction of Irish social security design as a liberal and male breadwinner welfare regime to

The author would like to acknowledge that the original research on which this chapter is based was funded by a Combat Poverty Agency PhD fellowship 2002–2005.

determine some of the direction of future Irish social security reform. However, path dependency does not explain the momentum or the distinctive style, pace and discourse of Irish reform, or why Irish social welfare reform has diverged from those countries with which it had previously had common development paths. Daly and Yeates (2003) point to a divergence between social security in Ireland and Britain and, reflecting on why this is the case, offer 'policy architecture' as a possible explanation. Hay (2004a) offers a three-dimensional framework to understand the process of change as an interaction of ideas, institutions and actors.

This chapter explores and analyses the policy process of the Irish social security policy community from 1987 to 2006. It concentrates on outlining the political and institutional factors that influence the trajectory of Irish social security and that domestically constrain the impact of globalisation. It first locates the Irish social security community within wider Irish political institutions, many of which act as veto points to change. It then analyses the policy institutions in which key social security decisions are mediated. It goes on to examine the power interests who mediate Irish social security. The chapter concludes by examining how such institutions, actors and ideational influences work together to constrain policy, mitigating threats associated with globalisation, but constraining possibilities of equitable reforms.

THE VETO POINTS OF THE IRISH STATE

While a lively literature contests different understandings of the Irish state, its capacity, level of autonomy and model of development (Allen 2000; Kirby and Murphy 2008; O'Hearn 1998; Adshead 2008, Ó Riain 2008; Taylor 2005), there is some consensus about key characteristics of the peculiar post-colonial institutions of the Irish state. Hay (2004a:205) differentiated states according to institutional characteristics that give rise to 'veto points'. A veto player or point can be understood as 'an individual or collective actor whose agreement is required for a policy decision' (Tsebelis 2002:209). The electoral regime is a key institution. Cousins (2005:124) concurs with Hay's (2004a:205) comment that 'centralised adversarial first-past-the-post and two-party systems are more prone to crisis induced policy-making than others which are more prone to incremental reforms'. In the context of globalisation Swank (2002:285) observed:

Central features of domestic institutions shape . . . promote or impede configurations of norms, values and behaviours embodied in national policy-making routines that favour or disfavour slow adaptation to the pressures of globalisation and the inclusion of all interests in that process.

Lijphart's (1999:255) map of shifts in democratic styles in twenty-six states since 1980 shows that Ireland moved from a barely majoritarian-style democracy to a consensus-oriented democracy. (Ireland is characterised by Lijphart (1999:67,

114–117, 189) as a unitary and centralised, two and a half-party, semi-presidential system with parliament and an elected president, a 'medium influencing' prime minister and 'weakish' in relation to judicial review and constitutional rigidity.)

This chapter argues that the Irish proportional representation through single transferable vote (PR-STV) electoral system combined with other veto points, such as a rigid constitution, coalition government, bicameralism and social partnership, creates an incremental policy culture that tends to mitigate both negative *and* positive reform and produce a frozen landscape for policy reform (Esping-Andersen 2003). Relative to other Anglo-Saxon regimes, Ireland has a higher, and an increasing, number of veto players. Multiple veto players lead to policy cultures dominated by policy avoidance (Pierson 2001), but also to a consensus culture and a more conservative policy predisposition (Lijphart 1999:301). Combined with a conservative early Irish state, which valued continuity of policy making and rejected policy innovation (Acheson *et al.* 2004; Ferriter 2004a; Kiam-Caudle 1967; Lee 1989), Irish veto players work to limit policy change. As the only English-speaking country and liberal welfare regime that fits the 'consensus' typology, the politics of mediating welfare reform in Ireland is likely to be different from that in other liberal welfare regimes. Ireland is more likely to be a 'consolidating' policy culture than an 'innovating' policy regime (Ditch and Oldfield 1999).

THE POLICY COMMUNITY: DOMESTIC AND INTERNATIONAL INSTITUTIONS

While it is difficult to bring order to complex, chaotic and ultimately unique policy processes it is helpful, nonetheless, to disaggregate policy processes into three discrete independent variables: 'interests', 'institutions' and 'ideas'. These variables determine the pace and direction of policy change in any policy community (Hay 2004a:204). The policy process is made even more complex by the transformational influence of globalisation towards more multi-level governance. A shortage of space means we are forced to focus in a general way on institutions and interests at the expense of examining the key role of ideas.

Domestic Institutions

Brewer and de Leon (1983) stressed the importance of decision-makers' subjective preferences. Senior membership of these institutions is stable and well networked. It is primarily male, middle-aged, third-level-educated, home-owning and white. Mainly indigenous Irish, the policy actors appear to share common Christian-based social and political values. Continuity and stability enables informal networking. While, internationally, Irish policy institutions are well regarded, in 2005 interviews conducted by the author, policy actors tended to share a common self-diagnosis of underdeveloped policy capacity and a weak policy learning capacity (Murphy 2006). Irish civil servants are powerful and can, and do, veto policy agendas. However, they now work in a more crowded and fragmented policy community and have to share space and, to some degree, access to power with social partners. Just as Ireland's lack of an effective national system of innovation was inimical to economic modernisation, the NESC (2005a) argues that there is a lack of effective infrastructure to support social innovation. The Irish civil service conservative culture has been slow to transform under the Strategic Management Initiative (NESC 2003; Pollit 2005). Still dominated by slow, incremental, path-dependent administrative considerations (Crotty 1998), it is marked by procrastination, policy paralysis or inertia (NESC 2005a). The civil service is not a monolithic interest group. Departments compete with each other. Departments, having devolved policy functions to numerous statutory agencies, are increasingly fragmented (Clancy and Murphy 2006; OECD 2008). While all departments have in common a weak policy capacity, they can still be differentiated by cultural and ideological differences.

In 2009 the main institution dealing with social security policy was the Department of Social and Family Affairs (DSFA); in 2010 this was renamed the Department of Social Protection. The department is heavily influenced by the priority it affords delivery. Preoccupied by administrative challenges, it is limited in its capacity to engage in policy making. This is not a simple resource issue, rather the pressures of guaranteeing delivery of weekly social welfare payments has influenced the department's own culture. The internal preoccupation with effective delivery of income supports was compounded by serious administrative failures in 1981 and 1989.

Divided into operational and policy divisions (the brawn and the brains), the policy division (the *Aireacht*) is small and under-resourced. Staff have fostered good relations in the policy community and engaged positively in social partnership. Over the past two decades, the DSFA has established a number of statutory organisations: the Citizens Information Board (previously Comhairle and National Social Services Board), which focuses on citizens' information and administrative and technical issues related to the delivery of welfare (Acheson *et al.* 2004); Combat Poverty Agency (in 2009 absorbed into the DSFA), which has a statutory function to advise the minister on poverty-related policy; the National Pensions Board (NPB) and the Family Support Agency (FSA). While these agencies institutionally strengthen the department's policy capacity and enhance policy debate, there is also overlap and duplication and a more complex, fragmented policy community. Most recently the Office for Social Inclusion (OSI) was established to support engagement with the various National Social Inclusion Action Plans and other policy processes associated with the European Union (EU) Open Method of Co-ordination (OMC) (explained later in this chapter). Within the department there is tension between those who believe it should take a leading role in social security debate and those who focus on its administrative role delivering policy developed elsewhere. It is curious that, for all the proliferation of government agencies over the period in question and despite the significant proportion of GDP spent on social security, there remains no single agency tasked with the overview of Irish social security policy.

The Department of Enterprise, Trade and Employment (DETE) leaves much of its social policy function to its statutory body, the training and employment agency An Foras Áiseanna Saothair (FÁS). Other agencies, the Industrial Development Authority (IDA) and the National Competitiveness Council (NCC), also influence national social security debate (Connolly 2007). Historically, the DETE had an obstructive working relationship with the DSFA. While the 'turf war' was more about institutional issues than policy, ideological differences are evident between the two departments. The underpinning attitude of the DETE often portrays social security as an obstacle to employment, and traditionally DETE civil servants are likely to promote the policy agendas of the Organisation for Economic Co-operation and Development (OECD) relating to activation and welfare-to-work-related social security policy. Various attempts to co-ordinate policy across the two departments include programme managers (1992), the Tax Strategy Group (1995), a Strategy Group on Long- and Short-Term Unemployment (1997) and a social partnership Labour Market Standing Committee focused on welfare-to-work and activation issues. Since 1998, the departments are required to work together under EU processes to deliver the National Employment Action Plan (NEAP). They also collaborate through the Senior Officials Group on Social Inclusion. The relationship is now more nuanced, but still characterised by conflicting positions and significant gaps in co-ordination and data sharing (Indecon 2005).

The senior Department of Finance (DoF) is ideologically and pragmatically associated with low public expenditure (Lee 1989). O'Connell and Rottman (1992:231) argue that it is 'opposed in principle to increases in state expenditure and taxes and in particular to increased commitments to social welfare'. This natural social conservatism of the Irish elites (Adshead 2008) and fear of escalating public expenditure was reinforced by the rise in spending of the 1990s. Compared, for example, to the employment policy focus of the United Kingdom Treasury, the DoF has an underdeveloped policy agenda and is more interested in keeping spending down than in how public money is spent. The Public Expenditure Unit (PEU), which links the DSFA to the DoF, is conservative about public spending. With a reputation for 'pouring cold water' over policy innovation, it vetoes spending in various ways, controlling the drafting of papers, refusing to adopt consensus reports and pressurising DSFA ministers to cut current expenditure. The key policy priorities of European Economic and Monetary Union (EMU), generating economic growth and avoiding borrowing, dominated the 1990s. While, to some degree, expenditure implications, rather than ideological positions, drove decision making, the DoF has a clear, pro-market ideological policy agenda. It vigorously resisted the National Anti Poverty Strategy (NAPS) and Active Labour Market Programmes (ALMPs) and contested proposals for refundable tax credits and using the revenue system to administer social protection.

While the DoF has remained dominant, power has shifted under various governments to the Department of the Taoiseach (DoT). This shift in power might perhaps explain the apparent loosening of controls over public expenditure in the last decade. The DoT has no specific policy responsibilities in the area of social security, but it co-ordinates government departments involved in social partnership and NAPS institutions. The general secretary to the government, the most powerful civil servant in the country, heads this department and attends all cabinet meetings, chairs the NAPS Inter-Departmental Committee, the National Economic and Social Council (NESC), the National Economic and Social Forum (NESF) and national wage agreements, and plays a key role linking political, civil service and social partnership actors. Two other institutions enjoy a type of monopoly role in Irish policy discourse. The National Economic and Social Development Office (NESDO) (which houses two social partnership institutions, the NESC and the NESF) and the Economic and Social Research Institute (ESRI) both influence debate towards a technical direction focused on statistical measurement and problem solving, rather than towards a more value-laden or political discourse.

International Institutions

While the Irish state appears to selectively filter its engagement with international social security discourse (Smith 2005:183), the international policy community is emerging as part of Ireland's social security policy architecture (Yeates 2002). New north/south bodies, the North/South Ministerial Council (NSMC) and the British-Irish Council (BIC), have been sites for administrative co-operation on issues relating to staff development, fraud control, migration and information technology. Ireland's colonial history is also evident in its participation in a social security policy exchange network of English-speaking countries, including the UK, USA, Canada, New Zealand and Australia. Limited policy shopping or transfer opportunities arise through membership of international institutions, including the United Nations-related social security institutions, the International Labour Organisation (ILO) and International Social Security Association (ISSA). The Organisation for Economic Co-operation and Development (OECD) and International Monetary Fund (IMF) also influence Irish policy discourse, but by far the most important international policy influence is the EU.

There is no commitment to EU-level social security convergence (Hay 2004b). The EU principle of subsidiarity means that social security policy is developed at domestic level and EU member states are protective of their domestic social security systems (Ó Cinnéide 2005). EU social security policy is driven by a free labour market ethos, which promotes the free movement of socially insured workers and those seeking employment. There is a more limited social inclusion agenda, which promotes fundamental human rights. There has been limited impact through EU legal directives and, while political and policy influence is harder to measure, it is likely that the EU was a very strong positive influence in moving Ireland from a traditional, Catholic anti-poverty ethos to a social policy that promoted social inclusion, if not equality. While social security is not a strategic policy area for Irish–EU relations, the Irish policy community does interact with relevant EU institutions. These include the Directorate General V (DGV), the Social Dialogue, the Social Policy Forum, the Structural Funds and Social Inclusion budgets, the Social Protection Committee, the Employment Committee and the Open Method of Co-ordination of monetary, pensions, employment and social inclusion policy. Each Commission Directorate (DG) has its own policy-making style, strategy and institutional features that influence policy-making patterns. DGV, the social policy and employment directorate, is characterised by a heterogeneous collection of mainly politically weak organisations arranged around social and civil dialogue (Ó Cinnéide 1993, 2005).

Figure 5.1 Irish social security policy formulation – domestic and international policy institutions

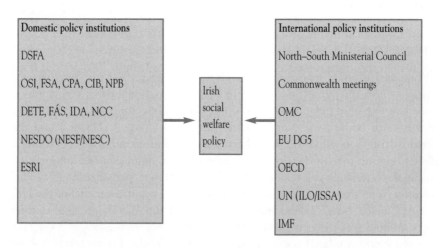

Source: Murphy (2006).

While the Lisbon Agenda promoted a three-legged strategy of competitiveness, job growth and social inclusion, its priority has shifted away from the social inclusion agenda in recent years. A policy process or governance process, known as the 'Open Method of Co-ordination' (OMC) (Ó Cinnéide 2005; O'Donnell and Thomas 1998), now dominates the EU social agenda (see Chapter 15). National states enter into a process of co-ordination, agreed at European Council level, of strategic action plans with long-term common objectives and short-term actions.

These are monitored by way of common indicators, joint EU evaluation, public accountability and the exchange of good practice. More a co-ordination of process than a co-ordination of policy, OMC is an increasingly dominant policy style across five policy areas, including social inclusion, pensions and employment-related social security issues. OMC processes do not have statutory power, but depend on the capacity of the domestic policy community to use the OMC as a political tool to lobby for improved domestic performance.

THE POLICY COMMUNITY: POWER AND POLITICS

This section examines power interests in the social security policy community. It first examines political power over the period 1986–2006. It then interrogates civil society power interests through the prism of elitist, corporatist and pluralist forms of power.

Political Influence

The historical origin of Irish political parties lies in a post-independence civil war intra-nationalist split, which dominated Irish politics and militated against a left–right ideological divide or a strong social democratic tradition in Irish politics (Mair 1992:389). It was discussed earlier how Ireland's distinctive post-colonial political institutions vetoed a culture of policy making (Smith 2005:186). It is not a difference in policy emphasis that differentiates political parties; rather, they are differentiated by the level of ambition and strategy for a planned approach to social security as an important part of national development.

Table 5.1 Social welfare ministers, 1987–2007

Year	Minister	Parties in Government
1987–1989	Woods (FF)	Fianna Fáil
1989–1992	McCreevy (FF)	Fianna Fáil and Progressive Democrats
1992–1994	Woods (FF)	Fianna Fáil/Labour
1994–1997	De Rossa (DL)	Fine Gael/Labour/Democratic Left
1997–2002	Ahern (FF)	Fianna Fáil/Progressive Democrats
2002–2007	Coughlan (FF) and Brennan (FF)	Fianna Fáil/Progressive Democrats

Table 5.1 above outlines who held political power and social welfare ministries over the period 1987 to 2007. The area under examination can be divided into three political periods: 1987–1992, 1992–1997 and 1997–2007. The stop-start nature of Irish social welfare activation strategies can be explained by inconsistent

policy across these stages, variations in political commitment to a fully developed welfare-to-work strategy and different degrees of emphasis on the degree to which policy should be offensive and supportive or defensive and punitive.

Fianna Fáil dominated the period in question (1987–2007), being in power for eighteen out of the twenty years. Being the most populist party, it is more cautious than other parties about negative changes, more likely to engage in short-term electoral budget cycles and less likely to have a planned approach to policy (Cousins 2005; Ferriter 2004b). The party's populist approach to policy development is a strong causal factor for the underdevelopment of various aspects of Irish social security policy and, over time, populist Fianna Fáil approaches to decision making permeate the thinking and practices of civil servants.

From 1987 to 1992, centre or centre-right governments held power. In this period of fiscal rectitude, the Fianna Fáil government had little social security ambition, but it understood the political expediency of protecting the incomes of the poorest. It readily accepted the consensus and expert analysis of the Labour Party-initiated Commission on Social Welfare (1986). This source of recommendations became the 'bible' for reform and guided future reform agendas. The period 1989–1992, when the Progressive Democrats (PDs) shared coalition with Fianna Fáil (FF), culminated in a period of cutbacks known as the 'dirty dozen'. In the second period, 1992–1997, covered by two different centre-left coalitions, government engaged with social democratic EU and UN dialogue in a reforming period marked by more ambitious policy processes, including the Tax Strategy Group, the Expert Working Group on Integration of Tax and Social Welfare and a NAPS. Labour's influence in government increased the pace and volume of policy debate about reform; however, resources for reform were limited. From 1994 to 1997, Minister De Rossa, from a small left-wing party, Democratic Left (DL), held the social security welfare ministry. He appeared more willing to expose his party to electoral risk and was more ideologically orientated towards gender reform and a more rigorous activation model. Actively engaging with the international policy community, this socialist minister looked to the EU social model and launched NAPS under the auspices of the UN Summit on Social Development in 1995.

From 1997 to 2002 and 2002 to 2007, centre-right governments engaged with a more neo-liberal, OECD-inspired rhetoric. The availability of resources and institutional capacity was not matched with political ambition for social security reform. The period was a missed opportunity, characterised by active resistance from the DoF to developing anti-poverty and income adequacy strategies under NAPS. The second half of this period was marked by fewer resources and, from 2002, a period of robust retrenchment under a more pronounced neo-liberal PD–Fianna Fáil (FF) coalition. There is evidence, consistent with smaller parties advocating more radical policy agendas, of the smaller right-wing party, the now defunct PDs, leading social security policy discourse in relation to non-Irish nationals, conditionality and lone parents. However, towards the end of this period, there was a distinctive softening of rhetoric by Fianna Fáil. This change of attitude to social security, reflected in higher social welfare rate increases in subsequent budgets, was attributed to the need to respond to significant electoral losses by Fianna Fáil in the 2004 local elections, evidence of the political power of the electorate.

ELITIST, CORPORATIST AND PLURALIST SOURCES OF POWER

Murphy (2004) identifies three coexisting principal patterns of organised civil society interests: elitism, corporatism and pluralism. This chapter now examines whether these forms of power have explanatory potential to account for the style of Irish social security reform.

Elite Power

What of elites and their influence on Irish social security policy? Strong globalisation theories (Cerny et al. 2005; Jessop 2002) expect the business elite to be increasingly influential. Hardiman (1998) argues that business elites are advantaged by the fact that governments are fully committed to a national model of development that promotes competitiveness over social policy and so prioritises business interests over redistributive policy agendas. The most powerful influence of the business elite is unlikely to be visible in policy institutions, but to happen through personal and social networking (Schmitt 1998). The establishment of the Pensions Board signified a governance shift that resulted in a partial privatisation of pensions. Domestic private industry and interests representing foreign direct investors also impacted on Pay Related Social Insurance (PRSI) rate-setting and broader PRSI policy. Employer lobbies have also influenced Irish labour market-led immigration policy.

The Catholic Church, long regarded an Irish elite, is now declining as a base of power. Pellion (2001:176) concludes that 'the church possesses no stake in social security, about which it has little to say' and it traditionally has had less direct influence in social security policy than in health and education policy, where it has had much more material and social capital. A recent trend has been to establish social justice interest groups (e.g. Conference of Religious of Ireland (CORI), Society of Saint Vincent De Paul (SVP), Bishops' Conferences, the justice desks of the Vincentians, the Jesuits and the Mercy orders). Catholic Church groups are not homogenous and there is ideological debate within and between Catholic groups. The dominant Church voice in the social security debate is CORI (formerly CMRS), which throughout the past two decades has focused on a basic income and adequacy lobby. CORI has been credited as the most effective lobby group and is judged to have had an impact on social security adequacy policy through creative long-term campaigning strategies (Acheson *et al.* 2004:87; Powell and Guerin 1997:16).

The Irish social security policy community is noticeably devoid of think tanks or a knowledge elite. The social security policy reading circle is small and dominated by the ESRI, the largest and most technically able think tank in the country, which is a key actor in policy debate and has a direct input into the senior Tax Strategy Group and key policy discussion. Other consultancy firms tend to be contracted on projects with narrow technical terms of reference determined by civil servants or politicians, or are small independent consultants hired by civil society actors. There is a small, under-developed social security academic community with few funding sources for social science research. There is little institutional social security expertise or serious analysis; rather, the media is used to campaign and lobby as groups try to influence decision making by influencing public opinion.

Corporate Power

What of corporate power? Irish corporatist structures were renewed in 1987, when government, facing into a difficult period of retrenchment, re-established social partnership (see Chapters 13 and 14), where trade unions, employers and farmers worked in several overlapping institutional spaces to develop consensus on policy strategies and to negotiate and monitor national wage agreements. This enabled governments to 'adopt reforms with reduced electoral and social risks' (Natali and Rhodes 1998:7). In 1994, Irish social partnership broadened to include the NESF, and in 1996 part of the community and voluntary sector was incorporated into partnership structures (Acheson *et al.* 2004). Some credit social partnership as the cause of Ireland's more humane welfare trajectory, relative to the UK or the USA (Daly and Yeates 2003; Kennelly and O'Shea 1998; Kiely *et al.* 1999). Others argue that social partnership can, through co-option, limit protest and smother the potential for more radical change (Broderick 2002; Murphy 2002; Ó Cinnéide 2000).

In other European national corporate institutions, both trade unions and employers directly manage and pay out social security benefits. This is not the case in Ireland, where social partners have little real expertise, interest in or ambition for social security (Hardiman 1998). Pellion (2001) and Cousins (2005) argue that employers use their political capital in social partnership more to curtail the general level of social expenditure than to look for specific social welfare changes. Trade union input in early national development programmes was significant, but by 1996 trade unions had begun to limit their input to issues directly impacting on members. Cousins (2005) and Hardiman (1998) argue that interests of employed union members primarily fuel the Irish Congress of Trade Unions' (ICTU) interest in social security policy, which focuses on low-paid/casual worker issues, equality issues around parenting and maternity, child income support as it relates to childcare, and pensions. There is less direct interest in a means-tested social security system basically serving the poor, although individual trade unions have developed specific social security policy interests because members are involved in the administration of social security or because members in low-paid or precarious employment have specific social security needs. Members of the agricultural and rural-based lobby groups focus primarily on rural-specific issues (pensions for farmers, Farm Assist and the social security needs of farming women).

The Community and Voluntary Pillar (CVP) is a social partnership participation mechanism comprising a large number of diverse organisations representing specific interest groups (Acheson *et al.* 2004:103). A limited number of individual organisations input directly into macro social security policy. Others interact on specific social security issues affecting their immediate membership. Given that government will manipulate policy differences between organisations, effective CVP participation has required collapsing individual organisational interests into coherent pillar-level policy positions. This causes tactical tensions, internal power struggles and strained internal relations within the pillar. CVP policy relevance has ebbed and flowed. High unemployment in the mid-1990s necessitated the problem-solving presence of unemployed/anti-poverty groups in national policy processes. However, as high unemployment decreased, such relevance diminished and the gaps between the CVP agenda and the business agenda widened (Larragy 2006) and the input of organisations representing the most disadvantaged is more likely to be residualised (Harvey 2009; Ó Broin and Kirby 2009).

In reality, scant social security policy change has been directly negotiated in social partnership and social partnership has not fundamentally changed Irish social security (Cousins 2005). However, to rest with this conclusion would underestimate the power of social partnership to provide an ideational framework for broader Irish policy (Connolly 2007). As discussed earlier, social partnership institutions in the NESDO play a powerful ideational role in developing and maintaining a consensual framework around a specific socio-economic model that subordinates social policy goals to the needs of the economy and employers. The impact of this influence on welfare has ebbed and flowed over the different stages of the political and partnership life cycles, but both Breathnach (2005) and Ó Riain (2008) identify three broadly similar stages, depicted in Table 5.2. It is striking that these three social partnership phases overlap with the political cycles outlined earlier. This suggests that the overall framework of social partnership agreements follows and reflects the dominant political policy mood. In other words, politics still matters hugely in determining national policy priorities.

Table 5.2 Social partnership life cycles, 1987–2007

Year	Breathnach (2005)	Ó Riain (2008)	Meaning of Phases
1987–1992	Early foundation phase	Macro-economic stabilisation	• Breaking the vicious socio-economic cycle and building a shared alternative future analysis • Foreign direct investment with tax incentives • Welfare characterised by cutbacks and stabilisation
1992–1997	Expansion phase	'Developmental network statism'	• Increased focus on social/equality and sharing of benefits social/equality and sharing of benefits • Extension of the partnership regime, a deepening of the innovation system and managing growth and inflation
1997–2007	Transition phase	Growth machine	• Refocuses on economics and a process of narrowing and controlling the agenda • Lower taxes and increasing domestic consumption • Narrowing of the development strategy and institutions and a reassertion of central state control

Source: Breathnach (2005); Ó Riain (2008:165–8).

Pluralist Power

What about pluralist forms of power? The community and voluntary sector's most powerful role is as a veto player – it has capacity to release the potential electoral power of sectoral lobby groups to act as vetoes on both regressive and progressive ambitious change agendas. However, the sector does not necessarily use this veto power strategically. McCashin (1992:5) accuses the sector of shying away from hard reform choices and critiques civil society groups' fear of grasping the nettle or engaging in controversial change.

Social security is distinguishable from the rest of the mixed welfare economy in that all social security income supports are state-delivered and tax- or PRSI-funded. Apart from direct civil service staff union interests, there are no large institutional insiders in the social security policy community. Most civil society or 'community and voluntary' sector organisations, even when they are social partners, continue to influence more through pluralist than corporate power relations and methods. A wide array of organisations operate from different power bases. Some larger national organisations maintain a coherent institutional engagement with government departments, including regular contact and bilateral meetings with both departmental officials and ministers, direct lobbying of politicians, circulation of policy literature, lobby days and attending political clinics in local constituencies. Others participate in consultation processes under the auspices of the NAPS, customer service initiatives or one-off departmental policy consultations. Most activity, however, is focused on DSFA-organised annual pre- and post-budget 'listening' forums, where up to forty groups submit social security budget submissions and engage in traditional forms of direct lobbying and campaigning.

While some groups have influenced delivery issues and income adequacy outcomes, much of this discourse has been 'voice without influence' (Lister 2004). The growing consultative voice of the sector 'has not proved enough to change policy priorities' (Hardiman 1998:142). Why is this? To echo Hardiman (1998:122): 'we may find that at least part of the explanation for the relative lack of progress in redressing these inequalities may be found in a closer analysis of the patterns of interest representation in the form of party policies and interest group formation'.

The sector does not have the policy-influencing power of a well-organised vested interest, and the absence of a national social security umbrella group dedicated to cross-sectoral campaigning on specific social security issues is noticeable (Murphy 2009). There is a perception in the policy community of duplication of work, inefficient use of resources and, relative to scale, ineffective impact (WRC 2001), fragmentation, and, at times, lack of trust and territorial dispute (Acheson et al. 2004). Like the contingent nature of the social security system, each group's social security agenda tends to be one-dimensional. While agendas are at times brought together through the mechanisms of the CVP and/or Community Platform, these joint agendas tend to be combined lists of demands collated for negotiation purposes, rather than coherent national campaigns. Distributional alliances, including Share the Wealth marches, anti-cuts campaigns, and Open Your Eyes to Child Poverty, have been successful but short term, and anti-poverty groups have not always demonstrated solidarity with each other (Ó Broin and Kirby 2009).

Acheson, Harvey and Williamson (2004:197) argue that the state plays a key role 'in structuring the civic space in which voluntary action occurs' and that 'interaction of state drivers with cultural and ideological forces' shapes voluntary action and development. Civil society's capacity to be an effective driver of change has been curtailed both by state strategies to control or limit the development of the sector (McCashin 2004) and by the sector's own failure to act cohesively (Acheson *et al.* 2004). Harvey (2009) observes how the Irish state, by way of funding, regulation and institutional reform, has proactively attempted to steer the community and voluntary sector (and hence civil society) away from networking and solidarity towards a particular development model marked by managerialism and service delivery. The shift illustrates how the state has attempted to manage domestic political tensions and mitigate societal reaction, as it subordinates social policy to the needs of the global economy.

CONCLUSION

How, then, can we explain the arrested development of Irish social welfare? What does this all-too-short review of the policy architecture, the interaction of Irish social security policy institutions and power interests tell us about Irish social security policy change over the last two decades? This chapter has highlighted how institutions and actors interacted over three distinct political phases. The overall impact of the policy architecture worked to constrain policy, mitigating threats associated with globalisation, but constraining possibilities of equitable reforms. Political power appears to have agency, but little ambition. In this complex area of policy, politicians work closely with civil servants, giving them power to progress or block the passage of policy or in furthering the agendas of certain lobby groups. Corporatist, pluralist and elitist power brokers are sometimes relevant. The Irish political system advantages groups able to organise and promote their interests. Groups with material and other resources to both organise members and articulate their interests have been more influential. Conversely, the least organised and most disadvantaged are residual and are least likely to voice their concerns in a way that influences the policy process and policy outcomes. Women are under-represented in all spaces of this policy community. Corporatist power is primarily ideational; pluralist power has ambition but little agency.

This chapter has explored how Irish institutional and cultural policy features domestically constrain global economic and political pressures on social security policy. The peculiar features of Irish political institutions can, at least partially, explain why the Irish experience has differed from other liberal regimes. This is the case whether the response is reactive to fiscal pressures associated with globalisation, or is proactive in attempting to strengthen social security in anticipation of new risks and challenges. In either case, there are strong domestic constraints on policy change that impede both positive and negative reforms.

A third aspect of policy architecture, the presence or absence of ideas and the type of ideological debate that takes place in a policy community, is also a factor with explanatory power. While we could not afford the space in this chapter, an analysis of the Irish social policy community's discursive practices could help us understand more about how social welfare knowledge and meaning is produced in this policy community and who has ideational influence. While institutions like the ESRI and NESDO have an ideational role, Irish political culture, the electoral system and the non-ideological nature of Irish political parties contribute to a weak tradition of political debate about social welfare values. Initiative for reform is dampened by absence of public debate (Cousins 2005; Kennelly and O'Shea 1998; NESC 2005b). This absence can be explained by the policy architecture, but also by the relative absence of policy crisis in the social security system. As at July 2009, it will be interesting to observe how the crisis invoked by the scale of social security recommendations in *An Bord Snip Nua* or the Report of the Special Group on Public Service Numbers and Expenditure Programmes (McCarthy 2009) provokes public debate about social security.

References

Acheson, N., Harvey, B. and Williamson, A. (2004) *Two Paths, One Purpose: Voluntary Action in Ireland North and South*. Dublin: Institute of Public Administration.

Adshead, M. (2008) 'State Autonomy, Capacity and the Patterning of Politics in the Irish State', in M. Adshead, P. Kirby and M. Millar (eds) *Contesting the State: Lessons from the Irish Case*, pp. 50–73. Manchester: Manchester University Press.

Alber, J. and Standing, G. (2000) 'Social Dumping, Catch-Up or Convergence: Europe in a Comparative Global Context', *Journal of European Social Policy* 10(2): 99–119.

Allen, K. (2000) *The Celtic Tiger: The Myth of Social Partnership in Ireland*. Manchester: Manchester University Press.

Breathnach, C. (2005) *Does the Concept of Social Capital Provide an Empowering Network for National Social Partnership?*, paper presented to Policy Institute, Trinity College Dublin, 25 May.

Brewer, G.D. and de Leon, P. (1983) *The Foundations of Policy Analysis*. Dorsey: Ridgewood.

Broderick, S. (2002) 'Community Development in Ireland: A Policy Review', *Community Development Journal* 37(1): 101–10.

Cerny, P.G., Menz, G. and Soederberg, S. (2005) *Internalising Globalisation: The Rise of Neo-Liberalism and the Decline of National Varieties of Capitalism*. Basingstoke: Palgrave.

Clancy, P. and Murphy, G. (2006) *Outsourcing Government – Public Bodies and Accountability*. Dublin: TASC/New Island.

Commission on Social Welfare (1986) *Report of the Commission on Social Welfare*. Dublin: Stationery Office.

Connolly, E. (2007) *The Institutionalisation of Anti-Poverty and Social Exclusion Policy in Irish Social Partnership*, Research Working Paper Series 07/01. Dublin: Combat Poverty Agency.

Cousins, M. (2005) *Explaining the Irish Welfare State*. Lewiston, NY: Edwin Mellen Press.

Crotty, W. (1998) 'Democratisation and Political Development in Ireland', in W. Crotty and D. Schmitt (eds) *Ireland and the Politics of Change*, pp. 1–26. London: Longman.

Daly, M. and Yeates, N. (2003) 'Common Origins, Different Paths: Adaptation and Change in Social Security in Britain and Ireland', *Policy and Politics* 31(1): 85–97.

Ditch, J. and Oldfield, N. (1999) 'Social Assistance, Recent Trends and Themes', *Journal of European Social Policy* 9(1): 65–76.

Esping-Andersen, G. (2003) *Towards the Good Society: Once Again*, paper presented to Fourth International Research Conference, International Social Security Association, Antwerp, 5–7 May.

Ferriter, D. (2004a) *The Transformation of Ireland, 1900–2000*. London: Profile Books.

— (2004b) 'Fianna Fáil Wary of Welfare', *The Village*, 30 October.

Hardiman, N. (1998) 'Inequality and Representation of Interests', in W. Crotty and D. Schmitt (eds) *Ireland and the Politics of Change*, pp. 122–55. London: Longman.

Harvey, B. (2009) 'Ireland and Civil Society: Reaching the Limits of Dissent', in D. Ó Broin and P. Kirby (eds) *Power, Dissent and Democracy: Civil Society and the State in Ireland*, pp. 9–25. Dublin: A&A Farmar.

Hay, C. (2004a) 'Ideas, Interests and Institutions in the Comparative Economy of Great Transformations', *Review of International Political Economy* 2(1): 204–26.

— (2004b) 'Common Trajectories, Variable Paces, Divergent Outcomes? Models of European Capitalism Under Conditions of Complex Economic Interdependence', *Review of International Political Economy* 2(2): 231–62.

Indecon (2005) *Review of the National Employment Action Plan Preventative Strategy*. Dublin: Indecon.

Jessop, B. (2002) *The Future of the Capitalist State*. Oxford: Blackwell.

Kearney, A.T. (2003) 'Measuring Globalization: Who's Up, Who's Down?', *Foreign Policy*, January/February, 60–72.

— (2004) 'Measuring Globalization: Economic Reversals, Forward Momentum', *Foreign Policy*, January/February, pp. 54–69.

— (2005) 'Measuring Globalization', *Foreign Policy*, May/June, 52–60.

— (2006) 'The Globalization Index', *Foreign Policy*, November/December, 74–81.

— (2007) 'The Globalization Index', *Foreign Policy*, November/December, 68–76.

Kennelly, B. and O'Shea, E. (1998). 'The Welfare State in Ireland: A European Perspective', in S. Healy and B. Reynolds (eds) *Social Policy In Ireland: Principles, Practice and Problems*, pp. 193–220. Dublin: Oak Tree Press.

Kiam-Caudle, P.R. (1967) *Social Policy in the Republic of Ireland*. London: Routledge and Kegan Paul.

Kiely, G., O'Donnell, A., Kennedy, P. and Quin, S. (eds) (1999) *Irish Social Policy in Context*. Dublin: University College Dublin Press.

Kirby, P. and Murphy, M. (2008) 'Ireland as a Competition State', in M. Adshead, P. Kirby and M. Millar (eds) *Contesting the State: Lessons from the Irish Case*, pp. 120–43. Manchester: Manchester University Press.

Larragy, J. (2006) 'Origins and Significance of the Community and Voluntary Pillar in Irish Social Partnership', *Economic and Social Review* 37(3): 375–98.

Lee, J. (1989) *Politics and Society in Ireland 1912–1985*. Cambridge: Cambridge University Press.

Lijphart, A. (1999) *Patterns of Democracy Government, Forms and Performances, in 36 Countries*. Yale, CT: Yale University Press.

Lister, R. (2004) *Poverty*. Cambridge: Blackwell/Polity Press.

Mair, P. (1992) 'Explaining the Absence of Class Politics in Ireland', in J. Goldthorpe and C. Whelan (eds) *The Development of Industrial Society in Ireland*, pp. 383–410. Oxford: British Academy.

McCarthy, C. (2009) *Report of the Special Group on Public Service Numbers and Expenditure Programmes*. Dublin: Stationery Office.

McCashin, A. (1992) 'A Future for Welfare', *Poverty Today* October/December: 4–6.

— (2004) *Social Security in Ireland*. Dublin: Gill & Macmillan.

McCoy, D. (2008) 'Making Choices, Choosing Futures: A Business Perspective', in S. Healy and B. Reynolds (eds) *Making Choices, Choosing Futures: Ireland at a Cross Roads*, pp. 1–16. Dublin: CORI Justice.

Murphy, G. (2004) 'Interest Groups in the Policy-making Process', in J. Coakley and M. Gallagher (eds) *Politics in the Republic of Ireland*, 4th edn, pp. 384–404. London: Routledge.

Murphy, M. (2002) 'Social Partnership: Is it the Only Game in Town?', *Community Development Journal* 37(1): 10–19.

— (2006) *Domestic Constraints on Globalisation: A Case Study of Irish Social Security Policy, 1985–2005*, unpublished PhD thesis, Dublin City University.

— (2009) 'What Impact Might Globalisation Have on Irish Civil Society', in D. Ó Broin and P. Kirby (eds) *Power, Dissent and Democracy: Civil Society and the State in Ireland*, pp. 34–51. Dublin: A&A Farmar.

Natali, D. and Rhodes, M. (1998) *New Politics of the Bismarckian Welfare State – Pension Reform in Continental Europe*. Florence: EUI.

NESC (National Economic and Social Council) (2003) *An Investment in Quality: Services Inclusion and Enterprise*. Dublin: Stationery Office.

— (2005a) *NESC Strategy 2006: People, Productivity, Purpose*, Report No.114. Dublin: Stationery Office.

— (2005b) *The Developmental Welfare State*. Dublin: Stationery Office.

NESF (National Economic and Social Forum) (2006) *Creating a More Inclusive Labour Market*, Report No. 33. Dublin: Stationery Office.

Ó Broin, D. and Kirby, P. (2009) *Power, Dissent and Democracy: Civil Society and the State in Ireland*. Dublin: A&A Farmar.

Ó Cinnéide, S. (1993) 'Ireland as the European Welfare State', *Policy and Politics* 21(2): 97–108.

— (2000) 'Programme Notes Understanding the PPF', *Poverty Today*, July/August, No. 47, pp. 4–5.

— (2005) *The EU and the Irish Welfare State*, paper presented to Colmcille Winter School, Gartan, Co. Donegal, 26 February 1993.

O'Connell, P. and Rottman, D. (1992) 'The Irish Welfare State in Comparative Perspective', in J. Goldthorpe and C. Whelan (eds) *The Development of Industrial Society in Ireland*, pp. 205–39. Oxford: British Academy.

O'Donnell, R. and Thomas, D. (1998) 'Partnership and Policy-Making', in S. Healy and B. Reynolds (eds) *Social Policy in Ireland*, pp. 117–46. Dublin: Oak Tree Press.

OECD (Organisation for Economic Co-operation and Development) (2008) *Ireland: A Public Services Review*. Paris: OECD.

O'Hearn, D. (1998) *Inside the Celtic Tiger: The Irish Economy and the Asian Model*. London: Pluto Press.

Ó Riain, S. (2008) 'Competing State Projects in the Contemporary Irish Political Economy', in M. Adshead, P. Kirby and M. Millar (eds) *Contesting the State: Lessons from the Irish Case*, pp. 165–86. Manchester: Manchester University Press.

Pellion, M. (2001) *Welfare in Ireland: Actors, Resources and Strategies*. London: Praeger.

Pierson, P. (2001) *The New Politics of the Welfare State*. Oxford: Oxford University Press.

Pollitt, C. (2005) 'International Experience of Public Management Reform', *Inside Government*, September, 4–6.

Powell, F. and Guerin, D. (1997) *Civil Society and Social Policy*. Dublin: A&A Farmar.

Schmitt, D. (1998) 'Conclusion: Continuity Change and Challenge', in W. Crotty and D. Schmitt (eds) *Ireland and the Politics of Change*, pp. 210–22. London: Longman.

Smith, N. (2005) *Showcasing Globalisation? The Political Economy of the Irish Republic*. Manchester: Manchester University Press.

Swank, D. (2002) *Global Capital, Political Institutions and Policy Change in Developed Welfare States*. Cambridge: Cambridge University Press.

Sweeney, J. and O'Donnell, R. (2003) *The Challenge of Linking Society and Economy in Ireland's Flexible Developmental Welfare State*, paper presented to the conference of the Society for the Advancement of Social Economics, Aix-en-Provence, France, 26–28 June.

Taylor, G. (2005) *Negotiated Governance and Public Policy in Ireland*. Manchester: Manchester University Press.

Tsebelis, G. (2002) *Veto Players: How Political Institutions Work*. Princeton, NJ: Princeton University Press.

WRC Social and Economic Consultants (2001) *Open Your Eyes to Child Poverty Initiative: An Interim Evaluation*. Dublin: WRC.

Yeates, N. (2002) *Globalisation and Social Policy*. London: Sage.

Chapter 6

Need the Irish Economic Experiment Fail?

William Kingston

INTRODUCTION

It was assumed throughout the struggle for self-government that Ireland would be able to handle the economic aspects of independence. However, with the centenary of the start of that experiment on the horizon, this assumption is now in serious doubt, because of fundamental structural weaknesses revealed by the world recession. The present chapter argues that the cause is the progressive replacement of economic activity which is based on individual property rights, regulated by generally applicable laws, by policies of intervention by the state.

The first part of this chapter explains the background to the country's present difficulties and discusses their impact, and the second part offers some suggestions for dealing with them. The basic argument is that democracy is a property rights system and can only be effective as long as a dynamic balance can be maintained between independent ownership on the one hand and the ballot box on the other; further, that the Irish electoral system works to undermine such a balance.

DIAGNOSIS

Property and Democracy

Historically, the wealth and prosperity of the western world has depended upon individual property rights. Not alone do these enable the widest possible range of human creative energy to express itself in economic ways, but they can also force self-interest to serve the public good – they are able to *civilise* it. Property rights make markets possible – without such rights, enforced by governments, there is only collectivism or the law of the jungle – and the kinds of market there will be depend upon the kinds of property rights there are (see Pipes 1999).

Because property rights and the markets they bring into being are human constructions, they are subject to imperfection, decay and manipulation. It does not take genius on the part of those who are being disciplined by market forces, resulting from property laws drafted with the public good in mind, to grasp the advantage they would gain if they could modify these laws to suit themselves. Pleas for free markets are invariably made by those who want markets to be shaped in ways from which they will benefit. The last thing business people want is a genuinely free market, since this would have no barriers to new entrants who would erode the incumbents' profits.

The Property/Voting Balance

The necessary balance of influence between the power of wealth and the power of numbers, as expressed in democratic societies by voting, is subject to constant undermining from both sides. Voters seek to divert the rewards of productive investment towards themselves through state interventionist policies and taxation. As the cost of getting elected increases, politicians become more dependent on those who provide their funding. Lobbying has consequently paralleled the extension of the franchise, so that property rights come into being through individual government decisions instead of being based on generally applicable laws.

This has been a worldwide phenomenon, and a cause of increasing concern. Usher's theoretical work, for example, shows that unless a significant proportion of income is independent of the state, democracy cannot survive, so that:

> somewhere between full public ownership of the means of production and extreme laissez-faire is a line that the liberal society cannot cross or a grey area within which politics becomes increasingly factious and unwieldy as the public sector expands, until eventually the liberal society dissolves into despotism. (Usher 1981:16)

Further, this expansion of the public sector is associated with growth in 'belief in the superior wisdom of the State . . . [that] breeds pathologies which deform, and at the limit destroy, the political economies based on it' (Skidelsky 1995:xiii). It is even being suggested that in many countries the death of democracy cannot now be discounted (Keane 2009).

The Banking Disaster

Nothing better illustrates how the property/voting balance can become corrupted than the present worldwide financial collapse. This is a direct result of allowing bankers to escape from the laws that used to discipline them, and this escape was made possible by their lobbying of politicians. What has been widely described as the failure of the free market system is actually the failure of markets based on property rights that have been distorted in this way. Capitalism can only operate to the extent that capitalists are denied the power to shape their own working conditions.

The laws that originally constrained bankers were those that forced them to be personally liable to their clients right up to the limit of their fortunes. These were not arbitrary, but were based upon understanding that money is fundamentally different from other tradeable commodities, and consequently needs different property rights. If a trader wants to expand his business beyond his existing resources, he must persuade someone else to invest or provide him with credit. A dealer in money can do it by and for himself, simply by making an entry in his books for which he does not have corresponding security. The ability to do this secretly is complete, and the temptation to do it is so great that only fear of the strictest sanction can prevent him from giving in to it. Historically, that sanction was bankruptcy, and it is the only one that has ever successfully disciplined bankers.

Maintaining unlimited liability for bankers made them careful about the quality of their loans, because of their fear of this powerful sanction. Over time, however, their lobbying of politicians got the law changed so that they could no longer lose more than they had invested in a particular financial institution. This allowed the original owners to issue shares to the public, so that banks increased enormously in size. Mergers then made them too big for governments to allow them to fail. This was a situation of what economists call 'moral hazard', because, in the knowledge that they would be bailed out by governments, bankers then took outrageous risks, and the credit and property bubbles were the result. Belief that bankers could be regulated by intervention instead of law proved completely illusory, because civil servants were not remotely a match for banking managements (see Kingston 2009a).

The Irish Electoral System

But why has the worldwide banking crisis borne most heavily on Ireland, out of all the developed countries? An important reason is that the degree of imbalance in Ireland between independent property and numbers in terms of voters, on which democracy and prosperity depend, is particularly high. This, in turn, is because the country's multiple-seat proportional representation electoral system filters out of the political process those who stand for anything other than what local 'numbers' want. The real rivals to a politician in a proportional representation through single transferable vote (PR-STV) system are not in another party, but in his own, and there have even been cases where politicians who moved to Dublin on being appointed as government ministers have lost their seats to others who 'worked' the constituencies in their absence.

Second, PR-STV makes significant parliamentary majorities impossible to achieve, so that any party with a few seats, or even a handful of independent deputies, can hold the balance of power. Again, this makes for short-term and 'populist' policies. Third, since the cabinet is formed from politicians elected in this way, their characteristics are carried through to the executive. Ministers with a record of failure can continue to top the polls in their local constituencies, and consequently cannot be removed from the cabinet. Such a cabinet is therefore intrinsically incapable of standing up to the local electorates' immediate wants, however damaging these may be to the long-term and true interests of the state. PR-STV therefore produces political parties and ministers whose electoral imperatives inevitably push them towards policies of intervention in every aspect of the national economy (for a fuller discussion see Kingston 2007: Chapter 2).

Other systems of representative democracy do not have the same results. In those that use a 'list' system, for example, up to half the members of parliament have no constituents at all, and consequently can look to the public interest instead of only to the local one. Even under the 'first past the post' arrangement, as used in Britain, rivalry within parties is finished once a candidate has been adopted. The system produces many 'safe' party seats where the member of parliament does not have to focus on his local electorate's concerns at the expense of broader policy issues.

Because PR in general greatly increases the weight on the 'numbers' side, all the more *independent* property would be needed to maintain a beneficial equilibrium. Switzerland, for example, has so much property of this kind that it is able to have many decisions taken through direct democracy in the form of referenda. But much of the private wealth that came into existence in Ireland since independence has been the result of specific intervention by the state in some way. Rights of property such as this, which result from the influence of interests on politicians, are not a counterweight to numbers – in fact, they reinforce the imbalance. Consequently, the country has more democracy than it is able to stand, leading to excessive intervention in the economy.

Max Weber (1930 [1904]: 180) showed us how what he called 'the tremendous cosmos of the modern economic order' depends upon those aspects of the Reformation that set the performance of tasks over social relationships. This, of course, is an exact inversion of how tribalism ranks them. In Ireland, PR-STV perpetuates tribal values. Awareness of this has begun to dawn, to the extent that the Oireachtas Joint Committee on the Constitution felt that it should study it, but concluded 'that there is not a compelling case for reforming the current electoral system at its most fundamental level' (Joint Committee on the Constitution 2010:15). In two referendums (1958 and 1968) and subsequent opinion polls, Irish voters have shown little interest in giving up the power this electoral system gives them over their local politicians. At the same time, they want to have a modern economy. Unfortunately, the two desires are incompatible.

Bureaucracy

Potentially harmful policies initiated by politicians could be tempered by quality in the civil service. The great economist Joseph Schumpeter had this in mind when he wrote:

> [D]emocratic government in modern industrial society must be able to command . . . the services of a well-trained bureaucracy of good standing and tradition [which] . . . must also be strong enough to guide and, if need be, instruct the politicians who head the ministries. In order to be able to do this it must be in a position to evolve principles of its own and be sufficiently independent to assert them. It must be a power in its own right. (Schumpeter 1950[1943]:293)

But the bureaucracy he was thinking of was that of the pre-First World War era, which at its best was 'supremely efficient, totally incorruptible, altogether independent of politics' (Schumpeter 1939:356). Their preference for law over intervention meant that these bureaucracies were responsible for much fruitful legislation. The culture shared by nineteenth-century civil servants and businessmen was conducive to economic innovation and entrepreneurship because it placed the emphasis on limited government. Law and property rights structured the economic environment within which individual creativity could be expressed. However, this is not the kind of bureaucracy that independent Ireland has had, because early attempts even to establish an officer corps in both the police and the civil service were quickly frustrated. The inability of those in charge to deal with corruption in the Gardaí in Donegal in the 1990s and early 2000s showed how damaging this has been in the first case, and in the second it is blindingly evident from the inability of those given responsibility for financial regulation to deal with bankers. The evolution of the Irish civil service has been towards making it more pliable in the hands of ministers – the exact opposite of what is required of it when these emerge from a PR voting system (see Kingston 2007:117ff.).

Responsibility

Individual property, independent of the state, is so economically successful because it allocates *responsibility*. Investment, either of time or money, made by individuals working within such a system will receive the utmost attention and analysis before it is made. Equally, an important reason why policies of intervention have such poor results is precisely because they remove individual responsibility from decision making.

After independence, the Irish civil service took over the British doctrine that the political head of a department is responsible for everything that happens in it, and those individuals who carry out the minister's wishes are responsible for nothing. This is why they can perform so poorly without sanction; above all, they do not face the danger of losing their jobs that is ever-present to those who work under the discipline of a market. Where results are important, one individual who can be fired for failure is worth an army of permanent employees. There are three results: first, the more the economy is run on the basis of intervention, the less anyone is responsible for anything. Second, tasks that can only be done properly if they are directed by people who will gain if they are successful and lose if they fail, are undertaken blindly and end in disaster. Third, what is misnamed the private sector increasingly reflects rent-seeking, which is primarily lobbying of politicians by business people in their own interest. Profits are a function of the strength of barriers to entry to a firm's market, and the strongest of all barriers is one granted specifically by the government. An Irish illustration of what this concept means is a government decision to build the M50 motorway with public money almost to each bank of the river Liffey and then to give a private firm the right to build the West Link bridge to join both parts *and toll the traffic*.

Public–Private Partnerships

The West Link toll bridge was a public–private partnership (PPP). Apart from their rent-seeking aspect, Irish governments have had a particular incentive to favour PPPs: they allow the European Union (EU) stability pact to be breached. Germany only gave up the Deutschmark in favour of the euro because other member countries of the Eurozone agreed not to borrow more than three per cent of their gross domestic product (GDP) in any year. In a PPP, the private capital does not count towards this stability pact limit.

In negotiating public–private arrangements of this kind, the interests of the country as a whole depend crucially on the quality of the civil servants who are acting on its behalf. An aspect of what Skidelsky (1995:xiii) called 'belief in the superior wisdom of the state' is over-estimation of the ability of the state's agents. The record of PPPs shows that this never measures up to that of the private sector side, primarily because of the differences between them in terms of responsibility and motivation.

A relevant economic term is 'information asymmetry', where one party in a negotiation knows more than the other. In PPP deals, the private partner will invariably be in such an advantageous situation, and even if the public negotiators could obtain the information they need, they will not be motivated to search for it. A few illustrations will make the point. In the West Link case, the deal was so good for the rent-seeking firm that when the tolls were eventually bought out by the state, the amount which had to be paid even after nineteen years of highly profitable operation was *sixty times* the original investment (Comptroller and Auditor General 2009; McDonald 1990). Another partnership where the public interest came off worst was between a mobile phone firm and Irish Rail, both of which needed to lay cables alongside the railway tracks. The phone firm took care to go first, and used mechanical diggers. When the railway company then wanted to lay the cables for its signalling, it had to do all the excavation manually at enormous cost, to avoid damaging the phone cables already laid. A third instance is that a number of schools were allowed to be built and run by PPPs, without any clause in the contract that they should be made available without charge to local clubs and societies for evening meetings, which had traditionally been the case when schools were built with public money only.

Quangos

Ministers will always be anxious to be seen to be doing something about the economy, and to take initiatives that can gain them publicity. Many such initiatives are beyond the capacity of public employees to do well, and sometimes even to do at all. Since failure is inevitable, avoidance of blame for it becomes a supreme value, and the main techniques for achieving this are the proliferation of committees with rapid mobility of individual members; employing consultants; and devolving power to quangos (quasi-autonomous non-governmental organisations).

The earliest of these bodies were the result of politicians' wish to intervene in the economy, coupled with realisation that traditional civil service constraints did not suit this. Later, they proliferated because of the inevitable tendency of governments to expand the bureaucracy as an alternative to taking action to solve a problem. Any proposal to provide a real correction will inevitably meet with opposition from vested interests. For the reasons already discussed, politicians elected under PR are particularly incapable of confronting anything that could make them unpopular, either with local constituents (who may turn to a rival within the same party) or with rent-seeking sources of party funding. The standard way of avoiding this is to institute or expand some form of regulatory regime.

Adding a new layer of bureaucracy to pretend to deal with a problem will also find civil service support, because some of the interests that could be affected by a real correction may be perceived to be able to affect senior public servants' career paths through political influence. Also, it will provide new opportunities for promotion and often escape from established operational constraints and pay levels. Not surprisingly, worldwide evidence is that such arrangements fall under the control of the interests they are meant to discipline – the process is called 'regulatory capture'. An obvious and singularly unfortunate Irish example is the way in which the Office of the Financial Services Regulator was staffed with people whose only experience had been gained in the Central Bank. Regulatory capture in this case left the country defenceless against unprecedented banking irresponsibility and incompetence.

However, great harm has also resulted from the existence of the two 'state agencies' that are concerned with industrial development, because this has provided politicians with an excuse for failing to try to stem the relentless decline in the country's international competitiveness over several years – or even to avoid policies that made it worse. Inward foreign investment depended on the 'natural' advantage Ireland had over many countries in the EU of the English language, coupled with the advantage it had given itself through low corporate taxation, at a time when its costs, especially wage costs, were not out of line with others. The first of these advantages has now largely gone, and (quite specifically because of interventionist policies) Irish costs have been progressively increasing compared with those in the Eurozone for the past ten years (National Competitiveness Council 2009). Not surprisingly, the country's share of both global and Eurozone foreign direct investment (FDI) has been dropping since 2002 (IMF 2009). Yet, to avoid the political unpopularity of at least trying to deal with the crucial problems of costs, policy has only been to increase promotional funding. This flies in the face of the fundamental marketing principle that no amount of advertising can sell a bad product.

The higher civil service also welcomed the foundation of quangos as a means of exporting responsibility for failures from their departments. Very many of those established during the Celtic Tiger period were of this type. They have added enormously to public service costs, while of course leaving the underlying problems, which are often their ostensible reasons for existence, largely untouched.

Politicians, Civil Servants and the Banking Collapse

These arguments find support in the two official reports on the banking crisis by Regling and Watson (2010) and Honohan (2010). Both reports make it clear that although the international credit crisis was the catalyst for the collapse of the Irish banking system, it was not its cause: 'it was in crucial ways "home-made"' (Regling and Watson 2010:5).

From the mass of evidence they provide, it emerges beyond doubt that the International Financial Services Centre (IFSC), which came to life under the Haughey regime that took office in 1987 and for which a physical area entitled to especially advantageous tax treatment was designated in the Finance Act of that year, has been an important element in this self-destruction (see Honohan 2010:108–9). Tax havens (of which the IFSC is one) are in competition to offer as little regulation as possible. In Ireland, this function had always been in the charge of the conservative Central Bank, so it was considered important to be able to signal to potential investors in the IFSC that they would not have to face this kind of regulation. Before Haughey left office in 1992, therefore, the ground had been laid for the fundamental transformation of the regulatory system that was brought about more than a decade later by the Central Bank and Financial Services Authority of Ireland (CBFSAI) Act 2003. It is no exaggeration to claim that there are strong roots of the country's banking troubles in this piece of legislation.

The CBFSAI Act 2003 charged the Central Bank 'to promote the development within the State of the financial services industry (but in such a way as not to affect the objective of the Bank in contributing to the stability of the State's financial system)' (Section 5) and established a regulator who was to be largely independent of the Bank. Nobody at the time grasped how far these two functions, of promotion and of regulation, are incompatible. In the Dáil debate on the CBFSAI Bill, the opposition economics spokesman failed to get a three-month postponement until the US investigation of the Enron case became available (Dáil Debates, vol. 553, col. 191, 18 June 2002). The government's position was expressed by one of its senators, who observed during the debate that foreign firms in the IFSC were very pleased with our 'light but effective regulation' (Seanad

Debates, vol. 172, col. 493, 7 March 2003). Advocacy of the IFSC soon dominated all regulatory considerations. To reassure potential foreign investors, the regulator's mission statement provided that its operation would be 'principles-based'. This meant that guidelines would be laid down, and the banks would be trusted to adhere to them, an assumption that, as events proved, was naive in the extreme. As Honohan (2010:108–9, emphasis added) describes it:

> A non-intrusive regulatory environment conducive to promoting the IFSC was considered important by Government. The Department of the Taoiseach took a lead role in coordinating support and the development of the international financial services industry. Partly, this was done through a consultation mechanism, the Clearing House Group at which senior Financial Regulator representatives as well as industry personnel were present to identify issues of major concern to the development of the sector. *The Chair and Chief Executive Officer of the Regulator participated in several roadshows to promote the IFSC.*

It would have been bad enough if this 'participation in roadshows' had been no more than passive, but this was not so. The Irish approach to regulation 'was characterised as being user-friendly in presentations aimed at expanding the export-oriented financial services sector' (Honohan 2010:9).

Whether regulation can ever be 'user-friendly' is moot, but, in any event, it could not apply to foreign banks in the IFSC without also becoming the norm for Irish banks. Not surprisingly, therefore, Honohan found that these now faced only 'a regulatory approach which was and was perceived to be excessively deferential and accommodating' (Honohan 2010:16). Regling and Watson (2010:41, 43) note that regulation 'was the opposite of hands-on or pre-emptive . . . the "light-touch" approach to supervision . . . sent wrong signals to banks and left supervisors poorly informed about banks' management and governance'. If, as argued earlier, it is an illusion to think that bankers can be regulated at all by bureaucrats rather than by laws, it was bordering on the insane to set up a regulatory system based on the assumption that they could be trusted to regulate themselves. Regling and Watson (2010:6) conclude that regulation was made all the more difficult because there was 'a socio-political context in which it would have taken some courage to act more toughly to restrain bank credit'. It was this 'socio-political context', of course, which had made it the Central Bank's statutory duty to promote the IFSC and which was articulated by the lead role in this taken by the Taoiseach's own department.

These two reports provide further evidence of the vulnerability of the Irish state to being captured by interests. The IFSC was born from lobbying, and once it proved to be lucrative for firms of auditors, lawyers and stockbrokers, they joined energetically in this. To take just one quite recent example, when the Revenue Commissioners proposed in 2006 to tax 'contracts for difference', a device operated by these firms to enable their clients to avoid stamp duty on share transactions, the

Minister for Finance removed the relevant clause from the Finance Bill at the behest of the Irish Stock Exchange (Cowen 2009; Quinn 2009). It may be remembered that it was 'contracts for difference' that enabled the huge individual stake to be built up by Seán Quinn in Anglo Irish Bank, which caused so much later trouble, both to Quinn and to the bank (Quinn 2009). Because of the inadequacy of the senior civil servants involved in regulation, the banks do not even appear to have needed to exert their pressure at the political level, since Honohan (2010:9, see also 73, note 96) reports that:

> intrusive demands from line staff could be and were set aside after direct representations were made to senior regulators. Also, attempts to formalise some of the principles (through Directors' Compliance Statements and a Corporate Governance Code) both came to naught following industry lobbying.

This shows how absolutely vital it is to have appropriate arrangements for 'whistle-blowing' in the public sector, which will be discussed below. Honohan's (2010:73–4) case studies of three banks show them as treating the regulator's observations about their behaviour with what can only be described as contempt.

The damage done to the country by virtually eliminating all regulation of Irish banks, so as to be able to offer little or no regulation to foreign ones in the IFSC, is now clear to all. What is much less widely known, and is not of course referred to in these reports, is how near these arrangements came to bankrupting the country, even apart from the local crisis. German banks took big advantage of the IFSC's freedom from regulation, and one of these, Depfa, actually moved its headquarters to Dublin, and became the largest buyer of last resort in the world, in effect offering insurance for bonds without hedging any of the risks involved. Fortunately for Ireland, Depfa was bought by Hypo Real Estate, a transaction that transferred responsibility for it back to the German regulator, only three months before it collapsed. The German authorities have had to bail out Hypo Real Estate through guarantees to the extent of €112 billion and counting (Stewart 2010:14–19). With its need to try to rescue its own banks, Ireland could not possibly have afforded such an additional amount to avoid facing multiple lawsuits by Depfa's customers for the failure of the country's 'light touch' regulatory system to protect them.

Law and Planning Enforcement

A report from the National Institute for Regional and Spatial Analysis (NIRSA 2010) shows convincingly that the failure of the planning system has been every bit as catastrophic as that of banking and its regulation. The report's detailed analysis shows that the over-zoning, the over-building and the 'ghost estates' will testify for generations to the unfitness for purpose of Irish local government. The authors blame 'clientelism, cronyism and low-level corruption' (NIRSA 2010:7 and *passim*), but there is nothing new about this except the level of damage. As early as 1924, bribery of councillors for jobs in their gift has reached such a level that the Local Appointments Commission had to be established. In 1940, further powers had to be taken away from elected representatives and given to county managers. However, councillors retained their power over spatial planning in the City and County Management (Amendment) Act 1955 and the Local Government Act 2001. It was the notorious Section 140 of the latter Act that enabled councillors to overrule whatever sane decisions their planners tried to make. Remarkably, there is no sanction against councillors acting as 'planning agents' or 'consultants' for developers. Central government's contribution to the building madness engendered by the unprecedented availability of credit was that it flouted 'its own principles as set out in the National Spatial Strategy (NIRSA 2010:4) and 'introduced tax incentive schemes, changed the parameters of stamp duty, lowered capital gains tax, allowed developers to forego their affordable and social housing obligations, and . . . in short, allowed the property sector to be driven by developers, speculators and banks' (NIRSA 2010:55).

PRESCRIPTIONS FOR IMPROVEMENT

Regulators were unable to control banks and planners were unable to control developers, proving that if we do not get the laws of property right, intervention (based as it is on 'belief in the superior wisdom of the state') cannot work. In contrast, even small legal improvements could have a quite disproportionate beneficial effect. One of the ways in which developers traditionally flouted the regulations, for example, was through 'retentions', but these could be dealt with by a simple change in the law, whereby a building contract would be enforced by the courts only if it was in exact correspondence with the relevant planning permission. 'Retentions' are cases where buildings are actually erected without permission, or in defiance of a permission, and they almost always involve political pressure being brought to bear on the planners. As a result, they have been the vehicle for some of the worst breaches of planning policies.

One of the most notorious of these was the Central Bank building in Dublin. The architects designed it thirty feet higher than its planning permission, no doubt expecting that retention would be granted through political influence once the work had already been done. At the time, the planners said they had too few staff even to be aware of what was happening until the roof was almost completed. Retention was, in fact, granted for the building in an incomplete state, which is why the exposed internal structure at the top was a feature of the Dublin architectural scene for many years. If the suggested amendment to the law had been in force then, it is quite unimaginable that one of the biggest builders in the country (Sisk) would have signed the contract to build according to the architects' specification, when the fact that this flouted the planning permission meant that it would not be enforceable through the courts. The Central Bank could not possibly have been built otherwise than in exact accordance with the approval it had been given by the planners. Of course, provision would have to be made in the legislation for special cases, such as where the developer is also the builder, but the broad principle should be clear: there are many instances where a simple change in the law, as it affects property, can deliver very much less expensive and better results than intervening directly in the economy.

Formal Departmental Law-Making Groups

A move towards ruling through appropriate laws, which would allow citizens to act on their own initiative, would need a small elite group in each government department with a quite new remit. This would be to suggest how changed or new legislation could contribute to solving a particular problem, before any decision is taken about it – and certainly before a decision to leave the problem untouched and superimpose some sort of intervention to pretend to deal with it. Such a group would be acting as a bureaucracy of the 'old' type, which independent Ireland has never had.

A partial model for it can be found in the Central Policy Review Staff (CPRS), known as the 'think tank', which was established in the British Cabinet Office at the instigation of a distinguished scientist, Lord Rothschild (see Blackstone 1990). This was intended to be a centre within the civil service that would plot initiatives unlikely to emerge from individual departments because of their necessary concern with routine work. Lord Rothschild's brief to the CPRS was therefore to 'think the unthinkable'. This was not popular with departmental heads, whose influence helped to persuade Mrs Thatcher to put an end to the experiment when she came to power. In Ireland, civil servants' opposition to an alternative to their power to intervene will be at least as strong as in Britain. Yet the advantages of such a change in the approach to policy making are so considerable that they might have to give ground. As a second example, consider some wider benefits of getting just one part of company law right.

Limited Liability and Unlimited Secrecy

General incorporation with limited liability is a social innovation of incalculable value in facilitating investment, and so bringing about economic development. It has underwritten enormous worldwide development of large-scale and professionally managed industry. It is not in any sense a right (though business people interpret it as a right and now take it for granted); it is simply a *privilege* granted by society for a public purpose. Secrecy forms no necessary part of the grant of this privilege, yet during the development of company law, no doubt through lobbying by special interests, the power to have absolute secrecy as to ownership has come to be included. Indeed, in many cases today, the *primary* objective in using a limited liability company for investment is to conceal the identity/identities of the true actor(s) in a business undertaking, something which countless examples show is not in the public interest (for illustrations see Kingston 2007:90–1).

Nor need this secrecy be even partially broken by the requirement for limited companies to file annual financial returns that are open to the public. They can in turn be owned by an *unlimited* company, which is not bound in this way. As this is the normal practice of Irish developers, the power to hide their activities, which they possess because secrecy has been allowed to become part of law that was never intended to include it and has no need for it, bears some responsibility for the property bubble. Further, the proposal to include a provision in the National Asset Management Agency (NAMA) legislation to prevent developers buying back their properties after the bank shareholders and taxpayers have accepted the losses on them is pointless as long as company law continues to allow beneficial ownership to be concealed.

There is no reason whatever why society should not require as a condition of granting the privilege of limited liability that the identity of anyone taking advantage of it should be publicly known. No investor in any honest project could have any basis for claiming that such a condition is in the slightest degree unreasonable, since they can invest co-operatively through a partnership if they wish. It would take only a minor amendment to the relevant law to remove much of the harm caused by the secrecy that now comes with limited liability. This would make any agreement in relation to a limited company non-justiciable, that is unenforceable through the courts, to the extent that it had the intention or effect of preventing the company's beneficial ownership from being known. Investors would then have to choose between having limited liability or keeping their identities secret, because they could no longer have both, legally endorsed.

Although intrinsically simple, making such a change would be politically difficult, because of the opposition it would raise from those who benefit from secrecy. Not surprisingly, therefore, politicians (to save loss of individual and party funding) and civil servants (to save themselves from trouble) have preferred to leave secrecy in place and to pretend to deal with some of the harms that result from it through bodies such as directorates for corporate enforcement, competition and the like. These can never be as effective as individuals operating in their own interest in a context of appropriate law, and, like all other quangos, they add to the cost of the public sector, making productive investment less attractive, so that the economy is less able to survive in a competitive world.

Whistleblowing in the Public Sector

The need for public sector reform has become more widely accepted with growth in public awareness of the numbers and scale of civil service failures. Up to now, however, the approach to it has been limited to trying to make the public service mimic private enterprise. This cannot work because, as noted above, it ignores the vital difference between them in terms of accepting responsibility. It is unimaginable that the sanction of dismissal for failure could ever be applied generally to civil servants. What could be done, however, is to introduce the fear both in them and in their political masters that wrongdoing, or gross incompetence, could be revealed to the public through arrangements for whistleblowing.

The besetting sin of every organisation is the cover-up, and the ability to conceal wrongdoing plays a large part in perpetuating poor, or even actually evil, decisions (as in the case of the Blood Transfusion Service Board's public sector performance (*Irish Times* 2009)). This ability owes almost everything to the viciousness with which organisations seek to harm those who would reveal the truth, by making the cost to them too great. Historically, whistleblowers have suffered much from the organisations they were trying to clean up, with loss of hope of ever being employed again as the almost certain penalty that few can risk. John Maynard Keynes resigned from the British delegation to the Versailles Treaty Conference in 1919 over the severity of the terms being imposed on Germany ('I work for a government I despise, in a cause I think criminal') – but as a fellow of a Cambridge college, he could afford to do so (Keynes 1919).

Since such public-spirited people are the most valuable and scarcest of all resources in public organisations, serious reform depends upon making what they do routine instead of exceptional (Kingston 2007:127–8). As Paul van Buitenen, whose revelations about EU corruption brought down the entire Santer Commission in 1999, put it: 'whistleblowing is not a necessary evil, it is a guarantee against the persistence of structurally endemic fraud and irregularities' (van Buitenen 2000:249). Although his courage won him a decoration from the Queen of the Netherlands (significantly, against the advice of her officials), it cost van Buitenen his EU job, as it cost Marta Andreasen hers in 2005 when, as the EU's chief accountant, she refused to sign off accounts she considered false (Andreasen 2009).

What is needed for whistleblowing in the public service is the establishment of an independent commission with power to relieve any civil servant from his or her obligation of secrecy when perception of wrongdoing requires it, and resources to provide proper protection against subsequent retaliation. The reaction of a few higher civil servants who have commented on this proposal has been strongly negative. They claim that it could destroy the cohesiveness of the service, which seems to be the supreme value for them. This ignores the extent to which this very cohesiveness has contributed to a very poor record of civil service performance (see Kingston 2007: Chapter 7). In practice, there should be extremely few cases where freedom to go public about an issue would need to be used, because the fear that it could happen would be such a powerful deterrent. Reverting to the discussion of banking regulation above (Honohan 2010:9), the regulator would surely have been less dismissive of the recommendations of his line managers if there was a danger that any of them could blow the whistle on him as well as the banks. An element of personal responsibility for outcomes would be introduced without affecting the permanent employment of civil servants. Any attempt at reform, therefore, which does not establish whistleblowing on a solid basis as a necessary component of public sector organisational discipline, will be no more than cosmetic.

Innovation

From its outset, the industrial economy of independent Ireland has never been an innovative one. The firms that came into being under its initial industrial protection policy were almost all subsidiaries of British parent companies. After the Second World War, West German firms set up here to take advantage of the Anglo-Irish free trade area, and eventually many US firms came to get access to the European Common Market. Indigenous industry, such as it was, typically avoided innovation, and an important reason was that it was never given the means of protecting investment in it through *appropriate* information protection laws. This is yet another illustration of the basic need to get laws right.

Nor does a rent-seeking economy produce entrepreneurs who are able to make it an innovatory one. Why would any investor face the risks, hard work and disappointments of innovation if he can persuade the government to provide him with a risk-free barrier against entry to his market by competitors, as the West Link case illustrates so convincingly?

At the present time, when it is beginning to be recognised officially that innovation is important, policy is to continue to look for it to come from foreign sources, rather than to devise laws for information protection which could deliver it from local initiatives. This is evident in government proposals for what they call the 'smart economy', and in the number of individuals from multinational firms on the Task Force for Innovation, both of which carry the stamp of the Industrial Development Authority (IDA). State agencies will always resist laws that replace intervention, as the IDA originally did in the case of a political initiative to replicate the British Business Start-up and Expansion Schemes (tax relief for equity investment) here (Kingston 2007:12, 134).

Law-making to suit indigenous innovation would require a high degree of creativity, because so little is to be learned from abroad. Just as bankers were allowed to escape from the only laws that could discipline them, and business interests were able to insert secrecy into limited liability, the laws of intellectual property (IP) have been progressively formulated by the large international firms in their own interest. Two illustrations are, first, the US Patent Act of 1952, whose provisions became the standard all over the world, and which was effectively written by the pharmaceutical industry. Second, the Trade-Related Aspects of Intellectual Property Rights (TRIPs) intellectual property annex to the 1994 World Trade Agreement was shaped by a committee of US multinational firms to such an extent as to justify the expert comment that 'twelve corporations made public law for the world' (Sell 2003:93).

Except for the interests that sponsor them, the world's resulting IP laws do a very poor job. For example, only one-third of all the profits attributable to patents accrue to industries other than chemical, broadly defined (Bessen and Meurer 2008:109). Moreover, intellectual property is a misnomer: the rights it grants are never clearly defined, nor are they enforced by the state, as property rights are. The cost of litigation to enforce them renders them worthless in many cases. Empirical research in the USA has led to the conclusion that 'for public firms in most industries today, patents may actually discourage investment in innovation . . . the average public firm outside the chemical and pharmaceutical industries would be better off if patents did not exist' (Bessen and Meurer 2008:264).

Irish Passivity

Ireland passively incorporated successive international IP changes into its own laws, even though they were quite unsuited to innovation by indigenous firms. In contrast, when India became independent in 1947, it took a diametrically opposite course, refused to join the international system, and formulated a patent law to suit itself, because it wanted to develop a native pharmaceutical industry. It has been outstandingly successful in this, to the extent of now being an important international player (Drahos 2009). The same industry in Ireland is overwhelmingly foreign-owned and, as happened to the Dell computer firm in Limerick in 2009, it could be moved at any time to countries with lower costs.

If policies had not been so completely committed to intervention, Ireland would have been able to formulate laws for information protection that suited its own circumstances, because the EU case law was to the effect that IP is a matter for individual states. But once the policy of trying to attract investment from abroad became dominant, there was no longer any question of Ireland having anything other than international IP arrangements, because these were considered necessary to persuade firms to locate here. In fact, the IDA acts as a lobbyist for the legal environment that multinational firms want.

An egregious example of this is what happened when Justice Costello followed British precedent in respect of new protection for small improvements in products. This was to the effect that to copy a three-dimensional object is to infringe the copyright in the drawings from which that object had been made. While this protection could have been very useful for some smaller Irish firms, it did not suit one of the IDA's clients, Hyster. This US multinational manufacturer had been diverted from establishing a plant to build its fork-lift trucks in Northern Ireland by a grant offer from the IDA which was so large that it was never published. The empty Ferenka factory in Limerick was a continuing embarrassment to the IDA since this manufacturer of radial tyre cord had abandoned it, so an offer from Hyster to take it over to make spare parts was very welcome. However, after the Costello judgment, the firm had to explain to the IDA that these spare parts were to be for their competitors' products, not their own. This of course would not be possible if they could be sued for infringement of the copyright in the drawings of these parts. The IDA responded by arranging a dramatic and urgent intervention by their minister to annul this case law by way of an insertion into a bill that was going through the Senate at the time (Copyright (Amendment) Bill 1984, Seanad Debates, vol. 105, cols 88–92, 13 September 1984). The bill lapsed when the Government fell before it had passed all its stages, and Hyster later abandoned its Irish operation and left the country.

Nonetheless, the proposed change in the law came up again in the new Dáil and was solemnly passed, to the continuing disadvantage of the indigenous firms the case law could have benefited. What should be noted particularly about this example is that for both the IDA and politicians, neither the property rights law nor the interest of indigenous firms seemed to count for anything. Nobody could admit that the Dáil was being asked to pass legislation whose only purpose was to benefit a specific company and for which there was no longer the slightest reason (Kingston 2007:62–3). This is a revealing example of law-making for individual cases, in contrast to law that applies to all citizens equally, which destroys the property/numbers balance, and, ultimately, democracy.

Better Information Protection

During the years when bankers were escaping from control, brainpower and energy in the wider society were sucked from technological into financial innovation, because that is where by far the highest rewards were to be attained (Philippon and Reshef 2009). The share of the finance sector in total US corporate profits, which throughout the years of very rapid growth in real wealth after the Second World War was about 10 per cent, grew to more than 40 per cent in the first half of the present decade, and its pay levels escalated correspondingly. A rebalancing towards non-financial forms of economic innovation is now likely, since financial institutions will no longer be able to pay so many talented people so much over the odds. This could offer an opportunity for any country ready to provide new kinds of information protection.

Some very valuable moves in this direction have been taken in the UK in recent years, but the Lisbon Treaty will inhibit or prevent national initiatives of this kind through its Article 118, which will take all power in respect of IP matters to Brussels. However, direct protection of innovation (DPI) would still remain a potentially valuable national option (see Kingston 2010: Chapter 11). This gives protection, not to a new idea, but to *investment* to turn a new idea into concrete reality. This new kind of protection, of innovations rather than inventions, could be applied to all the fields of technology where patents currently work badly. In Ireland, it would seem to be a necessary complement to the work of Science Foundation Ireland (SFI), since any successes with commercial potential from this body's funding are otherwise likely to be innovated abroad.

DPI has received powerful empirical endorsement from the results of the US Orphan Drug Act of 1982, which first put it into effect. The background to this is that there are diseases that affect too few people to justify research for relevant drugs by the major firms. Protection is therefore offered under this Act, not for the concept or formula of the new drug, nor even when laboratory proofs of its therapeutic value are available, but only for the fully developed and tested drug, ready to go on to the market. It has been spectacularly successful, resulting in twelve times more drugs of the kind required, with measurable declines in death rates (Grabowski 2005).

Protecting Ideas in the USA – What Ireland Could Do

The Lisbon Treaty will not affect national action relating to IP rights held in non-EU countries. Any serious indigenous innovation could not do without protection in the USA, but that country is notorious for infringement of foreigners' rights. For example, in a major EU study, it emerged that, without exception, every US patent that had any value and was owned by a small European firm was infringed there (EC 2001). However, there is a way for a country like Ireland to set up means to deal with this piracy (Kingston 2007:137).

What is known as 'contingency fee' litigation is legal in the USA, although not in Europe. In this, lawyers take cases on the basis that they will charge no fee if they lose, but will typically share 40–50 per cent of any awards they win for their client. Some competent legal practices specialise in this kind of work, so that a patentee with a good case has a much better chance of defending it in US courts than anywhere else. However, a serious drawback remains. Although in these cases the US legal firm is investing the expertise of its staff at its own risk, its client still has to pay all related costs, such as for discovery of documents, expert witnesses, court charges and the like. Infringers are very skilful at pushing up such charges as a way of intimidating opponents, although of course they are still only a fraction of the cost of the litigation itself.

A programme could be set up to fund such related costs for an Irish-based patentee who has found a US law firm to take a case on a contingency fee basis. This would not have the usual drawbacks of intervention, since it would be automatic. Such a condition puts it within the capacity of bureaucrats to administer, since they would not need to do any evaluation of projects or of a firm's chances of winning a case: no substantial firm of lawyers would invest its own valuable time and expertise unless it considered that it had a good chance of making money out of it. The only discretion the awarding body need have would therefore be in deciding on the list of law firms that could be used.

Such a programme could even tempt businesses that depend upon IP from abroad, even from the USA itself, to set up here, since unless their IP can be protected it is worthless. It would also attract genuine research and development (R&D) activity to Ireland (in contrast to the 'pseudo-research' encouraged by the current tax regime) (Kingston 2009b:77). And it could greatly improve the potential for joint applied research projects between Irish and foreign, especially US, universities, because the litigation support would presumably apply to anything that came out of their mutual efforts and the foreign university could not get it at home.

CONCLUSION

The above are only a few of the potential benefits of replacing intervention based on belief in the superior wisdom of the state by property rights derived from visions of the public good. John Stuart Mill (1848:159) observed that 'the laws of property have never yet conformed to the principles on which the institution of private property rests'. But they do not have to conform as badly as we have allowed lobbying by interests make them do. Searching for a better match between laws and principles, therefore, needs to be pursued with all the energy possible, now that the painful lesson is being learned that the alternative – intervention and the rent-seeking and public sector irresponsibility and incompetence that goes with it – is the way to ruin.

The scale of the challenges that now face the country is unprecedented, and it has to be accepted that if so much legislative power had not already been transferred from Dublin to Brussels, the day of reckoning would probably have come already. Nevertheless, credulity about what intervention can do still appears to be guiding such policy as there is for dealing with the crisis. The government's targets for reducing public expenditure over five years reflect nothing more than the hope that they will be enough to persuade foreign lenders to continue allowing the country to live beyond its means. The only plausible explanation for the proposal to bail out the banks through NAMA is that if foreign bondholders of these banks were allowed to suffer, it would militate against this level of borrowing.

Politicians and those who advise them are reluctant to face up to the reality that the external conditions that enabled the bureaucratic and property bubbles to develop have gone and will never return. Both bubbles were built on the ability of the Irish banks to obtain money in the international wholesale market on a huge scale, and this will not be repeated for the foreseeable future. This is all the more the case because in several countries – and certainly in Ireland – banking is now what has fairly been described as an 'off-balance sheet activity of governments'.

Consequently, if there is to be an economic future for the country, it cannot be built upon more of the same, 'the same' meaning interventionist policies. It can only result from abandoning these, just as protectionism had to be abandoned in the 1950s. But this time, it will be vastly more difficult. In the earlier case, the numbers in the public sector were very much smaller, they were paid nothing like as much as they are now, and they were less unionised. The cuts in both numbers and pay that are necessary may well be beyond the powers of any government made up of politicians who have been elected under multi-seat PR. If that proves to be so, the Irish economic experiment will indeed have failed.

References

Andreasen, M. (2009) *Brussels Laid Bare*. Yelverton, Devon: St Edward's Press.
Bessen, J. and Meurer, M.J. (2008) *Patent Failure: How Judges, Bureaucrats, and Lawyers Put Innovators at Risk*. Princeton, NJ: Princeton University Press.
Blackstone, T. (1990) *Inside the Think Tank: Advising the Cabinet, 1971–83*. London: Mandarin.

Comptroller and Auditor General (2009) *Annual Report: Accounts of the Public Services 2008* [online]. Available: http://www.audgen.gov.ie/documents/annualreports/2008/Annual_Report_2008_Eng.pdf (last accessed 17 September 2009).

Cowen, B. (2009) *Statement by the Taoiseach, Mr Brian Cowen TD, on the Issue of CFDs Raised by Deputy Gilmore on Leaders Questions Today Wednesday, 18th February 2009* [online]. Available: http://www.taoiseach.gov.ie/eng/Government_Press_Office/Taoiseach's_Press_Releases_2009/Statement_by_t he_Taoiseach,_Mr_Brian_Cowen_TD,_on_the_issue_of_CFDs_raised_by_De puty_Gilmore_on_Leaders_Questions_today_Wednesday,_18th_February_20 09.html (last accessed 14 June 2010).

Dáil Debates (1919–2009) [online]. Available: http://historical-debates.oireachtas.ie/en.toc.dail.html

Drahos, P. (2009) 'The Jewel in the Crown: India's Patent Office and Patent Innovation', in C. Arup and W. van Caenegem (eds) *Intellectual Property Policy Reform*, pp. 80–100. Cheltenham: Edward Elgar.

EC (European Commission) (2001) *Enforcing Small Firms' Patent Rights* [online]. Available: ftp://ftp.cordis.europa.eu/pub/innovation-policy/studies/studies_enforcing_firms_patent_rights.pdf (last accessed 7 September 2009).

Grabowski, H. (2005) 'Increasing R&D Incentives for Neglected Diseases: Lessons from the Orphan Drug Act', in K.E. Maskus and J.H. Reichman (eds) *International Public Goods and Transfer of Technology under a Globalized Intellectual Property Regime*, pp. 457–80. Cambridge: Cambridge University Press.

Honohan, P. (2010) *The Irish Banking Crisis: Regulatory and Financial Stability Policy, 2003–2008* [online]. Available: http://www.bankinginquiry.gov.ie/The%20Irish%20Banking%20Crisis%20Regulatory%20and%20Financial%2 0Stability%20Policy%202003-2008.pdf (last accessed 14 June 2010).

IMF (International Monetary Fund) (2009) *Staff Report for the 2009 Article IV Consultation Prepared by the Staff Representatives for the 2009 Consultation with Ireland.* Washington, DC: IMF.

Irish Times (2009) 'Hep C Scandal', 14 January [online]. Available: http://www.irishtimes.com/newspaper/opinion/2009/0114/1231738222559.ht ml (last accessed 14 September 2009).

Joint Committee on the Constitution (2010) *Fourth Report – Article 16 of the Constitution: Review of the Electoral System for the Election of Members to Dáil Éireann* [online]. Available: http://www.oireachtas.ie/documents/committees/30thdail/j-constitution/report_2008/20100722.pdf (last accessed 2 August 2010).

Keane, J. (2009) *The Life and Death of Democracy.* London: Simon and Schuster.

Keynes, J.M. (1919) *The Economic Consequences of the Peace.* London: Macmillan.

Kingston, W. (2007) *Interrogating Irish Policies.* Dublin: Dublin University Press.

— (2009a) 'Bankers Only Listen to Laws', *Regulation* 32: 4–5.

— (2009b) 'Interrogating Irish Policies Revisited', *Studies* 98(389): 71–9.

— (2010) *Beyond Intellectual Property: Matching Information Protection to Innovation*. Cheltenham: Edward Elgar.

McDonald, F. (1990) 'There is no Such Thing as a Free Road', *Irish Times*, 9 March 9, p. 11.

Mill, J.S. (1848) *Principles of Political Economy*, Book II, Chapter 1. New York, NY: Appleton.

National Competitiveness Council (2009) *Annual Competitiveness Report* [online]. Available: http://www.competitiveness.ie/media/ncc090818_acr_2009.pdf (last accessed 7 September 2009).

NIRSA (National Institute for Regional and Spatial Analysis) (2010) *A Haunted Landscape: Housing and Ghost Estates in Post-Celtic Tiger Ireland* (Working Paper No. 59) [online]. Available: http://www.nuim.ie/nirsa/research/documents/WP59-A-Haunted-Landscape.pdf (last accessed 2 August 2010).

Philippon, T. and Reshef, A. (2009) 'Wages and Human Capital in the US Financial Industry: 1909–2006', National Bureau of Economic Research working paper no.14644. Cambridge, MA: National Bureau of Economic Research, Inc.

Pipes, R. (1999) *Property and Freedom*. New York, NY: Knopf.

Quinn, E. (2009) 'The Power of One: How a 1% Tax on CFDs Could Have Saved the Banks', *Sunday Tribune*, February 1 [online]. Available: http://www.tribune.ie/business/article/2009/feb/01/the-power-of-one-how-a-1-tax-on-cfds-could-have-sa/ (last accessed 14 June 2010).

Regling, K. and Watson, M. (2010) *A Preliminary Report on the Sources of Ireland's Banking Crisis* [online]. Available: http://www.bankinginquiry.gov.ie/Preliminary%20Report%20into%20Ireland's%20Banking%20Crisis%2031%20May%202010.pdf (last accessed 14 June 2010).

Seanad Debates (1919–2005) [online]. Available: http://historical-debates.oireachtas.ie/en.toc.dail.html.

Schumpeter, J.A. (1939) *Business Cycles*. New York, NY: McGraw-Hill.

— (1950 [1943]) *Capitalism, Socialism and Democracy*, 3rd edn. London: Allen & Unwin.

Sell, S.K. (2003) *Private Power, Public Law: The Globalization of Intellectual Property*. Cambridge: Cambridge University Press.

Skidelsky, R. (1995) *The World After Communism*. London: Macmillan.

Stewart, J. (2010) 'Financial Innovation and Financial Crisis', paper presented at the International Joseph Schumpeter Conference, Aalborg, Denmark, 21–24 June.

Usher, D. (1981) *The Economic Prerequisite to Democracy*. Oxford: Blackwell.

van Buitenen, P. (2000) *Blowing the Whistle*. London: Politicos.

Weber, M. (1930 [1904]) *The Protestant Ethic and the Spirit of Capitalism* (trans. T. Parsons). London: Allen & Unwin.

Section II

Governance, Regulation and Justice

The chapters in this section deal with the issues of governance, regulation and justice. They examine Irish corporate governance, corporate social responsibility, white-collar crime, political corruption and the regulation of lobbying, as well as looking at the Celtic Tiger from a social justice perspective. Each of these chapters provides the reader with a particular theme that has been of growing public concern over the past decade. That the various topics overlap to some extent highlights how closely linked a variety of aspects of Irish society are, and provides this section of the book with a resulting synergy. In particular, this part of the book challenges the reader to appreciate the more general themes that run throughout its six chapters, encompassing aspects of openness, accountability, transparency and equality.

Chapter 7, by Niamh Brennan, provides an overview of corporate governance in Ireland. The chapter begins with a discussion of the definitions of corporate governance, as well as describing the internal and external mechanisms of such governance. The role of boards of directors, and theories explaining those roles, are considered. In order to provide an insight into the corporate governance research being conducted in Ireland, fifteen academic papers with an Irish focus are analysed by reference to theoretical perspective, governance mechanism studied, research method adopted and results obtained. This provides the reader with an overview of the range of research currently being undertaken into how businesses in Ireland are governed.

Rebecca Maughan focuses on the issues of corporate governance that fall under the rubric of corporate social responsibility (CSR) in Chapter 8. In recent decades, CSR has become a focal point for public attention and academic research. First, the concept of CSR and some of the most prevalent theories used to explain and understand CSR are considered. CSR in practice is then discussed, with an emphasis on current, as well as historical, practice and reporting in Ireland. Emergent areas of CSR research are also highlighted, and the final section of the chapter calls attention to CSR and private family firms as an important, but under-researched, area.

In Chapter 9, Roderick Maguire concentrates on how the law deals with the increasingly significant problem of white-collar crime. The chapter discusses the varieties of white-collar crime, and the historical and contemporary reactions to it in the legislative and political spheres. Explanations of the concept, and how it has been dealt with in the courts, are examined. The chapter looks at crimes perpetrated by employees in the course of their employment, as well as crimes perpetrated by businesses themselves.

Gillian Smith examines the issue of political corruption in Ireland in Chapter 10. She argues that, since at least the late 1980s, corruption has been a feature of Ireland's political landscape. As Ireland struggles to cope with failures in the national banking system, it appears that the failures of governance implicated in the current economic crisis have many parallels with past scandals. The chapter examines the structural and cultural factors in Ireland that inhibit the effectiveness of anti-corruption legislation and the importance of moral costs in reducing corrupt behaviour. Of particular interest is the chapter's provision of a unique insight into the attitudes of members of the Oireachtas to corrupt activities, and what this might mean for efforts to reduce corrupt behaviour in the future.

Taking another angle on the politics–business nexus, Chapter 11, by Conor McGrath, examines the issue of lobbying regulation from an Irish perspective. The chapter discusses the current absence of a law regulating the activities of lobbyists in Ireland, despite the fact that the lobbying industry here has been growing over the last two decades and that there has been a spate of major scandals centred on the relationships between politicians and business interests. This chapter considers how interest groups and lobbying operate in the Irish political context, it examines the proposals that have to date been put forward for lobbying regulation, and suggests what any future legislation might require of the industry.

Finally, in Chapter 12, Connie Ostwald provides a social justice perspective on the overall state of contemporary Ireland. This chapter discusses the fact that, although Ireland has recently been transformed by an economic boom, the level of income inequality remains a serious issue. The chapter analyses the results of this dramatic economic growth through a Rawlsian social justice lens, using Rawls' set of four 'primary goods' to analyse the impact of economic growth on Irish society: rights and liberty; equality of opportunity; income inequality; and the bases of self-respect. Using Rawls' principles of justice, including his 'Difference Principle', the chapter concludes that social justice was compromised during the Celtic Tiger period.

Chapter 7

A Review of Corporate Governance Research: An Irish Perspective

Niamh M. Brennan

INTRODUCTION

This chapter provides an overview of corporate governance, with particular emphasis on governance research with an Irish perspective. The chapter starts by examining various definitions of corporate governance, followed by a summary of the mechanisms of governance, both internal and external. Then the various theories applied in prior governance research are discussed. This is followed by a summary of prior empirical and other governance research. For reasons of space, only prior research with an Irish angle is reviewed. This is a fraction of the prior research on governance internationally, and governance researchers are encouraged to read more widely to obtain a more comprehensive view of prior governance research. The chapter concludes with some suggestions for further research.

DEFINING CORPORATE GOVERNANCE

Definitions of corporate governance are varied. Traditionally, the phrase corporate governance has been interpreted narrowly. Bradley *et al.* (1999) question the traditional and narrow view of governance, which tends to focus on the relation between firms (top managers as mediated by the board of directors) and their capital providers. A broader definition considers the relationships between various groups (in addition to capital providers) in determining the direction and performance of corporations (Markarian *et al.* 2007). Shleifer and Vishny (1997:737) define corporate governance as the process that 'deals with the ways in which suppliers of finance to corporations assure themselves of getting a return on their investment'. Denis (2001) and Denis and McConnell (2003) expand on this definition:

> Corporate governance encompasses the set of institutional and market mechanisms that induce self-interested managers (and controllers) to maximise the value of the residual cash flows of the firm on behalf of its shareholders (the owners). (Denis 2001:192)

> . . . the set of mechanisms – both institutional and market-based – that induce the self-interested controllers of a company (those that made the decisions on how the company will be operated) to make decisions that maximise the value of the company to its owners (the suppliers of capital). (Denis and McConnell 2003:1)

Johnson *et al.* (2000:142) refer to corporate governance as 'the effectiveness of mechanisms that minimise agency conflicts involving managers' and in so doing add 'effectiveness' as a criterion relevant to good governance. Keasey and Wright (1993:291) include accountability as a sub-set of governance in their definition:

> Corporate governance concerns the structures and processes associated with production, decision-making, control and so on within an organisation. Accountability, which is a sub-set of governance, involves the monitoring, evaluation and control of organisational agents to ensure that they behave in the interests of shareholders and other stakeholders.

Thus, the key elements of governance are reducing managerial self-interest, maximising shareholder value, ensuring governance mechanisms are effective and setting accountability through monitoring, evaluation and control.

MECHANISMS OF GOVERNANCE

Corporate structure has a major disadvantage arising from the separation of capital providers (shareholders) and capital users (management). Corporate governance mechanisms have evolved that help reduce – but never completely eliminate – the costs associated with the separation of ownership and control (Denis 2001). Mechanisms of governance are broader than might be expected and are often divided into two groups: those internal to and those external to the company.

Governance Mechanisms Internal to Company Operations

Agency theorists (Eisenhardt 1989; Fama 1980; Fama and Jensen 1983; Jensen and Meckling 1976) suggest that internal control mechanisms play an important role in aligning the interests of managers and owners. Internal governance mechanisms are the first line of protection of shareholders. The more effective these internal control mechanisms, the more likely managers are to pursue shareholder wealth. Internal governance mechanisms include (Daily *et al.* 2003; Denis 2001):

- effectively structured boards (with particular emphasis on director independence)
- compensation contracts designed to align managers' and shareholders' interests
- concentrated ownership holdings (including institutional shareholders) that lead to active monitoring of managers
- debt structures.

Added to these are the oversight role of auditors in relation to financial reporting, and the role of analysts in ensuring efficient markets.

Governance Mechanisms External to Company Operations

External governance mechanisms, which are activated when internal mechanisms do not work, include (Daily *et al.* 2003; Denis and McConnell 2003):

- the legal and regulatory system
- market for corporate control.

The legal and regulatory system. The legal system is a fundamentally important corporate governance mechanism. The key differentiation in different legal systems is the extent to which the law protects investors' rights, and the extent to which the laws are enforced. Recent international corporate governance research has identified systematic cross-country differences in the extent to which countries offer legal protection to minority shareholders. La Porta *et al.* (1997, 1998, 1999) assign a measure of investor protection to each of the forty-nine countries in their research, derived from variables related to shareholder and creditor rights. They find systematic cross-country differences in ownership concentration, capital market development, the value of voting rights, the use of external finance and dividend policies. These differences are related to the degree to which investors are legally protected from expropriation by managers and controlling shareholders.

The level of legal protection offered is in inverse proportion to ownership concentration. Countries with the highest legal protection (such as the USA and the UK) have the widest shareholder dispersion. Conversely, ownership concentration is highest in countries offering the least protection for minority investors (La Porta *et al.* 1998). Only legal systems that provide significant protection for minority shareholders can develop active equity markets. It is not clear whether it is the regulations themselves (law on the books) or the differences in enforcement of regulations (law in practice) that differentiates legal systems. However, common law systems seem to outperform civil law systems in providing superior protection to minority shareholders (Coffee 1999). Economies with a common law system and strong protection of minority shareholders have more dispersed shareholdings. Strong legal protection encourages investors to become minority shareholders. Thus, law does matter and regulation can somehow promote economic efficiency more than sole reliance on financial contracting.

While this section has focused on international variations in the legal rights of minority shareholders, there are other legal differences across countries influencing corporate governance, notably the requirement for two-tiered boards and worker directors in some countries. A further development of the research on majority and minority shareholders is the extraction of private benefits (disproportionately higher than the proportion of shares owned) by shareholders who (in various complex ways) can control companies. Such investors obtain control rights in excess of their cash flow rights. There are two ways in which this is done:

* tunnelling, whereby assets and profits are transferred out of firms for the benefit of controlling shareholders
* choosing the corporate managers (e.g. less well-performing family members instead of professional mangers).

In addition to legal regulations, corporate governance codes are now common. The best known is *The UK Corporate Governance Code* (Financial Reporting Council 2010), which applies to companies listed on the UK Stock Exchange. *The Irish Corporate Governance Code* is broadly similar and was issued by the Irish Stock Exchange in 2010. Like the corporate governance codes before them, the latest codes operate on a non-mandatory, voluntary 'comply-or-explain' basis. Thus, it is perfectly acceptable not to comply with the latest codes, so long as you explain non-compliance. Consequently, the codes remain a complete free-for-all; a smorgasbord of choice. No company is ever in breach of them. Until the banking crisis of 2008/9, there had been little or no oversight or enforcement of the corporate governance codes.

Market for corporate control. The central role of contracts and market transactions in agency theory extends beyond the internal workings of the firm, to include external market-based forces such as takeovers. Such external forces help ensure efficiency of internal forces. Inefficient contracting will be penalised by the market and these penalties promote self-correcting behaviour. Thus, poorly performing firms are more likely to be takeover targets. Takeovers create value in total. The combined value of the target and bidder increases as a result of the takeover. However, there is a negative side to takeovers. Takeovers can create additional conflicts of interest between managers and shareholders. While shareholders of target firms gain (on average) as a result of takeover, shareholders in bidding firms lose out (on average) by paying too much for the target. In some cases, the takeover premium exceeds the additional value created by the combination, causing the value of the bidder's shares to fall. Managers who are interested in maximising the size of their business empires can waste corporate resources by overpaying for acquisitions, rather than returning cash to shareholders (Denis 2001; Denis and McConnell 2003).

THEORIES OF BOARDS

Hermalin and Weisbach (2001) point out that there has been relatively little theorising about boards of directors, notwithstanding that they have been subject to a great deal of empirical research. No single theory to date fully explains corporate governance mechanisms, and multiple theories are necessary to take account of the many mechanisms and structures relevant to effective governance systems. Daily, Dalton and Cannella (2003) suggest that a multi-theoretic approach is necessary to understand the many mechanisms and structures that may enhance the way in which organisations are structured and function. Bonn and Pettigrew (2009) adopt such a multi-theoretic approach by integrating agency theory, decision-making theory and resource dependency theories, and suggest that board roles change over the life cycle of the firm.

Role of the Board

Although boards of directors are a legal mechanism, laws are generally silent on the purpose of boards of directors. Views on the role of the board are mixed, and differ across jurisdictions. This inconsistency may derive from differences in laws and other regulations specifying board roles. The role of the board is set out in a variety of regulatory sources, including: statute; common law (precedents set out in case law); and self-regulatory codes of practice.

Denis and McConnell (2003) observe that the role of the board in many European states is not specified in law. Where the role is specified, it is often couched in vague language, as this Canadian example illustrates: 'manage, or supervise the management of . . . the business and affairs of a corporation' (Leblanc 2001:6). Citing Wymeersch (1998), they note that in many European countries shareholder value is not the only, or even the primary, goal of the board of directors, stating that British, Swiss and Belgian systems are most focused on shareholder value.

Nor is the corporate governance literature consistent on the role of company boards. Applying a transaction cost economics perspective, Williamson (1985:316–17) defines the board's principal role as monitoring – to safeguard shareholders' investment in the firm. There are a number of ways to increase the likelihood that management acts in the interests of shareholders. One such is monitoring solutions. Monitoring solutions require effective monitors who present credible threats to managers. Shareholders are not capable of doing so, through lack of experience/expertise, and arising from their dispersion, making monitoring managers by small shareholders impractical. However, there are a number of alternatives by way of monitors. One such is boards of directors.

Denis (2001) identifies hiring, firing, compensating and advising top management as the key functions of a board. Denis and McConnell (2003) describe the role of the board as being to hire, fire, monitor and compensate management, with an eye to maximising shareholder value.

As part of its corporate governance project, the American Law Institute (ALI 1994, section 2.01) defines the objective and conduct of companies as follows:

(a) . . . a corporation should have as its objective the conduct of business activities with a view to enhancing corporate profit and shareholder gain.

(b) Even if corporate profit and shareholder gain are not thereby enhanced, the corporation, in the conduct of its business:
(1) Is obliged, to the same extent as a natural person, to act within the boundaries set by law;
(2) May take into account ethical considerations that are reasonably regarded as appropriate to the responsible conduct of business;
(3) May devote a reasonable amount of resources to public welfare, humanitarian, educational and philanthropic purposes.

Thus, although shareholder primacy is the general rule, subsection (b) allows for reasonable ethical and charitable considerations to supersede shareholder primacy. A company should conduct itself as a social, as well as an economic, institution (Eisenberg 1993). Williamson (1984) argues that shareholder value should be the sole criterion for firm effectiveness. The inclusion of other stakeholders' objectives compromises efficiency and invites tradeoffs. Cox (1993) expresses the view that directors' obligations should be more directly tied to shareholders, rather than to a more diffuse stakeholder group. A contrary opinion is that it is in the long-term interest of companies to engage in acts of corporate social responsibility as, in the long run, this increases shareholder value (Friedman 1970). Hayek (1969), more generally, discusses the importance of shareholders' interests in the operation of companies.

Duties of directors are also relevant here. Courts apply two broad principles against which to assess the conduct of directors:

• *Duty of care and skill*: this derives from the Roman term *mandatum* and requires directors to act in a reasonable, prudent, rational way, as expected of a similar person in his/her position. Courts apply the 'business judgment rule' (when conflicts of interest are absent), which provides directors with the benefit of the doubt when things go wrong. Failure to exercise such care amounts to negligence in common law countries.
• *Fiduciary duty*: this is a duty to act honestly and in good faith (sometimes referred to as a duty of loyalty) and specifically addresses situations of conflict of interest. Insiders should not profit at the expense of the company. Breach of fiduciary duty exposes a director to liabilities, and damages will arise where the interests of the company have been adversely affected.

To whom do directors owe their duty? This is another area of confusion in the literature. Strictly speaking, in law, directors owe their duty to the company, not to the shareholders. In most cases, this difference has no consequences in practice. However, in extreme cases (Enron in 2001, and Bear Sterns, AIG and Lehman Brothers in 2008 come to mind), where directors focus on shareholders/ shareholder value (in modern markets this is often an excessively short-term perspective), they may kill the company through misplacing their duty to shareholders instead of to the company. Thus, duty to company implies a longer-term perspective and a requirement for prudence in ensuring the survival of the company.

Accountability of directors is not a straightforward issue. In law (as outlined above), directors are accountable for their individual actions, yet they operate and make decisions collectively as a board (Pye 2002). Individuals may behave differently in a group. Thus, there is a tension between the analysis of individual and collective board actions. Directors (like other groups of people) may do things acting together that they would never do alone (Myers 1994). A board may be greater (or less) than the sum of its parts. Boards shape their organisations through all aspects of directors' communications, inside and outside the organisation, implicitly and explicitly (Pye 2002). Board roles most often emphasised are:

1   Strategy: the process by which directors shape the direction, future, vision and values of an organisation.
2   Monitoring and control of managers (including hiring and firing the chief executive officer (CEO)).
3   Residual/social roles such as the acquisition of scarce resources (Nicholson and Kiel 2004); providing support and wise counsel to the CEO (Westphal 1999).

The prior literature tends to focus on the monitor and control roles, rather than the strategy roles. Judge and Zeithaml (1992), Rindova (1999), Golden and Zajac (2001), Westphal and Fredickson (2001) and Carpenter and Westphal (2001) are exceptions.

Agency Theory

Under agency theory, firms are seen as a nexus of contracts negotiated among self-interested individuals. The company is a collection of explicit and implicit contracts that bind various stakeholder groups together. The objective of the company is seen as maximising the value of the firm's residual claims (i.e. not fixed claims), which typically is to maximise shareholder value. Shareholders are the residual risk-bearers. This means that they bear the discretionary risks and rewards, after all fixed contractual commitments to other participants in the enterprise are satisfied. The pre-eminence of shareholders under agency theory follows from their position as residual claimants. Only residual, rather than fixed, claimants have an incentive to maximise the firm's value.

Bradley et al. (1999) describe this agency perspective on governance as a contractarian paradigm. Voluntary contracting and market forces are relied upon to align the interests of managers and shareholders. Corporate managers facilitate the bargaining process by negotiating with each stakeholder group separately. This view, that individuals can freely enter mutually beneficial contracts, maximises individual freedom and, at the same time, economic efficiency.

Shareholders' interests are assumed to be purely financial – shareholders are seen as interested solely in the value of their shares. There are two directions in articulating the duties of managers: fiduciary and contractual. Fiduciary duties are duties of honesty and good faith, such that a court can void transactions if managers have not been fair in their dealings. According to Bradley *et al.* (1999), the fiduciary duties of corporate managers are to the firm's shareholders. This view could be disputed as, strictly speaking, under law, directors owe their fiduciary duties to the company, not to the shareholders.

Under their contracts, managers are assumed to have multiple self-interests. In addition to being interested in shareholder value, they will also value job security, personal power, recognition by society and the challenge of management. Managers may use entrenchment mechanisms to stay in power. They may be more risk averse than shareholders. They may want to keep free cash flow, instead of giving it back to the shareholders. They may also use their positions to shirk, or to consume extra perks. Berle and Means (1932) predicted that these conflicts, together with the increasing dispersion of ownership, would lead to the demise of companies. However, the reverse has been the case and this can only be explained by the benefits of companies outweighing the agency costs associated with the separation of ownership and control.

Daily, Dalton and Cannella (2003:372) suggest that agency theory is the dominant theory, with other theories acting as complements: 'In nearly all modern governance research, governance mechanisms [are] conceptualized as deterrents to managerial self-interest.' The view that the firm is a 'self-regulating contractual arrangement among independent bargaining groups' (Kaufman and Zacharias 1992, as quoted in Markarian *et al.* 2007:297) assumes that the internal mechanisms of control are able to effectively monitor management.

Agency Theory and Boards of Directors

How do investors get managers to return capital invested? Agency theorists argue that, in order to protect owners' interests, the board of directors must assume an effective oversight function, as an internal mechanism of control. In the event of failures in internal mechanisms of control, companies invite external governance interference, for example from hostile takeovers or shareholder activism.

The board is seen as a relatively low-cost monitoring device (Maher and Andersson 2002). Buckland (2001) comments that the board has evolved in a competitive environment as the lowest-cost means by which top managers are monitored. It is low cost because it fulfils the role of replacing or reordering top managers more efficiently than the market for corporate control. Mizruchi (1983) suggests that the exercise of control by boards may vary depending on the relative performance of the firm – boards being more active where performance is poorer.

Limitations of Agency Theory

There are a number of limitations of agency theory (Daily *et al.* 2003; Eisenhardt 1989; Shleifer and Vishny 1997):

- Agency theory assumes complete contracts (i.e. contracts that cater for all possible contingencies, such as ambiguities in language, inadvertence, unforeseen circumstances, disputes, etc). However, in practice, bounded rationality does not allow for complete and efficient contracts. Information asymmetries, transaction costs and fraud are insurmountable obstacles to efficient contracting
- Agency theory assumes that contracting can eliminate agency costs. The many imperfections in the market indicate that this assumption is not valid.
- Third party effects are not recognised. (Third parties are those who are affected by the contract but are not party to the contract.) Many boards are conscious of third party effects and adopt social, as well as financial, responsibilities. Thus, whereas maximum economic efficiency may (theoretically) be achieved under agency theory, it will not achieve maximum social welfare.
- Shareholders are assumed to be interested only in financial performance.
- Directors and management are assumed to owe their duty to shareholders. The law requires that duty to be owed to companies.
- Boards have a number of roles. Agency theory may be suitable for the monitoring-of-managers role of boards, but it does not explain the other roles of boards. Agency theory is not informative with respect to directors' resourcing, service and strategy roles.
- Much of the corporate governance research is conceptualised as deterrents to managerial self-interest. Agency theory treats managers as opportunistic, motivated solely by self-interest. Many would argue that this theory does not capture those who are loyal to their firms.
- Agency theory does not take account of competence. Thus, if even incompetent managers are honest (or are made honest by board control) they will still be limited in their ability to meet shareholder objectives. It is not enough to incentivise people to get a task done; they must have the ability to carry out the task (Hillman and Dalziel 2003).

Resource Dependence Theory

Under resource dependence theory, the role of the board of directors is seen as an effective means of obtaining scarce resources for the organisation, including advantageous contacts, enhancing the legitimacy of the organisation, and accessing other scarce resources. Researchers have classified this as one of the most important roles for boards of directors (Huse 2005; Johnson et al. 1996; Zahra and Pearce 1989).

The extent of a firm's need for resources may influence the mix of inside and outside directors. Directors are seen as 'boundary spanners' of the organisation and its environment (Dalton et al., 1998; Hillman et al. 2000; Johnson et al. 1996; Pfeffer and Salancik 1978). Outside directors can provide access to scarce resources. Outsiders might be useful when firms need enhanced inter-firm partnerships and legitimacy (Boyd 1994; Daily and Dalton 1994). Outside directors may be able to access borrowings (Stearns and Mizruchi 1993). In a crisis, greater outside representation on boards may help obtain valuable resources and information. Increasing the size and diversity of boards assists in linking the organisation and its environment in securing critical resources, including prestige and legitimacy.

Stewardship Theory

Davis, Schoorman and Donaldson (1997) provide a good overview of stewardship theory. Under stewardship theory, the board contributes to the stewardship of the company. Managers are seen as good stewards, diligently working towards good corporate performance with interests similar to those of shareholders. Management may see service to shareholders as serving their own interests (Lane *et al.* 1998). Managers' personal reputations, and career prospects, depend on how well they steward shareholders' assets. Thus, managers have incentives to operate the firm to maximise financial performance and shareholder returns. Stewardship theory implies a more collaborative approach between management and boards. Under this approach, empowering managers (stewards) of the firm to exercise unencumbered authority and responsibility enhances board–management ties and decision making.

As already noted, researchers are increasingly critical of the application of agency theory, which treats managers as opportunistic people motivated by self-interest. Stewardship theorists argue that many managers are stewards whose motives are largely aligned with the objectives of their principals (Donaldson 1990). When managers acting as stewards are treated as if they were opportunistic agents, they will feel frustrated and may not develop effective, co-operative working relationships with their boards. Donaldson and Davis (1994) caution against control-type theories that dominate thinking to the exclusion of other views.

As stated earlier, agency theory focuses exclusively on managerial self-interest, and ignores problems of competence. This raises serious questions for boards on the extent to which they nurture the development of the CEO's and senior managers' competencies, thus empowering them (stewardship perspective) and improving their competence. The issue of management competence is not a static concept. For example, Shen (2003) considers whether CEO competence and opportunism may vary over the CEO's tenure.

Class Hegemony Theory

Class-based theorists interpret boards of directors as ways of linking powerful elites into elite class networks (Pettigrew 1992; Stiles and Taylor 2001; Useem 1984). Thus, the power of an elite group is perpetuated by ensuring that members of the

ROUTING SLIP 02/01/15 11:02

Item SD000000216542
Irish business & society governing, part
icipatin /

Reservation for D4000000146658
Ms Ruth Callaghan

At TF/Ballyroan

Lapse 23/01/15
Web Reservation

board come from that one elite class. The primary function of the board is seen to be the maintenance of the power of those in authority.

Managerial Hegemony Theory

Under this theory, the ruling class elite is management (Kosnik 1987; Mace 1971; Stiles and Taylor 2001; Vance 1964). The board is a *de jure*, but not the *de facto*, governing body of the organisation. The real responsibility for running the organisation is assumed by corporate management. The board of directors is, in effect, a legal fiction and is dominated by management, making it ineffective in reducing agency conflicts between management and shareholders.

RESEARCH ON CORPORATE GOVERNANCE – AN IRISH PERSPECTIVE

Excellent reviews of corporate governance have been published (e.g. Becht *et al.* 2002; Huse 2005; Shleifer and Vishny 1997). In this section, prior corporate governance research is briefly reviewed (summarised in Table 7.1) from an Irish perspective – the theoretical perspectives adopted, the governance mechanisms studied, the methodologies applied; and the issues/sectors/contexts/variables are considered.

The fifteen papers summarised serve to illustrate the great variety in corporate governance research, in terms of theories applied, corporate governance mechanisms studied and methodologies adopted. The more traditional agency theory approach is illustrated by the work of Donnelly (Donnelly 2008; Donnelly and Kelly 2005; Donnelly and Mulcahy 2008). Corporate governance also lends itself to qualitative research methods including surveys (Brennan and Kelly 2007; O'Regan *et al.* 2005), in-depth interviews (Doyle 2007; Heneghan and O'Donnell 2007) and case studies (Dunne and Hellier 2002; Pierce 2003). A number of review papers point to opportunities for further research (Brennan 2003, 2006; Brennan and Solomon 2008). Annual reports, with their extensive corporate governance disclosures, also provide a research opportunity (Brennan and McCafferty 1997; Brennan and McDermott 2004; MacCanna *et al.* 1999).

It is hoped that the corporate governance research portrayed in this chapter will inspire researchers' imaginations to take the discipline into new territory, experimenting with new theoretical lenses through which corporate governance may be viewed and analysed, and with novel methodological approaches, techniques, contexts and timeframes.

Table 7.1 Prior corporate governance research reviewed

Paper (in chronological order)	Theory	Governance mechanism	Method	Issue researched	Result
Brennan and McCafferty (1997)	None identified	Disclosure of corporate governance compliance with Cadbury Code	Survey of annual reports	Practices surveyed include: • independence of boards • separation of role of chairman and chief executive • presence of board sub-committees • women on boards	Most Irish companies comply with the Cadbury Committee recommendations, with some evidence of non-compliance. Women are under-represented on boards of Irish companies.
MacCanna et al. (1999)	Network of interlocking directorates is structured, and not the result of random processes	Independence of directors	Social network analysis	Network of interlocking directorships of the top 50 financial and 200 non-financial companies in Ireland	Irish boards have a relatively loose connected network structure which is sparser and less dense than those of other countries. This is reflected in the relatively low percentage of multiple directors and the relatively fewer number of directorships per multiple directors. However, there is evidence of a thriving network of corporate power in Ireland.
Dunne and Hellier (2002)	None identified	Internal control and corporate governance procedures	Case study	Internal control and corporate governance failures in AIB plc in relation to fraud in US subsidiary	Lessons from previous high-profile scandals did not result in sufficient tightening of controls to prevent AIB fraud

Paper (in chronological order)	Theory	Governance mechanism	Method	Issue researched	Result
Brennan (2003)	None identified	Auditing, accounting, corporate governance and market failures	Conceptual/critical	Accounting scandals in the USA and Ireland around the time of Enron	Accounting scandals are the product of multiple failings of auditing, accounting, corporate governance and the market. In discussing the many factors that led to failure, the paper provides insights on regulatory inadequacies that contributed to these problems. At the centre is human failure – in particular greed and weakness.
Pierce (2003)	None identified	Financial reporting	Case study	Causes and consequences of financial reporting failure in Elan Corporation	Deficiencies in accountability and changes in investor and regulatory tolerance for financial reporting manipulation can seriously damage companies
Brennan and McDermott (2004)	None identified	Independence of directors	Survey of annual reports	Compliance with 7 independence criteria for non-executive directors of Irish listed companies prior to implementation of Higgs Report (2003)	61% of the companies sampled had one or more breaches of independence criteria set out in Higgs Report. If the Higgs Report's recommendations are implemented, many Irish listed companies will need to make considerable improvements for their boards to be judged fully independent.

Paper (in chronological order)	Theory	Governance mechanism	Method	Issue researched	Result
O'Regan et al. (2005)	Stakeholder theory (implicit)	• Board composition • Non-executive directors • Governance culture	Questionnaire of chief financial officers in Irish ICT SMEs	Governance regimes in a 'new economy' ICT sector	Governance structure is similar to other traditional firms and sectors. Critical importance of non-executive directors recognised.
Donnelly and Kelly (2005)	Agency theory	• Board size • Board composition • Ownership structure	Ordinary least squares regression	Substitution effects and bargaining effects between different mechanisms of governance	Findings support the bargaining hypothesis, with poor support of the substitution hypothesis
Brennan (2006)	Agency theory	Boards of directors	Conceptual/ critical	Relationship between boards of directors and firm performance	An expectations gap approach is applied for the first time to implicit expectations which assume a relationship between firm performance and company boards. Seven aspects of boards are identified as leading to a reasonableness gap. Five aspects of boards are identified as leading to a performance gap.
Doyle (2007)	None identified	Compliance requirements	In-depth interviews with 44 companies	Compliance requirements, tools to manage compliance, competitiveness barriers linked to compliance	Gap identified between regulations and application of requirements to maintain business advantage
Heneghan and O'Donnell (2007)	None identified	Legal regulations	In-depth and telephone interviews	Attitudes towards compliance, and compliance levels	Legal and regulatory changes contribute to a compliance culture

Paper (in chronological order)	Theory	Governance mechanism	Method	Issue researched	Result
Brennan and Kelly (2007)	None identified	Whistleblowing	Survey of trainee auditors	Factors influencing propensity or willingness to blow the whistle among trainee auditors	Trainee auditors in firms with adequate formal structures for reporting wrongdoing are more likely to report wrongdoing and have greater confidence that this will not adversely affect their careers. Training increases this confidence. Significant differences were found in attitudes depending on whether the reports of wrongdoing were internal or external. Willingness to report wrongdoing externally reduces for older (aged over 25) trainees.
Brennan and Solomon (2008)	• Agency theory • Stakeholder theory • Enlightened shareholder theory • Resource dependency theory • Stewardship theory • Institutional theory	• Governance regulations • Boards of directors • Transparency (financial reporting, disclosure) • Audit committees • External audit • Role of institutional investors	Review article	Reviews traditional corporate governance and accountability research	Encourages broader approaches to corporate governance and accountability research beyond the traditional and primarily quantitative approaches of prior research. Broader theoretical perspectives, methodological approaches, accountability mechanisms, sectors/contexts, globalisation and time horizons are identified.

Paper (in chronological order)	Theory	Governance mechanism	Method	Issue researched	Result
Donnelly (2008)	• Agency theory • Resource dependence theory	• Board size • Board independence • Non-executive chairman • Ownership structure	Regression analysis	Performance of well/badly governed Irish listed firms after the Elan scandal	Less well-governed firms lost more value after the Elan scandal than did well-governed firms
Donnelly and Mulcahy (2008)	Agency theory	• Board size • Board independence • CEO/chairman duality • Institutional investors • Management ownership	Poisson regression	Relation between voluntary disclosure and corporate governance	Voluntary disclosure increases with non-executive directors, but not other variables in the research

CONCLUDING COMMENTS

The term 'corporate governance' was first coined by Bob Tricker in 1984. The Cadbury Report in 1992 gave it impetus, as did subsequent reviews of corporate governance best practice. Nonetheless, corporate governance is a relatively new concept in business. Research on corporate governance is also at an early stage of development. Policy makers and regulators have few research findings on which to base their decisions. Much corporate governance research follows, rather than leads, regulatory change. Researchers ask questions after the event, such as: Did the regulatory change result in improved governance and added value for the firm? Researchers should search for opportunities to lead regulation, providing regulators with insights into the costs and benefits of regulatory change.

References

ALI (American Law Institute) (1994) *Principles of Corporate Governance*. St Paul, MN: ALI.

Becht, M., Bolton, P. and Röell, A. (2002) 'Corporate Governance and Control', National Bureau of Economic Research (NBER) working paper no. 9371, New York.

Berle, A.A. and Means, G.C. (1932) *The Modern Corporation and Private Property*. New York, NY: Harcourt, Brace & World.

Bonn, I. and Pettigrew, A. (2009) 'Towards A Dynamic Theory of Boards: An Organisational Life Cycle Approach', *Journal of Management and Organization* 15(1): 2–16.

Boyd, B.K. (1994) 'Board Control and CEO Compensation', *Strategic Management Journal* 15(5): 335–44.

Bradley, M., Schipani, C.A., Sundaram, A. and Walsh, J.P. (1999) 'The Purposes and Accountability of the Corporation in Contemporary Society: Corporate Governance at a Crossroads', *Law and Contemporary Problems* 62(3): 9–86.

Brennan, N. (2003) 'Accounting in Crisis: A Story of Auditing, Accounting, Corporate Governance and Market Failures', *Irish Banking Review* Summer: 2–17.

— (2006) 'Boards of Directors and Firm Performance: Is there an Expectations Gap?', *Corporate Governance: An International Review* 14(6): 577–93.

Brennan, N. and Kelly, J. (2007) 'A Study of Whistleblowing Among Trainee Auditors', *British Accounting Review* 39(1): 61–87.

Brennan, N. and McCafferty, J. (1997) 'Corporate Governance Practices in Irish Companies', *Irish Business and Administrative Research (IBAR)* 18: 116–35.

Brennan, N. and McDermott, M. (2004) 'Alternative Perspectives on Independence of Directors', *Corporate Governance: An International Review* 12(3): 325–36.

Brennan, N.M. and Solomon, J. (2008) 'Corporate Governance, Accountability and Mechanisms of Accountability: An Overview', *Accounting, Auditing and Accountability Journal* 21(7): 885–906.

Buckland, R. (2001) 'UK Board IPO Structures and Post-Issue Performance', working paper, available at http://ssrn.com/abstract=276049.

Cadbury Committee (1992) *Report on the Financial Aspects of Corporate Governance)* [Cadbury Report]. London: Gee Publishing.

Carpenter, M.A. and Westphal, J.D. (2001) 'The Strategic Context of External Network Ties: Examining the Impact of Director Appointments on Board Involvement in Strategic Decision Making', *Academy of Management Journal* 44(4): 639–60.

Coffee, J.C., Jr (1999) 'Privatization and Corporate Governance and its Implications', *Journal of Corporation Law* 25(1): 1–39.

Cox, J.D. (1993) 'The ALI, Institutionalization and Disclosure: The Quest for the Outside Director's Spine', *George Washington Law Review* 61: 1233–43.

Daily, C.M. and Dalton, D.R. (1994) 'Corporate Governance in the Small Firm: Prescriptions for CEOs and Directors', *Journal of Small Business Strategy* 5(1): 57–68.

Daily, C.M., Dalton, D.R. and Cannella, A.A. (2003) 'Corporate Governance: Decades of Dialogue and Data', *Academy of Management Review* 28(3): 371–82.

Dalton, D.R., Daily, C.M., Ellstrand, A.E. and Johnson, J.L. (1998) 'Meta-analytic Reviews of Board Composition, Leadership Structure, and Financial Performance', *Strategic Management Journal* 19: 269–90.

Davis, J.H., Schoorman, F.D. and Donaldson, L. (1997) 'Toward a Stewardship Theory of Management', *Academy of Management Journal* 31: 488–511.

Denis, D.K. (2001) 'Twenty-five Years of Corporate Governance Research . . . and Counting', *Review of Financial Economics* 10(3): 191–212.

Denis, D.K. and McConnell, J. (2003) 'International Corporate Governance', *Journal of Financial and Quantitative Analysis* 38(1): 1–36.

Donaldson, L. (1990) 'The Ethereal Hand: Organizational Economics and Management Theory', *Academy of Management Review* 15(3): 369–81.

Donaldson, L. and Davis, J.H. (1994) 'Boards and Company Performance: Research Challenges the Conventional Wisdom', *Corporate Governance: An International Review* 2(3): 151–60.

Donnelly, R. (2008) 'Accounting, Board Independence and Contagion Effects from Adverse Press Comment: The Case of Elan', *British Accounting Review* 40(3): 245–59.

Donnelly, R. and Kelly, P. (2005) 'Ownership and Board Structures in Irish plcs', *European Management Journal* 23(6): 730–40.

Donnelly, R. and Mulcahy, M. (2008) 'Board Structure, Ownership and Voluntary Disclosure in Ireland', *Corporate Governance: An International Review* 16(5): 416–29.

Doyle, E. (2007) 'Compliance Obstacles to Competitiveness', *Corporate Governance* 7(5): 612–22.

Dunne, T.M. and Hellier, C.V. (2002) 'The Ludwig Report: Implications for Corporate Governance', *Corporate Governance* 2(3): 26–33.

Eisenberg, M.A. (1993) 'An Overview of the Principles of Corporate Governance', *Business Law* 48: 1271–76.

Eisenhardt, K. (1989) 'Agency Theory: An Assessment and Review', *Academy of Management Review* 14(1): 57–74.

Fama, E.F. (1980) 'Agency Problems and the Theory of the Firm', *Journal of Political Economy* 88(2): 288–307.

Fama, E.F. and Jensen, M.C. (1983) 'Separation of Ownership and Control', *Journal of Law and Economics* 27: 301–25.

Financial Reporting Council (2010) *The UK Corporate Governance Code*. London: Financial Reporting Council.

Friedman, M. (1970) 'The Social Responsibility of Business is to Increase its Profits', *New York Times Magazine* 13 September: 32–3/122–6.

Golden, B.R. and Zajac, E.J. (2001) 'When Will Boards Influence Strategy? Inclination x Power = Strategic Change', *Strategic Management Journal* 22(12): 1087–111.

Hayek, F.A. (1969) 'The Corporation as a Democratic Society. In Whose Interest Ought it and Will it be Run?', in H.I. Ansoff (ed.) *Business Strategy – Selected Readings*, pp. 225–39. Harmondsworth: Penguin.

Heneghan, J. and O'Donnell, D. (2007) 'Governance, Compliance and Legal Enforcement: Evaluating a Recent Irish Initiative', *Corporate Governance* 7(1): 54–65.

Hermalin, B.E. and Weisbach, M.S. (2001) 'The Effects of Board Composition and Direct Incentives on Firm Performance', *Financial Management* 20(4): 101–12.

Hillman, A., Cannella, A. and Paetzold, R., Jr (2000) 'The Resource Dependence Role of Corporate Directors: Strategic Adaptation of Board Composition in Response to Environmental Change', *Journal of Management Studies* 37(2): 235–55.

Hillman, A.J. and Dalziel, T. (2003) 'Boards of Directors and Firm Performance: Integrating Agency and Resource Dependence Perspectives', *Academy of Management Review* 28(3): 383–96.

Huse, M. (2005) 'Accountability and Creating Accountability: A Framework for Exploring Behavioural Perspectives of Corporate Governance', *British Journal of Management* 16 (Supplement): S65–79.

Irish Stock Exchange (2010) *The Irish Corporate Governance Code*. Dublin: Irish Stock Exchange.

Jensen, M.C. and Meckling, W.H. (1976) 'Theory of the Firm: Managerial Behaviour, Agency Costs and Ownership Structure', *Journal of Financial Economics* 3(4): 305–60.

Johnson, J.L., Daily, C.M. and Ellstrand, A.E. (1996) 'Board of Directors: A Review and Research Agenda', *Journal of Management* 22 (September): 409–38.

Johnson, S., Boone, P., Breach, A. and Friedman, E. (2000) 'Corporate Governance in the Asian Financial Crisis', *Journal of Financial Economics* 58 (October): 141–86.

Judge, W. and Zeithaml, C.P. (1992) 'Institutional and Strategic Choice Perspectives on Board Involvement in the Strategic Decision Process', *Academy of Management Journal* 35(4): 766–94.

Keasey, K. and Wright, M. (1993) 'Issues in Corporate Accountability and Governance: An Editorial', *Accounting and Business Research* 23(91A) (Special Issue): 291–303.

Kosnik, R. (1987) 'Greenmail: A Study of Board Performance in Corporate Governance', *Administrative Science Quarterly* 32(2): 163–85.

Lane, P.J., Cannella, A.A., Jr and Lubatkin, M.H. (1998) 'Agency Problems as Antecedents to Unrelated Mergers and Diversification: Amihud and Lev Reconsidered', *Strategic Management Journal* 19(6): 555–78.

La Porta, R., Lopez-de-Silanes, F., Shleifer A. and Vishny R.W. (1997) 'Legal Determinants of External Finance', *Journal of Finance* 52: 1131–50.

— (1998) 'Law and Finance', *Journal of Political Economy* 106(6): 1113–55.

— (1999) 'Investor Protection and Corporate Governance', *Journal of Financial Economics* 58: 3–27.

Leblanc, R. (2001) *Getting Inside the Black Box: Problems in Corporate Governance Research*. Background paper for the Toronto Stock Exchange Joint Committee on Corporate Governance.

MacCanna, L., Brennan, N. and O'Higgins, E. (1999) 'National Networks of Corporate Power: An Irish Perspective', *Journal of Management and Governance* 2(4): 355–77.

Mace, M.L. (1971) *Directors: Myth and Reality*. Boston, MA: Harvard Business Review.

Maher, M. and Andersson, T. (2002) 'Corporate Governance: Effects on Firm Performance and Economic Growth', in J. McCahery, P. Moerland, T. Raaijmakers and L. Renneboog (eds) *Corporate Governance Regimes*, pp.386–418. Oxford: Oxford University Press.

Markarian, G., Parbonetti, A. and Previts, G.J. (2007) 'The Convergence of Disclosure and Governance Practices in the World's Largest Firms', *Corporate Governance: An International Review* 15(2): 294–310.

Mizruchi, M.S. (1983) 'Who Controls Whom? An Examination of the Relation between Management and Boards of Directors in Large American Corporations', *Academy of Management Review* 8(3): 426–35.

Myers, D.G. (1994) *Exploring Social Psychology*. New York, NY: McGraw-Hill.

Nicholson, G.J. and Kiel, G.C. (2004) 'A Framework for Diagnosing Board Effectiveness', *Corporate Governance: An International Review* 12(4): 442–60.

O'Regan, P., O'Donnell, D., Kennedy, T., Bontis, N. and Cleary, P. (2005) 'Board Composition, Non-Executive Directors and Governance Cultures in Irish ICT Firms: A CFO Perspective', *Corporate Governance* 5(4): 56–63.

Pettigrew, A.M. (1992) 'On Studying Managerial Elites', *Strategic Management Journal* 13(8): 163–82.

Pfeffer, J. and Salancik, G.R. (1978) *The External Control of Organizations*. New York, NY: Harper and Row.

Pierce, A. (2003) 'Elan Corporation: A Case Study in Corporate Obfuscation', *Corporate Governance International* 6(1): 5–23.

Pye, A. (2002) 'Corporate Directing: Governing, Strategising and Leading in Action', *Corporate Governance: An International Review* 9(3): 153–62.

Rindova, V.P. (1999) 'What Corporate Boards Have to do with Strategy: A Cognitive Perspective', *Journal of Management Studies* 36(6): 953–75.

Shen, W. (2003) 'Dynamics of the CEO–Board Relationship: An Evolutionary Perspective', *Academy of Management Review* 28(3): 466–76.

Shleifer, A. and Vishny, R.W. (1997) 'A Survey of Corporate Governance', *Journal of Finance* 52(2): 737–77.

Stearns, L.B. and Mizruchi, M.S. (1993) 'Board Composition and Corporate Financing: The Impact of Financial Institution Representation on Borrowing,' *Academy of Management Journal* 36(3): 603–18.

Stiles, P. and Taylor, B. (2001) *Boards at Work. How Directors View their Roles and Responsibilities*. Oxford: Oxford University Press.

Tricker, R.I. (1984) *Corporate Governance: Practices, Procedures and Powers in British Companies and their Boards of Directors*. Aldershot, Hants: Gower.

Useem, M. (1984) *Inner Circle: Large Corporations and the Rise of Business Political Activity in the U.S. and U.K.* Oxford: Oxford University Press.

Vance, S.C. (1964) *Boards of Directors: Structure and Performance*. Eugene, OR: University of Oregon Press.

Westphal, J.D. (1999) 'Collaboration in the Boardroom: Behavioural and Performance Consequences of CEO–Board Social Ties', *Academy of Management Journal* 42(1): 7–24.

Westphal, J.D. and Fredickson, J.W. (2001) 'Who Directs Strategic Change? Director Experience, the Selection of New CEOs, and Change in Corporate Strategy', *Strategic Management Journal* 22(12): 1113–37.

Williamson, O.E. (1984) 'Corporate Governance', *Yale Law Review* 93: 1197–219.

— (1985) *The Economic Institutions of Capitalism: Firms, Markets, Relational Contracting*. New York, NY: Free Press.

Wymeersch E. (1998) 'A Status Report on Corporate Governance Rules and Practices in some Continental European States', in K.J. Hopt, H. Kanda, M.J. Roe, E. Wymeersch and S. Prigge (eds) *Comparative Corporate Governance: The State of the Art and Emerging Research*, pp. 1045–200. Oxford: Clarendon Press.

Zahra, S.A. and Pearce, J.A., II (1989) 'Boards of Directors and Corporate Financial Performance: A Review and Integrative Model', *Journal of Management* 15(2): 291–334.

Chapter 8

Corporate Social Responsibility in Ireland: Current Practice and Directions for Future Research

Rebecca Maughan

INTRODUCTION

The idea that business has obligations to society and the practice of corporate philanthropy date back at least to the early part of the nineteenth century (Smith 2003). Then, as now, people were concerned about the amount of pollution companies were creating and the conditions in which employees were working and living. In the nineteenth century, family-run companies and businesses, such as Rowntree, Cadbury and Saltaire in the United Kingdom were often at the forefront of corporate social initiatives. During the same period, Irish family businesses, such as those run by the Richardson family in Newry and the Malcomson family in Waterford, pioneered the building of industrial villages, which provided better living conditions for their employees. However, Irish companies could now be accused of lagging behind their European counterparts in the field of corporate social responsibility (CSR).

While CSR may not be a new concept, recent decades have seen it become an increasingly prominent issue. The global nature of many corporations means that there are very few societies and communities that are not in some way affected by the activities of corporations. Human impact on the environment, in particular the threat of climate change, has become a focus of public, political and media attention, and many companies have become a focal point for this attention. Thus, a combination of environmental concerns, the global reach of corporations and numerous other factors, including corporate scandals and increased media scrutiny of corporate actions, has led to companies having to consider what responsibilities they have to society, and, conversely, society having to consider what it wants companies to be responsible for.

The next section provides an introduction to the concept of CSR, discusses how Irish managers have interpreted the concept, and briefly outlines some of the arguments for and against CSR. The second section provides an overview of some of the most prevalent theories used to explain CSR practice and reporting. The third section discusses CSR in practice, with an emphasis on CSR practice and reporting in Ireland. The final section highlights the paucity of research on CSR and family firms, and considers how the unique characteristics of family firms may (or may not) influence their engagement with CSR.

WHAT IS CSR?

While CSR has been the subject of much debate and a topic of academic study for several decades, there is no universally agreed definition of the term (McWilliams *et al.* 2006; Wood 1991). In fact, the term itself is often used interchangeably or in conjunction with other related terms, such as corporate citizenship, corporate social responsiveness, corporate philanthropy, corporate social performance and sustainability (Silberhorn and Warren 2007). A commonly cited definition of CSR is Wood's (1991:695) suggestion that the 'basic idea of corporate social responsibility is that business and society are interwoven rather than distinct entities: therefore, society has certain expectations for appropriate business behaviour and outcomes'. This definition follows an ethical or normative conception of CSR (often called CSR1) that suggests companies are an integral part of society (Sethi 1979:64) and have responsibilities that go beyond economic, technical and legal requirements (Carrol 1991; Davis 1973; Fredericks 1986; Jones 1980; Preston 1975). These responsibilities extend not just to shareholders, but also to other groups in society (Jones 1980), that are usually termed stakeholders (Donaldson and Preston 1995; Jones and Wicks 1999). Implied in this conception of CSR is the idea of a social contract (Gray *et al.* 1988; Wartick and Cochran 1985), an implicit agreement between the members of society and business, in which society allows business to operate in return for certain benefits (Hasnas 1998:29), provided it operates in a manner that society views as responsible (Davis 1973).

However, CSR1 has been criticised as being vague and ambiguous (Clarkson 1995), and a second concept of CSR, termed corporate social responsiveness (CSR2), emerged with a focus on companies' responses to social pressures (Fredericks 1986). This conception of CSR focuses on 'society's impact on business rather than business's impact on society' (O'Dwyer 2003:527) and treats CSR as an operational and management issue (Ackerman and Bauer 1976). From this perspective, a company's social responsibilities are secondary to its economic objectives, and a company's engagement in CSR is primarily motivated by a desire to protect or improve its economic performance (Fredericks 1986).

Perhaps unsurprisingly, given the debate over the meaning and nature of CSR, studies of CSR in Ireland have found that executives in both large and small companies have difficulty providing a precise definition of CSR (O'Dwyer 2003; Sweeney 2007). O'Dwyer (2003) found that senior managers in Irish publicly listed companies (plcs) had difficultly in articulating exactly what CSR might mean. In general, O'Dwyer's interviewees (twenty-nine senior managers) tended to interpret CSR in a manner consistent with a CSR2 perspective, suggesting that CSR was primarily motivated by a company's economic self-interest. The effective management of social issues and stakeholders was seen as helping companies to fulfil their primary objective of maximising shareholder value. However, some managers maintained that their personal view of CSR was not consistent with this narrow corporate perspective and was based on a broader, more societally concerned perspective. Sweeney (2007), in a study using a sample of both large and small firms, found that interviewees in large firms tended to define CSR by reference to the company's responsibility to a variety of stakeholders, including customers, employees, the environment and the community. Interviewees in the small firms were perceived as providing quite a vague definition of CSR, describing it as conducting business in a responsible manner. Generally, interviewees in smaller firms perceived the wider community as their company's most important stakeholder.

Both the CSR1 and CSR2 approaches have attracted many critics and proponents (Brickson 2007; also see Davis (1973) or Wartick and Cochran (1985), for a summary of the arguments for and against CSR). Proponents of CSR1 argue that business has a moral imperative to 'do the right thing' (e.g. Bowie 1991; Fredericks 1986; Mintzberg et al. 2002; Preston 1975). Proponents of CSR2 tend to focus on the business case for CSR, arguing that being a socially responsible company can lead to increased shareholder wealth. While there is mixed evidence for the link between CSR and a company's financial performance (Aupperle et al. 1985), advocates of the business case for CSR suggest that engaging strategically in CSR is important for the long-term success of a company (McElhaney 2008).

Critics of CSR pose a variety of arguments, which reflect a broad spectrum of views on the role of business in society. Some critics, most notably Friedman (1962, 1970), argue that CSR is a distraction from the fundamental economic role of business to maximise shareholder value. However, there is growing acceptance that, whether it is an appropriate objective or not for business, companies are involved in a wide variety of CSR activities and reporting. Critics at the other end of the spectrum argue that business is ill-equipped to advance the interests of society as a whole. CSR is criticised for being an attempt by business to avoid regulation, manipulate public opinion and maintain the status quo (Everett and Neu 2000; Newton and Harte 1997; Tinker et al. 1991). Companies' CSR activities and reports are perceived as either greenwashing, that is to say misleading the public about a product's environmental benefits or a company's environmental practices (Terrachoice 2009), or part of a public relations strategy aimed at gaining, maintaining or repairing a company's reputation and social acceptance without having to adjust its behaviour.

PREVAILING THEORIES

Just as there is no one universally accepted definition of CSR, neither is there one predominant theory used to explain and analyse CSR. The most commonly used theories include accountability theory, legitimacy theory and stakeholder theory (Buhr 2007; Moir 2001). These theories are not all mutually exclusive, but can be seen as overlapping and mutually enriching (Deagan 2002; Gray, Kouhy and Lavers 1995). The following section provides a brief outline of each theory and its relationship to CSR.

Accountability Theory

Gray (2001) suggests that accountability, in its simplest form, is about providing an explanation of one's conduct, usually to someone in authority. In a similar vein, Roberts and Scapens (1985:447) suggest that it is 'the giving and demanding of reasons for conduct'. However, agreement on what companies are accountable for, and to whom they are accountable, is elusive. Proponents of CSR, particularly CSR1, would argue that companies should be accountable not just for their economic performance, but also for their social impacts, to a wider range of groups in society beyond their shareholders (Davis 1973; Fredericks 1986; Gray *et al.* 1996; Preston 1975; Preston and Post 1975; Sethi 1979). CSR reporting could be perceived as a mechanism to fulfil accountability relationships concerning a company's social impacts (Buhr 2002; Gray 1992).

Legitimacy Theory

Legitimacy theory considers the need for corporations to convince the public that they are acting within the boundaries of social norms (de Villiers and van Staden 2006; Guthrie and Parker 1989). The most frequently cited definitions suggest that legitimacy involves a company adhering to the values, norms, rules and meanings of the society in which it operates and that a company's actions are perceived by society as appropriate and proper (Deephouse and Carter 2005; Lindblom 1994; Suchman 1995). Woodward, Edwards and Birkin (1996) suggest that companies use corporate social reporting as a method of communicating their legitimacy to a wider audience in a manner that is easily understood. A company seeking to maintain or restore its legitimacy may use CSR activities, and in particular, reporting on those activities, as a tool to change how the company is perceived in an effort to legitimise its actions (Buhr 1998; Deegan *et al.* 2002; Guthrie and Parker 1989; Milne and Patten 2002; Neu *et al.* 1998). If a company's legitimacy has been damaged by certain events, for example an environmental incident such as an oil spill, it may provide greater information about its corporate social responsibility activities in an effort to restore its legitimacy (Cho 2009; O'Donovan 2002).

Studies of organisational legitimacy as an explanation for CSR reports have produced mixed results. While several studies have found evidence consistent with legitimacy theory as an explanatory factor for CSR (Buhr 1998; Cho 2009; Deegan *et al.* 2002; Deegan *et al.* 2000; Gray, Kouhy and Lavers 1995; Milne and Patten 2002; Neu *et al.* 1998; O'Donovan 2002), others have contested the explanatory power of legitimacy theory (Campbell 2000; de Villiers and van Staden 2006; O'Dwyer 2003; Wilmhurst and Frost 2000). In an Irish context, O'Dwyer (2002) found that CSR reporting was not perceived as an effective tool for Irish companies seeking to maintain or repair their legitimacy. O'Dwyer (2002) found that a sample of senior managers in Irish plcs perceived CSR reporting as potentially counterproductive when trying to achieve organisational legitimacy, as CSR reporting, particularly on environmental issues, could attract unwanted attention from activists and could increase, rather than diminish, public scepticism.

Stakeholder Theory

Freeman's (1984:46) widely cited definition of a stakeholder is 'any group or individual who can affect or is affected by the achievement of the organization's objectives'. This broad definition allows for a very wide set of stakeholders for any particular company. However, the company itself may take a more limited view of who it wants to recognise as its stakeholders. As with legitimacy theory, stakeholder theory and CSR are frequently linked. There is a substantial body of literature on the relationship between stakeholder theory and CSR, including work on corporate philanthropy, community relations, ethical investment, responses to pressure groups and international stakeholder management (Wood 1991). Mirroring the divisions in the conception of CSR, stakeholder theory can be divided into two main concepts: a managerial perspective and a normative or ethical perspective (Hasnas 1998).

From the managerial perspective, stakeholder support is seen as a vital component in a company's continued existence (Gray, Kouhy and Lavers 1995; Ullmann 1985). Taking a managerial perspective when formulating a CSR strategy means that a company will focus on meeting the demands of its economically powerful stakeholders (Gray, Walters, Bebbington and Thomson 1995). Consequently, this may mean that the needs of its less influential stakeholders are ignored. On the other hand, if stakeholder theory is viewed from a normative or ethical perspective, all stakeholders could be viewed as having an equal right to information. Taking an ethical perspective, a company would view its stakeholders as any group or individual affected by its practices, policies or actions (Hummels 1998). Moreover, a company would be involved in meaningful dialogue with all stakeholders, regardless of their economic influence over the company, as part of an overall process of accountability to stakeholders (Gray, Walters, Bebbington and Thomson 1995). In practice, however, companies seem to take a managerial approach to stakeholder engagement (Owen *et al.* 2001).

CSR IN PRACTICE

In keeping with the wide variety of theories used to explain and analyse CSR, companies in practice adopt a variety of approaches and attitudes to CSR. Some companies view CSR as an integral part of the way that they do business (for instance, fair trade companies such as Traidcraft or the Irish company Heart of Africa), while for others it is an ancillary activity, a 'nice to do' rather than a 'must do'. As well as a range of approaches, there are a multitude of CSR-type activities in which companies can engage. Companies may focus on minimising their environmental impacts, get involved in a broad range of community, charitable or workplace initiatives, or incorporate social or environmental considerations into the products they produce, for example biodegradable plastics (McWilliams et al. 2006).

As well as a variety of approaches to CSR, companies communicate their CSR activities and policies through a wide variety of channels. CSR-related information is most frequently reported in a company's annual report, in a stand-alone CSR report, or on its website. If companies produce a stand-alone report, they might be titled as CSR reports, sustainability reports or triple bottom line reports (Milne and Gray 2007). CSR reporting is not yet regulated or audited in the same way as financial reporting. There are, however, a number of reporting guidelines that have been developed to serve as frameworks for CSR reporting and auditing. The most prominent standards include the Global Reporting Initiative's Sustainability Reporting Guidelines, AccountAbility's AA1000 standard, the European Eco-management and Auditing Standard (EMAS) and the ISO 14000 environmental management standard.

While the advent of standards for CSR reporting is a recent event, a company reporting on its CSR activities is not a new phenomenon. Studies by Hogner (1982) and Guthrie and Parker (1989) provide examples of the long history of CSR reporting by two steel companies, US Steel and Broken Hill Proprietary (BHP). The Australian company BHP had been reporting CSR-type information since 1885 (Hogner 1982).

A company's approach to CSR and the focus of its activities and reporting can change over time, as it responds to external pressure or internal factors, such as changes in senior management (Gray, Kouhy and Lavers 1995; Silberhorn and Warren 2007). While CSR is a relatively new term, as already noted, the practice of corporate philanthropy has its antecedents in the early nineteenth century (Smith 2003). For instance, leading industrialists often built towns for their employees. Smith (2003) cites the examples of Bourneville (founded by George Cadbury), Port Sunlight (founded by William Lever) and Saltaire (founded by Sir Titus Salt), all founded during the nineteenth century in Britain. These towns included not just housing, but also parks, schools, churches and hospitals. In Ireland, the Richardson family built a village for the employees of their linen mill near Newry in the 1840s. One of the earliest examples of an industrial village is

Portlaw in County Waterford, which was built by the industrialist David Malcomson for his employees in the early nineteenth century. It is claimed that British towns such as Bourneville owe their conception partly to Portlaw. While much of this philanthropic activity has been linked to the personal, often religious, beliefs and values of the founding families of these companies, there is also an argument that they were in part motivated by enlightened self-interest. By providing facilities for their employees, these philanthropists were ensuring that they had a stable and healthy population of employees when, for example, during the 1850s in Britain riots were common in factory towns and the average life expectancy in one British industrial town, Bradford, was only twenty years (Smith 2003).

Notwithstanding these early examples of corporate philanthropy, recent surveys of corporate donations to the voluntary sector have found that Irish companies now contribute considerably less than their British and American counterparts (Donoghue et al. 2000; Donoghue 2000). In the field of CSR reporting, Irish companies could also be accused of lagging behind some of their European neighbours (O'Dwyer 2001; O'Dwyer and Gray 1998). This could be due to the fact that a lot of CSR-type activity is not reported, especially in the case of small and medium-sized enterprises (SMEs) that may be involved in CSR activities but do not categorise these activities as CSR (Sweeney 2007). However, there is a gradual increase in the number of publicly quoted companies publishing CSR-related information in either their annual reports or stand-alone reports (Maughan 2006, 2007; Sweeney 2008). Irish plcs generally use their websites or annual reports to disclose CSR-related information, and only a small number of these companies produce stand-alone CSR reports (Maughan 2006, 2007; Sweeney 2008). The most common types of disclosure relate to employees, health and safety, community involvement, the environment, customers and corporate governance. The majority of companies that disclose CSR information tend to disclose positive information of a qualitative nature, and many companies simply report their CSR policies (Maughan 2006, 2007; Sweeney 2008).

However, some Irish firms do outline their objectives for CSR and their progress towards achieving these objectives, including both their achievements and their challenges (Sweeney 2008). Examples of best practice in CSR reporting in an Irish context include reports from Musgrave Group, ESB, CRH plc and Irish Life and Permanent. Each of these companies has produced stand-alone CSR reports that have in recent years won the Association of Chartered Certified Accountants' (ACCA) Irish sustainability reporting awards.

On the regulatory side, there is legislation covering areas of practice that would be encompassed in the concept of CSR, such as the vastly increased body of environmental legislation now in force in Ireland (Wynn 2003). However, the mandatory disclosure requirements in relation to reporting CSR data are minimal (O'Dwyer 2002). Currently, company legislation in Ireland requires disclosure of the average number and type of staff employed by the company. All other mandatory disclosures relate to financial data. In some countries, such as Sweden,

France, Denmark and the UK, there are legal requirements for CSR reporting and auditing, but this is not the case in Ireland. Currently, there does not seem to be any intention to introduce any further mandatory disclosure requirements in relation to CSR information (Sweeney 2008).

CSR AND FAMILY COMPANIES

While there are a small number of studies and surveys of CSR in Ireland, such research has focused on either plcs (Maughan 2006, 2007; O'Dwyer 2001, 2002, 2003; O'Dwyer and Gray 1998; Sweeney 2007), or SMEs (Sweeney 2007). While it is likely that family companies were among the SMEs studied by Sweeney (2007), this was not the study's focus. This is in line with the overall trends in empirical research on CSR, where the vast majority of work has focused on plcs' CSR activities and reporting. There is also a growing body of research looking at CSR and SMEs. However, little is known about family companies and CSR (Vyakarnam et al. 1997). The deficit of research on CSR and family firms could be due to a lack of CSR reporting on the part of these companies, but a lack of reporting does not necessarily mean a lack of involvement in CSR. Interestingly, in an Irish context, one of the leading CSR reporters is Musgrave Group, a large, private family company.

Defining Family Firms

Family companies can be defined using a number of characteristics. Smith (2007) suggests three broad criteria for identifying family companies: first, a self-selection criterion, where members of the company perceive their firm as being a family company; second, where a company's managers are drawn from a single dominant family group; and, third, where a controlling stake in the company is owned by a single family. The family company represents the dominant form of economic entity globally (Chrisman et al. 2003). For example, in the USA, family-owned or controlled companies make up 40 per cent of the Fortune 500, account for half of US GDP and employ about half of the US labour force (Chami 1999). In Ireland, in 2005, family businesses accounted for 46 per cent of all businesses in the annual survey of the service industry produced by the Central Statistics Office (CSO 2008). In 2005, the total turnover for family businesses in the Irish services sector alone was €49bn (CSO 2008). Despite their economic importance, there is a deficit of studies of CSR and family-owned companies. Yet ownership may have a significant influence on the attitudes of senior managers to CSR issues and reporting (Adams and McNicolas 2007).

Are Family Firms Distinctive?

While traditional theories of corporate control and management, such as agency theory, are based on a model of the corporation where ownership and control are separated, in the case of family companies, family members are often involved as managers or directors as well as being owners of the company (Braun and Sharma 2007; Johannisson and Huse 2000; Uhlaner *et al.* 2007; Vilaseca 2002). Much of the literature on family companies argues that they have distinct characteristics that influence the way in which they are managed and controlled (Chami 1999; Chrisman *et al.* 2003; Cromie *et al.* 1999; Ibrahim *et al.* 2004; James 1999; Mishra *et al.* 2001). The differences between family-owned and non-family-owned companies are most frequently attributed to the dual nature of family companies (Chrisman *et al.* 2003; James 1999; Smith 2007). Lansberg (1983) suggests that, within family companies, two distinct subsystems coexist: the family system and the business system. The family system differs from the business system in areas such as the reasons for the existence of the firm, culture, decision making and acceptable behaviour rules (Sharma *et al.* 1996). Family performance expectations could include, for example, the need to provide employment for family members or maintain the family's reputation in the community (Mitchell *et al.* 2003).

It is claimed that the existence of the family system can have a significant influence on the decision-making process of managers and employees. Andrews (1971) contends that strategic decisions are rarely made on economic grounds alone; the values and aims of both the owners and the top executives also play a significant role. It is suggested that the decision-making process may be quicker and more flexible within family companies, while the timeframe for decision making is generally longer than in non-family companies (Bartholomeusz and Tanewski 2006; James 1999; Mishra *et al.* 2001). Mitchell, Morse and Sharma (2003) suggest that employees in family companies face more complex decision-making processes than employees in non-family companies, as they have to be cognisant of both business performance expectations and family-related performance expectations.

How do Family Firms Engage with CSR?

How might the distinctive characteristics attributed to family companies affect their engagement with CSR? Recent work by Basu and Palazzo (2008) and Brickson (2007) suggests that CSR results not directly from external demands but is instead primarily influenced by internal factors, including a company's own ethos or identity. A company's identity consists of its members' (employees and managers) shared perceptions of their company's central, distinctive and enduring qualities (Albert and Whetten 1985; Dutton and Dukerich 1991; Hatch and Schultz 1997). Family ownership could be an important component in the construction of a company's identity. This identity can guide a company's action and will influence how a company manages its internal and external relationships (Brickson 2007). Taking this perspective, a company's internal identity or character will influence how it engages in CSR. If, as Basu and Palazzo (2008) and Brickson (2007) suggest, CSR results not directly from external demands, but instead is primarily influenced by a company's own ethos or identity, will family companies' engagement in CSR differ substantially from that of non-family companies?

According to much of the existing literature, the culture within family companies is different from that within non-family companies (Sharma *et al.* 1996). Among other differences, it is suggested that family companies want to maintain the family's reputation and take a longer-term view when making decisions (Bartholomeusz and Tanewski 2006; James 1999; Mishra *et al.* 2001). These attributes could support a positive attitude to CSR. Given the unique characteristics accorded to them, it might be tempting to suggest that family companies may be more willing than non-family-owned companies to accept their social and environmental responsibilities. However, it is difficult to find convincing evidence to support such an argument. Also, while the literature on family companies argues that there are a raft of differences between family and non-family companies, a recent Australia-based study by Smith (2007) suggests that there are actually fewer differences between family and non-family companies than has been suggested by much of the extant literature.

A review of the literature on family companies and CSR found only one empirical study: an examination of forty-two small and medium-sized Danish family companies (Uhlaner *et al.* 2004). This survey-based pilot study focused on whether the respondents perceived the family aspect of their business as influencing their relationship with a variety of stakeholders. The study found that the respondents perceived the family character of the business most frequently impacted on employee and client relationships (Uhlaner *et al.* 2004: 190). The study also found that the companies in question were involved in a limited amount of CSR activity, which in most cases could be described as 'small acts of kindness' (Uhlaner *et al.* 2004). However, while the study provides some insight into how family companies view their relationship with stakeholders and the type of CSR activities they engage in, it is limited in both scale and methodology.

Directions for Future Research

The literature on family companies often treats them as a homogenous group; however, Smith (2007) suggests that in many cases family companies are more similar to other companies in their industry than to family companies in different industries. Thus, it could be the case that family companies will differ very little from non-family companies in their approach and attitude to CSR. It is also possible, given the overlapping roles of owner, manager and director often played by family members, that if family members are concerned only with the economic performance of the company, the company's managers could actually have less opportunity and discretion to engage in CSR activities than in a non-family-owned company. The existing literature on family companies supports a wide range of suppositions as to how and why family companies could approach and engage in CSR. Given the proliferation of family companies, both globally and in Ireland, and their corresponding social and economic impacts, much more research is needed to explain and analyse how these companies actually engage in CSR.

CONCLUDING COMMENTS

The role of business in society is contested, dynamic, and continually evolving. CSR practices and reporting have been the focus of much academic, media and public debate. A vast body of CSR-related research, informed by a variety of theoretical perspectives, now exists. This chapter has provided a brief introduction to this extensive literature. Within this body of work, a number of studies have examined current CSR practice and reporting in Ireland and provided insights into Irish managers' attitudes to CSR. Drawing on these studies, this chapter provides an overview of CSR in Ireland.

While Irish companies are not generally at the forefront of CSR practice and reporting, there seems to be a growing awareness of CSR issues in the Irish business community. Even though Irish managers struggle with defining CSR, and are somewhat sceptical of the pragmatic benefits of CSR reporting, there has been a gradual increase in the number of Irish plcs disclosing CSR-related information. There are also a number of pioneering Irish companies who produce stand-alone, independently audited CSR reports. However, even with the gradual increase in CSR reporting, it is difficult to gauge the overall level of CSR-type activity in Irish companies, as many companies still do not disclose this kind of information.

Despite the extensive body of research on CSR, some areas remain under-researched. This chapter has highlighted the paucity of research on CSR and family companies. Different forms of ownership could have a significant influence on a company's engagement with CSR. The existing literature on family firms suggests that they have distinctive characteristics that influence the way in which they are managed and controlled. These characteristics could have a significant influence on family companies' engagement with CSR. Given the economic significance of family firms, both domestically and internationally, the nature and extent of their engagement with CSR warrants greater academic attention.

References

Ackerman, R.W. and Bauer, R.A. (1976) *Corporate Social Responsiveness: The Modern Dilemma*. Reston, VA: Reston Publishing.

Adams, C.A. and McNicholas, P. (2007) 'Making a Difference: Sustainability Reporting, Accountability and Organisational Change', *Accounting, Auditing and Accountability Journal* 20(3): 382–402.

Albert, S. and Whetten, D. (1985) 'Organizational Identity', *Research in Organizational Behaviour* 7: 163–95.

Andrews, K.R. (1971) *The Concept of Corporate Strategy*. Homewood, IL: Dow Jones-Irwin.

Aupperle, K.E., Carrol, A.B. and Hatfield, J.D. (1985) 'An Empirical Examination of the Relationship between Corporate Social Responsibility and Profitability', *Academy of Management Journal* 28(2): 446–63.

Bartholomeusz, S. and Tanewski, G.A. (2006) 'The Relationship between Family Firms and Corporate Governance', *Journal of Small Business Management* 44(2): 245–67.

Basu, K. and Palazzo, G. (2008) 'Corporate Social Responsibility: A Process Model of Sensemaking', *Academy of Management Review* 32(1): 122–36.

Bowie, N.E. (1991) 'Challenging the Egotistic Paradigm', *Business Ethics Quarterly* 1(1): 1–21.

Braun, M. and Sharma, A. (2007) 'Should the CEO also be Chair of the Board? An Empirical Examination of Family Controlled Public Firms', *Family Business Review* 20(2): 111–26.

Brickson, S.L. (2007) 'Organizational Identity Orientation: The Genesis of the Role of the Firm and Distinct Forms of Social Value', *Academy of Management Review* 32(3): 864–88.

Buhr, N. (1998) 'Environmental Performance, Legislation and Annual Report Disclosure: The Case of Acid Rain and Falconbridge', *Accounting, Auditing and Accountability Journal* 11(2): 163–90.

— (2002) 'A Structuration View on the Initiation of Environmental Reports', *Critical Perspectives on Accounting* 13(1): 17–38.

— (2007) 'Histories of and Rationales for Sustainability Reporting', in J. Unerman, J. Bebbington, and B. O'Dwyer (eds) *Sustainability Accounting and Accountability*, pp. 57–69. London: Routledge.

Campbell, D.J. (2000) 'Legitimacy Theory or Managerial Reality Construction? Corporate Social Disclosure in Marks and Spencer Plc Corporate Reports, 1969–1997', *Accounting Forum* 20(1): 80–100.

Carrol, A.B. (1991) 'The Pyramid of Corporate Social Responsibility: Toward the Moral Management of Organizational Stakeholders', *Business Horizons* 34(4): 39–48.

Chami, R. (1999) 'What's Different about Family Business?', Working Paper, International Monetary Fund, Washington DC.

Cho, C.H. (2009) 'Legitimation Strategies Used in Response to Environmental Disaster: A French Case Study of Total Sa's *Erika* and *AZF* Incidents', *European Accounting Review* 18(1): 33–62.

Chrisman, J.J., Chua, J.H. and Lloyd, P.S. (2003) 'An Introduction to Theories of Family Business', *Journal of Business Venturing* 18(4): 441–8.

Clarkson, M.B.E. (1995) 'A Stakeholder Framework for Analyzing and Evaluating Corporate Social Performance', *Academy of Management Review* 20(1): 92–117.

Cromie, S., Adams, J., Dunn, B. and Reid, R. (1999) 'Family Firms in Scotland and Northern Ireland: An Empirical Investigation', *Journal of Small Business and Enterprise Development* 6(3): 253–66.

CSO (Central Statistics Office) (2008) *Family Business in Ireland – Services Sectors 2005.* Dublin: CSO.

Davis, K. (1973) 'The Case for and against Business Assumption of Social Responsibility', *Academy of Management Journal* 16(2): 312–22.

Deegan, C. (2002) 'The Legitimising Effect of Social and Environmental Disclosures – A Theoretical Foundation', *Accounting, Auditing and Accountability Journal* 15(3): 282–311.

Deegan, C., Rankin, M. and Tobin, J. (2002) 'An Examination of the Corporate Social and Environmental Disclosures of BHP from 1983 to 1997: A Test of Legitimacy Theory', *Accounting, Auditing and Accounting Journal* 15(3): 312–43.

Deegan, C., Rankin, M. and Voght, P. (2000) 'Firms' Disclosure Reactions to Major Social Incidents: Australian Evidence', *Accounting Forum* 24(1): 101–30.

Deephouse, D.L. and Carter, S.M. (2005) 'An Examination of Differences between Organizational Legitimacy and Organizational Reputation', *Journal of Management Studies* 42(2): 329–60.

de Villiers, C. and van Staden, C. (2006) 'Can Less Environmental Disclosure Have a Legitimating Effect? Evidence from Africa', *Accounting Organizations and Society* 31(8): 763–81.

Donaldson, T. and Preston, L.E. (1995) 'The Stakeholder Theory of the Corporation: Concepts, Evidence and Implications', *Academy of Management Review* 28(1): 363–6.

Donoghue, F. (2000) *Philanthropy or Advertising? Corporate Giving to the Non-Profit Sector in Ireland.* Dublin: Policy Research Centre, National College of Ireland.

Donoghue, F., Ruddle, H. and Mulvhill, R. (2000) 'Warm Glow in a Cool Climate? Philanthropy in Ireland', paper presented at the International Society for Third Sector Research (ISTR) Fourth International Conference, Dublin: ISTR.

Dutton, J.E. and Dukerich, J.M. (1991) 'Keeping an Eye on the Mirror: Image and Identity in Organizational Adaptation', *Academy of Management Review* 33(3), 517–54.

Everett, J. and Neu, D. (2000) 'Ecological Modernization and the Limits of Environmental Accounting?', *Accounting Forum* 24(1): 5–29.

Fredericks, W.C. (1986) 'Toward CSR3: Why Ethical Analysis is Indispensable and Unavoidable in Corporate Affairs', *California Management Review* 28(2): 126–41.

Freeman, R.E. (1984) *Strategic Management: A Stakeholder Approach.* Boston, MA: Pitman Publishing.

Friedman, M. (1962) *Capitalism and Freedom*. Chicago, IL: University of Chicago Press.

— (1970) 'The Social Responsibility of Business is to Increase its Profits' [online]. Available: http://www.umich.edu/~thecore/doc/Friedman.pdf (last accessed 30 November 2009).

Gray, R.H. (1992) 'Accounting and Environmentalism: An Exploration of the Challenge of Gently Accounting for Accountability, Transparency and Sustainability', *Accounting, Organizations and Society* 17(5): 399–425.

— (2001) 'Thirty Years of Social Accounting, Reporting and Auditing: What (if Anything) have We Learnt?', *Business Ethics: A European Review* 10(1): 9–15.

Gray, R.H., Kouhy, R. and Lavers, S. (1995) 'Corporate Social and Environmental Reporting: A Review of the Literature and a Longitudinal Study of UK Disclosure', *Accounting, Auditing and Accountability Journal* 8(2): 47–77.

Gray, R.H., Owen, D. and Adams, C. (1996) *Accounting and Accountability: Changes and Challenges in Corporate and Social Reporting*. London: Prentice Hall.

Gray, R.H., Owen, D.L. and Maunders, K.T. (1988) 'Corporate Social Reporting: Emerging Trends in Accountability and the Social Contract', *Accounting, Auditing and Accountability Journal* 1(1): 6–20.

Gray, R.H., Walters, D., Bebbington, J. and Thomson, I. (1995) 'The Greening of Enterprise: An Exploration of the (NON) Role of Environmental Accounting and Environmental Accountants in Organisational Change', *Critical Perspectives on Accounting* 6(3): 211–39.

Guthrie, J. and Parker, L.D. (1989) 'Corporate Social Reporting: A Rebuttal of Legitimacy Theory', *Accounting and Business Research* 19(76): 343–52.

Hasnas, J. (1998) 'The Normative Theories of Business Ethics: A Guide for the Perplexed', *Business Ethics Quarterly* 8(1): 19–42.

Hatch, M. and Schultz, M. (1997) 'Relations between Organizational Culture Identity and Image', *European Journal of Marketing* 31(5/6): 356–65.

Hogner, R.H. (1982) 'Corporate Social Reporting: Eight Decades of Development at US Steel', *Research in Corporate Social Performance and Policy* 4: 243–50.

Hummels, H. (1998) 'Organising Ethics: A Stakeholder Debate', *Journal of Business Ethics* 17(13): 1403–14.

Ibrahim, A.B., McGuire, J., Soufani, K. and Poutziouris, P. (2004) 'Patterns in Strategy Formation in a Family Firm', *International Journal of Entrepreneurial Behaviour and Research* 10(1/2): 127–40.

James, H.S. (1999) 'Owner as Manager, Extended Horizons and the Family Firm', *International Journal of the Economics of Business* 6(1): 41–55.

Johannisson, B. and Huse, M. (2000) 'Recruiting Outside Board Members in the Small Family Business: An Ideological Challenge', *Entrepreneurship and Regional Development* 12(4): 353–78.

Jones, T.M. (1980) 'Corporate Social Responsibility Revisited, Redefined', *California Management Review* 22(2): 59–67.

Jones, T.M. and Wicks, A.C. (1999) 'Convergent Stakeholder Theory', *Academy of Management Review* 24(2): 206–79.

Lansberg, I.S. (1983) 'Managing Human Resources in Family Firms: The Problem of Institutional Overlap', *Organizational Dynamics* 12(1): 39–46.

Lindblom, C.K. (1994) 'The Implications of Organizational Legitimacy for Corporate Social Performance and Disclosure', paper presented at the Critical Perspectives on Accounting Conference, New York.

Maughan, R. (2006) *European Sustainability Reporting Association Report for Ireland* [online]. Available: http://www.sustainabilityreporting.eu/esra/ireland/ (last accessed 30 November 2009).

— (2007) *European Sustainability Reporting Association Report for Ireland* [online]. Available: http://www.sustainabilityreporting.eu/esra/ireland/ (last accessed 30 November 2009).

McElhaney, K.A. (2008) *Just Good Business: The Strategic Guide to Aligning Corporate Responsibility and Brand*. San Francisco, CA: Berrett-Koehler.

McWilliams, A., Siegel, D.S. and Wright, P.M. (2006) 'Corporate Social Responsibility: Strategic Implications', *Journal of Management Studies* 43(1): 1–18.

Milne, M.J. and Gray, R. (2007) 'Future Prospects for Corporate Sustainability Reporting', in J. Unerman, J. Bebbington and B. O'Dwyer (eds) *Sustainability Accounting and Accountability*, pp. 184–207. London: Routledge.

Milne, M.J. and Patten, D.M. (2002) 'Securing Organizational Legitimacy: An Experimental Decision Case Examining the Impact of Environmental Disclosures', *Accounting, Auditing and Accountability Journal* 15(3): 372–404.

Mintzberg, H., Simmons, R. and Basu, K. (2002) 'Beyond Selfishness', *Sloan Management Review* 44(1): 67–74.

Mishra, C.S., Randoy, T. and Jenssen, J.I. (2001) 'The Effect of Founding Family Influence on Firm Value and Corporate Governance', *Journal of International Financial Management and Accounting* 12(3): 235–59.

Mitchell, R.K., Morse, E.A. and Sharma, P. (2003) 'The Transacting Cognitions of Nonfamily Employees in the Family Businesses Setting', *Journal of Business Venturing* 18(4): 533–51.

Moir, L. (2001) 'What Do We Mean by Corporate Social Responsibility?', *Corporate Governance* 1(2): 16–22.

Neu, D., Warsame, H. and Pedwell, K. (1998) 'Managing Public Impressions: Environmental Disclosure Content Analysis', *Accounting Organizations and Society* 23(3): 265–82.

Newton, T. and Harte, G. (1997) 'Green Business: Technicist Kitsch?', *Journal of Management Studies* 34(1): 75–98.

O'Donovan, G. (2002) 'Environmental Disclosures in the Annual Report: Extending the Applicability and Predictive Power of Legitimacy Theory', *Accounting, Auditing and Accountability Journal* 15(3): 344–71.

O'Dwyer, B. (2001) *The State of Corporate Environmental Reporting in Ireland.* London: ACCA.

— (2002) 'Managerial Perceptions of Corporate Social Disclosure: An Irish Story', *Accounting, Auditing and Accountability Journal* 15(3): 406–36.

— (2003) 'Conceptions of Corporate Social Responsibility: The Nature of Managerial Capture', *Accounting, Auditing and Accountability Journal* 16(4): 523–57.

O'Dwyer, B. and Gray, R.H. (1998) 'Corporate Social Reporting in the Republic of Ireland: A Longitudinal Study', *Irish Accounting Review* 5(2): 1–34.

Owen, D., Swift, T. and Hunt, K. (2001) 'Questioning the Role of Stakeholder Engagement in Social and Ethical Accounting, Auditing and Reporting', *Accounting Forum* 25(3): 264–82.

Preston, L.E. (1975) 'Corporation and Society: The Search for a Paradigm', *Journal of Economic Literature* 13(2): 434–53.

Preston, L.E. and Post, J.E. (1975) *Private Management and Public Policy: The Principle of Public Responsibility.* Englewood Cliffs, NJ: Prentice Hall.

Roberts, J. and Scapens, R. (1985) 'Accounting Systems and Systems of Accountability: Understanding Accounting Practices in their Organizational Contexts', *Accounting Organizations and Society* 10(4): 443–56.

Sethi, S.P. (1979) 'A Conceptual Framework for Environmental Analysis of Social Issues and Evaluation of Business Response Patterns', *Academy of Management Review* 4(1): 63–74.

Sharma, P., Chrisman, J.J. and Chua, J.H. (1996) *A Review and Annotated Bibliography of Family Business Studies.* Boston, MA: Kluwer Academic.

Silberhorn, D. and Warren, R.C. (2007) 'Defining Corporate Social Responsibility: A View from Big Companies in Germany and the UK', *European Business Review* 19(5): 352–72.

Smith, M. (2007) '"Real" Managerial Difference between Family and Non-Family Firms', *International Journal of Entrepreneurial Behaviour and Research* 13(5): 278–95.

Smith, N.C. (2003) 'Corporate Social Responsibility: Whether or How?', *California Management Review* 45(4): 52–76.

Suchman, M.C. (1995) 'Managing Legitimacy: Strategic and Institutional Approaches', *Academy of Management Review* 20(3): 571–610.

Sweeney, L. (2007) 'Corporate Social Responsibility in Ireland: Barriers and Opportunities Experienced by SMEs when Undertaking CSR', *Corporate Governance* 7(4): 516–23.

— (2008) *European Sustainability Reporting Association Report for Ireland* [online]. Available: http://www.sustainabilityreporting.eu/esra/ireland/ (last accessed 30 November 2009).

Terrachoice (2009) *The Seven Sins of Greenwashing: Environmental Claims in Consumer Markets* [online]. Availabe: www.sinsofgreenwashing.org (last accessed 30 November 2009).

Tinker, A.M., Lehman, C. and Neimark, M. (1991) 'Falling Down the Hole in the Middle of the Road: Political Quietism in Corporate Social Reporting', *Accounting, Auditing and Accountability Journal* 4(1): 28–54.

Uhlaner, L., van Goor-Blak, H.J.M. and Masurel, E. (2004) 'Family Business and Corporate Social Responsibility in a Sample of Dutch Firms', *Journal of Small Business and Enterprise Development* 11(2): 186-94.

Uhlaner, L., Wright, M. and Huse, M. (2007) 'Private Firms and Corporate Governance: An Integrated Economic and Management Perspective', *Small Business Economics* 29(3): 225–41.

Ullmann, A.A. (1985) 'Data in Search of a Theory: A Critical Examination of the Relationships among Social Performance, Social Disclosure, and Economic Performance of U.S. Firms', *Academy of Management Review* 10(3): 540–57.

Vilaseca, A. (2002) 'The Shareholder Role in the Family Business: Conflict of Interests and Objective between Non-employed Shareholders and Top Management Team', *Family Business Review* 15(4): 299–320.

Vyakarnam, S., Bailey, A., Myers, A. and Burnett, D. (1997) 'Towards an Understanding of Ethical Behaviour in Small Firms', *Journal of Business Ethics* 16(15): 1625–35.

Wartick, S.L. and Cochran, P.L. (1985) 'The Evolution of the Corporate Social Performance Review', *Academy of Management Review* 10(4): 758–69.

Wilmhurst, T. and Frost, G.A. (2000) 'Corporate Environmental Reporting: A Test of Legitimacy Theory', *Accounting, Auditing and Accountability Journal* 13(1): 10–26.

Wood, D.J. (1991) 'Corporate Social Performance Revisited', *Academy of Management Review* 16(4): 691–718.

Woodward, D., Edwards, P. and Birkin, F. (1996) 'Organizational Legitimacy and Stakeholder Information Provision', *British Journal of Management* 7(4): 329–47.

Wynn, M. (2003). 'The Irish Waste Management Industry's Response to EU Waste Legislation', paper presented at the European Federation of Waste Management and Waste Services (ESA/FEAD) Conference, London, UK.

Chapter 9

White-Collar Crime: The Business of Crime

Roderick Maguire

INTRODUCTION

Though previous writers such as the American sociologist Ross (1907:6) had drawn attention to the 'darling sins that are blackening the face of our time', and scholars such as the Dutch Marxist Bonger (1916) had highlighted crime by the privileged and those with high social status, it was not until Sutherland's (1937, 1939, 1940, 1947, 1949) work that the study of white-collar crime gained a surer footing in the literature. However, as Croall (2001:6) notes, the research in this area is small in comparison to other areas of crime, though 'its critical role is considerable although it remains a highly contested concept'.

This chapter addresses the 'darling sins' that are white-collar crime. It does this by first tackling the issue of how white-collar crime is defined. Next, various types of white-collar crime are discussed. This is followed by a discussion of how white-collar crime is or, as is often the case, is not prosecuted. Some explanations of white-collar crime are then discussed. The question of how regulation and deregulation define what is held to be white-collar crime is dealt with in the next section, before concluding the chapter.

DEFINING WHITE-COLLAR CRIME

The first problem faced in any discussion on white-collar crime is the definition of the concept. While over the past thirty years the term has become widely accepted, there is no agreement between criminologists, or lawyers or sociologists, as to what exactly encompasses white-collar crime. Though Sutherland coined the phrase in his presidential address to the American Sociological Society in December 1939 (Sutherland 1940), he himself did not proffer a definition until his monograph ten years later (Sutherland 1949). The initial definition propounded by Sutherland (1949:9) was a crime 'committed by a person of high status during the course of his employment'.

Sutherland (1949) argued that, taking criminal statistics at face value, it could be extrapolated that most crime is committed by the poorer sections of society.

However, this is in fact a bias, he argued, that originates in the unequal application of the criminal law. He stated that:

> persons of the upper socio-economic class engage in much criminal behavior; that this criminal behaviour differs from the criminal behaviour of the lower socio-economic class principally in the administrative procedures which are used in dealing with the offenders; and that variations in administrative procedures are not significant from the point of view of the causation of crime. (Sutherland 1949:9)

Later commentators, such as Nelken (1994), have argued that Sutherland's definition lacks coherence and leaves questions unanswered: should the social status of the offenders or the context of the offending be the focus of study? How should the social status of the individual be defined, and how should similar crimes by individuals not falling within that definition be treated? Should only large organisations be considered, as was done by Sutherland himself? Should only criminal infractions be considered, and if not (as Sutherland held), what should the definitional limits be?

Durkheim famously said that society considers dangerous those behaviours it considers criminal, not the other way round: 'We do not condemn it because it is a crime, but it is a crime because we condemn it' (Giddens 1972:123–4). White-collar crime, in a myriad of forms, has harmed people greatly. But that has never been enough to elevate it in the common consideration to criminal behaviour. Durkheim's (1895) work in functionalist theories of crime suggests that, far from deviance in criminal behaviour being a bad thing, it is found in all societies and is normal (Giddens 1972:38). He theorised that it performs four functions in our society. First, the constancy of criminal or abhorrent behaviour gives an indispensable counterpoint to fixing notions of justice and morality. Second, it follows that the defining of deviance serves to mark out social and moral boundaries. Third, it then follows that a response to deviance can promote social unity: through expressions of collective outrage, the social and moral ties that bind communities are strengthened. Fourth, Durkheim argued that deviance actually encourages social change – today's deviance becomes tomorrow's morality: crime has an 'indirect utility' (Carrabine et al. 2004:47; Durkheim1895:71).

Croall (2001) highlighted a number of features of white-collar crime that differ from other forms of criminal activity: it generally takes place in private; the perpetrators are usually legitimately at the scene; it normally involves an abuse of trust in an occupational role; it tends to have an aspect of 'insider' knowledge; there is generally no complaint, or, if there is a complaint, it is often made a long time after the event; because there is no immediate physical threat, white-collar crime is generally less a source of fear or anxiety than some other forms of crime; determining responsibility may prove difficult due to the organisational setting of white-collar crime; and there is generally an ambiguous legal and criminal status.

White-collar crime has, arguably, never gained the status in criminology that Sutherland sought for it (see the discussion by Tombs and Whyte (2007a)). It has often been seen as an aberration and contrasted with street criminals and common crimes. However, recent developments in criminological literature may be very helpful to the study of white-collar crime. Traditionally, the actor in criminological terms, whether an individual or a corporation (the focus of much of Sutherland's work), was viewed in a binary fashion: they were either criminal or they were not. Research tended to focus on why certain people committed crimes and others did not; why one person was genetically disposed to commit crime, while another was not; why one had a personality suited to crime, while another did not; why one had the social background that predicted criminal behaviour, while another did not. Certain recent studies (e.g. Weisburd *et al.* 2001) have suggested that the immediate context of crime has a much more powerful effect than previously considered, and what has been termed 'opportunistic' crime is more prevalent than heretofore believed.

Certain elements of the literature in this area distinguish between corporate crime or organisational crime, on the one hand, and the crime of the individual working within the corporation or occupational crime, on the other. The former would encompass breaches of competition law, environmental crime and health and safety crime, where the latter would include fraud and embezzlement by the employee on the organisation. For the purposes of business understanding of the area, the net should be cast as wide as possible, and the discussion in this chapter will encompass both elements; however, given the non-exacting nature of definitions that describe white-collar crime, there will inevitably be a cross-over between the different strands.

TYPES OF WHITE-COLLAR CRIME

Though there is no agreed definition of what white-collar crime is, and what it encompasses, a list of the main types of crime was developed by Croall (2001).

Theft at Work

This type of crime can vary from the small-scale nature of 'fiddling' to large-scale embezzlement. Studies in this area tend to show that theft at work is often seen as a perk of work, and not considered criminal by the perpetrators (see the historical discussion by Elmsley 2005). The British Retail Consortium (2010) found that seven per cent of all retail losses in UK shops in 2009 were due to theft by employees, and that four employees per thousand engaged in this behaviour. The value per incident of employee theft was £872, almost twenty times the value per incident of customer theft (British Retail Consortium 2010). A likelihood of significant under-reporting was noted.

Fraud

This covers a wide range of activity from social welfare fraud to cheque fraud to counterfeit goods to gaming frauds (e.g. race 'fixing'). 'Fixing' markets through insider dealing or market abuse, where sensitive information is used to manipulate and make personal gain from the markets, is also included in fraud, as is tax fraud on an individual basis, such as the bogus non-resident bank account scandal (Baer and Le Borgne 2008:60) and the value added tax (VAT) frauds that are uncovered on a regular basis. Traditional embezzlement – keeping money that you handle, whether from an employer or a client – is also part of fraud.

Many more large-scale frauds and embezzlements have been uncovered during the recent financial crisis, due to the fact that falling markets make individuals want their money in their hands, and make it more difficult to hide losses. Bernie Madoff embezzled €65bn in a 'Ponzi' scheme, where new investors paid the premium to existing clients, while the original funds were spent by the principal (for how Madoff operated, see Creswell and Thomas (2009)).

Ponzi schemes were named after an Italian immigrant in New York in the 1920s, and have a long history. Charles Ponzi's scheme was to buy postal International Reply Coupons with debased currencies, redeem them in America and then sell the stamps at a sizeable profit. In December 1919, Ponzi launched a firm called the Securities Exchange Company and promised investors 50 per cent returns on their money in forty-five days. By 1929, he was taking in a million dollars weekly. As Ponzi paid off old clients with money from new ones, the press became suspicious and eventually published the news that the US Post Office denied selling large quantities of postal coupons to Ponzi. It turned out that Ponzi had never actually bought many postal coupons. Ponzi was convicted by a Massachusetts jury on sixty-eight counts of larceny on 11 September 1920 (see Chernow 2009; Matulich and Currie 2009).

In Madoff's case, his most audacious innovation was to pretend to fend off investors, rather than openly courting them. He made it seem impossibly difficult to invest with him and his mystique led prominent personalities, including film director Steven Spielberg, to invest with him direct or through charities they established. One of the hard lessons to be learnt in investment is that relationships do not trump due diligence (see Agarwal 2009).

Ivar Kreuger was another fraudulent financier. He was a genuine businessman in Sweden with the ambition in the 1920s to monopolise the sale of boxes of matches (Partnoy 2009). Through his holding company, Kreuger & Toll, he offered a dividend worth 25 per cent, which blinded investors. Kreuger lent money to governments at very low interest rates, in exchange for domestic monopolies on matchbox production. In order to pay his dividends, he took secret loans, believing them to be only temporary, but these spiralled, and led ultimately to his suicide in 1932. Ivar Kreuger presents a credible explanation of how giant Ponzi schemes come about: not as sudden inspirations of criminal masterminds, but rather as a culmination of minor compromises or wrong turns made by financial operators who are not quite as brilliant as they might think.

In recent times, Nick Leeson, a rogue trader for Barings Bank in Singapore, took huge positions in futures contracts, and hid losses in a secret bank account. He increased his exposure exponentially in the hope of covering previous losses with future gains. In early 1995, Leeson took positions that depended on Japanese stock prices rising. Over a short period of time, he concluded contracts that he would buy very large amounts of Japanese shares, though he had no formal authorisation from his superiors in London. By February 1995, Leeson was no longer able to hide the losses accumulating and fled, subsequently being jailed in Germany. The losses of over $1.4bn brought about the collapse of the bank (see Drummond 2008).

Leeson's breaking of Barings Bank was then unprecedented (Levi 2006), but was subsequently dwarfed by the French trader Jerome Kerviel, a 31-year-old who accumulated losses of €4.9bn, or over $7.1bn, by the time his activity was uncovered in January 2008 (Hosking et al. 2008). Kerviel worked for the bank Société Générale in France and was a trader in European futures. In 2007 he had major success betting that stocks would fall. However, he was hedging more than $73bn, far in excess of Société Générale's market capitalisation of $52.6bn. He had bypassed five levels of control in order to trade at such high and unapproved levels, and successfully avoided controls for two years. It has been suggested that the lax monitoring of star performers within the bank, just as with Leeson, was tacit approval for his position (see Comstock 2009). There was also lax monitoring of the apparently successful John Rusnak, a rogue trader in Allfirst Bank in Maryland in the USA, a subsidiary of Allied Irish Bank (AIB). Rusnak was first hired in 1993 and made large losses on futures contracts for yen. He hid these losses through creating fake futures options and falsifying supporting documentation, bypassing more and more controls. He had been hired when he told the then Allfirst treasurer that he would 'consistently make more money by running a large option book hedged in the cash markets, buying options when they were cheap and selling them when they were expensive' (Cole and Ring 2006:249). By the time he was sentenced in 2003 to ninety months in prison, he had accumulated losses of more than $300 million. Rusnak had earned $650,000 in bonuses because he appeared to have such profitable trades (Salinger 2005:704).

These types of crime accord with the general perception of crime, and differ only in the context in which they occur – theft and fraud are essentially the same animal in different forms. However, other types of white-collar crime do not have direct parallels in traditional notions of crime.

Employment Offences

There is extensive legislation in Ireland regulating the relationship between employers and employees. Much of this stems from the raft of European Union

(EU) legislation regulating employment since the 1970s. This legislation tends to centre on regulating the relationship between the employer and the employee – from directives on employment equality (Directive 2000/78/EC) to the maximum hours that can be worked by employees (the Working Time Directive (Council Directive 93/104/EC)). While these can result in the criminalisation of treatment in each member state, depending on the method of incorporation into domestic law and the extension of the relevant principles, the regulation of the health and safety of employees more directly in the workplace was the starting point of this development. Over the decades, EU law has developed through particular initiatives controlling the safety of the workplace. The legislation is also designed to stop corporate behaviour that has a detrimental effect on individuals and the environment outside the workplace.

In relation to employment crimes, the most notable is corporate killing, and the figures presented by Newburn (2007:380) suggest that the largest numbers of those injured and killed at work are from lower socio-economic backgrounds. Research for the UK's Health and Safety Executive indicates that self-employed people are 28 per cent more likely to suffer workplace injury, and that those working in larger establishments are more likely to have had a reportable workplace injury (Davies and Jones 2005:57). Men are almost twice as likely to be injured in the workplace than women (Davies and Jones 2005:49), but this was almost entirely attributable to the fact that men are more likely to be employed in the more hazardous occupations.

Environmental Crimes

Environmental crimes account for another category of crimes in Croall's (2001:40) taxonomy. Often, legislative initiatives are spurred on by a particular incident or incidents. For example, Directive 2003/105/EC amending Directive 96/82/EC on the control of major-accident hazards involving dangerous substances, the 'Seveso II' Directive, cites the reasons for its inception in its preamble:

> In the light of recent industrial accidents and studies on carcinogens and substances dangerous for the environment carried out by the Commission at the Council's request, the scope of Directive 96/82/EC should be extended . . . The cyanide spill that polluted the Danube following the accident at Baia Mare in Romania in January 2000 has demonstrated that certain storage and processing activities in mining, especially tailings disposal facilities, including tailing ponds or dams, have potential to produce very serious consequences. The Commission communications on the safe operation of mining activities and on the sixth environment action programme of the European Community have therefore highlighted the need for an extension of the scope of Directive 96/82/EC. In its resolution of 5 July 2001(5) on the Commission Communication on the safe operation of mining activities, the

European Parliament also welcomed the extension of the scope of that Directive to cover risks arising from storage and processing activities in mining. (EU 2003)

State-Corporate Crime

The seven main types of crime that were identified by Croall (2001) have been added to by Michalowski and Kramer (2006), who list 'state-corporate crime' as another heading. Michalowski and Kramer (2006:3) argue that since the enquiries started by Sutherland into the area of white-collar crime, the division between economics and politics in such an examination 'has remained largely unquestioned'. They seek to 'breach the conceptual wall between economic crimes and political crimes in order to create a new lens through which we can examine the ways crimes and social injuries often emerge from intersections of economic and political power' (Michalowski and Kramer 2006:3).

Michalowski and Kramer (2006) use the case of the *Challenger* space shuttle and argue that the disaster in which it exploded soon after take-off in 1986 was the result of interaction between the US National Aeronautics and Space Administration (NASA) and Morton Thiokol, Inc., a private corporation. They examine budgetary restraints that led to safety compromises and the organisational culture that led to unacceptable risk-taking. They highlight the conclusions of the US House of Representatives Committee on Science and Technology (1986:3) that '[p]ressures within NASA to attempt to evolve from an R&D agency into a quasicompetitive business operation caused a realignment of priorities in the direction of productivity at the cost of safety'. The committee also stated 'that NASA's drive to achieve a launch schedule of 24 flights per year created pressure throughout the agency that directly contributed to unsafe launch operations'. The *Challenger* space shuttle blew apart because of a failure in a joint seal (called an O-ring) on the right solid rocket booster (SRB). The Committee found that 'the failure of the joint was due to a faulty design, and that neither NASA nor Thiokol fully understood the operation of the joint prior to the accident. Further, the joint test and certification programs were inadequate, and neither NASA nor Thiokol responded adequately to available warning signs that the joint design was defective' (Committee on Science and Technology 1986:4). This, in turn, caused the committee to conclude:

Information on the flaws in the joint design and on the problems encountered in missions prior to 51-L was widely available and had been presented to all levels of Shuttle management. Despite the presence of significant amounts of information and the occurrence of at least one detailed briefing at Headquarters on the difficulties with the O-rings, the NASA and Thiokol technical managers failed to understand or fully accept the seriousness of the problem.

There was no sense of urgency on their part to correct the design flaws in the SRB. No one suggested grounding the fleet, nor did NASA embark on a concerted effort to remedy the deficiencies in O-ring performance. Rather, NASA chose to continue to fly with a flawed design and to follow a measured, 27-month, corrective program. (Committee on Science and Technology 1986:5)

PROSECUTING CORPORATE CRIME

Corporations have for a relatively long time, back to the early part of the twentieth century, been held to be liable for crimes in Ireland. For instance, the Factory and Workshop Act 1901 and the Companies (Consolidation) Act 1908 both allowed for the prosecution of companies for offences (Law Reform Commission 2005:3). However, the reluctance to prosecute can be attributed to the notion of what a crime is, and the specific requirements that have developed in relation to a crime.

At law, most crimes require two elements: the *actus reus*, or guilty act, accompanied by the *mens rea*, or guilty mind. There is a limited category of crimes that are strict liability, or require only the proof of the act by the accused in order to secure a conviction. These are mainly confined to regulatory or relatively minor offences, but there have been instances in Ireland, as well as other countries, such as in relation to the Criminal Law (Amendment) Act 1935, and the charge of statutory rape, where statutes have been passed that do not require proof of *mens rea* in relation to each element of the crime. That particular Section of the Act was subsequently found to be unconstitutional by the Supreme Court in the case of *C.C. v. Ireland & Ors*, delivered on 23 May 2006, the Court declaring that S. 1(1) of the Criminal Law (Amendment) Act 1935 was inconsistent with the provisions of the Constitution. The usual requirement is that a crime requires *mens rea*. However, this is a presumption that can be rebutted by clear statutory words to the contrary. Such crimes are generally limited, in Ireland, to:

1   acts that are not criminal in any real sense, but which, in the public interest, are prohibited under a penalty;
2   some, and perhaps all, public nuisances; and
3   cases that, although criminal in form, are really only a method of enforcing a civil entitlement.

There has been a development in recent times in relation to corporate crime in Ireland, and now the position is that certain Acts, such as the Criminal Justice (Theft and Fraud Offences) Act 2001, the Competition Act 2002 and the Prevention of Corruption (Amendment) Act 2001 provide for liability of corporate bodies in circumstances where there is a requirement for a mental element for conviction. There is also provision in these Acts for criminal liability of managers in corporate bodies who contributed to the corporate offence.

Tombs and Whyte (2007b) use a variety of case studies to illustrate what they divine as the shared characteristics of these types of criminal behaviour. They explore such workplace disasters as the sinking of the P&O *Herald of Free Enterprise* in Zeebrugge in 1987, which resulted in 188 people dying. The report of the official inquiry into that incident was highly condemnatory of the company, stating that 'the body corporate was infected with the disease of sloppiness' (Sheen 1987:14). The court case that followed (*R v. P&O European Ferries (Dover) Ltd* (1991) 93 Cr App R 72) failed to result in the company being found criminally liable, because no particular person could be found liable for manslaughter. Ironically, the lack of a system of responsibility, which led to the disaster of the doors of the ferry remaining open as it left the port and led directly to the deaths aboard, resulted in the dismissal of the case.

Tombs and Whyte (2007b) also analyse the case of the chemical leak in Bhopal, India in 1984. The Union Carbide of India Limited (UCIL) plant used highly toxic chemicals to make pesticides. On one evening, the plant leaked and released a cocktail of gases and chemicals, including up to forty tons of methyl isocyanate (MIC) into the atmosphere. The leak, in the estimate of Amnesty International (2004), caused the acute deaths of 7,000 people and long-term deaths of 15,000. This is arguably a corporate crime in the sense that its origins lie in a lack of correct corporate structures, yet it is clearly environmental in its impact, and therefore should perhaps be considered under that heading of Croall's (2001) analysis. In their analysis of this case, along with many other 'safety crimes', Tombs and Whyte (2007b) argue that when businesses put people at risk of serious injury – whether it is the public at large or their own workers – they should be more closely regulated by governments.

Croall (2001) also lists consumer offences, food offences and corruption as other types of white-collar crime. Inevitably, there is a crossover between areas within this taxonomy. For instance, the release of the Ford Pinto in 1970 in the USA, and the ensuing deaths and injuries caused, can be characterised as emanating from the ethics and practices of the workplace, and seen as employment offences, or within the notion of consumer offences.

The Ford Pinto, which went on the market in 1970, was designed to compete with new imported models of cars in the domestic US market, particularly Japanese cars and the Volkswagen Beetle, and, as such, was designed to be a smaller and cheaper car than the corporation had traditionally built. The decision to build the car itself domestically and the nature of the project were internal areas of conflict within Ford, and paved the way for Lee Iacocca, then vice-president, to become president of Ford in 1970, when Henry Ford Jr backed Iacocca's suggestion of building a sub-compact domestically, and this led to the resignation of the then president of Ford, Semon Knudsen (Birsch and Fielder 1994:6). The new design had the petrol tank placed behind the rear axle of the car, and in tests it was shown that in every crash-test at over twenty-five miles per hour, there would be a rupture of the tank and the petrol would ignite. For $11 per vehicle, there was a remedy for this design flaw, and an elimination of any threat of fire, but Ford decided not to issue a recall. An internal cost-benefit analysis estimated that a recall would cost the company in the region of $138 million, and 180 burn deaths resulting from the design of the car would only cost the company $49.5 million (Birsch and Fielder 1994).

Throughout the 1970s, there were a number of accidents in which cars were involved in collisions and the petrol tank ignited, resulting in passengers dying in flaming vehicles. In 1980, the Ford Motor Company was indicted in Indiana following the deaths of three teenagers when the Pinto they were travelling in was rear-ended and burst into flames. The company was charged with reckless homicide under Indiana state law, building a dangerous vehicle and ignoring the company's duty to protect its customers from known dangers. Though the trial resulted in a jury verdict of not guilty, it did establish that a corporation could face criminal charges because of its actions. Civil cases followed and the company recalled the vehicles, though it continued to publicly defend the car (Punch 1996:23; Slapper and Tombs 1999:142).

Slapper and Tombs (1999:142) have argued that the cost-benefit analysis, putting human life below the considerations of profit, is an endemic feature of systems of commerce. However, other commentators have cautioned against this approach and warned that whatever information is to hand *ex post facto* will not accurately depict the motives and interactions of executives in a boardroom meeting (Punch 1996).

EXPLANATIONS OF WHITE-COLLAR CRIME

Explanations of white-collar crime have developed since Sutherland (1939, 1947) wrote in the area (for a critique of its development see Sutherland *et al.* 1992:91). Sutherland (1947:5–9) put forward the idea of differential association as explanatory of this type of criminal behaviour:

> Criminal behaviour is learned in interaction with other persons in a process of communication . . . When criminal behaviour is learned, the learning includes (a) techniques of committing the crime, which are sometimes very complicated, sometimes very simple; (b) the specific direction of the motives, drives, rationalizations and attitudes.

This idea is not by any means universally accepted, and classic works by, for instance, Clinard (1946) and Cressey (1953) cast doubt on such learning in activities such as price regulation and embezzlement. However, Sutherland's theory does invite questions about the nature of the corporate environment that are still being wrestled with (e.g. Michalowski and Kramer 2006:210).

Other theories that have been advanced to explain white-collar crime include self-control theory, neutralisation and critical theory. Self-control theory is advanced by Gottfredson and Hirschi (1990) and is applicable to a variety of crimes. Its central thesis is that individuals pursue self-interest, immediate gratification and the avoidance of pain. To this end, criminal behaviour is a way of maximising pleasure and minimising pain, and white-collar crime is no different from any other type of crime. The criminality of certain individuals is explained by their lack of 'social attachment' stemming from, in the first instance, their upbringing, which results in less weight than is proper being given to the feelings of others (Gottfredson and Hirschi 1990:94). The theory has been criticised in that two of the major supporting claims made by the authors – that the demographic distribution of conventional and white-collar crimes is the same, and that white-collar crime is relatively rare – are false (see Koletar 2003:66; Larson and Garrett 1996:106; Steffensmeier 1989). Therefore, the notion of a single unifying theory of all crime is disputed.

The theory propounded by Sykes and Matza (1957) is that certain 'techniques of neutralisation' are learned. These techniques are five-fold and are all centred on ways to deflect blame. They are: the denial of responsibility – 'it wasn't my fault'; the denial of the victim – 'I was just borrowing it' or 'they can well afford it'; the denial of the injury – perhaps seeing the crime as rightful retaliation; the condemnation of the condemners – police are corrupt, teachers show favouritism and parents always blame their children; and the appeal to higher loyalties – 'always help a buddy' and 'never squeal on a friend'.

Critical theory takes the view that the structure of contemporary capitalism is an explanatory factor in an examination of corporate crime (Pearce 1976; Punch 1996; Slapper and Tombs 1999). Crime and misconduct are seen as endemic to business and the key to understanding any notion of white-collar crime in the corporate world lies in recognising the structure that the business environment gives to misconduct. That structure is to be viewed both in terms of opportunities and in terms of how misconduct is managed (Clarke 1990).

REGULATING AND DEREGULATING

In the recent past, following the financial crisis, corporate regulation has been thrown into sharp relief. Corporations are no longer seen as the energy that drives all things good in a developed country, as perhaps they were when Sutherland first explored the area of white-collar crime (see, e.g., McQuaid 1986:212). It is dangerous to label corporations as responsible in some way, and innately so, for the failings of their employees, or to see them resolutely and only as possibly amoral features of an economy that must be tolerated. Much criminological literature has focused on the misinterpretation of the Smithian idea in philosophy of the exchange in the market as the thesis of western civilisation – rather, as powerfully argued by Sen (2009), Adam Smith also saw that there were higher concerns than the market and that these needed to be accommodated (Smith 1976 [1759]).

The corporate scandals in the early years of the twenty-first century have raised again, and forcefully, some of Sutherland's basic points, particularly the fact that white-collar crimes are much more damaging than traditional street crime. The 2001 collapse of Enron (Berkowitz 2002; Fox 2003; Nordstrom 2007), and the 1989 US Savings and Loan (Barth *et al.* 2004) and 2002 Worldcom (Jetter 2003) scandals highlighted the damage that well-dressed men in expensive suits can inflict without using a threatening word, and it is likely that the ultimate fall-out of the current financial crisis will again require a recalibration of criminal law and regulatory oversight, which will alter long-held assumptions.

In the last twenty years, there have been major shifts in policy at two levels of worldwide commerce. The first shift was an institutional rowing-back of the regulatory restraints imposed in the wake of the Wall Street Crash in 1929. The second has been a flowering of high-profile and public regulation, often spearheaded by individual politicians or judges (e.g. Kotkin and Sajó 2002; Richards 1995), and focused in particular on financial institutions. It would seem that the second of these shifts was too little too late to restrain the dangers to society of unbridled capitalism in the form of the global financial collapse of 2008 (for a general review, see Mathiason 2008).

The cutting edge of the conceptualisation of white-collar crime is the expansion into regulation and criminalisation of previously accepted or tolerated practice. To that extent, the nature and effect of white-collar crime is political and not criminal or judicial, and the business student should note that this landscape is constantly evolving. The critical arguments about whether these actions are harmful or not, and criminal or not, take place in government cabinet rooms, rather than courts.

The Pendulum of Regulation

Following the Great Crash of 1929, one of every five banks in the USA failed. Many believed that market speculation engaged in by banks during the 1920s was a cause of the crash. In 1930, the Bank of United States failed, reportedly because of activities of its security affiliates that created artificial conditions in the market. In March 1933, newly inaugurated President Franklin D. Roosevelt closed all the banks throughout the country for a four-day period, and four thousand banks closed permanently. The breathing space provided by this period was used to announce and implement a new macroeconomic policy.

In 1933, Senator Carter Glass, a Democrat from Virginia, and Congressman Henry Steagall, a Democrat from Alabama, introduced legislation that bore their name (also known as the Banking Act of 1933 (48 Stat. 162)), seeking to limit the conflicts of interest created when commercial banks are permitted to underwrite stocks or bonds. Previously, individual investors had been taken advantage of by banks that were trying to promote particular stocks that were of benefit to the banks themselves, and not to the investors. This conflict of interest, between the interests of the bank and the investor customer, was a significant problem. The Glass–Steagall Act banned commercial banks from underwriting securities, and therefore forced the banks to decide whether they were going to be straightforward lending institutions or become underwriting institutions of stocks and shares. The Act also created the Federal Deposit Insurance Corporation (FDIC), which insures bank deposits with money levied from banks, and was part of President Roosevelt's New Deal programme. The aim of the legislation was to create confidence in the banking system. It was followed by the Bank Holding Company Act in 1956, which extended the restrictions on banks, including that bank holding companies owning two or more banks could not engage in non-banking activity and could not buy banks in another state.

Many historians believe that the commercial bank securities practices of the time had little actual effect on the already devastated economy and were not a major contributor to the Depression of the 1930s (e.g. Effros 1992:286; Drucker and Puri 2007:196). Some legislators and bank reformers argued that the Act was never necessary, or that it had become outdated and should be repealed (Engerman and Gallman 1996).

Congress responded to these criticisms in passing the Gramm–Leach–Bliley Act of 1999, which made significant changes to the Glass–Steagall Act. The former Act repealed Glass-Steagall's restrictions on bank and securities firm affiliations and 'represented several decades worth of legislative jockeying by different financial and congressional interests to modernize the US financial services statutory framework' (Mullineux and Murinde 2003:629). The new law sought this financial modernisation by removing the barriers that the Glass–Steagall Act had erected. It opened the door for bigger and more complex financial institutions. At the same time as a variety of individuals and institutions were trying to have Glass–Steagall changed and to liberate a wave of banking innovation, others were seeking to restrain bank criminality that was seen as widespread and inextricably linked to the larger multi-faceted nature of modern financial institutions.

The Attorney General of New York elected in 1999, Eliot Spitzer, campaigned to regulate more strictly a number of these institutions (Gitlow 2007). From 2002 onwards, he uncovered bankers who pressurised analysts to inflate certain stocks. He also investigated mutual funds and their after-hours and 'timing' trades that were contrary to regulations. The method of charging fees for certain mutual funds was also questioned. Spitzer successfully prosecuted Merrill Lynch, the mutual funds industry, and insurance brokers, forcing a number of companies to remove their CEOs and pay millions of dollars in fines, with Citigroup alone paying $300m (Nelson and Trevino 2006). His method in doing this was commended, and with the national regulator, the Securities and Exchange Commission (SEC), following his lead, he was seen as an exemplary public activist (e.g. Richter and Burke 2007:230). However, the 1999 passage of the Gramm–Leach–Bliley Act fully reversed the prohibitions in Glass–Steagall, and completed work begun by the

Federal Reserve in 1987 in their interpretation of Section 20 of the Act. The new Act was not expected to increase the pace of acquisition or give opportunities for consolidation (Mathieson and Schinasi 2000). However, it is now seen as having contributed to the financial crisis that began in 2008, at least insofar as the loosened regime under Glass–Steagall was not replaced with a comprehensive new framework (for contemporary US reaction see Leonhardt 2008).

The liberalisation of international finance that stemmed from the relaxation of US regulation brought the Irish Financial Services Centre (IFSC) to Dublin's docklands in 1987. While this political decision to attract international finance was successful, it was the political decision to keep regulation light that ultimately caused problems for Ireland (see Chapter 6). Regulation continued to be light for the next twenty years, with the then Minister for Enterprise, Trade and Employment 'addressing administrative burdens which can genuinely be identified as disproportionate' (Martin 2005). In relation to compliance statements that had been deemed necessary by legislation enacted in 2003, the minister at the time stated:

> The review of the Directors' Compliance Statement undertaken by the Company Law Review Group (CLRG) was instituted due to unhappiness in the business sector at the degree and extent of obligations imposed by the directors' compliance statement obligations set out in Section 45 of the Companies [Auditing and Accounting] Act 2003 (45/2003). The Government has now agreed to progress into law the proposed new model for the Directors' Compliance Statement as proposed by the CLRG on foot of its intensive review of the proportionality, efficacy and appropriateness of 45/2003. This means that Section 45 of the 2003 Act will never be commenced. The new model of the Directors' Compliance Statement which will replace it differs from existing 45/2003 in restricting and clarifying the obligations on which directors must report, in being less prescriptive about the methods a company uses to review its compliance procedures, and in not requiring review of the compliance statement by an external auditor. Thus we should help embed good corporate governance without increasing costs. (Martin 2005)

Thus, the government was responding to what it saw as a need for 'light-touch' regulation:

> The Financial Regulator is particularly conscious of the need to balance an efficient and effective regulatory regime while, at the same time, encouraging a competitive and expanding market of high reputation. I know that it is also very conscious of the need to avoid being over-prescriptive to the extent of stifling legitimate innovation and development. This, indeed, is the core of its principles-based approach to regulation. (Martin 2005)

As Palma (2009:829) has stated:

> The current financial crisis is the outcome of something much more systemic, namely an attempt to use neo-liberalism (or, in US terms, neo-conservatism) as a new technology of power to help transform capitalism into a rentiers' delight. In particular, into a system without 'compulsions' on big business, i.e., one that imposes only minimal pressures on big agents to engage in competitive struggles in the real economy (while doing the opposite to workers and small firms).

Ireland exploited that lack of compulsion on big business through its exceptionally low corporate tax regime under the Finance Act 1987, which established a tax rate of 10 per cent for corporations, and this increased in 2002 to 12.5 per cent. Protecting the more than twenty thousand jobs that were created due to this became paramount, and the Irish government was not going to jeopardise those jobs and the attendant tax revenues by unilaterally raising the internationally low standards of regulation reflected in the comments of then-minister Martin. The pendulum is now swinging away from this type of regulatory pandering, and what replaces it remains to be seen.

The Irish Position Today

While the era of the industrial revolution in Britain, approximately 1750–1850, has been credited with many watersheds in the development of our ontology of white-collar crime, with the emergence of financial offences and the restructuring of workplace crime (Locker and Godfrey 2006), recent happenings on the world scale, and even more so in Ireland, may lead to just as important a sea change. The lobbyist Frank Dunlop was sentenced to two years' imprisonment in May 2009 for corruption of public officials in the planning process (see Chapter 11). The Criminal Assets Bureau has recommended that this should be followed by prosecution of a 'handful' of politicians (Cullen and Lally 2009). This is, in one way, the culmination of the long-running Tribunal of Enquiry into Certain Planning Matters and Payments (also known as the Mahon Tribunal), which was established on 4 November 1997 and has not yet finally reported.

At the same time as Dunlop was awaiting the imposition of his two-year sentence, based solely on his own evidence, the final report of the Commission to Inquire into Child Abuse (also known as the Ryan Commission, after its chairman, Mr Justice Sean Ryan) (2009) was published. The report detailed the systematic and institutionalised physical, psychological and sexual abuse of children in state institutions from 1936 to the present day. The main part of the report concerned the period 1936–1970, between the publication of the Cussen Report (Cussen 1936) and the Kennedy Report (Kennedy 1970), a period when industrial and reformatory schools were widespread. The definition of white-collar crime offered by Geis (1992:47) as 'abuse of power by persons who are situated in high places where they are provided with the opportunity for such abuse' characterises this behaviour as white-collar crime, and indeed, it is hard not to think that the lessons that Sutherland sought to teach cannot be learned through the examination of even this report.

The third and final recent event that may affect a sea change in Ireland, and more widely, is the recent behaviour of certain individuals and corporations in the financial services industry. Irish banks, which recklessly loaned monies to persons without adequate security (Joint Committee on Economic Regulatory Affairs 2009) and purposely ensured that their financial records did not adequately reflect the true situation (e.g. non-disclosure of director's loans by Anglo Irish Bank (see Labanyi 2009)), have been considered at length in the media, though there has been little talk of criminal repercussions for those responsible.

CONCLUSION

The ambiguity of the concept of white-collar crime can, in some way, be avoided, but its fundamental lesson should be heeded: criminal activity can occur in boardrooms as well as in back alleys, and the same caution and judgment should be employed in both situations. The criticisms that were levelled against Sutherland in his work in this area are still extant. There are certain fundamental problems with the concept of white-collar crime (see the discussion by Sutherland, Cressey and Luckenbill 1992:93). The notion that 'socially injurious' (Sutherland 1937:180) actions constituted criminal behaviour bypassed the criminal justice system. This area of study led the criminologist to sit in judgment on what was criminal activity, and therefore who was criminal.

In Ireland, as in many other countries, the vast majority of people who end up before the courts on criminal charges are not white-collar workers. This may display the prejudice of the system or the difficulties of enforcement, but it no longer indicates that improper behaviour by those in business is not criminal.

The steady tide of regulation in Ireland is now heading towards increasing criminalisation of improper conduct for those in business. The reprieve won in 2003 for company directors to personally stand over their annual returns is now to be re-considered by the Company Law Review Group. It seems likely that there will be no strong voices against imposing increased obligations on corporate entities to explain, in readily understandable form, all information that could affect the investor. While the first legal developments to emerge from this financial crisis will be regulatory in nature, the logical next step is to criminalise those who fail in this obligation or who wilfully mislead the public. The expansion of criminal law has to go hand-in-hand with the expansion of such obligations. Just as in competition law, with our Competition (Amendment) Act 1996, expanded with the Competition Act 2002, there was criminalisation of anti-competitive behaviour at a national level, the ultimate sanction of opprobrium, and the threat of the deprivation of liberty by way of a prison sentence, will be necessary to give effectiveness to any major development in regulatory law (OECD 2000, 2003).

The apparent reluctance to prosecute individuals in relation to the white-collar crimes in Ireland referred to above may be explained by a wish not to upset any future criminal trial by adverse publicity at the stage of investigation, or it may be that the inadequate regulatory oversight has left a gaping hole in our criminal justice armoury – the criminal justice system is simply not fit for purpose. Either way, the direct correlation between the economic downturn, increase in unemployment, reduction of wages and public services, and mounting public debt, on the one hand, and the actions required by the government to rescue what have been deemed 'systemic' financial institutions in the state, will have to have an impact on criminal legislators. While earlier accounting scandals, such as the overcharging of bank customers by AIB for the ten years prior to 2004 (RTÉ 2004, 2009) raised eyebrows, there was not a similar and readily identifiable link between the loss to the public at large and these actions.

The confluence of recent events in Ireland discussed above invites a reconsideration of the criminal law in Ireland. As with all political changes, there will be many factors to consider in the development of the law in this area, but the fact that pursuing criminal assets, under our innovative Criminal Assets Bureau Act of 1996, netted the exchequer more than €10m in 2007 (An Garda Síochána 2007) indicates that the government may be able to make major strides in this area without increasing its spending hugely. Whether it has the political will to do so remains to be seen.

In any recalibration of the market and the views of corporations, the benefits of the corporate structure and the corporation generally should be remembered. That is to say, the good that corporations do can be done in different regimes, without dismantling the whole way that our society works. Strong regulation is needed, not banking regulation dreamt up by the bankers themselves as was done in Basel II (the regulatory code developed by the Bank for International Settlements, an organisation of central banks, in 2004). Rather, measures are needed that are akin to the Canadian code that has seen those banks survive and prosper in these volatile times. Strong regulation can and will redeem these sectors. Perhaps it will not place them back at the apex of our cultural hierarchy, but they can survive and contribute to the economy.

References

Agarwal, M. (2009) *The Future of Hedge Fund Investing: A Regulatory and Structural Solution for a Fallen Industry*. Hoboken, NJ: Wiley & Sons.

Amnesty International (2004) *Clouds of Injustice: Bhopal Disaster 20 Years On*. London: Amnesty International Publications [online]. Available: http://www.amnesty.org/en/library/asset/ASA20/015/2004/en/fa14a821-d584-11dd-bb24-1fb85fe8fa05/asa200152004en.pdf (last accessed 10 November 2009).

An Garda Síochána (2007) *Annual Report of the Criminal Assets Bureau* [online]. Available: http://www.justice.ie/en/JELR/CAB%20Complete%20Report%202007.pdf/Files/CAB%20Complete%20Report%202007.pdf (last accessed 10 November 2009).

Baer, K. and Le Borgne, E. (2008) *Tax Amnesties: Theory, Trends, and Some Alternatives*. Washington, DC: International Monetary Fund.

Barth J., Trimbath, S. and Yago, G. (eds) (2004) *The Savings and Loan Crisis: Lessons from a Regulatory Failure*. Norwell, MA: Klewer Academic Publishers.

Berkowitz, A.L. (2002) *Enron: A Professional's Guide to the Events, Ethical Issues and Proposed Reforms*. Chicago, IL: CCH.

Birsch, D. and Fielder, J.H. (eds) (1994) *The Ford Pinto Case: A Study in Applied Ethics, Business and Technology*. New York, NY: State University of New York Press.

Bonger, W. (1916) *Criminality and Economic Conditions* (trans. H. Horton). Boston, MA: Little, Brown.

British Retail Consortium (2010) *Retail Crime Survey 2009*. London: British Retail Consortium [online]. Available: http://www.brc.org.uk/downloads/BRCCrimeSurvey2009.pdf (last accessed 7 February 2010).

Carrabine, E., Iganski, P., Lee, M., Plummer, K. and South, N. (2004) *Criminology: A Sociological Introduction*. London: Routledge.

Chernow, R. (2009) 'Annals of Finance, "Madoff and his Models"', *New Yorker*, 23 March, p. 28.

Clarke, M. (1990) *Business Crime: Its Nature and Control*. Cambridge: Polity Press.

Clinard, M.B. (1946) 'Criminological Theories of Violations of Wartime Regulations', *American Sociological Review* 11: 258–70.

Cole, E. and Ring, S. (2006) *Insider Threat: Protecting the Enterprise from Sabotage, Spying and Theft*. Rockland, MA: Syngress Publishing.

Commission to Inquire into Child Abuse (2009) *Report of the Commission to Inquire into Child Abuse* [online]. Available: http://www.childabusecommission.com/rpt/ (last accessed 10 November 2009).

Committee on Science and Technology (USA) (1986) *Investigation of the Challenger Accident*, Washington DC, US Government Printing Office [online]. Available: http://www.gpoaccess.gov/challenger/64_420.pdf (last accessed 19 January 2010).

Comstock, C. (2009) 'The Adventures of Jerome Kerviel', *Forbes*, 2 September [online]. Available: http://www.forbes.com/2009/09/02/jerome-kerviel-fraud-societe-generale-markets-faces-legal.html (last accessed 17 January 2010).

Cressey, D.R. (1953) *Other People's Money: A Study in the Social Psychology of Embezzlement*. Glencoe, IL: Free Press.

Creswell, J. and Thomas, L. (2009) 'The Talented Mr Madoff', *New York Times*, 24 January [online]. Available: http://www.nytimes.com/2009/01/25/business/25bernie.html (last accessed 10 November 2009).

Croall, H. (2001) *Understanding White-Collar Crime*. Buckingham: Open University Press.

Cullen, P. and Lally, C. (2009) 'Some Politicians Set to Face Corruption Charges', *Irish Times*, 27 May [online]. Available: http://www.irishtimes.com/newspaper/ireland/2009/0527/1224247503189.html (last accessed 10 November 2009).

Cussen, G.P. (1936) *Report of the Commission into the Reformatory and Industrial School System, 1934–1936*. Dublin: Stationery Office.

Davies, R. and Jones, P. (2005) *Trends and Context to Rates of Workplace Injury*, Research Paper 386, Health and Safety Executive (UK), Coventry: Warwick Institute for Employment Research, University of Warwick [online]. Available: http://www.hse.gov.uk/research/rrpdf/rr386.pdf (last accessed 7 February 2010).

Drucker, S. and Puri, M. (2007) 'Banks in Capital Markets', in B.E. Eckbo (ed.) *Handbook of Corporate Finance: Empirical Corporate Finance*, pp. 190–221. Amsterdam: North Hollander.

Drummond, H. (2008) *The Dynamics of Organizational Collapse: The Case of Barings Bank*. Abingdon: Routledge.

Durkheim, E. (1895) *On the Normality of Crime*. New York, NY: Free Press.

Effros, R.C. (1992) *Current Legal Issues Affecting Central Banks*, Vol. 1. Washington DC: International Monetary Fund.

Elmsley, C. (2005) *Crime and Society in England 1750–1900*, 3rd edn. Harlow: Pearson Education.

Engerman, S.L. and Gallman, R.E. (eds) (1996) *The Cambridge Economic History of the United States, Vol. 1: The Colonial Era*. Cambridge: Cambridge University Press.

EU (European Union) (2003) *Directive 2003/105/EC of the European Parliament and of the Council* [online]. Available: http://eur-lex.europa.eu/LexUriServ/LexUriServ.do?uri=CELEX:32003L0105:EN:HTML (last accessed 10 November 2009).

Fox, L. (2003) *Enron: The Rise and Fall*. Hoboken, NJ: John Wiley & Sons.

Geis, G. (1992) 'White-Collar Crime: What Is It?', in K. Schlegel and D. Weisburd (eds) *White-Collar Crime Reconsidered*, pp. 31–52. Boston, MA: Northeastern University Press.

Giddens, A. (1972) *Emile Durkheim: Selected Writings*. Cambridge: Cambridge University Press.

Gitlow, A.L. (2007) *Corruption in Corporate America*, 2nd edn. Lanham, MD: University Press of America.

Gottfredson, M.R. and Hirschi, T. (1990) *A General Theory of Crime*. Stanford, CA: Stanford University Press.

Hosking, P., Bremner, C. and Sage, A. (2008) 'Jerome Kerviel Named in €5bn Bank Trading Fraud', *Times Online*, 24 January. Available: http://business.timesonline.co.uk/tol/business/industry_sectors/banking_and_finance/article3242996.ece (last accessed 10 November 2009).

Jetter, L. (2003) *Disconnected: Deceit and Betrayal at Worldcom*. Hoboken, NJ: Wiley & Sons.

Joint Committee on Economic Regulatory Affairs (2009) 'Anglo Irish Bank: Discussion with Financial Regulator', Parliamentary Debates, Office of the Houses of the Oireachtas [online]. Available: http://debates.oireachtas.ie/ DDebate.aspx?F=ERJ20090113.xml&Node=H2#H2 (last accessed 10 November 2009).

Kennedy, E. (1970) *Reformatory and Industrial Schools Systems Report, 1970*. Dublin: Stationery Office [online]. Available: http://www.lenus.ie/hse/ bitstream/10147/77793/1/Reformatory%26IndusSchoolSys.pdf (last accessed 20 January 2010).

Koletar, J.W. (2003) *Fraud Exposed: What You Don't Know Could Cost Your Company Millions*. Hoboken, NJ: Wiley & Sons.

Kotkin, S. and Sajó, A. (2002) *Political Corruption in Transition: A Skeptic's Handbook*. Budapest: Central European University Press.

Labanyi, D. (2009) 'ICAI Appoints Purcell to Inquire into Anglo's Director Loans', *Irish Times*, 20 February [online]. Available: http://www.irishtimes. com/newspaper/breaking/2009/0220/breaking32.htm (last accessed 20 January 2010).

Larson, C.J. and Garrett, G.R. (1996) *Crime, Justice and Society*. Lanham, MD: General Hall.

Law Reform Commission (2005) *Report on Corporate Killing*. Dublin: Law Reform Commission [online]. Available http://www.lawreform.ie/ Corporate%20Killing%20Report.pdf (last accessed 10 November 2009).

Leonhardt, D. (2008) ' Washington's Invisible Hand', *New York Times*, 26 September [online]. Available: http://www.nytimes.com/2008/09/28/ magazine/28wwln-reconsider.html (last accessed 10 November 2009).

Levi, M. (2006) 'The Media Construction of Financial White-Collar Crimes', *British Journal of Criminology* 46(6): 1037–105.

Locker, J.P. and Godfrey, B. (2006) 'Ontological Boundaries and Temporal Watersheds in the Development of White-Collar Crime', *British Journal of Criminology* 46(6): 976–92.

Martin, M. (2005) 'Speech by the Minister for Enterprise, Trade and Employment', IFSC Annual Lunch, Dublin Castle, 9 December [online]. Available: http://www.entemp.ie/press/2005/20051209.htm (last accessed 19 January 2010).

Mathiason, N. (2008) 'Three Weeks that Changed the World', *The Observer*, 28 December [online]. Available: http://www.guardian.co.uk/business/ 2008/dec/28/markets-credit-crunch-banking-2008 (last accessed 10 November 2009).

Mathieson, D.J. and Schinasi, G.J. (2000) *International Capital Markets: Developments, Prospects and Key Policy Issues*. Washington, DC: International Monetary Fund.

Matulich, S. and Currie, D.M. (2009) *Handbook of Frauds, Scams and Swindles: Failures of Ethics and Leadership*. Boca Raton, FL: CRC Press.

McQuaid, K. (1986) *A Response to Industrialism: Liberal Capitalism and the Evolving Spectrum of Capitalist Reform, 1886–1960*. Washington, DC: Beard Books.

Michalowski, R.J. and Kramer, R.C. (eds) (2006) *State-Corporate Crime: Wrongdoing at the Intersection of Business and Government*. Piscataway, NJ: Rutgers University Press.

Mullineux, A.W. and Murinde, V. (eds) (2003) *Handbook of International Banking*. Cheltenham: Edward Elgar.

Nelken, D. (1994) 'White-Collar Crime', in M. Maguire, R. Morgan and R. Reiner (eds) *The Oxford Handbook of Criminology*, 1st edn, pp. 355–92. Oxford: Oxford University Press.

Nelson, K. and Trevino, L. (2006) *Managing Business Ethics*, 4th edn. Hoboken, NJ: Wiley & Sons.

Newburn, T. (2007) *Criminology*. Collompton: Willan Publishing.

Nordstrom, C. (2007) *Global Outlaws: Crime, Money, and Power in the Contemporary World*. Berkeley, CA: University of California Press.

OECD (2000) *Annual Report on Competition Policy Developments in Ireland* [online]. Available: http://www.oecd.org/dataoecd/52/13/39554071.pdf (last accessed 10 November 2009).

— (2003) *Annual Report on Competition Policy Development in Ireland* [online]. Available: http://www.oecd.org/dataoecd/37/3/34720597.pdf (last accessed 10 November 2009).

Palma, J.G. (2009) 'The Revenge of the Market on the Rentiers. Why Neo-liberal Reports of the End of History Turned Out to Be Premature', *Cambridge Journal of Economics* 33: 829–69.

Partnoy, F. (2009) *The Match King: Ivar Krueger, the Financial Genius Behind a Century of Wall Street Scandals*. New York, NY: Public Affairs.

Pearce, F. (1976) *Crimes of the Powerful: Marxism, Crime and Deviance*. London: Pluto Press.

Punch, M. (1996) *Dirty Business: Exploring Corporate Misconduct*. London: Sage.

Richards, C. (1995) *The New Italians*. London: Penguin.

Richter, W.L. and Burke, F. (eds) (2007) *Combating Corruption, Encouraging Ethics: A Practical Guide to Management Ethics*. Lanham, MD: Rowman & Littlefield.

Ross, E.A. (1907) *Sin and Society: An Analysis of Latter-Day Iniquity*. Boston, MA: Houghton Mifflin Company.

RTÉ (Raidió Teilifís Éireann) (2004) 'AIB Overcharging Forex Customers', 6 May [online]. Available: http://www.rte.ie/business//2004/0506/aib.html (last accessed 20 January 2010).

— (2009) 'AIB Overcharging: Regulator Responds', 24 March [online]. Available: http://www.rte.ie/business/2009/0324/aib.html (last accessed 20 January 2010).

Salinger, L.M. (2005) *Encyclopedia of White-collar and Corporate Crime*, Vol. 2. Thousand Oaks, CA: Sage.

Sen, A. (2009) *The Idea of Justice*. Cambridge, MA: Harvard University Press.

Sheen, B. (1987) *Herald of Free Enterprise: Report of Court No. 8074 Formal Investigation*. London: HMSO for Department of Transport.

Slapper, G.J. and Tombs, S. (1999) *Corporate Crime*. London: Addison Wesley Longman.

Smith, A. (1976 [1759]) *The Theory of Moral Sentiments*. Oxford: Clarendon Press.

Steffensmeier, D. (1989) 'On the Causes of "White-Collar" Crime: An Assessment of Hirschi and Gottfredson's Claims', *Criminology* 27(2): 345–58.

Sutherland, E.H. (1937) *The Professional Thief*. Chicago, IL: University of Chicago Press.

— (1939) *Principles of Criminology*, 3rd edn. Philadelphia, PA: J.B. Lippincott.

— (1940) 'White-Collar Criminality', *American Sociological Review* 5 (1): 1–12 [online]. Available: http://www2.asanet.org/governance/PresidentialAddress1939.pdf (last accessed 20 January 2010).

— (1947) *Principles of Criminology*, 4th edn. Philadelphia, PA: J.B. Lippincott.

— (1949) *White Collar Crime*. New York, NY: Dryden Press

Sutherland, E.H., Cressey, D.R. and Luckenbill, D.F. (1992). *Principles of Criminology*, 11th edn. Lanham, MD: General Hall.

Sykes, G.M. and Matza, D. (1957) 'Techniques of Neutralization: A Theory of Delinquency', *American Sociological Review* 22(6): 664–70.

Tombs, S. and Whyte, D. (2007a) 'Researching Corporate and White-Collar Crime in an Era of Neo-Liberalism', in H. Pontell and G. Geis (eds) *International Handbook of White Collar and Corporate Crime*, pp. 125–47. New York, NY: Springer.

— (2007b) *Safety Crimes*. Collompton: Willan Publishing.

Weisburd, D., Waring, E. and Chayet, E. (2001) *White-Collar Crime and Criminal Careers*. Cambridge: Cambridge University Press.

Chapter 10
Political Corruption in Ireland: A Downward Spiral
Gillian Smith

INTRODUCTION

The global liquidity crisis of 2008, combined with the collapse of the domestic property market, pushed Irish banks to the brink of collapse. As the true situation within Irish banks emerged, the public was scandalised by the revelations of improper behaviour by high-ranking bank officials and the lack of supervision by the Financial Regulator (Carswell 2008; Weston 2009). It appears that this lack of oversight allowed top bankers to engage in irregular lending practices, which increased the institutions' exposure to the global crash. Investigations by the Garda Fraud Squad and the Office of the Director of Corporate Enforcement (ODCE) (Brady 2009) might be able to shed light on any corrupt activities of bankers. Fuelled by tax incentives for developers and investors, the property boom also relied on easy access to credit. The close relationship between politicians (who relied heavily on donations from the construction sector), property developers and bankers, resulted in a prolonged property boom in Ireland, beyond that seen in the United States or the United Kingdom.

The opposition parties have called for an end to the 'crony capitalism' that encouraged the property bubble (McGee 2009a). Costs associated with this type of crony capitalism are borne by the shareholders of the banks and by the Irish taxpayer. The government rescue package for the banks includes funds for recapitalisation and the creation of a new body, the National Asset Management Agency (NAMA), to take on 'toxic assets' from the banks; this may ultimately be paid for by the taxpayer.

Suspicion of 'crony capitalism' is not a recent development in Ireland. Both property developers and banks were the subject of investigations in the 1990s. The Planning Tribunal (the Flood/Mahon Tribunal, 1997 to date) was set up to investigate the connection between developers' 'donations' to individual politicians and bureaucrats and certain planning decisions in Dublin. The McCracken Tribunal (1997) investigated payments to former Taoiseach Charles Haughey. In its wake, the Financial Regulator was set up to ensure proper supervision of foreign exchange controls and to monitor offshore accounts. In the course of the McCracken Tribunal, it became clear that the Central Bank was not fulfilling this role adequately and significant tax evasion through offshore accounts (the Ansbacher deposits) had occurred as a result of inadequate oversight (McCracken 1997:25). The Public Accounts Committee also investigated the banks in the 1990s and reported that there was 'a particularly close and inappropriate relationship between banking interests and government' (Murphy 2005:380).

The introduction of ethics legislation was a policy priority for the rainbow coalition government of Fine Gael, the Labour Party and Democratic Left (1994–1997). The scandals that emerged from the end of the 1980s highlighted the close relationship between high-ranking government officials and businessmen and made it clear that existing legislation was insubstantial (Smith 2008). The rainbow coalition government introduced the first laws on ethics since the foundation of the state with the Ethics Acts (1995) (Murphy 2006a). The McCracken (1997), Moriarty (1997 to date) and Flood/ Mahon (1997 to date) tribunals exposed intricate networks of secret payments to politicians and public officials. The tribunals repeatedly questioned the motivation of businessmen giving large, covert donations to politicians (McCracken 1997; O'Halpin 2000). This created the impetus for more regulation to combat corruption.

An official from the Standards in Public Office Commission (SIPO) stated that Irish politics has been irrevocably changed by the revelations of the tribunals and the regime created by the ethics legislation (Smith 2008:3). This would imply that the corrupt activities that are the subject of recent tribunals will not be repeated; it appears no senior politicians have been involved in the scandals emerging from the banks in 2008 and 2009. The emerging details of bank practices during the Celtic Tiger era suggest that the casual approach to ethical behaviour that existed across politics and business in Ireland prior to the tribunals and ethics legislation of the 1990s persisted into twenty-first-century century Ireland (McCarthy 2009; Slattery 2009).

This chapter examines the definitions and costs of corruption and investigates the institutional and cultural factors that influence corruption in the Irish context. The influence of political leadership on the level of moral costs is then examined. A recent study by Smith (2008) surveyed the attitudes of Irish legislators to corrupt activities. The results of this study are discussed in order to assess both the effect of the new ethics legislation introduced since 1995 and the prospects for change.

PERSPECTIVES ON CORRUPTION

There are several approaches to defining corruption. Nye's (1970:567) definition is based on legality, stating that corruption 'violates rules against the exercise of certain types of private-regarding influence'. Rogow and Lasswell's (1963:132) definition, that 'a corrupt act violates responsibility toward at least one system of public or civil order and is in fact incompatible with (destructive of) any such system', sees corruption as acts against the public interest. A third approach to defining corruption is public opinion: 'how the people in a nation define corruption' (Gardiner 2002: 32).

The first two definitions present obstacles to the researcher (Peters and Welch 2002; Smith 2008). The public opinion definition is valuable when examining why anti-corruption laws have failed. Perceptions of corruption play an important role for, if the general public's perceptions of corruption diverge from a nation's laws on corruption, it is likely that these laws will be ignored and local norms and customs will be followed instead. Heidenheimer (1970) developed a corruption scale based on elite and public opinions of certain types of activity in certain types of society. The scale indicates the likelihood of activities occurring and/or being prosecuted. Heidenheimer (1970:27) evaluates 'black corruption' as an action 'which a majority consensus of both elite and mass opinion would condemn and would want to see punished as a matter of principle'. 'Grey corruption' describes an action that the elites want to see punished, that some find tolerable and on which the majority view may be ambiguous. 'White corruption' is tolerated by a majority of elite and public opinion.

The formal definition of corruption that this chapter will employ is that used by Transparency International (TI), an NGO created to highlight and reduce corruption internationally, who define corruption as 'the misuse of entrusted power for private gain' (TI 2009:13). This definition is based on principal agent models (Bull and Newell 2003:3), where, motivated by personal reward, the agent (corrupt actor) violates a contract by acting against the interests of the principal (Della Porta and Vannucci 1999). Utilising the principal agent model, political corruption includes both corruption by public representatives and by bureaucrats (Della Porta and Vannucci 2005).

This chapter is primarily concerned with political corruption. The opportunity for political corruption generally exists within Heidenheimer's (1970) 'grey zone' and comprises conflict of interest and constituency service situations. Constituency service is one category of activity where the line between legitimate and illegitimate activity can become blurred (Johnston 2005:11). Politicians engage in constituency service in the hope of attracting more support in the form of votes that will help them to win the next election. Thompson (1995) insists that political gain is a legitimate reward and does not demean the democratic process.

Conflict of interest is defined by Mancuso (1995:39) as 'a situation that arises when an individual MP's legislative autonomy is compromised by personal concerns'. It is possible to eliminate conflicts of interest either by divesting the concern that creates the conflict or by recusal from the decision-making process. In Ireland, the preferred method for removing conflict of interest has been increased transparency, achieved through the Freedom of Information Acts (1997, 2002) and the Register of Members' Interests. By examining Irish legislators' attitudes to these types of activity, Smith (2008) was able to assess where the potential for corruption exists in Ireland.

Costs of Corruption

The 1990s witnessed the re-emergence of corruption as a global concern. Increased globalisation of the world economy made experts realise that 'widespread corruption threatens the very basis of an open, multilateral world economy' (Glynn et al. 1997:7). Empirical research reinforced the view that corruption is inherently harmful to society (Nazario 2007; Tverdova 2007). Mauro (1997:92) has shown that corruption levels have a direct effect on levels of investment, particularly where corruption is high. He has also shown that corrupt countries spend less on educational investment, instead diverting funds to construction projects. This will have long-term societal, economic and political effects. Corrupt activities such as bribery increase inefficient exchanges between the state and private enterprise (Elliott 1997; Rose-Ackerman 1999). As economists search for answers to the crisis that began unfolding in 2008, international experts such as TI have asserted that Ireland's perceived tolerance for corruption has contributed to its economic downfall. A recent TI report estimated that political corruption could cost the Irish economy as much as €3bn per year in foreign investment (TI 2009).

Thompson states that legislative ethics is 'more important than any single policy because all other policies depend on it' (Thompson 1995:17). An acceptance of corrupt activities by Oireachtas members will have a detrimental effect on the legislative and policy output from the legislature. If members of the Oireachtas are engaging in corrupt acts, the laws and policies that are formulated may not benefit the country as a whole.

Corruption also has implications for political development, as it rewards the haves at the expense of the have-nots and can create a system of patronage that discourages political opposition (Johnston 2005:29). Machine politics, patron client networks, cronyism and nepotism are described by Johnston (1986:468) as being 'integrative' to varying degrees. As they include many individuals in the process, they are more sustainable. As leaders of a newly formed democracy, Irish legislators needed to confirm their legitimacy in the face of internal and external opposition. The patronage and clientelism that developed from the 1920s may have had an integrative effect that contributed to the success of Irish democracy in a period when fascism was sweeping through the fledgling democracies of Europe (Smith 2008).

Bull and Newell (2003:240) recognise the negative economic and political effects of corruption; they also note the 'significant self-generating mechanism' that is built into corruption. The more common corrupt exchanges become, the lower the costs associated with them. Viewed from an economic perspective, as an exchange between rational actors, corruption will only occur where the utility derived is greater than the costs, as corruption spreads the risks of being caught and hence the costs diminish. Moral costs represent a loss of utility from 'engaging in illegal actions' (Rose-Ackerman 1978:113). Moral costs are affected by individual actors' values, which are in turn influenced by the cultural and institutional setting in which they act (Della Porta and Vannucci 2005). As corruption becomes more widespread, it is normalised and the moral costs associated with corrupt activity are reduced. Moral costs can also be viewed from a macroeconomic perspective as an effect (Della Porta and Vannucci 2005). Both aspects of moral costs combine to contribute to the self-generating nature of corruption.

Causes of Corruption in the Irish Context

The scandals emerging from the banks since late 2008 appear fundamentally different from the cases that were previously tackled by the tribunals. However, they all have similar causes. The evidence that has emerged indicates that a 'cosy cartel', a relaxed and co-operative culture, existed within which some of the financial institutions were able to flexibly apply the rules to help each other, while the Financial Regulator cast a cursory glance over the proceedings. This is eerily similar to the evidence that emerged from the Beef Tribunal (1991–1994), where it was alleged that a large company was able to bend export rules due to a close relationship with high-ranking state officials (Hamilton 1994).

These examples show that Klitgaard's (1988) formula, that corruption is equal to monopoly plus discretion minus accountability (corruption = monopoly + discretion - accountability), holds true in the Irish case. In the case of the Beef Tribunal (1991–1994), the near monopoly of Goodman Meats in the meat processing business, combined with ministerial discretion, created the opportunity for corruption. In the more recent banking scandal, the failure of the Financial Regulator to hold the banks accountable facilitated activities that appeared both ethically and legally questionable (Brady 2009; Weston 2009).

Interestingly, the 1940s saw three tribunal reports on political corruption in Ireland. These included the Transport Tribunal, the Locke Distillery Tribunal and the Ward Tribunal. They investigated the close links between high-level politicians and businessmen (Brennan and Kerrigan 1999). The emergence of clusters of tribunals may be explained by a long period of government by the same party (Bull and Newell 2003; Byrne 2006). Johnston (1986) explains that when certain groups or individuals are kept outside the spoils system for too long, complaints and reactionary reform may result. The last three Fianna Fáil Taoisigh have appeared before various tribunals (Murphy 2006b). The long tenure of leaders who exhibited little regard for ethical probity may have reduced the moral costs associated with unethical activity among Fianna Fáil members. As Johnston (1986) explains, when an exchange occurs frequently, it becomes more acceptable. Patronage, cronyism and nepotism became normalised under successive Fianna Fáil leaders and appeared to peak with Ahern (Molony 2008).

Corruption can assume a positive moral value when it achieves private organisational aims (Della Porta and Vannucci 2005). The attitude of political parties to campaign fundraising is a good example of this. Members achieve status by helping the party achieve financial goals, regardless of the source of these funds.

This occurred in Ireland with senior political figures who achieved status within their party based on a machine that was built around their ability to raise funds (Cullen 2002; McCarthy 2007).

It has been suggested by commentators that party members were outraged, not at the significant sums of money that were received in exchange for favourable political decisions by ministers from their party, not at the potential tax evasion, but only when it became clear that the funds in question were not all handed over to the party (Cullen 2002:272–4; Mitchell 2006). Taoiseach Bertie Ahern appointed Ray Burke to his cabinet in 1997, despite allegations of corruption. Ten years later, Bertie Ahern was himself granted a reprieve by Fianna Fáil members, despite allegations of corruption that were emerging from the Mahon Tribunal. This is the 'immoral cost' described by Della Porta and Vannucci (2005). Corrupt actors are expected to act 'ethically' within the corrupt norms of their organisation. When these norms become established within an organisation, corruption becomes entrenched.

The close relationship between Fianna Fáil and Irish businessmen was initiated by Seán Lemass and formalised by Jack Lynch through an organisation called Taca (Brennan and Kerrigan 1999). Despite warnings from George Colley of 'low standards in high places', Charles Haughey became leader of Fianna Fáil and was Taoiseach in the 1980s and early 1990s (Dwyer 1997:153). During Haughey's reign, the links between business and politics were cemented and a 'Golden Circle' of the rich and powerful emerged (Brennan and Kerrigan 1999). Fluid interaction between businessmen and politicians was completely normalised within Fianna Fáil. The activities of Burke, Ahern and Liam Lawlor, which became fodder for the Flood and Moriarty Tribunals (Flood 2002; Murphy 2006b), were within the norms created by Haughey (Moriarty 2006).

Collins and O'Shea (2003) consider a lack of moral leadership as a cause of corruption in Ireland. When Della Porta and Vannucci's (2005) consideration of moral costs is taken into account, it becomes clear that without moral leadership, institutions can turn to corrupt practices to achieve their own aims. Over time an acceptance of corrupt means of achieving organisational goals becomes instilled into organisational culture and behaviour. It also results in the goals of the institution becoming dominant over the goals of the principals. In the case of corrupt political parties, their goal of achieving power overrides the national interest. In the case of financial institutions, their goal to maximise short-term market share and enhance directors' salaries prevails over the long-term interests of shareholders.

Corrupt institutions are maintained by shared beliefs, which reinforce the informal rules under which they operate. If legislation undermines the ability of institutions to act within these informal rules, or if the groups share a dislike for legislation, they can act together to circumvent formal rules (Aoki 2001:13). A former minister and long-serving TD stated that Oireachtas members are 'always scheming' to get around campaign finance limitations. They share ideas and openly discuss loopholes in the system (Smith 2008:44). Considerations of moral costs are still being eroded by party members who wish to socialise all members and reduce the risks associated with engaging in corrupt activity. Della Porta and Vannucci (2005) conclude that corruption will become the norm where moral costs are reduced by pressures from above (from the leaders of institutions) and from below, due to cultural factors. Organisations such as political parties and corporations do not act in a vacuum; they are subject to the institutional and cultural environment within which they function.

The next two sections examine the effect of Irish political structures and culture on the ethical outlook of politicians and political parties; this in turn influences the level of moral costs in society.

The Influence of Political Structures on Perceptions of Corruption

Ireland has a bicameral parliament. Parliamentary systems are seen as effective checks on executive abuse, particularly where one party does not control both chambers (Johnston et al. 2006). In Ireland, the Seanad is not directly elected and always comprises a government majority, as eleven senators are the Taoiseach's nominees. It has been described as a 'talking shop', as the Dáil can overrule it in the area of legislation (Gallagher 2005:234). This reduces its effectiveness in combating corruption, as it cannot act autonomously of the Dáil or the government.

Ireland operates under the Westminster system, where the legislature mainly acts as a rubber stamp for the government (the executive). The role of parliaments in curbing corruption is vital; a 'separation of powers . . . helps prevent abuses of authority with different government bodies disciplining each other in the citizens' favour' (Lederman et al. 2006: 29). MacCarthaigh (2005:25) questions the value of alternative forms of holding the government to account and says, 'when parliament cannot fulfil its role of holding Government to account, the value of its existence and the democratic legitimacy of its decisions may be called into question'. Collins and O'Shea (2003:172) point out that 'the appointment of tribunals and inquiries in the wake of media revelations of corruption amounts to recognition that the established means of accountability have been deficient'. Ineffectual accountability structures provide increased opportunities for corruption to both the government and the legislature as a whole.

The electoral system in Ireland is proportional representation with single transferable vote (PR-STV) with multi-seat constituencies. This electoral system contributes to the 'constituency orientation' of Teachtaí Dála (TDs), which leads to a system of brokerage (Sinnott 2005:123). TDs prioritise constituency work ahead of their legislative role, as the goal of most TDs is to get re-elected. Marsh et al. (2008) have shown that personal contact between voter and candidate plays a crucial role in voter choice. This personal contact before an election is extended into a 'welfare officer' role once a TD or senator is elected, which involves members acting as intermediaries between the organs of the state and constituents. Gallagher and Komito (2005:243) point out that 'for some observers constituency work has negative associations because it is regarded as using undue influence to give particular people unfair advantage'. It also affects popular conceptions of corruption. As political access is afforded to many, it can be seen as acceptable to ask a local representative for favours; this may be viewed elsewhere as corrupt (Collins and O'Shea 2003:166). As described by Johnston (1986), these local norms must be taken into account when assessing perceptions of corruption. These norms may reduce the moral costs associated with corrupt activities, as they create an ill-defined line between inappropriate and appropriate behaviour.

Another role adopted by Irish TDs as a result of their close constituency ties is that of 'local promoter'. Thus, the TD is 'expected to advance the interests of the constituency generally' (Gallagher and Komito 2005: 242). This role, combined with close personal contact between voters and representatives, diminishes the desire of the electorate to hold politicians accountable for unethical activities by removing them from office. Michael Lowry TD still tops the poll in his north Tipperary constituency as an Independent candidate, after allegations of corruption pushed him to resign from the rainbow coalition cabinet and led to the Fine Gael leadership refusing his nomination as a Fine Gael candidate in that constituency (Murphy 2006b).

PR-STV, combined with weak local government, has led to a situation where 'the parish pump dominates all politics and most politicians' and the national interest may suffer due to this preoccupation (Tierney 1982:9). This leads us to part of the problem with defining corruption. If representatives are acting in the interest of their constituency, which will further their efforts to be re-elected (and, as such, is also in their own interest), but are not acting in the national interest, is this corrupt? Are they not meant to serve those who elected them (Thompson 1995)? This is a problem common to many representative democracies. It is accentuated in Ireland by the voting system, the weakness of local government, and the high ratio of TDs to citizens.

It has been noted that Fianna Fáil are acutely aware of constituency seat issues when making ministerial appointments and spending decisions. In April 2009, Taoiseach Brian Cowen appointed the recently elected (June 2008) TDs Áine Brady (North Kildare) and Dara Calleary (Mayo) as junior ministers to maximise Fianna Fáil exposure and support in areas where electoral support is not guaranteed (McGee 2009b). Such action leaves the party concerned open to being accused of putting its interests (in terms of future electoral success) before the national interest. While this is not corruption in its pure form, it can add to an organisational culture that is fertile for corruption.

Some, on surveying the history of Fianna Fáil, suggest that the party's main motivation has been a desire for power, rather than a dedication to the achievement of a policy programme (Carty 2008:219; Mair and Weeks 2005:144). Such a hunger for the trappings of political office, rather than an urge to serve the public interest, can make political parties more tolerant of corrupt activities (Della Porta and Vannucci 2002). Irish party competition has traditionally offered voters a choice of Fianna Fáil or 'the rest'. Mair and Weeks (2005) suggest that, since the 1980s, the structure of the party system has changed, and has become more unstable. This change in the structure of the system has made all parties more vulnerable, which may explain the willingness of the larger parties to accept large donations to help fight elections in the 1980s and early 1990s, and also their eagerness to distance themselves from corrupt activity since then.

Legislation can also affect perceptions of corruption. As shown by Mancuso (1995), a lack of defined rules can lead to the development of unethical norms within parliament. Until the 1990s, no anti-corruption legislation pertaining to members of the Oireachtas had been passed. The 1976 Local Government (Planning and Development) Act introduced disclosure requirements for councillors in an effort to reduce corruption in the planning process (Cullen 2002). The range of laws introduced since 1995 concerning corruption, election funding and expenditure, and transparency should help to change the attitudes of legislators as a group and contribute towards the creation of a consensus of views among the legislative elite (Atkinson and Mancuso 1985). A *Prime Time* (RTÉ 2007) investigation into local councillors found that most ignored the requirements of the legislation on disclosure. Legislation alone cannot change deep-seated habits, but, if accompanied by strict enforcement, which would generate political, economic and moral costs, it may curtail the motivation of politicians to engage in corrupt exchanges. Changes in legislation may also encourage a change in Irish political culture. The influence of political culture on corruption and moral costs is discussed below.

The Influence of Political Culture on Perceptions of Corruption

Johnston (1983) lists political culture as one of the factors influencing the type and extent of corruption within a state. He describes political culture as pointing towards a complex balance of public conduct and private values. Thus, the political culture within a state acts as a guide to what is perceived as corrupt behaviour. As political culture changes, so do the parameters of what is considered good conduct.

Political culture can also explain the differing reactions in different countries to types of corruption (Johnston 1989). Della Porta and Vannucci (2005) state that political culture influences the moral costs associated with corruption and will contribute to the prevalence of corruption within a society. Coakley (1993:27) states that 'the pattern of political activity in any society is . . . a product of the political culture of that society; and political culture is, in turn, a product of a complex interplay of more fundamental societal factors'. In order to properly examine attitudes to corruption in Ireland, it is necessary to understand the political culture within the state.

Ireland's political culture has been influenced by its colonial past and struggle for independence, by the dominance of Catholicism and by the isolationist policies followed by governments up until the 1960s (Garvin 1998). This, combined with low levels of industrialisation, resulted in a culture that was characterised by 'authoritarianism, nationalism, anti-intellectualism and personalism and individualism' (Coakley 2005:39). This culture resulted in an unquestioning attitude toward political and religious elites and a tendency to mistrust unfamiliar or 'foreign' ideas (Coakley 2005; Garvin 1998). Personalism and individualism combine to undermine democratic values and can contribute to an acceptance of corrupt activities (Coakley 2005; Johnston 1983).

Catholicism has been positively correlated to increased levels of corruption by studies in the USA and Europe (Elazar 1970; Johnston 1983; Treisman 2000). Elazar's (1970) and Johnston's (1983) research indicates that Roman Catholicism results in an individualistic political culture. Elazar predicted that corruption would be common where an individualistic culture is dominant, as in these cultures politics is a marketplace in which self-interest comes first. He points out that corruption in individualistic areas produces little public outcry (Elazar 1970). Ireland fulfils the religious requirements for Elazar's (1970) individualistic political culture; Catholicism was practised by over 90 per cent of the Irish population for most of the twentieth century (CSO 2006).

Ireland began its transition from an isolated, clericalist society to an industrialist, pluralist society in the 1970s with membership of the European Economic Community (EEC) (Coakley 2005:60). Ireland has been transformed since then; the end of the 'Troubles' in the North, increased secularisation and net immigration have resulted in Irish political culture becoming less authoritarian and nationalistic and more conservative on public policy issues (Coakley 2005:67). The increased education levels and wealth of the electorate have changed attitudes toward elites and, combined with the political and Church scandals, have resulted in a reduction of trust in the institutions of democracy (Anderson and Tverdova 2003; Hardiman and Whelan 1998). These changes in political culture influence the attitudes of the public towards corruption; the recent tribunals and legislative changes may be indicative of this change in political culture. Political culture has been transformed, not so fundamentally as to eradicate corruption, but to the point where corrupt activities cause an outcry among certain sectors of the public. The difficulty of measuring the changes that have occurred in Ireland, as well as the current level of corruption, is the subject of the next section.

MEASURING CORRUPTION IN IRELAND

The Group of States against Corruption (GRECO) Evaluation Report (2001:27) commends the legislative measures taken by the Irish government to combat corruption and concludes: 'Ireland appears to belong to the group of those

GRECO members that are least affected by corruption.' However, anti-corruption laws may not be enough to combat the existence and perception of corruption. McCarthy (2003:14) argues that 'greater attention needs to be paid to the 'corruption proofing' of policies and institutional arrangements, in addition to the 'vigorous pursuit of wrongdoers' in order to prevent the occurrence and perception of corruption in Ireland.

TI has developed a measurement of corruption called the Corruption Perceptions Index (CPI). This uses a poll of polls to rank countries' corruption levels based on the opinions of a panel of experts familiar with the country. The index scores countries on a scale of 1 to 10, with 10 being the least corrupt. According to this index, the level of corruption in Ireland increased between 1995 and 2002. From 2002 onwards the level of corruption gradually decreased. Ireland's score and ranking on the CPI for the years 1995–2008 is shown in Table 10.1. A country ranked 1 on this scale would be considered least corrupt or not corrupt. This table also shows the number of countries included in the index, as well as the number of surveys used to compile the score. Murphy (2006a) points out that the significant increase of countries included in the CPI, from 41 to 180, renders Ireland's drop in ranking less meaningful.

As discussed by Johnston (2005), the CPI provides a useful snapshot of individual countries, despite having limitations that include the subjective nature of the measurement and the narrow focus of the type of corruption it includes. McCarthy (2003) and Murphy (2006a) both explain that Ireland's falling CPI scores may be due to an increased awareness of the level of historical corruption owing to the publicity received by the investigations of several tribunals of inquiry in the late 1990s.

The CPI is well publicised internationally and any indication of an increase in corruption has the potential to negatively affect inward investment to the Irish economy (McCarthy 2003). As corruption is inherently a hidden act and difficult to discover until after it has occurred, the CPI is a useful measure for companies and international bodies, such as the World Bank, that want to gain insight into levels of corruption in different countries.

Perceptions of elite corruption can undermine the legitimacy of regimes and reduce interpersonal trust (Anderson and Tverdova 2003). Levels of trust towards the government and institutions can serve not only as an indicator of perceptions of corruption, but also, as described by Della Porta and Vannucci (2005), as an influence on moral costs. Where trust in the state is low and there is a low 'sense of state' (Della Porta and Vannucci 2005:6), moral costs are reduced among citizens and the potential for corruption is increased. Falling trust among the public, combined with declining economic conditions, can contribute to a decline in moral costs and an increase in corruption. As legitimate structures fail to satisfy citizens' needs, they will seek to circumvent formal rules. Table 10.2 shows the level of trust Irish citizens had for their national government and parliament in 1993 and 2008, according to the Eurobarometer results in those years (EC 1993, 2008). The table shows that trust levels dropped almost 50 per cent in the period.

Table 10.1 Ireland's score on the Corruption Perceptions Index, 1995–2009

Year	Ranking	Score	No. of countries	Surveys used
1995	11	8.57	41	6
1996	11	8.45	54	6
1997	12	8.28	52	6
1998	14	8.2	85	10
1999	15	7.7	99	10
2000	19	7.2	90	8
2001	18	7.5	91	7
2002	23	6.9	102	8
2003	18	7.5	133	9
2004	17	7.5	145	10
2005	19	7.4	159	10
2006	18	7.4	163	7
2007	17	7.5	180	6
2008	16	7.7	180	6
2009	14	8	180	6

Source: Transparency International Corruption Perceptions Index, 1995–2009.

This may be attributed to the exposure of the body politic by the tribunals during this period. Interestingly, the gap between trust in parliament and government widened from a 1 per cent gap in 1993 to a 3 per cent gap in 2008. This may indicate increasing disillusionment with a long-serving government (by 2008 Fianna Fáil had been in power continuously for eleven years).

Table 10.2: Change in trust levels in Ireland between 1993 and 2008

	1993 Tend to Trust (%)	2008 Tend to Trust (%)
National government	59	33
National parliament	60	36

Source: EC (1993, 2008).

While the Irish trust levels remain higher than those of the countries of Eastern Europe, they are still far below those countries with high CPI scores, such as Finland. Table 10.3 shows the CPI scores for the three countries with the highest trust in their institutions and the three with the lowest, according to TI (2008) and Eurobarometer (EC 2008). Ireland's scores are included for comparison.

Table 10.3: Trust in national institutions (in descending order of CPI scores)

Country	Trust in National Parliament (%)	Trust in National Government (%)	Score on CPI
Denmark	75	60	9.3
Finland	71	68	9.0
Netherlands	64	66	8.9
Ireland	36	33	7.7
Latvia	9	16	5
Lithuania	11	16	4.6
Bulgaria	8	15	3.6

Sources: TI (2008) and EC (2008).

This table shows that, even before the revelations of the tribunals, Irish citizens had less trust in their parliament and government than current high-trust countries, such as the Netherlands. It also shows that low levels of trust are correlated with high levels of corruption; Bulgaria, which has the lowest trust levels in the EU, also has high levels of corruption, as shown by the low CPI score of 3.6. Denmark, which has the highest level of trust in its political institutions, has the top score on the CPI: it is considered the least corrupt country in the TI poll.

The recent TI National Integrity Systems report on Ireland (2009:16) states that 'Ireland is regarded by domestic and international observers as suffering high levels of "legal corruption".' This report gives thirty recommendations aimed at reducing the levels of legal corruption and improving Ireland's image abroad, thus aiding with FDI and improving economic recovery. By examining the attitudes of legislators to different types of corruption, it is possible to assess the likelihood of these reforms occurring. Legislative attitudes may also offer an explanation as to why the ethics laws enacted since 1995 have not been completely effective in combating political corruption in Ireland.

A study by Smith (2008) assessed Oireachtas members' attitudes to corruption based on their responses to a questionnaire. This type of attitudinal study has been used in the past by Peters and Welch (1978) in the United States and Mancuso (1995) in the United Kingdom, as well as in Canada (Atkinson and Mancuso 1985) and Australia (Smith 1998).

The Irish study (Smith 2008) surveyed TDs and senators in December 2007 to establish their opinions on a range of scenarios. The sample used for the survey was the universe of Oireachtas members, including government ministers. Sixty-eight completed surveys were returned, representing a response rate of thirty per cent (Smith 2008). This meets the requirements for a representative sample, which will give validity to the findings and enable generalities to be extrapolated from the findings (Schofield 1996). Survey evidence was supplemented by interviews of a cross-section of TDs and senators. From the responses to the scenarios presented in the study, certain generalities were found, namely:

- Oireachtas members are more likely to condemn an activity that is specifically against the law or which has been investigated by the tribunals. Over 90 per cent of respondents considered bribing a garda to be corrupt. This scenario is blatantly against the law. The granting of state licences to political donors was considered corrupt by 88 per cent of respondents. This issue was considered by the Moriarty Tribunal in its investigation of Communications Minister Michael Lowry (Fine Gael TD) granting a mobile phone licence to Denis O'Brien's ESAT consortium. The negative attention focused on this practice by the tribunal may have influenced members' attitudes towards it. The tribunals can have an indirect effect on corruption by influencing legislators' attitudes to certain activities.
- Oireachtas members are more likely to condemn an act that involves large amounts of money, which conforms to findings in other studies. One former minister commented that 'it is more likely to be effective if it's a bigger bribe' (Smith 2008:50).
- The warnings of the SIPO Commission do not have a significant impact on members; this implies that a change of tactics would be beneficial. This is shown in the response to the scenario concerning a civil servant giving advice to a parliamentary party on particular policy issues. The SIPO Commission gave a clear ruling on this in its 2006 annual report (SIPO 2007). Only 28 per cent of respondents ranked this scenario as corrupt. This indicates that they were unaware of the SIPO report and creates the impression that the activities of the SIPO Commission have little impact on the everyday activities of Oireachtas members. This suggests that accountability is diminished.
- The most accepted forms of corruption are patronage and nepotism. This may suggest that the influence of Catholicism on the political culture is still prevalent, as politicians are treating politics as a marketplace: 'winning benefits is more important than obeying the rules of the game' (Johnston 1982:25). When discussing patronage an independent member stated (Smith 2008:53):

> One of the greatest abuses in Irish political life is that you can identify on any semi-state board people who are the political party cronies and friends of ministers or come from the constituency. They are not chosen on merit at all.

- There is little political will to change this system, as coalition government gives all parties potential to have access to the spoils of government at some point (Smith 2008:66).
- It was expected that longer-serving Oireachtas members would be more tolerant of corrupt activities than more recently elected Oireachtas members, due to the recent changes in the law and the evolving political culture in Ireland. However, of the respondents, longer-serving Oireachtas members were significantly more intolerant of corrupt activities than their junior colleagues. One possible explanation for this is that the breakdown of the party system (Mair and Weeks 2005) has caused greater competition for votes and that newer members are more willing to bend the rules to benefit their constituents in order to garner more support (Smith 2008).

The findings indicated that Oireachtas members have divergent perceptions of what constitutes corrupt behaviour. Agreement exists in responses to 'very corrupt' acts and 'not corrupt' acts; however, there is a significant grey area where opinion is divided on what constitutes corruption. It is within this area that scope for future corruption exists. The existence of this 'grey zone' and the lack of consensus among members indicate that the ethics laws are not having the desired effect of rendering corrupt activities completely intolerable to legislators (Smith 2008).

CONCLUSION

Della Porta and Vannucci (2005) concluded that the persistence of corruption in Italy was due to a reduction in moral costs associated with corrupt activities. The level of moral costs is influenced by the behaviour of the leadership within institutions and by pressure from the masses. By examining the interplay of these factors in Ireland, with particular reference to Fianna Fáil (which has been in power for nineteen of the last twenty-two years), it appears that legislation alone has been and will be ineffective in combating political corruption. Survey and interview evidence (Smith 2008) indicates that Oireachtas members are still accepting of certain types of corrupt activity. The continuing evolution of Irish political culture (Coakley 2005), combined with the pressures presented by the current financial crisis, may create the conditions for a dual change at the top and bottom of the political process. If this occurs, the ethics legislation may become more effective. If it is enforced with greater rigour, under a new regime, it will increase moral costs, which will in turn reduce the attractiveness of corrupt behaviour.

International perceptions of Ireland as a corrupt country have the potential to reduce FDI (TI 2009). While corruption is not endemic in Irish society, if it is not tackled effectively it may spiral out of control (Bull and Newell 2003; GRECO 2001). Widespread corruption has more serious costs, such as a reduction in education and equality, and environmental degradation (Mauro 1997; UNDP

2008). Tackling corruption will improve Ireland's attractiveness to multinational corporations, while improving the ability of the government to implement economic policies that benefit a broad spectrum of Irish society. The hard decisions required to map Ireland's way out of the financial doldrums require the electorate to trust the leadership of elected representatives. Evidence points to falling trust levels, which damages the prospects of rallying the country to communal action. Combating corruption and developing a political culture that is intolerant of corruption will empower politicians to tackle future national crises more effectively.

References

Anderson, C.J. and Tverdova, Y.V. (2003) 'Corruption, Political Allegiances, and Attitudes toward Government in Contemporary Democracies', *American Journal of Political Science* 47(1): 91–109.

Aoki, M. (2001) *Toward a Comparative Institutional Analysis*. Cambridge, MA: MIT Press.

Atkinson, M. and Mancuso, M. (1985) 'Do We Need a Code of Conduct for Politicians? The Search for an Elite Political Culture of Corruption', *Canadian Journal of Political Science*, 28(3): 459–80.

Brady, T. (2009) 'Gardaí Poised to Quiz Key Anglo Figures in Bank Probe: Extra Officers Are Drafted in as Inquiry Focuses on Loans', *Irish Independent*, 9 September [online]. Available: http://www.independent.ie/business/irish/gardai-poised-to-quiz-key-anglo-figures-in-bank-probe-1881292.html (last accessed 22 October 2009).

Brennan, P. and Kerrigan, G. (1999) *This Great Little Nation: The A–Z of Irish Scandals and Controversies*. Dublin: Gill & Macmillan.

Bull, M. and Newell, J. (eds) (2003) *Corruption in Contemporary Politics*. London: Palgrave Macmillan.

Byrne, E. (2006) 'The Moral and Legal Development of Corruption: Nineteenth and Twentieth Century Political Corruption in Ireland', unpublished PhD thesis, University of Limerick.

Carswell, S. (2008) 'Regulator Stumbled on Loans During Inspection of Rival Bank's Books', *Irish Times*, 20 December, p.18.

Carty, R.K. (2008) 'Fianna Fáil and Irish Party Competition', in M. Gallagher and M. Marsh (eds) *How Ireland Voted 2007: The Full Story of Ireland's General Election*, pp. 218–31. New York, NY: Palgrave Macmillan.

Coakley, J. (1993) 'Society and Political Culture', in J. Coakley and M. Gallagher (eds) *Politics in the Republic of Ireland*, pp. 25–48. Dublin: Folens.

— (2005) 'Society and Political Culture', in J. Coakley and M. Gallagher (eds) *Politics in the Republic of Ireland*, 4th edn, pp. 36–71. London: Routledge.

Collins, N. and O'Shea, M. (2003) 'Corruption in Ireland', in M. Bull and J.

Newell (eds) *Corruption in Contemporary Politics*, pp. 164–75. London: Palgrave Macmillan.

CSO (Central Statistics Office) (2006) *Census Results* [online]. Available: http://beyond2020.cso.ie/Census/TableViewer/tableView.aspx?ReportId=7464 0 (last accessed 6 August 2009).

Cullen, P. (2002) *With a Little Help from My Friends: Planning Corruption in Ireland*. Dublin: Gill & Macmillan.

Della Porta, D. and Vannucci, A. (1999) *Corrupt Exchanges*. New York, NY: Aldine.

— (2002) 'Corrupt Exchanges and the Implosion of the Italian Party System', in J. Heidenheimer and M. Johnston (eds) *Political Corruption: Concepts and Contexts*, pp. 717–38. New Brunswick, NJ: Transaction.

— (2005) 'Corruption as a Normative System', paper presented at the International Conference on Corruption Control in Political Life and the Quality of Democracy: A Comparative Perspective Europe – Latin America, Lisbon, 19–20 May [online]. Available: http://home.iscte.pt/~ansmd/CC-DellaPorta.pdf (last accessed 24 November 2009).

Dwyer, T.R. (1997) *Fallen Idol: Haughey's Controversial Career*. Cork: Mercier Press.

EC (European Commission) (1993) *Eurobarometer: Public Opinion in the European Union* (EB 40) [online]. Available: http://ec.europa.eu/public_opinion/archives/eb/eb40/eb40_en.pdf (last accessed 2 August 2009).

— (2008) *Eurobarometer: Public Opinion in the European Union* (EB 70) [online]. Available: http://ec.europa.eu/public_opinion/archives/ebs/ebs_303_brut_en.pdf and http://ec.europa.eu/public_opinion/archives/eb/eb70/eb70_ie_nat.pdf (last accessed 2 August 2009).

Elazar, D.J. (1970) *Cities of the Prairie: The Metropolitan Frontier and American Politics*. New York, NY: Basic Books.

Elliott, K.A. (1997) 'Corruption as an International Policy Problem: Overview and Recommendations', in K.A. Elliott (ed.) *Corruption and the Global Economy*, pp. 175–236. Washington, DC: Institute for International Economics.

Flood, F. (2002) *The Second Interim Report of the Tribunal of Enquiry into Certain Planning Matters and Payments*. Dublin: Stationery Office.

Gallagher, M. (2005) 'Parliament', in J. Coakley and M. Gallagher (eds) *Politics in the Republic of Ireland*, 4th edn, pp. 211–42. London: Routledge.

Gallagher, M. and Komito, L. (2005) 'The Constituency Role of Dáil Deputies', in J. Coakley and M. Gallagher (eds) *Politics in the Republic of Ireland*, 4th edn, pp. 242–71. London: Routledge.

Gardiner, J. (2002) 'Defining Corruption', in A. Heidenheimer and M. Johnston (eds) *Political Corruption: Concepts and Contexts*, pp. 25–40. New Brunswick, NJ: Transaction.

Garvin, T. (1998) 'Patriots and Republicans: An Irish Evolution', in W. Crotty and D. Schmitt (eds) *Ireland and the Politics of Change*, pp. 144–55. London: Longman.

Glynn, P., Kobrin, S.J. and Naim, M. (1997) 'The Globalization of Corruption', in K.A. Elliott (ed.) *Corruption and the Global Economy*, pp. 7–30. Washington, DC: Institute for International Economics.

GRECO (Group of States against Corruption) (2001) *Evaluation Report on Ireland* [online]. Available: http://www.coe.int/t/dghl/monitoring/greco/ evaluations/round1/GrecoEval1(2001)9_Ireland_EN.pdf (last accessed 13 August 2009).

Hamilton, L. (1994) *Report of the Tribunal of Inquiry into the Beef Processing Industry*. Dublin: Stationery Office.

Hardiman, N. and Whelan, C. (1998): 'Changing Values', in W. Crotty and D. Schmitt (eds) *Ireland and the Politics of Change*, pp. 66–85. London: Longman.

Heidenheimer, A.J. (1970) *Political Corruption: Readings in Comparative Analysis*. New York, NY: Holt, Rinehart and Winston.

Johnston, M. (1982) *Political Corruption and Public Policy in America*. Monterey, CA: Brooks/Cole.

— (1983) 'Corruption and Political Culture in America: An Empirical Perspective', *Publius* 13(1): 19–39.

— (1986) 'The Political Consequences of Corruption: A Reassessment', *Comparative Politics* 18(4): 459–77.

— (1989): 'Corruption and Political Culture in Britain and the United States', *Innovation* 2(4): 417–36.

— (2005) *Syndromes of Corruption: Wealth, Power, and Democracy*. Cambridge: Cambridge University Press.

Johnston, N., Pelizzo, R. and Stapenhurst, R. (2006) *The Role of Parliament in Curbing Corruption*. Washington, DC: World Bank Institute.

Klitgaard, R. (1988) *Controlling Corruption*. Berkeley, CA: University of California Press.

Lederman, D., Loayza, N. and Soares, R. (2006) 'On the Political Nature of Corruption', in N. Johnston, R. Pelizzo and R. Stapenhurst (eds) *The Role of Parliament in Curbing Corruption*, pp. 27–38. Washington, DC: World Bank Institute.

MacCarthaigh, M. (2005) *Accountability in Irish Parliamentary Politics*. Dublin: Institute of Public Administration.

Mair, P. and Weeks, L. (2005) 'The Party System', in J. Coakley and M. Gallagher (eds) *Politics in the Republic of Ireland*, 4th edn, pp. 135–59. London: Routledge.

Mancuso, M. (1995) *The Ethical World of British MPs*. Montreal: McGill–Queens University Press.

Marsh, M., Sinnott, R., Garry, J. and Kennedy, F. (2008) *The Irish Voter*. Manchester: Manchester University Press.

Mauro, P. (1997) 'The Effects of Corruption on Growth, Investment, and Government Expenditure: A Cross-Country Analysis', in K.A. Elliott (ed.)

Corruption and the Global Economy, pp. 83–108. Washington, DC: Institute for International Economics.

McCarthy, C. (2003) 'Corruption in Public Office in Ireland: Policy Design as a Countermeasure', *Economic and Social Research Institute* [online]. Available: http://www.esri.ie/pdf/QEC1003SA_McCarthy.pdf (last accessed 21 September 2009).

McCarthy, J. (2007) 'Bertie's Real Cabinet: The Taoiseach's Electoral Machine', *Sunday Tribune*, 25 March, p. N16.

— (2009) 'How Anglo Cash Flowed Through DDDA's Life', *Sunday Tribune*, 19 April, p. N12.

McCracken, B. (1997) *Report of the Tribunal of Inquiry (Dunne's Payments)*. Dublin: Stationery Office.

McGee, H. (2009a) 'Gilmore Urges Limit on Number of Directorships to End "Crony Capitalism"', *Irish Times*, 16 April, p. 9.

— (2009b) 'Cowen Says Government Making Sacrifices', *Irish Times*, 23 April p. 9.

Mitchell, S. (2006) 'Bertie's Banker', *Sunday Business Post*, 8 October, p. N23.

Molony, S. (2008) 'Over 100 Plum Jobs Filled During Ahern's Last Days', *Irish Independent*, 19 May [online]. Available: http://www.independent.ie/national-news/over-100-plum-jobs-filled-during-aherns-last-days-1379554.html (last accessed 25 October 2009).

Moriarty, M. (2006) *Report of the Tribunal of Inquiry into Payments to Politicians and Related Matters Part I*. Dublin: Stationery Office.

Murphy, G. (2005) 'Interest Groups in the Policy Making Process', in J. Coakley and M. Gallagher (eds) *Politics in the Republic of Ireland*, 4th edn, pp. 356–83. London: Routledge.

— (2006a) 'Assessing the Relationship Between Neoliberalism and Political Corruption: The Fianna Fáil-Progressive Democrat Coalition, 1997–2006', *Irish Political Studies* 27(3): 297–317.

— (2006b) 'Payments for No Political Response? Political Corruption and Tribunals of Inquiry in Ireland, 1991–2003', in J. Garrard and J. Newell (eds) *Scandals in Past and Contemporary Politics*, pp. 91–105. Manchester: Manchester University Press.

Nazario, O. (2007) 'A Strategy for Fighting Corruption in the Caribbean', paper presented at Conference on the Caribbean: A 20/20 Vision, Washington DC, June 19–21 [online]. Available: http://siteresources.worldbank.org/INTOECS/Resources/NazarioPaper.pdf (last accessed 11 July 2009).

Nye, J.S. (1970) 'Corruption and Political Development: A Cost Benefit Analysis', in A.J. Heidenheimer (ed.) *Political Corruption: Readings in Comparative Analysis*, pp. 564–78. New York, NY: Holt, Rinehart and Winston.

O'Halpin, E. (2000) '"Ah, They've Given Us a Good Bit of Stuff . . ." Tribunals and Irish Political Life at the Turn of the Century', *Irish Political Studies* 15(1): 183–92.

Peters, J.G. and Welch, S. (1978) 'Political Corruption in America: A Search for Definitions and a Theory, or If Political Corruption is in the Mainstream of American Politics why is it not in the Mainstream of American Politics Research?', *American Political Science Review* 72(3): 974–84.

— (2002) 'Gradients of Corruption in Perceptions of American Public Life', in J. Heidenheimer and M. Johnston (eds) *Political Corruption: Concepts and Contexts*, pp. 155–72. New Brunswick, NJ: Transaction.

Rogow, A. and Lasswell, H. (1963) *Power, Corruption and Rectitude*. Englewood Cliffs, NJ: Prentice Hall.

Rose-Ackerman, S. (1978) *Corruption: A Study in Political Economy*. New York, NY: Academic Press.

— (1999) *Corruption and Government: Causes, Consequences and Reform*. Cambridge: Cambridge University Press.

RTÉ (Raidió Teilifís Éireann) (2007) *Prime Time Investigates*, 27 November [online]. Available: http://www.rte.ie/news/2007/1126/primetime.html (last accessed 28 July 2009).

Schofield, W. (1996) 'Survey Sampling', in R. Sapsford and V. Jupp (eds) *Data Collection and Analysis*, pp. 32–55. London: Sage.

Sinnott, R. (2005) 'The Rules of the Electoral Game', in J. Coakley and M. Gallagher (eds) *Politics in the Republic of Ireland*, 4th edn, pp. 105–34. London: Routledge.

Slattery, L. (2009) 'Anglo Writes Off Loans of €308m to 10 Clients', *Irish Times*, 30 May, p. 18.

Smith, G. (2008) 'Corruption: The View from the Oireachtas', unpublished MA thesis, Dublin Institute of Technology.

Smith, R. (1998) 'Strange Distinctions: Legislators, Political Parties and Legislative Ethics Research', in N. Preston and C. Sampford, with C.-A. Bois (eds) *Ethics and Political Practice: Perspectives on Legislative Ethics*, pp. 41–51. London: Routledge.

SIPO (Standards in Public Office Commission) (2007) *Annual Report 2006*. Dublin: Stationery Office.

Thompson, D.F. (1995) *Ethics in Congress: From Individual to Institutional Corruption*. Washington, DC: Brookings Institution.

TI (Transparency International) (2008) *Corruption Perceptions Index* [online]. Available: http://www.transparency.org/news_room/latest_news/press_releases_nc/2008/2008_09_23_ireland_cpi (last accessed 23 July 2009).

— (2009) *National Integrity Systems: Transparency International Country Study – Ireland 2009* [online]. Available: http://www.transparency.ie/news_events/nispr09.htm (last accessed 20 August 2009).

— (2010) *Corruption Perceptions Index 2009* [online]. Available: http://www.transparency.org/policy_research/surveys_indices/cpi_2009_table (last accessed 14 August 2010).

Tierney, M. (1982) *The Parish Pump*. Dublin: Able Press.

Treisman, D. (2000) 'The Causes of Corruption: A Cross-National Study', *Journal of Public Economics* 76(2): 399–457.

Tverdova, Y. (2007) 'How Widespread is Corruption? A Cross-National Study', paper presented at the Annual Meeting of the American Political Science Association, Chicago, IL, 30 August–2 September [online]. Available: http://www.allacademic.com//meta/p_mla_apa_research_citation/2/1/1/4/1/pages211419/p211419-1.php (last accessed 24 November 2009).

UNDP (United Nations Development Programme) (2008) *Primer on Corruption and Development* [online]. Available: http://www.undp.org/governance/docs/Corruption_and_Development_Primer_2008.pdf (last accessed 10 August 2009).

Weston, C. (2009) 'Damning Report on Anglo Spells End for Financial Regulator', *Irish Independent*, 10 January [online]. Available: http://www.independent.ie/national-news/damning-report-on-anglo-spells-end-for-financial-regulator-1597823.html (last accessed 25 October 2009).

Chapter 11

Lobbying Regulation: An Irish Solution to a Universal Problem?

Conor McGrath

INTRODUCTION

Lobbying and lobbyists have never been held in high regard by the general public, although they often provide invaluable (and legitimate) services to policy makers. Over 120 years ago, an American political dictionary opined that, '*Lobby, The,* is a term applied collectively to men that make a business of corruptly influencing legislators. The individuals are called lobbyists' (Brown and Strauss 1888:253). The phrase 'lobbying' tends to conjure up in the public's imagination a notion that influencing public policy is inherently improper and unethical – indeed, this (mis)perception appears to be quite common in most nations. In Ireland, 'lobbying' is often thought of as, if not synonymous with corruption, then certainly related to it: here, lobbying features in the public consciousness largely in terms of the various financial scandals which have been exposed through official tribunals. Lobbyists themselves argue that they 'are a vital link between government and the private sector, and provide a great service to the state' (Fallon 2006:211).

In common with most other nations, Ireland currently has no statutory regulation of lobbying activities. Equally, though, lobbying regulation is becoming a more prominent subject of political debate. This chapter examines the nature of the relationship between the state and interest groups in Ireland, charts the development of the lobbying industry, and notes the pervasive context of political corruption and scandal over the last twenty years. It then analyses suggestions for lobbying regulation that have been proposed, and concludes with a potential reform agenda. The opportunity exists for Ireland to take a lead in producing a comprehensive, and meaningful, regulatory regime – genuine and principled reform, rather than a muddled compromise.

LOBBYING REGULATION IN A GLOBAL CONTEXT

It is useful to briefly outline the state of lobbying regulation around the world so as to give context to the Irish situation. The most detailed such survey is that by

Chari, Hogan and Murphy (2010), while Pross (2007) and the OECD (2006, 2008) also provide useful summaries of the initiatives taken in a number of countries. Most nations have no specific regulation of lobbying. A number have recently considered proposals to regulate lobbying activity, but have not yet enacted any official mechanism: these include France, Scotland, Italy, Norway, Korea, Croatia, Latvia, Romania, Slovakia, Brazil and Chile. Ireland also falls into this category, as is discussed in detail below. Next, there are countries in which some form of voluntary self-regulation by (a minority of) the lobbying industry has been attempted, most notably, perhaps, the United Kingdom (McGrath 2009). There are several nations that have enacted significant lobbying reforms, including the establishment of a register of lobbyists, which nevertheless have substantial flaws in their subsequent implementation, such as Hungary, Poland and Lithuania (McGrath 2008). Finally, the most rigorous forms of statutory regulation of lobbying exist in the United States (at both federal and state levels), Canada and Australia. In these systems, regulation is mandatory, strictly defined and subject to significant penalties for non-compliance.

Chari, Murphy and Hogan (2007) put forward a three-step typology of regulatory systems – low, medium, and highly regulated systems. At present, Ireland would not rate as even a low-regulated system, given the complete absence of any lobbyist registration scheme. However, in considering how a future regulatory programme here might be crafted, an assessment of the existing models used around the world leads to a number of pertinent observations. Most fundamentally, the perfect lobbying regulation does not exist, but some regulation is better than none. No means of regulating lobbyists can be devised that absolutely guarantees the impossibility of future scandals, but regulation does, at least, allow for the retrospective punishment of unethical behaviour. Finally, the best regulation is that which is sufficiently flexible to ensure amendments over time as new issues emerge and as lobbying practice develops.

INTEREST GROUP–STATE RELATIONS IN IRELAND

One particular feature of the Irish policy-making process, which provides the backdrop for interest group activity and influence, is the system of social partnership that has operated formally since 1987. Prior to that, it was possible to clearly identify specific groups and organisations that exerted considerable influence over the political process, both sectional interests (including employers' associations, trade unions, vintners and farmers) and cause-centred interests (such as the Catholic Church, the GAA, pro- and anti-abortion groups). In Ireland, as in every political system, there have always been interests that seek to influence policy decisions. The beginnings of an organised and structured dialogue between those groups and the state can be traced, though, to the 1960s, when Ireland started planning in earnest its application to join what was then the European Economic Community (EEC) (Murphy 2003).

Since 1987, the major economic interest groups (employers, unions and farmers) have negotiated directly with government through the system of social partnership, dealing with a range of socio-economic policy issues, including pay rises, tax cuts and social welfare benefits. In 2000, this model was broadened to include some representatives of the voluntary sector. While this development of a social pillar was generally welcome, in practice many of the third-sector groups newly brought into the process began to feel over time that their concerns were not accorded the same level of attention as the employers and unions enjoyed. FitzGerald (2007:14) agreed that their inclusion 'has extended the social aspect of policy making', but went on to note that it is nevertheless 'difficult to resist an impression that what emerges from the process consists more of policies that the government would in any event have been introducing, rather than new ideas emanating from civic society'. Moreover, it is possible to view social partnership as a mechanism whereby government seeks simultaneously to 'capture' significant interest groups by limiting their capacity to lobby outside that process, and to minimise the input of smaller groups that have not been given a seat at the table.

LOBBYING AND THE IRISH POLITICAL SYSTEM

The Irish political system has a number of distinguishing characteristics that tend to encourage lobbying. It is simultaneously poorly resourced and overloaded; TDs and senators receive relatively little in the way of public funding for researchers/policy advisers, yet have relatively high demands placed upon them by their constituents (see Gallagher (1987) for a discussion of the volume of voter representations to TDs). This creates an opportunity for external interests to fill the financial and informational vacuums, and thus gives politicians a significant incentive to make themselves available to interest groups. While the relative ease with which Irish policy makers can be accessed and contacted is admirable in some respects, it does bring with it the danger that they can be unduly influenced behind closed doors by lobbyists. Policy makers have a real need for sources of detailed information about the practical implications of the policy options they consider, and often this means that they are reliant on outside interest groups. In addition, Irish politics is undoubtedly clientelistic – crudely put, who you know can often be at least as important as what you know. Writing in a different context, Garvin (1981:199) asserted that, 'Many Irish people are pessimistic about the possibility of government being honest and impersonal. . . . The pattern of individualistic responses to political problems is far more pronounced in Ireland than in other western liberal democracies.' In terms of lobbying, this impulse towards personalised decision making accounts, to a great extent, for the tendency (discussed below) for interest groups and lobbying firms to rely upon former party staffers.

The prevailing culture of secrecy in policy making also reinforces the perceived need by many organisations to hire lobbyists. Even with a Freedom of Information Act, it can be enormously difficult for someone outside the political elite to discern how any particular issue is being considered within government, thus creating an air of mystique around the policy-making process, which can help drive client recruitment for lobbying firms. Moreover, one further element of Irish politics, which helps drive the lobbying market, is the reality that the last general election to produce a single-party government was that of 1977. Coalition government has been a fact of life for a generation now, to the point where it is difficult to imagine the country's electoral system producing a future single-party administration. Indeed, the 2007 election campaign was dominated more by debate on who would coalesce with whom than by any substantial policy disagreements between the parties. As one senior lobbyist notes (Fennell 2007), coalition government offers 'multiple opportunities for clients to pursue their political objectives'. Allied to this is the presence of a number of independent TDs not beholden to a party whip, who can often be crucial to the maintenance of the governing coalition and who are thus highly attractive targets of lobbying activity. Indeed, it is not uncommon for independent TDs to rise to elected office as a result of having built up a local grassroots support base through their involvement with an organised interest group (Murphy 2005:371–2; O'Halpin and Connolly 1999).

Ireland's membership of the European Union (EU) has also had a considerable impact upon the lobbying industry in two ways, as Laffan and Tonra (2005: 449–53) note. First, much of Ireland's policy agenda is, in fact, set in Brussels such that the national implementation of EU legislation creates an enormous need for a wide variety of organisations to lobby in Dublin. And second, the major Irish interest groups will routinely work with the government in order to influence EU policy in Brussels.

Development of the Irish Lobbying Industry

In the early 1980s, there were very few people working as self-employed lobbying consultants, although the major economic interests certainly had employees whose role included talking to government. It would have been difficult for an observer to discern an Irish lobbying industry. While the industry today is by no means sizeable in absolute numbers (perhaps something in the order of 100–200 consultants and 500–600 in-house lobbyists), it has certainly matured into a distinctive and recognisable specialism. One atypical, and generally unfortunate, feature of Irish lobbying is that it operates predominantly as a sub-sector of the broader public relations industry, rather than having developed as an independent profession. This has, to some extent, retarded its ability to present itself to the public as a reputable and legitimate activity, not because public relations is in any way dishonourable, but because lobbyists have not themselves generated a vigorous and proactive leadership willing to promote and defend the industry.

We see in many other countries trade associations that specifically represent individual lobbyists and/or lobbying firms, such as the American League of Lobbyists, the UK Association of Professional Political Consultants, the

Government Relations Institute of Canada, and the Association of Accredited Lobbyists to the European Parliament. Such groups exist, also, in less well-established democracies, including the Association of Professional Lobbyists in Poland, the Croatian Lobbyist Association, and the First Hungarian Lobby Association. No such grouping has been developed to date in Ireland. I have argued elsewhere that, 'The central question facing all lobbyists in all countries over the next decade is whether lobbying can be transformed from the vibrant and thriving industry it certainly is today into a more mature and confident, more accepted and acceptable, profession' (McGrath 2005:134). The solution to this challenge is for lobbyists, in Ireland as much as elsewhere, to become more secure in their professional identity, to build an infrastructure of organisations, norms and values, and to communicate more positively with the public about the legitimate and valuable contribution which lobbying makes to society. That agenda, though, is for the future.

Lobbying Consultancies

The Irish lobbying industry has historically emerged from the communications sector, in particular public relations and journalism, with its pioneers often bringing additional partisan political experience. Many of the early lobbying consultancies in the 1980s were single-handed, or very small, operations. The backgrounds of a few are typical: P. J. Mara was a Fianna Fáil strategist and government press secretary who twice served in the Seanad before establishing his own consultancy; Frank Dunlop, a Raidió Teilifís Éireann (RTÉ) journalist and government press secretary before becoming a director of a public relations firm, similarly set himself up as a lobbyist; Brendan Halligan served successively as Labour Party general secretary, senator, then TD, and Member of the European Parliament (MEP) before establishing Consultants in Public Affairs; and Myles Tierney served as a Fine Gael councillor in Dublin and, while not as high-profile as some others, is said to have been the first professional lobbying consultant in Ireland.

A similar profile can be seen among many of those who launched themselves as lobbyists in a larger wave in the 1990s: Nuala Fennell was a Fine Gael TD, minister and senator before establishing Political Communications; Paul Allen, who worked at RTÉ and was a Fianna Fáil activist, has an eponymous agency; Fergus Finlay joined Wilson Hartnell PR after a career as a senior Labour Party adviser; Stephen O'Byrnes, a founder member of the Progressive Democrats and assistant government press secretary, established Business Insight and then MRPA Kinman; and Pat Montague was Labour Party Youth Officer before setting up Montague Communications.

Lobbying units within commercial consultancies are 'a relatively new phenomenon in Ireland but appear to be growing with some speed' (Allen 2007:64), so the larger public relations consultancies in Ireland all now offer a lobbying service, although it is more generally couched in less explicit terms, such as 'public affairs' or 'parliamentary affairs'. These for-hire teams are almost invariably staffed by figures who can boast close personal contacts in the political system. Among the best known are: Alan Dukes (former Fine Gael leader and minister, now at Wilson Hartnell PR); Gerard Howlin (a special adviser to Bertie Ahern, now at MKC Communications); Iarla Mongey (a senior staffer in the Progressive Democrats, now at Drury Communications); Michael Parker (former Progressive Democrats general secretary, now at Insight Consultants); and Jackie Gallager, a former special adviser to Bertie Ahern, and Martin Mackin, former Fianna Fáil general secretary (both at Q4 Public Relations).

Associations

As one journalist recognises, 'while there has always been a focus on private public affairs consultancies, the most effective lobbying continues to come from interest groups and non-governmental organisations' (Reid 2007:5). Indeed, some interest groups have historically had intimate 'links to various political parties going back many years' (Murphy 2005:372), and persist in exerting substantial influence over government. While battles may be won or lost, there are some seemingly eternal interests active in Irish politics. One such interest is that of vintners: pubs have long been central to politics at a local level in Ireland, with many politicians holding their surgeries in pubs. The author of perhaps the most detailed case study of how interest groups have competed over a policy issue (the 2003–2004 debate over the introduction of a ban on workplace smoking) remarks, 'the pub trade had long been amongst the strongest lobby groups in the country' (Gilmore 2005:15). While publicans were ultimately unable to prevent the smoking ban, they recovered sufficiently to block government plans in 2005 to permit European-style café bars.

Another major organised interest has been construction and property development (McCarthy 2008), a sector intimately connected with several lobbying scandals in recent years. Much of the Celtic Tiger's socio-economic transformation was based upon a booming construction industry, which, in the mid-1990s, represented around 20 per cent of the nation's entire economic activity.

Sporting organisations, such as the GAA, have exercised considerable influence over the years, and are often welcomed by politicians as they provide an opportunity for association with a populist and feel-good sector (plus many notable politicians began their public careers as sportsmen). Trade unions clearly have strong ties to the Labour Party in particular (indeed, the party was created by the Irish Congress of Trade Unions (ICTU)), as do environmental groups to the Green Party. Although its then president, Tom Parlon, decided in 2002 to join the Progressive Democrats, the Irish Farmers' Association (IFA) has traditional connections to Fine Gael, several of whose leading figures have come from the IFA ranks.

It is also important to bear in mind that within all of these large sectional associations, there will additionally be individual companies, unions or groups that separately undertake their own lobbying efforts.

Causes

Engagement with cause-centred organisations has historically given the Irish government perhaps most difficulty. This could be because causes tend to generate widespread emotional responses, or because they cut across the lines of party politics, or because they are led, on the whole, by citizens rather than professional lobbyists. One distinguishing feature of many causes is that they campaign on social, rather than economic, issues, which are often hugely divisive at the time, for example abortion (O'Reilly 1992), contraception, gay rights, feminism, divorce, or immigration (although McDermott (2008) relates, from an insider's perspective, the controversial pro- and anti-nuclear campaigns, which were more business/economic than social in focus). O'Halpin and Connolly (1999) note that while in 1970 the Commission on the Status of Women received forty submissions to its inquiry, its successor in 1990 received over two hundred (see Levine (1982) for an account of the early days of the women's movement). The proliferation of what are sometimes erroneously referred to as single-issue groups has been remarkable in Irish politics over the last three decades, and they can be more willing than the major economic interests to undertake the politics of pressure rather than of compromise. While some causes generate intense media interest for relatively short periods (e.g. Rossport 5 2006), there are also well-established and highly respected charities and non-governmental organisations (NGOs), such as Barnardos and Greenpeace, that are consistently engaged in lobbying and advocacy efforts in a lower-key manner over many years.

IRISH LOBBYING SCANDALS

Ireland has historically been seen as being relatively free from major political corruption, but that underlying trust in politicians and institutions has been steadily eroded over the last two decades, as a number of allegations have been made about the probity of individual TDs, in particular about their financial relationships with businesspeople. As Murphy (2006:94) has put it, without hyperbole, 'revelations about the increasingly muddy links between business and politics have created something of a crisis of confidence in Irish political life'. To discuss the details of each scandal would require many volumes in itself, but it is worth briefly noting how several have touched upon lobbying.

The Revolving Door

One area of particular concern in recent years has been the so-called 'revolving door', the practice whereby an individual will move, over the course of his or her career, between a variety of public and private sector posts. In essence, the issue here is that of potential conflicts of interest. Stated at its baldest, there is a danger that a former politician or civil servant will be able to use the contacts and knowledge they have gained at taxpayers' expense in their official position and translate those assets into a valuable commodity when moving into a new role as a lobbyist to advance the narrow self-interest of the new lobbying employer (potentially against the interests of Irish companies and employers). This is by now a well-established career path in the United States (Revolving Door Working Group 2005; Santos 2004) and the United Kingdom (Alexander 2008), and is not uncommon in Ireland. Speaking in the Seanad on the Registration of Lobbyists Bill 1999, Joe Costello stated that, 'Most of the lobbyists within the confines of this House are former Members. . . . we see such people everywhere in the House as they have privileged access' (Seanad Debates, vol. 160, col. 113, 30 June 1999).

As the name suggests, the revolving door involves circular movement. There are examples of lobbyists becoming politicians, such as John Deasy, who began his political career as a legislative assistant for US Senator John Heinz in 1990–1991, went on to work as a lobbyist for a waste management company in America in 1991–1992 and, having moved back to his native Ireland, was elected to the Dáil at the 2002 general election. Of more concern, though, is when former politicians and officials become lobbyists, as this scenario can present more opportunities for conflicts of interest to arise. And, in fact, quite a number of former politicians have made this transition (see above). Without doubt, however, the instance that has received most attention is that of Tom Parlon. Parlon was president of the IFA from 1997 to 2001, before being elected as a Progressive Democrat TD at the 2002 general election and being immediately appointed Minister of State at the Department of Finance. When he lost his seat five years later, he was appointed director general of the Construction Industry Federation (CIF) at a reported salary of €250,000 (McKenna 2007). This move was particularly controversial, in part because one of Parlon's ministerial responsibilities had been to oversee the Office of Public Works (OPW), which negotiated large public construction projects, thus raising the question of why politicians are allowed to move straight into private sector roles that relate to their former public duties. It has been suggested that the absence of any 'cooling-off' or 'decontamination' period for former ministers contravenes Ireland's obligations under Article 12 of the UN Convention Against Corruption, which requires states to impose restrictions on public officials moving to private sector jobs that relate directly to their previous functions (McMorrow and Frawley 2007).

One slightly atypical scandal (in that it involved a civil servant, rather than a politician) in 1999 highlighted the problems which can occur when public servants mix too closely with private interests. Paddy Duffy was forced to resign as a special adviser to Taoiseach Bertie Ahern when it emerged that he was being listed as a director of Dillon Consultants (Kerrigan and Brennan 1999:87–9). The company had as one of its clients NTL, which was then in the process of buying Cablelink, a state-owned company, for £535m. Duffy's position became untenable, despite his claims that he had no involvement in either the Cablelink sale or in advising NTL, and that he was unaware that his appointment to the board of

Dillon Consultants had been made while he was still in the public service. Since resigning, Duffy runs a public affairs consultancy, The Right Word.

The government does recognise the potential for conflicts of interest caused by the revolving door, such that since 2004, senior civil servants (but not yet politicians or special advisers) must obtain permission from an independent Outside Appointments Board if they want to take up a private sector post or consultancy within a year of leaving the public sector. The board is able to impose restrictions, such as that someone can take a job but not engage in lobbying activities for a twelve-month period.

Tribunals of Inquiry

In 1991, a new term entered Irish public consciousness, 'Tribunals of Inquiry'. That year, the Hamilton Tribunal was established as a judicial inquiry into allegations that certain companies in the beef sector had received government favouritism. While the resulting report revealed 'staggering irregularities . . . a massive, systematic tax-evasion scheme' (Collins and O'Shea 2003:171), it nevertheless concluded that there was nothing improper in the relations between political leaders and corporate executives. One lasting consequence of the so-called 'Beef Tribunal', however, was to shine some light on the funding by private businesses of politicians and political parties. It thus set the scene for the establishment of the McCracken Tribunal in 1997, which reported on financial contributions given by businessman Ben Dunne to both Charles Haughey (former Taoiseach) and Michael Lowry TD. McCracken uncovered substantial evidence against both politicians, to the point where Lowry had to resign from the Cabinet and was forced to leave Fine Gael, and Haughey faced criminal charges (until it was ruled that a call by the then Tánaiste Mary Harney for him to be convicted prejudiced any future trial). The McCracken report was explicit in its view that politicians who received significant private donations in secret ran the risk of exposing themselves to accusations of bribery, yet concluded that neither Haughey nor Lowry had actually allowed their private financial affairs to influence their public behaviour or decisions. This apparent judicial ambiguity was countered by waves of public and political pressure, and all the dominos began falling.

In September 1997, the Moriarty Tribunal was created to further inquire into payments to Haughey, Lowry and other public office holders. At the time of writing (June 2010), the tribunal has not yet completed its work, but it did, at the end of 2006, publish its first report, which unpicked in extraordinary detail Haughey's personal finances from 1979 to 1996 and concluded that he had received in the region of £9m in personal donations (equivalent to 171 times his 1988 salary as Taoiseach). Moriarty again found little evidence that these payments had influenced Haughey's official decisions, but was careful to warn that he had by no means been able to exhaustively probe all of the politician's public actions. Two close observers of Irish corruption summarised the tribunals' difficulty:

Whenever a politician was caught taking a chunk of money from wealthy interests we were assured that 'no favours were sought or given', so everything was okay. . . . Short of uncovering a piece of paper on which the politician promises to make a certain decision on foot of receiving a bribe, the task of proving a link between donations and favours is next to impossible. . . . Failure to produce such absolute evidence leads to the politician claiming he has been investigated and vindicated. (Kerrigan and Brennan 1999:101–2)

Lobbying came into centre stage of the tribunal arena with the establishment in November 1997 of the Flood Tribunal (although, since Feargus Flood's retirement, it has actually been chaired by Judge Alan Mahon), the final report of which is currently (July 2010) being drafted. The Flood Tribunal initially focused on allegations that politicians had been bribed in relation to planning permissions and land rezoning around Dublin in the 1990s, but its remit was substantially broadened as evidence of further corruption came to light (Cullen 2002). In response to a newspaper advertisement placed by a firm of solicitors, which offered a reward for information about planning corruption, James Gogarty (a retired executive in a building firm) alleged that a former Fianna Fáil minister, Ray Burke, had received a bribe of £80,000 from a property developer to help secure land rezoning; in 2005, Mr Burke was sentenced to six months in prison. Another Fianna Fáil TD, Liam Lawlor, was jailed on three occasions for refusing to co-operate with the Flood Tribunal. And, perhaps most dramatically, Bertie Ahern resigned as Taoiseach in May 2008 after his personal finances were subjected to forensic scrutiny by the tribunal in the course of its investigation into allegations that Ahern had received payments from a property developer.

Lobbying really moved to the forefront of public consciousness when Frank Dunlop was called to give evidence to the Flood Tribunal in April 2000. Dunlop was a Fianna Fáil press officer before being appointed in 1978 as the first person to hold the title of Government Press Secretary, later setting up Frank Dunlop & Associates as a lobbying firm. Dunlop's initial testimony to Flood was less than frank – he denied making any payments to politicians in relation to land rezoning – but the tribunal had evidence from his bank accounts which suggested otherwise. Cautioned by Feargus Flood to go home and reflect overnight on the accuracy of his evidence, Dunlop appeared again on 19 April 2000 and sensationally began to name Dublin county councillors whom he now admitted to having bribed in return for their votes on rezoning land on which the Liffey Valley shopping centre was later built.

In November 2008, Dunlop was arrested and charged with sixteen counts of corruption under laws dating from 1889 and 1916, as well as the 1995 Ethics in Public Office Act. Dunlop pleaded guilty to five sample charges in January 2009, thus avoiding a protracted trial, which would have led to further delays in the final publication of the Flood/Mahon report (Cullen 2008:1). Having been found guilty,

Dunlop was sentenced on 26 May 2009 to two years in prison with six months suspended, and fined €30,000. Just as lobbying regulation was tightened in America following the Jack Abramoff affair (McGrath 2007), so too should Frank Dunlop's testimony provide an impetus to serious lobbying reform in Ireland. If it does, Dunlop will indeed, belatedly, have done the state some service.

EFFORTS TO REGULATE IRISH LOBBYING

The Labour Party stands alone in Irish politics in having actually introduced legislation designed to regulate lobbying. Indeed, it has done so on five occasions – twice in 1999, then again in 2000, 2003 and 2008. By contrast, Fianna Fáil has consistently opposed all efforts to regulate lobbying, while Fine Gael has been largely mute on the issue until recently. Both coalition partners – the Progressive Democrats and the Green Party – have called for lobbying reform from time to time, but neither has translated that into action.

The Labour Party's first 1999 bill and that in 2000 were introduced in the Seanad, and are the only bills to have been debated at second stage. It is worth examining in some detail the legislation as it was originally proposed in 1999, as it was thorough and innovative in some respects, and it has remained substantially intact throughout the various iterations. To begin with, it stated that anyone would be engaged in lobbying activities (and thus would be regarded as a lobbyist) when they either communicated directly 'with an office holder' or arranged a meeting 'between an office holder and any other person' in 'an attempt to influence' a legislative proposal by a minister, TD or senator or the 'passage, defeat or amendment of any Bill or resolution that is before either House of the Oireachtas', or the 'making, revocation or amendment' of a statutory instrument. In addition, lobbying activities were defined as including any attempt to influence the 'development or amendment of any policy or programme of a public body' or the 'awarding of any contract, grant, contribution or other benefit by or on behalf of a public body' (Registration of Lobbyists Bill 1999:4–5). The 1999 bill defined an 'office holder' as a minister, the attorney general, TDs and senators, staff employed by the Dáil or Seanad or by a political party, a director or employee of a public body, and a member of the Defence Forces and the Garda Síochána (Registration of Lobbyists Bill 1999:4). A 'public body' is defined as including government departments, local authorities, health boards, organisations established by statute and organisations appointed by ministers (Registration of Lobbyists Bill 1999:12–13).

The 1999 bill required both commercial lobbyists and in-house lobbyists to register, although it prescribed slightly different information that each would have to provide. It should be noted that it applied only to paid professionals acting for someone else and not to volunteers or citizens lobbying on their own behalf. In essence, lobbyists would have been required to declare: their name and business address and those of their client or employer, plus those of any parent company;

any funding received by the client or employer from government; the 'subject matter' or policy area in relation to which any lobbying is being undertaken; the precise 'legislative proposal, Bill, resolution, regulation, policy, programme, grant, contribution, benefit or contract' towards which the lobbying activity was directed; and the public body in which any office holder who is being lobbied serves (Registration of Lobbyists Bill 1999:6, 8). This is broadly typical of the nature of the information lobbyists are required to give under similar registration schemes in other jurisdictions. One very novel suggestion, however, was also included in the Labour Party bill. Had it passed, lobbyists in Ireland would additionally have been obliged to:

> identify any communication technique (including appeals to members of the public through the mass media or by direct communication that seek to persuade members of the public to communicate directly with an office holder in an attempt to place pressure on the office holder to endorse a particular opinion) that the person has used or expects to use in an attempt to influence that matter. (Registration of Lobbyists Bill 1999:6)

This appears to have been the first legislative attempt anywhere in the world that would have made the process of grassroots lobbying transparent to policy makers and the general public.

Under the Registration of Lobbyists Bill 1999, the Public Offices Commission would have been responsible for maintaining the register of lobbyists and for reporting annually on its operation; in the 2003 and 2008 iterations of the legislation this was changed to the Standards in Public Office Commission, which was set up by the 2001 Standards in Public Office Act. Crucially, the Commission would have been given power to 'verify the information contained in any return or other document submitted to it' by lobbyists (Registration of Lobbyists Bill 1999:9), and, equally important, the register would have been open and available to the public. The commission could proactively investigate any suspected breach of the legislation, and, if the investigation concluded that a criminal offence had been committed, the commission would issue a report to the Director of Public Prosecutions; the maximum penalties for intentionally making 'any false or misleading statement in any return or other document submitted to the Commission' would have been a fine of up to £1,500 and/or up to twelve months' imprisonment for summary conviction, or a fine and/or imprisonment for up to two years following a conviction on indictment (Registration of Lobbyists Bill 1999:12).

Finally, the 1999 bill contained a schedule that detailed a proposed Lobbyists' Code of Conduct, which was intended to underpin the provisions of the legislation. It began by describing lobbying as 'a legitimate activity' and affirmed that 'free and open access to government is an important matter of public interest', but also stated that 'it is desirable that public office holders and the public be able to know who is attempting to influence government' and cautioned that 'a system for the registration of paid lobbyists should not impede free and open access to government' (Registration of Lobbyists Bill 1999:13). The 1999 Code (Registration of Lobbyists Bill 1999:14) expressed three basic principles: integrity and honesty (that lobbyists should essentially behave properly towards 'public office holders, clients, employers, the public and other lobbyists'); openness (they should be 'frank about their lobbying activities, while respecting confidentiality'); and professionalism (they should act ethically and 'conform fully with not only the letter but also the spirit' of the Code of Conduct and all relevant legislation). It went on to set out eight specific rules, which instructed lobbyists, among other things, to disclose to policy makers the identity of their client or employer on whose behalf lobbying is being undertaken; to ensure that information they provide is accurate; and not to reveal confidential information without the permission of their client or employer. Under that code, lobbyists were also told to refrain from simultaneously representing conflicting or competing interests without the agreement of all parties involved, and to avoid anything which would improperly influence an office holder (Registration of Lobbyists Bill 1999:14–15).

SELF-REGULATION AND THE POLITICAL DEBATE

In October 1999, the Public Relations Institute of Ireland (PRII) and its sister organisation, the Public Relations Consultants Association Ireland (PRCA), published a joint report on lobbying regulation. While it welcomed any effort that would improve the transparency of the lobbying process (PRII and PRCA 1999:3), it asserted that this goal could best be achieved through an industry-based code of conduct, ethics reform in the public sector, and restrictions on those moving from public office to private sector jobs. So far as the Labour Party bill was concerned, the PRII/PRCA report came out as being firmly opposed to the 1999 text, stating that the bill was 'excessive' on a number of fronts. In the PRII/PRCA's view, the bill was essentially an over-reaction 'in relation to the level of lobbying activity which occurs in Ireland'; would require lobbyists to register a burdensome 'level of information'; and was too wide-ranging as it could potentially require not just lobbyists to register, but also 'solicitors, accountants, economic consultants, public relations companies and commercial, educational, social, cultural, sporting representative bodies' (PRII and PRCA 1999:2).

Another four years passed before the PRII adopted, in December 2003, a Code of Professional Practice for Public Affairs and Lobbying. Compliance with this code was made a mandatory condition of PRII membership. The code was relatively basic and not particularly restrictive. Members of the PRII:

- are obliged to act according to the law, and forbidden to 'improperly influence the decision-making processes of government' (PRII 2003: article 1);
- must 'ensure that all information supplied, and representations made, by them to third parties is factually accurate and honest' (PRII 2003: article 2);

- are to disclose to policy makers the 'identity of clients on whose behalf they are making representations' (PRII 2003: article 3);
- may not offer bribes to public servants (PRII 2003: article 4); and
- must not 'bring professional public affairs and public relations practice into disrepute' (PRII 2003: article 19).

Under the code, lobbyists need not make any information at all available to the public, and thus it does nothing whatever to increase general transparency or accountability in the lobbying process. Hence, the PRII code, while well-intentioned, fails to enhance the public acceptability of lobbying or public trust in the policy-making process.

Over the last decade, there has been considerable political pressure for lobbying regulation, but one critical stumbling block has not yet been overcome: Fianna Fáil's opposition thus far to reform. It was reported in May 2000 that the Cabinet had instructed the Attorney General, Michael McDowell, to draft a bill to establish a lobbyists' register, which could then be considered by the Dáil Committee on Members' Interests (Donohoe 2000), but nothing came of this. Hopes rose following the 2007 general election that the government would take action. A report (Chari and Murphy 2006), which had been commissioned by the Department of the Environment, Heritage and Local Government, and which had suggested a lobbyists' register, appeared to be preaching to the converted when the Green Party leader, John Gormley, became minister, as the Green Party's election manifesto in 2007 included a pledge to 'establish a national register of lobbyists . . . detailing the company, clients and interests being represented' (Green Party 2007:31). In March 2009, a report by Transparency International Ireland found that while Ireland is ranked as the sixteenth least corrupt nation out of 180 countries, it nevertheless suffers from relatively high levels of what was termed 'legal corruption'. The report urged the government to bring forward proposals for a register of lobbyists 'as a matter of priority' (Transparency International Ireland 2009:23). Whether this call to action yields results where others have failed in the past remains to be seen.

CONCLUSION: IRISH LOBBYING REGULATION

Lobbying reform is an idea whose time has come around the world, and this is no less true of Ireland. It is by no means an exaggeration to assert that it is an essential precondition to a well-functioning democracy. The reality is that lobbying in Ireland is currently secretive and closed to external scrutiny, even at the same time as it exerts a significant influence over the formulation and implementation of public policy. The public, media and academics are largely excluded from the lobbying world, and thus find it difficult to assess its scale, effectiveness and probity. As one scholar has noted: 'Lobbying remains an area of political life that has not been penetrated by either parliamentary or public forms of accountability. . . . This is an issue that the Dáil must pursue' (MacCarthaigh 2005:262).

Irish policy makers can learn important lessons from an initiative currently under way in the United Kingdom. At the start of 2009, the House of Commons Public Administration Select Committee issued a report on the regulation of lobbying there (PASC 2009a, 2009b; also see McGrath 2009). That body has covered much of the ground that would need to be investigated in the Irish context (while of course there are particular institutional and cultural differences which are important), and its work repays close scrutiny, as do the OECD-commissioned reports by Pross (2007) and Holman and Susman (2009). Among its key conclusions were that lobbyists should establish a 'single umbrella organisation with both corporate and individual membership, in order to be able to cover all those who are involved in lobbying as a substantial part of their work' (PASC 2009a:42). The group must apply more rigorous ethical standards to its members (including some degree of independent and external accreditation), and should establish 'an externally assessed and validated standard – a kind of kite mark – which its members should be required to meet' (PASC 2009a:43). The report recommended that a mandatory register of lobbying activity be created, which need not involve substantial financial disclosure, and which should be framed in such a way as to require only that information which can be provided with relative ease, and only that which is 'of genuine potential value to the general public, to others who might wish to lobby government, and to decision makers' (PASC 2009a:52). The register ought in addition to provide details of contacts between lobbyists and policy makers, so that the public can 'see what contacts are taking place, and to reach a reasonably informed judgement as to whether decision makers are receiving a balanced perspective from those they are meeting' (PASC 2009a:54).

A rigorous and comprehensive regulatory system for lobbying in Ireland should be enacted as a matter of urgency, following widespread and open consultation by an independent expert group that would be empowered to produce proposals as a starting point for legislative drafting by the government. Such a system could include some or all of the following elements.

- Some statutory component is required, because all paid professional lobbyists in Ireland must be subject to the same rules. The scheme must be explicitly based on clear and sensible definitions of who is and is not a lobbyist and what is and is not meant by lobbying – perhaps based on how much time a person, or how much money an organisation, spends on lobbying (McGrath 2009:104–11). It should, though, apply to all who are professional lobbyists – consultants, in-house employees, NGOs, corporations, lawyers, and so on.
- The operation of any new regulatory framework must be independent of the lobbying industry, so as to encourage public trust in its impartiality.
- All lobbyists should be subject to the same requirements as apply to the holding of parliamentary passes, and, in particular, some lobbyists must not enjoy privileged access because they were formerly TDs or senators.

- All information registered by lobbyists should be freely available and accessible through a searchable, web-based system.
- All government departments and public bodies should be required – and parliamentarians should be encouraged – to post on their websites copies of all correspondence to and from registered lobbyists.
- A requirement that lobbyists register all grassroots campaigns which they have been involved in organising would enable Ireland to set a new benchmark in lobbying regulation.
- Ultimately, all regulatory requirements under which lobbyists must operate in their dealings with central government must be translated into similar mechanisms applying to local government and other public bodies.
- Tailored training programmes should be organised for policy makers (and their staff) in order that public officials are entirely clear on the standards required of lobbyists, how their relationships with lobbyists should be conducted, and the mechanisms available to them should they wish to make a complaint about a lobbyist's behaviour.
- Stricter provisions are needed to slow down the 'revolving door', particularly in respect of former parliamentarians and special advisers.
- Finally, a range of penalties – from censure to more substantial measures – must be available to the regulatory authority and/or the criminal courts for non-compliance with the system.

Assuming that some new system which approximates to the agenda above does emerge, Ireland will have what Chari, Murphy and Hogan (2007:428) would categorise as a medium-regulated system: it would be mandatory rather than voluntary; lobbyists would register the issue/legislation which they seek to influence and the policy maker/institution their lobbying is targeted at, but they might not be required to register financial information; registration could be done online, and certainly there should be relatively easy public access to the register; an enforcement mechanism would be capable of imposing penalties for non-compliance. Indeed, it is conceivable (and would be desirable) that some elements of the system would be sufficiently rigorous as to constitute high regulation – for instance, if relatively extensive information was provided about the contact of lobbyist/policy maker communication, and the enforcement process could potentially be more proactive than is true in other jurisdictions.

Michael McDowell (2003) (then Minister for Justice, Equality and Law Reform) once stated that the consequence of lobbying regulation here should be that 'professional ethical lobbyists' take the place of 'fly-by-night secretive intermediaries with dubious motives and ethics'. That would indeed enable the Irish lobbying industry to take its first real steps towards professionalisation; rather than the traditional Irish fudged compromise, the government could decide to take measures to regulate lobbying, which would be a model for future reform around the world.

References

Alexander, A. (2008) '69 Lobbyists Turned Legislators', *Public Affairs News*, November, pp. 26–31.

Allen, K. (2007) *The Corporate Takeover of Ireland*. Dublin: Irish Academic Press.

Brown, E. and Strauss, A. (1888) *A Dictionary of American Politics: Comprising Accounts of Political Parties, Measures and Men*. New York: A.L. Burt.

Chari, R., Hogan, J. and Murphy, G. (2010) *Regulating Lobbying: A Global Comparison*. Manchester: Manchester University Press.

Chari, R. and Murphy, G. (2006) *Examining and Assessing the Regulation of Lobbyists in Canada, the USA, the EU Institutions, and Germany: A Report for the [Irish] Department of the Environment, Heritage and Local Government*. Dublin: Department of the Environment, Heritage and Local Government.

Chari, R., Murphy, G. and Hogan, J. (2007) 'Regulating Lobbyists: A Comparative Analysis of the United States, Canada, Germany and the European Union', *Political Quarterly* 78(3): 422–38.

Collins, N. and O'Shea, M. (2003) 'Political Corruption in Ireland', in M.J. Bull and J.L. Newell (eds) *Corruption in Contemporary Politics*, pp. 164–77. Basingstoke: Palgrave Macmillan.

Cullen, P. (2002) *With a Little Help From My Friends: Planning Corruption in Ireland*. Dublin: Gill & Macmillan.

— (2008) 'Dunlop Not to Contest 16 Charges of Bribery to Rezone Land', *Irish Times*, 22–23 November, p. 1.

Donohoe, M. (2000) 'Work on Lobbyist Register Bill has Started', *Irish Times*, 2 May [online]. Available: http://www.ireland.com/newspaper/ireland/2000/0502/pfarchive.00050200016.html (last accessed 5 May 2006).

Fallon, J. (2006) *Party Time: Growing Up in Politics*. Cork: Mercier Press.

Fennell, G. (2007) 'Three in a Row', *Public Affairs News*, July, p. 28.

FitzGerald, G. (2007) 'Flaws Emerge in Social Partnership Model', *Irish Times*, 14 July, p. 14.

Gallagher, M. (1987) 'Does Ireland Need a New Electoral System?', *Irish Political Studies* 2(1): 27–48.

Garvin, T. (1981) *The Evolution of Irish Nationalist Politics*. Dublin: Gill & Macmillan.

Gilmore, N. (2005) *Clearing The Air: The Battle Over the Smoking Ban*. Dublin: Liberties Press.

Green Party (2007) *Manifesto 2007: It's Time*. Dublin: Green Party.

Holman, C. and Susman, T. (2009) *Self-Regulation and Regulation of the Lobbying Profession*, GOV/PGC/GF(2009)5. Paris: OECD.

Kerrigan, G. and Brennan, P. (1999) *This Great Little Nation: The A–Z of Irish Scandals and Controversies*. Dublin: Gill & Macmillan.

Laffan, B. and Tonra, B. (2005) 'Europe and the International Dimension', in J. Coakley and M. Gallagher (eds) *Politics in the Republic of Ireland*, 4th edn, pp. 430–61. Abingdon: Routledge.

Levine, J. (1982) *Sisters: The Personal Story of an Irish Feminist*. Swords: Ward River Press.

MacCarthaigh, M. (2005) *Accountability in Irish Parliamentary Politics*. Dublin: Institute of Public Administration.

McCarthy, J. (2008) 'How to Build a Fortune with Bricks, Mortar, Money, Influence and Power', *Sunday Tribune*, 14 September, p. 13.

McDermott, V. (2008) *Going Nuclear: Ireland, Britain and the Campaign to Close Sellafield*. Dublin: Irish Academic Press.

McDowell, M. (2003) 'McDowell Endorses Role for Ethical Lobbyists', press release [online]. Available: http://www.michaelmcdowell.ie/releases/23_09_03.html (last accessed 20 January 2005).

McGrath, C. (2005) 'Towards a Lobbying Profession: Developing the Industry's Reputation, Education and Representation', *Journal of Public Affairs* 5(2): 124–35.

— (2007) 'Lobbying and the 2006 U.S. Midterm Elections', *Journal of Public Affairs* 7(2): 192–203.

— (2008) 'The Development and Regulation of Lobbying in the New Member States of the European Union', *Journal of Public Affairs* 8(1/2): 15–32.

— (2009) 'Access, Influence and Accountability: Regulating Lobbying in the UK', in C. McGrath (ed.) *Interest Groups and Lobbying in Europe*, pp. 53–123. Lewiston: Edwin Mellen Press.

McKenna, G. (2007) 'PDs Facing Wipeout as Parlon Quits for €1/4m Job', *Irish Independent*, 11 July, pp. 1–3.

McMorrow, C. and Frawley, M. (2007) 'Parlon Sues State in New Job After Career U-Turn', *Sunday Tribune*, 15 July, p. 1.

Murphy, G. (2003) 'Towards a Corporate State? Sean Lemass and the Realignment of Interest Groups in the Policy Process, 1948–1964', *Administration* 51(1/2): 105–18.

— (2005) 'Interest Groups in the Policy-Making Process', in J. Coakley and M. Gallagher (eds) *Politics in the Republic of Ireland*, 4th edn, pp. 352–83. Abingdon: Routledge in association with PSAI Press.

— (2006) 'Payments for no Political Response? Political Corruption and Tribunals of Inquiry in Ireland, 1991–2003', in J. Garrard and J.L. Newell (eds) *Scandals in Past and Contemporary Politics*, pp. 91–105. Manchester: Manchester University Press.

OECD (Organisation for Economic Co-operation and Development) (2006) *Governance Arrangements to Ensure Transparency in Lobbying: Comparative Overview*. Paris: OECD [online]. Available: http://www.olis.oecd.org/olis/2006doc.nsf/ENGDATCORPLOOK/NT00000D5A/$FILE/JT00197349.PDF (last accessed 2 October 2008).

— (2008) *Lobbyists, Governments and Public Trust: Building a Legislative Framework for Enhancing Transparency and Accountability in Lobbying.* Paris: OECD [online]. Available: http://www.oecd.org/dataoecd/5/41/41074615.pdf (last accessed 11 December 2008).

O'Halpin, E. and Connolly, E. (1999) 'Parliaments and Pressure Groups: The Irish Experience of Change', in P. Norton (ed.) *Parliaments and Pressure Groups in Western Europe*, pp. 124–44. Abingdon: Routledge.

O'Reilly, E. (1992) *Masterminds of the Right.* Dublin: Attic Press.

PASC (Public Administration Select Committee) (2009a) *Lobbying: Access and Influence in Whitehall – Volume I Report*, HC 36-I. London: Stationery Office [online]. Available: http://www.publications.parliament.uk/pa/cm200809/cmselect/cmpubadm/36/36i.pdf (last accessed 6 January 2009).

— (2009b) *Lobbying: Access and Influence in Whitehall – Volume II Oral and Written Evidence*, HC 36-II. London: Stationery Office [online]. Available: http://www.publications.parliament.uk/pa/cm200809/cmselect/cmpubadm/36/36ii.pdf (last accessed 6 January 2009).

PRII (Public Relations Institute of Ireland) (2003) *Code of Professional Practice for Public Affairs and Lobbying.* Dublin: PRII [online]. Available: http://www.prii.ie/show_content.aspx?idcategory=1&idsubcategory=1 (last accessed 27 May 2009).

PRII (Public Relations Institute of Ireland) and PRCA (Public Relations Consultants Association Ireland) (1999) *Report on the Regulation of Lobbying in Ireland.* Dublin: PRII and PRCA.

Pross, A.P. (2007) *Lobbying: Models for Regulation.* Paris: OECD [online]. Available: http://www.oecd.org/dataoecd/17/50/38944782.pdf (last accessed 10 October 2008).

Registration of Lobbyists Bill (1999), No. 36 of 1999. Dublin: Stationery Office.

Registration of Lobbyists (No. 2) Bill (1999), No. 43 of 1999. Dublin: Stationery Office.

Registration of Lobbyists Bill (2000), No. 29 of 2000. Dublin: Stationery Office [online]. Available: http://www.oireachtas.ie/documents/bills28/bills/2000/2900/b2900.pdf (last accessed 15 May 2009).

Registration of Lobbyists Bill (2003), No. 62 of 2003. Dublin: Stationery Office [online]. Available: http://www.oireachtas.ie/documents/bills28/bills/2003/6203/b6203d.pdf (last accessed 15 May 2009).

Registration of Lobbyists Bill (2008), No. 28 of 2008. Dublin: Stationery Office [online]. Available: http://www.oireachtas.ie/documents/bills28/bills/2008/2808/b2808d.pdf (last accessed 15 May 2009).

Reid, L. (2007) 'May I Introduce You ...', *Irish Times* ('How We Are Governed' Supplement), 17 April, p. 5.

Revolving Door Working Group (2005) *A Matter of Trust: How the Revolving Door Undermines Public Confidence in Government – And What to Do About It.* Washington: Revolving Door Working Group.

Rossport 5 (2006) *Our Story*. Magheramore: Small World Media.

Santos, A. (2004) 'The Role of Lobbying on Legislative Activity when Lawmakers Plan to Leave Office', *International Social Science Review* 79(1/2): 44–55.

Seanad Debates (1919–2005) [online]. Available: http://historical-debates.oireachtas.ie/en.toc.dail.html.

Transparency International Ireland (2009) *National Integrity Systems – Country Study: Ireland 2009*. Dublin: Transparency International Ireland.

Chapter 12

A Social Justice Perspective on the Celtic Tiger

Connie Harris Ostwald

INTRODUCTION

As Ireland follows its European neighbours into a serious recession, one asks the question whether or not the dramatic economic growth of the past two decades was really a period of gain and glory for all of the Irish, or whether perhaps there was a shadow side to the economic phenomenon that gave birth to the Celtic Tiger. Going beyond the economic data of gross domestic product (GDP) growth rates to look at the Irish economy through a social justice lens, one can see clearly that there were both 'winners' and 'losers' in the Tiger economy. The purpose of this chapter is to analyse Ireland's relatively high level of income inequality during the years of the Celtic Tiger, and the consequences of this, through a social justice lens.

Ireland was completely transformed by the economic boom that impacted all sectors and social classes of Irish society while labelling Ireland with the nickname of the Celtic Tiger in an attempt to compare the period of rapid economic expansion with that of the four Asian Tigers (Hong Kong, Singapore, South Korea and Taiwan). From independence in 1922 until 1987, the country struggled to find a path of economic development that would bring to its citizens a standard of living comparable to its Western European neighbours (Cantillon and O'Shea 2001; Nolan and Maitre 2008; Ó Gráda 1997; O'Hagan 1995). Finally, a combination of circumstances and policy decisions came together in the late 1980s that gave Ireland the fastest-growing economy in the world during the last decade of the twentieth century while launching an economic boom that would last for the next twenty years (OECD 2003, 2008; Sweeney 1999).

The benefits of this period of rapid economic growth were not distributed in an equitable manner among the people of the Irish Republic. Although many Irish people enjoyed an increased standard of living, there were a number who were left behind. Data on income distribution shows that income inequality continued to be an issue during the period of the economic boom (CSO 2006; Nolan and Maitre 2008). The distribution of income will be analysed through the theoretical lens of Rawls' 'theory of justice' to gain a deeper understanding of the changes in economic and social well-being during this period of rapid economic expansion.

RAWLSIAN JUSTICE

Since the publication of *A Theory of Justice* in 1971, John Rawls' ideas have had a profound influence on the concept of social justice, even though Rawls is hardly known beyond the walls of academia. Although various elements of his theory have been used by a variety of political theorists and economists, the major focus has been on his Difference Principle, which concerns maximising the welfare of the least advantaged individuals in a society. Rawls' complete theory of justice, more comprehensive than just the Difference Principle, is actually composed of two principles of justice. The first principle concerns equal rights and liberties for all, and the second concerns the equitable arrangement of social and economic goods of which the Difference Principle is a key element.

Rawls has summarised his two principles of justice into what he calls the following 'general conception':

> All social primary goods – liberty and opportunity, income and wealth, and bases of self-respect – are to be distributed equally unless an unequal distribution of any or all of these goods is to the advantage of the least favored. (Rawls 1971:73)

This general conception of his principles of justice will be used as the framework for the analysis of the changes that took place in Ireland during the two decades of rapid economic expansion. The Difference Principle will be used as the lens through which to analyse the changes in income distribution, but since the Difference Principle cannot be taken out of the context of the more comprehensive theory of justice, the notions of individual rights and liberties, opportunities, and the bases of self-respect will also be addressed to fully assess whether or not Ireland became more just with the emergence of the Tiger economy. Rawls was chosen for this analysis because he has provided a thoughtful, comprehensive treatment of the subject of fairness and equity in which he systematically addresses these important issues. His work has become a foundation for others concerned with egalitarian issues of social justice, such as Amartya Sen and Robert Nozick (Edgren 1995; Nozick 1979; Sen 1980).

Rawls suggests that to understand his theory, we enter into a thought experiment. He asks us to imagine ourselves in what he calls the 'original position'. People in this 'original position' are denied knowledge of everything that makes them who they are, including their social class, knowledge and skills, age, gender, religious views and conception of 'the good life'. This situates people behind what Rawls calls a 'veil of ignorance'. It is only from behind this veil of ignorance that people would choose to regulate their relationships with one another in a truly just manner that is not distorted by one's own interests.

Rawls posits that from behind a veil of ignorance, a committee of rational but not envious persons will adopt a concept of what is right that is general in form, universal in application, publicly recognised, a final authority, and able to prioritise conflicting claims (Edgren 1995; Rawls 1971). He claims that the rational committee will adopt such principles of justice without knowing anything about their own personal situations. Personal knowledge would only tempt them to manipulate the situation to give themselves unfair advantage. Such unbiased human beings would pursue a low-risk strategy and agree to principles that are basically egalitarian. These agreed-upon principles would guarantee the highest possible minimum levels of freedom, wealth and opportunity, even at the cost of lowering the average levels (Rawls 1971).

Two Principles of Justice

Rawls claims that this committee of rational people behind the veil of ignorance would choose to be governed by two principles of justice.

The first principle of justice on which men and women in the original position would agree is the importance of guaranteeing their freedom to live their lives as they choose. Rawls' first principle states that each individual should have a right to the most extensive basic liberties such as the right to vote, freedom of thought, and so on. The basic liberties of the individual are compatible with a like liberty for all in society. Rawls argues that the state should remain neutral between different concepts of what is a 'good life', and simply protect the freedoms that allow us to live according to our own choices of what makes life worthwhile.

The second principle of justice, Rawls' famous Difference Principle, is much more original. The Difference Principle concerns the distribution of wealth and power in society. It states that social and economic inequalities are acceptable only in so far as they benefit the least advantaged. Social and economic inequalities are to be arranged so that they are to the greatest benefit of the least advantaged, a statement that addresses the distribution of income and wealth. However, Rawls adds to this notion by stating that the social and economic inequalities will be arranged so that they are attached to offices and positions open to all under conditions of fair equality of opportunity, this phrase thus addressing the equitable distribution of power (Rawls 1971:73). He goes on to develop this notion of equal opportunity by clarifying that the formal rules related to hiring use only criteria related to competence in the job. He claims that excessive accumulation of wealth and unequal access to educational opportunities that would give some an unfair advantage should also be precluded (Rawls 1971:73). These assertions of Rawls concerning equality of opportunity are very significant in the Irish case and will be discussed further in the final section of this chapter.

The best way to understand this second principle of justice, the Difference Principle, is to contrast it with the traditional notion of 'equality of opportunity'. The proponents of equality of opportunity posit that people who have the same abilities, along with a similar willingness to use them, should enjoy the same prospects of success in a market society. In contrast, Rawls argues that it is clearly wrong that our destinations in life, our chances for success, be determined by our educational opportunities or our social class. It is equally unjust that our success be determined by our talents or abilities. These characteristics of our personal lives, in the same way as the social class of our parents, are the outcome of what Rawls calls the 'natural lottery', a circumstance over which we have no control (Rawls 1971).

Rawls uses the Difference Principle to clarify his notion of efficiency. His concept of efficiency is associated with the notion of 'Pareto optimality' in the field of economics, which states that no system can be called 'efficient' if there is an alternative arrangement that improves the situation of some people with no worsening of the situation of the rest of the people. Of course, there are many conditions that are 'efficient' in this sense, but not all of them are equally just, according to Rawls. This is where he applies his principles of justice, and especially the Difference Principle. 'The Difference Principle is a strongly egalitarian conception in the sense that unless there is a distribution that makes both persons better off (limiting ourselves to the two-person case for simplicity), an equal distribution is to be preferred' (Rawls 1971:76).

The next section describes the period of rapid economic development in Ireland, a critique of using GDP growth as a measure of success and, finally, an analysis of Ireland's Tiger economy through the social justice lens of Rawls.

THE BIRTH OF THE CELTIC TIGER

Ireland had historically lagged behind its neighbours in the economic development process, subjecting the majority of the population to significantly lower living standards than its more developed Western European neighbours. Ireland fell into the role of a peripheral or semi-peripheral country relative to the stronger core of Western Europe while under the shadow of British imperialism (Munck 1993; Ó Gráda 1997). Even after independence in 1922, Ireland suffered from poverty while striving to rise above its reputation as an undeveloped 'Third World' outpost of Western Europe (O'Hagan 1995; O'Hearn 1998).

The first wave of focused economic development began in the 1970s, bringing to the forefront the consequences of the development process on the distributive justice question. Then in 1987, a new wave of economic development, financed by multinational corporations, began to significantly change the social and economic landscape (FitzGerald 2009; Nolan et al. 2000; Sweeney 1999). The country was finally able to shake off its status as a peripheral European country because of its success in imitating the four Tiger economies of Asia in an internationally financed economic development strategy (O'Hearn 1998).

The 'Tiger' label stuck, and Ireland began to enjoy its new status as a legitimate contender in the international economic system. The economic growth rates were the highest among the then fifteen European Union (EU) countries, as well as the twenty-nine OECD member states, for most of the 1990s, and were even higher than those of the four Asian Tigers before their financial collapse in 1997 (OECD 1999, 2003; Sweeney 1999).

Growth of the Irish economy, measured by increases in GDP per annum, was greater than 11 per cent in 1995, reached almost 10 per cent during the next two years, exceeded 9 per cent in 1998, and finally levelled off after 2000 at about 6 per cent per annum, but remained higher than the growth rates of its EU neighbours until the beginning of the current recession in 2008 (OECD 2003, 2008). During this period, employment rose by more than 40 per cent and emigration was no longer an issue. In fact, there was increased demand for immigrants to fuel the economy (see Chapters 1 and 23) (MacSharry and White 2000).

The Fallacy of Misplaced Concreteness

The use of GDP figures to calculate the economic and social welfare of the Irish people blinded the Irish and the world to many of the negative consequences of that growth. The growth of GDP has become the most watched economic indicator of a capitalist economy, and the key indicator of everything that is right or wrong in an economy (Daly and Cobb 1994). In the Irish case, it was the publication of the phenomenal GDP growth rates that brought Ireland into the international spotlight. The extremely high figures for GDP growth signalled to the Irish, and to the world, that all was well in the Irish economy. This turned out to be a false signal.

The practice of using GDP growth rates to measure economic well-being has given economists and politicians a very neat way to operationalise economic well-being. Since the concept of economic well-being is such a nebulous idea, with different meanings to different people, the GDP growth rate has become a poor substitute for a more rounded theory of economic well-being.

GDP is often correlated with other economic indicators, such as unemployment figures, to 'prove' that it measures the health of the economy. Yet, even if GDP correlates with certain other economic indicators, there are many social conditions intricately woven into economic well-being that are adversely affected by GDP growth. Just because GDP is increasing does not mean that society is enjoying a higher level of economic and social welfare. Also, greater economic and social well-being for individuals may not be reflected in a growing GDP.

Policy makers, journalists, academics and society as a whole have grown accustomed to the use of the GDP as a simplified, abstract model of economic and social well-being without even realising that there are faulty conclusions woven into the findings when applied to the real world. Alfred North Whitehead called this practice the 'fallacy of misplaced concreteness' (Daly and Cobb 1994; Whitehead 1925). This analysis will show that the Irish policy makers misplaced their trust in a faulty 'concreteness' of the GDP as an indicator of economic and social well-being during the growth of the Celtic Tiger.

The Cost of Economic Growth to the Irish People

The Celtic Tiger did not develop without costs to Irish society. One of the greatest costs was that of increased income inequality (CSO 2006; Nolan and Maitre 2008; O'Hearn 1998). A close look at Ireland reveals that the rewards of the economic boom were not distributed fairly, or equally, among the population. Relative poverty still plagued Irish society, and seemed to be embedded in the socio-economic system.

The dramatic growth in Ireland was dominated by the export share of industry, primarily computer software and pharmaceuticals. This rising share of export surplus resulted in significant profits for the multinational corporations, most of which were taken out of Ireland due to the lenient corporate tax policies used to entice corporations to locate there in the first place. These multinational corporations demanded Irish labour with specific high-tech skills, which led to a dual labour market structure and perpetuated income inequality (Cantillon and O'Shea 2001).

The service sector also grew considerably in support of industry, yet for the most part, the new employment opportunities in the service sector were primarily low-paying jobs, perpetuating the dual labour market structure. The poor in Ireland were categorically excluded from participating in the rapidly industrialising economy financed by foreign direct investment (FDI) (FitzGerald 2009; MacSharry and White 2000; Sweeney 1999). An assessment of social justice brings deeper understanding to these issues.

AN ASSESSMENT OF SOCIAL JUSTICE IN THE CELTIC TIGER

Once again, Rawls summarises his theory of justice in the following statement: 'All social primary goods – liberty and opportunity, income and wealth, and the bases of self-respect – are to be distributed equally unless an unequal distribution of any or all of these goods is to the advantage of the least favored' (Rawls 1971:73). Because Rawls presents his principles of justice with lexicographic significance (clarifying Rawls' absolute preference for the least favoured) the analysis of social justice begins with a discussion of liberty and rights in Ireland. The following section is an analysis of equality of opportunity. The concept of opportunity is multifaceted; therefore the concept has been defined in terms of educational achievement and social mobility in the Irish case. Recent studies on both of these indicators of opportunity will be discussed in order to assess the concept of equal opportunity in Ireland.

After presenting the notion of opportunity in his list of social primary goods, Rawls addresses the concepts of income and wealth equality. A summary review of the increase in income inequality indicates a decrease in social justice in Irish society over the period of rapid economic development from 1987 to 2007.

Rawls concludes his list of primary goods with a broad category of goods that provide the 'social bases of self-respect'. In this section, the starting point will be Adam Smith and his leather shoes, and then a discussion of what this means in modern Ireland, using the concepts of deprivation and social exclusion to provide the foundation for what constitutes the social bases of self-respect.

A progression emerges in that the Celtic Tiger appears to be a 'just' society in terms of rights and liberty, yet the notion of social justice fades as the analysis of primary goods continues. Within the discussion of opportunities, the first evidence emerges that justice and fairness are compromised. The discussions of income inequality, deprivation and social exclusion will show how social justice became a lost concept during the years of the Celtic Tiger economy.

Rights and Liberty: Political Culture

In Rawls' *Theory of Justice*, he clearly establishes the priority of liberty. His concept of liberty includes personal liberties comprised of basic political and civil rights, yet more confined than the rights proposed by libertarian theorists. In establishing the priority of liberty, Rawls posits that these basic rights cannot be compromised by the force of economic needs, and believes that these basic political and civil rights are necessary to provide one with personal advantage in pursuing economic objectives. According to Rawls, a strong constitutional political system provides a foundation for one to pursue one's own view of what constitutes a 'good life' (Rawls 1993).

In applying Rawls' views on personal liberties to Ireland, it is clear that the Irish Constitution has provided the framework for the protection of individual and civil rights. Because the Irish are afforded a full spectrum of civil rights, there is no doubt that this aspect of Irish society is just. A deeper look at the changes in the political culture of Ireland throughout the last decade shows how changes in attitudes have brought legislative changes that affect certain rights of individuals within Irish society, leading to an increase of social justice in this category.

Equality of Opportunity

Rawls' 'equality of opportunity' comes from the idea that positions and offices should be reasonably open to all (Edgren 1995; Rawls 1971). More specifically, his equality of opportunity requires that the formal rules related to hiring use only criteria related to the competencies required in the job. Rawls (1971:72) calls for the 'same legal rights of access to advantaged social positions' with no discrimination based on race, gender or religious beliefs. This system of rights leading to equal opportunity becomes in Rawlsian terminology 'natural liberty' (Rawls 1971:72). Ireland clearly has a firm set of employment laws in place that provide equality of opportunity as defined by Rawls.

However, Rawls expands his notion of equality of opportunity when he states that 'excessive accumulation of wealth and unequal access to educational opportunities that would give some an unfair advantage are also precluded' (Rawls 1971:73). Have certain social classes had unfair advantage in the Irish case due to excessive accumulation of wealth or unequal access to educational opportunities? To answer this question, recent studies on social mobility and educational achievement will be discussed to determine whether Irish society has become more just and fair during the growth of the Celtic Tiger. Increasing social mobility might indicate an increase in opportunity. Increases in educational achievement could help both horizontal and vertical social mobility. This social mobility might indicate that the Irish are taking advantage of equal opportunities in the educational system.

Layte and Whelan (2000) published a study that set out to answer the following questions:

1   Did equality of opportunity rise?
2   Did a more meritocratic society emerge?

The study examined trends in social mobility from the early 1970s to the mid-1990s. The changes in class origin and destination distributions reflect the economic transformation from an agrarian to a post-industrial society. The speed of transition from a pre-industrial society to a post-industrial society had a significant impact on the structural change within the economy and the society.

Layte and Whelan (2000) found that over time, there was no decrease in the impact of class origin on education level. The relative access for those from professional and managerial family backgrounds to third-level education increased. Even though a substantial number of working-class children took advantage of increased educational opportunities, this was overshadowed by the larger increase in the number of children of professional and managerial backgrounds going on to university. The substantially greater educational opportunities for working-class children have been accompanied by increases in class inequality. The concept of 'maximally maintained inequality' is significant here: the changes in the social structure are a consequence of the expansion in opportunities rather than the distribution of opportunities. The maximally maintained inequality is evidence that social justice did not increase with the increase in educational opportunities (Layte and Whelan 2000).

During the development of the Tiger economy, there was a rapid increase in educational participation among young people in Ireland. It has been commonly assumed that these educational increases have been beneficial to all young people. Since educational participation was already high for the middle class, it has been assumed that the increases in educational participation for the working class have 'closed the gap'. Smyth and Hannan (2000) found that this was not true, and that educational participation and achievement remained strongly differentiated in terms of social class background.

It is interesting to note that Ferdinand von Prondzynski, President of Dublin

City University, called in August 2008 for a reinstatement of third-level fees to meet the 'cash crisis' of the university, even though it would decrease the ability of the working classes to attend university (McDermott 2008). In 1995, the Irish government tried to equalise the opportunity to participate in third-level education by providing university tuition as a public good to all who met the entrance requirements. The reinstatement of fees would completely undo this policy to make access to university more affordable for all, and thus decrease social justice.

Most second-level schools prepare students for university and white-collar work, while vocational schools are mainly for the working class and the unemployed. Social segregation between the two types of school leads to social class inequality. The presence of active parental choice and the lack of state intervention in the school systems further leads to social class inequality in that parents tend to choose the school (vocational or academic) and the level of education for their children according to their social class background. Without involvement of the state in local school issues, there is considerable difference between schools according to ability groupings, discipline, parent involvement, pupil–teacher interaction and academic climate. These differences lead to significant differences in educational attainment and drop-out rates between schools (Smyth and Hannan 2000).

Because of the association between education and labour market outcomes, young people in Ireland who do not achieve educational qualifications are more likely to experience labour market marginalisation in terms of unemployment, insecure jobs and low pay. Since educational outcomes are associated with social class background, labour market marginalisation is more prevalent among working class youth. Also, Smyth and Hannan (2000) found that there is evidence that family background factors have a direct effect on the early labour market career, even controlling for education, therefore further disadvantaging young people without employment networks or social capital.

Layte and Whelan (2004) updated their analysis of the impact of the economic boom on social mobility closer to the end of the boom. In this study, they found that increases in social mobility, evident in the second half of the Tiger economy, were a result in the short term of a tight labour market in which employers were willing to hire those with perhaps fewer educational qualifications when labour shortages occurred. Layte and Whelan (2004) found no relationship between social mobility and economic growth, or between social mobility and educational level. Evidence from the EU Survey on Income and Living Conditions (CSO 2006) shows that poverty levels continued to correlate with the education level of the head of household, nearly two decades into the period of rapid economic growth. These findings confirm that increases in educational opportunity did not lead to higher levels of opportunity, social mobility or increased social justice from a Rawlsian perspective.

To deepen a social justice analysis of the relationship of equality of opportunities, Svallfors (2005) suggests that more longitudinal studies be done concerning family effects on stratification, and also that subjective aspects of inequality such as identity, aspirations and norms be added to the traditional aspects of inequality such as income and wealth. He noted that the European Social Survey (ESS), developed in the second half of the Celtic Tiger period, adds attitudinal sub-themes to its research on inequality, and will become a valuable tool in the future to bring a normative analysis into the study of economic growth. His work highlights the importance of fairness and social justice in the issue of inequality (Svallfors 2005).

Income Inequality

Income and wealth are the most measurable of Rawls' primary goods for which he calls for a commitment to an equal distribution. The only deviations permitted from equality in the distribution of income and wealth are those that increase the well-being of the least advantaged people in society. Even though Ireland became increasingly wealthy through the combination of internal policy changes, external environmental conditions and the huge impact of FDI, it continued to have one of the highest levels of income inequality in the EU throughout the growth of the Tiger economy (OECD 1999, 2003, 2008). Those households that were already better off gained from the economic boom to a greater extent than those that were less well off. Rawls was concerned that any change in the equitable distribution of primary goods should be to the advantage of the least advantaged, the foundational concept of his Difference Principle. What happened in Ireland was the exact opposite of this principle of social justice. This fact supports the notion that economic growth had not been able to bring a better standard of living to all Irish people, or for the 'rising tide to lift all boats' – in the words of the former Taoiseach Seán Lemass – in an equitable manner.

The dispersion in Irish earnings data was relatively high by European criteria during the early years of the Tiger economy. However, the dispersion increased from 1987 through the next decade, directly correlating with high levels of GDP growth. This increase was greater than for any other OECD country for which data were available. By the second half of the 1990s, the rate of increase in earnings inequality slowed, but the top of the distribution continued to move away from the middle. In the last half of the Tiger economy (the early 2000s), income distribution had stabilised with the levelling off of GDP growth, yet Ireland remained one of the most unequal countries in the EU in terms of income distribution (OECD 1999, 2003, 2008).

Another key finding was that older households moved down in the distribution of income while younger households moved up in the distribution during the Tiger economy. Households headed by someone under age thirty-five were concentrated in the top two deciles of the distribution. Large families were concentrated at the bottom of the distribution. Households headed by someone aged thirty-five to sixty-five were spread evenly across the distribution (Callan and Nolan 1999; CSO 2006).

Data on income distribution from the Living in Ireland Surveys (LIIS) show the income share of the top decile rose significantly during the 1990s while the share going to the bottom three deciles decreased significantly. There was also a gain in the middle shares of deciles five, six, seven and eight. These facts alone show an increase in income inequality with the benefits going to the middle and top deciles, leaving those in the bottom deciles worse off, a clear contradiction of Rawls' Difference Principle (Callan and Nolan 1999).

After the year 2000, similar income distribution data using household surveys were collected by the EU's Survey on Income and Living Conditions (SILC) which continued to show a high level of income inequality throughout the second decade of the Tiger economy (CSO 2006). The Economic and Social Research Institute (ESRI) completed a survey for the Luxembourg Income Study Database, a comprehensive study of income distribution in OECD countries, and found similar results to those of the LIIS and the SILC surveys. The Luxembourg Wealth Study has started collecting comparative data on wealth distribution, another aspect of inequality on which Rawls based his social justice analysis (Svallfors 2005).

The growing gap between rich and poor was damaging to society in a number of important ways. First of all, greater inequality brought greater poverty, and poverty of a different kind. Severe income inequality that leads to greater relative poverty destroys social cohesion and inclusion. This leads to an alienation of marginalised groups, which imposes high social costs because income inequality hinders the ability of those on low incomes to participate fully in the political, social, cultural and economic life of society. There are limits to the diversity of choices for those at the lower end of the income distribution in such a society.

These factors point to the last of Rawls' primary goods used in his analysis of social justice: the bases of self-respect.

The Bases of Self Respect

During the time of Adam Smith, a man needed a linen shirt and a pair of leather shoes to command self-respect. In modern Ireland, the issue is considerably more complicated, yet the concept remains a very important factor in determining whether or not society has become more just. Lack of self-respect has become a pivotal issue in modern notions of deprivation and social exclusion. In the days of Adam Smith, a man without leather shoes and a linen shirt had no self-respect because he was too poor to afford such basic needs. Although statistics show that absolute poverty has decreased over the past two decades, the increase in relative poverty focuses on the deprivation of resources that one needs to attain the self-respect to fit into a rapidly changing society (Cantillon and O'Shea 2001).

Wren (2000), columnist for the *Irish Times*, used the story of four-year old Mary and a tricycle to illustrate how the bases of self-respect have changed in Ireland. Wren admits that tricycles 'don't rank when politicians and sociologists compile lists of the basic necessities of life', but that look of longing on little Mary's face when playing with a borrowed tricycle illustrates the sense of deprivation felt by many Irish people in her situation. Mary's mother, a single parent, was on a waiting list for public housing, and prayed for the opportunity for Mary to get into a national school, even though she could not afford the uniform for her child. Mary's mother was ashamed that she could not provide the school uniform, but worried more about what form social exclusion would take in Mary's future. The deprivation of a tricycle was only a shadow of what Mary would feel ten years from now when her middle-class schoolmates will all have computers with access to the Internet while Mary will still not even have a phone line (Wren 2000).

Wren criticised the government's claim that absolute poverty decreased during the growth of the Celtic Tiger because what really mattered was that relative poverty had actually increased during the same time period. Wren argued that it is relative poverty that leads to feelings of deprivation and social exclusion. Because of the government's focus on absolute poverty, Wren claimed that it ignored the truth about the increases in deprivation and social exclusion.

The concept of social exclusion elaborates on the concept of deprivation as a basis for self-respect. Social exclusion has been at the heart of the economic, social and political debates of the EU, including Ireland, throughout the past two decades. New forms of poverty, deprivation and exclusion have emerged as a result of the structural changes in the economy and society necessitated by increased globalisation of domestic economies (Bhalla and Lapeyre 1999; Nolan and Maitre 2008). Ireland is a prime example of this increased participation in the global economy through the impact of the multinational corporations operating in the country, and is also suffering from new forms of deprivation and exclusion, directly affecting the bases of self-respect, and thus social justice, in the Irish socio-economic system.

Walker and Walker (1987:2) posit that social exclusion is not poverty as defined by a lack of material resources, but is a 'more comprehensive formulation which refers to the dynamic process of being shut out, fully or partially, from any of the social, economic, political, or cultural systems which determine the social integration of a person in society'. Levitas (1996:8) argues that 'the cause of exclusion is not the fundamental nature of capitalism (which never gets discussed) but the "contemporary economic and social conditions" that tend to exclude some groups from the cycle of opportunities'. The rapid economic changes brought about by the growth of the Celtic Tiger have led to the type of economic and social conditions that exclude certain groups and individuals, such as the uneducated, from Levitas' (1996) 'cycle of opportunities', and have thereby eroded their bases for self-respect.

It can be argued that with the growing income inequality in the Irish economy, social exclusion has become more prevalent than absolute poverty. The increase in relative poverty as a result of growing income inequality has taken away the bases of self-respect. This change in the socio-economic structure has resulted in an issue of social justice in Irish society throughout the period of rapid economic growth.

CONCLUSION

As has been shown, social justice from a Rawlsian perspective did not increase in Ireland during the growth of the Celtic Tiger. Is the New Ireland really better off because of the dramatic growth in GDP? It depends on whom you ask. When the author interviewed a top financial executive and member of one of Dublin's wealthiest families, he made it very clear that 'No one wants to talk about the losers' in the new economy, and proceeded to expound on the benefits for the winners (Ostwald 2000). The least advantaged were left out of the discussions, the 'losers' left behind in many regards, as has been shown in this analysis of social justice.

However, in 2007, the Irish government launched the National Action Plan for Social Exclusion 2007–2016: Building an Inclusive Society. This plan is based on an initiative for social policy developed by the ESRI that looks at relative poverty measures and deprivation of specific necessities of life related to food, clothing and shelter, as well as social needs (CSO 2006). These issues that constitute the bases of self-respect, one of Rawls' primary goods, were finally acknowledged from a policy perspective.

Perhaps the full range of issues concerning inequality and social justice will be addressed at the national policy level. The days of the Celtic Tiger are quickly becoming history as the business cycle has clearly taken a downward trend, with GDP growth rates falling into the negative range (OECD 2009). Economic pessimism is spreading across Europe, but when the business cycle turns the corner again and economic expansion returns, the Irish will have the opportunity to carefully manage the trade-off between economic growth and social justice. The question is, will they?

References

Bhalla, A.S. and Lapeyre, F. (1999) *Poverty and Social Exclusion in a Global World*. London: Macmillan Press.

Callan, T. and Nolan, B. (1999) 'Income Inequality in Ireland in the 1980s and 1990s', in F. Barry (ed.) *Understanding Ireland's Economic Growth*, pp.167–92. London: Macmillan.

Cantillon, S. and O'Shea, E. (2001) 'Social Expenditure, Redistribution and Participation', in S. Cantillon, C. Corrigan, P. Kirby and J. O'Flynn (eds) *Rich and Poor: Perspectives on Tackling Inequality in Ireland*, pp.81–110. Dublin: Oak Tree Press.

CSO (Central Statistics Office) (2006) *EU-SILC: European Union Survey on Income and Living Conditions*. Dublin: Stationery Office.

Daly, H. and Cobb, J. (1994) *For the Common Good*. Boston, MA: Beacon Press.

Edgren, J. A. (1995) 'On the Relevance of John Rawls' Theory of Justice to Welfare Economics', *Review of Social Economy* 53(3): 332–49.

FitzGerald, J. (2009) *Two Failures and a Success: Ireland 1970–2009*. Dublin: ESRI.

Layte, R. and Whelan, C.T. (2000) 'The Rising Tide and Equality of Opportunity: The Changing Class Structure', in B. Nolan, P. O'Connell and C.T. Whelan (eds) *Bust to Boom? The Irish Experience of Growth and Inequality*, pp. 90–108. Dublin: Institute of Public Administration.

— (2004) 'Economic Boom and Social Mobility: The Irish Experience', Working Paper 154. Dublin: ESRI.

Levitas, R. (1996) 'The Concept of Social Exclusion and the New Durkheimian Hegemony', *Critical Social Policy* 16(1): 5–20.

MacSharry, R. and White, P. (2000) *The Making of the Celtic Tiger: The Inside Story of Ireland's Boom Economy*. Dublin: Mercier Press.

McDermott, J. (2008) 'Funding Deficit Threatens our University's World Standing' *Irish Times*, 8 August, p. 2.

Munck, R. (1993) *The Irish Economy: Results and Prospects*. London: Pluto Press.

Nolan, B. and Maitre, B. (2008) 'Economic Growth and Income Inequality: Setting the Context' in T. Fahey, H. Russell, and C.T. Whelan (eds) *Quality of Life in Ireland: Social Impact of Economic Boom*, pp. 28–43. Amsterdam: Springer Publications.

Nolan, B., Whelan, C.T. and O'Connell, P. (2000) *Bust to Boom? The Irish Experience of Growth and Inequality*. Dublin: Institute of Public Administration.

Nozick, R. (1974) *Anarchy, State, and Utopia*. Oxford: Blackwell.

OECD (Organisation for Economic Co-operation and Development) (1999, 2003, 2006, 2008) *Economic Surveys of Ireland*. Paris: OECD.

— (2009) *Economic Outlook for Ireland*. Paris: OECD.

Ó Gráda, C. (1997) *A Rocky Road: The Irish Economy Since the 1920s*. Manchester: Manchester University Press.

O'Hagan, J.W. (ed.) (1995) *The Economy of Ireland: Policy and Performance of a Small European Country*, 6th edn. London: Macmillan Press.

O'Hearn, D. (1998) *Inside the Celtic Tiger: The Irish Economy and the Asian Model*. London: Pluto Press.

Ostwald, C. (2000) Personal interviews at Davy Stockbrokers. Dublin, 20 July.

Rawls, J. (1971) *A Theory of Justice*. Cambridge, MA: Harvard University Press.

— (1993) *Political Liberalism*. New York, NY: Columbia University Press.

Sen, A. (1973) *On Economic Inequality*. Oxford: Clarendon Press.

Smyth, E. and Hannan, C. (2000) 'Education and Inequality', in B. Nolan and P. O'Connell and C .T. Whelan (eds) *Bust to Boom: The Irish Experience of Growth and Inequality*, pp. 109–12. Dublin: IPA and ESRI.

Svallfors, S. (2005) *Analyzing Inequality: Life Chances and Social Mobility*. Stanford, CA: Stanford University Press.

Sweeney, P. (1999) *The Celtic Tiger: Ireland's Continuing Economic Miracle*. Dublin: Oak Tree Press.

Walker, A. and Walker, C. (1997) *Britain Divided: The Growth of Social Exclusion in the 1980s and 1990s*. London: Child Poverty Action Group.

Whelan, C.T. (1999) 'Social Mobility in Ireland in the 1990s: Evidence from the 1994 Living in Ireland Survey', *Economic and Social Review* 30(2): 133–58.

Whitehead, A.N. (1925) *Science and the Modern World*. New York, NY: Macmillan.

Wren, M. (1999) 'Government Turning a Blind Eye to the Truth about Poverty', *Irish Times*, 18 August, p. 26.

Section III

Partnership and Participation

The chapters comprising this section are concerned with the fact that business is done, policy making is performed, and disputes are resolved with people and groups who have contributions to make, rights to respect and emotions to manage. The contributors here examine the resulting partnerships and participations at various levels, in various settings and from a variety of perspectives.

John Hogan, in Chapter 13, analyses the politics of partnership at the national level. From the late 1950s, when the trade union movement was invited into the policy-making process by a government desperate to revive a sclerotic economy, to the emergence of partnership at the national level in response to the crises of the 1980s, the chapter examines how economic crises have led to changes in the trade union movement's influence on public policy.

Emerging from the framework of national social partnership agreements was the policy of enterprise-level partnership, which sought to extend the new-found levels of co-operation that had developed between the social partners at national level to the level of the local firm. In Chapter 14, Kevin O'Leary compares the competing employee voice strategies offered by human resource management on the one hand and the trade union movement on the other. Enterprise-level partnership as a third option is reviewed and its development is considered.

Chapter 15, by Jesse Norris, analyses four forms of partnership governance focused on combating social exclusion on a local area basis. The four forms – open method of co-ordination, County/City Development Boards (CDBs), Area Partnerships (APs), and the Revitalising Areas by Planning, Investment and Development (RAPID) programme – have all had positive effects on substantive policies and policy-making processes. However, they have also failed to bring about transformations in social inclusion policy or governance. The chapter argues that a more sophisticated governance architecture, and the abandonment of a conflict-averse approach to partnership, would improve effectiveness.

In Chapter 16, Olive McCarthy, Robert Briscoe and Michael Ward examine the co-operative approach to doing business and the structural characteristics of co-operatives. In Ireland, there is a range of very successful co-operative businesses in agriculture, finance, housing and community development. The authors argue that the co-operative approach holds out the promise of giving people, and society in general, ownership and control of the ways in which their needs are met.

Helen Chen and Patrick Phillips, in Chapter 17, explore the relationship between managers' emotional intelligence and conflict resolution in the workplace. Evidence from their own empirical work suggests that generalising too quickly that managers have to be disagreeably tough to succeed may underestimate the need for mastery of the emotions. They argue that in-depth analysis of the utility of particular components of emotional intelligence in specific situations is needed, if the potential of the approach is to be realised.

In Chapter 18 Mary Faulkner provides a guide to the complex regulatory framework and associated fora governing employee–employer relations. This offers a picture of the legal rights and duties that allow workplace partnerships and participation to be built, but that also constrains them and acts as the final resort when they fail.

The multidimensional nature of participation and partnership is revealed in this section of the book. The authors here have provided important challenges and insights for readers. These challenges and insights are needed as, whatever partnership arrangements are used, Irish business and society face a future requiring both co-ordination and co-operation between its various constituents.

Chapter 13

Economic Crises and the Changing Influence of the Irish Congress of Trade Unions on Public Policy

John Hogan

INTRODUCTION

Over the last half century, there has been a series of dramatic changes in the influence of the Irish Congress of Trade Unions (ICTU) on public policy. This chapter examines those changes, highlighting the circumstances under which they occurred and the kinds of influence the ICTU gained and lost as a result of its fluctuating fortunes.

By the late 1950s, the Irish economy was in serious difficulty and a mood of despair pervaded society. Into this environment came Seán Lemass, the new Taoiseach and leader of the largest party, Fianna Fáil. Lemass introduced new ideas on how to manage the economy and how to reform the country's relationship with the world. His ideas and influence transformed economic policies and had a profound influence on the role of trade unions in the formulation of public policy.

The growing economic openness of the 1960s produced incentives for new patterns of collective bargaining. Ireland had come to rely on foreign direct investment (FDI) to promote industrialisation and employment. In response, from the 1970s onwards, public policy was directed towards minimising strikes and restraining pay increases: 'the then Fianna Fáil government of Jack Lynch brought the trade union movement into the policy-making process as a way of ensuring economic stability' (Murphy and Hogan 2008:578).

However, by the early 1980s, the economy had deteriorated. Although centralised agreements between the employers, the government and the ICTU were the hallmark of industrial relations during the 1970s, they were not achieving the unions' objectives. This led to reluctance on the part of the ICTU to continue participating in these agreements. Irrespective of the unions' attitude, they were excluded from the policy-making environment by the Fine Gael and Labour coalition government (1982–1987) as economic decline gathered momentum.

By 1987, the economy had reached a historic nadir. In response, a new Fianna Fáil minority administration sought a centralised pay agreement with the ICTU and the employers, bringing the unions' influence directly back into the corridors of power. This was to be the first of a series of such agreements. The social partnership born of these agreements contributed to the transformation of society over the following decades.

This chapter is divided into four sections, each one of which deals with a particular period – the late 1950s–mid-1960s; mid-1960s–late 1970s; the early 1980s; and the late 1980s – that saw the ICTU's influence on public policy transformed. Each section begins with a discussion on the economy at that time and the impact that this had upon government thinking. Thereafter, the section moves on to examine how economic circumstances impacted upon the relations and interactions between the government and the trade union movement.

THE TRANSFORMATION OF THE TRADE UNIONS' ROLE IN SOCIETY (LATE 1950s–MID-1960s)

The trade union movement expanded with industrialisation in the 1930s (Boyd 1985:108). However, with industrialisation came inter-union rivalry. During the 1940s Seán Lemass, then Minister for Industry and Commerce, sought to encourage trade union rationalisation (McCarthy 1973:42). However, efforts to rationalise the unions created tensions that fissured the movement. In April 1945, fifteen Irish-based unions withdrew from the Irish Trades Union Congress (ITUC) and established the Congress of Irish Unions (CIU) (Nevin 1994:94). The existence of two rival congresses weakened the movement's efforts, dissipated resources and rendered a common front against employers impossible. However, in 1956 a Provisional United Trade Union Organisation was set up to co-ordinate the activities of both congresses, with a view to reunification.

The general election of 1957 resulted in a Fianna Fáil victory, and saw its seventy-five-year-old leader, Éamon de Valera, form his final administration. The year '1957 is conventionally thought of as the end of an era, marking the final exhaustion of the ideas of the first generation of political leaders' (Garvin 1982:37). Two years later, de Valera was succeeded as Taoiseach by Seán Lemass. Lemass, although almost sixty, and a lifelong follower of de Valera, was nevertheless to stand for a clean break with the policies of the past and was to oversee the opening of the country's economy. The transformative impact of his innovative leadership, upon a then poor and insular Ireland, was to constitute the foundations upon which modern Ireland is built.

The Economic Stagnation of the 1950s

From the late 1940s onwards, the Irish economy stagnated (Hillery 1980:46). Ó Gráda and O'Rourke (1995:214) argue that 'in the 1950s, Ireland's relative [economic] performance was disastrous, poorer than the European average'. The benefits from protection had been reaped by the industrial expansion of the 1930s. The post-war economic boom petered out at the end of the 1940s (Ó Gráda 1997:23). By the 1950s, Irish industry was supplying as much of the domestic market as it could.

Analysis by the Organisation for Economic Co-operation and Development (OECD) (1961:8) showed that agricultural production was abnormally low, while industrial output was faltering. Per capita gross national product (GNP) grew at 2.4 per cent throughout the 1950s, but only because of 'the exceptional demographic experience during this period when net migration averaged forty-one thousand persons a year' (OECD 1962:6). However, this growth rate was among the lowest in the OECD (OECD 1962:6). Although employment in the economy was falling, the cost of living was still high (*Irish Times* 1959a). The impact of these disastrous figures upon the populace at large cannot be underestimated.

> By the middle of the 1950s a serious crisis of confidence developed, caused by widespread anxiety that the performance of the economy was so poor the country was falling behind Western European standards, not only in productivity, but in the social benefits that productivity might confer. (Lyons 1973:618)

In 1957, manufacturing output was no higher than it had been in 1953, while building activity declined. Between 1951 and 1958, GDP rose by less than one per cent per annum, employment declined by 12 per cent, unemployment rose and half a million people emigrated (Haughton 1995). By the late 1950s, the outlook for the economy was depressing, while Europe was achieving strong and sustained growth (MacSharry and White 2001:14–19).

The Government's Response to the Economy

On his appointment as Minister for Industry and Commerce, in the new Fianna Fáil government of 1957, Lemass began implementing policies opening the state to foreign investment (Girvin 1994:125). Despite fears over the competitiveness of protected Irish industry, the pressure for change increased (DoF 1958a). By the end of the decade, both the government and the opposition recognised the crisis facing the country. During the Dáil debate on Lemass's nomination as Taoiseach, Daniel Desmond of the Labour Party argued that it was time for the political establishment to realise that solving the problems with the economy superseded their own struggles for power (*Irish Times* 1959b). On becoming Taoiseach in 1959, Lemass stated that the task was to consolidate the economic foundations of independence (*Irish Times* 1959c). He brought to government vigorous entrepreneurial leadership (McCarthy 1973:22).

The crisis in the economy prompted a fundamental reappraisal of the policies pursued up to that time. Into this pessimistic environment came T. K. Whitaker's report, *Economic Development*, in 1958. Whitaker, then secretary of the Department of Finance, was committed to export-led growth. He advanced a strategy within the finance department of more planning, fewer tariff barriers and greater emphasis on productive investment: 'It was in the atmosphere of a new government and a more active and interventionist Department of Finance, that *Economic Development* was born' (Murphy 2003:61).

This document was 'a watershed in the modern economic history of the country' (Lyons 1973:628). It proposed the gradual transition to free trade, stimulation of private investment, the reorientation of government investment towards more productive uses, the introduction of grants and tax concessions to encourage export-oriented manufacturing and the inducement of FDI-oriented manufacturers (DoF 1958b). The document advocated abandoning the protectionism Fianna Fáil had pioneered since the 1930s. These measures were incorporated into the First Programme for Economic Expansion in November 1958. This White Paper, based on Whitaker's document, 'was drawn up by Charles Murray of the Department of Finance, supervised by a four-member Government subcommittee headed by Lemass' (Horgan 1997:177). The fact that Lemass was involved in the White Paper ensured that the essence of *Economic Development's* recommendations remained intact:

> While there were some significant differences between *Economic Development* and the [First] *Programme for Economic Expansion*, which arose out of their different parentage, such differences were for the most part cosmetic as the main thrust of both documents was the same. (Murphy 2003:72)

The ICTU Brought in from the Cold

The ITUC and CIU eventually reunited after fifteen years apart. The absence of ideological and organisational differences between the congresses made the process of reunification easier. Additionally, the existence of two separate congresses had only weakened the trade union movement as a whole. Thus, February 1959 saw the ITUC and CIU unite to form the ICTU (Nevin 1994:96). Trade union unity provided Lemass with an opportunity to embark on national bargaining on wages policy, as there was now a chance that the unions and employers could be brought together in a new framework to achieve industrial progress without disputes (Horgan 1997:190).

Soon after Lemass became Taoiseach he sought a meeting with the ICTU to discuss the challenges facing the economy and how co-operation might be fostered between the various economic interests (Girvin 1994:125). The number of meetings between the new Taoiseach and the unions increased thereafter (ICTU 1960), whereas there had been little interaction with de Valera (ICTU 1959).

These meetings covered a range of issues, from the economy to the prospects of Ireland joining the European Economic Community (EEC). This development was in line with the calls for consultation between state, unions and employers contained in the First Programme for Economic Expansion (DoF 1958c).

The Fianna Fáil government's 1958 and 1959 budgets reflected a change in fiscal policy (OECD 1961:12). Lemass's speeches in 1959 often paralleled the positions adopted by the ICTU (Girvin 1994:125). These included the need for state involvement in development and the expansion of the state sector (Dáil Debates, vol. 176, 21 July 1959). The ICTU argued that the government should pump-prime the economy for growth and that capital investment should not be pursued to the detriment of social spending (ICTU 1959). Within a year of Lemass becoming Taoiseach, budgets began expanding (DoF 1960, 1961, 1962), with increased investment in areas identified by Congress (DoT 1959). By 1961, the reshaping of public capital expenditure, to give increased emphasis to directly productive investment, something for which the trade unions had argued, stimulated economic growth. A policy of grants and tax exemptions attracted foreign capital (OECD 1961:10) and the government also pursued an increasingly liberal trade policy (OECD 1962:12).

The Unions and their Role in Policy Development

Until the 1950s, the unions' influence was largely indirect (Allen 1997:181). However, during the late 1950s, the government's policies began to reflect those of the unions. Lemass's perspective on economic development was close to that of Congress. In June 1959, Lemass remarked on the need for change in industrial development policy (Dáil Debates, vol. 175, 3 June 1959). The government began to regard the trade union movement in general, and the united Congress in particular, as both an ally and supporter of its programme for national development (McCarthy 1980:32). The task of adjusting industries to competition led public policy into the realms of labour practices, industrial relations and pay bargaining. In return, Lemass was prepared to offer the unions an integral part in the development of economic and social programmes (McCarthy 1980:32):

> He [Lemass] clearly understood that the government would have to play a more active, even hegemonic, role in the Irish economy, but he also realised that the success of government strategy assumed a new partnership with different interest groups, which would (in time) become players in the policy game. (Murphy 1997:58)

In 1961, the ICTU and the Federated Union of Employers (FUE) reached agreement on the formation of the Employer–Labour Conference (ELC), which the government subsequently facilitated (ICTU 1961). This body became central to corporatist control (Lalor 1982:80). The unions' increasing influence was visible in all areas of government policy. For instance, the 1961 budget saw increases in social welfare payments at the behest of Congress (DoF 1961; ICTU 1961).

Lemass argued that social progress would follow from economic development (Bew et al. 1989:83). With the move towards the liberalisation of trade and economic planning, Lemass was instrumental in creating consultative bodies involving the unions and employers (Lee 1989:401). This was government recognition of the importance of unions to economic management and provided the ICTU with more avenues through which to influence policy.

Union membership, declining throughout the 1950s, increased after 1959 and would go on rising for the next 21 years (see Table 13.1 at the end of this chapter). After 1959, the number of committees on which the ICTU was represented expanded. The Irish National Productivity Committee (INPC) was a joint consultative body charged with improving productivity (ICTU 1963). The Committee on Industrial Organisation (CIO) was set up in 1961 to examine the ability of Irish industry to compete within the EEC (Murphy 1997:62). The National Industrial Economic Council (NIEC) was established in 1963 as a consultative body in economic planning (ICTU 1964). These bodies, paralleling 'the state's commitment to economic planning as contained in the first two programmes for economic expansion' (Girvin 1994:127), permitted the unions to co-operate with the state on a range of problems posed by economic expansion. Thus, the period between 1959 and 1965 witnessed a new pattern of Congress participation in state institutions (Girvin 1994:127), such that '[t]he institutional setting soon became largely tripartite, with the representatives of business, of labour and of government discussing the issues of employment, output, prices and trade' (Pratschke 1979:43).

THE MOVE TO CENTRALISED BARGAINING (MID-1960s– LATE 1970s)

In the 1960s, the economy performed well, real gross domestic product (GDP) increased by 4.4 per cent per annum, economic openness grew by 23 per cent, while unemployment averaged 5.05 per cent (Mitchell 1993). Economists attribute this success to export-led growth based upon trade liberalisation and FDI.

The Institutionalisation of the ICTU/Government Relationship

Congress's attitude to EEC entry was initially cautious, but by 1962 it was willing to support Lemass's plans. Congress, recognising free trade as inevitable, decided to embrace it from a position of influence with the government through membership of the CIO and NIEC (Murphy 1997:65). Dialogue between the state and major socio-economic groups acquired an institutional character (Peillon

1995:370). However, the limitations of relying on a web of collaborative bodies to oversee economic adjustment, while collective bargaining remained unregulated, became clear (Roche 1994:155).

The government's attitude towards collective bargaining was influenced by its increasing economic significance (Roche 1994:199). As more workers became unionised (see Table 13.1 at the end of the chapter), bargaining exerted a major influence on macroeconomic policies. Industrial development's pride of place in national policy influenced the government's stance towards centralised collective bargaining.

Lemass had urged a corporatist strategy towards industrial relations following the Second World War. Corporatism (or, as it is sometimes called, neo-corporatism) is an inclusive bargaining approach involving the unions, employers and government (Schmitter and Lehmbruch 1979). However, the employers' and unions' preference for the status quo – free collective bargaining – prevented the introduction of corporatism. As Roche (1994:220) puts it, 'The eventual move towards some form of neo-corporatist accommodation with unions and employers was influenced initially by the policy of industrialisation in the context of an open economy.'

The pay rounds of the 1960s prompted attempts to again centralise collective bargaining. Growing trade union power, rising industrial conflict and wage pressures impelled governments to adopt a more interventionist stance. The dangers of economic crisis from industrial unrest and an unprecedented pay-round increase in 1969 were the catalysts for the move towards corporatism. This resulted in the unions' influence over public policy increasing substantially. Throughout the following decade, pay determination became increasingly politicised and public policy was directed towards minimising strikes and restraining pay.

Economic Stagnation at the Beginning of the 1970s

Economic expansion and decentralised collective bargaining were viewed as incompatible in the NIEC's (1970) *Report on Incomes and Prices Policy*. To compound matters, economic growth slowed (OECD 1971:5). Statistics for output, employment, imports and sales all indicated a stagnating economy (ESRI 1970:1). Industrial production and construction activities were affected by strikes, while investment was depressed by a six-month bank strike (Central Bank of Ireland 1970:5). Inflation was running at 8.5 per cent, its highest level since 1952 (*The Economist* 1970:80). The OECD (1971:5) argued that the high level of inflation was due partly to the labour disputes. The Central Bank warned that the penalty for high and prolonged inflation would be declining sales, followed by a fall in production and employment (Central Bank of Ireland 1971:7). The improvements in living standards in the 1960s were in danger of being lost to inflation (Devine 1970). At this time, economic openness declined, while the total number of days lost through economic disputes peaked at over one million (Mitchell 1993).

The Government's Deepening Relations with the Unions

'The chief lesson emerging from the operation of collective bargaining in the 1960s was that decentralised wage rounds were by their nature unstable and prone to inflation' (Gunnigle *et al.* 1999:193). The government's economic policy, traditionally geared to long-term growth and industrialisation targets, from 1969 became increasingly concerned with inflation (OECD 1971:5). Demand and output were depressed by the government's anti-inflationary policy and the recession in the United Kingdom (UK) (OECD 1973:5). The combination of relatively slow growth, inflation and a large external deficit in 1970 presented a dilemma. As prices became a primary concern, budgetary strategy was aimed at moderating government spending so as not to contribute to inflation (OECD 1972:15). In response, the government's policies towards organised labour changed.

The NIEC (1970) viewed economic expansion and decentralised collective bargaining as incompatible. The 1970 budget argued, 'the principal need at present is for a more orderly development of incomes if we are to bring the present inflationary situation under control' (DoF 1970:12). Another lesson from the 1960s was the need for a joint body to administer national pay agreements (NIEC 1970). It was against this background of industrial strife and economic difficulties that the NIEC prepared its *Report on Incomes and Prices Policy*. A consequence was the reconstitution in May 1970 of the ELC (which had become defunct during the early 1960s), a significant event in restructuring the adversarial approach to industrial relations (McGinley and Filby 1997:202). The government became a participant in the ELC with the intention of influencing wages. Then Minister for Finance, George Colley, stated that the economy could not afford wage increases unrelated to productivity increases (*Irish Independent* 1970:11). Following the collapse of talks at the ELC in the autumn of 1970, the government threatened statutory controls on wages and salaries with a Prices and Incomes Bill (OECD 1971:16).

The threatened bill resulted in the first national agreement for six years in December 1970; this in spite of the ICTU's opposition to being coerced into a deal and its advocacy of free collective bargaining (Weinz 1986:98). However, it should be noted that the ICTU refused to ratify the agreement until the government withdrew its Prices and Incomes Bill (ICTU 1971). The 1970 agreement marked the beginning of a decade of engagement in centralised collective bargaining, a significant change in the politics of pay determination (DoF 1971). Between 1972 and 1978, six National Wage Agreements (NWAs) were reached through bipartite negotiations between the ICTU and employers. A further two agreements reached in 1979 and 1980, referred to as National Understandings (NUs), were arrived at through tripartite negotiation with the involvement of the government.

By the mid-1970s, the new collective bargaining was marked by quid pro quo arrangements on taxation between the unions and the state and the integration of government budgetary policy into national pay determination. The linkage between the national pay agreements and government budgetary policy was 'the most profound change in the nature, functions and prerogatives of democratic government in the history of the state' (O'Brien 1981:144). With active state involvement in industrial relations came union involvement in policy making. The relationship between the ICTU, the FUE and the government had changed significantly.

Trade Union Representation and Government Policies

According to Roche (1989:121), following the 1970 agreement the boundary between politics and industrial relations was dismantled by the state and unions. ICTU representation on government committees, in the economic and social fields, expanded. All centralised pay agreements were drafted and concluded by employer and trade union representatives in the reconstituted ELC and thereafter adopted as state policy (Hardiman 1988:53). Membership of the ELC consisted of an equal number of representatives from the employers and unions. The institutionalisation of pay bargaining through the ELC enhanced the political leverage of Congress.

The 1970s saw union membership expand (see Table 13.1 at the end of this chapter). Throughout that decade the unions' and employers' federations became major actors in policy formulation. Meetings between representatives of the social partners (as the unions and employers came to be called) and ministers were commonplace. From 1970 onwards, there was a marked change in the level of ICTU policies incorporated into the government's policies. The Industrial Relations Act of 1971 largely followed the proposals of the ICTU, and the National Prices Commission was established by the then Minister for Industry and Commerce in line with Congress's proposals (ICTU 1972). The NWA of 1975, although concluded without establishing the principle of a trade-off between pay and public policy commitments, created a degree of expectation that the NWAs and budgets to follow would be linked. By the end of the 1970s, formal tripartite agreements were concluded. The government went from using budgetary policy to underwrite national pay deals, to placing a range of policy issues on the negotiation table. The ICTU, through dialogue with the government, gained influence over the most important economic policy instruments in the state (Roche 1994:165).

Industrial relations difficulties – attributed to the wage round system and free collective bargaining – along with inflation, the loss of competitiveness and industrial conflict, impelled the centralisation of collective bargaining (Roche 1994:177). With the conclusion of the NU in 1979, the government acknowledged a new role for pressure groups in an important sector of economic policy making and incurred commitments to them; they, in turn, incurred reciprocal obligations involving the conduct of their members (Chubb 1992:127). However, by 1978, the ICTU had grown strong due to the state's willingness to grant it concessions. This became clear in 1980, when the main decisions concerning the second NU were taken by the ICTU and government before being communicated to the employers (Weinz 1986:99). This left the employers disgruntled and questioning their place in social partnership.

THE COLLAPSE OF CENTRALISED BARGAINING (EARLY 1980s)

By the close of the 1970s, centralised agreements had become policy agreements. However, by the time the second NU expired in 1981, the unions and employers were disillusioned. The sought-after economic stability had not materialised. Unemployment continued to rise, despite commitments to full employment. The national debt was growing at an unsustainable rate, while the onset of another international recession offered the prospect of worsening conditions.

The Economy Crisis and Economic Policy

The centralised agreements implemented as solutions to the economic and industrial relations problems of the 1960s were increasingly relied upon to address the problems of the 1970s (Hardiman 1992:329). The late 1970s saw the economy recover from the downturn following the 1973 oil crisis. Inflation and unemployment began to fall, while strong growth returned (Leddin and Walsh 1998:26). Real GDP increased by 5.3 per cent annually from 1976 to 1979 (OECD 1982:8). However, the Fianna Fáil government of 1977 employed an expansionist fiscal policy when the economy was already growing unsustainably (OECD 1982:10). Strong pro-cyclical policies led to deterioration in fiscal balances, with the public sector borrowing requirement (PSBR) rising from 13 per cent of GNP in 1976 to 17 per cent by 1979. The structural problems highlighted by the first oil crisis remained unresolved when the second crisis struck in 1979 (OECD 1983).

Adjustment to the European Monetary System (EMS), entered in 1979 after severing the link with sterling to reduce inflation, proved problematic and inflation fell more slowly in Ireland than in the UK. The average rate of consumer price increase in 1980 was 18.25 per cent (Central Bank of Ireland 1981:15). Although high levels of current expenditure produced a budgetary over-run in 1979, the government continued its expansionary policies due to the worsening international economic climate resulting from the second oil crisis and the increasing level of unemployment (OECD 1982:50).

Following rapid growth in the second half of the 1970s, demand fell in the early 1980s. 'The second oil shock, the protracted international recession and the failure to achieve the fiscal policy of retrenchment led to a worsening of [economic] imbalances' (OECD 1983:10). With a slowdown in growth, unemployment rose to historic levels (OECD 1982:10). The increase in fiscal deficit, intended to be temporary, became impossible to eliminate as the economy declined. By 1981, the national debt reached £10.195bn (Leddin and Walsh 1998:155–6). The PSBR peaked at 20.1 per cent of GNP, while the current budget deficit stood at 7.3 per cent (Leddin and O'Leary 1995:167). Government spending was so high that the total amount budgeted for 1981 had been used by June (Bacon *et al.* 1982:6).

The Unions and the Ending of the National Agreements

New taoiseach Charles Haughey, who came to power after winning a divisive party leadership contest within Fianna Fáil in December 1979, needed to prove his authority to a divided party with an election victory (Murphy and Hogan 2008:591). In this context, the government was reluctant to adopt measures that could prove unpopular. In September 1980, as talks on a second NU entered their final stages, they collapsed, resulting in government intervention. 'The Taoiseach managed to press the FUE national executive into resuming negotiations by pledging guarantees on the content of the 1981 budget' (Lalor 1982:83). The second NU was subsequently ratified, but the FUE resented the pressure placed upon it (O'Brien 1981:154).

Centralised bargaining was not meeting the FUE's objectives. For employers, particularly in indigenous companies in exposed sectors, the agreements imposing similar wage norms across the economy undermined competitiveness. For the unions, the agreements were not transforming pay restraint into jobs at a sufficient level to meet the labour supply, nor were they reducing social inequality. The state looked to the agreements to restrain pay increases, preserve competitiveness and deliver economic growth. However, these objectives were compromised by extensive bargaining below national level. The result was a second tier of pay determination developed in the 1970s (Fogarty *et al.* 1981:32). Although the agreements had procedures for containing industrial conflict, this was historically high during the 1970s (Brannick and Doyle 1994:260–161).

Irish governments have tended to appease interest groups through ad hoc policy concessions. This worked against enduring agreements between the state and interest groups found in continental neo-corporatism. Additionally, close ideological affinity between the unions and government, a feature of stable neo-corporatist arrangements, was absent in Ireland. The social partners' failure to share similar views on the policies needed for tackling economic problems compounded the difficulties. Employers warned that spiralling wages fuelled inflation and contributed to rising unemployment. The unions argued that unemployment was a consequence of deficient demand. Their solution was expansionary fiscal policy. Employers resisted the demands for public sector job creation on the grounds that it would have a crowding-out effect. These divergent approaches complicated the process of reaching a national pay agreement. Although talks opened on a new NU in 1981, an impasse on pay was soon encountered (ICTU 1981).

Political and Economic Instability

The general election of 1981 saw a minority Fine Gael and Labour coalition government come to power. At a most inopportune time, Ireland was condemned to a period of unstable government (*Irish Times* 1981:12).

Prior to the election, the Central Bank (1982:8) stated the 'fundamental problem is that the community still does not realise that it must adjust its living standards and expectations downwards in the face of deteriorating terms of trade and the need to commit resources to servicing the increased external debt'. The new coalition government was determined to bring order to the public finances. According to the National Economic and Social Council (NESC) (1986:43), a spiralling current budget deficit, PSBR and national debt precipitated a new approach to economic management. Regaining control of the public finances would entail constraining public service pay (FitzGerald 1991:385). The supplementary budget, in July 1981, sought to reduce the central government borrowing requirement and the balance of payments deficit (ESRI 1981:15).

Government ministers saw little merit in tripartite agreements (Redmond 1985). When discussions on a new NU broke down, the government was unwilling to intervene to save the talks. It considered the terms under consideration incompatible with economic correction. Unrealised expectations and undelivered commitments ended national bargaining. From late 1981 onwards, with worsening economic conditions, wage rounds became decentralised (Cox 1983). By 1982, all political parties were committed to curbing public spending, which was incompatible with the terms of the NUs. Union influence on public policy was drastically reduced during the first half of the 1980s, as the ICTU was pushed out of the policy-making process. The Fine Gael wing of the coalition decided that social partners had no right to influence policy (O'Brien 1982:1).

Political and economic instability peaked in 1981–1982 (Mjøset 1992:381). With the national debt and budget deficit spiralling out of control, a coherent policy approach was essential (CSO 1986:298). However, the governments of 1981/1982 lasted such a short time that no clear policies emerged. When the second Fine Gael–Labour coalition came to power in November 1982, the national debt was almost on par with GNP (Leddin and Walsh 1998). By then, all the parties agreed on the need to stabilise the debt/GNP ratio (Mjøset 1992:381).

The state's strategy for much of the 1980s was to exclude the unions from the policy-making process (Roche 1994:172). State policy changed from focusing on employment to balancing budgets, export growth and international competitiveness. Persistent turbulence over public service pay, and government disinclination to return to tripartism, meant meetings between the government and the ICTU were formal, tense and unproductive (FitzGerald 1991:454).

The Changed Influence of the Unions

After expanding for two decades, union membership peaked at 545,200 in 1980 and then declined thereafter (see Table 13.1 at the end of this chapter). During the late 1970s, the unions' polices had been finding their way into legislation. However, by January 1982, the ICTU was at loggerheads with the Fine Gael–Labour coalition over their budget. Determined to cut government expenditures, the subsequent Fianna Fáil government ignored ICTU proposals (Dáil Debates, vol. 363, 6 February 1986). The Fine Gael–Labour coalition budget of February 1983 saw the tax burden on pay as you earn (PAYE) workers increase and social welfare cut (DoF 1983). Thereafter, it was clear that on taxes, wages and welfare, the government and the ICTU were in disagreement. Between 1982 and 1987, the ICTU's relations with the Labour Party grew strained (Collins 1993). The party's shared responsibility for government spending cuts distanced it from the ICTU.

The coalition government of November 1982 to February 1987 experienced considerable difficulties in righting the economy (O'Byrnes 1986:219). As McCarthy (1999:5) put it, 'an attempt to achieve fiscal correction and disinflation through increased taxation, rather than expenditure reduction, completed the economic picture'. However, the stabilisation of the debt required sharp cuts in borrowing and, consequently, in current spending. Control over current spending proved difficult to achieve with high unemployment and population growth. Government spending on social services jumped from 28.9 per cent of GNP in 1980 to 35.6 per cent in 1985 (Leddin and Walsh 1998:302). As noted by Kennedy (1981:140), 'the inescapable consequence of sustained heavy borrowing to finance expenditure which does not contribute adequately to developing productive potential is that the service of past borrowing absorbs a large and growing proportion of tax revenue'. With investment and productivity capacity depressed by high taxes and interest rates, the economy entered a downward spiral.

THE REINSTITUTION OF CENTRALISED BARGAINING (LATE 1980s)

The 1980s saw a stagnating economy, deteriorating public finances and unprecedented unemployment. By the mid-1980s, the level of unemployment was being offset by emigration (OECD 1986:12). Between 1981 and 1986, 75,000 people left the country (NESC 1986:304), and, for the first time in a quarter of a century, 1986 saw the population decrease (Munck 1993:37). By 1987, the economy reached its lowest point ever.

The State of the Economy

By 1986, most economic indicators had reached historic lows, while national economic and political commentators, the media and domestic and international organisations all regarded the economy to be in crisis. The policies introduced to shelter the economy from the oil shocks of the 1970s led to unsustainable macroeconomic imbalances. Between 1982 and 1987, the national debt doubled to over 130 per cent of GNP (Jacobsen 1994:161). The government borrowed to spend on welfare services that could be sustained only by more borrowing (*The Economist* 1987:53). Economic commentators advocated debt repudiation (*Irish Times* 1987a). Although inflation had fallen, the borrowing requirement stood at 13 per cent of GNP in 1986 (Jacobsen 1994:160). Unemployment reached 17.7 per cent in 1987 (Daly 1994:122), with 254,526 people out of work (CSO 1991). The numbers in work had fallen from 1,145,000 in 1979 to 1,095,100 by 1986, shrinking the tax base (Leddin and Walsh 1998:320).

The Central Bank (1987:7) viewed the situation with pessimism, as it would not permit for improvements in welfare benefits to the needy (O'Morain 1987:8). The business community was extremely concerned and leading businessman and entrepreneur Tony O'Reilly warned of the dangers of International Monetary Fund (IMF) intervention in the economy (Keenan 1987:8). If the IMF were to intervene in the operation of the Irish economy, it would signal to the international financial community the diminution of Irish economic sovereignty and be widely perceived as confirmation that the Irish government was incapable of righting the economy on its own.

The NESC Report: A Strategy for Development

In this context, the government became interested in building support among the economic and social interests for a national recovery strategy. Through the involvement of the major economic interests, the NESC acted as a forum for discussing the crisis. In the autumn of 1986, it produced a report, *A Strategy for Development, 1986–1990*, in which it noted that '[t]he argument against a continuation of present policies is based on the consideration that discretion over economic and social policy would ultimately be removed from [Irish] control' (NESC 1986:304).

The NESC report emphasised a plan, requiring an integrated medium-term strategy, that would command acceptance throughout society to tackle the crisis in public expenditure. The report was conceived as a means of supporting the coalition government's recovery plans. While still in opposition, Fianna Fáil proposed building on the NESC's report and its 1987 manifesto, *The Programme for National Recovery*, absorbed much of *A Strategy for Development* (Breen *et al.* 1990:220).

The 1987 General Election

By 1986, Fianna Fáil, in opposition, was aware that the unions were disillusioned with the government, especially the Labour Party (Allen 1997:169). In the absence of political links, the union movement faced the prospect of continued marginalisation from policy debates. Spotting an opportunity, Fianna Fáil sought to woo the unions through its willingness to involve them in policy discussions if elected to government. It did not regard the arm's-length dealings with the unions employed by the coalition government as ideal for imposing fiscal discipline upon the troubled economy. Haughey (1986) also denounced the Thatcherite policies of the Fine Gael–Labour government, supporting the calls of union leaders for a return to social partnership.

Labour Party ministers struggled in cabinet to maintain social benefits (NESC 1990:199), imposing considerable strains on the coalition (FitzGerald 1991:640). Yet the Labour ministers' stance had not made their relationship with the unions easier (Collins 1993). The coalition government collapsed in 1987, when Labour resigned in disagreement over budget cuts (Mjøset 1992:382).

The election of 1987 saw all party leaders proposing fiscal rectitude (Ford 1987:2). The Fine Gael election manifesto, *Breaking out of the Vicious Circle*, proposed reduced public spending and borrowing (Fine Gael 1987). Fianna Fáil campaigned on a platform of opposition to cuts in social spending and advocated a return to centralised pay agreements.

The election saw a shift of urban working-class support towards Fianna Fáil, in protest at the harshness of the measures proposed by the coalition (Laver *et al*. 1987:104). The new Fianna Fáil minority administration was considered likely to want to avoid the risks of implementing severe spending cuts. However, after Haughey visited the Department of Finance for a briefing on the national finances, Fianna Fáil recanted on its manifesto promises (O'Halpin 1993: 202), making it clear that it proposed little modification to the outgoing government's plans (Carnegy 1987:2). The budget introduced in March 1987 sought greater fiscal adjustment than had been achieved in preceding years. This marked a clear shift in policy emphasis and a determination to reduce the deficit (OECD 1989:16). Expenditure was reduced by £250m, while tax revenue increased by £117m (OECD 1987:21).

The Unions and the Programme for National Recovery

The new government's actions appeared unpromising from the ICTU's perspective. However, Fianna Fáil wanted to avoid confrontation with the unions, especially in the public service. Within a few months of assuming office the government promoted talks on a national pay agreement – the Programme for National Recovery (PNR) – in accordance with the principles in the NESC report (Jacobsen 1994:177). The administration was interested in securing a three-year tripartite agreement throughout the economy (Allen 1997:170). 'The Taoiseach invited the unions, along with the other social partners, to take part in an effort to spur recovery by means of consensus' (Mjøset 1992:383). To facilitate agreement, the government was willing to modify its stance on public service pay and discuss tax concessions, job creation and welfare (Coghlan 1987:1).

By supporting a centralised pay agreement for industrial peace and union commitment to spending cuts (*Irish Times* 1987b:6), Fianna Fáil revealed a preference for defusing, rather than inflaming, industrial conflict and for seeking union support, rather than excluding them from policy deliberations (Hardiman 1988:237). By 1987, the unions favoured a return to centralised pay determination (Roche 1994:180). The prospects of agreement on a moderate pay rise, combined with tight control over second-tier bargaining, also drew in the employers.

The union movement entered negotiations in a weaker position than it had occupied in the 1970s. Although the unions had not been consulted on policy by the coalition government, they still possessed leverage in the Dáil with the Labour Party and Fianna Fáil. However, with Fine Gael now in opposition and operating under its Tallaght Strategy of not opposing the government's measures to revive the economy, many of which had ironically been proposed by Fine Gael in the run-up to the election, the unions had few options besides doing a deal (MacSharry and White 2001:75).

Talks were built on the NESC (1986) report. The ICTU executive argued that the PNR would prevent Ireland going down the Thatcherite road, which had utterly marginalised the UK Trades Union Congress (TUC) (Allen 1997:170). Thus, the PNR restored social partnership, as well as bringing considerable benefits for capitalism (Allen 1997:169). The PNR resembled the NUs in scope, but not content. The central issue was an agreement on wages in the public and private sectors for three years. However, the PNR, and its successor agreements, also encompassed a wide range of economic/social policy commitments on job creation and welfare benefits. Unlike the situation in the 1970s, these agreements were based on shared understanding of the problems facing the economy and the policies required to address them (NESC 1996:14).

The Unions and Policy Developments

Following the recommendations of the NESC (1986), the government's objective was to reduce the debt/GNP ratio to a sustainable level. The change in government economic policy, first encapsulated in its March 1987 budget, as a determination to reduce the deficit, was elaborated in the PNR. In contrast with earlier attempts, the targets for 1987 were achieved. Subsequent budgets were designed in harmony with the PNR and the agreements thereafter (DoF 1988, 1989, 1990) and they provided for implementation of policies into which the unions had direct input.

Three joint government–ICTU working parties – on employment and development measures, taxation, and social policy – were established and chaired by the Secretary of the Department of the Taoiseach. More committees were formed following subsequent national agreements (ICTU 1988). A ministerial–ICTU group also met monthly to review progress (ICTU 1988). The unions had secured input into policy making through their position as an essential constituency with rights of representation on state boards, committees and policy forums.

From 1987 onwards, Congress policies on pay, tax and social welfare found their way into government policy. Ireland had embarked on a tripartite approach to income policy (von Prondzynski 1992:82), marking 'a fundamental change in [the] approach to social partnership between that practised up to the early 1980s and that practised from 1987 onwards' (Teahon 1997:53). The agreements of the 1980s and 1990s were not confined to wages, but encompassed a range of socio-economic policies. The focus of these agreements was economic stability, greater equity in the tax system and enhanced social justice, with the result that 'in the decade after 1987, interest group activity in Ireland attained centre stage, with the tripartite agreements of the 1990s cementing social partnership' (Murphy 1999:291). Ireland's political economy shifted from a British towards a European mode of consensus between social partners. 'These arrangements re-established a reciprocal relationship between Congress, the government, and employers on a much stronger institutional footing than heretofore' (Girvin 1994:130).

Social partnership continued to function up until the collapse of talks on a new national agreement in 2008, as a new economic crisis took hold. It remains to be seen whether Ireland will witness a return to the decentralised collective bargaining of the early 1980s, or if the social partnership arrangements can be revived. In this respect, the current situation in some ways mirrors conditions in 1981. This decision will have huge implications for the role of trade unions in Irish society, and for the performance of the economy, over the coming decade.

CONCLUSION

This chapter examined the four periods in which the trade union movement's influence over Irish public policy changed dramatically during the latter half of the twentieth century. In each of these cases, extant economic circumstances had a significant role to play. Thus, the unions' changing influence was examined in the context of the broader Irish political economy.

The 1950s was a depressing decade. However, after Lemass came to power in 1959, the Fianna Fáil administration sought to open the economy to competition and FDI. Lemass regarded trade union involvement as critical in this attempt to revive the economy. As a result, ICTU access to the Taoiseach, representation on government committees, government economic policies and policies towards organised labour changed in the unions' favour.

Fear that industrial unrest might frighten off FDI led to centralised collective bargaining between the state, unions and employers throughout the 1970s. The NWAs and, later, NUs provided the ICTU with unprecedented access to government, its policies and their formulation. These centralised collective bargaining arrangements were linked to government budgets. Thus, the state came to play a role in industrial relations, in return for which the unions gained influence over economic policy. By the end of the 1970s, wage agreements were being concluded in a tripartite context.

The early 1980s were a time of economic turmoil and political instability. The national agreements of the 1970s, a solution to the industrial relations problems of the late 1960s, were no longer addressing the needs of the economy. The employers had become disillusioned with the agreements' failure to control wage inflation, while the unions felt pay restraint was not resulting in job creation. In 1981, the government abandoned centralised bargaining, as it sought to bring public spending under control. As a consequence, the ICTU was excluded from directly influencing policy.

By 1987, with the country on the verge of bankruptcy and unemployment at almost 20 per cent, the political establishment recognised the need for a new consensual approach to the economy (Tansey 1998). A new Fianna Fáil administration, building on an NESC (1986) report and determined to impose fiscal discipline, sought to involve the unions in policy consultation to avoid the dangers of open confrontation. For the weakened ICTU, fearful of permanent marginalisation, the prospect of reinstituted centralised bargaining was a welcome lifeline. The unions saw this as an opportunity to regain influence over taxation, unemployment and social welfare policy. From 1987 onwards, a tripartite approach to managing the economy developed, wherein the social partnership agreements encompassed a range of economic and social issues. The ICTU, through involvement on numerous committees and working parties, secured an input into state policies that endured up to 2008.

However, with the collapse of social partnership in 2008, a large question mark hangs over the whole process. If the impact of the current recession was sufficient to collapse the social partnership process, this raises questions as to the underlying strength of the agreements. Did Irish social partnership hold together from 1987 onwards because of an underlying societal commitment to what the agreements represented? Or, did partnership exist primarily due to a very favourable set of economic circumstance that, once ended, made it an unsustainable proposition? The answer to these questions will determine the future of Irish social partnership, and that of the wider political economy, over the next decade.

Table 13.1 Level of trade union membership (1957–1961; 1968–1972; 1979–1983; 1985–1989)

Year	Membership	Annual Rate of Change (%)	Employment Density (%)	Workforce Density (%)
1957	308,200	-2.5	46.5	42.3
1958	306,800	-0.4	46.9	42.4
1959	313,700	+2.2	47.9	43.7
1960	325,500	3.8	50.2	45.8
1961	335,600	+3.1	52.4	48.2
1968	389,800	+3.2	55.1	50.8
1969	409,200	+5.0	57.0	52.9
1970	424,100	+3.6	59.1	54.2
1971	427,100	+0.7	59.2	54.5
1972	433,900	+1.6	59.5	54.4
1979	534,200	+4.2	63.9	57.8
1980	545,200	+2.1	63.5	57.4
1981	542,200	-0.4	62.9	54.9
1982	536,900	-0.9	62.4	53.2
1983	530,400	-1.1	63.5	52.1
1985	501,500	-3.1	62.5	48.8
1986	482,700	-3.7	59.0	46.1
1987	468,600	-2.8	57.5	44.8
1988	470,500	+0.40	57.7	45.4
1989	476,800	+1.3	58.8	47.1

Sources: Bean (1989); DUES (2004); Ebbinghaus and Visser (1999).

References

Allen, K. (1997) *Fianna Fáil and Irish Labour: 1926 to the Present.* London: Pluto Press.

Bacon, P., Durkan, J. and O'Leary, J. (1982) *The Irish Economy: Policy and Performance 1972–1981.* Dublin: ESRI.

Bean, R. (1989) *International Labour Statistics: A Handbook, Guide, and Recent Trends*. London: Routledge.

Bew, P., Hazelkorn, E. and Patterson, H. (1989) *The Dynamics of Irish Politics*. London: Lawrence and Wishart.

Boyd, A. (1985) *The Rise of the Irish Trade Unions*. Dublin: Anvil Books.

Brannick, T. and Doyle, L. (1994) 'Industrial Conflict', in T.V. Murphy and W.K. Roche (eds) *Irish Industrial Relations in Practice*, pp. 251–75. Dublin: Oak Tree Press.

Breen, R., Hannan, D.F., Rottman, D.B. and Whelan, C.T. (1990) *Understanding Contemporary Ireland: State, Class, and Development in the Republic of Ireland*. London: Macmillan.

Carnegy, H. (1987) 'Ireland's Budget Aims to Bolster Public Finances', *Financial Times*, 1 April, p. 2.

Central Bank of Ireland (1970) *Quarterly Bulletin*, Autumn. Dublin: Central Bank of Ireland.

— (1971) *Quarterly Bulletin*, Autumn. Dublin: Central Bank of Ireland.

— (1981) *Annual Report*. Dublin: Central Bank of Ireland.

— (1982) *Annual Report*. Dublin: Central Bank of Ireland.

— (1987) *Quarterly Bulletin*, Summer. Dublin: Central Bank of Ireland.

Chubb, B. (1992) *The Government and Politics of Ireland*, 3rd edn. London: Longman.

Coghlan, D. (1987) 'Cabinet Offers Pay Deal for Union Support', *Irish Times*, 5 August, p. 1.

Collins, S. (1993) *Spring and the Labour Story*. Dublin: O'Brien Press.

Cox, B. (1983) 'The Impact of Recession on Industrial Relations', *Industrial Relations News Review* 2(4): 217–40.

CSO (Central Statistics Office) (1986) *Statistical Abstract of Ireland, 1982–1985*. Dublin: Stationery Office.

— (1991) *Statistical Abstract of Ireland 1990*. Dublin: Stationery Office.

Dáil Debates (1919–2005) [online]. Available: http://historical-debates.oireachtas.ie/en.toc.dail.html (last accessed 11 February 2010).

Daly, A. (1994) 'Representing Employers: The Irish Business and Employers' Confederation', in T.V. Murphy and W.K. Roche (eds) *Irish Industrial Relations in Practice*, pp. 110–25. Dublin: Oak Tree Press.

Devine, J. (1970) '"Time is Ripe" for Action on Inflation', *Irish Independent*, 12 October, p. 7.

DoF (Department of Finance) (1958a) *Budget 1958*. Dublin: Stationery Office.

— (1958b) *Economic Development*. Dublin: Stationery Office.

— (1958c) *First Programme for Economic Expansion*. Dublin: Stationery Office.

— (1960) *Budget 1960*. Dublin: Stationery Office.

— (1961) *Budget 1961*. Dublin: Stationery Office.

— (1962) *Budget 1962*. Dublin: Stationery Office.

— (1970) *Budget 1970*. Dublin: Stationery Office.

— (1971) *Budget 1971*. Dublin: Stationery Office.

— (1983) *Budget 1983*. Dublin: Stationery Office.

— (1988) *Budget 1988*. Dublin: Stationery Office.

— (1989) *Budget 1989*. Dublin: Stationery Office.

— (1990) *Budget 1990*. Dublin: Stationery Office.

DoT (Department of the Taoiseach) (1959) 'Meeting with the Taoiseach 1959', *ICTU Archive*, Box 42 Economic Policy, 4002.

DUES (2004) *Data Series on Trade Unions in Ireland*. Department of Industrial Relations, University College Dublin, and University of Mannheim Centre for European Social Research, Germany.

Ebbinghaus, B. and Visser, J. (1999) *Development of Trade Unions in Western Europe, 1945–1995*. Basingstoke: Macmillan.

Economist, The (1970) 'Early Frost', 24–30 October, p. 80.

— (1987) 'How the Government Spent the People into a Slump', 24–30 January, p. 53.

ESRI (Economic and Social Research Institute) (1970) *Quarterly Economic Commentary*, No. 3. Dublin: ESRI.

— (1981) *Quarterly Economic Commentary*, No. 3. Dublin: ESRI.

Fine Gael (1987) *Breaking out of the Vicious Circle: Election '87*. Dublin: Fine Gael.

FitzGerald, G. (1991) *All in a Life: An Autobiography*. Dublin: Gill & Macmillan.

Fogarty, M., Egan, D. and Ryan, W.L.J. (1981) *Pay Policy for the 1980s*. Dublin: FUE.

Ford, R. (1987) 'FitzGerald Suffers Election Setback', *The Times*, 7 February, p. 2.

Garvin, T. (1982) *The Evolution of Irish Nationalist Politics*. Dublin: Gill & Macmillan.

Girvin, B. (1994) 'Trade Unions and Economic Development', in D. Nevin (ed.) *Trade Union Century*, pp. 117–32. Cork: Mercier Press.

Gunnigle, P., McMahon, G. and Fitzgerald, G. (1999) *Industrial Relations in Ireland: Theory and Practice*, 2nd edn. Dublin: Gill & Macmillan.

Hardiman, N. (1988) *Pay, Politics and Economic Performance in Ireland 1970–1987*. Oxford: Clarendon.

— (1992) 'The State and Economic Interests: Ireland in Comparative Perspective', in J.H. Goldthorpe and C.T. Whelan (eds) *The Development of Industrial Society in Ireland*, pp. 229–258. Oxford: Oxford University Press for the British Academy.

Haughey, C. (1986) *The Spirit of the Nation: The Speeches and Statements of Charles J. Haughey (1957–1986)*. Cork: Mercier Press.

Haughton, J. (1995) 'The Historical Background', in J.W. O'Hagan (ed.) *The Economy of Ireland: Policy and Performance of a Small European Country*, pp. 1–48. Dublin: Gill & Macmillan.

Hillery, B. (1980) 'Industrial Relations: Compromise and Conflict,' in D. Nevin (ed.) *Trade Unions and Change in Irish Society*, pp. 39–52. Dublin: Mercier Press.

Horgan, J. (1997) *Seán Lemass: The Enigmatic Patriot*. Dublin: Gill & Macmillan.

ICTU (Irish Congress of Trade Unions) (1959) *Annual Report 1959*. Dublin: ICTU.

— (1960) *Annual Report 1960*. Dublin: ICTU.

— (1961) *Annual Report 1961*. Dublin: ICTU.

— (1963) *Annual Report 1963*. Dublin: ICTU.

— (1964) *Annual Report 1964*. Dublin: ICTU.

— (1971) *Annual Report 1971*. Dublin: ICTU.

— (1972) *Annual Report 1972*. Dublin: ICTU.

— (1981) *Annual Report 1981*. Dublin: ICTU.

— (1988) *Annual Report 1988*. Dublin: ICTU.

Irish Independent (1970) 'Colley's Income Threat', 9 October, p. 11.

Irish Times (1959a) 'Lemass Announces his New Government', 24 June, p. 9A.

— (1959b) 'Lemass Opposed as Taoiseach', 24 June, p. 1.

— (1959c) 'Lemass Elected Taoiseach by 73 Votes to 51', 24 June, p. 1.

— (1981) 'Politicians' Choice', 15 June, p. 12.

— (1987a) 'Bruton Wants Wider Base of Corporation Tax', 12 February, p. 10.

— (1987b) 'Economic Plan "A Major Achievement"', 10 October, p. 6.

Jacobsen, J.K. (1994) *Chasing Progress in the Irish Republic*. Cambridge: Cambridge University Press.

Keenan, B. (1987) 'It's Easier to Run a Big Company than a Small Country', *Irish Independent*, 14 February, p. 8.

Kennedy, K. (1981) 'The State of the Public Finances', *Administration* 29(2): 137–52.

Lalor, S. (1982) 'Corporatism in Ireland', *Administration* 30(4): 74–97.

Laver, M., Mair, P. and Sinnott, R. (1987) *How Ireland Voted: The Irish General Election 1987*. Dublin: Poolbeg Press.

Leddin, A.J. and O'Leary, J. (1995) 'Fiscal, Monetary, and Exchange Rate Policy', in J.W. O'Hagan (ed.) *The Economy of Ireland: Policy and Performance of a Small European Country*, pp. 159–195. Dublin: Gill & Macmillan.

Leddin, A.J. and Walsh, B.M. (1998) *The Macroeconomy of Ireland*, 4th edn. Dublin: Gill & Macmillan.

Lee, J.J. (1989) *Ireland, 1912–1985: Politics and Society*. Cambridge: Cambridge University Press.

Lyons, F.S.L. (1973) *Ireland Since the Famine*. London: Fontana.

MacSharry, R. and White, P. (2001) *The Making of the Celtic Tiger: The Inside Story of Ireland's Boom Economy*. Cork: Mercier Press.

McCarthy, C. (1973) *The Decade of Upheaval: Irish Trade Unions in the 1960s*. Dublin: Institute of Public Administration.

— (1980) 'The Development of Irish Trade Unions', in D. Nevin (ed.) *Trade Unions and Change in Irish Society*, pp. 26–38. Dublin: Mercier Press.

McCarthy, D. (1999) 'Building a Partnership', in B. Reynolds and S. Healy (eds) *Social Partnership in a New Century*, pp. 4–20. Dublin: CORI Justice Commission.

McGinley, K.J. and Filby, I.L. (1997) 'From Sidelines to Centre Stage: The Role of Government in Relation to Wage Policy in Ireland, 1970–1997', in J. Browne (ed.) *The Role of the State in Industrial Relations*, Vol. 3, pp. 201–31. Dublin: Oak Tree Press.

Mitchell, B.R. (1993) *International Historical Statistics. Europe 1750–1988*, 3rd edn. Hong Kong: Stockton Press.

Mjøset, L. (1992) *The Irish Economy in a Comparative Institutional Perspective*. Dublin: NESC.

Munck, R. (1993) *The Irish Economy: Results and Prospects*. Pluto Press: London.

Murphy, G. (1997) 'Government, Interest Groups and the Irish Move to Europe', *Irish Studies in International Affairs* 8(1): 57–68.

— (1999) 'The Role of Interest Groups in the Policy Making Process', in J. Coakley and M. Gallagher (eds) *Politics in the Republic of Ireland*, 3rd edn, pp. 271–93. New York, NY: Routledge.

— (2003) *Economic Realignment and the Politics of EEC Entry: Ireland 1948–1972*. Bethesda, MD: Academica Press.

Murphy, G. and Hogan, J.W. (2008) 'Fianna Fáil, the Trade Union Movement and the Politics of Macroeconomic Crises, 1970–1982', *Irish Political Studies* 23(4): 577–98.

NESC (National Economic and Social Council) (1986) *A Strategy for Development 1986–1990: Growth, Employment and Fiscal Balance*, Report No. 83. Dublin: NESC [online]. Available: http://www.nesc.ie/publications.asp (last accessed 11 February 2010).

— (1990) *A Strategy for the Nineties: Economic Stability and Structural Change*, Report No. 89. Dublin: NESC [online]. Available: http://www.nesc.ie/publications.asp (last accessed 11 February 2010).

— (1996) *Strategy into the 21st Century*, Report No. 99. Dublin: NESC [online]. Available: http://www.nesc.ie/publications.asp (last accessed 11 February 2010).

Nevin, D. (1994) 'Decades of Dissension and Division 1923–1959', in D. Nevin (ed.) *Trade Union Century*, pp. 85–98. Cork: Mercier Press.

NIEC (National Industrial Economic Council) (1970) *Report on Incomes and Prices Policy*. Dublin: NIEC.

O'Brien, J.F. (1981) *A Study of National Wage Agreement in Ireland*. Dublin: ESRI.

O'Brien, K. (1982) 'Queries on Cost of Plan Declined', *Irish Times*, 3 February, p. 1.

O'Byrnes, S. (1986) *Hiding Behind a Face: Fine Gael Under FitzGerald*. Dublin: Gill & Macmillan.

OECD (Organisation for Economic Co-operation and Development) (1961) *Ireland 1961*. Paris: OECD.

— (1962) *Ireland 1962*. Paris: OECD.

— (1970) *Ireland 1970*. Paris: OECD.

— (1971) *Ireland 1971*. Paris: OECD.

— (1972) *Ireland 1972*. Paris: OECD.

— (1973) *Ireland 1973*. Paris: OECD.

— (1982) *Ireland 1982*. Paris: OECD.

— (1983) *Ireland 1983*. Paris: OECD.

— (1986) *Ireland 1986*. Paris: OECD.

— (1987) *Ireland 1987*. Paris: OECD.

— (1989) *Ireland 1989*. Paris: OECD.

Ó Gráda, C. (1997) *A Rocky Road*. Manchester: Manchester University Press.

Ó Gráda, C. and O'Rourke, K. (1995) 'Economic Growth: Performance and Explanations,' in J.W. O'Hagan (ed.) *The Economy of Ireland: Policy and Performance of a Small European Country*, pp. 198–227. Dublin: Gill & Macmillan.

O'Halpin, E. (1993) 'Policy Making,' in J. Coakley and M. Gallagher (eds) *Politics in the Republic of Ireland*, 2nd edn. Dublin: PSAI Press.

O'Morain, P. (1987) 'Threats and Promises: The Economics of the Election', *Irish Times*, 2 February, p. 7.

Peillon, M. (1995) 'Interest Groups and the State in the Republic of Ireland', in P. Clancy (ed.) *Irish Society: Sociological Perspectives*, pp. 360–78. Dublin: Institute of Public Administration.

Pratschke, J.L. (1979) 'Business and Labour in Irish Society, 1945–70', in J.J Lee (ed.) *Ireland 1945–70*, pp. 38–47. Dublin: Gill & Macmillan.

Redmond, V. (1985) 'An Analysis of the Breakdown of National Agreements and Understandings', unpublished MBS thesis, University College Dublin.

Roche, W.K. (1989) 'State Strategies and the Politics of Industrial Relations in Ireland since 1945', in T. Murphy (ed.) *Industrial Relations in Ireland: Contemporary Issues and Developments*, pp. 115–32. Dublin: Department of Industrial Relations, University College Dublin.

— (1994) 'Pay Determination and the Politics of Industrial Relations', in T.V. Murphy and W.K. Roche (eds) *Irish Industrial Relations in Practice*, pp. 126–205. Dublin: Oak Tree Press.

Schmitter, P.C. and Lehmbruch, G. (1979) *Trends Towards Corporatist Intermediation*. London: Sage.

Tansey, P. (1998) *Ireland at Work: Economic Growth and the Labour Market, 1987–1997*. Dublin: Oak Tree Press.

Teahon, P. (1997) 'The Irish Political and Policy Making System', *Administration* 45(4): 49–58.

von Prondzynski, F. (1992) 'Ireland: Between Centralism and the Market', in A. Ferner and R Hyman (eds) *Industrial Relations in the New Europe*, pp. 69–87. Oxford: Basil Blackwell.

Weinz, W. (1986) 'Economic Development and Interest Groups', in B. Girvin and R. Sturm (eds) *Politics and Society in Contemporary Ireland*, pp. 87–101. Aldershot: Gower.

Chapter 14

Partnership at Enterprise Level in Ireland

Kevin O'Leary

INTRODUCTION

Enterprise-level partnership, as an employee voice mechanism in the individual enterprise, can trace its origins to the series of national social partnership agreements that have operated continuously in Ireland since 1987. The extension of the partnership principle to the enterprise level was promoted as a natural development of the emerging levels of consensus and co-operation achieved by the social partners under national-level agreements. This extension was to be a significant component of the fourth agreement, Partnership 2000 for Inclusion, Employment and Competitiveness (DoT 1996), which operated from 1997 to 2000, and in the agreements that followed.

This chapter will consider the political and economic influences that have informed this employee relations practice, particularly the influence of European models of corporate governance. Parallel developments in human resource management (HRM) and the conceptual similarities and ideological differences between those developments and European models of corporate governance will be explored. The failure of the enterprise-level model to win acceptance as a best practice model in Ireland, despite its active promotion in the context of successive national social partnership agreements, is also examined. Insights from two authoritative and influential surveys that are viewed as reliable indicators of the degree of partnership uptake in private sector organisations are also considered.

THE BACKGROUND TO THE NATIONAL SOCIAL PARTNERSHIP AGREEMENTS

National social partnership emerged as a pragmatic response to the economic crisis that had confronted the country during the mid-1980s. The Programme for National Recovery (PNR) (DoT 1987) became the first agreement in the present round of national social partnership agreements. The agreement was a direct response to an economy on the verge of collapse in the face of burgeoning inflation, high unemployment, excessive interest rates and out-of-control government borrowing. The series of agreements between government, employers and trade unions that followed, which began with the PNR, were to be substantially different from and significantly more far-reaching than the earlier tripartite National Understandings of 1978 and 1980. These earlier agreements were essentially centralised wage agreements which had attempted to fix levels of pay increase during their lifetime. The parties to these agreements were also the government, employers and trade unions. However, in these earlier agreements, government participation focused mainly on its role as a public sector employer. The significant new development in the PNR and subsequent partnership agreements was that government took on a much broader agenda for itself in terms of using its leadership of the agreements to address far-reaching economic and social policy decision making in consultation with the social partners. Hardiman (2000:288) contends that the earlier National Understandings 'had never really approximated to the continental European model of societal corporatism'. Corporatism as a political model is defined by O'Donnell and Thomas (2002:176) as 'institutional bargaining between peak associations of labour and capital and the government in which the state becomes a partner in collective bargaining and in return assigns a role in the policy making process to the social partners'.

In the PNR (1987–1990), concessions by government on taxation, initiatives to tackle inflation and job creation were traded against agreement from the trade unions to accept levels of wage increase at 2.5 per cent per annum during the period 1988–1990 at a time when the Central Statistics Office (CSO) reports inflation standing at 3.2 per cent (CSO 2009) at the commencement of the agreement. Wage levels, which had chased inflation rates ranging from 3.2 to 20.4 per cent during the 1980s (CSO 2009), represented a significant component of the inflationary spiral that demanded urgent attention. While centralised pay bargaining remained as an essential component of the partnership arrangement, the scope of the PNR and subsequent agreements became much more far-reaching and influential in determining economic and social policy.

An initial sense of reticence was evident in that not all participants had embraced the proposed model with enthusiasm. Employers had become disillusioned with the previous round of centralised agreements and had consequently negotiated pay agreements on a firm-by-firm basis during the period 1982–87. Earlier experiences with national agreements during the 1960s and 1970s had thus led to the eventual collapse of the model in 1982. On both the employer and trade union sides, Hardiman (2000:290) observes:

> . . . considerable misgivings were expressed within ICTU [Irish Congress of Trade Unions]. IBEC [Irish Business and Employers' Confederation] was initially reluctant to become involved and sceptical that the agreement would hold. . . . Undoubtedly the shared sense of economic crisis helped to bring union and employer leaders together, patriotism and a sense of

responsibility to the wider community played an important part in shaping the participants' views.

On the political side, there was more enthusiasm, though this was hardly surprising given the scale of the crisis and the prospect of facing the electorate. According to Hastings, Sheehan and Yeates (2007:53), 'initial scepticism in 1987 of anything that smacked of the National Understandings had been overcome by a mixture of persuasion, and perhaps a degree of subtle pressure, particularly by the Haughey-led Fianna Fáil minority government of 1987'.

Looking back, almost a decade later, at the birth of the PNR, Phil Flynn, the outgoing President of the ICTU, talked of Taoiseach Charles Haughey's crucial and influential part in securing acceptance for the PNR: 'The initiative came from us, we drove it but we could have been pushing till doomsday. The employers opposed it and it was Haughey more than anyone else who dragged the employers into the process, he saw the potential' (Yeates 1995:4). Flynn's perception of Haughey's far-seeing intervention is interpreted somewhat differently by O'Connor (2002:164), who perceived it as:

> another example of Fianna Fáil seeking a special relationship with labour to cover an electoral flank. Crucial to the deal was the determination of Fianna Fáil leader Charles J. Haughey to neutralise trade union opposition to the swingeing cuts introduced by his minority government in 1987.

Whatever Haughey's rationale or ambition for the partnership process, the threat of impending economic collapse had forced a departure from the old adversarialism to a new corporatist and consensual approach with the involvement of business and trade unions in the making of public policy at the macro level. This would eventually evolve to include the concept of partnership at local enterprise level.

PARTNERSHIP 2000 AND THE DEVELOPMENT OF ENTERPRISE-LEVEL PARTNERSHIP

Partnership 2000 for Inclusion, Employment and Competitiveness (DoT 1996) was the fourth social partnership agreement and it identified an aspiration for the deepening of the partnership concept in the promotion of its extension for the first time to local enterprise level.

European Influences

The inspiration for the extension of partnership to the local enterprise level had its roots in the various models operating in a number of European states where more inclusive corporate governance structures operate. Two-tier board structures, with fixed levels of worker representation and works councils enjoying powers of co-determination and veto, became a norm in early post-war West Germany and were underpinned there by a series of legislative provisions. Co-determination for employees means the right to participate in decisions that affect them and also the right to crucial background information about the organisation. Co-determination in this context refers specifically to joint decision making, rather than simply consultation. These institutional arrangements are replicated to a lesser extent in other European states and provided an impetus for Ireland to consider its own response.

Irish governments had historically remained uncertain and tentative as to how this European model could be incorporated into the Irish voluntarist industrial relations tradition. The voluntarist approach, inherited from the British practice of free collective bargaining and non-interference by government in the employment relationship, seemed incompatible with the high level of regulation and institutional supports seen in Europe. Ireland, in following Europe's lead, had enacted the Worker Participation (State Enterprises) Act 1977, which provided for worker representation at board level in eleven state bodies. The subsequent Worker Participation (State Enterprises) Amendment Act 1988 extended the benefits of the 1977 Act to an additional forty semi-state organisations and incorporated the principle of sub-board participation, without, however, the powers of co-determination and veto. It should be noted, of course, that the legislation applied to state enterprises only and did not impact on the private sector. Subsequent EU directives required a response from the Irish government, which proceeded to enact the Transnational Information and Consultation of Employees Act 1996. This Act applied only to transnational or multinational organisations that employed 1,000 or more employees across two or more states of the EU and where there was a minimum of a 150 employees in each state. The subsequent Employees (Provision of Information and Consultation) Act 2006 provided rights to workers in organisations employing in excess of fifty people within the state. It must be noted that both these Acts provide rights to information and consultation, but not to co-determination or co-decision making.

In 1980, the then Department of Labour (currently Enterprise and Employment) published a discussion paper entitled *Worker Participation*. The purpose was to stimulate debate on worker participation in the private sector. The discussion paper (Department of Labour 1980) was published against a backdrop of significantly well-developed worker participation models in other then European Economic Community (EEC) countries where employee participation at board level and at works council level had become the norm. It asserted a belief that worker participation would be the basis for a new social order with the potential to escape the old conflicts of capital and labour:

> In a rapidly developing industrial society we must find a new order, not based
> on the old class concept, but designed to reconcile the demands for social

justice and individual freedom with modern industrial development and technology. Worker participation is a step in this direction. (Department of Labour 1980:15).

Some form of employee participation was also identified as being a panacea to the high level of conflict that had been a feature of industrial relations throughout the 1970s. Industrial action during this period accounted for almost 600,000 days lost annually due to industrial disputes (LRC 2003:17). The new order envisaged foresaw the worker as an important organisational stakeholder, an ambition that would have to wait a further seventeen years before achieving at least explicitly stated acceptance by the social partners in the Partnership 2000 agreement.

Following on from the Department of Labour's (1980) discussion paper a 1985 government initiative saw the Minister for Labour set up an advisory committee on worker participation where 'the majority considered that legislation should be introduced with reference to organisations in the private sector employing more than 100 people' (Meenan1999:275).

It is difficult to identify a national consensus between the relevant stakeholders on what the Department of Labour's 'new order' in its 1980 discussion paper might represent. Prior to the return to centralised pay bargaining in 1987 it would appear that the employers and unions were in no hurry to focus their minds on the challenge posed by the 1980 discussion paper. In 1991, the Federation of Irish Employers (FIE), which in 1993 merged with the Confederation of Irish Industry to become IBEC, and ICTU published the *Joint Declaration on Employee Involvement in the Private Sector*. The joint declaration was a response to a 1990 request from the Minister for Labour to both parties to discuss worker participation in the private sector. The FIE/ICTU declaration is a slim document running to all of eight pages and appears to be little more than a discussion paper without any road map identifying the way forward or any further commitment or agreement on the next stage in advancing this particular agenda. O'Leary (2006:12) contends:

> It could be argued that employers saw participation as a substantial threat to a long-standing world view regarding their right to manage. They were simply not ready for what they considered to be a significant dilution of their control and what they perceived as the inevitable democratisation of the workplace.

The unions were similarly uncomfortable with the possible erosion of their traditional power base in representing workers' rights and acting as the direct interface with the employer within the accepted adversarial model of industrial relations.

New Developments in Human Resource and Manufacturing Management Practice

Simultaneously, new developments in HRM and manufacturing management practice, borrowing from US and Japanese models, were becoming a concern for the trade union movement. The significantly increased levels of employee involvement in work systems offered by these approaches were representing a challenge for the trade union movement, which commissioned a report to inform its response.

In 1993, ICTU published a report entitled *New Forms of Work Organisation* (ICTU 1993), which had been commissioned from independent consultants by its executive council to identify the strategic options open to unions in responding to new forms of work organisation in manufacturing industry. The new forms of work in question included such practices as total quality programmes, self inspection, cell-based manufacturing and team-working initiatives. Innovations in HRM practice such as employee involvement programmes, communication programmes, reward system changes and an increased commitment to training and development similarly required a response.

These changes demanded new levels of skill, initiative and flexibility from employees. Many of these employees had carried out largely de-skilled jobs where high levels of demarcation traditionally supported by trade unions limited their opportunity for creativity and the exercise of initiative. The trade union movement would also have perceived new forms of direct communication and consultation as usurping their role. Thus, unions were unsure as to their response to this changing environment.

The ICTU (1993) report, in its conclusions and recommendations, considered five possible options and advised against those choices that proposed opposition. The report suggested that opposition to these initiatives could be counter-productive on the grounds that it would cause damage to the perception and credibility of unions and would likely lead to their increased marginalisation. An alternative strategy of not taking a formal policy stance and leaving the decision to local shop stewards and union officials on a case-by-case basis was also rejected.

In contrast to such defensive options, the authors of the ICTU (1993) report argued strongly for a positive and proactive approach, advocating that the trade union should – depending on the particular business context – engage by embracing either or both of the following alternatives.

- Adopting a proactive approach on the basis that it is in the best interests of members that unions are seen to respond positively so as to have as much input as possible in the introduction and monitoring [of the new forms of work organisation].
- Actively promoting the introduction [of the new forms of work organisation] with the unions' own agenda. This would place unions in a position from which

they can actively influence the nature and form of the initiatives in the best long-term interest of their members. (ICTU 1993:42)

Though this was an ICTU report, it was written by independent consultants. However, if the views of Des Geraghty, then Vice President of the Services, Industrial, Professional and Technical Trade Union (SIPTU), Ireland's largest trade union, are considered representative, it must be accepted that the trade union leadership's response has been unequivocal in supporting the recommendations set out in the ICTU (1993) report. Geraghty (1995:14) remarked that:

SIPTU's approach to enterprise partnership is based on the view that employees' involvement in joint employer/union initiatives is intended to ensure that goods and services are delivered to the highest possible standards, thereby helping to secure employment and improve the living standards for our members. We believe that the partnership approach offers the best prospect for successful enterprise in this era combined with job satisfaction, personal fulfilment and rising living standards.

Furthermore, Peter Cassells, then General Secretary of the ICTU, endorsed Geraghty's views when proposing that many companies were operating industrial relations practices 'dating back to the industrial revolution' by denying employees 'any real say in the organisations which they had helped to create'. He sounded a warning that the national consensus achieved in the national social partnership process 'could only be maintained on the basis of a full partnership at company level' (Yeates 1998:4).

The other social partners appear to have accepted this principle in the negotiations for a new national agreement to succeed the Programme for Competitiveness and Work (PCW, 1994–1996). The Partnership 2000 Agreement (DoT 1996:51), which operated from 1997 to 2000, gave expression to ICTU's ambition thus:

9.1 An objective of this Partnership is to extend partnership arrangements at enterprise level . . . International and domestic experience suggest that further development of the partnership approach at enterprise level will enhance the competitiveness of firms, the quality of the work environment and the access of employees to lifelong learning.

The phraseology of the statement is noteworthy insofar as the objective is couched in the language of business efficiency rather than as an ideological principle of extending employee voice. This view is reaffirmed by section 9.5, which stated, 'The NESC (National Economic and Social Council) has concluded that competitiveness can be greatly assisted by partnerships at enterprise level which can provide "a potentially powerful means for accelerating innovation'" (DoT 1996:51).

The objective, as stated in section 9.1, is careful to avoid any compulsion on employers to engage with the ambition, or to define a commitment to transpose into legislation a requirement to set up European-style works councils with powers of co-determination. Such a compulsion for powers of co-determination seems to have been a bridge too far for Irish employers.

Section 9.2 of Partnership 2000 outlines the NESC's suggestion that the challenge is to 'encourage the development of new models' and again to 'encourage firms, employees and unions to advance from experiment to comprehensive innovation' (DoT 1996:51). Partnership therefore becomes an option for employers and the wording recognises the difficulties to be confronted: 'For some employers, employees and their representatives, the move to a partnership culture requires a radical change in current attitudes and approaches' (DoT 1996:52).

In the subsequent agreement, the Programme for Prosperity and Fairness (PPF), which ran from 2000 to 2002, a commitment is set out by government that the changes required in modernising the public service would be undertaken and 'advanced through the participative structures put in place under Partnership 2000 to involve all public servants in the change process' (DoT 2000:131). These commitments effectively institutionalise enterprise-level partnership as part of the public sector model. Government, as the employer, can exercise its capacity and capability to establish this model for the public sector, but a parallel initiative for the private sector would require the enactment of legislation. Consequently, enterprise-level partnership, as defined by Partnership 2000, remained as an option for private sector employers.

CONTESTING THE DEFINITION OF ENTERPRISE-LEVEL PARTNERSHIP

It is clear from the above discussion that a variety of employee voice mechanisms are capable of being described as partnership. The challenge of definition is complicated by the partnership concept being grounded in the language of industrial relations and simultaneously in the HRM rhetoric. This gives rise to a number of terms related to how enterprise-level partnership is conceived. It is worth discussing some of these terms in some detail.

Industrial Democracy

The term 'industrial democracy' appears to be one of the earliest used in the developing language of the employee voice principle. The term, which was commonly used in the 1970s, has obvious political resonance and is largely rooted in a time when labour politics in the UK and Ireland would have had significant leanings toward socialism and the rhetoric of the left. The real expectation of the socialist ambition was famously articulated by Brendan Corish, leader of the Irish Labour Party and Tánaiste in the coalition government of 1973, who had earlier predicted that 'the 70s will be Socialist' (O'Connor and O'Halloran 2008:70). The UK shared a similar political and industrial relations landscape, according to Brannen (1983:670):

> In the 1970s interest was centred around the notion of power sharing through industrial democracy and an influential role was seen for the unions, even though such ideas were contested by employers and also a subject of controversy within the union movement.

As the political landscape began to change, Labour softened its socialist aspiration and joined Fine Gael in the coalition government of 1973–1977. The ambitions of industrial democracy in that particular incarnation began to recede. However, there were more tentative efforts to advance the industrial democracy agenda, albeit under a different identity. The 1977/1980 Worker Participation (State Enterprises) Acts were followed in 1980 by the Department of Labour's (1980) discussion paper *Worker Participation* (discussed above) to stimulate debate on advancing the concept of worker participation to private sector firms. However, the ideals of worker democracy did not find significant approval from employers given its terminology rooted in the language of a political ideology, with implications of the power of veto, collective decision making and the imagined vista of worker co-operatives, all of which were largely inimical to the employers' perception of their right to manage.

Employee Involvement

Marchington *et al.* (1992:42) define employee involvement as 'those practices which are initiated principally by management and are designed to increase employee information about and commitment to the organisation'. Armstrong (2001:280) states, in relation to involvement, that it is where the employer gives employees the opportunity to become involved in their work and their organisation beyond the simple performance of their contracted duties and obligations. Marchington (1995:283) makes clear the distinction between involvement and industrial democracy in that involvement presumes that management should be free to choose when and how to involve employees, while democracy assumes that employees should have rights over those who manage their working lives. Bratton and Gold (1999:328) identify the concerns of some commentators and practitioners, that employee involvement and joint consultative procedures might be used by managers to circumvent established collective bargaining machinery.

Employee Participation

Marchington (1995:284) uses the term 'participation' to cover employee influence that may be exercised through bargaining and negotiation over a wide range of issues associated with the organisation, conduct of work and the terms and conditions of employment. Armstrong (2006:808) sees participation as being about employees playing a greater part in the decision-making process 'by being given the opportunity to influence management decisions'. Salamon (2000:66) extends the range of activities or scale of engagement of participation from the operational level of employee involvement initiatives to the more strategic level:

> Employee participation denotes a distinct evolutionary development which is aimed at extending collective employee influence beyond the traditional remit of collective bargaining into much wider areas of organisational planning and decision making at both the operational and more importantly the strategic level.

It could be said that the primary difference between employee involvement and participation is that the former applies to simple operational involvement while the latter refers to involvement at a higher level in strategic level decision making. Participation is not only grounded in the collective bargaining tradition, it also represents a major extension of the representational process. Bratton and Gold (1999:301) see participation as 'workers exerting a countervailing and upward pressure on management control, which may not imply unity of purpose'.

Partnership

Partnership as a concept is not exclusive to the Irish context and it features in the international industrial relations and HRM literature. In a report commissioned by the British Department of Trade and Industry (DTI), Knell (2000:5) observes that 'partnership is not a term that carries with it any precise theoretical or practical connotation'. In attempting to establish some general meaning, Knell (2000:5) observes that 'definitions of partnership have tended to focus more on the cultural values and aspirations that are seen to underpin partnership, rather than on precise empirical definitions of partnership approaches and outcomes'.

Ackers and Payne (1998:532), in seeking definition of partnership, talk about the need to find conceptual tools to 'decipher the various semantic threads and crisscrossing definitions' and that the best guide to meaning is 'the rhetorical usage by the major political and social actors', particularly for a term that 'combines seductive rhetoric with ambiguous and shifting meaning'. The challenge of definition is reflected in the Involvement and Participation Association's (IPA) (a UK organisation dedicated to the promotion of partnership) identification of seven main conceptualisations of partnership in operation in that jurisdiction alone (IPA 2004).

Roche (1999:12) identifies partnership as a component of 'new industrial relations'. New industrial relations 'encapsulates . . . a wide range of industrial relations and human resource practices which commentary and research suggests have become common during the 1980s and 1990s'. Partnership is not exclusively a natural evolution of industrial democracy principles in unionised organisations; rather, it is a product of a more general shift in the management of employee relations:

> Many of the practices in question, for example, forms of direct employee involvement, performance related pay or profit sharing, are not confined to unionised firms and appear to have become common across the board. . . . When occurring in combination or in bundles, new practices are usually regarded – certainly in the Anglo Saxon literature – as the basis of a new model of industrial relations, also variously described as 'mutual gains', 'jointist', 'partnership', 'joint governance' or 'joint management model'. (Roche 1999:12)

Guest and Peccei (2001:208), in the search for a definition of partnership, where different writers emphasise 'different elements and dimensions', identify partnership as falling within 'three broad intellectual traditions and theoretical perspectives'. These traditions, they claim, can be pluralist, unitarist or what they term hybrid. The pluralist incarnation has its roots in the European debate on workplace representation and is grounded in discussions on worker democracy and worker participation as viewed from a pluralist perspective. Guest and Peccei (2001:208) cite the German model, where legislation sets out rights of co-determination, consultation and communication, which is defined as including a representative participation perspective built around legislation and grounded in a pluralist tradition.

The unitarist framework seeks to integrate employer and employee interests, while at the same time maximising employee involvement in and commitment to the organisation. Guest and Peccei (2001:208) identify two broad strands of the unitarist framework. One is where financial involvement through share ownership arrangements is seen as the 'principal method of reconciling and aligning employer and employee interests' (Guest and Peccei 2001:210). The second strand sees direct employee participation and involvement in day-to-day operational, rather than strategic issues, but with a view to increasing employee commitment. Guest and Peccei (2001:208) see this as a rather one-sided form of partnership implying a low level of trust. The second strand identified here has much in common with HRM employee involvement strategy.

The third, or hybrid, model, combines elements of the first two. It is based on 'pluralist assumptions and recognises the importance of direct forms of employee involvement and participation as well as the benefits of management and employees working together to ensure gains for all the parties concerned' (Guest and Peccei 2001:210).

So, as the discussion above makes clear, the literature recognises the difficulties in establishing universally accepted definitions for the terminology of the various employee voice mechanisms. Table 14.1 endeavours to summarise the above discussion and establish some form of categorisation.

Table 14.1 Employee voice mechanisms

	Participation	Involvement	Partnership
Perspective	Pluralist	Unitarist	Hybrid
Major influences	Industrial relations Industrial democracy European models of corporate governance	HRM and new forms of work organisation	Attempts to integrate both sets of major influence
Economic standpoint	Corporatist	Neo-liberal	Corporatist
Role for trade unions	Institutionalised	Peripheral or none in non-union firms	Institutionalised
Level of engagement	Operational and strategic	Operational only	More strategic than operational
Preoccupations	Extending employee voice	Maintaining the right to manage	Establishing a sense of mutuality

PARTNERSHIP IN IRELAND

In terms of the categorisation discussed above, the Irish social partnership model falls most comfortably into the hybrid type. This can be seen in discussing some details concerning the model.

In the Irish context it is necessary to refer to the *Partnership 2000* document for the accepted definition agreed by the social partners:

> Partnership is an active relationship based on recognition of a common interest to secure the competitiveness, viability, and prosperity of the enterprise. It involves a continuing commitment by employees to improvements in quality and efficiency, and the acceptance of employees as stakeholders with rights and interests to be considered in the context of major decisions affecting their employment. (DoT 1996:63)

The agreement is cautious to avoid the more politically loaded terms 'worker democracy', 'worker participation' or 'employee involvement' and offers a carefully crafted definition so neutral as to be acceptable to all the parties.

While the official face of IBEC (a signatory to the agreement) has consistently been a willing and enthusiastic participant in social partnership at national level, different perceptions do appear to exist about the certainty of this position – that the membership may not entertain the same dedication to the extension of partnership to local level. Geary and Roche (2002:12) comment that the agreed definition of enterprise-level partnership in the agreement is 'broad and general' and allows for both representative participation and direct employee participation. Direct employee participation was:

> designed to meet the concerns of the employer's organisation, Irish Business and Employers' Confederation whose varied membership, which includes unionised and non unionised firms, had very different perceptions of the merit or otherwise of cultivating close relations with trade unions. (Geary and Roche 2002:12)

Partnership 2000 avoided imposing a prescriptive template for partnership itself. The agreement clearly sets out an acceptance that establishing a single template for partnership is inappropriate and that different employment settings must find an application of partnership that is adapted to their organisational context:

> The National Framework for Partnership for Competitive Enterprise does not attempt to impose any single structure or model of partnership. The parties to this National Framework accept that there is a need to tailor the approach to different employment settings. (DoT 1996:63)

The possibility of imposing a model or legislating for the introduction of partnership was considered counter-productive by John Dunne, Director General of IBEC in 1997, who is reported as stating that 'Statutorily based mandatory representation for employees would not help real employee involvement in companies' (Yeates 1997:9).

Partnership Penetration in Ireland

The National Centre for Partnership and Performance (NCPP) stated that:

> while there has been a significant level of innovation and experimentation with partnership-based approaches to decision making in Irish companies, there is little compelling evidence that Partnership has become part of a mainstream approach to change in an Irish context. (O'Connell 2002)

This view was confirmed by the NCPP's own surveys (O'Connell et al. 2003). As can be seen from Table 14.2, the survey examining employers' experience reports that only 4.3 per cent of organisations in the private sector have explicitly stated partnership agreements with their trade unions.

Table 14.2 Partnership involvement – 2003

Formal partnership arrangements involving union and employees	4.3%
Informal partnership-style arrangement between management and employee representatives	19.3%

Source: abstracted from O'Connell *et al.* (2003:17).

The figure of 4.3 per cent for explicitly declared partnership arrangements is at significant odds with an earlier survey which quotes a figure of 22 per cent for this type of agreement (IBEC 2002:71). If, however, the figure for informal partnership arrangements (19.3 per cent) from the NCPP survey is added, the total (23.6 per cent) approximates closely to the IBEC finding. The IBEC survey did not, however, differentiate between explicit and informal partnership arrangements. This was because the IBEC survey was designed to measure the diffusion of HRM practice rather than to quantify the level of private sector uptake of the partnership concept advocated by Partnership 2000. O'Connell *et al.* (2003:17) offer further data (see Table 14.3), as reflecting partnership activity, but it could more properly be identified as being indicative of HRM innovation.

Table 14.3 Partnership or HRM innovation?

New work practices such as team work/multitasking/quality circles	20.8%
Information to and consultation with staff on change in the company	61.5%
Arrangement for direct involvement of employees in decision making and problem solving	62.4%
Employee discretion in the way their work is organised	70.0%

Source: abstracted from O'Connell *et al.* (2003:17).

A significant feature of this table is the fact that 62.4 per cent of organisations in the sample had direct involvement of employees in decision making and problem solving compared to only 4.3 per cent having explicitly stated partnership arrangements. Again, it is important to draw the distinction between employee involvement (existing at the operational level) and partnership (which is considered to be employee participation at a strategic level). It must also be recognised that employee involvement has already been identified as a management-led initiative as opposed to being driven by the industrial relations process. It is likely that many of the initiatives referred to in the NCPP 2003 survey were informed and influenced by an emerging body of innovative HRM practice.

Roche (2007:203) confirms the view that partnership has not become a best practice model and that progress has been patchy insofar as it 'remains more a guiding vision than reality' and may have even 'dropped off significantly after early experimentation'. O'Connell *et al.* (2003) report significantly higher levels of partnership arrangements, at 46 per cent in the public sector. However, it must be noted that this experience is underpinned by government, as employer, committed to driving the sectoral strategies developed under the Strategic Management Initiative on 'a participative basis between management and staff' (DoT 2000:131). Subsequently these strategies were advanced through 'participative structures put in place under Partnership 2000 to involve all public servants in the change process' (DoT 2000:131). Therefore, it is not surprising that higher levels of participation are demonstrated for this sector.

Geary and Roche (2002:13) state that government, while having been sympathetic to trade union concerns that partnership at enterprise level is significantly less conspicuous in the private sector,

> has avoided adopting a directive approach in deference to employers' reservations. Certainly the option of legislating for union participation in management decision-making was not seen as a feasible option. To pursue such a course would have endangered, government officials and industrial development agencies argued, 'capital flight' amongst foreign owned enterprises. As a consequence the government has adopted a largely exhortative and non-interventionist position.

The non-interventionist policy largely mirrors the view that has been taken by successive governments on the issue of mandatory trade union recognition, an issue which has consistently been on the agenda at the negotiations of successive national agreements. The trade unions have looked to the possibility of mandatory recognition as a means of shoring up declining density levels. (Trade union density refers to the percentage of the workforce who are trade union members.) Though the decline is clear, precise figures for trade union membership have differed, with Roche (2008:21) showing estimates from a number of surveys indicating a reduction from 62 per cent in 1980 to 39 per cent by 2006. Other data from the CSO Quarterly National Household Survey identify trends of decline from 46 per cent in 1996 to 33 per cent by 2006 (CSO 2007). Dobbins (2005:12) offers rates of membership for the private sector at 21 per cent and 80 per cent for the public sector. It is important to note that while density levels are in decline, membership numbers have increased. Dobbins (2005:12) reports that, for the ten-year period 1994–2004, membership grew from 423,900 to 521,400, but given a total increase in numbers employed of 562,000 during this period, the estimated trade union density levels declined from 45.8 per cent to 34.7 per cent.

Government and the employer bodies have steadfastly refused in national agreements to concede the principle of mandatory recognition as a means of arresting the decline. This would be clearly inimical to government's policy of promoting Ireland as a low-tax and low-regulation destination for foreign direct investment (FDI), given our dependency on this sector for job creation.

It is ultimately ironic that, while the national social partnership process extended dramatically the influence of the trade union movement (with a direct voice in influencing social and economic policy), representation levels in the private sector have fallen so significantly. Roche (2008:41) asserts that the advent of partnership at local enterprise level 'might have been expected to provide the kind of extended union influence and supports to organisations associated with works council arrangements in continental European countries'. However, as already demonstrated, this has not happened and has no doubt been undermined by an apparent reluctance at organisation level to engage with the process.

CONCLUSION

The establishment of the enterprise-level partnership model as a method of expanding the sense of mutuality of interest between employers and their workforces has experienced low levels of uptake. The influences that have driven the model have been a mixture of politics, pragmatism and vested interest rather than a real commitment to the values of partnership, or at least its accepted recognition as possible best practice. Declining levels of trade union density in the private sector and the rise of management-led employee involvement initiatives as part of HRM strategy have presented a significant challenge.

Government's strategy to attract FDI, in offering a destination of low regulation and low corporate taxation, has conditioned a reticence to legislate for corporate governance strategies that parallel European structures. Instead, government has adopted a policy of relying on collective agreements at national level rather than legislative enforcement. The enactment of the Employees (Provision of Information and Consultation) Act 2006, which gives employees new rights to be informed and consulted about issues that affect their employment and the prospects of the business, appears somewhat light in comparison to European models. Roche (2008:41), referring to the views of some commentators who consider the provisions of the new Act 'minimalist', considers that 'it is unlikely to enhance union influence at workplace level'.

The voluntarist model, characterised by the lack of legal intervention in the industrial relations process, presents a tradition of less, rather than more, regulation. An expanding body of HRM practice largely influenced by US multinational organisations and conditioning employee relations strategy in indigenous Irish organisations, has created a model inspired more by Boston than Berlin. In this context, it should not be surprising that a felt need within the private sector to maintain the 'right to manage' has most likely presented the single greatest impediment to the diffusion of the enterprise-level partnership principle.

A further obstacle is created by Ireland's deepening economic troubles and by SIPTU's leader, Jack O'Connor's, prediction of the demise of national agreements in his assertion that 'there is no potential for concluding a social partnership deal with the government on economic recovery' and that 'the process is over' (Wall

2009:1). The absence of a consensus at national level poses a more significant and potentially fatal challenge to the aspiration of local enterprise-level partnership in a collapsing economy where the possibility of mutual gains for employees and employers is seriously eroded.

References

Ackers, P. and Payne, J. (1998) 'British Trade Unions and Social Partnership: Rhetoric, Reality and Social Myth', *International Journal of Human Resource Management*, 9(3): 529–50.

Armstrong, M. (2001) *A Handbook of Human Resource Management Practice*, 8th edn. London: Kogan Page.

— (2006) *A Handbook of Human Resource Management Practice*, 10th edn. London: Kogan Page.

Brannen, P. (1983), *Authority and Participation in Industry*. London: Batsford.

Bratton, J. and Gold, J. (1999) *Human Resource Management*. London: Macmillan.

CSO (2007) *Quarterly National Household Survey*, Union Membership Quarter 2, 2007 [online]. Available: http://www.cso.ie/releasespublications/documents/labour_market/current/qnhsunionmembership.pdf (last accessed 8 December 2009).

— 'Annual Percentage Change in Consumer Price Index by Year and Commodity' [online]. Available: http://www.cso.ie/quicktables/GetQuickTables.aspx?FileName=CPA01C3.asp&TableName=Annual+Percentage+Change&StatisticalProduct=DB_CP (last accessed 8 December 2009).

Department of Labour (1980) *Worker Participation – a Discussion Paper*. Dublin: Stationery Office.

Dobbins, T. (2005) 'Union Density Decline Driven by Global Economic Factors', *Industrial Relations News*, 14 September, p. 12.

DoT (Department of the Taoiseach) (1987) *Programme for National Recovery*. Dublin: Stationery Office.

— (1996) *Partnership 2000 for Inclusion, Employment and Competitiveness*. Dublin: Stationery Office.

— (2000) *Programme for Prosperity and Fairness*. Dublin: Stationery Office.

Geary, J.F. and Roche, W.K. (2002) 'Workplace Partnership and the Theory of the Displaced Activist'. EUI Working Paper, SPS NO, 2002/3.

Geraghty, D. (1995) 'No Going Back to Hand-to-Hand Combat in Industry', *Irish Times*, 6 January, p. 14.

Guest, D. and Peccei, R. (2001) 'Partnership at Work: Mutuality and the Balance of Advantage', *British Journal of Industrial Relations* 39(2): 207–37.

Hardiman, N. (2000) 'Social Partnership, Wage Bargaining and Growth', in B. Nolan, J.O'Connell and T. Whelan (eds) *Bust to Boom*, pp. 286–339. Dublin: IPA.

Hastings,T., Sheehan, B. and Yeates, P. (2007) *Saving The Future – How Social Partnership Shaped Ireland's Economic Success*. Dublin: Blackhall.

IBEC (Irish Business and Employers' Confederation) (2002), *Human Resource Management Survey*. Dublin: IBEC.

ICTU (Irish Congress of Trade Unions) (1993) *New Forms of Work Organisation*, Dublin: ICTU.

IPA (Involvement and Participation Assocation) (2004) 'Key Themes – Partnership – Definition of Partnership' [online]. Available: http://www.ipa-involve.com/60/61/64/71/index.php (last accessed 17 June 2004).

Knell, J. (2000) 'Partnership at Work', *Employment Relations Research* series, No. 7. London: Industrial Society/Department of Trade and Industry.

LRC (Labour Relations Commission) (2003) *Annual Report 2003*. Dublin: LRC.

Marchington, M. (1995) 'Employee Involvement', in J. Storey (ed.) *HRM: A Critical Text*, pp. 280–308. London: Routledge.

Marchington, M., Goodman, J., Wilkinson, A. and Ackers, P. (1992), *New Developments in Employee Involvement*. London: HMSO.

Meenan, F. (1999) *Working within the Law*, 2nd edn. Dublin: Oak Tree Press.

O'Connell, L. (2002) Speech at the launch of *Working Together – Towards a Modern Workplace*, NCPP, 24 July 2002 [online]. Available: http://www.ncpp.ie/press_detail.asp?newsId=126&zoneId=6&catId=291 (last accessed 15 November 2009).

O'Connell, P.J., Russell, H., Williams, J. and Blackwell, S. (2003) Forum on the Workplace of the Future, *The Changing Workplace: A Survey of Employees Views and Experiences*. Dublin: NCPP.

O'Connor, E. (2002) 'Ireland in Historical Perspective', in S. Berger and H. Compston (eds) *Policy Concertation and Social Partnership in Western Europe*, pp. 155–66. Oxford: Berghahn Books.

O'Connor, T. and O'Halloran, A. (2008) *Politics in a Changing Ireland*. Dublin: Institute of Public Administration.

O'Donnell, R. and Thomas, D. (2002) 'Ireland in Historical Perspective', in S. Berger and H. Compston (eds) *Policy Concertation and Social Partnership in Western Europe*, pp.167–90. Oxford: Berghahn Books.

O'Leary, K. (2006) 'An Exploration of Enterprise Level Partnership and the Influences Informing Private Sector Organisations' Choice of this Model In the Republic of Ireland', unpublished MPhil thesis, Dublin Institute of Technology.

Roche, W.K. (1999) 'The End of New Industrial Relations', *EUI Working Paper*, SPS No. 99/8 European University Institute, Florence .

— (2007) 'Social Partnership and Workplace Regimes in Ireland', *Industrial Relations Journal* 38(3): 188–209.

— (2008) 'The Trend of Unionisation in Ireland since the Mid-1990's', in T. Hastings (ed.) *The State of the Unions*, pp. 17–46. Dublin: Liffey Press.

Salamon, M. (2000) *Industrial Relations Theory and Practice*, 4th edn. London: FT/Prentice Hall.

Wall, M. (2009) 'SIPTU Leader Sees no Potential for Deal on Social Partnership', *Irish Times*, 4 August, p. 1.

Yeates, P. (1995) 'Phil Flynn: A Committed and Articulate Champion of Centralised Bargaining', *Irish Times*, 3 July, p. 4.

— (1997) 'Work Partnership Could Be Enforced, Says Flynn', *Irish Times,* 13 September, p. 9.

— (1998) 'Sharing Required for Real Partnership – ICTU', *Irish Times,* 24 April, p. 4.

Chapter 15

From Ballymun to Brussels: Forms of Partnership Governance in Irish Social Inclusion Policy

Jesse J. Norris

INTRODUCTION

The Frankfurt school theorist Hannah Arendt was uncomfortable with the idea of a welfare state. To her it entailed the death of participatory democracy at the hands of the technocratic administrative state (Arendt 1958). Now that various policy forums at the European, national and local levels are devoted to broadly participatory, strategic deliberation on welfare policy, this view may seem hopelessly outdated. After all, no one today would argue that technocrats should be the sole decision makers on social policy, insulated from democratic debate and non-state participation.

Yet, in Ireland today, a roughly analogous critique is still widespread, based on a deep dissatisfaction with public deliberation on the welfare state. According to this view, partnership governance is a sham, meant to impose state power on a compliant civil society by luring non-state parties into consensus-based, participatory, but state-dominated processes. This chapter presents reasons to doubt the most extreme version of this critique. But ultimately the onus is on both the government and the community and voluntary sector to prove the critique mistaken, in ways this chapter explains.

Several features of Irish governance besides social partnership – the open method of co-ordination (OMC), County/City Development Boards (CDBs), Area Partnerships (APs) and the Revitalising Areas by Planning, Investment and Development (RAPID) programme – can be described as partnership governance. In all these processes, various interests are represented, including among others labour, business, the community and voluntary sector, and statutory agencies. For all their differences, the processes share a common objective: to determine in a participatory, collaborative and strategic way how best to combat poverty and social exclusion, and to take initial steps to do so through co-ordination and policy innovation.

This chapter provides a brief analysis of the impacts and challenges of the OMC, CDBs, APs and RAPID. The OMC, an EU process requiring member states to create strategies to achieve commonly agreed goals, has had important substantive and procedural impacts on policy making, but suffers from a lack of transparency. The CDBs co-ordinate local policies through broad-based collaboration. They have begun to enhance the co-ordination of social inclusion policy, but insufficient monitoring, transparency and funding, among other problems, has inhibited their effectiveness. APs are organisations devoted to solving social problems in an innovative, participatory way. The most successful partnership governance mechanism, APs have made numerous impacts on national and local policy, but national policy makers still have not learned from their work in a systematic way. RAPID, which brings additional resources and initiatives to the most disadvantaged neighbourhoods through local collaboration, has brought about significant improvements, but a lack of funding and national responsiveness has limited its impact. While each of these mechanisms has had positive effects, they require key governance reforms, as well as the adrenalin shot of adversarial policy campaigns, to achieve their goals. This would involve a comprehensive strategy for allowing partnership governance to work, and recognising the value of conflict in partnership.

PARTNERSHIP GOVERNANCE AND DEMOCRATIC EXPERIMENTALISM

A sense of crisis has long haunted the welfare state and the traditional bureaucratic state, which are seen as ineffective, outdated and in need of broad reforms (Esping-Andersen *et al.* 2002; Peters 2001). Over the last decade, a number of new governance mechanisms have arisen to address these concerns. Governance reforms in the 1980s tended to have a market or consumer focus, seeking to make government more efficient. Reforms during the last decade, however, have been based on a partnership model that develops innovative solutions and better integrates existing efforts through a collaborative, participatory approach involving social partners and disadvantaged groups (Bovaird and Löffler 2003). This 'good governance' philosophy is highly influential in the European Union (EU), which has created or funded numerous forms of partnership governance across Europe, including the OMC and local partnerships.

Within governance theory, democratic experimentalism is a particularly well-developed perspective (Dorf and Sabel 1998). The democratic experimentalist approach promotes governance arrangements that encourage local units to innovate in pursuit of revisable central objectives. It places emphasis on rigorous central monitoring, mutual learning processes such as peer review, transparency, widespread participation and local flexibility. Such experimentalist governance can stimulate effective problem solving, diffuse innovative practices and foster a dynamic form of accountability. Criticism of the government, especially when informed by comparative data generated by governance processes, is considered a major source of dynamism (Sabel and Zeitlin 2008).

THE OPEN METHOD OF CO-ORDINATION

In the OMC, EU member states establish common goals in a particular policy area, and commit to work towards them by implementing detailed national plans. The OMC is a collaborative, consensual system for encouraging policy reform in areas where it is inappropriate for the EU to directly regulate member states. Though the results have been mixed, the OMC has had significant effects on national policy thinking, substantive policies, governance procedures and the participation of non-state actors (Zeitlin 2005).

There are several OMC processes, but the most influential across the EU have been the OMC for employment policy and the OMC for social inclusion. After a 'relaunch' in 2005, the processes were consolidated so that the employment plan became a chapter in a broader national reform programme, and the social inclusion plan was incorporated in a social protection plan encompassing pensions and health care. This relaunch diminished important facets of the OMC, making less use of peer review and common indicators, and requiring less comprehensive reports (Zeitlin 2007).

To explain the process in more detail, all member states periodically agree on a set of common goals towards which they will seek to orient their policies. Each member state composes regular national action plans, which describe the country's current policies and future strategies, as well as implementation reports. Along with exchanging good practices, countries evaluate each others' plans through a peer review process. The European Commission (EC) issues evaluations of countries' progress, suggesting areas for improvement.

The Employment OMC

The employment OMC (launched in 1997 as the European Employment Strategy (EES)) has had a considerable impact in Ireland, even if social partnership has detracted somewhat from its importance. It stimulated the creation of the Preventative Strategy, a successful active labour market policy begun in 1998 that now provides all unemployed persons with employment assistance within three months of receiving jobseeker's benefits. The EES seems to have prompted greater attention to lifelong learning, resulting in the creation of a lifelong learning strategy. It also brought heightened attention to gender issues in employment policy (O'Donnell and Moss 2005). Beyond this, it is difficult to identify particular policy changes prompted by the process, as social partnership is where the government typically commits to new employment policies.

EC reactions to Ireland's participation in the employment OMC have generally been positive, but it has sometimes criticised the lack of comprehensive statistics in the action plans, the lack of budgetary detail, the lack of information on progress towards targets, and the lack of data on policy impacts, all of which make the plans difficult to evaluate. Such problems are pervasive in partnership governance, and are discussed below in terms of operational transparency, or the lack of clarity in how a governance process works or will work in practice (Norris 2007:168–80).

The Open Method of Co-ordination for Social Inclusion

Ireland's National Anti-Poverty Strategy (NAPS) began in 1997 as a ten-year strategy, influenced by the United Nations World Summit for Social Development in 1995. Similar in structure to social partnership, the NAPS involved consultations with various stakeholders, who together monitored the strategy's implementation. The EU launched the OMC for social inclusion in 2001, apparently influenced by the Irish approach.

Concerns with operational transparency have been pervasive in both the NAPS and the OMC for inclusion. The EC, the National Social and Economic Council (NESC), and the community and voluntary sector in Ireland have all criticised the plans' vagueness on 'concrete steps, policies and resources' (O'Donnell and Moss 2005:333). More substantively, the European Anti-Poverty Network (EAPN) Ireland also criticised the NAPS' weak targets (which were met quite easily), lack of impact on the budget, inadequate resources, and the lack of data on the effects of its policies (Hanan 2002).

The first (2001–2003) national inclusion plan for the OMC was submitted during a mid-term review of the NAPS, and was roundly critiqued for containing nothing new or particularly useful. The revised NAPS, published in 2002, contained more ambitious targets, and further provisions for the strategy's governance. The second (2003–2005) action plan for the inclusion OMC, published just one year later, mainly incorporated material from the revised NAPS, effectively merging the two processes. Because of the new targets, more elaborate monitoring and consultation, and improved analysis, the EC responded more positively, but urged attention to various issues, arguing that adequate resources needed to be committed to social inclusion policy. EAPN Ireland and NESC made the same operational transparency criticisms as before, but EAPN Ireland also drew attention to policies actually worsening poverty, and noted that despite far-reaching consultation their input failed to influence the plan (Daly 2003; EAPN Ireland 2003).

The implementation report for the second plan, and the 2006–2008 social protection plan, leave ambiguous whether the OMC process added anything to what was agreed through social partnership. They did include, however, considerable material on immigration and racial concerns, including a National Action Plan Against Racism. EC pressure to address these issues may well have prompted this new emphasis.

Dissatisfied for various reasons with the 2008–2010 social protection plan, EAPN Ireland released its own shadow report (EAPN Ireland 2008). The shadow report included a detailed critique of the plan and numerous recommendations, based partially on extensive consultation with people experiencing poverty.

Though it is no longer required after the OMC relaunch, Ireland published a National Action Plan for Social Inclusion (2007–2016). This plan, with the same timeframe as the Towards 2016 agreement, provides a more detailed description of the social inclusion-related commitments of the agreement. Thus, despite the abolition of the stand-alone inclusion OMC, the Irish adapted the report to deepen the social inclusion dimension of social partnership, which was seen as less developed in the previous agreement.

What difference has the inclusion OMC made? It has influenced national policy thinking and procedural arrangements for policy making and implementation, including increases in non-state participation. It has also probably affected substantive policies. Procedural shifts are the most prominent. An elaborate set of institutions, from the Senior Officials Group on Social Inclusion to local Social Inclusion Units, has been created to promote a co-ordinated approach to combating social exclusion. This has resulted in a greater commitment to social inclusion among various government actors, more rigorous monitoring, and new opportunities for non-state involvement (even if the fruits of this involvement are difficult to ascertain). The Office for Social Inclusion (OSI) has taken on a disciplinary function, pressuring departments to implement social inclusion policies. The OMC has enabled a stronger role for the social affairs department in policy making and co-ordination, beyond merely administering social programmes.

The inclusion OMC has affected policy thinking by enhancing the importance of relative income poverty, by pressuring all departments to systematically consider their impact on social exclusion, and by broadening the discourse on poverty to encompass social inclusion (Norris 2007:115–24). The significantly redistributive nature of the 2005 and 2006 budgets may have been influenced by the increased salience of relative income poverty (CPA 2006). Such changes are important because the state has long resisted inequality-based poverty definitions, which show poverty rates in Ireland to rank among Europe's highest.

Strategic planning has also improved (Norris 2007:113–14). Officials have become more careful in composing targets for national plans, and more attentive to developing data sources for evaluating progress, resulting in a more rationalised planning process (see Zeitlin 2005:248). Targets have become more numerous and specific, with precise timeframes and quantitative commitments.

While it is difficult to identify policy changes caused by the inclusion OMC, it probably affected substantive policies. OSI and non-state actors both reported using the OMC process strategically to affect policy. As noted above, greater awareness of income inequality may have affected budgets' distributive effects, and the process may have spurred more attention to racism.

LOCAL PARTNERSHIPS

Local welfare systems are often as troubled as their national counterparts, with high concentrations of poverty, social problems and long-term unemployment. Governance is also problematic at the local level, where a multiplicity of private, state and semi-state organisations provide similar services with little co-ordination. Since the late 1980s, local partnerships have been created in various countries to meet these challenges, uniting all the relevant entities in reflexively co-ordinating local employment and welfare policies (Geddes and Benington 2001). It is useful to divide local partnerships into two categories: policy co-ordination partnerships; and project-management partnerships (Norris 2007).

Local co-ordination partnerships are designed to foster co-ordination of local policies in a given policy area. CDBs are a wide-ranging local co-ordination partnership, which collaboratively produce plans for social, economic and cultural development. The RAPID programme co-ordinates policy responses for the most disadvantaged neighbourhoods, through cross-agency co-operation and grassroots participation.

Project-management partnerships may encourage co-ordination, but unlike co-ordination partnerships, they are heavily involved in the actual management of projects, usually time-limited collaborative ventures. These partnerships may implement projects themselves, or more indirectly manage them by providing funding, technical assistance and guidance to other groups. Especially for member states receiving significant EU aid, project-management partnerships are of great importance, since they deliver much of this funding. Ireland's APs are among the oldest and most well-known examples in Europe.

Area Partnerships

APs were created in 1991 to address long-term unemployment with a multidimensional, experimental approach. The programme started with twelve pilot partnerships, and was expanded in 1994 to thirty-eight partnerships. After a cohesion process meant to consolidate different kinds of local partnership to cover the entire Republic without overlap, there are now thirty-seven Integrated Local Development Companies and seventeen Urban Partnerships. Though this classification no longer distinguishes between APs and other partnerships, APs maintain their identity through their national network (called Planet, the Partnerships Network). APs are independent companies governed by a board of directors with representation from state agencies, the local community, social partners and local councillors. They are funded by EU and national funds, and Pobal, a semi-state body, plays an administrative and monitoring role. APs often have sections devoted to enterprise, employment, youth or education and community development, with a number of projects in each section ongoing at any given time.

The participation of APs in projects varies widely, and can include taking a leading role in certain stages of a project, mentoring those running the project, providing technical assistance, dispensing small grants for feasibility studies and providing funds for community development workers. Pobal distinguishes APs' roles into a delivery approach, in which the AP delivers a project itself; an agency approach, in which APs arrange for other actors to implement projects; and a brokerage approach, in which APs develop experimental projects that are delivered within state agencies (Pobal 2006b). All three occur to some extent, but the delivery approach is less favoured and is becoming less common.

Policy and Governance Impacts

Of the partnerships discussed in this chapter, the APs have had the strongest impacts on policy. Through what is called mainstreaming, many of the projects developed by APs have gone on to receive more regular funding, or have been generalised into new national programmes. Examples of national programmes mainstreamed from AP projects include, among others, Community Employment, the Back to Work Allowance, and the Money Advice and Budgeting Service. Numerous projects have also been mainstreamed by receiving government funding to continue after the time-limited project expired. Among them are a Traveller health project, an educational initiative for young mothers and a programme assisting small farmers.

Besides mainstreaming their innovations, APs have also managed to persuade the government to change policies, for example by expanding eligibility requirements for certain social services or benefits (Sabel 1996:84). This lobbying, based on needs identified in their work on the ground, has borne fruit on a number of occasions (Norris 2007:338).

APs have had a number of other concrete impacts. These include widening local participation, increasing the resources available locally, shifting the priorities of state agencies to better meet local needs, creating innovative training and job placement approaches, and giving rise to various targeted projects, from community policing to participatory housing estate management (Haase and McKeown 2003; Pobal 2006a; Teague 2006; Turok 2001; Walsh 2001).

Accountability: Problematic or Advanced?

Based on concerns that APs were unaccountable and distant from electoral democracy, elected councillors now sit on the boards. The same concerns drove the creation of the CDBs, which after the cohesion process now have to approve APs' plans. Yet there are indications that APs are remarkably accountable, particularly in comparison to government agencies, and have actually enhanced the accountability of state groups. First, Pobal monitoring and evaluation has become increasingly rigorous and multi-faceted, prompted in part by the arguments that evaluations could be more comprehensive and outcome-focused (Haase and McKeown 2003). Second, APs are responsive to members of disadvantaged groups, whom they continually consult and involve at various levels. Finally, APs have contributed to the accountability of state groups, prompting them to listen more closely to community voices, through consultations and other forms of participation (Turok 2001). As an example, one AP worker described how a large part of her work was convincing the local regeneration planner to improve its consultation practices (see interview in Norris 2007:345).

A Community Development Approach

Rather than co-opting combative local groups into passive service delivery, APs are often focused on trying to get local groups – many of which would not exist without the APs – to think beyond their immediate aims and funding needs to understand how to influence government policy. AP workers, like RAPID and CDB workers, are strong believers in a version of community development principles focused not just on capacity building but on showing local groups how to counter all kinds of inequality and fight for local policy changes. Definitions vary, but community development principles tend to support a radical approach, dedicated to social justice and fighting all forms of oppression. These principles are constantly invoked by AP workers, Combat Poverty Agency (CPA) personnel, and even Pobal officials, all of whom have participated in a strategic shift toward community development (Pobal 2006b).

The shift toward community development has had several important consequences, including growth in the number and strength of community groups involving disadvantaged populations, more sophisticated structures for involving community members in APs, and a proliferation of courses teaching community development and leadership skills to community members, who often go on to become community development workers or activists. APs often fund community development workers for particular groups, helping them to organise and grow until they can obtain funding from another source (what one worker termed 'staff capitalism') (see interview in Norris 2007:353). The overwhelming focus of these activities is enhancing the ability of disadvantaged groups to accomplish policy changes to improve their lives.

Reform and Challenges

In reaction to evaluations, APs have strengthened networking, monitoring and mainstreaming mechanisms. This effort includes the development of various channels for APs to affect policy, the rise of a national network (Planet), more than twenty national policy committees and working groups with partnership or Pobal representation, and greater efforts to publicise and mainstream best practices. It has also featured an increased level and intensity of Pobal monitoring, a larger number of evaluations (both quantitative and qualitative), and an increase in informal networking activities among APs.

Although APs' governance infrastructure is better developed than in other partnerships, challenges remain. Pobal has acknowledged a need for 'enhanced mechanisms . . . to capture the policy implications' of AP work, and that 'continuing effort is needed to strengthen mechanisms for both horizontal and vertical learning' (Pobal 2006b:4, 66). An evaluation identified a need for a 'more proactive and ongoing communications strategy at the national level' (Fitzpatrick Associates 2007:160). For all the APs' efforts, it has been difficult to get national policy makers to pay attention to them in a systematic way.

COUNTY/CITY DEVELOPMENT BOARDS

In the year 2000, CDBs were created in all counties and major cities in Ireland. Their goal is to better co-ordinate state and non-state services to the public, by addressing duplication and gaps in services, and more generally to promote social inclusion and integrated social, cultural and economic development. The impetus for creating the CDBs was the sense of a proliferation of overlapping local initiatives, partnerships and agencies, with no forum to promote their strategic co-ordination, and often little role for elected councillors.

In addition to councillors, CDBs include representatives of local authorities, statutory agencies, local development groups, social partners and the community. The CDBs are headed by a councillor and co-ordinated by local authority staff in the Departments of Community and Enterprise, who are sometimes called community, enterprise and development officers (CEDOs). Social inclusion measures (SIM) groups, committees within the CDBs that are focused on social inclusion, are considered quite active and effective (Indecon 2008:43).

By 2002 the CDBs had all published ten-year strategies for economic, social and cultural development. In addition to describing the existing interventions ongoing in each policy area, the strategies often include collaborative initiatives for addressing gaps and other deficiencies in local policy identified through the CDB process. Despite problems with securing new funding, many of the initiatives have been implemented with the participation of various agencies and local groups. Examples include projects to provide tailored services for Travellers and other target groups, increase the accessibility of transportation and other services for the disabled, create educational programmes in rural areas lacking universities, and develop community development projects for disadvantaged youth. CEDOs tend to take the lead in organising these activities, in addition to planning networking events, training local state actors in social inclusion issues and consultation, teaching community development skills, and helping to mentor community representatives and community forums.

CDBs have begun to effect a cultural change in state actors, towards a willingness to collaborate across agencies, listen to and consult with the public and citizen groups, and recognise that social inclusion applies to all departments and agencies. CEDOs report that state agencies are more likely to be transparent, openly seek advice and willingly take criticism, and are more appreciative of social inclusion and community involvement (see interview in Norris 2007:239–40).

CDBs, Civil Society and Democracy

Some suggest that the CDBs function mainly to allow elected councillors to increase their power vis-à-vis community groups (Geoghegan and Powell 2009:104). Yet, while CDBs increase the involvement of councillors in local governance, they also increase community involvement. Councillors' roles in CDBs have encouraged to some degree a shift from traditional patronage politics to a more collaborative and strategic orientation. This was one of the main purposes of the Strategic Policy Committees (SPCs) that preceded the CDBs. The advent of the CDBs meant more opportunities for community involvement, which were relatively weak in the SPCs.

The CDB process sometimes results in the formation of disciplinary mechanisms, through which local activists hold officials accountable by regularly compelling them to respond publicly to requests, ideas and complaints. When officials promise anything, even that they will look into an issue, community activists take them to task at every opportunity, demanding to know what they have done and what they will commit to do.

Such mechanisms suggest the potential existence of a new form of accountability, based not on electoral approval and top-down commands, but on the continual responses of state actors to bottom-up participation by non-state actors, and to opportunities for cross-sectoral collaboration (Norris 2007:291–6). Regardless, this kind of pressure can lead to policy change. Councillors' political survival may depend on it. Indeed, in at least two cases, community sector representatives on CDBs were later elected as councillors (see O'Leary 2004:231). The natural response to this competition is for councillors to become more engaged with and responsive to community groups.

Depictions of partnerships as imposing state power on civil society fall flat when one listens to partnership workers (APs, CDBs, and RAPID included). Their passion for an egalitarian, radical version of community development principles drives their work, which is focused on helping disadvantaged groups learn to affect policy in every way possible, from consultation to confrontation. Some CEDOs work with the community forum as one of their main activities, and are delighted when it is aggressive and demanding (Norris 2007:236–7, 240–1).

Challenges Facing CDBs

While CDBs have had positive effects, the process has been beset by difficulties. A lack of national co-ordination and responsiveness to the CDBs' needs and ideas has resulted in wide variation, with some CDBs having little to show for their efforts. The new funding needed to accomplish the CDBs' aims has been in short supply. The cohesion process, which aimed to introduce greater coherence to local governance, antagonised local development groups such as APs by requiring CDB approval of their plans, even though state entities – whose accountability problems are, if anything, more acute – were not subjected to additional scrutiny. CDBs have also suffered after the local authorities' departments of community and enterprise shifted from recruiting staff from outside local authorities, which allowed a unique infusion of community development idealism into local government, to traditional in-house hiring. This has not always caused disaster, but as one source told the author, 'You can't make a community development worker of somebody who's been doing pure administration all their lives' (see interview in Norris 2007:245–6).

An evaluation identified a need to ensure and highlight national government commitment to CDBs, establish a mechanism for national government to consider CDBs' advice and recommendations when making decisions, introduce incentives for officials to actively engage in the process, and increase mutual exchange of best practices among CDBs and between CDBs and state agencies (Indecon 2008). It also recommended establishing a national co-ordinative group to 'give impetus to the work of CDBs, to inform the Cabinet on key emerging issues, and to address any obstacles which exist' (Indecon 2008:62). If these suggestions are implemented, along with increased funding, local flexibility and greater government openness to non-state participation, the CDBs would closely approximate the democratic experimentalist ideal, and would be capable of far greater accomplishments.

THE RAPID PROGRAMME

RAPID is a partnership programme that was initiated in 2001 in twenty-five disadvantaged urban neighbourhoods and expanded a year later to twenty lower-population areas. Arising from a commitment in the Programme for Prosperity and Fairness (2000–2003) agreement, RAPID has three aims: to increase investment in RAPID areas; to 'improve the delivery of public services through integration and co-ordination'; and to foster communities' participation in the 'strategic improvement of their areas' (Pobal 2009).

Each RAPID area has a co-ordinator, and an Area Implementation Team (AIT) composed of elected representatives, statutory agencies, local development groups and community representatives. The programme is monitored nationally by a monitoring group chaired by the Minister for Community, Rural and Gaeltacht Affairs, and locally by the CDBs' SIM groups, and is administered by Pobal. RAPID co-ordinators, in collaboration with the AIT and community members, organise the drafting of a plan for implementing RAPID in their area. RAPID results in increased funding for communities, by arranging for the financing of new initiatives, and through prioritising RAPID areas in national funding streams.

Impacts of RAPID

The increased funding brought about by RAPID has included, among many other things, community development projects, infrastructural projects such as new community centres, educational and training initiatives, security measures, and more services and activities for youth. For example, after discovering needs for adult education in Tallaght and Clondalkin, the RAPID partnerships in those areas each arranged the hiring of an adult education worker serving the RAPID areas exclusively. The Department of Education and Science agreed to fund the workers, in response to RAPID-generated pressure (Cosgrove 2004).

An evaluation identified several strengths of RAPID. The programme has brought about new local development projects, multi-stakeholder partnerships leading to new funding and more efficient service delivery, an increase in local and national government spending in RAPID areas, innovative methods of community participation, the elimination of duplication, and structures for 'disadvantaged communities to identify needs, influence policy and develop projects for the first time' (Fitzpatrick Associates 2006:6).

RAPID has sometimes resulted in a greater appreciation among government actors for collaboration, stronger commitment to the RAPID areas, and community members' greater capacity for engaging with government programmes. RAPID co-ordinators spend large amounts of time both in encouraging government actors to be closely involved, and in cultivating the skills and involvement of community representatives. This has fostered an identification with the RAPID areas among government actors, who often became 'champions' within their organisation for the RAPID areas and developed personal ties with local residents, who would then feel comfortable contacting them with community problems. Community representatives have occasionally assumed a more assertive role, driving RAPID-area actions by determining local priorities and securing government commitments to address them.

Residents have, at times, used RAPID to exert pressure on state actors to make positive changes and follow through on their commitments. By taping meetings, preparing minutes and keeping close track of even the smallest commitments, community representatives are sometimes able to impose a certain level of discipline on state actors, ensuring that their concerns are addressed in a timely, direct and public manner. RAPID co-ordinators enthusiastically help residents establish such relationships.

Challenges Facing the RAPID Programme

While there have been some positive results, RAPID suffers from fundamental weaknesses, and took years to recover from an initial funding crisis. Based on RAPID's public presentation – which then Taoiseach Bertie Ahern personally launched in 2001 with much fanfare – RAPID areas were expecting billions of euros in new funding. This was supposed to happen through 'frontloading' social inclusion expenditures in the 2000–2006 National Development Plan. This turned out to be impossible, because these expenditures had been planned in advance by numerous statutory agencies, and could not be delivered early in any co-ordinated way. The results on the ground were dire. For years, RAPID co-ordinators desperately struggled to keep residents engaged, despite the complete absence of new funds, by cobbling together local resources for modest improvements.

RAPID's biggest weakness is the lack of any mechanism to compel national government departments to focus their mainstream spending on RAPID areas, or to actively engage in the RAPID process (see Murphy and Ó Broin 2008). New funding arises mainly through national leverage funding, small amounts of resources made available locally, and project funding aided by prioritisation of RAPID areas in competitive funding streams. Leverage schemes, arranged through the personal negotiations of the resourceful Minister Éamon Ó Cuív in the Department of Community, Rural and Gaeltacht Affairs, enabled certain projects (traffic calming measures are one example) to be implemented across various RAPID areas.

Central to the funding problems is a lack of government responsiveness. Leverage schemes may be arranged with local input, but they rarely correspond to the priorities of individual RAPID areas, even though this was a key purpose of the programme. RAPID co-ordinators were highly appreciative of Minister Ó Cuív for bringing about the leverage funds. However, the government as a whole needs to commit to making RAPID work, by providing funding for priority needs and compelling all the participants to be fully engaged. This would of course be difficult to achieve with the financial crisis, which has led to sharp cuts to social expenditures in the 2008 and 2009 budgets (CPA 2009).

IMPROVING PARTNERSHIP GOVERNANCE

Despite the differences between these governance processes, they have much in common. They all seek to promote innovative approaches to combating social exclusion, and to do so through collaboration, mutual learning, strategic planning and bottom-up participation. All have had partial success, even if the magnitude of effect varies widely among the mechanisms. Yet it is clear that they have ushered in neither a new welfare state configuration nor a new era of partnership governance. Ireland still suffers from widespread inequality and exclusion, still has nearly the same 'anorexic' welfare regime (Boyle 2005:113–15), and is still governed mainly through traditional bureaucracy and politics.

Continuing their current trajectory, these mechanisms will stimulate additional improvements, but are unlikely to effect a genuine transformation in policy and governance. If more fundamental change is to occur, shifts in partnership governance are necessary. This would involve important governance reforms. But it would also involve changing how both the government and the civil society conceive of partnership governance.

Table 15.1 Local partnership processes – a summary

	County/City Development Boards	Area Partnerships	RAPID Programme
Objectives	Promote integrated social, cultural and economic development; co-ordinate inclusion policies	Promote innovative, collaborative approaches to fighting social exclusion	Increase investment in poorest areas through a collaborative and participatory approach
Areas covered	Counties/cities	Counties/cities	Disadvantaged neighbourhoods
Support provided	Analyse and co-ordinate policies; eliminate duplication; address gaps; support community involvement	Develop, fund, and manage collaborative projects; promote community development	Analyse and co-ordinate policies; eliminate duplication; address gaps; support community involvement
Challenges	Funding; agency involvement; national responsiveness; co-ordination	Government mainstreaming; systematically learning from APs	Funding; agency involvement; national responsiveness

The Missing Politics in Partnership Governance

One of the most important things the government could do to enhance governance in the social inclusion field would be to recognise that partnership governance should not be free of conflict and contestation. Trying to maintain a quiet consensus alienates participants and limits effectiveness. The community and voluntary sector could also contribute by systematically promoting ambitious policy alternatives.

A striking feature of Irish governance is the community and voluntary sector's deep distrust of the government's motives. Sector activists were dismayed that the government not only expelled the Community Platform from the social partnership process, from 2003 to 2006, after it refused to endorse the Sustaining Progress agreement, but also excluded it, and its members, from various other governance forums (Norris 2007:63, 348–9). The sector depicted the government's transfer of the CPA to the Department of Social Welfare as an attempt to silence its independent, critical perspective on government policy (Kirby and Murphy 2009:152–3). The withdrawal of funding from the Community Workers' Co-operative in 2005 was widely interpreted as retribution for its outspoken criticisms of the government, including during the Sustaining Progress negotiations (Community Workers' Co-operative 2005). The withdrawal of funding from other vocal groups, and indications that the government expected organisations receiving government funds to refrain from policy campaigns, were also seen as an attempt to confine non-state groups to passive service delivery (Harvey 2009). These and other events have left many in the sector feeling that the state is against them and wants nothing more than to silence and co-opt them into compliant agents of a neo-liberal state (Kirby and Murphy 2009; Murphy 2009).

The government should address the sector's concerns. At a minimum, the government should commit itself to ensuring that no one is denied funding or excluded from governance processes for criticising the government. Going further, the government should acknowledge the great importance of community development work – even though it can lead to activism against the state – and dispel fears that it seeks to confine the sector to passive service delivery. In doing so, the government would in effect alter its semi-corporatist, conflict-averse governance philosophy, to a more democratic model that recognises the inherent legitimacy of contested politics and dissent, even in partnership governance (Geoghegan and Powell 2009). It is arguably in the state's interest to do so. As an example, the NESC's ambitious plans for a 'developmental welfare state' – which include a 'radical development of services' and a 'tailored universalism' – seem impossible without more pressure from below and will from above (NESC 2005:159, 203).

The community and voluntary sector could also help break this impasse. Sector activists have long dwelt on the state's supposed hostility, and on the evils of being dependent on and thus potentially co-opted by the state. Yet, despite the risks, it is still possible to combine constructive involvement in partnership governance with actively challenging state policies. As one activist told the author, working in partnership never stopped him protesting – one just has to be 'smart' or strategic (see interview in Norris 2007:345). With feasible alternatives to state funding nowhere in sight, sector members would be well advised to follow their hearts and start a broad-based, popular movement for a comprehensive, community development-oriented welfare state (Kirby and Murphy 2009:148–59; National Women's Council of Ireland 2009).

This may well come to pass. As a sign of its increasing sophistication, the Community Platform recently published a thorough and engaging critique of current trends in Irish welfare state development – including the idea of a developmental welfare state – and presented an alternative vision for a far stronger welfare system (Kirby and Murphy 2008; see EAPN Ireland 2008). While it is encouraging to see the NESC's complex proposal become a subject of public debate, the Platform seems to understand that a more realistic topic for debate is a simpler question: does Ireland want to continue with more or less of its minimalist welfare regime, or shift towards a more generous, equality-promoting model? (See Murphy 2007:17–19.)

If a welfare movement can convince the public that it wants the latter (with a community development twist), then partnership governance – from social partnership and the OMC-linked processes down to local partnerships – would be well suited to pragmatically hammer out the details of the resulting political mandate, and co-ordinate implementation. Yet, without a vigorous political push from above and below, partnership governance is unlikely to dramatically diminish poverty and social exclusion. Partnership in a political and media vacuum, all sound and no fury, can be virtually directionless.

In democratic experimentalist thought, one way to avoid incrementalism is by mainstreaming local innovations (Dorf and Sabel 1998:412). However, without policy campaigns, grassroots lobbying, or a more vigorous government commitment, it seems unlikely that mainstreaming would result in any large-scale policy shift. Experimentalist theory does provide a method for making partnership political: in what are called democratising destabilisation effects, activists use information obtained through the governance processes (such as through comparisons between countries through the OMC) to challenge policies (Sabel and Zeitlin 2008). Similarly, non-state actors have often used the OMC process strategically to obtain results (Zeitlin 2009:17–19). Partnership governance seems to have the biggest impact when stimulated by activism.

It is a mistake to regard partnership governance as inherently neo-liberal or apolitical, or as having any fundamental essence. The good-governance partnership ethos is not unique to Ireland, but rather pervades European politics. It is susceptible to incorporation within any political perspective. Ireland's history of catch-all, centrist, political parties and growth-oriented deal-making through social partnership, need not define partnership governance. More progressive currents run deep as well, and can be tapped.

Enhancing the Governance Architecture

Several improvements in the governance architecture would go a long distance in improving the results of partnership governance. This would include a government commitment to partnership governance, a multi-dimensional strategy to make it work, a central forum for national/local co-ordination, adequate funding, local flexibility and enhanced transparency.

The vital ingredient is a real government commitment to fully allowing the partnerships to succeed, by providing for ample funding, sophisticated monitoring, and the continual attention of leaders in the civil service, cabinet and the Oireachtas. Partnership governance cannot be effective if is only a half-forgotten side project of the government. It has to be part of state actors' everyday world, influencing their decision making and general style of governance.

This will not happen without the state devising and implementing a great co-ordinated effort, a continually re-examined, multi-dimensional strategy to make governance processes effective. Among other things, such a strategy would promote vigorous bottom-up participation and regular national/local communication, and ensure that state actors are engaged, through informal pressure, the promotion of a culture of new governance, and official means, such as new regulations or department circulars (Norris 2007:436–6).

As part of such a strategy, a central body responsible for monitoring, co-ordinating, learning from and communicating with the partnerships could have great benefits. Such an arrangement could raise partnerships' profile, help mainstream local innovations, ensure national actors address local implementation problems, consolidate monitoring data, and host mutual learning or peer-review practices. It could also enhance the OMC by providing a central forum to communicate with partnerships about implementing national priorities. As the CPA (2007:1–2) recognised, 'What is needed is a process for receiving and deliberating on information' from partnerships and 'more importantly, reacting to that information through transparent responses to those providing it', while also ensuring that 'national expectations will be delivered and reported on' by local actors.

The design of a central governance body could be informed by governance theory, the ideas of stakeholders, and analogous structures in other countries. As an example, President Obama, the first US president with a past as a community development worker, is establishing a White House Office on Social Innovation, intended to monitor and promote policy experimentation (Perry 2009). Present governance arrangements such as those supporting the OMC could of course serve as models or building blocks for any reforms.

Regardless of whether a new central body is created, it is critical to establish some kind of vertical co-ordination mechanism that continually relays partnerships' concerns and ideas to national decision makers. Otherwise the government responds slowly, if at all, to the experience on the ground. This is not just a problem with partnership governance, but is a common feature of the gap between law on the books and law in action, which socio-legal scholars have long documented. Closing this communication gap is all the more crucial for partnership governance, which involves not just implementing policies, but also developing new ones while attempting to solve complex problems in an innovative and deeply collaborative way.

Ensuring that all actors are truly engaged in partnerships is of crucial importance, above all for co-ordination partnerships. In RAPID and the CDBs, there is no regular mechanism for pressuring or giving incentives to recalcitrant partners. The lack of participation and prioritisation by certain agencies is a major obstacle, particularly for RAPID. When certain actors are not contributing, the government needs to vigorously experiment with methods to induce them to do so.

Adequate funding and local flexibility are also key. Among the mechanisms discussed in this chapter, APs have had the largest impact on policy and governance. What explains this, besides the fact they have existed for so long, is probably that they have always had ample resources and the flexibility to experiment. A chief impediment to new initiatives in CDBs and RAPID is the scarcity of funds not already tied to particular projects, and agencies' difficulties in departing from existing spending plans.

An increase in transparency – in all its dimensions – would also make partnership governance more effective. Transparency is more than simply releasing documents (see Chapter 11). Certainly, the government should release documents, and do so in a more systematic and complete way. Indeed, for some governance entities – like the promising-sounding Local Government Social Inclusion Steering Group – virtually no information is publicly available. At the very least, websites should reveal a group's members, meeting dates and rudimentary meeting minutes, and officials should refrain from making decisions without publicly justifying them. But this is only the beginning.

It is also crucial to enhance transparency about the content and operation of governance mechanisms, including, for example, clarifying exactly what is new in OMC and CDB plans and how these plans will be accomplished. Problems with operational transparency are pervasive in partnership governance, and sometimes quite harmful. For example, the vain promise that the NDP would front-load its funds in RAPID areas was probably inspired by misunderstandings about the NDP process. Moreover, most criticisms of the OMC relate to deficits in operational transparency. Enhancing operational transparency could enable a stronger role for the OMC and CDBs in policy making, allowing them to fulfil their original missions. When plans simply list all policies without identifying what is new, virtually no one can understand their significance.

Partnership processes could also foster openness about the results of their efforts, by conducting and releasing more research ('substantive transparency'). The current norm of commissioning a comprehensive evaluation every few years is too slow and inexact. Recognising this, the APs have begun producing more evaluations, qualitative as well as quantitative. A central governance mechanism could develop a more continual evaluation process, which could also be aided by mutual learning or peer review exercises.

CONCLUSION

This chapter argues that while the partnership governance processes discussed here – the OMC, CDBs, RAPID and the APs – have had significant successes, their current trajectory is unlikely to lead to transformative impacts on social exclusion or governance. While the OMC has not led to widespread policy changes, it has had some important effects on governance and national policy thinking. It has also created a range of useful governance structures, upon which a more effective governance architecture could be built. The APs, CDBs and RAPID have fostered a culture of collaboration among local actors, given a greater voice to disadvantaged groups, created new initiatives to address neglected problems, and prioritised the neediest areas. Yet social exclusion as a whole has scarcely diminished, and partnership governance remains peripheral to traditional bureaucracy and closed-door politics.

For partnership governance to decisively tackle poverty and social exclusion, two things need to occur. First, the state needs to fully commit to partnership governance, by providing the necessary attention and funds, and to a reformed governance system that monitors and guides partnerships effectively and is continually responsive to their successes, ideas and concerns.

Second, the state and the community and voluntary sector need to overcome their fears about partnership governance, integrating it with the politics of contestation and big ideas. The state should stop expecting partnership governance to be free from discord and outspoken dissent, and steadfastly refrain from punishing critics with less access or funding. This would mean recognising the valid role of conflictual politics in and alongside partnership, instead of seeing partnership as a way to eliminate open conflicts. The government should also resist the temptation to consider partnership governance a substitute for a more well-developed welfare state. Partnerships may, at times, eliminate duplication and solve problems in less costly ways, but a much higher level of spending is needed to substantially reduce poverty and social exclusion.

For its part, the community and voluntary sector should continue the pragmatic work of collaborative problem solving, while at the same time abandoning the fear that larger policy campaigns for fundamental change might result in retribution. Rather than being distracted by a paralysing angst about the state's supposedly sinister intentions, the sector should take the initiative to start a broad-based, transformative campaign for an egalitarian Ireland. If the sector convinces the public of the need for a stronger welfare state devoted to eliminating poverty and promoting community development, its increased leverage in partnership governance – from local partnerships to social partnership and the OMC, from Ballymun to Brussels as it were – could allow it to help design and implement the new policies.

Finally, observers should be careful in evaluating the success of partnership governance, and drawing conclusions from this about its ultimate worth. Co-ordination partnerships like the CDBs and RAPID and processes like the OMC have existed for only a few years. The challenges they are meant to address – all forms of social exclusion and the failings of traditional bureaucracy – are enormously complex and deep-seated. Against the sheer scale of what they are up against, it is remarkable that these political novelties accomplish anything at all. This is especially so, given the fact that the government is often not very supportive of these experiments after founding them, and the fact that the processes can operate in a virtual vacuum, with little awareness diffused outside their participants. Whether or not these problems are completely addressed, partnership governance will need time to work, and it deserves the chance to finish what it started.

References

Arendt, H. (1958) *The Human Condition*. Chicago: University of Chicago Press.

Bovaird, T. and Löffler, E. (2003) 'Evaluating the Quality of Public Governance: Indicators, Models and Methodologies', *International Review of Administrative Sciences* 69(3): 313–28.

Boyle, M. (2005) *FÁS and Active Labour Market Policy 1985–2004*. Dublin: Policy Institute.

Community Workers' Co-operative (2005) *Government Censures Dissent (Funding to Community Workers' Co-operative Axed)*, press release [online]. Available: www.december18.net/web/docpapers/doc2319.doc (last accessed 25 August 2009).

Cosgrove, S. (2004) *Case Study Research into the Implementation of the RAPID Programme at Government Department and Agency Level*. Dublin: Area Development Management Ltd.

CPA (Combat Poverty Agency) (2006) *Action on Poverty Today Supplement: Analysis of Budget 2006* [online]. Available: http://www.cpa.ie/publications/povertytoday/2006 _AoPT_12_Supp_BudgetAnalysis.pdf (last accessed 21 August 2009).

— (2007) *Linking Local and National Structures: Tackling Poverty and Promoting Social Inclusion* [online]. Dublin: Combat Poverty Agency. Available: http://www.cpa.ie/publications/policystatements/2007_Policy_LinkingLocalA ndNationalStructures.pdf (last accessed 21 August 2009).

— (2009) *Analysis of Poverty Impact of Budget 2009* [online]. Available: http://cpa.ie/publications/povertytoday/2009_AoPT_23_Supp_Budget Analysis.pdf (last accessed 4 August 2009).

Daly, M. (2003) *NAP/INCL 2003: First Background Report on Ireland* [online]. Available: http://ec.europa.eu/employment_social/social_inclusion/docs/ireland_1st_report_final_en.pdf (last accessed 21 August 2009).

Dorf, M. and Sabel, C. (1998) 'A Constitution of Democratic Experimentalism', *Columbia Law Review* 98(2): 267–473.

EAPN (European Anti-Poverty Network) Ireland (2003) *Anti-Poverty Groups on the New National Action Plan Against Poverty and Social Exclusion (NAPincl): Is the Government Serious about Ending Poverty?* [online]. Available: http://homepage.eircom.net/~esosc/2003_2/NAPS.htm (last accessed 22 July 2009).

— (2008) *Shadow Report on Ireland's NAP Inclusion 2008–2010* [online]. Available: http://www.eapn.ie/documents/1_EAPN Ireland Shadow Report on NAP Incl 2008-2010-Final.pdf (last accessed 22 July 2009).

Esping-Andersen, G., Gallie, D., Hemerijck, A. and Myles, J. (2002) *Why We Need a New Welfare State*. Oxford: Oxford University Press.

Fitzpatrick Associates (2006) *Evaluation of the RAPID (Revitalising Areas through Planning, Investment and Development) Programme: Final Report* [online]. Available: http://www.pobal.ie/media/06.01EvaluationofRAPID ProgrammeFinalReport.doc (last accessed 21 August 2009).

— (2007) *Value-for-Money review of the Local Development Social Inclusion Programme 2000–2006* [online]. Available: http://www.pobail.ie/en/ CommunityLocalDevelopmentProgrammes/LocalDevelopmentSocialInclusio nProgrammeLDSIP/textfile,9585,en.doc (last accessed 21 August 2009).

Geddes, M. and Benington, J. (eds) (2001) *Local Partnerships and Social Exclusion in the European Union: New Forms of Local Social Governance?* London: Routledge.

Geoghegan, M. and Powell, F. (2009) 'Community Development, the Irish State and the Contested Meaning of Civil Society', in D. Ó Broin and P. Kirby (eds) *Power, Dissent and Democracy: Civil Society and the State in Ireland*, pp. 95–110. Dublin: A&A Farmar.

Haase, T. and McKeown, K. (2003) *Developing Disadvantaged Areas through Area-Based Initiatives: Reflections on over a Decade of Local Development Strategies* [online]. Available: http://www.pobal.ie/Documents/DevelopingDisadvantagedAreasthroughArea BasedInitiatives.pdf (last accessed 21 August 2009).

Hanan, R. (2002) 'Addressing the Weaknesses of the Irish NAPs/Incl?', *Poverty Today* 54: 7 [online]. Available: http://www.combatpoverty.ie/publications/ povertytoday/ 2002_PT_54.pdf (last accessed 25 August 2009).

Harvey, B. (2009) 'Ireland and Civil Society: Reaching the Limits of Dissent 2009', in D. Ó Broin and P. Kirby (eds) *Power, Dissent and Democracy: Civil Society and the State in Ireland*, pp. 25–33. Dublin: A&A Farmar.

Indecon (2008) *Indecon Review of County/City Development Board Strategic Reviews and Proposals for Strengthening and Developing the Boards* [online]. Available: http://www.cdb.ie/pdf/taskfrcdocs/Indecon_Report_CDBs-FINAL.pdf (last accessed 22 July 2009).

Kirby, P. and Murphy, M. (2008) *A Better Ireland is Possible: Towards an Alternative Vision for Ireland. Galway*: Community Platform [online]. Available: http://eprints.nuim.ie/1128/1/MMBetter_Ireland_is_Possible.pdf (last accessed 13 February 2010).

— (2009) 'State and Civil Society in Ireland: Conclusions and Mapping Alternatives', in D. Ó Broin and P. Kirby (eds) *Power, Dissent and Democracy: Civil Society and the State in Ireland*, pp. 143–59. Dublin: A&A Farmar.

Murphy, M. (2007) 'The Emerging Irish Workfare State and its Implications for Local Development' in D. Jacobson, P. Kirby and D. Ó Broin (eds) *Taming the Tiger: Social Exclusion in a Globalised Ireland*, pp. 85–112. Dublin: TASC [online]. Available: http://eprints.nuim.ie/1192/1/MMemerging.pdf (last accessed 22 July 2009).

— (2009) 'What Impact Might Globalisation Have on Irish Civil Society?' in D. Ó Broin and P. Kirby (eds) *Power, Dissent and Democracy: Civil Society and the State in Ireland*, pp. 34–47. Dublin: A&A Farmar.

Murphy, M. and Ó Broin, D. (2008) *Square Pegs and Round Holes: Dublin City's Experience of the RAPID Programme*, paper presented at Metropolitan

Governance Work Shop, European Consortium for Political Research, Rennes, France (April) [online]. Available: http://eprints.nuim.ie/1164/1/MMSquare_pegs.pdf (last accessed 22 July 2009).

National Women's Council of Ireland (2009) *Social Welfare Reform* [online]. Available: http://www.nwci.ie/our_work/economic_equality/social_welfare_reform (last accessed 22 July 2009).

NESC (National Economic and Social Council) (2005) *The Developmental Welfare State*. Dublin: NESC.

Norris, J.J. (2007) 'Searching for Synergy: Governance, Welfare and Law in Two EU Member States', unpublished PhD dissertation, University of Wisconsin-Madison.

O'Donnell, R. and Moss, B. (2005) 'Ireland: The Very Idea of an Open Method of Co-Ordination', in J. Zeitlin and P. Pochet (eds), *The Open Method of Co-ordination in Action: The European Employment and Social Inclusion Strategies*, pp. 311–50. Brussels: P.I.E.-Peter Lang.

O'Leary, E. (2004) 'Local Governance in Action: A Case Study of the Cork City Development Board', unpublished PhD dissertation, University College Cork.

Perry, S. (2009) *White House Appoints Head of Social Innovation Office* [online]. Available: http://philanthropy.com/news/government/7874/appointment-of-white-house-office-of-social-innovation-head-confirmed (last accessed 4 August 2009).

Peters, B.G. (2001) *The Future of Governing*. Lawrence: University Press of Kansas.

Pobal (2006a) *Working Together, Working for Change: The Achievements of the Local Development Social Inclusion Programme 2000–2006* [online]. Available: http://www.pobal.ie/ media/Publications/Working%20Together%20 Working%20for%20 Change%2006.pdf (last accessed 22 July 2009).

— (2006b) *Partnership Dynamics: Key Lessons for Local Partnership in Practice* [online]. Available: http://www.pobal.ie/funding%20programmes/ ldsip/informationforbeneficiaries/publications/partnership%20dynamics%20-%20key%20lessons%20from %20local%20partnership%20in%20practice% 202006.pdf (last accessed 22 July 2009).

— (2009) *RAPID* [online]. Available: http://www.pobal.ie/Funding% 20Programmes/ Rapid/Pages/Background.aspx (last accessed 21 August 2009).

Sabel, C. (1996) *Ireland: Local Partnerships and Social Innovation*. Paris: OECD.

Sabel, C. and Zeitlin, J. (2008) 'Learning from Difference: The New Architecture of Experimentalist Governance in the European Union', *European Law Journal* 14(3): 271–327.

Teague, P. (2006) 'Social Partnership and Local Development in Ireland: The Limits to Deliberation', *British Journal of Industrial Relations* 44(3): 421–43.

Turok, I. (2001) 'Area-Based Partnerships in Ireland: Collaborative Planning in Practice?', Paper for EURA conference, Copenhagen, Denmark (May) [online]. Available: http://www.sbi.dk/eura/workshops/papers/workshop5/turok.pdf (last accessed 21 August 2009).

Walsh, J. (2001) 'Catalysts for Change: Public Policy Reform through Local Partnership in Ireland', in M. Geddes and J. Benington (eds), *Local Partnerships and Social Exclusion in the European Union: New Forms of Local Social Governance?*, pp. 111–33. London: Routledge.

Zeitlin, J. (2005) 'The Open Method of Co-ordination in Action: Theoretical Promise, Empirical Realities, Reform Strategy', in J. Zeitlin and P. Pochet (eds), *The Open Method of Co-ordination in Action: The European Employment and Social Inclusion Strategies*, pp. 447–503. Brussels: P.I.E.-Peter Lang.

— (2007) 'The Lisbon Strategy, the Open Method of Co-ordination, and the Future of EU Governance', Paper presented at workshop on Social Europe and the Future of the Welfare State, March, Madison, Wisconsin.

— (2009) 'The Open Method of Co-ordination and Reform of National Social and Employment Policies: Influences, Mechanisms, Effects', in M. Heidenreich and J. Zeitlin (eds), *Changing European Employment and Welfare Regimes: The Influence of the Open Method of Co-ordination on National Reforms*. London: Routledge.

Chapter 16

People in Control: The Promise of the Co-operative Business Approach

Olive McCarthy, Robert Briscoe and Michael Ward

INTRODUCTION

Co-operatives are an innovative business form set up, owned and controlled by their users. These people-centred businesses are intended to involve the users of the product or service they provide in the design and often delivery of those products and services. They frequently emerge in a context where public or private interests have failed to meet particular needs in society. In Ireland, there is a range of very successful co-operative businesses in agriculture, finance, housing and community development. Internationally, co-operatives have been proven in these and a far wider range of activities, including the provision of effective solutions to major organisational problems in the provision of childcare, eldercare, disability services, and environmental protection, issues that are also key concerns in Irish society. Co-operatives are invaluable organisational tools for enabling communities to build unique solutions to their own special problems, as well as making it possible for local businesses to participate creatively in the global economy. This chapter examines the special nature of the co-operative form of organisation and argues that, while it is not without its own problems and challenges, it has a renewed relevance for business in Irish society.

MEANING AND ORIGINS OF CO-OPERATIVES

A co-operative can be defined as 'a self-help business owned and democratically controlled by the people who use its services and share in its benefits' (Briscoe and Ward 2005:10). While this is a simple definition, it does focus on a number of the key features of the co-operative approach. First of all, a co-operative is a self-help organisation, owned and controlled by the people who use its services. It has been set up for the purpose of helping its members address their own needs and problems. Second, it is designed to serve its users. They are the people who use the

319

co-operative's services on a day-to-day basis. Third, co-operatives are democratically controlled, and each member has one vote. Things are done very differently in the typical business, where votes are allocated according to the number of shares owned.

Clearly co-operatives are unusual businesses and they tend to arouse strong feelings, both positive and negative. For some, the word co-operative may have pleasant connotations, to do with people taking charge of their own lives and democratically controlling the organisations that meet their needs. For others, it may have negative images of inefficiency, conflict and misplaced idealism. Many more will have heard of co-operatives, but cannot quite pinpoint what it is that makes them different from more conventional forms of business. For many, the word also summons up images of one particular kind of business. In Ireland, most people associate co-operatives with the dairy industry, even though Ireland has a wide range of co-operatives, including credit unions, housing co-operatives and so on. In Britain and continental Europe, many people associate co-operatives with food retailing.

Not surprisingly, our image of a co-operative is shaped and limited by our own experience. One of the reasons co-operatives have not reached their full potential is that people tend to have a very narrow view of the kinds of task co-operatives can perform. Depending on where they live, they will see a co-operative as just a creamery or a retail store, and be totally unaware of other possibilities. As we will see in the next section, co-operatives can, in fact, be adapted to many different kinds of purpose.

The design of the formal co-operative form is attributed to a group of textile workers in Rochdale near Manchester, England in the 1840s. At that time, incomes were low, prices high and jobs hard to come by. The workers had tried to improve their lot by organising a trade union and threatening to strike. But all to no avail, as there were plenty of unemployed people ready to take the places of the strikers. When all else failed, citizens of Rochdale began to think about an alternative way of increasing their spending power. By pooling their purchasing power and buying in bulk to meet their basic needs, they would be able to get more food for their money. They set up their co-operative to be as inconspicuous as possible, selling its goods at market prices rather than trying to undercut directly the prices in company stores. The financial benefits to the members would come in the form of a refund, paid at the end of the year, in proportion to each member's purchases from the co-operative.

Yet it would be a mistake to assume that co-operatives are products of desperation and misery alone. Co-operatives have also been motivated by powerful visions of a better world. Even in the gloomy world of Rochdale in the 1840s, desperation was not the sole or even the main motivation of the co-operative pioneers. Their idealism and vision showed in the catalogue of ambitious objectives, such as a store selling provisions and clothing, the erecting of houses for members and the purchase of land for cultivation. They operated under a list of businesslike rules to ensure that the store would be operated efficiently and in the best interests of all its members. These rules, which we shall discuss below, formed the foundation of the co-operative principles as we know them today.

The Rochdale co-operators had developed a successful co-operative model, which stimulated the development of large-scale co-operative movements in country after country. But long before Rochdale, the Irish economist William Thompson of Cork had developed a vision of a co-operative system. According to Tucker (1983), his ideas influenced the Welsh social reformer Robert Owen, who, in turn, influenced the Rochdale pioneers. In the early part of the nineteenth century, Thompson had developed not only a powerful critique of the existing economic system, but also a positive vision of a better future.

Senge (1990), a leading systems theorist, argues that the kind of positive vision shared by Thompson and the Rochdale Pioneers is a much more powerful and reliable motivator than the desperate desire to avoid distress. According to Senge (1990), people learn through aspiration and through desperation, but there is a great difference in the quality of that learning. If a co-operative is a child of desperation alone, it learns only as long as it must, stopping when the external pressures are removed. This is exactly what happens in co-operatives that have lost their original sense of purpose and are finding it difficult to develop a new reason for existence. Senge (interviewed by di Carlo 1996:229) emphasises the importance of a compelling, positive vision:

> The purpose of thinking about and articulating the vision is to generate energy for change – to create a focus, enthusiasm, a sense of what might be possible. Now who knows what will actually develop? Who knows the ways in which it will develop? It may be as we imagine it, or it might also be in a way that is completely unimaginable today. The important thing is that it produces change in the right direction.

'Change in the right direction' was the immediate outcome of the vision formulated by the Rochdale Pioneers in 1844. Their inspiring vision of the self-supporting, co-operative community was never achieved, but it did move things in the right direction toward the unimaginable worldwide co-operative movement of today, involving more than 800 million people and providing jobs to 100 million people (ICA 2007). The top 300 co-operatives worldwide had a turnover in excess of US$1.1 trillion in 2008 (ICA 2008). This equates to about the size of the Spanish economy.

Today, the significance and importance of co-operatives continues to be widely recognised, both in Ireland and internationally. Forfás (2007) notes that the co-operative way of doing business, whereby people work together and share equally in the benefits of this work, fits well with wider societal objectives, such as social cohesion and increasing the stock of social capital. The European Commission (EC 2004) recognised the increasingly important and positive role of co-operatives as vehicles for the implementation of many European Union (EU) objectives. The International Labour Organisation (ILO) (2002), in a recommendation adopted by all EU member states, acknowledged the significant impact of co-operatives in improving social and economic well-being. The United Nations (UN 1992) highlighted the importance of co-operatives in capital-scarce conditions and, in 2006, the important employment creation opportunities provided by co-operatives in the face of unemployment and underemployment. Most recently, the ILO (2009) has reported that the co-operative approach to business is a sustainable form of enterprise, which is able to withstand and survive economic crisis and can, indeed, avert future crisis.

RANGE AND SCOPE OF CO-OPERATIVE ACTIVITY

Co-operatives are best categorised according to five main types of user/member.

Consumer Co-operatives

Consumer co-operatives are owned and controlled by consumers. The most successful example of this kind of co-operative in Ireland is the credit union, which serves the consumers of financial services and is owned and democratically controlled by its borrowers and savers. Housing co-operatives (owned by their tenants) also fit into this category. In the USA, health care co-operatives (health care centres and hospitals owned by their patients), electricity supply co-operatives and telephone co-operatives (owned by the people who use the electricity and the phone services) are all commonplace. Consumer co-operatives hold the promise of giving consumers access to services at terms and conditions that suit their needs and circumstances and control over the way in which these services are delivered. For example, credit unions are extremely important players in promoting and enabling financial inclusion of those who may have been turned away by the conventional banking system.

Producer Co-operatives

Producer co-operatives are owned and controlled by independent producers who use their co-operative to help improve their own individual businesses, such as farmers, fishermen and artisans, as well as other small business operators as varied as taxi drivers, pharmacists, hauliers and plumbers. The purpose of this kind of co-operative is to help producers improve the effectiveness and profitability of their own individual business. For example, a dairy co-operative can help its farmer-members get a better price for their milk by processing and marketing it for them. Agricultural producer co-operatives can also provide a range of other services, including the supply of farm inputs (such as fertilisers and seeds), and access to equipment and machinery. Ocean Spray is a familiar brand in Ireland and few consumers here realise that this is a co-operative comprised mainly of cranberry growers who pool their cranberries for processing into juices and sauces. Handicraft co-operatives help members get a better price for their artefacts by providing training to improve members' skills and productivity, as well as marketing services and the supply of raw materials. For example, Carrickmacross Lace in Co. Monaghan is a co-operative of lace makers. A new field for producer-owned co-operatives in Ireland is the rapidly growing field of wind power, where co-operatives are being established by farmers to help them combine their resources and give them collective scope that would not exist if they remained as individual wind producers.

Producer co-operatives hold the promise of maximising prices and minimising costs. For example, the impact of agricultural producer co-operatives in Ireland, especially in the face of global economic crisis, has been in cushioning farmers from declining prices as they adjust to changing economic circumstances. Irish agricultural co-operatives have maintained milk prices for farmers when more conventional businesses could not compete at the same level. This is because they were in a position to subsidise milk prices from the surpluses of previous years. This scenario would never arise in a conventional business, where maximum returns must be paid to outside investors annually.

Workers' Co-operatives

Workers' co-operatives are less common in Ireland than elsewhere, but this business model is attracting increasing interest as a useful means of job creation and small business development. A workers' co-operative is a business owned and democratically controlled by its workers (e.g. a furniture factory, owned and controlled by the cabinet-makers). A well-known example of a workers' co-operative is the Quay Co-operative in Cork, which runs a successful vegetarian restaurant, organic food store and in-house bakery. Workers' co-operatives are very popular in countries such as Italy and Spain, which are more heavily industrialised.

Workers' co-operatives tend to succeed best in times of recession and high unemployment and the ILO (2009) expects considerable growth in this co-operative sector in the future. Workers' co-operatives often provide a vehicle for workers to take over an ailing business in order to preserve their jobs, even if this means wage cuts and longer hours while the new co-operative business recovers.

Community Co-operatives

Community co-operatives are owned and democratically controlled by the people living in a particular community. Often, these communities are in remote areas that have been neglected by the state. The purpose of such a co-operative is to improve the viability of a community by creating jobs, marketing the community's assets and providing needed services. Many of Ireland's islands, particularly the Irish-speaking islands, have established community co-operatives. For example, a co-operative was established on Tory Island off the coast of Co. Donegal to encourage economic, cultural and social development on the island. Community co-operatives are also prolific in remote parts of Scotland, bringing much-needed supplies of food, hardware and other necessities.

The future promise of community co-operatives lies in the fact that social enterprises, providing much-needed local services that have heretofore been supported by government funding, may face severe funding cuts. The most effective response in such a scenario lies in communities working together through co-operative action to provide local services. This is the same context in which many of the existing community co-operatives were first formed in the 1960s and 1970s.

Multi-Stakeholder Co-operatives

Finally, multi-stakeholder co-operatives are owned and controlled by two or more of the groups of users described above. It might be a business owned jointly by its customers and workers (e.g. the Eroski supermarket chain in the Basque region of Spain; or American health care co-operatives, some of which are owned jointly by medical staff and patients). Another possibility is a producer/consumer co-operative owned jointly by farmers and shoppers (such as the multi-stakeholder consumer/farmer/fisherman co-operatives of Iceland). Social economy co-operatives often use the multi-user structure. For example, a child care co-operative is often jointly owned and controlled democratically by both the parents of the children being looked after and the workers providing the care services. This form of co-operative is not evident in Ireland to date. And of course, there are second-tier co-operatives, which are co-operatives owned and controlled by a group of similar co-operatives. For example, the Irish Dairy Board (IDB) is a co-operative of agricultural co-operatives, which markets Irish dairy produce abroad. The Kerrygold label is one of the best known brands employed by the Irish Dairy Board.

THE CO-OPERATIVE MOVEMENT IN IRELAND

In total, Ireland has about 1,500 registered co-operatives, including credit unions. For a variety of reasons, some organisations choose to register as companies, but include co-operative principles in their memorandum and articles of association and in their modus operandi. Therefore, in examining the statistics on co-operatives, we are limited to those that are formally established and registered as co-operatives, even though this may not present the most accurate picture. We do know that well over half of the Irish population are members of a co-operative, many of whom may not realise they are members and part-owners of the business which serves them. Agricultural co-operatives dominate most Irish minds when they think about co-operatives, despite the fact that the credit union movement is far more widespread. Fishing co-operatives, housing co-operatives, water co-operatives and community co-operatives are also at the forefront of the co-operative movement in Ireland.

Of course, opportunities for co-operative development in Ireland abound, particularly in meeting newly emerging needs. For those wishing to establish a co-operative, the Irish Co-operative Organisation Society (ICOS) and the Registry of Friendly Societies are usually the first ports of call. ICOS acts as an umbrella body for co-operatives in Ireland and provides a range of services to co-operatives. It also provides specialist advice to groups planning on setting up a co-operative. The Registry of Friendly Societies, under the auspices of the Companies Registration Office and the Department of Enterprise, Trade and Employment, registers co-operatives and maintains records from the statutory annual returns made by each co-operative.

CO-OPERATIVE GOVERNANCE

Co-operatives differ from more conventional business structures primarily in terms of ownership, control and profit distribution. They also emphasise social as well as economic goals, while most conventional businesses are more concerned with economic goals alone. Co-operatives are owned by their customers/users and are open to membership by anyone who wishes to use the services offered. Conventional firms tend to restrict ownership to a limited elite of wealthy owners. Member control in a co-operative is organised according to the democratic principle of one member, one vote. In conventional firms, voting rights are weighted according to the number of shares held. Profits are shared equally in co-operatives, more usually according to member usage of the co-operative, rather than shareholding. Conventional firms distribute profits according to shareholding.

Earlier we used a general working definition of a co-operative as a self-help business owned and democratically controlled by the people who use its services. This definition gives us a useful general picture, but it is very incomplete. Co-operatives in most parts of the world are required by legislation to abide by a number of so-called 'co-operative principles'. These principles were originally set out by the co-operative pioneers in Rochdale, but have been revised and updated a number of times since then to reflect experience and a changing society. The seven principles are as follows:

1   *Voluntary and open membership.* Membership in a co-operative is open to anyone who can make use of its services. We are probably all privileged enough to think that this principle is rather innocuous. In considering this principle, however, one must reflect on the experiences of people in non-democratic countries, where 'co-operative membership' and sharing of resources was forced, rather than voluntary. For example, in Romania under the Ceauçescu

regime (1974–1989), farmers were forced to hand over their livestock, farm machinery and land to so-called 'co-operatives' set up by the government. They then had to work what was, in effect, their own land and assets on behalf of the government-owned and controlled 'co-operative' for little pay or benefits. Farmers who did not comply suffered horrific consequences.

2   *Democratic member control.* Co-operatives should be democratically controlled and administered. All members have an equal say in the co-operative's annual general meeting and in elections for the board of directors. The board, in turn, appoints the manager and oversees the running of the co-operative. Voting rights go with membership, not with the size of capital invested or number of shares owned (as would happen in a conventional company). The rule is one member, one vote. In other words, you cannot buy more votes in a co-operative by investing more money. To become a member in a co-operative, you usually have to buy at least one share. Some co-operatives will let you buy more than one share, many will require that you buy more, but these additional shares will not provide you with more votes.

3   *Member economic participation.* Members should contribute equitably to, and control democratically, the capital of their co-operative. At least part of that capital is usually the common property of the co-operative. A number of approaches are used to ensure that capital is controlled democratically and equitably.

- Limited return on share capital: typically, co-operatives are required to pay only a limited return on shares. In a conventional company, profits are distributed in proportion to the number of shares owned; not so in a co-operative. In co-operatives, members are paid no more than a fixed rate of interest on the money they have invested in shares.

- Co-operatives distribute profits in proportion to members' use of the co-operative: instead of distributing profit according to shares owned, which is what happens in the conventional business, co-operatives typically distribute profits according to how much members have used the business. A credit union, for example, might pay a rebate of interest paid on loans, as well as a return on savings.

- Issue bonus shares: some co-operatives, when distributing profits according to use, issue those payments in the form of bonus shares. Typically, these shares cannot be redeemed for cash immediately, but must be retained within the co-operative for an agreed period. This enables the co-operative to reward members for their use of the co-operative, while continuing to have the use of the allocated capital.

- Reinvest profits in the co-operative: of course, co-operatives are not obliged to distribute any profits at all. It all depends on the wishes of the members and the financial state of the business. Members may choose to reinvest all the profits in their co-operative to help build the business and expand its range of services.

4   *Autonomy and independence*. Co-operatives are autonomous, self-help organisations controlled by their members. When they deal with other organisations, they should do so on terms that ensure democratic control by their members and maintain their co-operative autonomy.

5   *Education, training and information*. Co-operatives should invest in building the abilities and capacities of their members and employees. Because co-operatives exist to encourage the development of people, they should spend some of their profits on developing their members (to improve their ability to run their own affairs). For example, many credit unions now try to educate their members on the costs and other dangers of money lending. Co-operatives should also try to inform the general public to show them how the techniques of co-operation can be applied to the solution of societal problems.

6   *Co-operation among co-operatives*. Co-operatives should co-operate with other co-operatives and are much more likely to prosper if they do. This is why you find credit unions working together to set up a central body to provide affordable services to them all, and small retail co-operatives co-operating to run a wholesaling organisation so that they can enjoy the cost advantages of bulk buying.

7   *Concern for community*. While focusing on members' needs and wishes, co-operatives also work for the sustainable development of their communities through policies approved by their members.

The first three of the co-operative principles (open membership; democratic control; member economic participation) are typically used by governments to define the legal structure within which a co-operative must operate. In Ireland, co-operatives are primarily legislated for under the Industrial and Provident Society Acts 1893–1978. Uniquely among Irish co-operatives, credit unions operate under their own distinctive legislation, the Credit Union Act 1997, and enjoy differentiated regulation under the Irish Financial Services Regulatory Authority's (IFSRA) Credit Union Regulator.

Our discussion of governance so far has emphasised the structural characteristics of co-operatives, rather than the quality of the process carried out within that structure. While the principles and the legislation define aspects of the structure of a co-operative, they give us little help in understanding the process of how to operate an effective co-operative within that structure. This has led to the peculiar tendency to regard organisations as fully functioning co-operatives 'simply because they abide by minimal structural requirements, without ever considering the quality of the relationship between members, their co-operative and the community at large' (Briscoe *et al.* 1982:39). Briscoe *et al.* (1982) stressed the need for process guidelines (such as participation in decision making, openness in operations and communications and social responsibility to the wider community), as well as structural guidelines (such as open membership and democratic control). In addition, the principles cannot be treated in isolation from one another. They work together. Leave some of them out and the whole structure does not work properly. For example, it is not much use having a democratic voting structure if no effort is put into the education needed to build the skills and capacity of members to question the opinions and assess the performance of their managers and officials.

The co-operative process is likely to be most effective when the following three practices are put into place. (These concepts are discussed in detail in Briscoe *et al.* 1982.)

1   *Activation of users.* The people experiencing problems and needs are actively involved in the process of designing services, activities and structures to address those problems; they are treated as origins of action, not passive objects to be serviced and manipulated. In other words, people are encouraged to do things for themselves, and to acquire the skills needed to run their own affairs. Instead of being passive objects, they become origins of action. The assumption behind this is that things get done more effectively when the people using the organisation are knowledgeable, conscious of the nature of their needs and problems, and actively involved in seeking effective solutions.

2   *Mutual aid.* Those experiencing the problems and needs pool their efforts and resources to help one another develop collective solutions to their mutual problems. In other words, things are likely to work more efficiently if we work together to develop collective solutions. The underlying assumption is that co-operation and mutual support produce better solutions than the attempts of isolated people. For example, we can solve our housing problems individually by buying or renting our own house. Collectively, we could set up a housing co-operative, combine our skills and resources to do the work more cheaply and even design our own neighbourhood to meet our needs.

3   *Design for use.* The organisation itself, its products, services and activities are self-consciously designed for use, i.e. to be helpful to the people who use its products and services (instead of being designed around the goals of a limited elite). The people with the needs and the problems are actively involved in this design process. If the prime purpose of a co-operative organisation is to promote the well-being of its users, it would seem logical for every aspect of the organisation to be tailored self-consciously to people's needs. Everything about it, its structure and management styles, its products and services, its facilities and location, its member education programmes, should all be designed to address the key problems experienced by the organisation's users.

COMPETITIVE ADVANTAGES

So what is really so special about a co-operative? What are its competitive advantages in the marketplace? Because co-operatives are controlled by their members/customers, it follows that the services and products they provide will be precisely tailored to people's needs. Their single-minded focus on the end user is predominant over any focus on profit maximisation and ensures that services and products are continually relevant and competitive in the marketplace.

Co-operatives, as we have seen, are a very different kind of business. They seem to turn the world of commerce upside down:

- they are controlled democratically by the people who use their services, rather than by absentee investors
- they share the profits on the basis of use, rather than investment
- they emphasise social, as well as business, goals.

All of this means that co-operatives do not have the single-minded focus on profits that is seen by many as the key strength of the conventional business approach.

A closely related competitive advantage over conventional businesses is that co-operatives do not have to pay substantial portions of their profits to outside investors. This helps provide the co-operative with extra resources for meeting the interests and needs of its users. According to Thirkell (1998), it is the single-minded focus of agricultural co-operatives on the needs of farmers and the freedom from the requirement to reward rich investors which give these co-operatives a substantial competitive edge over conventional business.

Empowering Users to Take Conscious Control

Some co-operatives have been very successful at involving a large number of members in their decision-making processes. If consumers are to be empowered to get involved in designing solutions to their needs and problems, education has a vital role to play. Enthusiasm and good intentions are no substitute for education and training in the knowledge and skills needed to manage a democracy and make a business work.

Successful co-operatives have always invested heavily in the education and development of their members. The vigorous co-operative movement that developed in the Atlantic provinces of Canada (credit unions, agricultural, consumer, fishery, housing and community co-operatives) grew out of a revolutionary adult education programme initiated by the Extension Division of St Francis Xavier University in Antigonish, Nova Scotia. This educational programme and the co-operatives that developed from it have become known collectively as the Antigonish Movement. This was unlike any university programme that had ever been heard of. Extension workers took the programme out into the scattered communities. First mass meetings were used to spark interest. Then, in kitchen meetings around the region, the real work began of focusing on the economic and social problems that confronted people in their own locality, and devising practical ways of addressing those problems.

Empowering people to take control of their own community organisations and businesses is not something that should be left to chance. However, the type of education that seems to work best is not the traditional approach of imposing structure from on high. What has seemed to work well in many different parts of the world is a co-operative approach to education, in which the learner participates actively with other learners in the design of a learning process tailored to their changing needs.

Marketing Advantages

Webb (1998) points out that consumers have a favourable view of co-operatives (including credit unions) in spite of their failure to invest in marketing their unique values and special relationships with users. He argues that co-operatives are in an excellent position to capitalise on two widely acclaimed marketing concepts: relationship marketing (i.e. creating a relationship between a business and its customers, thereby building loyalty and market share, for example store loyalty cards and frequent flyer points) and character marketing (i.e. convincing customers that a business has a good character, such as being environmentally friendly, defenders of human rights, pillars of the community).

Webb (1998) maintains that co-operatives should be in an unrivalled position to develop unique selling points (USPs) in terms of relationships and good character. He goes on to argue that while most businesses are focused on only one bottom line (maximising returns on investor capital), co-operatives have multiple bottom lines, which focus on the values that people consider to be important. He states that '[s]uch values include trust, community support, democracy, justice and fairness. Co-operatives are blessed with two USPs, their ownership structure and the values they hold. These unique selling points would be difficult to match without becoming a co-operative' (Webb 1998:94).

The Co-operative Bank in the UK is a prime example of a co-operative that has built a strong relationship with its customers. Since 1992, it has regularly consulted its customers to identify their ethical concerns on what the bank will and will not finance. It has drawn up an ethical policy statement reflecting these concerns, covering issues such as human rights, international development and fighting poverty, ecological impact and animal welfare. Since it launched its ethical policy, it has turned away more than Stg£1bn in what is deemed unsuitable business. Despite this, it has grown its total commercial lending by an average of 14 per cent per year (Co-operative Bank 2009). The Co-operative Bank was awarded Best Financial Services Provider at the *Which?* Awards 2009 based on the quality of its products and services, as well as on customer feedback. It has won numerous other consumer and business awards (*Which?* 2009).

Economies of Scale

Collective solutions developed through mutual aid are often demonstrably less costly and of higher quality than individual solutions. For example, people in remote areas can combine with their neighbours to pool shopping orders, thereby reducing the cost of home deliveries and the costs of shopping by buying in greater bulk. Co-operatives in remote communities are often organised around this need.

Another pertinent example of achieving economies of scale through collective action is of a group of twenty-three credit unions in Ireland that were recently each faced with a similar difficulty requiring complex legal advice. The cost of this advice was in the region of €45,000. Had each credit union sought this advice individually, they would have had to bear the full costs and the likelihood would have been that the advice would have differed from credit union to credit union. Instead, they agreed to share the cost of the advice from one solicitor, reducing the cost to under €2,000 each and ensuring that all proceeded jointly on the basis of the same advice.

Mutual Aid – A Different Kind of Competition

A new generation of businesses is finding that they can compete in the marketplace by offering consumers ethical options. A UK electricity company called Unit(e) is selling electricity that costs consumers more, but guarantees that its power comes from renewable sources.

A UK gas company called Ebico has designed its pricing structure to help its less wealthy customers by charging all its customers a flat rate, no matter how they pay their bills. This approach was designed to help the poorest consumers who pay the most for their gas because they normally use pre-pay meters and do not have access to a bank account.

The Phone Co-op is a rapidly growing Oxfordshire co-operative which applies co-operative principles to discount phone services. Not only do user-members enjoy substantial discounts on their phone calls, they can also share in the profits. Some of the profits are distributed as refunds to members on the basis of their phone use, but some are allocated as grants to charities/voluntary organisations. Members currently enjoy discounts of 33 per cent on daytime national phone calls.

Trustworthiness as a Competitive Advantage

Fukuyama (1996) has argued that trust is a key factor in economic development and is crucial for the effective functioning of the information economy of the twenty-first century. Clearly, the business that is seen as trustworthy ought to have a competitive advantage over those whose customers view them with suspicion. Recent Canadian research suggests that consumer co-operatives in Canada are indeed seen as more trustworthy than conventional firms. According to Webb (1998), the vast majority of Canadian consumers expressed positive attitudes toward the values and principles of co-operation. More than 30 per cent went so far as to say that they would be prepared to pay a little more to shop at a co-operative.

CHALLENGES AND OPPORTUNITIES OF THE CO-OPERATIVE BUSINESS MODEL

Despite the clear benefits of the co-operative model, it is not without its problems. Inactive or poorly represented membership, difficulties in raising finance and demutualisation are some of the issues it must contend with.

Inactive or Poorly Represented Membership

Zeuli and Cropp (2004: 49) assert that the most important responsibility of co-operative members is 'participation in the governance of the co-operative'. They point out that co-operatives depend on the active participation of all members. However, Hoyt (2003:8–9) points to weak practice in co-operatives (an issue Birchall (2001:203) refers to as a 'democratic deficit' in co-operatives). She contends that many co-operative boards are

> woefully uninformed about their members. They may be in close contact with relatively few members, who are much like them both demographically and philosophically. They may not be aware of the massive changes that are taking place in their membership, many of which mirror the changes in the population as a whole. The question is, what do these members want, need, and expect from a co-operative? What do they understand about what the co-operative provides for them? What do they understand about the board's work and the important responsibility some members have assumed for the group when they agree to be directors? And most fundamentally, how can the board determine the best use of members' resources if they are not intimately aware of their members' needs and expectations?

Furthermore, Meister (1978) discusses the degeneration thesis, whereby co-operatives become less involving as they grow in size. There is also a tendency for some co-operative boards to become less representative of their membership as a whole. Hoyt (2003:9) asserts that co-operatives do not know who their members are as individuals and that if co-operatives are to be competitive in the market, they must 'unbundle the membership as a whole and figure out how to communicate the co-operative's message to each member as an individual'.

It might be argued that democracy is not compatible with sound business management because democratic control could be beset by the following kinds of problem:

- a possible lack of confidentiality in decision-making processes;
- slowness in reaching decisions;
- the possibility that major decision-making power may be in the hands of people who do not understand the realities of running a business; and

- the possibility that directors might be elected on the basis of their popularity, rather than their business acumen.

If ever there was a false dilemma, it is the notion that democratic control is incompatible with efficient management. Perhaps it all depends upon how democracy is defined. If it means that all members must be involved in taking every decision, then it is likely to be inefficient as soon as the number of members exceeds about a dozen. Larger organisations can implement democratic control through a system of representative democracy, with different kinds of decision being delegated to different groups of people under the overall supervision of a board of directors, elected and reviewed by the total body of the membership.

Raising Finance

One of the most serious dilemmas faced by co-operatives is how to raise adequate business finance while observing co-operative principles. The principles stipulate that only a limited rate of return can be paid on capital and that profits should be distributed according to use of the business (rather than on the amount of capital invested). This makes co-operatives less attractive to people with money to invest. As a result, co-operatives may have more problems raising adequate capital.

Because of the above problems, co-operatives will be more dependent (compared with conventional firms) on debt capital than on share capital (equity capital). This increases the riskiness of the co-operative because of the costs of servicing this additional debt. However, most co-operatives have found ways of resolving these dilemmas. Some of their strategies are as follows.

- Make sure that the co-operative is designed to provide services that are in great demand, and that there are tangible benefits for members.
- Distribute profits in the form of bonus shares, which have to be retained within the co-operative for an agreed period of time. This approach enables the co-operative to reward members for their use of the co-operative, while continuing to have the use of the allocated capital.
- Many co-operatives raise adequate capital by requiring a more substantial investment. Many producer co-operatives require an investment in proportion to the member's use of the business. Some workers' co-operatives require a substantial initial investment from members, but help the worker find the money by guaranteeing a loan, which is repaid in instalments from wages earned at the co-operative.

Demutualisation

Pfimlin (1998) suggests that co-operatives with a growing focus on technical aspects of their business and a reducing focus on social relations (a spirit of solidarity and responsibility among the members and a rich network of human relations) face a very real threat of demutualisation. Demutualisation threatens the very existence of co-operatives and credit unions by removing ownership and control of the organisation from the members and placing it in the hands of private investors whose main objective is to maximise profits. In order to overcome the threat of demutualisation, co-operatives need to reassess the value they are giving to their members. They can do this by reconnecting with their members, as recommended by Hoyt (2003), focusing on improving member relations and emphasising the benefits of co-operatives. The Oliver Wyman Consultancy (2008) report emphasises the need to explain the benefits of co-operative membership to individuals and to society as a whole, to correct any misconceptions or misunderstandings of the co-operative model, to recognise the different needs of different kinds of members, and to ensure broad representation in the membership. In essence, we can see that education of members and of society in general on the benefits of co-operatives will be essential in building the co-operative movement and in preventing potential demutualisation.

CONCLUSION

The co-operative approach to business has impacted positively all over the world, but perhaps its full potential and promise have yet to be realised, particularly in Ireland, where the adoption of the co-operative model has been largely confined to agriculture and finance. And even within these sectors, there is scope for further use of the model in meeting societal needs. National priorities in Ireland focus on agriculture, the rural economy and food, health, environmental sustainability, marine and energy (DETE 2006: Chapter 6; Government of Ireland 2007: Chapters 4 and 6). The sustainable development of each of these sectors is seen as crucial to Ireland's economy. Worldwide, co-operatives have been to the fore in each of these sectors and the co-operative model is one that needs to be explored further in Ireland, drawing on our rich tradition and experiences of co-operative action. The co-operative approach to business has proved to be a resilient one, surviving and thriving in both recession and boom. In an era when ownership of and control over decisions affecting local, national and global communities are more important than ever, the co-operative has renewed relevance and offers a viable and sustainable alternative business model.

References

Birchall, J. (2001) 'Member Participation in Mutuals: Towards a Theoretical Model' in J. Birchall (ed.) *The New Mutualism in Public Policy*, pp. 202–25. London: Routledge.

Briscoe, R., Grey, S., Hunt, P., Linehan, M., McBride, H., Tucker, V. and Ward, M. (1982) *The Co-operative Idea*. Cork: Centre for Co-operative Studies, University College Cork.

Briscoe, R. and Ward, M. (2005) 'From the Cradle to the Grave and Beyond!', in R. Briscoe and M. Ward (eds) *Helping Ourselves: Success Stories in Co-operative Business and Social Enterprise*, pp. 7–27. Cork: Oak Tree Press.

Co-operative Bank (2009) *Why We have Ethical Policies* [online]. Available: http://www.goodwithmoney.co.uk/why-do-we-need-ethical-policies/ (last accessed 8 March 2010).

EC (Commission of the European Communities) (2004) *On the Promotion of Co-operative Societies in Europe*, COM(2004)18 [online]. Available: http://eur-lex.europa.eu/LexUriServ/LexUriServ.do?uri=COM:2004:0018:FIN:EN:PDF (last accessed 12 August 2009).

DETE (Department of Enterprise, Trade and Employment) (2006) *Strategy for Science, Technology and Innovation 2006–2013*. Dublin: Stationery Office.

di Carlo, R. (ed.) (1996) *Towards a New World View: Conversations on the Leading Edge*. Edinburgh: Floris Books.

Forfás (2007) *Ireland's Co-operative Sector*. Dublin: Forfás.

Fukuyama, F. (1996) *Trust: The Social Virtues and the Creation of Prosperity*. London: Penguin.

Government of Ireland (2007) *National Development Plan: Transforming Ireland – A Better Quality of Life for All*. Dublin: Stationery Office.

Hoyt, A. (1995) *Marketing Member Involvement: The American Experience*. Madison, WI: University of Wisconsin Centre for Co-operatives.

ICA (International Co-operative Alliance) (2007) *Statistical Information on the Co-operative Movement* [online]. Available: http://www.ica.coop/members/member-stats.html#members (last accessed 12 August 2009).

– (2008) *Global 300 List*. Geneva: ICA.

ILO (International Labour Organisation) (2002) *Promotion of Co-operatives Recommendation*, R193. Geneva: ILO.

— (2009) *Resilience of the Co-operative Business Model in Times of Crisis*. Geneva: ILO.

Meister, A. (1984) *Participation, Associations, Development, and Change*. New Brunswick: Transaction.

Oliver Wyman Consultancy (2008) *Co-operative Bank: Customer Champion* [online]. Available: http://www.oliverwyman.com/ow/pdf_files/OW_En_FS_2008_CooperativeBank.pdf (last accessed 31 July 2009).

Pfimlin, E. (1998) 'Demutualisation of Financial Co-operatives', *Review of International Co-operation* 91(3): 47–53.

Senge, P. (1990) *The Fifth Discipline: The Art and Practice of the Learning Organisation*. London: Century Business.

Thirkell, D. (1998) 'Ignorance Abounds on the Worth of Farmer Co-ops', *Irish Farmers' Journal*, 7 November, p. 25.

Tucker, V. (1983) 'Ireland and the Origins of the Co-operative Movement', in C. Keating (ed.) *Plunkett and Co-operatives: Past, Present and Future*, pp. 14–32. Cork: Centre for Co-operative Studies, University College Cork.

UN (United Nations) (1992) *Report of the Secretary-General*. Document a/47/216-E/1992/43.

— (2006) Expert Group Meeting on Co-operatives and Employment – Aide Memoire [online]. Available: http://www.un.org/esa/socdev/poverty/subpages/coop_egm2.htm (last accessed 31 July 2009).

Webb, T. (1998) 'Marketing Co-operation in the Global Economy', *Review of International Co-operation* 91(1): 92–5.

Which? (2009) *Which? Awards 'The Best of the Best' in Products and Services* [online]. Available: http://www.which.co.uk/about-which/what-we-do/which-awards/index.jsp (last accessed 8 March 2010).

Zeuli, K. and Cropp, R. (2004) *Co-operatives: Principles and Practices in the 21st Century*. Madison, WI: University of Wisconsin-Extension.

Chapter 17

Emotional Intelligence Components and Conflict Resolution

Helen Chen and Patrick Phillips

INTRODUCTION

Given the changing nature of society and the demanding nature of work in developed economies such as Ireland, organisations will increasingly rely on the productivity and creativity of highly autonomous employees. However, these individuals will need to work in teams within the workplace, where personal contacts are ubiquitous and conflicts so often arise among and between employees and managers (Mayer *et al.* 2008). Conflicts are emotionally charged events and, as Fulmer and Barry (2002:247) argue, 'emotional expression is pervasive in human communication, and it is reasonable to assume that people routinely bring their emotions with them to the bargaining table'. Therefore, assessing the role that emotional intelligence (EI) plays in conflict resolution, while complex, could be invaluable for managers when engaging with employees. If managers do not have the skills to manage conflicts, stalemate among conflicting parties could have a potentially negative influence on an organisation operating in today's competitive environment.

Despite the potential for understanding the role of EI, Irish business and society continue to stress more traditional intelligences. Schools and universities in Ireland have long emphasised academic learning. Yet we all know of students with average academic performance who go on to be chief executive officers (CEOs) or managing directors (MDs) in their future jobs, while those with high academic achievement may languish at middle management level or lower. As Cooper (1997:32) notes, '[r]esearch suggests that people with high levels of emotional intelligence experience more career success, build stronger personal relationships, lead more effectively, and enjoy better health'. Therefore, we are compelled to ask ourselves, what is missing in the curriculum? If EI is the suggested missing link in the educational curriculum, we should consider the influence of emotions more closely: 'EI even provides the medium by which educational reform can, and finally will, reach its full potential, across primary, secondary, and tertiary levels of schooling' (Zeidner *et al.* 2004:372). To have such a radical transformation in education, and for EI to have its full effect on business and society, we need to know more. This chapter, by addressing a specific issue in EI and its impact on the particularly important issue of conflict management, shows the importance of such knowledge and illustrates an addition to that body of knowledge.

The rest of the chapter is organised as follows. The next section gives the reader some background by looking at the emergence of EI and its introduction to the field of management. Next, we provide an overview of some of the difficulties and controversies involved in defining EI. Some of the issues in defining EI are discussed in greater detail in the following section, which looks at how various researchers have broken down EI into its components. With a greater knowledge of EI and its components, we are able to proceed to look, in a little more detail, at how EI is regarded in business and management. We then argue that in order to study EI in business and management there is a need to focus on the detailed components of EI and their particular effects in a specific way. In the next section, we report on a particular study where we looked at the extent to which Irish managers working in hotels and clinics/hospitals in Dublin acknowledge the existence of the components of EI, and analyse how the different components of EI play a role in effective conflict resolution in the workplace. Finally, we conclude in a way that we hope will allow more managers to consider the use of the EI components to effectively resolve conflict and help increase employee productivity.

THE EMERGENCE OF EI

Though works as early as Thorndike (1920), Guilford (1956) and Gardner (1983) on social intelligence point out the importance of emotions to intellectual functioning, the term EI was not brought into mainstream psychology until the 1990s (Mayer *et al.* 1990; Salovey and Mayer 1990). The original definition of EI refers to the understanding of our own thoughts and feelings and the capability to understand and empathise with the thoughts and feelings of others (Salovey and Mayer 1990). Some academics describe EI as processes that include 'the appraisal and expression of emotions, assimilation of emotions in thoughts, understanding emotion, and the regulation and management of emotions' (Matthews *et al.* 2004:372).

In the field of management, EI is being explored in the general context of human interaction, as academics such as Fulmer and Barry (2002) understand that people do bring emotions to workplace communication and negotiation. Wallace and Rijamampianina (2005:84) argue that while 'technical skills are necessary for productivity', they 'are insufficient to explain the difference between high and mediocre performers'. They go on to explain that EI is relevant because emotionally intelligent managers 'have a deep understanding of their own emotions, strengths, weaknesses, needs and drives', and that 'in their drive for self improvement, they create a culture of constructive feedback that fosters growth' (Wallace and Rijamampianina 2005:84). This is an important strength:

individuals who are aware of their strengths and weaknesses and, in addition, can accept constructive criticism, can learn to constantly improve themselves. McPhail (2003:630) argues that 'a developed emotional intelligence is crucial for critically engaging with the world' and Goleman (1995:105) posits that 'market forces that are reshaping our work life are putting an unprecedented premium on emotional intelligence for on-the-job success'. Research on EI has shown that managers with high EI are likely to facilitate productive working relationships (Rosete and Ciarrochi 2005) and that managers with higher EI have a greater capacity to unite employees to work towards the common objectives of the organisation (Côté and Miner 2006).

EI: PERSONAL TRAITS OR INTELLIGENCE?

The argument as to whether EI is a form of intelligence or simply an array of personal traits is much debated. Davies, Stankov and Roberts (1998) argue that EI is not intelligence in the same sense as IQ and that it should be studied as a group of personality traits. Accordingly, EI is defined as a personal trait, a constellation of emotion-related, self-perceived abilities and dispositions located at the 'lower' levels of personality hierarchies (Petrides and Furnham 2001), or an eclectic mix of personal traits, such as happiness, self-esteem, self-management, etc. (Bar-On 2000). While the debate continues, a third set of voices argue that there is no way to prove the existence of EI, claiming that 'a thorough search of the scientific literature' fails to reveal 'any studies which demonstrated the criterion-related validity of EI for any specific occupational area' (Robertson and Smith 2001:444).

However, this relative lack of progress in validating the criteria of EI may reflect the fact that EI is a more elusory form of intelligence to measure than is IQ. A solution offered by major EI theorists, such as Goleman (1995), is to define EI in more general terms as representing all positive qualities that are *not IQ*. Bar-On (1997:151) characterises EI as 'an array of non-cognitive capabilities, competencies, and skills that influence one's ability to succeed in coping with environmental demands and pressures'. In sum, little agreement exists over whether EI represents a cognitive ability for processing emotional stimuli, attributes of personality, such as integrity and character, or some facility for adapting to challenging situations (Matthews *et al.* 2004).

COMPONENTS OF EI

Whereas IQ provides for a more tangible form of measuring an individual's ability by excluding the complexity of emotions, EI dares to ask the questions 'what about emotions?' and 'to what extent does emotional awareness in ourselves and in others lead to success in life?' However, academics find it difficult to agree on specific descriptions of EI, for 'examination of the literature suggests there is no clear, consensual definition of EI' (Matthews *et al.* 2004:180). As a result, the multitude of qualities, when a detailed description is proposed, causes an outcry of disagreement; the reason for this debate quite possibly revolves around the fact that no accurate method for measuring EI currently exists.

Theories of EI range from a capacity for processing information that is applied to emotions (Mayer *et al.* 2000) to the complex interaction of emotions, mood, personality and social orientation in both interpersonal and intrapersonal situations (Bar-On 2000). These theories propose different components that EI should include. The main models of EI, in the existing literature, include: the multifactor EI scale (MEIS) (Mayer *et al.* 1999); the Mayer-Salovey-Caruso EI test (MSCEIT) (Mayer *et al.* 2000); the emotional competency inventory (ECI) (Goleman 1998); the emotional quotient inventory (EQ-I) (Bar-On 1997); the EI quotient (EIQ) (Dulewicz and Higgs 2000); the EI test (SREIT) (Schutte *et al.* 1998); the Swinburne EI test (SUEIT-Genos EI Assessment) (Palmer and Stough 2001); the trait meta mood scale (TMMS) (Salovey *et al.* 1995); and the workgroup EI profile (WEIP) (Jordan *et al.* 2002). In an effort to provide the reader with a guide to the at times bewildering range of EI components, we present a summary of the components of each model in Table 17.1.

Table 17.1 Components of EI in different models

Model	Components	References
Trait Meta-Mood Scale (TMMS)	• Attention • Clarity • Repair	Salovey *et al.* 1995
Emotional Quotient Inventory (EQ-I)	• Intra-personal components • Inter-personal component • Adaptability • Stress management • General mood	Bar-On 1997
Emotional Competence Inventory (ECI 360)	• Awareness of emotions in self • Awareness of emotions in others • Management of emotions in self • Management of emotions in others	Goleman 1998
Self Report Emotional Intelligence Test (SREIT)	• Monitor and discriminate between emotions • Use emotions in thought and reactions	Schutte *et al.* 1998
Multi-factor Emotional Intelligence Test (MEIS) Mayer-Salovey- Caruso Emotional Intelligence Test (MSCEIT)	• Emotion perception • Using emotion to facilitate thought • Understanding emotion • Emotion management	Mayer, Caruso and Salovey 1999; Mayer, Salovey and Caruso 2000

Model	Components	References
Emotional Intelligence Questionnaire (EIQ)	• Self-awareness • Emotional resilience • Motivation • Interpersonal sensitivity • Influence • Intuitiveness • Conscientiousness	Dulewicz and Higgs 2000
Swinburne University Emotional Intelligence Test (SUEIT)/Genos EI Assessment	• Incorporates the predominant models and measures of EI	Palmer and Stough 2001
Work Group Emotional Intelligence Profile (WEIP)	• Awareness of emotions • Ability to discuss emotions • Using emotions to prioritise thinking • Application of own emotions to facilitate thinking • Ability to recognise emotions in others • Ability to read others' false display of emotion • Managing others' emotional states • Ability to encourage positive emotions in self and others	Jordan *et al.* 2002

Source: derived from Bar-On (1997), Dulewicz and Higgs (2000), Jordan *et al.* (2002), Mayer, Caruso and Salovey (1999), Mayer, Salovey and Caruso (2000), Palmer and Stough (2001), Schutte *et al.* (1998) and Salovey *et al.* (1995).

All the above models seem to emphasise different components, but a closer examination suggests that all the models agree on the key components of EI, namely understanding oneself and others, and managing oneself and others. This is the key argument in Goleman (1998, 2001) and Boyatzis, Goleman and Rhee (2000). These authors identify the following primary components of EI: awareness of emotions in self; awareness of emotions in others; management of emotions in self; and management of emotions in others. In the same light, Mayer and Salovey (1997) interpret EI as the ability to reason about emotions. For Matthews, Roberts and Zeidner (2004), EI includes our ability to: accurately perceive, appraise and express emotions; access or generate feelings that facilitate thought; understand emotions and emotional knowledge; and regulate emotions to promote emotional and intellectual growth.

EI IN BUSINESS AND MANAGEMENT

Although EI has received an increasing amount of attention from both academics and practitioners, there are different views in the literature with regards to whether emotionality, even when intelligent, is appropriate in business. Max Weber (1922), for example, argues that if managers use emotions at work, efficiency and effectiveness are adversely affected. His argument was that emotions are irrational, so there could not be intelligent emotions in rational organisations. Weber's view that EI is opposed to reasoning has influenced many scholars in the study of EI (McPhail 2003). Even Zeidner, Matthews and Roberts (2004:380) recognise that some otherwise desirable elements of EI may not be appropriate to the aims of some organisations: 'qualities of agreeableness such as empathy, altruism, and interpersonal sensitivity are central to conceptions of EI, but these qualities may mitigate against effective performance in jobs requiring ruthlessness, toughness, and individual initiative'. Nonetheless, some researchers argue that EI should be considered in business and management, as 'we are paying a drastic price, in our personal lives and organizations, for our attempts to separate our hearts from our heads and our emotions from our intellect. It can't be done. We need both, and we need them working together' (Cooper 1997:32).

There exists a body of literature supporting the argument proposed by Cooper (1997) that EI is needed within organisations and across working life. Goleman (1998) and Huy (1999) suggest that EI can have a substantial impact on not just the organisation but also the individual and the society as a whole. Cooper (1997:31) observes that 'research shows that emotions, properly managed, can drive trust, loyalty, and commitment and many of the greatest productivity gains, innovations, and accomplishments of individuals, teams, and organizations'. In a similar fashion, other research work, for example Rosete and Ciarrochi (2005), discovered that managers with higher EI scores are more capable of demonstrating greater personal integrity and are therefore able to facilitate productive working relationships among employees. The stream of EI literature suggests that the significance of EI exists in a wider context:

> From a macro perspective, one would expect that a society comprised of individuals high in emotional intelligence would tend to have low rates of aggressiveness and violent crime as well as a variety of other mental health problems . . . [and] . . . the overall physical health of such a society would most likely be superior to a society comprised of individuals low in emotional intelligence. (Vandervoort 2006:5)

Since research links EI to every facet of an individual's life, it does not need to be localised to the workplace. Thus, developing EI will benefit the person as a whole and result in progression in both career and private life: 'We found that individuals reporting higher EI reported higher levels of life satisfaction, self-acceptance, and self-esteem than individuals who are relatively low in emotional intelligence' (Carmeli *et al.* 2009:72). This provides for a suitable answer to the question set at the beginning of the chapter regarding the missing curriculum in colleges and universities.

RESEARCHING EI IN BUSINESS: THE NEED TO GET SPECIFIC

Cooper and Sawaf (1997) describe effective management as relying to some degree on an understanding of emotions and abilities associated with EI. As with research on the effects of IQ, when the effects of EI are researched there is a tendency to use the overall rating of EI (e.g. Lenaghan *et al.* 2007; Suliman and Al-Shaikh, 2007). Yet '[t]here appears from the literature to be some debate about what constitutes the domain of emotional intelligence, about terminology used to describe the construct and about methods used to measure it' (Cooper 1997:32). Zeidner, Matthews and Roberts (2004) argue that the definition proposed by Goleman, Boyatzis and McKee (2002) does not allow for the distinct abilities and personality traits that may influence recognition and regulation of emotions separate from EI. It is apparent that the primary components of EI, as described by Goleman (1998), are seen to be too narrow (Zeidner *et al.* 2004). Therefore, there are reasons to believe that examining the separate impact of different components of EI may be useful. After all, every component of EI may not be equally important in all contexts. There might be some components that are effective in one management situation, with other components effective in managing another situation. Decomposing EI, therefore, is likely to be a useful method for generating interesting results in researching the effects of EI, and to provide a plausible approach to the ongoing debate on how to contextualise the subject.

There are clearly many components of EI, as can be seen from our earlier discussion of Table 17.1. However, the management of conflict is a vital task in the context of contemporary Ireland. It is therefore the components of EI that relate particularly to the management of conflict to which we now give special attention. The different models in Table 17.1 suggested that, among the different components, some might be more significant than others in effective conflict resolution.

Conflict occurs every day wherever a group of people gather to pursue objectives: for example, in organisations. Sanhole and van de Merwe (1993:6) describe conflict as 'a situation in which at least two parties, or their representatives, try to pursue their perceptions of mutually incompatible goals by undermining, directly or indirectly, each other's goal seeking capability'. Obeidi, Hipel and Kilgour (2003:785) give a more comprehensive description of conflict as 'an antagonistic social situation among people who perceive incompatibilities over issues like goals, values, interests, or beliefs, and attempt either to control each other or to prevent each other from attaining or pursuing its aspirations'.

While contrasting ideas can be helpful to an organisation, it is up to the managers to ensure that differing opinions do not disintegrate into prolonged conflict scenarios, as this is counterproductive. Therefore, it is reasonable to assert that conflict management is fundamental to the successful running of an organisation. Managers must become mediators and negotiators. They often must attempt to pacify numerous parties, while ensuring that the goals of the organisation are achieved. It can be extremely difficult for employees at any level to admit when they are wrong and seek assistance in improving so as not to repeat the same mistake or create conflict through stubbornness. The practical relevance of EI to business is apparent in this context, as Wallace and Rijamampianina (2005:86) explain: 'reasonable people create an environment of trust and fairness' and 'self regulators cope well with ambiguous situations'. Rosete and Ciarrochi (2005) found that managers with high EI are able to demonstrate greater personal integrity and, therefore, to facilitate productive working relationships among employees. Côté and Miners (2006) noted that managers with higher EI are more likely to unite employees to achieve the common objectives of organisations. Therefore, Huy (1999) argues that EI is the key to understanding others' perspectives and needs, resolving conflicts, and wielding influence.

There are different approaches to the study of conflict management. One stream of research focuses on the styles of conflict management. For example, Rahim and Psenicka (2002) posit five specific styles of handling conflict: integrating (high concern for self and others); obliging (low concern for self and high concern for others); dominating (high concern for self and low concern for others); avoiding (low concern for self and others); and compromising (intermediate in concern for self and others). Kolb and Putnam (1992) propose another set of conflict management styles: self-help, avoidance, lumping it (best described as a capacity for tolerating a particular situation without drawing attention to it or complaining), negotiation, and the involvement of third-party mediators, arbitrators and adjudicators.

Another stream of research focuses on the personal traits and skills that managers possess that enable them to resolve conflicts effectively. For example, Sheppard et al. (1994) posit there are three different types of conflict resolution: fair, effective and satisfactory. To effectively resolve a conflict, a manager needs to get at the facts to analyse the situation; s/he needs to take the dispute out of the hands of the conflict parties; s/he needs to maintain a level of seriousness, etc. (Sheppard et al. 1994:60). These methods could prove useful to management in identifying their own strengths and weaknesses when it comes to mediating conflict effectively.

Managing conflict involves the manager's knowledge of the situation and their skills in handling interpersonal conflicts (Goleman 1998). A manager's knowledge of a conflict situation is built through constant learning and experience (Suliman and Al-Shaikh 2007), in which the EI of the manager plays a critical role. As was discussed above, the models proposed by Bar-On (1997), Goleman (1998), Salovey and Mayer (1990) and Dulewicz and Higgs (1999) make clear that EI need not be considered a single, monolithic variable; rather, it can be viewed as consisting of a few main components. Key questions in considering the relationship between conflict management and emotional capabilities thus emerge:

- Are managers who appreciate the role of self-improvement likely to use more effective conflict resolution skills?
- Are managers who can better understand their own and other people's feelings more likely to use more effective conflict resolution skills?

EVIDENCE FROM AN IRISH CONTEXT ON EI AND CONFLICT MANAGEMENT

While there is still a need for more empirical research that addresses these questions, we can discuss some findings from work in an Irish context that we report more fully in Chen and Phillips (2007). A questionnaire was administered to managers working across hotels and clinics/hospitals in Dublin and the responses were analysed using a combination of factor analysis (to identify the main factors of EI and of effective conflict resolution) and regression analysis (to examine the contribution of the identified components of EI on effective conflict resolution). For the purpose of the study, we chose to use the hotel and hospital/clinic environments since in these service sectors people are the key element. This means that in these workplaces conflicts are unlikely to be avoidable as a result of the high level of human interaction, and as people compete for jobs, resources, power, acknowledgement and security (Suliman and Al-Shaikh 2006).

Identifying Important Components of EI

Through the study of the hotels and clinics/hospitals in Dublin, eight important components of EI were identified in Chen and Phillips (2007: Table 2). These were:

1   intuitiveness
2   assertiveness
3   conscientiousness
4   consistency
5   empathy
6   motivation
7   interpersonal sensitivity
8   resilience.

We will now discuss each of these eight important EI components in more detail.

Intuitiveness

A former editor of *Fortune*, who has written extensively on intuitive management, contends that 'the last step to success frequently requires a daring intuitive leap, as many chief executives who control the destinies of America's biggest corporations will reluctantly concede' (Rowan 1986:1). Intuitiveness was identified in the Irish context as one of the components of EI. To be intuitive, managers need to be able to: work through a depressed state; maintain a rational disposition; make decisions by using reason and intuition; and disregard standard procedures in failure (Chen and Phillips 2007). The findings conform to those of Goleman (1998), Mayer, Caruso and Salovey (1999), Mayer, Salovey and Caruso (2000), and other EI theorists.

Assertiveness

Goleman (1995) identifies the importance of assertiveness, as do other researchers in the field, such as Mayer, Caruso and Salovey (1999) and Bar-On (1997). This is also the finding in our study in the Irish context, in which assertiveness is defined as being able to influence others to accept one's words, having the abilities to motivate people and persuading people to achieve common goals (Chen and Phillips 2007). The capacity for assertiveness allows a manager the confidence to convert planning into action. Such ability would prove valuable in a competitive market when decisions must be made efficiently and with confidence.

Conscientiousness

To be conscientious is to be aware of people's feelings when angry (Dulewicz and Higgs 2000; Goleman 1998). It may be extremely difficult for a manager to remain aware of the feelings of subordinates when failure is encountered. Lacking awareness of subordinates' feelings may allow a manager to develop a strong desire to blame and belittle. However, this could have negative effects on the morale of employees (Rosete and Ciarrochi 2005). Therefore, it is necessary for those in a managerial role to be aware of what effect their words might have on others. Research carried out by Boyatzis, Goleman and Rhee (2000) demonstrated that conscientiousness had a significant role to play in effective management, which is defined in the Irish context as the ability to be aware of other people's feelings when angry and to behave according to prevailing ethical standards (Chen and Phillips 2007).

Consistency

The consistency trait requires that a manager be capable of identifying how he or she is feeling at any given moment (Matthews *et al.* 2004). Consistency is a vital aspect of successful management and coping with pressure scenarios (Mayer *et al.* 2008), for example completing an important project on schedule and within budget. To be able to conduct an assessment of one's own emotional state and respond appropriately and consistently has been identified as an important trait, the reason being that operating under pressure involves controlling one's emotions (Jordan *et al.* 2002). In addition, being consistent instils faith and peace of mind in subordinates, as they will feel they understand their manager (Côté and Miner 2006). In the Irish context, Chen and Phillips (2007) classified being consistent with words and actions, maintaining performance under pressure and being able to identify what upsets oneself.

Empathy

Empathy requires that an individual be aware of other people's feelings and emotions. Possessing empathy shows a keen emotional awareness and strong capacity for EI generally (Goleman 1998; Jordan *et al.* 2002; Mayer *et al.* 1999). The benefits of management at all levels demonstrating empathy can have a positive effect on staff and result in 'personal feelings of attachment toward the organisation and translates into such attachment behaviours as loyalty, defence of the organisation's name and reputation even outside work boundaries, or abstention from demanding immediate compensation for extra efforts' (Huy 1999:337).

Motivation

A further finding suggests that having the emotional spirit to tackle challenging goals is vital for managers in organisations (Chen and Phillips 2007). Motivation is defined in the Irish context as people's drive and energy to attain challenging goals or targets and interest and passion in life (Chen and Phillips 2007). Managers who know what they wish to accomplish are focused and passionate, indicating strong motivation.

Interpersonal Sensitivity

Interpersonal sensitivity is defined as being sensitive to other people and being a good listener (Chen and Phillips 2007). To understand the position of a colleague or subordinate, a manager must have the capacity to listen, which demonstrates that the manager cares about the opinion of others and reflects a sense of interpersonal sensitivity. The capacity to display sensitivity towards others follows on from being a good listener. Sensitivity towards others refers more to an ability to communicate on a emotional level with others and demonstrating this capacity as a manager can, for example, act as a powerful tool in uniting with subordinates as they will feel that their manager cares and identifies with them (Dulewicz and Higgs 2000).

Resilience

In a competitive market, regrouping after failure is a must (Salovey *et al.* 1995). This again is a component of EI found in Chen and Phillips (2007). Resilience refers to the ability of a manager to 'rally the troops' after a setback and to try again. In addition, a manager must be capable of lifting their own spirits after a perceived defeat, and coping with pressures applied from above requires resilience. As Lubit (2004:6) argues, 'enhancing your EI is preventative medicine, a vaccine against the development of toxic relationships as well as a suit of armour limiting the damage that toxic managers can do'.

Identifying Aspects of Successful Conflict Resolution

As shown in the previous section, factor analysis generated eight components of EI in Chen and Phillips (2007), which were used as the independent variables. The same analysis was used to generate the different aspects of successful conflict resolution, which were the dependent variables in Chen and Phillips (2007). From the results of the study of hotels and hospital/clinics in Dublin (Chen and Phillips 2007: Table 3), four aspects of effective conflict resolution were identified. These four factors were:

- successful handling of others in conflict
- successful handling of oneself in conflict
- appropriate post-conflict behaviour
- leadership in conflict resolution.

We will now discuss each of these four factors in more detail.

Successful Handing of Others in Conflict

To resolve a conflict effectively, managers must be capable of listening with an open mind to alternative opinions (Huy 1999). As Huy (1999:339) argues, 'in front of powerful persons, individuals are likely to restrict the range of displayed emotions . . . (and) . . . such restricted emotional sharing and expression limit the higher level of learning'. In addition, Wallace and Rijamampianina (2005) found that accepting criticism from others can be helpful in resolving conflict, as managers may demonstrate a self-oriented position; this inability to see beyond one's own perspective will serve merely to escalate the confrontation. Third, Chen and Phillips (2007) argue that agreeing on specific issues in a disagreement is a necessary conflict resolution skill. According to Jehn (1997), any perceived disagreement among different parities on important issues inflames intense emotions. Therefore, managers' ability to shorten the process of a conflict is desirable.

Successful Handling of Oneself in Conflict

Chen and Phillips (2007) identified four items in relation to the successful handling of oneself in conflict. First, according to Huy (1999), ensuring that a reasonable response is provided in a conflict scenario is an effective strategy in avoiding further agitation, thereby ensuring that the involved parties will be in a better position to rethink the context and the conflict (Fulmer and Barry 2002). Second, discussion of the conflict has to be done within the sphere of the manager's knowledge (Huy 1999). Exposing a manager to a scenario beyond the confines of what s/he may be familiar with is problematic. Third, it is believed that the positive attitude of a manager will influence the conflicting parties to shift their positions towards the positive side of the situation: 'those leaders who considered themselves to motivate and inspire subordinates to work toward common goals (inspirational motivation), reported that they monitored and managed emotions both within themselves and others' (Palmer *et al.* 2001:8). Finally, if a manager possesses the capability to influence conflicting parties in order to achieve a common objective, this will prevent further escalations and thereby limit future damage (Huy 1999).

Appropriate Post-Conflict Behaviour

According to Goleman (1998), effective conflict resolution does not stop when the conflict is over. At the end of a dispute, different parties will have different perceptions with regards to how a conflict should be resolved and what the outcome should be. A successful manager should be able to adjust those biased perceptions towards the conflict or the resolution (Leban and Zulauf 2004). This is because, in the future, the conflicting parties may need to work together again. Any misconceptions regarding the dispute outcome may lead to future conflict if not addressed properly today. Therefore, it is essential that managers take the time to ensure that all parties get out of dispute as quickly as they can and that there is a thorough understanding of what is meant by the agreement made; this requires the particular skills of an emotionally intelligent manager (Goleman 1998).

Leadership in Conflict Resolution

In Chen and Phillips (2007), two items are discovered to contribute to this factor. To resolve a conflict successfully, a manager must demonstrate leadership qualities by requesting that the differing parties explain their positions to ensure that all opinions are considered (Huy 1999). Taking the responsibility to address a conflict has been found to 'subdue' conflict quickly (Jordan and Troth 2002). Furthermore, a leader needs to approach the conflict from a perspective that is above the interests of a specific party; s/he must demonstrate complete impartiality (Goleman 1998). The decisions made by managers in an unbiased manner seem to be primarily important to employees involved in conflicts (Niehoff and Moorman 1993). To be unbiased, a manger needs to ensure that 'accurate and unbiased information' (Niehoff and Moorman 1993: 528) is collected to assess the situation, which is linked to the first factor identified in Chen and Phillips (2007), i.e. successfully handling others in conflict.

Effect of EI Components on Aspects of Successful Conflict Resolution

By using four different regression models, in which the eight components of EI were the independent variables and each of the four aspects of effective conflict resolution was the dependent variable, our analysis was able to provide some evidence on the effects of the eight components of EI towards the four aspects of effective conflict resolution. While the study produced interesting findings on these relationships, we will focus on the EI components that have statistically significant effects in Chen and Phillips (2007).

Intuitiveness – on leadership in conflict resolution

The analysis suggests that intuitiveness, one component of EI, has a significant effect on the leadership aspect, which is so important in conflict resolution (Chen and Phillips 2007: Table 4). Given the fact that maintaining leadership performance under pressure is crucial to conflict resolution, possessing strong intuition appears to be significant in terms of leadership performance. The ability to maintain a rational disposition when dealing with conflict and to make decisions using reason would also seem to be critical in shaping leadership for effective conflict resolution. The finding corresponds with Anderson (1999), who points out that managers with a high degree of intuition are more effective than those who possess low intuition, since employing reason and intuition requires a calm mind. It can therefore be concluded that one of the EI components – intuition – is very important in effective conflict resolution.

Interpersonal sensitivity – on successful handling of others

Chen and Phillips (2007: Table 4) also show that interpersonal sensitivity is a component that has a significant impact on two aspects of effective conflict resolution: the successful handling of others in conflict; and appropriate post-conflict behaviour. Our work shows that the more sensitive a manager is towards other people's feelings, the more likely it is that the manager will listen with an open mind to alternative options put forward by others, and that the manager will accept constructive suggestion and sometimes criticism. Thus, personal sensitivity can help conflict to be resolved successfully. It has to be pointed out that our findings on personal sensitivity seem to disagree with some extant literature, which has some criticisms of this component of EI. It will be recalled, from our earlier discussion of the role of EI in business, that Zeidner, Matthews and Roberts (2004:380) counted interpersonal sensitivity as one of the qualities of agreeableness that might reduce the effectiveness of performance in management jobs. We found, in the Irish context, the opposite.

Interpersonal sensitivity – on post-conflict behaviour

In addition, we found that the same component, interpersonal sensitivity, has a significant effect on appropriate post-conflict behaviour. Being able to be aware of the influence of negative and positive self-perceptions and being able to meet other people's needs at the end of the conflict are considered in Sheppard *et al.* (1994) as appropriate post-conflict behaviour in effective conflict resolution. In the context we studied, those managers who are able to demonstrate interpersonal sensitivity are likely to reduce the negative effects of the conflict in the lives of the conflict parties so that when they work together in the future, they can do so with a fresh perspective (Chen and Phillips 2007).

CONCLUSION

Conflict occurs every day, not just in Irish organisations but in all organisations worldwide. Management must have the capacity to cope effectively with the various issues that arise and to possibly convert a conflict into a beneficial result, for:

> [o]rganizations in which functional conflict is a part of the culture tend to be more creative and responsive to clients and have higher employee job satisfaction. In line with this, it is conceivable that an organization that encourages constructive conflict, allowing both parties to express their needs and opinions to reach a collaborative solution or compromise tends to be more successful. (Jordan and Troth 2002:63)

We have seen that EI, and, in particular, certain aspects of its components, are important in effective conflict resolution. It is important to note that, despite the progress made to date on researching EI, there remains much more to learn. EI is still in its infancy and there remains 'scant, and sometimes highly controversial, empirical evidence used to support the importance of EI in the workplace' (Zeidner *et al.* 2004:372). In considering the significance of EI in the workplace and the scarcity of accurate information on it that is available for dissemination, it is of particular importance that the role of EI in a business environment is better understood. We know that humans are inherently complex beings and that trying to understand the self is complicated. Trying to comprehend the actions and thoughts of others is even more so. Yet this is the challenge facing managers in today's organisational structures. The potential for conflict is always present in the workplace, with the potential for deadlines and targets to cause stress and frustration. In order to appreciate the position of the people they wish to motivate and inspire, it is helpful for managers to begin with an honest self-assessment of their own strengths and weaknesses to determine where they might improve their own managerial skills.

Chen and Phillips's (2007) findings of Irish managers working in hotels and hospitals/clinics stress the importance of specific, rather than all, components of EI in effective conflict resolution. In particular, maintaining leadership performance in a conflict requires managers to: be able to work through a depressed state; maintain a rational disposition; make decisions by using reason and intuition; and disregard standard procedures in failure. Higher levels of intuitiveness enhance higher levels of leadership performance. Another finding in the study was with regards to the two successful conflict resolution skills: handling others; and appropriate post-conflict behaviour. Interpersonal sensitivity has a positive impact on these two aspects, which suggests that being a good listener and showing empathy and sensitivity towards people could help managers to be more effective in conflict resolution by means of handling others and displaying appropriate post-conflict behaviour.

While the theories of EI explored in this chapter, and specific findings such as Chen and Phillips (2007), may well be revised and enriched by further work in this growing field, it seems certain that current trends in business and society will result in an increasing need to appreciate the importance of EI in the workplace. As business needs more and more of the whole individual to be able to engage in more and more complex work, the '[c]onventional dichotomy between reason and emotion cannot be sustained under close analysis and that contrary to the prevailing view, emotions are central in all rational decision making processes' (McPhail 2003:630). It is our hope that this chapter clearly illustrates the need for further research on specific aspects of EI, both for the continued success of Irish business and for the successful handling of conflicts in Irish society.

References

Anderson, J.A. (1999) 'Intuition in Managers: Are Intuitive Managers More Effective?', *Journal of Managerial Psychology* 15(1): 46–63.

Bar-On, R. (1997) *The Emotional Intelligence Inventory (EQ-i): Technical Manual.* Toronto: Multi-Health Systems.

— (2000) 'Emotional and Social Intelligence: Insights from the Emotional Quotient Inventory (EQ-i)', in R. Bar-On and J.D.A. Parker (eds) *Handbook of Emotional Intelligence*, pp. 363–88. San Francisco, CA: Jossey-Bass.

Boyatzis, R.E., Goleman, D. and Rhee, K.S. (2000) 'Clustering Competence in Emotional Intelligence: Insights from the Emotional Competence Inventory (ECI)', in R. Bar-On and J.D.A. Parker (eds) *Handbook of Emotional Intelligence*, pp. 343–62. San Francisco, CA: Jossey-Bass.

Carmeli, A., Yitzhak-Halevy, M. and Weisberg, J. (2009) 'The Relationship Between Emotional Intelligence and Psychological Wellbeing', *Journal of Managerial Psychology* 24(1): 66–78.

Chen, H. and Phillips, P. (2007) 'Emotional Intelligence and Conflict Resolution', paper presented at the Irish Academy of Management

Conference, Belfast, 3–5 September.

Cooper, R.K. (1997) 'Applying Emotional Intelligence in the Workplace', *Training and Development* 51(12): 31–8.

Cooper, R.K. and Sawaf, A. (1997) *Executive EQ: Emotional Intelligence and Organisations.* New York, NY: Perigee.

Côté, S. and Miner, C.T.H. (2005) 'Emotional Intelligence, Cognitive Intelligence and Job Performance', *Administrative Science Quarterly* 51(1): 1–28.

Davies, M., Stankov, L. and Roberts, R.D. (1998) 'Emotional Intelligence: In Search of an Elusive Construct', *Journal of Personality and Social Psychology* 75(4): 989–1015.

Dulewicz, S.V. and Higgs, M.J. (1999) 'Can Emotional Intelligence be Measured and Developed?', *Leadership and Organization Development Journal* 20(5): 242–52.

— (2000) '360 Degree Assessment of Emotional Intelligence: A Study', *Selection and Development Review* 16(3): 3–8.

Fulmer, I.S. and Barry, B. (2002) 'The Smart Negotiator: Cognitive Ability and Emotional Intelligence in Negotiation', *International Journal of Conflict Management* 15(3): 245–72.

Gardner, H. (1983) *Frames of Mind: The Theory of Multiple Intelligences.* New York, NY: Basic Books.

Goleman, D. (1995) *Emotional Intelligence: Why It Can Matter More Than IQ.* London: Bloomsbury.

— (1998) *Working with Emotional Intelligence.* New York, NY: Bantam.

— (2001) *The Emotionally Intelligent Workplace.* San Francisco, CA: Jossey-Bass.

Goleman, D., Boyatzis, D.R. and McKee, A. (2002) *Primal Leadership: Realising the Power of Emotional Intelligence.* Boston, MA: Harvard Business School Press.

Guilford, J. (1956) 'The Structure of Intellect', *Psychological Bulletin* 53(4): 267–93.

Huy, Q. (1999) 'Emotional Capability, Emotional Intelligence and Radical Change', *Academy of Management Review* 24(2): 325–45.

Jehn, K.A. (1997) 'A Qualitative Analysis of Conflict Types and Dimensions in Organizational Groups', *Administrative Science Quarterly* 42(3): 530–57.

Jordan, P., Ashkanasy, N., Hartel, C. and Hooper, G. (2002) 'Workgroup Emotional Intelligence: Scale Development and Relationship to Team Process, Effectiveness and Goal Focus', *Human Resource Management Review* 12(2): 195–214.

Jordan, P.J. and Troth, A.C. (2002) 'Emotional Intelligence and Conflict Resolution: Implications for Human Resource Development', *Advances in Developing Human Resources* 4(1): 62–79.

Kolb, D.M. and Putnam, L.L. (1992) 'The Multiple Faces of Organizational Conflict', *Journal of Organizational Behavior* 13(3): 311–24.

Leban, W. and Zulauf, C. (2004), 'Linking Emotional Intelligence Abilities and Transformational Leadership Styles', *Leadership and Organization Development Journal* 25(7): 554–64.

Lenaghan, J.A., Buda, R. and Eisner, A.B. (2007) 'An Examination of the Role of Emotional Intelligence in Work and Family Conflict', *Journal of Managerial Issues* 19(1): 76–94.

Lubit, R. (2004) 'The Tyranny of Toxic Managers: Applying Emotional Intelligence to Deal with Difficult Personalities', *Ivey Business Journal* March/April: 1–7.

Matthews, G., Roberts, R.D. and Zeidner, M. (2004) 'Seven Myths about Emotional Intelligence', *Psychological Inquiry* 15(3): 179–96.

Mayer, J.D., Caruso, D.R. and Salovey, P. (1999) 'Emotional Intelligence Meets Traditional Standards for an Intelligence', *Intelligence* 27(4): 267–98.

Mayer, J.D., DiPaolo, M. and Salovey, P. (1990) 'Perceiving Affective Content in Ambiguous Visual Stimuli: A Component of Emotional Intelligence', *Journal of Personality Assessment* 54(3/4): 772–81.

Mayer, J.D. and Salovey, P. (1997) 'What Is Emotional Intelligence?', in P. Salovey and D.J. Sluyter (eds) *Emotional Development and Emotional Intelligence: Educational Implications*, pp. 3–31. New York, NY: Basic Books.

Mayer, J.D., Salovey, P. and Caruso, D.R. (2000) 'Models in Emotional Intelligence', in R.J. Sternberg (ed.) *Handbook of Intelligence*, pp. 396–420. Cambridge: Cambridge University Press.

— (2008) 'Emotional Intelligence: New Ability or Eclectic Traits', *American Psychologist* 63(6): 503–17.

McPhail, K. (2003) 'An Emotional Response to the State of Accounting Education: Developing Accounting Students' Emotional Intelligence', *Critical Perspectives on Accounting* 15(4): 629–48.

Niehoff, B.P. and Moorman, R.H. (1993) 'Justice as Mediator of the Relationship between Methods of Monitoring and Organizational Citizenship Behavior', *Academy of Management Journal* 36(3): 527–56.

Obeidi, A., Hipel, K.W. and Kilgour, D.M. (2003) 'Emotion: The Missing Ingredient in Conflict Analysis', in *Proceedings of the IEEE International Conference on Systems, Man, and Cybernetics*, pp. 3322–9. Piscataway, NJ: IEEE.

Palmer, B.R. and Stough, C. (2001) 'The Measurement of Emotional Intelligence', *Australian Journal of Psychology* 53 (Supplement): 85.

Palmer, B.R., Walls, M., Burgess, Z. and Stough, C. (2001) 'Emotional Intelligence and Effective Leadership', *Leadership and Organization Development Journal* 22(1): 5–10.

Petrides, K.V. and Furnham, A. (2001) 'Trait Emotional Intelligence: Psychometric Investigation with Reference to Established Trait Taxonomies', *European Journal of Personality* 15(6): 425–48.

Rahim, M.A and Psenicka, C. (2002) 'A Model of Emotional Intelligence and Conflict Management Strategies: A Study in Seven Countries', *International*

Journal of Organisational Studies 10(4): 302–26.

Robertson, I.T. and Smith, M. (2001) 'Personnel Selection', *Journal of Occupational and Organizational Psychology* 74(4): 441–72.

Rosete, D. and Ciarrochi, J. (2005) 'Emotional Intelligence and its Relationship to Workplace Performance of Leadership Effectiveness', *Leadership and Organization Development Journal* 26(5): 388–99

Rowan, R. (1986) *Intuitive Managers*. New York, NY: Little, Brown.

Salovey, P. and Mayer, J.D. (1990) 'Emotional Intelligence', *Imagination, Cognition and Personality* 9(1): 185–211.

Salovey, P., Mayer, J.D., Goldman, S., Turvey, C. and Palfai, T. (1995) 'Emotional Attention, Clarity and Repair: Exploring Emotional Intelligence Using the Trait Meta-Mood Scale', in J.W. Pennebaker (ed.) *Emotion, Disclosure, and Health*, pp. 125–54. Washington, DC: American Psychological Association.

Sanhole, D. and van de Merwe, H. (1993) *Conflict Resolution Theory and Practice: Integration and Application*. Manchester: Manchester University Press.

Schutte, N.S., Malouff, J.M., Hall, L.E., Haggerty, D.J., Cooper, J.T. and Golden, C.J. (1998) 'Development and Validation of a Measure of Emotional Intelligence', *Personality and Individual Differences* 25(2): 167–77.

Sheppard, B.H., Blumenfeld-Jones, K., Minton, J.W. and Hyder, E. (1994) 'Informal Conflict Intervention: Advice and Dissent', *Employee Responsibilities and Rights Journal* 7(1): 53–72.

Suliman, A.M. and Al-Shaikh, F.N. (2007) 'Emotional Intelligence at Work: Links to Conflict and Innovation', *Employee Relations* 29(2): 208–20.

Thorndike, E.L. (1920) 'A Constant Error in Psychological Ratings', *Journal of Applied Psychology* 4(2): 25–9.

Vandervoort, D.J. (2006), 'The Importance of Emotional Intelligence in Higher Education', *Current Psychology* 25(1): 3–7.

Wallace, E. and Rijamampianina, R. (2005) 'Strategic Decision Making with Corporate Emotional Intelligence', *Problem and Perspectives in Management* 8(3): 83–91.

Weber, M. (1922) 'Legitimate Authority and Bureaucracy' in L.E. Boone and D.D. Bowen (eds) (1987) *The Great Writings in Management and Organizational Behavior*, pp. 5–19. Boston, MA: Irwin.

Zeidner, M., Matthews, G. and Roberts, R.D. (2004) 'Emotional Intelligence in the Workplace: A Critical Review', *Applied Psychology: An International Review* 53(3): 371–99.

Chapter 18

Regulatory Framework: Irish Employment Law

Mary Faulkner

'Oh what a tangled web we weave'
(Sir Walter Scott, *Marmion*, Canto VI, Stanza 17)

INTRODUCTION

The Irish workplace can be quite a confusing landscape to negotiate for both employee and employer when contentious workplace issues arise. For employees, it is important to know what protections they are entitled to, which remedies are available should the need arise and where they may be sought. For employers, it is equally important to know what claims they may face, where these claims may be aired and the possible extent of the liability to be incurred. As the Irish workplace has become more regulated, the number of fora providing for the resolution of contentious employment issues has increased significantly, a development that has not escaped some criticism. The regulatory fora are many and varied; the functions and powers of the various bodies range from advisory only to quasi-judicial with decisions binding on the parties. In addition to these regulatory fora, there are the civil courts, which also provide a means of redress in employment law issues.

With over eight fora, a myriad of laws from statutes, statutory instruments, sectoral employment agreements and codes of practice to European Union (EU) directives and regulations, the regulatory landscape can be a difficult place to navigate. I propose to outline these fora and some of the laws that obtain. The next section will describe the functioning of the Labour Court and the evolution of its role in its sixty-four-year history. Then the Employment Appeals Tribunal is examined. The following section concerns the Labour Relations Commission. The establishment of the Equality Tribunal and its development is then discussed. The next four sections deal with some employment implications of InjuriesBoard.ie, the Safety Authority, data protection and the civil courts, before drawing the chapter to a close with some pertinent observations.

THE LABOUR COURT

Established under the Industrial Relations Act 1946, the Labour Court is an independent body consisting of employers' and employees' representatives participating on an equal basis. Since its establishment, its role has evolved considerably, keeping pace with the significant developments in national and European employment legislation.

Initially established and designed to assist in the resolution of industrial relations issues, its role has now evolved to include an adjudicative role in the area of employment rights under various employment laws. Referrals under various employment rights statutes now account for 25 per cent of cases coming before the Court (Labour Court 2009:4). The court has come under scrutiny recently, most notably in the Ryanair case (*Ryanair Ltd v Labour Court and IMPACT* 2007), and has been required to adapt its procedures to reflect the legal principles and procedures inherent in the determination of legal rights and responsibilities.

According to the court's mission statement, its purpose is to provide fast, fair, informal and inexpensive arrangements for the adjudication and resolution of trade disputes (Labour Court 2009:2). When first established, it did not have the power to make legally binding decisions, except in relation to certain collective agreements. It now enjoys an increased jurisdiction and has the power to make legally binding determinations under a range of Acts.

Structure of the Labour Court

The Labour Court consists of nine full-time members: a chairperson, two deputy chairpersons and six ordinary members (three employer members and three employee members). The Minister for Enterprise, Trade and Employment appoints the chairperson and deputy chairpersons; the employers' members are nominated by the Irish Business and Employers' Confederation (IBEC), while the employees' members are nominated by the Irish Congress of Trade Unions (ICTU). A legal adviser (registrar) is also appointed by the minister. Hearings generally take place in private before a court of three, comprising a chairperson, an employers' member and an employees' member.

The Labour Court is not a court of law in the strict sense, though it should be noted that it has become more legalistic over the years. In trade disputes, the court acts as a tribunal, hearing both sides and making non-binding recommendations. In cases under legislation relating to the following issues, the court has the power to make legally binding decisions:

- employment equality
- pensions
- organisation of working time
- industrial relations (amendment)

- protection of employees (part-time or fixed term)
- national minimum wage.

The court received 1,179 referrals in 2008, showing an increase of 28 per cent over 2007 (Labour Court 2009). The main reason for the increase in referrals was a rise in the number of cases alleging breaches of Registered Employment Agreements (REA). These complaints accounted for 30 per cent of cases coming to the Court. An REA is an agreement on pay and conditions of employment concluded by the two sides in an industry or enterprise. Once registered with the Labour Court, the provisions of the REA are legally enforceable in respect of every worker and employer to which it is expressed to apply, even if such worker or employer is not a party to the agreement. Currently, there are sixty-eight such agreements registered with the court (Labour Court 2009). A number have, in the recent past, proved controversial and are being challenged in the High Court as to their constitutionality, most notably the REA concerning the electrical contracting industry. While the overall number of referrals has increased in the court, it is interesting to note that equality referrals in 2008 showed a reduction of 26 per cent on the previous year (Labour Court 2009).

An important Supreme Court decision on procedures and other issues relating to the Labour Court was that reached in *Ryanair Ltd v Labour Court and IMPACT* (2007). The background to the case was that Ryanair had tried to enter into various agreements with its pilots concerning re-training and repayment of the cost of that training should they leave the company within five years. The Irish Airline Pilots' Association (IALPA) wished to enter into negotiations with Ryanair. The company refused to negotiate directly with unions, stating that it was negotiating with Employee Representative Committees. The pilots refused to negotiate with Ryanair where they could not be represented by their trade union. The matter was referred to the Labour Court. In order to deal with the dispute, the Court had first to establish whether or not it had jurisdiction: were the preconditions in Section 2(1) of the Industrial Relations (Amendment) Act 2001, satisfied that:

- a trade dispute existed?
- it was not the practice of the employer to engage in collective bargaining?
- internal dispute resolution procedures had failed to resolve the dispute?

Ryanair argued that the Labour Court lacked jurisdiction in the matter, that there was no dispute and that the referral was part of the applicant's strategy to compel union recognition. It also contended that it had engaged in extensive collective bargaining through its Employee Representative Committees in town hall meetings, though it did not negotiate with unions.

The Labour Court found that it did have jurisdiction to hear the case. Ryanair sought to quash that decision by means of judicial review to the High Court on the basis that the preconditions had not been met and that the procedures followed in the Labour Court had been unfair. The High Court refused the order and the matter came before the Supreme Court. In quashing the Labour Court decision, the Supreme Court noted that it had failed to properly investigate the internal dispute resolution mechanism that Ryanair executives claimed it had to resolve disputes. A unilateral withdrawing from a process did not mean that there were no collective bargaining arrangements. The Labour Court had erred in its interpretation of what constituted collective bargaining in the company in respect of the group in dispute. The Supreme Court also held that the failure to take sworn or unsworn evidence was a fundamentally unfair procedure. The fact that there had not been disclosure of the identities of the pilots being represented by the union was also deemed unfair.

Though established initially to deal with the resolution of industrial relations issues, the Labour Court's role as an adjudicative body in individual employment rights continues to grow. When there is already a well-established body of agencies dealing with individual employment rights, it could be questioned whether it is the appropriate forum for such matters.

In 2009, one of the largest individual awards by the Labour Court was made under the National Minimum Wage Act 2000. Generally, such awards are in the low to mid-thousands. In this case, it was alleged the complainant, Surinder Singh, worked seven days a week for up to eighteen hours a day over a period of many years at below the minimum wage rate for his employer, Mr Puri. A rights commissioner determined in March 2009 that Mr Singh be paid €204,352. According to media reports, that decision was not implemented and the case came before the Labour Court again in November 2009 (Rogers 2010).

EMPLOYMENT APPEALS TRIBUNAL

The Employment Appeals Tribunal (EAT) was set up under Section 39(18) of the Redundancy Payments Act 1967. It is a quasi-judicial tripartite body. Originally set up to adjudicate in disputes relating to redundancy, with the passage of legislation its scope has been extended considerably over the years. The EAT now deals with disputes relating to individual employment rights under the following legislation and statutory instruments:

- Adoptive Leave Acts 1995–2005
- Carer's Leave Act 2001
- Competition Act 2002
- European Communities (Protection of Employees' Rights on Transfer of Undertakings) Regulations 2003
- European Communities (Protection of Employment) Regulations 2000
- Maternity Protection Acts 1994–2004
- Minimum Notice and Terms of Employment Acts 1973–2001

- Organisation of Working Time Act 1997
- Parental Leave Acts 1998–2006
- Payment of Wages Act 1991
- Protection of Employees (Employers' Insolvency) Acts 1984–2003
- Protection for Persons Reporting Child Abuse Act 1998
- Protection of Young Persons (Employment) Act 1996
- Redundancy Payments Acts 1976–2003
- Terms of Employment (Information) Acts 1994–2001
- Unfair Dismissals Acts 1977–2001.

The tribunal is also an appellate body adjudicating on appeals from the decisions of rights commissioners made under a number of pieces of employment legislation. According to its mission statement,

> The Employment Appeals Tribunal is an independent body established to provide a speedy, inexpensive and relatively informal means for the adjudication of disputes on employment rights under the body of legislation that comes within the scope of the Tribunal. (EAT 2009:4)

Although the intention is to provide a more informal approach to dispute resolution, the increasingly complex nature of employment law, the rise in the number of parties opting for legal representation before the tribunal, and the use of legal conventions and rules has somewhat diluted the informal nature of the EAT.

Structure of the Employment Appeals Tribunal

The tribunal comprises a chairperson who is a practising barrister or solicitor and three panels: a panel of vice-chairpersons, each member legally qualified and appointed by the Minister for Enterprise, Trade and Employment; an employers' panel, with members nominated by employer organisations; and an employees' panel, nominated by the ICTU. The tribunal ordinarily acts in divisions consisting of the chairperson or vice-chairperson and two other members, one drawn from each of the two panels.

Adjudicating on unfair dismissals cases continues to be the core activitiy of the tribunal, accounting for approximately 85 per cent of its workload in terms of time taken up at hearings (EAT 2009). The number of cases referred to the tribunal increased by 72 per cent to 5,457 in 2008, while the tribunal disposed of 1,111 cases of unfair dismissal in that same year (EAT 2009). It is likely that 2009 figures across all areas will reflect a continuing increase in the tribunal's caseload because, as Ireland continues to experience an economic downturn, it is expected that redundancy and unfair dismissal cases will feature prominently in that caseload. The average waiting period to have a claim heard in 2008 was sixteen weeks in Dublin and thirty-one weeks in provincial areas (EAT 2009).

An interesting case where the issue of the jurisdiction of the Tribunal arose was *Patricia Mayland v H.S.S. Ltd T/A Citywest Golf & Country Club* UD 1438/2004. Following a dismissal, the claimant suffered from panic attacks and was on medication as a result. The claimant asked the tribunal to take into account the psychological injuries she had suffered after the dismissal. The tribunal, however, determined that the matter was not within its jurisdiction. Note: the House of Lords case, *Johnson v Unisys Ltd* (2001), where the Law Lords held that the statutory provision in the UK, which governs unfair dismissal compensation and provides for compensation of 'such amount as the Tribunal considers just and equitable in all the circumstances having regard to the loss sustained by the complainant in consequence of the dismissal insofar as that loss is attributable to action taken by the employer', was not confined to financial loss. It was open to a tribunal to award compensation, in an appropriate case, for distress, humiliation, damage to reputation in the community or to family life. Clearly, the EAT chose a more confined role for itself.

LABOUR RELATIONS COMMISSION

The Industrial Relations Act 1990 provided for important changes in relation to industrial action, as well as the industrial relations procedures for dealing with industrial disputes. The Labour Relations Commission (LRC) was established under Section 24 of the Act, and came into being in January 1991 with the purpose of promoting good industrial relations. The Conciliation Service and Rights Commissioner Service heretofore provided by the Labour Court were transferred to the LRC under the 1990 Act. Trade disputes were to be referred to the LRC in the first instance, rather than to the Labour Court. The intention was to make the Labour Court a court of last resort. The function of the LRC is as follows:

> To promote the development and improvement of Irish industrial relations policies, procedures and practices through the provision of appropriate, timely and effective services to employers, trade unions and employees. (LRC 2009:4)

The LRC provides the following services:

- an industrial relations conciliation service
- industrial relations advisory and research services
- a rights commissioner service
- a workplace mediation service
- assistance to Joint Labour Committees and Joint Industrial Councils.

The LRC also has a role to play in reviewing developments in the area of industrial relations, establishing codes of practice and engaging in research.

Conciliation Services Division

Conciliation is a voluntary mediation process. It is a very effective means of facilitating the resolution of disputes. When a dispute is referred to the LRC under this process, the LRC assigns an industrial relations officer (IRO) to mediate. The process is informal and non-legalistic. Parties may be represented by trade unions or employer organisations. Settlement of a dispute is by consensus: it is not an outcome that is imposed by the LRC mediator. This service is generally available to all employees and employers, with the exception of the defence forces, gardaí and prison officers. Its services are free of charge to employers, employees and their representatives. Over 80 per cent of disputes referred to the division in 2008 were resolved at the conciliation stage (LRC 2009).

Advisory Services Division

The Advisory Services Division is involved in non-dispute situations and its function is to develop effective industrial relations practices and structures. It works in partnership with employers and employees. Services provided include conducting an industrial relations audit in a workplace, providing preventative mediation and preparing codes of practice. Examples of codes of practice cover such issues as grievance and disciplinary procedures, Sunday working in the retail trade and procedures for addressing bullying in the workplace.

Rights Commissioners

Rights commissioners were first established under the Industrial Relations Act 1969. Section 13(2) sets out the functions of the office as being to investigate and to make recommendations in a trade dispute. The definition of a trade dispute did not include disputes concerned with rates of pay, hours or times of work or annual holidays.

The role of the rights commissioner has expanded considerably since the 1969 Act and in recent years has included an important and often mandatory role in the resolution of very complex legal issues under seventeen separate pieces of legislation and statutory instruments (Faulkner 2008:16). The Protection of Employees (Fixed-Term Work) Act 2003, demonstrates such complexity, where the issues are not confined to Irish domestic law, but also encompass European case law involving, for example, questions of the direct effect of an EU directive. Rights commissioners now investigate disputes and grievances referred by individuals in relation to such issues as leave, employee permits, maternity protection, minimum wage, part-time work, fixed-term work, safety, health and welfare, transfer of undertakings and unfair dismissals. In many instances, the rights commissioner is the first stop when an individual seeks redress.

Rights commissioners are appointed by the Minister for Enterprise, Trade and Employment, on the recommendation of the LRC. Hearings are generally held in private. They are formal but not adversarial, and parties may be represented if they wish. A trade union, employer's organisation, solicitor, friend or family member may act as the representative.

In 2008, referrals to the Rights Commissioner Service rose by 20 per cent to 10,900 (LRC 2009:29). As in previous years, the highest number of referrals concerned grievances under the Payment of Wages Act 1991. The other main sources of grievance concerned Terms of Employment (Information) Acts 1994–2001 (1,722 referrals); Unfair Dismissals Acts 1977–2005 (1,566 referrals); Organisation of Working Time Act 1997 (1,516 referrals); and the Industrial Relations Acts 1969–1990 (1,470 referrals) (LRC 2009:29). Complaints referred to the service concerned, among other issues, underpayment of wages, non-payment of holiday pay, holiday entitlement, maximum working hours, written statements of terms of employment and fair procedures in the case of dismissals.

Workplace Mediation Service

Workplace mediation is a service available to individuals or small groups of workers in situations of conflict, dispute or disagreement in a workplace to enable the parties to arrive at a resolution of the difficulties concerned. The type of situation where mediation can be used includes interpersonal differences, issues arising from a disciplinary procedure or certain industrial relations matters. It is a voluntary process.

Joint Labour Committees

The LRC provides industrial relations officers to act as chairpersons to a number of councils and committees. The purpose of the Joint Labour Committees is to draw up proposals in relation to setting minimum rates of pay and conditions for employees in certain sectors. There are sixteen sectors involved, ranging from agricultural workers to catering, contract cleaning, law clerks and tailoring (Faulkner 2008:17). When the proposals are confirmed by the Labour Court in the form of an Employment Regulation Order, they become the statutory minimum pay and conditions of employment for the sector concerned. The Joint Labour Committees operate in areas where collective bargaining is not well established.

Joint Industrial Councils

These councils were established under the 1946 Industrial Relations Act. The Act provided that they were associations of employers and employees representatives whose function was to bring about harmonious relations between the parties and to facilitate industrial peace. The Act also provided that if a trade dispute arose, the parties would agree not to undertake strike action before such dispute had been referred to the council for its consideration.

EQUALITY TRIBUNAL

The Equality Tribunal was set up under the Employment Equality Act 1998. It is an independent body which hears complaints of alleged discrimination under equality legislation. Cases before it come under the Employment Equality Acts 1998–2004, Equal Status Act 2000, and certain sections of the Pensions Acts. The tribunal is a quasi-judicial body whose decisions are legally binding.

The tribunal saw a 26 per cent increase in employment cases brought in 2008, with race the main ground for referral in 359 of the 842 cases (Equality Tribunal 2009:11). Disability accounted for just over ten per cent of cases brought, and age for slightly fewer. It would appear that the level of referrals will have been similar in 2009. As in previous years, the majority of claims were not upheld, with only 36 per cent being successful. The average award was €11,755, and the highest €60,000 (Equality Tribunal 2009:14).

As employment equality claims become more specialised, choice of forum becomes crucial. Outcomes may vary depending on whether the case is brought to the Equality Tribunal, the EAT or the Circuit Court. A case in point is the situation obtaining in certain dismissals cases, particularly those involving a claim of discrimination. Compensation for an unfair dismissal before a rights commissioner or the EAT is limited to financial loss attributable to the dismissal. However, an award from the Equality Tribunal or the Labour Court (on appeal) can include financial loss, as well as other loss, such as upset, caused by the discriminatory acts in question. Indeed, there have been several cases where substantial awards have been made when the employee had suffered no financial loss whatsoever.

INJURIESBOARD.IE

The Personal Injuries Assessment Board, now called the InjuriesBoard.ie, is an independent statutory body set up by government to assess the level of compensation due to an injured party, such injury having resulted from a workplace, motor or public liability accident. Since July 2004, all personal injuries claims, with the exception of medical negligence, must be submitted to the InjuriesBoard.ie.

The InjuriesBoard.ie was set up under the Personal Injuries Assessment Board Act 2003, which was an

> Act to enable, in certain situations the making of assessments, without the need for legal proceedings to be brought in that behalf, of compensation for personal injuries (or both such injuries and property damage), in those situations to prohibit, in the interests of the common good, the bringing of legal proceedings unless any of the parties concerned decides not to accept the particular assessment or certain other circumstances apply, to provide for the enforcement of such an assessment, for those purposes to establish a body to be known as the Personal Injuries Assessment Board and to define its functions and to provide for related matters. (Personal Injuries Assessment Board Act 2003)

Section 3 of the Act states that the Act applies to civil actions:

a) by an employee against his or her employer for negligence or breach of duty
b) by a person against another arising out of that other's ownership, driving or use of a mechanically propelled vehicle
c) by a person against another arising out of that other's use of land or building.

In essence, the only personal injuries actions not dealt with are those arising from alleged medical negligence. When a person is making a claim for assessment (i.e. an assessment as to the amount of damages the claimant is entitled to) the following must be submitted:

- a document notifying the other side of the claim and seeking compensation
- copies of any correspondence between the parties
- medical reports in respect of the personal injury
- receipts, vouchers or other documentary proof in relation to the loss or damage.

The board has discretion not to make an assessment in a number of circumstances, including the following.

- If, in its opinion, there is not a sufficient body of case law or settlements to which the assessors could refer for the purpose of making an assessment.
- If, in its opinion, it would not be appropriate to do so because of the complexity of the issues involved.
- The injuries consist wholly or in part of psychological damage.

One of the functions of the board is to publish a Book of Quantum containing general guidelines as to amounts that may be awarded in respect of specified types of injury.

The Act sets out the membership of the board, which cannot number more than eleven. They comprise the chairperson and the chief executive, two members nominated by ICTU, one member nominated by IBEC, one member nominated by the Irish Insurance Federation (IIF), the Director of Consumer Affairs (DCA) and the Consumer Director of the Irish Financial Services Regulatory Authority (IFSR).

In setting up the Board, and thereby removing personal injuries claims from the courts, the intention was to lower insurance costs and reduce delay and legal costs/fees involved in such claims. Awards made comprise general damages for pain and suffering caused by the injury, current and into the future, and special damages for financial loss to date and into the future. Financial loss includes loss of income as well as medical costs. In 2008, compensation totalling €217m was awarded in respect of 8,845 personal injuries claims (InjuriesBoard.ie 2009:7).

SAFETY AUTHORITY

Employers owe wide-ranging duties to their employees under both statutory and common law. Issues of safety and welfare in the workplace had been covered by common law for many years, but it was not until 1989 that a legal framework was set down establishing, for the first time, minimum standards for all workplaces. Before 1989 the approach was quite fragmented, with minimum standards established for only 20 per cent of the workforce. Calls for reform led to the establishment in 1983 of the Barrington Commission, comprising employers, trade unions, government representatives and other interests. The report that issued led ultimately to the passing of the Safety, Health and Welfare at Work Act 1989. In 2005, a new Safety, Health and Welfare at Work Act was passed, which represents an expanded version of the earlier 1989 Act. It sets out duties not only of employers and employees, but also of other parties associated with the workplace, such as designers of workplaces and workplace equipment and suppliers of goods for use in the workplace. Enforcement procedures have been strengthened, with significant increases in penalties available.

The Safety, Health and Welfare at Work Act 2005 sets out the general framework of rules aimed at preventing accidents and ill health in the workplace. The protection afforded under the 2005 Act is supplemented by the 2007 regulations. Under the 2005 Act, an employer has a duty to 'ensure, so far as is reasonably practicable, the safety, health and welfare at work of his or her employees' (Safety, Health and Welfare at Work Act 2005).

The phrase 'in so far as is reasonably practicable' is noteworthy. The employer is not an insurer and thus is not expected to prevent all accidents from happening. Interestingly, the Act contains the first ever statutory definition of the term 'reasonably practicable'. Section 2(6) Part 1 of the 2005 Act states:

For the purposes of the relevant statutory provisions, 'reasonably practicable', in relation to the duties of an employer, means that an employer has exercised all due care by putting in place the necessary protective and preventive measures, having identified the hazards and assessed the risks to safety and health likely to result in accidents or injury to health at the place of work concerned and where the putting in place of any further measures is grossly disproportionate having regard to the unusual, unforeseeable and exceptional nature of any circumstance or occurrence that may result in an accident at work or injury to health at that place of work. (Safety, Health and Welfare at Work Act 2005)

Courts' interpretation of the term 'reasonably practicable' is that 'the law does not require an employer to ensure in all circumstances the safety of his workmen. He will have discharged his duty of care if he does what a reasonable and prudent employer would have done in the circumstances' (Mr Justice Henchy in *Bradley v CIE* (1976)). One of the best statements of this general principle is to be found in *Stokes v Guest, Keen and Nettlefold (Bolts & Nuts)* (1968), where Mr Justice Swanwick stated:

[T]he overall test is still the conduct of the reasonable and prudent employer, taking positive thought for the safety of his workers in the light of what he knows or ought to know; where there is a recognised and general practice which has been followed for a substantial period in similar circumstances without mishap, he is entitled to follow it, unless in the light of common sense or newer knowledge it is clearly bad; but where there is developing knowledge, he must keep reasonably abreast of it and not be too slow to apply it; and where he has in fact greater than average knowledge of the risks, he may be thereby obliged to take some more than the average or standard precautions. He must weigh up the risk in terms of the likelihood of injury occurring and the potential consequence if it does; he must balance against this probable effectiveness of the precautions that can be taken to meet it and the expense and inconvenience they involve. If he is found to have fallen below the standard to be properly expected of a reasonable and prudent employer in these respects he is negligent.

In this case, the plaintiff, Stokes, contracted cancer of the scrotum from exposure at work over a long period to mineral oil, which saturated his clothing and came into contact with his skin on a daily basis. The factory doctor was aware of the cancer risk, but no steps were put in place to address the risk. Stokes eventually died from the cancer (Faulkner 2008).

Employees are obliged under the Act not to put themselves in a position where they might be a danger to themselves and to others in the workplace. They must co-operate with the employer or others to enable compliance with relevant statutory provision, not engage in improper behaviour likely to endanger others, attend safety training, make proper use of safety equipment, submit to appropriate tests for intoxicants and report dangers posed to health and safety.

The Health and Safety Authority (HSA), established under the Act, has the authority to enforce the Act and will do this in a number of ways. Section 64 of the Act provides that the first line of enforcement rests with the inspectorate, which, on foot of an investigation, may direct improvements to a workplace or, in cases of a likely risk of serious injury, close a workplace. Where the risk to safety is considered to be so serious that use of the workplace should be immediately restricted or prohibited, the HSA, or an approved person, may approach the High Court for an injunction so restricting or prohibiting. Where prosecutions are taken for breaches of the Act, the penalties can be severe. Minor infringements could attract fines of €3,000 and/or imprisonment up to six months, while more serious infringements can incur fines up to €3m and/or imprisonment up to two years.

DATA PROTECTION

The Data Protection Acts 1988–2003 have a significant impact on how employers can deal with employees' personal data (see Chapter 30). Employers must ensure that personal data is obtained and processed fairly, that it is accurate, retained only for legitimate purposes and is not excessive in relation to the purpose for which it was collected. Particular care needs to be taken in relation to the processing of sensitive data. Such data would include information on racial or ethnic origin, religious beliefs, trade union membership, and the physical or mental health of the data subject. Failure to comply with the obligations under the Acts could result in a complaint to the Data Protection Commissioner, who has wide powers under the Acts. Penalties include fines and /or imprisonment.

CIVIL COURTS

Civil courts also offer a means of redress in employment law issues or disputes, depending on the nature of the matter in question. The principal courts in this regard are the Circuit Court, the High Court and, on rare occasions, the Supreme Court and European Court of Justice (ECJ).

In the High Court case of *Minister for Justice, Equality and Law Reform & Commissioner of An Garda Síochána v Director of the Equality Tribunal* (2009), the Minister for Justice, Equality and Law Reform brought judicial review proceedings challenging the Equality Tribunal's authority to hear a case on the issue of age discrimination in An Garda Síochána. The case concerned three individuals aged between thirty-six and forty-eight years of age, whose applications to join the force had been turned down because they were over the age limit of thirty-five. Entry to training in An Garda Síochána was governed by the Garda Síochána (Admissions and Appointments) (Amendment) Regulations of 1988, 2001 and 2004. They brought their complaint to the Equality Tribunal and the Minister for Justice challenged its authority to hear the matter.

In a letter dated 5 April 2006, the Equality Authority had stated its view that the Garda Síochána (Admissions and Appointments) Regulations were not consistent with the Employment Equality Acts and, further, that any exemption of An Garda Síochána from the general prohibition on age discrimination was removed by the Equality Act 2004.

In his judgment, Mr Justice Charleton stated there was no principle of European law that allowed an administrative body or a court of limited jurisdiction to exceed its own authority where it believed that a European law had not been properly implemented at national level. He went on to state:

> The respondent does not have the authority to make a binding legal declaration of inconsistency or insufficiency on a comparison of European and national legislation. The High Court has that power as this has been expressly reserved to it by Article 34 of the Constitution. The respondent is bound by S.I. No. 749 of 2004 fixing the upper age for admission to training as a member of An Garda Síochána at 35 years. (*Minister for Justice, Equality and Law Reform & Commissioner of An Garda Síochána v the Director of the Equality Tribunal* (2009))

An important decision dealing with two areas of law that are increasingly a source of litigation – the contractual duty to act with mutual trust and confidence, and employer's liability in contract or tort for psychiatric injury caused by work-based stress – arose in the 2009 Supreme Court case of *Berber v Dunnes Stores Ltd* (2009). The case arose out of the appeal by Dunnes Stores of an earlier High Court decision (*Berber v Dunnes Stores Ltd* 2006). The facts of the case are that Berber commenced working for Dunnes Stores in 1980 and until 1988 was employed as a store manager in various locations. In 1988 he moved to buying, where he remained until 2000, gradually moving up the promotion ladder to men's 'ready-mades' buyer.

During 2000, the situation changed considerably in that, unlike previous years, where as many as fifty days were spent abroad sourcing and buying merchandise, only one trip was taken to a clothing show in Germany. There also appeared to be a new interest in his health, which was given as a reason for not sending him on a buying trip to the Far East. The plaintiff had suffered from Crohn's disease since his late teens and he was also colour blind. In August, the plaintiff was requested to report to the human resources department on his medical condition. In late 2000, he was requested by management to move from buying back to store management, which he viewed as a demotion. Based on assurances from the managing director that he would be fast-tracked to store manager or regional manager within six to twelve months, he agreed to return to store management, starting in the flagship Blanchardstown store in ladies' wear. On arrival at the defendant's head office on 27 November, he discovered that he was being directed to home wares. He did not go to Blanchardstown. After three meetings with the director of stores' operations, he was suspended from work with pay. He was subsequently certified as being unfit for work until December.

The plaintiff's final day at work was 15 May 2001, during which a heated argument developed that resulted in an alleged abusive verbal attack on the plaintiff within the hearing of other management staff. Legal proceedings were instituted. The plaintiff's claim fell under two main headings:

1   For breach of contract, in that he was constructively and wrongfully dismissed.
2   For personal injuries formulated both in contract and in tort.

On the plaintiff's submission that there was a series of breaches of contract amounting to repudiation, Miss Justice Laffoy did not agree:

> The correct interpretation of what happened is that the manner in which the defendant dealt with the plaintiff in the knowledge of the precarious nature of his physical and psychological health viewed objectively amounted to oppressive conduct. It was likely to seriously damage their employer/employee relationship and it did so. Accordingly, the defendant breached its obligation to maintain the plaintiff's trust and confidence . . . A breach by an employer of its implied obligation to maintain trust and confidence of an employee is a breach which goes to the root of the contract. (*Berber v Dunnes Stores Ltd* (2006))

It was decided that the defendant had indeed unlawfully repudiated the contract of employment.

On the personal injuries claim, Miss Justice Laffoy did not consider it necessary to distinguish between the two causes of action in contract and in tort and made reference to the English High Court case *Walker v Northumberland County Council* (1995), where Mr Justice Colman pointed out, 'the scope of the duty of care owed to an employee to take reasonable care to provide a safe system of work is co-extensive with the implied term as to the employee's safety in the contract of employment'. This statement was approved of later by the Court of Appeal in *Gogay v Hertfordshire County Council* (2000).

On the question of liability, Miss Justice Laffoy believed that the questions identified by Mr Justice Clarke as the relevant questions in *Maher v Jabil Global Services Limited* (2005) were the proper approach:

a)   Has the plaintiff suffered an injury to his or her health as opposed to what might be described as ordinary occupational stress?
b)   If so, is that injury attributable to the workplace?
c)   If so, was the harm suffered to the particular employee concerned reasonably foreseeable in all the circumstances?

The plaintiff was awarded €72,622, comprising €40,000 in general damages and €32,622 in special damages/damages for breach of contract.

The case was appealed to the Supreme Court and came up for hearing in 2009. The High Court decision of Miss Justice Laffoy was overturned. In its decision, the Supreme Court did affirm that

> there is implied in a contract of employment a mutual obligation that the employer and the employee will not without reasonable and proper cause conduct themselves in a manner likely to destroy or seriously damage the relationship of trust and confidence between them. (*Berber v Dunnes Stores Ltd* (2009))

It went on to note that, with regard to the mutuality of the obligation, the impact of an employee's behaviour is also relevant. It stated that an employee has obligations to obey the lawful and reasonable orders of his employer. The legal consequences of not obeying such orders was dismissal. Objectively, Berber's behaviour had been unreasonable, yet the employer had not dismissed him. The Supreme Court stated that the employer had not acted unreasonably and had not been in breach of the implied term of mutual trust and confidence. On the personal injuries element of the case, the Court held that the employer had not acted unreasonably or in breach of its duty of care, as the injury to Berber was not foreseeable. In this regard, it affirmed the Hatton principles as set out by Lady Justice Hale (*Sutherland v Hatton* (2002), discussed below).

The original award of damages was set aside, except for the sum of €9,079, which was in respect of a Christmas and annual bonus. The case represents a significant clarification of the law in relation to mutual trust and to workplace stress. In respect of the latter, it would appear that a higher burden of proof is now placed on claimants.

In the UK, one of the most important cases in the area of work-related stress was the Hatton case. The *Sutherland v Hatton* (2002) case concerned four conjoined appeals in which the employer was appealing against the finding of liability for the employee's psychiatric injury. Two of the plaintiffs were teachers in a comprehensive school, the third person was an administrative assistant at a local authority training centre and the fourth was a raw material operative in a factory. In this case, the tests to be applied in determining an employer's liability for stress-related psychiatric injury were set down. They may be summarised as follows.

- The ordinary principles of employer's liability apply.
- The threshold question is whether this kind of harm to this particular employee was reasonably foreseeable. This has two components: (a) an injury to health (as distinct from occupational stress) which (b) is attributable to stress at work (as distinct from other factors).
- Foreseeability depends upon what the employer knows (or ought reasonably to know) about the individual employee. Because of the nature of mental disorder,

it is harder to foresee than physical injury, but may be easier to foresee in a known individual than in the population at large. An employer is usually entitled to assume that the employee can withstand the normal pressures of the job unless he knows of some particular problem or vulnerability.

- The test is the same whatever the employment: there are no occupations which should be regarded as intrinsically dangerous to mental health.
- The employer is generally entitled to take what he is told by his employee at face value, unless he has good reason to think to the contrary. He does not generally have to make searching enquiries of the employee or seek permission to make further enquiries of his medical advisers.
- The employer is only in breach of duty if he has failed to take the steps which are reasonable in the circumstances, bearing in mind the magnitude of the risk of harm occurring, the gravity of the harm which may occur, the costs and practicability of preventing it, and the justifications for running the risk.
- An employer who offers a confidential advice service, with referral to appropriate counselling or treatment services, is unlikely to be found in breach of duty.
- If the only reasonable and effective step would have been to dismiss or demote the employee, the employer will not be in breach of duty in allowing a willing employee to continue in the job.
- The claimant must show that that breach of duty has caused or materially contributed to the harm suffered. It is not enough to show that occupational stress has caused the harm. (*Sutherland v Hatton* (2002))

CONCLUSION

As can be seen from the foregoing, it is indeed the case that the Irish regulatory environment can be difficult to negotiate for both employees and employers when it comes to workplace conflict and attempts at resolution. Not alone is there a significant body of law, including domestic legislation, regulations, codes of practice and case law, but also, increasingly, there are policy decisions at EU level that require implementation. Added to the mix is a myriad of regulatory fora, making for a complex and somewhat fragmented approach to dispute resolution. This complexity, though arising from the welcome development of labour law over the last thirty years, poses a number of challenges. First is the obvious complexity and fragmentation of the labour law processes that makes it difficult for parties to access the processes. Second, there is also the danger of what might be called 'fora shopping', i.e. the possibility that parties may be tempted to choose particular fora to maximise the outcome. Consolidation of the legislation in this area would mitigate these difficulties. A streamlining of the functions of the various fora would also be of benefit. Perhaps as industrial relations faces into the uncertain waters of recession, some consolidation of labour law and a merging of regulatory functions could be considered.

REFERENCES

Berber v Dunnes Stores Ltd (2006) IEHC 327 [online]. Available: http://www.
bailii.org/ie/cases/IEHC/2006/H327.html (last accessed 13 February 2010).

Berber v Dunnes Stores Ltd (2009) IESC 10 [online]. Available: http://
www.bailii.org/ie/cases/IESC/2009/S10.html (last accessed 13 February 2010).

Bradley v CIE (1976) IR 217.

EAT (Employment Appeals Tribunal) (2009) *Forty-First Annual Report, 2008*
[online]. Available: http://www.eatribunal.ie/en/annual_reports.aspx (last
accessed 13 February 2010).

Employment Equality Act 1998 [online]. Available: http://www.acts.ie/
en.act.1998.0021.1.html (last accessed 13 February 2010).

Equality Act 2004 [online]. Available: http://www.acts.ie/en.act.2004.0024.1.
html (last accessed 13 February 2010).

Equality Tribunal (2009) *Annual Report 2008* [online]. Available:
http://www.equalitytribunal.ie/uploadedfiles/AboutUs/Annual%20Report%20
2008%20-%20Final2.pdf (last accessed 13 February 2010).

Faulkner, M. (2008) *Essentials of Irish Labour Law*. Dublin: Gill & Macmillan

Gogay v Hertfordshire County Council (2000) IRLR 703 [online]. Available:
http://www.bailii.org/ew/cases/EWCA/Civ/2000/228.html (last accessed 13
February 2010).

Industrial Relations Act 1946 [online]. Available: http://www.acts.ie/
en.act.1946.0026.1.html (last accessed 13 February 2010).

Industrial Relations Act 1969 [online]. Available: http://www.acts.ie/
en.act.1969.0014.1.html (last accessed 13 February 2010).

Industrial Relations Act 1990 [online]. Available: http://www.acts.ie/
en.act.1990.0019.1.html (last accessed 13 February 2010).

Industrial Relations (Amendment) Act 2001 [online]. Available: http://
www.acts.ie/en.act.2001.0011.1.html (last accessed 13 February 2010).

InjuriesBoard.ie (2009) *Annual Report and Accounts 2008* [online]. Available:
http://www.injuriesboard.ie/eng/Forms_and_Publications/Annual_Reports/Inj
uriesBoard_ie_Annual_Report_2008_PDF.pdf (last accessed 13 February
2010).

Johnson v Unisys Ltd. (2001) IRLR 279 [online]. Available: http://www.bailii.org/
uk/cases/UKHL/2001/13.html (last accessed 13 February 2010).

Labour Court (2009) *Annual Report 2008* [online]. Available:
http://www.labourcourt.ie/labour/labour.nsf/LookupPageLink/HomeAnnualRe
port (last accessed 13 February 2010).

LRC (Labour Relations Commission) (2009) *Annual Report 2008* [online].
Available: http://www.lrc.ie/documents/annualreports/2008/LRC_AR08.pdf
(last accessed 13 February 2010).

Maher v Jabil Global Services Limited (2005) IEHC 130 [online]. Available:
http://www.bailii.org/ie/cases/IEHC/2005/H130.html (last accessed 13
February 2010).

Minister for Justice, Equality and Law Reform & Commissioner of An Garda Síochána v Director of the Equality Tribunal (2009) IEHC 72 [online]. Available: http://www.bailii.org/ie/cases/IEHC/2009/H72.html (last accessed 13 February 2010).

National Employment Rights Authority (2010) *Review of 2009* [online]. Available: http://www.employmentrights.ie/en/media/ NERA%20Review%20of%202009.pdf (last accessed 13 February 2010).

National Minimum Wage Act 2000 [online]. Available: http://www.acts.ie/en.act.2000.0005.1.html (last accessed 13 February 2010).

Personal Injuries Assessment Board Act 2003 [online]. Available: http://www.acts.ie/en.act.2003.0046.1.html (last accessed 13 February 2010).

Protection of Employees (Fixed-Term Work) Act 2003 [online]. Available: http://www.acts.ie/en.act.2003.0029.1.html (last accessed 13 February 2010).

Redundancy Payments Act 1967 [online]. Available: http://www.acts.ie/en.act.1967.0021.1.html (last accessed 13 February 2010).

Rogers, S. (2010) 'Labour Court Awards €204k to Man Over 7 Years' Work', *Irish Examiner,* 8 January [online]. Available: http://www.irishexaminer.com/ ireland/labour-court-awards-euro204k-to-man-over-7-years-work- 109203.html (last accessed 13 February 2010).

Ryanair Ltd v Labour Court and IMPACT (2007) IESC 6 [online]. Available: http://www.bailii.org/ie/cases/IESC/2007/S6.html (last accessed 13 February 2010).

Safety, Health and Welfare at Work Act 1989 [online]. Available: http://www.acts.ie/en.act.1989.0007.1.html (last accessed 13 February 2010).

Safety, Health and Welfare at Work Act 2005 [online]. Available: http://www.acts.ie/en.act.2005.0010.1.html (last accessed 13 February 2010).

Stokes v Guest, Keen and Nettlefold (Bolts & Nuts) (1968) 1 WLR 1776 [online]. Available: http://oxcheps.new.ox.ac.uk/new/casebook/cases/Cases% 20Chapter%2025/Stokes%20v%20Guest%20Keen%20and%20Nettlefold%2 0(Bolts%20and%20Nuts)%20Ltd.doc (last accessed 13 February 2010).

Sutherland v Hatton (2002) 2 ALL ER 1 [online]. Available: http://www.bailii. org/ew/cases/EWCA/Civ/2002/76.html (last accessed 13 February 2010).

Walker v Northumberland County Council (1995) 1 ALL ER 737 [online]. Available: http://www.bailii.org/ew/cases/EWHC/QB/1994/2.html (last accessed 13 February 2010).

Section IV

Whither Irish Borders? Ireland, Europe and the Wider World

What unites the chapters in this section of the book is the general theme of borders, be they between Ireland and the European Union (EU), Ireland North and South, those that distinguish Ireland culturally in the realm of tourism, or the borders of migration. Indeed, the picture that emerges is one of borders that have become more permeable, but that could just as easily become unyielding should circumstances alter. In this context, readers will encounter chapters dealing with the Irish debate on the Lisbon Treaty, and whether the Irish wished to be 'in' or 'out' of Europe, the Europeanisation of public policy in Ireland, and the evolving relationship between the Republic of Ireland and Northern Ireland. Migration also comes into focus from two different perspectives: the move from economic migration towards lifestyle migration for those with international careers; and the risk the Irish economy faces through recession-induced net emigration. Finally, coming from the perspective of tourism development, we have a chapter that looks at capitalising on cultural borders in terms of what makes Ireland and the Irish different.

Following Ireland's two rounds of voting on the EU's Lisbon Treaty, in Chapter 19 John O'Brennan reflects on Ireland's relationship with the wider Europe. Arguing that since the economic impact on Ireland of EU membership has been almost universally accepted as positive, recent rejections of EU referendums are somewhat paradoxical. Some explanation can be found in the exclusive nature of Irish national identity, but also in an increasing chasm between elite and popular opinion on the matter. Despite Ireland's acceptance of the second Lisbon referendum, there are likely to be more twists and turns in Ireland's future relationship with Europe.

Turning to Chapter 20, Mary C. Murphy traces the evolution of the relationship between Northern Ireland and the Republic of Ireland since the introduction of partition in 1920. A once troubled relationship has changed to the point where a variety of economic, political, social, cultural and sectoral links now exist between North and South. More specifically, where cross-border co-operation is deemed mutually beneficial, there exists a strong practical and functional logic towards co-operation. The institutionalisation of North–South relations, as per the terms of the 1998 Belfast Agreement, provides an important context within which this relationship has been pursued.

Breda McCarthy, in Chapter 21, looks at cultural tourism development in Irish towns and villages. Beginning with an outline of the factors that facilitate the development of cultural tourism in regional Ireland, she moves on to propose a model of cultural tourism development that argues that stocks of social, cultural and tourist capital are important to the development of the industry, in addition to emphasising the notion of authenticity in the cultural encounters and experiences of tourists and local actors. Through case study research on a selection of Irish villages, towns and hinterland, the chapter demonstrates that tourism development is strongly rooted in the local social and cultural environment. While noting that the obvious starting-point for cultural tourism development is the possession of cultural resources, the chapter argues that cultural capital becomes more valuable when it is combined with social capital, since it assists wealth creation.

Positing twenty-first-century international careers as witnessing a move from economic to lifestyle migration, in Chapter 22 Marian Crowley-Henry explores international careers in contemporary society from a critical and individual perspective. With the increasing internationalisation of trade and careers, and an increasingly multicultural workforce, the chapter argues that it is important to consider the stories of individuals living international careers, so as to better inform policy and practices in organisations and wider society. Built around the findings from a qualitative exploratory research undertaking, the chapter emphasises a focus on a more comprehensive systems approach to careers, encompassing subjective and objective career dimensions, as well as structural influences and life stage elements. Implications of the findings for Ireland's changing multicultural society are discussed, particularly for those Irish who voluntarily choose to embark on an international life and career experience as lifestyle migrants.

Taking Ireland's history of emigration and seeing lessons from Irish economic history for achieving growth in a regional economy, John McHale in Chapter 23 considers the risk the Irish economy faces through recession-induced net emigration. The chapter begins with a brief overview of Ireland's post-Famine demographic history, along with consideration of distinct phases of demographic development and their correlations to economic performance. While the effects of emigration on Ireland have been thought damaging to the development of industries where economies of scale are important, recent international literature on the links between skilled migration and development leans to more optimistic conclusions than the earlier work on the 'brain drain', highlighting the dynamic benefits of 'brain circulation'. Arguing that emigration will make it harder to achieve competitive advantage in the innovation-intensive sectors the government is targeting in its new growth strategy, the chapter concludes by briefly considering possible implications for three policy areas: fiscal, labour market activation and immigration.

Finally, in Chapter 24, Kate Nicholls considers some of the factors that might explain the Europeanisation of public policy in Ireland. She starts out by reviewing the development of the concept of 'Europeanisation', along with a number of theories developed by political scientists in order to identify the conditions under which policy Europeanisation takes place. She then moves on to argue that the best way to pinpoint the factors that either facilitate or hinder policy Europeanisation is to place Ireland in comparative context. By comparing Ireland with 'most similar' cases, such as Portugal and Greece, the chapter highlights the role of policy-making institutions and processes capable of balancing functions of consultation and incorporation. In the final analysis, the chapter reasons that Ireland's consensus-oriented democratic tradition has provided a good basis on which to construct such institutions and processes.

Chapter 19

Ireland and the European Union: Mapping Domestic Modes of Adaptation and Contestation

John O'Brennan

INTRODUCTION

When Professor Lee (1989) wrote his magisterial history of twentieth-century Ireland, one of the most important issues he addressed was the apparent economic failure of the Republic of Ireland. The main reasons advanced for this failure included slow and erratic patterns of economic growth, low productivity in key economic sectors, high and persistent levels of unemployment, exceptionally high emigration rates, and a preponderance of enduring social problems. That this remained the case after more than a decade of European Union (EU) membership seemed to call into question the wisdom of the Irish decision in 1973 to join the then European Economic Community (EEC). Two decades later Ireland's membership of the EU was thrown into serious question by the Irish electorate's rejection in June 2008 of the Lisbon Treaty. This was the third such referendum on Europe held in Ireland since the millennium and the second referendum in three to result in a rejection of an EU Treaty following the failed Nice poll in 2001 (O'Brennan 2003, 2004).

The debate on the Lisbon Treaty offers the opportunity to look back at and reflect on Ireland's membership of the EU, to examine whether and to what extent membership has been good for Ireland, and the fundamental changes that European integration has wrought. And, although the 'No' to Lisbon was reversed in a second referendum held in October 2009, it remains the case that European integration is now seriously questioned in Ireland. This chapter examines the Irish experience of European integration. It assesses the impact of the EU on key aspects of Irish economic and political life and the different modes of adaptation and contestation that have characterised the Irish experience of membership.

ECONOMIC ADAPTATION

It is in the economic sphere where one can most readily observe the striking changes that Irish membership of the EU has produced. The Irish economic journey in the period in question has been somewhat of a rollercoaster, with bouts of significant growth (the 1970s, 1990–2007) and equally periods of retrenchment and stagnation (the 1980s, 2008–2010). For better or worse, it is undoubtedly the case that the European integration process has had more impact than any other factor (internal or external) on the shape and performance of the Irish economy. This in turn has had a pronounced impact on the Irish social and political landscape.

The most significant indicator of economic performance is the rate of annual economic growth or gross domestic product (GDP) achieved by a country. When one examines Irish GDP growth (1973–2010), the most striking characteristics are the rise in both the absolute and the comparative level of GDP. It is worth examining the figures in some detail. When Ireland joined the EEC in 1973, it had a GDP per capita of 53 per cent, the lowest average GDP of the then nine-member Community. By 2008, Irish GDP per capita had reached 135 per cent of the EU average, the second highest level after Luxembourg (Eurostat 2010).

Although one can point to twenty years of strong growth between 1987 and 2007, it is really the period 1994–2007 that stands out as impressive. Economic growth averaged a very high 7.4 per cent in those years, reaching as high as 12 per cent in some years (O'Toole and Dooney 2009:392–3). By any standard, this change represents a fundamental shift. It is especially impressive when compared with the performance of states that were similarly poor and under-performing in the 1970s – Greece, Portugal and Spain all advanced much more slowly than Ireland, even though in receipt of EU subvention. And, although the financial and fiscal crisis of 2008–2010 undoubtedly presented major difficulties for Ireland, there is no denying that the country's membership of the EU has coincided with a historic increase in wealth and prosperity. To what extent can that change be attributed to membership of the EU?

It seems clear that EU membership alone cannot explain the Irish economic renaissance (or, indeed, the periods of crisis). Other significant reasons advanced for Ireland's changed position include: investment in secondary and higher education, a flexible labour force, low rates of corporate taxation, demographic advantages, relatively low interest rates, a commitment to fiscal discipline, increased productivity, and a social partnership model which delivered a benign industrial relations climate. All these reasons help to explain why Ireland's position within the EU has changed so dramatically during the course of membership. But it is worth noting that when Professor Lee (1989) made his criticisms of Irish economic under-performance, the country had been a member of the EEC for more than a decade. And it would be another ten years before the economic upswing, which would become known as the Celtic Tiger, became a reality.

However, the European dimension is also noteworthy. During the negotiations on the Single European Act (SEA) in the mid-1980s, Ireland aligned itself with the poorer Mediterranean states to argue that a deepening of market-based integration should be accompanied by redistributive measures which would help them compete better with the wealthier member states of the EU. The aim of economic and social cohesion was there from the beginning of the EEC in 1957, but only became salient after successive enlargements had made the Community less homogenous. The Delors Package of 1988 significantly expanded the existing redistributive arrangements, and Ireland – as a so-called Objective 1 country – became a high priority for regional subvention as the enlarged aid programme became operational. Similar pressure during the Maastricht negotiations yielded the Cohesion Fund, which provided financial assistance for projects in the fields of environment and transport to member states whose gross national product (GNP) per capita was less than 90 per cent of the overall EU average.

Over the next twenty years, Ireland would benefit from a supranational transfer of wealth unprecedented in history: there was a doubling of resources in the EU budget for the Structural Funds between 1988 and 1992, and a doubling of the transfers to the Cohesion states, including Ireland, by 1993 (Laffan and O'Mahony 2008:139). EU Structural and Cohesion Funds effectively delivered a mini-Marshall Plan to Ireland, precisely at a time when the Irish government was being forced to cut capital spending as an imperative in tackling a bloated budget deficit and challenging fiscal climate. Between 1989 and 1999, regional aid to Ireland amounted to approximately three per cent of GDP per annum; in some years the receipts amounted to in excess of five per cent of GDP (O'Donnell 2001). Comparison with aid distributed to the other Cohesion states suggest that the money was relatively well spent in Ireland, in developing the country's physical infrastructure, notably the road system and telecommunications, and, through the European Social Fund (ESF), in re-training workers who had been made unemployed in the harsh economic landscape of the late 1980s. Irish negotiators were very successful in arguing their case during successive EU budget negotiations, with the result that, as late as 2008, Ireland was still a net recipient from the EU budget, despite years of impressive economic growth (O'Toole and Dooney 2009:392).

The consensus among economists is that, although EU structural aid was not sufficient of itself to contribute decisively to recovery, the timing of the programmes, combined with indirect effects on public policy making, both played a part in changing the fundamentals of Irish economic performance. Measuring the exact impact on the economy of this subvention is difficult, not least because of the influence of other macro effects. Research conducted by the Economic and Social Research Institute (ESRI) concludes that EU funds added a long-term two per cent growth to the economy above the level it would have reached without them (O'Donnell 2001). This was significant, but only an element in the overall strong economic performance after 1987.

A second significant area for economic analysis lies in the Irish trade performance since 1973. Ireland's adjustment to European market integration involved striking changes in the level, composition and geographic concentration of trade (McAleese 1998), and, notwithstanding the financial hurricane of 2008–2010, contributed to a quantifiable leap in prosperity. Most commentators agree that EU membership provided the bedrock for enduring Irish economic success in a volatile global economic arena. Because of the small scale of its home market and a lack of natural resources, Ireland is heavily dependent on trade. Nevertheless, there has been a remarkable increase in the openness of the economy, to a point where Ireland is regularly cited as one of the most open economies in the world (e.g. Kearney/*Foreign Policy* 2002, 2003, 2004, 2005, 2006, 2007).

Ireland's trade performance has benefited most crucially from participation in the Single European Market (SEM) and, more recently, membership of Economic and Monetary Union (EMU). From a position in 1973 where exports represented 38 per cent of GDP, Ireland went to a position where, by 2002, exports were 94 per cent of GDP (Haughton 2008:22). During the Celtic Tiger years, Ireland's export performance continued to astound commentators with impressive growth rates compared to its European partners (Cassidy and O'Brien 2005:77–8). There are many important factors that might explain Ireland's exporting success, but EU membership, including, crucially, Ireland's attractiveness as a location for inward foreign direct investment (FDI), underpinned by secure access to an expanding EU market of twenty-seven member states and 500 million consumers, has to rank as very significant.

It is clear that Ireland has benefited disproportionately from the surge in FDI evident worldwide from the late 1980s: FDI going into Europe rose substantially in this period and FDI going into Ireland increased by substantially more. One of the great advantages of the Single Market Programme was that it put an end to the stultifying and bewildering regime of state aids prevalent in Europe up to the late 1980s, and created (at least potentially) a level playing field for all member states regarding incentives and disincentives to inward investment. Prior to 1992, some member states would literally do anything to prevent other member states selling into 'their' home markets. As Peter Sutherland (2008:16) argues, the 1992 Programme created the conditions under which Ireland was as good a place as France for selling goods into the French market.

Irish industrial development policy over the last two decades has been to target specific sectors for investment: information and communication technology (ICT), pharmaceuticals, engineering, international financial services and consumer products. In 2008, there were almost one thousand foreign multinational companies in operation in Ireland, employing over 136,000 people directly and many more indirectly (IDA Ireland 2009:23). This compared with a total foreign multinational employment figure in Ireland of around 110,000 in the early 1990s (Leddin and Walsh 2003:422).

Amazon, Apple, Boston Scientific, Dell, IBM, Intel, Google and Microsoft are among the household names that set up in Ireland after 1987, and all cite access to the largest single market in the world as central to their investment decisions. Pharmaceutical companies in Ireland include Wyeth Merck, Pfizer, Allergan Wyeth, GlaxoSmithKlein and Bristol-Myers Squibb; today six out of ten of the world's top-selling drugs are produced in Ireland, including Lipitor and Viagra (Sweeney 2008:208–9). Ireland has also become a destination for FDI in the medical technology sector and attracted eight of the world's top ten companies, including Abbott, Johnson and Johnson, and Tyco Healthcare. By the mid-2000s, the stock of inward FDI in Ireland (in investment in factories, plant and offices) stood at almost €200bn, or 106 per cent of Irish GDP. This constituted the highest relative level of FDI in Europe and almost triple the EU average; the Netherlands came in second with 74 per cent, Sweden and the Czech Republic followed with 48 per cent and the UK lagged behind with 37 per cent (Sweeney 2008:169).

Although the eastern enlargement of the EU in 2004 heralded a shift in the preferences of some multinational corporations (confirmed by Dell's decision in 2008 to switch most of its manufacturing activity from Limerick to Lödz, Poland), Ireland continued to remain an attractive location for FDI within the EU. One other interesting result of eastern enlargement has been the greater propensity of Irish companies to invest in Poland, Hungary, Bulgaria and other new member states. Thus, Ireland has also become an external agent of FDI in the developing economies of Central and Eastern Europe.

As the analysis of FDI patterns indicates, the commodity or product composition of Irish exports has also changed markedly during the period of EU membership (McAleese 1998). In 1961, at the time of the first (unsuccessful) application for membership, 61 per cent of Irish merchandise trade exports consisted of food and 20 per cent of manufactures (McAleese and Hayes 1995: 267). By 1992, the relationship had been reversed, with food accounting for only 23 per cent of merchandise trade exports; by 2003, food exports' share had fallen to under eight per cent (Cassidy and O'Brien 2005:80). Services sector exports also ballooned in size from 2000, almost trebling by 2006 (Sweeney 2008:168–9). After the establishment of the International Financial Services Centre (IFSC) in 1987, this sector grew in Ireland, so that by 2008 the country had become, as Sweeney (2008:209) puts it, 'home to half of the world's top fifty banks and one of the main European locations for insurance and for the funds industry'. Thus, the period of Irish membership of the EU has coincided with a historically unprecedented expansion in, and diversification of, the country's underlying trade patterns.

The geographical pattern of exports has also changed radically (McAleese 1998). From accounting for 75 per cent of Irish exports in 1960, and 61 per cent in 1971, the UK market share fell steadily to under 20 per cent in 2008 (CSO 2010). In parallel with this, we have seen exports to EU states (excluding the UK) rise from just 13 per cent in 1970 to 41 per cent in 1990, to 43 per cent in 2003 (Cassidy and O'Brien 2005:82) and nearly 44 per cent in 2008 (CSO 2010).

Market diversification away from the UK and towards other continental partners has continued apace. But whilst almost 70 per cent of the total value of exports is to the EU (including the UK), the UK remains the single largest export destination for Irish goods, accounting for almost twice the value of exports to our second largest markets (Belgium and Germany). And crucially, many indigenous Irish firms are particularly dependent on the UK market (Ruane and Uğur, 2005: 176–7). In 2008, for example, the UK accounted for fully 45 per cent of exports from the Irish agri-foods industry (Bord Bia 2009). This was one element of the debate on whether Ireland should enter the Single Currency (the Euro) without the UK also doing so; it was feared that Irish companies, which were much more exposed to the UK market, would be particularly vulnerable to currency volatility.

Entry into the Single Currency was facilitated by a hugely significant landmark in Irish economic history: the break with sterling in 1979. Analysts tend now to view the break as significant primarily in a psychological sense. It seems certain, however, that without the historic rupture, it is highly unlikely that Ireland would have had the know-how and institutional self-confidence to contemplate EMU without the participation of the UK. Abstention from EMU might also have weakened governmental commitment to fiscal responsibility and a lower debt/GDP ratio as recovery took off in the 1990s (McAleese 1998). At the very least, one can argue that EU membership has resulted in a dramatic geographic recalibration of Irish exports.

A third significant area deserving of attention is the extent to which European integration has changed the dynamics of competition in the private sector in Ireland. Safeguards for 'sensitive' sectors threatened by the prospect of foreign competition absorbed an inordinate amount of diplomatic energy at the time of accession, when there was a real fear that Irish companies would not be able to compete effectively against their leaner continental rivals. The same fears were present during negotiation of the SEA in the mid-1980s. Despite the spilling of vast quantities of negotiating blood, import-substitution industries, such as motor assembly, footwear, and textiles, were effectively destroyed by competition from cheaper foreign-owned entities. Irish policy towards safeguards and towards intra-sectoral competition has tended to be rather conservative and cautious, perhaps a legacy of the highly protected economy of the pre-EU period (McAleese 1998). The Irish authorities in the 1970s and 1980s repeatedly sought extended transitional periods and exemptions from Brussels as new legislation was introduced. In this sense, Ireland tended to side more with the protectionist stance of the Mediterranean member states than with the liberalism of the UK. With the passing of time, these safeguards have diminished greatly in importance.

The liberalisation of the services sector was forced upon Ireland by Brussels. Irish policymakers were not inclined to rock the boat in protected public utilities where producers' priorities, mainly the trade unions and management, ruled supreme. Brussels' initiatives tended to be resisted and liberalisation labelled 'Thatcherite' and automatically condemned (McAleese 1998). This was no more than an extension of the dominant logic in Ireland's domestic political economy, one in which the 'possessor principle' had historically trumped the 'performance principle' as Professor Lee (1989) memorably put it.

Competition was under EU pressure reluctantly introduced into airline transport, telecoms, banks and insurance. One clear example can be cited as evidence of the huge impact of EU-inspired liberalisation of the transport sector: the enormous increase (fivefold) in air passenger traffic between London and Dublin, at one-fifth the price (see Chapter 2). Actions taken to enforce competition have tended to be undertaken rather apologetically, and because Brussels requires such measures rather than because they benefit the economy. The first Irish legislation to combat anti-competitive practices came into force only in 1991, almost a hundred years after the equivalent law, the Sherman Act, in the USA. Essentially the 1991 Act extended the principles of EU competition law to the domestic economy and established a competition authority. The level playing field also required restraints on state aids (McAleese 1998). Thus, although Irish governments retained complete autonomy over much of the economy, it can be demonstrated that in some crucial areas EU membership provided Ireland with the instruments necessary to provide a more competitive and pluralistic impulse in previously bounded and state-dominated markets.

THE COMMON AGRICULTURE POLICY

Prior to accession, the most important reason advanced for membership was the anticipated benefits to be accrued through membership of the Community's fledgling Common Agriculture Policy (CAP). For the Irish government, this held out the prospect of unlimited market access leading to substantial price increases and a rise in farm incomes. As important was the denationalisation of agricultural spending. At the time of accession, the agricultural sector accounted for 50 per cent of net exports and 25 per cent of all employment (McAleese 1998). In the 1970s, the CAP guaranteed markets for unlimited output of Irish agricultural produce at relatively high prices (considerably higher than Irish agricultural prices of the period). An added bonus was the fact that Irish farmers would no longer be dependent on selling into the British market, where prices were lower than the Community average and, indeed, world prices. Increased production could easily be accommodated within the CAP intervention schemes, and price rises would aid farm incomes.

Membership of the EU delivered a historic transfer of income to the Irish farmer, from both the European consumer and European and Irish taxpayers (Matthews 2005). Although the massive boom in agricultural land prices at the time of accession proved short-lived (as in other later entrant states also), the farming sector has been the recipient of massive transfers ever since. From 1973 to 2002, CAP receipts to Ireland totalled over €31bn (Leddin and Walsh 2003: Table 24.5). In 2003, the EU contributed €1.9bn of Ireland's €2.8bn total public expenditure on agriculture (Laffan and O'Mahony 2008:160). Between 1973 and 2001, Ireland's net receipts from the EU averaged nearly four per cent of GNP, and much of this went to Irish farming (Leddin and Walsh 2003: 475–8). Agriculture-related receipts accounted for about two-thirds of Ireland's EU transfers (Haughton 2008:22–3).

CAP receipts have resulted in a complete transformation in living standards in rural areas. But, like protection of so many sensitive sectors, it has not led to the regeneration of economic activity in agriculture. Employment in agriculture declined over two and half per cent per year from 1971 to 2001 (Leddin and Walsh 2003:425). So why has Ireland continued to experience such a dramatic 'flight from the land' if receipts from the CAP have remained so buoyant? The most telling statistic reveals that about 30 per cent of Europe's farmers receive about 70 per cent of CAP payments, an indication of the trend towards concentration of agricultural land in larger (more productive) units. When the Department of Agriculture finally published the figures for dispersal of CAP funds in Ireland, it was revealed that 550 farmers and companies received more than €100,000 each in 2008 (Minihan 2009:2). But what is remarkable about these figures is that the distribution of CAP funds in Ireland is completely dominated by agri-food companies, rather than individual farmers (MacConnell 2008:2). Figures for 2008 show the Greencore Group topping the list with payments of €83.4m, with the Irish Dairy Board Co-op coming second with payments of over €6.5m and Kerry Ingredients Ireland third with over €5m (Minihan 2009:2). Other companies listed among the top twenty-five CAP beneficiaries were: RA Bailey Ltd, €2,861,538; Commercial Mushroom PRS Co-op, €2,851,824; Ashbourne Meat Processors, €1,164,792; Rosderra Irish Meats Group, €715,218; Wyeth Nutritionals Ireland, €698,123; Abbott Ireland, €680,898; Oliver McAvinia Ltd, €664,911; and Glanbia Foods Society Ltd, €558,182 (Minihan 2009:2). At the other end of the scale, people working the average family farm were increasingly forced to take employment away from the farm as, even by 2006, their annual farm income amounted to under €17,000 (Matthews, 2008:267–8). Thus, it seems clear that, in the Irish context, the CAP has disproportionately benefited very large production units and accelerated the flight from the land.

From the early 1990s, the CAP system came under significant pressure; to some extent it proved the victim of its own success. The EU's main paymaster, Germany, became increasingly preoccupied with absorbing its eastern regions, while World Trade Organisation (WTO) pressures also contributed to new thinking about the wasteful and protectionist elements of the CAP. EU enlargement to the east in particular acted as a catalyst for significant change, with a reduction in price supports and compensation through a direct payments instrument. By 2002, direct payments accounted for up to 70 per cent of farm income in Ireland (Matthews 2005:223). This decoupling of payment from farm production was accompanied by a growing emphasis on rural development policies and agri-environmental measures, such as the Rural Environment Protection Scheme (REPS), which sought to induce farmers to pay as much attention to the environment as to production priorities. Further reviews of the CAP made compliance with REPS a condition for receipt of the single farm payment. It must be pointed out that, of all the 'successes' enjoyed by Ireland in Europe, agriculture remains the most significant. Irish ministers for agriculture and their officials proved very savvy negotiators in successive rounds of CAP talks and the Irish Farmers' Association (IFA) and the Irish Creamery and Milk Suppliers' Association (ICMSA) developed sophisticated lobbying arms to protect agricultural interests. More often than not, Ireland aligned with France and other more protectionist states to defend national prerogatives and protect CAP receipts from the more reformist member states, such as the UK and the Netherlands.

THE LISBON REFERENDUMS

The debates on the Lisbon Treaty referendums in 2008 and 2009 produced evidence of new economic dividing lines in Ireland's relationship with the EU. The protection of Ireland's corporate tax regime assumed a central place in the campaign of those on the right of the political spectrum, such as Cóir and Libertas (but also, curiously, Sinn Féin, which styles itself as a socialist party), who were particularly eager to stress the competitive threat facing Ireland if Lisbon were to be ratified. It was frequently asserted that a large number of EU states, but particularly France and the Benelux countries, would push for a common consolidated corporate tax base (CCCTB), on the basis of enhanced co-operation procedures, which would effectively circumvent an Irish veto on corporate tax. With fiscal autonomy constrained by Ireland's membership of the Eurozone, tax policy was presented as the key contemporary instrument of sovereign economic power (O'Brennan 2009:14). The impact of these arguments can be gauged by the government's decision to seek a legally binding protocol prior to the 2009 referendum asserting the primacy of national decision making on taxation.

In marked contrast, the left critique of the European integration process focused in both campaigns on the alleged neo-liberal bias of the EU and the ongoing attacks on 'Social Europe' by the European Commission (EC), corporate Europe and the European Court of Justice (ECJ), whose policy agenda invariably produces negative distributional asymmetries in Ireland. But whereas social and economic issues dominated the 2005 French campaign and arguments about EU market failure penetrated thoroughly through different sections of society, in Ireland this remained difficult for the left. After all, the Irish social model is a much more minimalist one than the French and so there is much less to 'defend' than in France when arguing against EU competition policy or open markets. Nevertheless, for a good part of the left's opposition to Lisbon in both 2008 and 2009, resistance to the rampantly neo-liberal ideology of 'Brussels' – said to become even more entrenched with new articles in the Lisbon Treaty – was a key element in the propaganda battle, with the spectre of Commission-led globalisation presented as an existential threat to the interests and welfare of Irish workers. A particular target of attack was the ECJ, which, despite its record of robust interventionism on the side of workers' rights, was routinely presented as a friend of the market, rather than of the worker (O'Brennan 2009:264).

What the economic elements of the Lisbon Treaty debates reveal is that, after a long period of agreement on the economic benefits of Irish membership of the EU, there is now significant contestation from both right and left of the supposed pole of attraction the EU is said to constitute. Despite the fact that the great majority of trade unions and business groups align themselves with the pro-European side, the space in which contestation of EU economic norms takes place has broadened considerably. If indeed the Lisbon referendum was 'rescued' the second time around by the collapse in the Irish economy experienced since September 2008, it may prove a pyrrhic victory for the 'Yes' side. Clearly, the circumstances in which the second referendum was held were exceptional and it may be that the gap between exponents and opponents of the integration process is much closer than the 2009 referendum result demonstrated. What is clear is that the old cosy consensus in the economic sphere – EU membership as an unvarnished economic good for Ireland – has gone for ever and we will now see a more 'normal' dividing line between right and left as the economic dimension of membership is contemplated in the future.

POLITICAL INSTITUTIONS – EXECUTIVE AND BUREAUCRATIC POLITICS

Membership of the EU brought considerable change to the domestic political order in Ireland, and, in particular, to the executive and bureaucratic functions of government. Adaptation to a dynamic and evolving rule system required a great degree of flexibility and adaptability; compliance with EU directives and regulations would place great pressure on individual government ministries and the civil service, as the deepening of the European integration process really gained momentum after the enactment of the SEA.

The 'European' layer of governance in Ireland has over time become a domestic layer as the boundaries of what previously were thought of as discrete national and supranational areas of competence have gradually dissolved. This phenomenon of a 'Europeanisation' of Irish public policy has been managed from the centre, by what Laffan terms the 'holy trinity' of Irish government – the Department of Foreign Affairs (DFA), the Department of Finance and the Department of the Taoiseach (Laffan and O'Mahony 2008:64). From the earliest days of membership, the day-to-day business of managing Ireland's relations with Brussels fell to Foreign Affairs, which relied to a great extent on the Irish Permanent Representation in Brussels. Over time, we have seen a subtle re-balancing of responsibilities between Foreign Affairs and Finance, which from the beginning of formal statehood in 1922 had been the pre-eminent government department. The twin processes of deepening and widening of the EU triggered a significant change in the relationship between the two departments, with DFA taking on more responsibility (and status). For example, one important element of DFA's response to the successive enlargements of the EU is that Ireland now has direct diplomatic representation across all twenty-six partner states: eastern enlargement in 2004 was the catalyst for the most significant expansion of DFA's scope and influence since the post-war period. This is important because, in the enlarged EU of twenty-seven member states, alliances and coalition building take on a whole new significance that simply was not there in the 1970s and 1980s. The DFA is thus at the hub of a network of relationships critical to Irish success in Brussels. When, in 2009, the McCarthy report (Special Group on Public Service Numbers and Expenditures 2009) proposed a significant reduction in Ireland's diplomatic representation abroad, there was considerable disquiet at the suggestion that some of the new embassies in Central and Eastern Europe would be targeted for closure. Embassies in the other twenty-six member states provide important information and intelligence on the policy positions and potential bargaining stances of partners and rivals within a fluid system of inter-governmental relations. This is particularly significant where policy proposals of particular interest to Ireland are being debated and framed as legislation: coalition building becomes an imperative in the effort to defend the national interest. This dynamic is also in evidence during inter-governmental conferences (IGCs), where constitutional reform is discussed in advance of possible treaty changes, and, on a day-to-day level, where disputes threaten the overall cohesiveness of EU policy making. Knowledge and information are everything in the diplomatic arena, and especially so in a union as diverse and interest-driven as the EU.

The Irish Permanent Representation in Brussels is the pivotal institution amongst the constellation of DFA entities involved in EU policy making. It is the key site for gathering intelligence on the policy process, and, more generally, on the broad thrust of politics and decision making in the European integration process. The importance of the Permanent Representation is reflected in its budget, which is one of the largest enjoyed by any Irish diplomatic representation abroad, and by the calibre of officials posted to Brussels as Permanent Representative. Among the officials to serve as Permanent Representative, outstanding individuals like Noel Dorr and Bobby McDonagh have performed with particular distinction and have been acknowledged as world-class diplomats.

Within DFA, the EU Division co-ordinates Ireland's approach in the EU. The Political Division is responsible for international political issues and has responsibility for managing Ireland's participation in the EU's Common Foreign and Security Policy (CFSP) and defence structures. This separation of responsibilities reflects the fact that security, defence and foreign affairs remain policy areas where an inter-governmental approach to policy prevails. That is to say, the member states themselves zealously protect their prerogatives in the foreign policy arena and remain masters of their own destiny, with the right to veto any proposal they find contrary to their national interests. This is in marked contrast to the economic realm of the European integration process where, after the enactment of the Lisbon Treaty in late 2009, collective decision-making norms mean that majority voting has replaced unanimity as the default mode of decision making.

Although it played second fiddle to DFA during the first two decades of Irish membership of the EU, the Department of Finance has become much more important to Ireland's EU decision making since the late 1980s. This is because the deepening of the European integration process through the Single Market Programme and, later, EMU brought national finance ministries much more influence over collective EU decision making; the importance of the Council of Finance Ministers (ECOFIN) has been greatly enhanced as the euro has become established as a global reserve currency to rival the dollar. Similarly, management of the accelerated programme of structural funding from the early 1990s also enhanced the power of Finance within the domestic policy-making structure.

Finally, one should note that the Department of the Taoiseach has also assumed enhanced responsibilities in the domestic sphere of EU policy making, though its role is more one of strategic co-ordination of government departments and the civil service than a hands-on management of EU business. The Department of the Taoiseach is especially important in the context of European Council summits, which have become more frequent over the last two decades and have taken on a significance not envisaged in the original institutional structure of the EU. The importance of the European Council as a locus of debate and strategic decision making was acknowledged when its institutional position and status was given formal recognition for the first time in the Lisbon Treaty; the introduction of a new post – President of the European Council – is also an indication of its new elevated status in the pecking order. In the Irish case, the Department of the Taoiseach has been especially important during Ireland's periods as President of the rotating Council of the European Union. The department first assumed importance during the presidency of 1990, when Taoiseach Charles Haughey acted as an intermediary between France and Germany in talks on German reunification. At the same time, Haughey played a key role in shaping the twin IGCs – on political union and economic and monetary union – that paved the way for the Maastricht Treaty. A similarly intensive six-month period of diplomacy followed in 2004, when Bertie Ahern engaged in an extended bout of trans-European diplomacy in order to get agreement on the EU's Constitutional Treaty. Ahern's department, in conjunction with DFA, also took responsibility for the symbolic enlargement ceremony at Áras an Uachtaráin on 1 May 2004, which welcomed ten new member states into the EU.

POLITICAL INSTITUTIONS – POLITICAL PARTIES AND THE OIREACHTAS

There are two distinct dimensions to Irish parliamentary party participation in EU politics. The first takes place at the national level, where 'Europe' has become an important part of the domestic political order, not least the work of the Oireachtas. The second level is the European level, where Irish parties compete with each other for seats in the European Parliament, and formally attach themselves to the political groupings (or 'Euro-families') within the Parliament's institutional and organisational structure. The key question here is whether these different vehicles for participation in 'Europe' have led to an internalisation of the EU in the parliamentary system in Ireland. Have Irish political parties changed their identities as a result of prolonged exposure to EU modes of decision making? Can we evince a process of 'socialisation' whereby, over time, Irish parliamentarians have engaged intensively with the EU? Have the attitudes and behaviour of Irish public representatives towards Europe changed much in the period of Irish membership of the EU?

We can state quite emphatically that despite almost forty years of membership of the EU, the Irish political landscape remains resolutely focused on local and national issues and attached to more or less exclusively national modes of behaviour and engagement. Direct elections to the European Parliament, formally instituted in 1979 as a vehicle for enhancing the legitimacy of the EU, have made little difference to this pattern of apathy and disengagement, despite the fact that the European Parliament has accrued more and more formal powers since the SEA of 1987. Political scientists refer to European Parliament elections in Ireland as so-called 'second-order elections', meaning that they are electoral contests dominated by local and national issues; EU issues, to the extent that they feature at all, tend to be of a secondary nature. Campaign literature and rhetoric pays little attention to Brussels and Strasbourg, and where candidates incorporate Europe in their campaigns, it tends to be in a materialist/utilitarian framework where the candidate promises to 'deliver for the constituency' by bringing back financial and material rewards.

There is little evidence of Irish political parties being socialised into more 'European' modes of behaviour. This is despite the fact that all the main political parties belong to specific 'Euro-groups' within the European Parliament. Fine Gael has been a long-time member of the centre-right European People's Party (EPP) and Labour resides in the Party of European Socialists (PES). Fianna Fáil, however, has had a much more difficult time finding a natural home in the ideologically framed EP political groupings. Because Fine Gael was first to claim a place in the EPP, Fianna Fáil was forced to seek a place in an alternative grouping. In the early 1980s, it joined with the French Gaullists to form the European Democratic Alliance (EDA) and later the United European Nation (UEN) group. But after the Gaullists departed in 2002, Fianna Fáil was left with a less than wholesome range of partners, including Italy's neo-fascist National Alliance and Poland's Law and Justice Party. Later, Fianna Fáil would depart for the Alliance of European Democratic Liberal (ALDE) grouping, but this has proved an extremely uncomfortable arrangement for many Fianna Fáil MEPs. In October 2009, Taoiseach Brian Cowen had to suffer the indignity of being harangued by the ALDE leadership after a number of Fianna Fáil MEPs voted against the ALDE block in a plenary vote in the European Parliament.

In a broad context, parliaments are central institutions in European systems of government. They elect and control the government, approve legislation, and, as the bodies responsible for amending the constitution, hold the ultimate power in society (O'Brennan and Raunio 2007:12). Parliaments also represent the most important checks on the power of untrammelled executive authority, especially when they exercise functions of oversight and scrutiny. Yet such constitutional perspective is arguably increasingly divorced from reality in the European context. National parliaments are almost without exception portrayed as reactive institutions, as 'victims' of the European integration process, casting rather modest influence on policy initiatives coming from the executive. Understanding the role of the Oireachtas seems particularly compelling in the light of the rejection of the Lisbon Treaty in the referendum of June 2008, even if that decision was reversed in October 2009. Although it is frequently alleged that the failure of the first Lisbon referendum can be attributed to a so-called 'democratic deficit' at EU level, I argue that there exists a much more important *domestic democratic deficit*, in that the political representatives charged with the responsibility of holding executive authority to account seem disengaged from the European integration process and unable or unwilling to properly scrutinise governmental action in the EU sphere: 'Europeanisation' has coincided with 'deparliamentarisation'. According to the so-called deparliamentarisation thesis, the development of European integration has led to an erosion of parliamentary control over executive office holders. Powers that were previously under the jurisdiction of national legislatures have been shifted upwards to the European level.

In the Irish case, as previous sections of the chapter make clear, EU policy making has been dominated by the executive and, over time, a process of centralisation of authority within the 'holy trinity' of the Departments of Foreign Affairs, the Taoiseach and Finance has come to dominate European affairs. In combination with top officials in the civil service and the Permanent Representation in Brussels, the executive arm has left little room for any substantive engagement by the Oireachtas, which has become increasingly reactive in its stance toward Europe. It was only in the early 1990s that the Oireachtas finally set up a Joint Committee on European Affairs (JCEA), which, for much of its life, has played second fiddle to the executive. In particular, the JCEA has failed to insist on the introduction of a robust system of oversight and scrutiny of executive activity in European affairs. TDs remain completely detached and disengaged from EU policy making; indeed, the vagaries of Ireland's PR electoral system are such that any TD who voluntarily seeks to play a role in EU decision making is taking the risk of a backlash in his/her constituency, where the real emphasis lies on representation of citizens' local concerns, rather than control over executive power (O'Brennan 2009:276).

The institution by the JCEA of a Sub-Committee on European Scrutiny after 2002 was supposed to bridge the gap between Ireland and other member states, such as Denmark, where parliament has much more significant control over Danish decision making in Brussels. But, in truth, the sub-committee has neither the resources nor the capacity to carry out this demanding role in a way that would help reverse the deparliamentarisation pattern. TDs seem to know very little about the EU institutions or the EU legislative process; recent referendum campaigns have clearly demonstrated the paucity of knowledge on Europe that exists within the Oireachtas, emphasising how Europeanisation has had a perverse impact on the national parliament's ability to contribute to the policy process.

Finally, the transformation of Irish foreign policy during the period of EU membership also warrants analysis (Tonra 2006). Among the most important changes, those relating to the EU presidency stand out. For small states, the responsibility of representing the EU globally has offered the possibility of achieving visibility on the world stage and strengthening their position in the European power structure. Irish presidencies have been identified as particularly successful over the years. Membership has also broadened the horizons of Irish diplomacy, moving it away from the traditional post-independence fixation with the UK, and led to a distinctive process of modernisation of the bureaucratic machinery that supports the diplomatic arm of government.

The foreign policy dimension of membership has not been uncontroversial, however. The issue of an emerging European defence and security policy has featured strongly in Ireland's European debates since at least the Maastricht Treaty and was a significant concern among voters in the 2001 and 2002 Nice polls and again in the 2008 and 2990 Lisbon referendums. A number of political parties, including Sinn Féin, along with a range of civil society groups, such as the Irish Peace and Neutrality Alliance (PANA), have coalesced around this theme and argued that successive treaties have steadily eroded Irish neutrality. In effect the 'No' side has sought to paint a picture of untrammelled 'movement' in the area of defence and security policy, arguing that the government and 'establishment' could not be trusted to protect neutrality and, indeed, was suspected of colluding with other EU member states in the 'creeping militarisation' of the EU. Those making the militarisation argument continually seek to link the EU to a militarist agenda, and, despite all the evidence to the contrary, specifically to an American militarisation agenda. 'Yes' campaigners have struggled in recent years to convince voters that Ireland's veto on foreign and security policy remains and that the EU constitutes no threat to Irish sovereignty and institutional autonomy.

CONCLUSIONS

Membership of the EU has been good for Ireland, but perhaps not quite in the ways expected in the early 1970s. It has produced distinct patterns of adaptation and contestation at the domestic level, as the European integration process has both deepened and widened over the years. In the economic sphere, foreign investment played a more vital role than anticipated, and most of it came from the United States, not from the affluent countries of Europe (McAleese 1998). Even so, it is clear that access to the SEM proved of enduring importance. Another unexpected turn was that bad domestic policy came near to wrecking the Irish economy's capacity to utilise the advantages of market access provided by integration in the 1980s: the EU could not, of itself, constitute a panacea to poor domestic economic management. EMS and then the Maastricht criteria, however, acted as a fiscal lode star, an acceptable target to both left and right of the political spectrum, around which politicians could rally popular support for otherwise unpalatable economic measures. EU membership provided very substantive support for Irish agriculture, and, at a critical period in the 1990s, structural funding helped ease the Irish economy on to a firm growth trajectory. Later, the Celtic Tiger era would see the Irish economy reach a level of development similar to those of partner countries in the EU, before the destructive crash of 2008–2010 induced a new path of austerity. In sum, there are few who would argue that EU membership has not been good for Ireland in almost every aspect of economic life.

The outcome of recent referendums may seem paradoxical to some in that Eurobarometer opinion polls of attitudes to the EU continue to demonstrate that Irish people are strong supporters of the integration process. While the decisive 'Yes' vote in the second Lisbon referendum in October 2009 seemed to herald a return to normal voting patterns on EU issues, one cannot ignore the fact that two of the three previous referendums were rejected by the Irish people. Thus, the latest referendum result may constitute an aberration, reflecting as it did the very unusual economic circumstances in which the referendum was held.

Eurobarometer polls also demonstrate an Irish attachment to an overwhelmingly exclusivist national identity, rather than a more open and fluid (including 'European') identity. This means that a space exists where issues such as neutrality, sovereignty and Ireland's relative influence in the EU institutional matrix can be readily exploited by opponents of the European integration process and where any changes in the EU constitutional order can be emotively presented as an existential threat to Ireland's values and interests. The absence of any effort by government to provide and promote a civic education programme or sufficient information channels that explain how and why Ireland's EU membership matters means that EU 'debates' in Irish political culture are frequently characterised by apathy, confusion and ignorance, with an increasingly wide chasm between elite and popular opinion. Thus, 'lack of knowledge and information' emerge as a key variable in explaining voting behaviour across recent referendums (O'Brennan 2009:276–7).

In this sense, the rejection of the Nice Treaty in 2001 can be viewed as a watershed in Ireland's relationship with the EU. What it signalled was not just the end of the era of 'permissive consensus' on EU issues, but that, in the absence of substantive welfare-enhancing measures which can be effectively communicated to citizens, the EU space in Ireland is one where the pro-integration side finds it increasingly difficult to persuade voters to match the overwhelming support for Ireland's EU membership with active consent for changes to the EU constitutional order and policy agenda. Irish citizens, and even committed political party members, are now quite prepared to disregard party loyalty when confronted with EU referendums. Increasingly confrontational (largely British-based) Euro-hostile media fan the flames of anti-integration sentiment at every opportunity and provide a valuable platform for the Euro-sceptic lobby to disseminate their views. Thus, although victory for the pro-European side in the October 2009 referendum seems to have settled the question of Irish commitment to the European integration process for the foreseeable future, it may turn out to have been a pyrrhic victory for the 'Yes' side: we will undoubtedly witness many more twists and turns in the Irish relationship with the EU in the years to come.

References

Adshead, M. and Tonge, J. (2009) *Politics in Ireland: Convergence and Divergence in a Two-Polity Island.* Basingstoke: Palgrave.

Bord Bia (2009) *Factsheet on the Irish Agriculture and Food and Drink Sector,* September [online]. Available: http://www.bordbia.ie/industryinfo/agri/pages/default.aspx (last accessed 10 February 2010).

Cassidy, M. and O'Brien, D. (2005) 'Export Performance and Competitiveness of the Irish Economy', *Central Bank of Ireland Quarterly Bulletin* 3: 75–95.

CSO (Central Statistics Office) (2010) *Main Trading Partners – 2008 €m* [online]. Available: http://www.cso.ie/statistics/botmaintrpartners.htm (last accessed 10 February 2010).

Eurostat (2010) *GDP Per Capita in Purchasing Power Standards (PPS)* [online]. Available: http://epp.eurostat.ec.europa.eu/tgm/table.do?tab=table&init=1&plugin=1&language=en&pcode=tsieb010 (last accessed 10 February 2010).

Haughton, J. (2008) 'Historical Background', in J. O'Hagan and C. Newman (eds) *The Economy of Ireland: Policy Issues for a Regional Economy*, 10th edn, pp. 2–28. Dublin: Gill & Macmillan.

IDA (Industrial Development Authority) Ireland (2009) *Annual Report 2008.* Dublin: IDA Ireland.

Kearney, A.T./*Foreign Policy* (2002) 'Globalization's Last Hurrah?', *Foreign Policy* January/February: 38–51.

— (2003) 'Measuring Globalization: Who's Up, Who's Down?', *Foreign Policy* January/February: 60–72.

— (2004) 'Measuring Globalization: Economic Reversals, Forward Momentum', *Foreign Policy* January/February: 54–69.

— (2005) 'Measuring Globalization: The Global Top 20', *Foreign Policy* May/June: 52–60.

— (2006) 'The Globalization Index: The Global Top 20', *Foreign Policy* November/December: 74–81.

— (2007) 'The Globalization Index: The Global Top 20', *Foreign Policy* November/December: 68–76.

Laffan, B. and O'Mahony, J. (2008) *Ireland and the European Union*. Basingstoke: Palgrave.

Leddin, A.J. and Walsh, B.J. (2003) *The Macroeconomy of the Eurozone: An Irish Perspective*. Dublin: Gill & Macmillan.

Lee, J.J. (1989) *Ireland, 1912–1985: Politics and Society*. Cambridge: Cambridge University Press.

MacConnell, S. (2008) 'Agriculture Businesses Top CAP List for Payouts', *Irish Times*, 4 September, p.2 [online]. Available: http://www.irishtimes.com/newspaper/ireland/2008/0904/1220372097517.html (last accessed 12 February 2010).

Matthews, A. (2005) 'Agriculture, Rural Development and Food Safety', in J. O'Hagan and C. Newman (eds) *The Economy of Ireland: National and Sectoral Policy Issues*, 9th edn, pp. 215–42. Dublin: Gill & Macmillan.

McAleese, D. (1998) 'Twenty-Five Years A-growing: The Economic Impact of EU Membership', paper presented to the Institute of European Affairs, Dublin, 19 November.

McAleese, D. and Hayes, F. (1995) 'European Integration, the Balance of Payments and Inflation', in J.W. O'Hagan (ed.) *The Economy of Ireland: Policy and Performance of a Small European Country*, 6th edn, pp. 265–95. Dublin: Gill & Macmillan.

Minihan, M. (2009) 'Over €2bn Paid to Farmers and Companies under EU CAP Scheme', *Irish Times*, 1 May, p.2 [online]. Available: http://www.irishtimes.com/newspaper/ireland/2009/0501/1224245764614.html (last accessed 12 February 2010).

O'Brennan, J. (2003) 'Ireland's Return to "Normal" EU Voting Patterns: The 2002 Nice Treaty Referendum', *European Political Science* 2(2): 5–14.

— (2004) 'Ireland's National Forum on Europe: Elite Deliberation meets Popular Participation', *Journal of European Integration* 26(2): 167–82.

— (2009) 'Ireland Says No (Again): The 12 June 2008 Referendum on the Lisbon Treaty', *Parliamentary Affairs* 62(2): 258–77.

O'Brennan, J. and Raunio, T. (2007) *National Parliaments within the Enlarged European Union: From 'Victims' of Integration to Competitive Actors?* Abingdon: Routledge.

O'Donnell, R. (2001) 'To Be a Member: The Experience of Ireland', public lecture delivered at the Dublin European Institute, University College Dublin, 26 September.

O'Toole, J. and Dooney, S. (2009) *Irish Government Today*, 3rd edn. Dublin: Gill & Macmillan.

Ruane, F. and Uğur, A. (2005) 'Trade and Foreign Direct Investment in Manufacturing and Services', in J. O'Hagan and C. Newman (eds) *The Economy of Ireland: National and Sectoral Policy Issues*, 9th edn, pp. 162–87. Dublin: Gill & Macmillan.

Special Group on Public Service Numbers and Expenditures (2009) *Report of the Special Group on Public Service Numbers and Expenditures* (McCarthy Report). Dublin: Stationery Office.

Sutherland, P. (2008) 'Chapter Two' (untitled), in P. Sweeney (ed.) *Ireland's Economic Success: Reasons and Lessons*, pp. 13–25. Dublin: New Island Press.

Sweeney, P. (2008) 'All Changed, Changed Utterly', in P. Sweeney (ed.) *Ireland's Economic Success: Reasons and Lessons*, pp. 1–4. Dublin: New Island Press.

Tonra, B. (2006) *Global Citizen and European Republic: Irish Foreign Policy in Transition*. Manchester: Manchester University Press.

Chapter 20

Northern Ireland and the Republic of Ireland: A Changed Relationship

Mary C. Murphy

INTRODUCTION

Northern Ireland and the Republic of Ireland are separated by an international border, which divides the island of Ireland between two sovereign states. Northern Ireland's position is somewhat unusual in that it is geographically detached from the rest of the United Kingdom (UK), but directly borders the Irish state.

For nationalists, the border came to symbolise the unjust partition of the island, while for Unionists it was a line of protection and security from an antagonistic neighbour. Relations between Northern Ireland and the Republic of Ireland have inevitably been affected by these different interpretations of the border's function. Such polarised views, however, have evolved and changed over time. Where once their depth and intensity sullied relations between North and South, in recent times they have become less intense, and thus less troublesome and obstructive to the development of closer links between the two parts of the island. The result has been the gradual growth and expansion of pre-existing and sometimes tenuous relationships, as well as the emergence of new contacts, networks and relations between North and South. These interactions embrace a range of political, economic, sectoral and civil society activities. Where once it was possible to speak of the 'permeability of the United Kingdom–Irish border' (Whyte 1983a:300), today it is perhaps more appropriate to characterise the border between North and South as porous. Relations between the neighbours have effectively been transformed. This transformation has been gradual and, crucially, has largely been guided by 'intergovernmental political will' (see Tannam 1999:199), which has used practical and functional considerations as the basis for the emergence of constructive and mutually beneficial relations.

This chapter traces the evolution of the political relationship between Northern Ireland and the Republic of Ireland since the introduction of partition in 1920. It determines the extent to which traditional interpretations of the conflict exacerbated delicate political relations between North and South. The troubled relationship was eventually alleviated by revised analyses of partition among political actors on both sides of the Irish border and by the political drive on the part of key figures to enhance North–South relations via the development of practical and functional cross-border links. Political contact between North and South during the period 1922 to the 1950s may have been limited, but some communication did exist. A more open and visible period of contact followed from the 1960s, and in particular during the 1980s and 1990s. Often difficult and problematic, cross-border co-operation did nevertheless precede the development of a more measured and constructive relationship between Northern Ireland and the Republic of Ireland. The high point of this relationship was arguably reached during the 1990s in the context of the peace process and the signing of the 1998 Belfast Agreement. Today, the totality of relations between North and South are multi-faceted and multi-sectoral. Cross-border relations remain close and demonstrate a strong practical and functional logic. The institutionalisation of relations, as per the terms of the Belfast Agreement, is an important context in this regard. The formalisation of structures for cross-border co-operation has produced political and economic benefits, though some sectors, such as tourism, have benefited more than others.

THE HISTORY OF NORTH–SOUTH RELATIONS

The partition of Ireland has historical roots that arguably date back to the seventeenth century. The official partition of the island, however, was ultimately realised by the Government of Ireland Act in 1920. The Act was preceded by the first Home Rule Bill for Ireland, tabled in 1886, which proposed a hybrid form of federalism and devolution for the island of Ireland as a whole. It was defeated by Westminster, but was followed some years later by a second similar Home Rule Bill in 1893. It, too, was rejected, although on this occasion it was passed by the House of Commons before being rejected by the House of Lords. The outbreak of the First World War suspended the imposition of the third Home Rule Bill (1912), which was due to be introduced by default after four years, despite its rejection by the House of Lords three times in succession. The failure of the British government to act within the agreed timespan led to violence in Ireland, as proponents of home rule sought to achieve home rule by physical force. The 1916 Easter Rising in Dublin, which the British government decisively quelled, was a direct response to the inactivity of the government on the Irish home rule question. The brutal manner in which the British authorities dealt with the Irish combatants hardened Irish public opinion against the British government and led to an increase in support for the home rule cause. The seeds of dissent had thus been sown and the following decade was to be a violent and bloody period in the history of Ireland.

The response of the British government to the subsequent serious and violent political and civil disorder in Ireland was the partition of the island. The

Government of Ireland Act of 1920 formed the basis for partition. Specifically, it contained provisions for two parliaments on the island of Ireland: a Belfast parliament, with jurisdiction over the six counties of Northern Ireland; and a Dublin parliament, with powers to legislate for the remaining twenty-six counties of Ireland. The political arrangements only came into being in Northern Ireland. The south of Ireland secured first dominion, then free state status, before eventually becoming the Republic of Ireland in 1949. Unlike the Republic of Ireland, however, the new Northern entity was a less than cohesive unit. The six counties of Northern Ireland contained a Protestant majority and a sizeable Catholic minority (approximately one-third). (The link between religion and political ideology in Northern Ireland generally suggests Protestant support for unionism, i.e. maintenance of the union between Britain and Northern Ireland, and Catholic support for nationalism, i.e. the creation of a united Ireland. The connection is, admittedly, crude but nevertheless represents a broadly acceptable shorthand for describing the primary political cleavage in Northern Ireland society, both then and today.)

The Government of Ireland Act also contained provisions for all-Ireland institutions. The proposed Council of Ireland never met and, by the mid-1920s, any formal attempts to develop North–South political relations were effectively abandoned. For the following four decades, relations between the two jurisdictions were largely confined to areas where cross-border co-operation was unavoidable. The period was marked by relations between Northern Ireland and the then Irish Free State that can readily be characterised as 'sour' (Tannam 1999:43). The animosity between the administrations North and South was most directly apparent in the 1937 Irish constitution. The original versions of Articles 2 and 3 of the Irish Constitution included an explicit territorial claim to Northern Ireland. Their tone and content offended Unionists and posed 'a powerful ideological challenge to the existence of Northern Ireland' (Girvin 1999:222). Relations between North and South were inevitably poor during this period.

A Brief North–South Rapprochement

The 1960s witnessed an attempt by Taoiseach Seán Lemass and Northern Ireland Premier Terence O'Neill to normalise relations between North and South. Such moves were both politically and economically motivated. Economic relations between Northern Ireland and the Republic of Ireland underwent considerable change with the signing of the Anglo-Irish Free Trade Agreement in 1965. The Agreement paved the way for the eventual achievement of complete free trade between the UK and the Republic of Ireland. It also permitted accelerated tariff reduction in favour of Northern Ireland goods exported to the Republic of Ireland. The initiative was largely deemed to be economically favourable for both parts of the island and was broadly welcomed (see Kennedy, M. 2000:258–9). The introduction of free trade, however, was also politically sensitive. For Unionists in particular, the 1965 Agreement treated Northern Ireland differently and separately from other parts of the UK (and thus potentially undermined their position within the UK). Conversely, political leaders in the Republic of Ireland were well disposed to such arrangements, which they viewed as possibly laying the basis for Irish unity in the long term. Differing political perspectives regarding the impact of free trade, however, should not diminish the extent to which this period 'appeared to be the beginning of a new epoch in cross-border relations after the half-century-long cold war between the North and the South' (Kennedy, M. 2000:260).

Despite promising signs of a more favourable relationship between North and South, however, political efforts to foster and nurture co-operation were ultimately futile. By the late 1960s, civil unrest erupted on the streets of Northern Ireland, community relations degenerated and political relations on the island began to cool. As the decade approached its end, the intensification of the conflict was to have profound economic consequences. The 1970s and 1980s witnessed 'a dramatic reversal of fortune' for the Northern Ireland economy (Rowthorn and Wayne 1988:79). A prolonged industrial crisis, coupled with serious political instability, resulted in long-term economic stagnation, the seeds of which had arguably been sown many years previously.

The Outbreak of the Conflict

During the period 1921–1972, the Ulster Unionist Party (UUP) remained in power continuously and was perceived by nationalists as presiding over a political regime that facilitated discrimination and unfair treatment for Catholics: 'The most serious charge against the Northern Ireland government is not that it was directly responsible for widespread discrimination, but that it allowed discrimination on such a scale over a substantial segment of Northern Ireland' (Whyte 1983b:31). The Northern Ireland civil rights movement emerged in the late 1960s to oppose the political system they saw as discriminating against the minority community. Espousing a largely moderate character, the movement was nevertheless prepared to 'extend earlier pressure-group activity into civil disobedience' (Tonge 2002:37). Confrontations with the Royal Ulster Constabulary (RUC) and counter-demonstrators ensued and the peaceful civil rights movement gradually assumed a more sectarian character, with the civil rights agenda giving way to a more politicised nationalist rhetoric. Inter-communal violence and elements determined to execute change by violent means became more apparent. This resulted in serious and widespread civil unrest and a critical security situation. By 1972, the system of devolution came to an abrupt end when the Northern Ireland parliament was suspended, in response to a situation that was threatening to edge Northern Ireland towards the brink of civil war.

The years from the late 1960s to the early 1970s arguably mark the lowest point in relations between North and South. Relations between Dublin and Belfast were, at this time, severely strained. Naturally allied to the nationalist cause, the Dublin government pursued an approach to the Northern Ireland question that was paradoxical (to say the least):

> At one level Jack Lynch's Fianna Fáil Government in Dublin sought to build bridges between South and North and to develop a working relationship between Ireland and Britain. But at another level the Irish Government prepared for military intervention in Northern Ireland in conjunction with the IRA. (Hennessey 2005:337–8)

In addition to plans to intervene in Northern Ireland should circumstances warrant it, Irish government finances supported and nurtured the young and emerging Provisional Irish Republican Army (PIRA). Little wonder, then, that the Northern Ireland Unionist community viewed the Irish government with immense suspicion and distrust. The character of North–South relations during this period was highly politicised. Irish government support for nationalists (and Republicans) alienated Unionists and contributed to a skewed and antagonistic North–South relationship.

Some attempt to remedy this situation came in 1973 with the signing of the Sunningdale Agreement, which contained proposals for Northern Ireland's future governance. Based on power-sharing principles, it included a cross-border dimension. The Council of Ireland was to be a free-standing, independent executive institution with extensive powers, which could conceivably be viewed as 'having the makings of an all-Ireland parliament' (Dixon 2008:139). The cross-border dimension to the Sunningdale Agreement was clearly considerable, and it was therefore no surprise that it motivated an extensive, orchestrated campaign of Unionist opposition. Northern Ireland was brought to a standstill by protests, strike action, intimidation and serious violence. The agreement, the Northern Ireland administration and, in particular, the Unionist leadership were seriously undermined by this bitter and hostile public opposition. UUP leader Brian Faulkner resigned and, with this, the legitimacy of the power-sharing arrangement was fatally challenged, such that, eventually, the agreement was abandoned.

Political relations between North and South were to remain strained for some time to follow. By the mid-1980s, however, a thaw in relations between the Republic of Ireland and the UK began to develop and it was to change the dynamic of North–South relations. The 1985 Anglo-Irish Agreement (AIA) – an international treaty signed by the governments of the Republic of Ireland and the UK – was (despite its emphasis on the principle of consent) greeted with dismay and alarm by the Northern Ireland Unionist community. The AIA effectively granted the Republic of Ireland a limited role in Northern Ireland politics. Most significant was the creation of the Anglo-Irish Conference (AIC), which brought together on a regular basis the secretary of state for Northern Ireland and the Irish foreign minister to promote cross-border co-operation and to discuss political and security matters of mutual interest. The AIC had a permanent secretariat in Belfast staffed by civil servants from Northern Ireland and the Republic of Ireland. Unionist resistance to the AIA was severe and, as had been the case after the signing of the Sunningdale Agreement, a massive and extensive campaign of opposition was mounted. On this occasion, however, Unionist objections did not succeed in destroying the AIA. The so-called 'Irish dimension' to the Northern Ireland conflict was thus politically recognised and secured and was to be further strengthened during the years that followed.

Although violence continued to scar the Northern Ireland political landscape, by the end of the 1980s the beginnings of a peace process were under way. Secret talks between the leaders of the Social Democratic and Labour Party (SDLP), John Hume, and Sinn Féin, Gerry Adams, were contributing to a reassessment of the traditional Republican position. New political leadership in London and Dublin signalled a greater willingness to accommodate the interests of both communities in Northern Ireland. Political initiatives, including the 1993 Downing Street Declaration and the 1995 Frameworks Documents, emphasised the importance of consent in determining Northern Ireland's constitutional position. They also made it clear that any final settlement in Northern Ireland would incorporate a cross-border, North–South dimension. Although both documents were initiatives of the Irish and British governments, they nevertheless contributed in the longer term to normalising and stabilising relations between North and South.

THE CONTEXT OF NORTH–SOUTH RELATIONS

Understanding the dynamics of North–South political relations requires a broad overview of the context within which relations have developed. Cross-border co-operation on the island of Ireland is influenced (and sometimes dictated) by indirect factors. In the case of North–South political relations, a key obstacle to their pursuit has been public attitudes in Northern Ireland and the Republic of Ireland.

Public Attitudes to North–South Relations

Opposition to the advancement of North–South relations was clearly politically motivated and apparent on both sides of the border. For Northern Ireland Unionists, hostility to the Southern state was based on a range of views, including:

The South is a third world country; its economy is bankrupt; its politics are those of 'banana republic'; it is dominated by the Roman Catholic Church; its people are manipulative, devious and untrustworthy; its culture is parochial, introverted and backward; it is a 'very sick country'; Southern Protestants have been denied a real say in public life and their numbers have been reduced to a fraction of their original size; Southern Catholics have an

ingrained hostility to Northern Protestants and will defeat and destroy them
if ever they get the opportunity. (Ruane and Todd 1996:257)

In this context, traditional Unionist reluctance to engage in cross-border relations
is unsurprising. Although clearly less hostile to North–South relations, nationalists
in Northern Ireland were largely ambivalent to the Republic of Ireland. Wounded
by Southern indifference to their plight, they were nevertheless reliant on the
Southern state to defend their minority status. For its part, the Southern public
was frustrated by what was perceived as unreasonable Unionist opposition to Irish
unity. With respect to their Northern nationalist counterparts, they resented the
damage done to Ireland by Republican violence, but also experienced guilt in
relation to their indifference to the conflict.

These public perceptions of communities, North and South, clearly acted as an
obstacle to the pursuit of cross-border relations. Cultural and political perspectives
on the 'dangers' of cross-border co-operation and a wider sense of ambivalence
towards such a relationship limited the extent to which meaningful co-operation
could be achieved. A changed Republican strategy from the 1980s onwards led to
the calling of paramilitary ceasefires in 1994 and was accompanied by a new
rational civic form of unionism, which adopted a more pragmatic approach to the
constitutional question (see English 2002). The UUP, in particular, engaged with
political developments on the basis that being involved was preferable to self-
exclusion from what was judged to be an inevitable drive to agree a peace
settlement for Northern Ireland. The political context north of the border was
thus substantially transformed and the seeds were sown for the eventual signing of
the 1998 Belfast Agreement – a document that contains a developed cross-border
dimension (see below).

Attitudes to North–South relations on both sides of the border changed during
the 1990s as a consequence of these developments. Public opinion surveys during
this period suggest less opposition to cross-border relations than previously,
particularly amongst Unionists. This is markedly so in relation to functional and
practical areas of co-operation, such as transport, health, agriculture and tourism.
On the question of Northern Ireland's political future, however, Protestant support
for North–South co-operation was decidedly less positive (see Murphy and Totten
2000:308–11).

Public attitudes to North–South co-operation inevitably influence political
leaders. Unionists have not been overtly predisposed to the development of cross-
border relations and, in any case, were not willing to antagonise or alienate
sceptical voters. Nationalists generally support cross-border links. Political and
cultural considerations of this nature may be to the forefront in explaining the
difficulties involved in developing North–South cross-border relations, but
economic factors also contribute important explanatory detail.

Cross-Border Economic Co-Operation

In addition to political and cultural factors, opposition to cross-border co-operation was also driven by practical economic considerations. Tannam (1999:200) characterises the economic cross-border relationship as a complex one, in that '[t]here are grounds for co-operation, but there are also differences which may impede co-operation'. The very different nature of the economies north and south of the border has been a substantial obstacle to co-operation. Indeed, some authors, such as Birnie and Hitchens (2001:15), suggest that 'the economic benefits of North–South co-operation have been and are likely to remain relatively small'. Similarly, some business groups believe that pursuing closer economic co-operation may undermine immediate economic interests.

The traditional reticence displayed by both the economic interests and the civil administrations, North and South, is evident with reference to the low levels of cross-border trade between North and South. Prior to the 1998 Belfast Agreement (which institutionalised some elements of cross-border economic co-operation), cross-border trade levels were low (see Birnie and Hitchens 2001). In 2008, North to South trade was worth €1.3bn and South to North trade was worth €1.6bn. These figures compare favourably with their equivalent 1995 figures of €826.9m and €997.1m respectively. The total all-island trade figure for 2008 stood at €2.8bn – €1bn higher than the equivalent figure for 1995 (InterTradeIreland 2009). These increased levels of North–South trade have occurred in the context of a broader debate about the development of an all-island economy. A more nuanced consideration of the North–South economic link began to develop during the 1990s and arguably was influenced by wider political developments, including the formalisation of links between Northern Ireland and the Republic of Ireland. The all-island economy idea has generated support among a number of leading business and political leaders north and south of the border (see McCartney 2000; Michie and Sheehan 1998). According to Coakley and O'Dowd (2007:882), 'even prominent figures from a unionist background [extol] the virtues of cross-border cooperation, *especially as regards the economy*' (emphasis added).

The signing of the 1998 Belfast Agreement and the institutionalisation of cross-border relationships have allowed this objective to be pursued with greater vigour than heretofore by the Irish and British governments. In 2006, both governments jointly published a *Comprehensive Study on the All-Island Economy*. The report highlights an intention to create 'a world-class all-island economy which manifests itself in comparable levels of economic dynamism and performance in both parts of the island' (InterTradeIreland 2006:6). This study was conducted within the context of the *Irish National Development Plan (2007–2013)*, which contains an All-Island Co-operation chapter. Areas targeted for economic co-operation include infrastructure, trade, tourism, enterprise promotion and the environment. Plans for economic co-operation are not all-encompassing. There is recognition by both governments that:

From a purely economic perspective, appropriate areas for Government action arise where there is market failure or where the Government is involved in the provision of public goods, such as infrastructure, or public services such as health and education. The case for an all-island approach is made where the market failure arises from the existent of the border or where the public goods and services could be more efficiently provided on a co-ordinated basis. (InterTradeIreland 2006: 4)

This responds to the obvious sensitivities that surround questions of cross-border economic co-operation. Such co-operation is only pursued in the context of it being mutually beneficial to both parts of the island. For Unionists, this is a vital context – their suspicion of political attempts to promote all-island economic co-operation is only slowly dissolving (Adshead and Tonge 2009:191). Unionist wariness in relation to economic co-operation is grounded in very real fears about the possible 'spill-over effect' that such co-operation might have. Neo-functionalist interpretations of economic co-operation posit that increased levels of economic co-operation on the island of Ireland will diminish the significance of the border between North and South and, in time, cement the case for Irish unity. Studies have failed to prove that such a logic exists (see Tannam 2006), but Unionists remain cautious in their support for such endeavours.

What is clear in relation to the development and evolution of cross-border economic relations is that they are heavily influenced by a practical and functional logic. This logic is determined by notions of mutual benefit, and, more crudely, self-interest. The growth in cross-border economic co-operation in recent years is closely related to political developments and the creation of new cross-border institutions. The provision of an institutional format within which cross-border economic relations can be pursued has altered the character and extent of co-operation.

European Union Context

In contrast to the obstructive effect of public opposition to cross-border co-operation, wider European political developments have created a context more conducive to the development of North–South relations. Laffan and O'Mahony (2008) are of the view that British and Irish EU membership has been an important context within which North–South relations have evolved.

Initially, neither Irish nor UK authorities viewed accession to the EU as having any significant direct impact on the Northern Ireland conflict (see Kennedy, D. 2000). Indeed, the experience of membership since 1973 does not point to the EU having had any effective impact on resolving the conflict, or on diminishing the resilience of the border (as some had predicted). As the peace process developed in Northern Ireland during the 1990s, greater cognisance of the EU was incorporated into domestic initiatives aimed at resolving the conflict. The 1995

Frameworks Documents were particularly interesting in this respect. Teague (1996:550) interprets their provisions as indicating that 'both the Irish and British governments have signalled . . . that EU programmes and activities could be a key way to deepen political and economic ties between the North and South of the island'.

In less overtly political domains of activity, the impact of the EU on North–South relations has been tangible. EU-sponsored financial aid programmes to Northern Ireland have nurtured and cultivated cross-border relations: 'Despite criticisms of the outcomes and achievements of [the Peace] programmes . . . the European Commission amongst others has welcomed their contribution to a new, inclusive, cross-border and bottom-up decision-making' (Murphy 2007:297).

The EU's Interreg programmes have a more explicitly cross-border character. The initiative funds and supports strategic cross-border, transnational and inter-regional co-operation aimed at promoting the development of a more prosperous and sustainable border region. Both the Interreg and Peace programmes have been welcomed for their positive contribution to cross-border relations:

> I think it is very important to emphasise the positive impact of the cross-border nature of the Interreg and Peace Programmes. The fact that they are cross-border programmes has helped to change the mindset of people on both sides of the border. They have helped to forge new links between communities and they have encouraged greater tolerance for diversity. Thousands of projects have been supported and many thousands of people have engaged at grass roots level in the job of peace building and reconciliation. (Cowen 2008)

In practice, elements of the Interreg programme have been criticised (see study by Laffan and Payne 2001). Notwithstanding this, there is a recognition of the constructive role the EU has played in assisting the development of cross-border relations: 'Cross-border trade and partnership have been a good "trial run" for EU-fostered networks and programmes because they are seen as having clear, beneficial and neutral ends (i.e. economic development)' (Hayward 2007:691).

THE BELFAST AGREEMENT

The domestic context for North–South relations changed substantially during the 1990s. The 1998 Belfast Agreement was clearly a political development of historic proportions, but it was preceded and ultimately occasioned by earlier developments. Political relations between the Republic of Ireland and the UK developed a more co-operative and constructive character during this period. The evolving peace process in Northern Ireland (and, in particular, the 1994 paramilitary ceasefires) provided a backdrop against which the Irish and British governments could pursue and facilitate political progress.

Throughout the 1990s, the two governments produced a series of documents, declarations and statements, which hinted at the eventual achievement of a peace settlement that would acknowledge the 'Irish dimension'. This would inevitably require the creation of cross-border bodies and the institutionalisation of North–South relations.

For Unionists in Northern Ireland, the prospect of formalised relations between North and South was less than appealing. The UUP reaction to the likelihood of such a development forced a reappraisal of traditional unionism. What emerged from this process was a form of 'new unionism' based on a pragmatic approach to domestic and international political engagement. This reformulation of unionism and its development along rational civic lines was not grounded in any strong ideological outlook; rather, it was grounded in a perception that Unionist interests are best protected by supporting the pluralist dimensions of the 1998 Agreement, accepting the legitimacy of constitutional nationalism and tolerating power-sharing with cross-border bodies (Tonge 2005:74). Practically, this involved 'a fundamental change in relationships between Ulster Unionists and nationalist Ireland, as the party leadership began to engage with the Republic of Ireland' (Coakley 2009:402).

The political form of engagement between North and South is detailed in the Belfast Agreement. In the context of North–South relations, the removal of the Irish Constitution's territorial claim to Northern Ireland, and its replacement with a commitment that Irish unity could only be achieved by *consent*, was especially significant. The changes to Articles 2 and 3 of the Irish Constitution that resulted fundamentally altered the political environment for Unionists and ultimately allowed that community to accept North–South co-operation. In addition to this key provision, the Belfast Agreement contains three strands which detail the institutional arrangements for governing Northern Ireland. Strand 1 of the document outlines internal institutional arrangements, including the power-sharing Northern Ireland Assembly and Executive. Strand 2 establishes North–South institutions and Implementation Bodies and provides a means by which to develop and advance cross-border relations. Strand 3 creates an 'East–West' dimension. The British–Irish Council brings together representatives of the Irish and British governments and the devolved administrations in the UK. Its functions and powers are less extensive than its North–South equivalent.

Strand 2 of the Agreement, which contains the 'Irish dimension', was the most difficult and fraught component of the talks process that eventually led to the signing of the 1998 Agreement. Unionists harboured serious reservations about the institutionalisation of North–South relations and were keen to limit the powers and scope of any new cross-border institutions.

The Agreement creates a series of institutions, including the North South Ministerial Council (NSMC) that meets in both plenary and sectoral formats and is assisted by a North–South secretariat. When meeting in plenary format, the NSMC brings together the taoiseach and the Northern Ireland first minister and deputy first minister. In practice, plenary meetings are attended by all Irish and Northern Ireland ministers and focus on long-term North–South plans for cross-border co-operation (Coakley 2009: 398). Sectoral meetings of the NSMC bring together the relevant Irish minister and her Northern Ireland equivalent, plus a minister representing the 'other' community in Northern Ireland. In sectoral guise, the NSMC oversees the activities of six Implementation Bodies and supervises work in areas where formal co-operation exists between the Northern Ireland and Republic of Ireland administrations. The Implementation Bodies formalise and institutionalise co-operation in dedicated functional fields of activity. In addition, both governments pursue co-operation in additional areas, but through existing government departments (see Table 20.1). All areas of cross-border co-operation have a clear functional logic, which makes them palatable and acceptable to the Unionist community. Indeed, some are simply a formalised continuation of existing co-operation and were presented as such by leading Unionists:

> It was David Trimble, the UUP leader, who pointed out to sceptics in his party that a large amount of cross-border co-operation was largely being carried out, particularly in the form of EU programmes such as Interreg. These programmes were there already and required to be carried on. (Alcock 2001:175)

Table 20.1 North–South co-operation (Strand 2, Belfast Agreement)

North–South Implementation Bodies	North–South Areas of Co-operation
Waterways Ireland	Agriculture
Food Safety Promotion Board	Education
Trade and Business Development Board (IntertradeIreland)	Environment
Special European Union Programmes Body	Health
Language Body/An Foras Teanga / Tha Boord o Leid	Tourism, including Tourism Ireland
Foyle, Carlingford and Irish Lights Commission	Transport

Source: North South Ministerial Council (2006).

The operation of the North–South dimension of the Belfast Agreement has not been without difficulties. The sporadic suspensions of devolution between 1999 and 2007 impacted negatively on the operation of North–South institutions. Political non-participation by the Democratic Unionist Party (DUP) during the period 1999–2002 was also problematic. Notwithstanding these obstacles, 'the Strand 2 institutions seem to be functioning effectively, providing a useful mechanism for discussion and negotiation between North and South in some of the areas where this makes most practical sense' (Coakley 2005:127). In this respect, their value is inherently practical. The pursuit of functional co-operation in areas of mutual interest has produced important outputs. According to a 2006 study of cross-border co-operation:

> The Good Friday Agreement and its Strand 2 components, the North–South Ministerial Council, cross-border implementation bodies and areas of cooperation, have provided a supportive framework and a political space for a great variety of cross-border projects. (O'Dowd et al. 2006:18)

Some areas of cross-border activity have proved more successful than others. The creation of Tourism Ireland, for example, formalises cross-border co-operation in this area of activity and has been deemed one of the more successful examples of North–South co-operation: 'Overall, tourism co-operation has succeeded relatively well, given the international obstacles it faced, in increasing numbers of visitors to Northern Ireland and the Republic of Ireland, but particularly in increasing communication channels and in facilitating harmonious agreement' (Tannam 2006:270).

In contrast, the cross-border body InterTradeIreland has not experienced the same degree of success, with levels of cross-border business co-operation not altering substantially. The creation of a dedicated cross-border institution has not fully eliminated the practical and perceived obstacles faced by firms considering cross-border co-operation (Roper 2007:569–70). Nevertheless, although the impact of cross-border institutions may be uneven, they have produced some tangible results.

The value of cross-border co-operation, however, is more than merely practical; it is also, and perhaps more importantly, symbolic. The bringing together of ministers, officials and networks from both sides of the border is indicative of the diminishing sensitivity of cross-border relations and bears witness to the enormous changes in the character and tone of political and community relations on the island of Ireland. Unionist fears that new relationships of this nature would hasten the charge towards a united Ireland have not materialised. The border may well be less of an obstruction to North–South co-operation than it was hitherto, but this has not compromised its integrity or existence. This is manifest in the attitudes of Unionists towards cross-border activities: 'The success of the bodies is reflected in the extent to which, by 2004, they appear to be largely taken for granted as part of the institutional landscape' (Coakley 2005:131).

The practical and symbolic dimensions of cross-border activity have produced positive and tangible outputs. However, this should not obscure the challenges which cross-border co-operation faces in the longer term. The Belfast Agreement may well provide a useful framework for North–South co-operation, but, in the absence of long-term and consistent high-level political commitment and adequate funding, cross-border co-operation may well suffer (see O'Dowd *et al.* 2006).

NORTH–SOUTH RELATIONS TODAY

Today, North–South relations are of a very different tenor and character from those that prevailed for much of the twentieth century. Cross-border activities and relations have been transformed, with contact between North and South evident across a range of political, economic, social, cultural and sectoral activities. The development of new forms of cross-border co-operation and networks of contact has produced tangible outcomes. The positive benefits that have accrued from these activities are largely indisputable; not alone have many produced practical advantages but, perhaps more significantly, they have also been of symbolic value and have contributed to changing the extent and nature of cross-border relationships in Ireland.

The most remarkable feature of cross-border relations in recent years has been the rapprochement that has occurred between the Unionist community and the Republic of Ireland. Of particular significance has been the previously unthinkable engagement between the DUP and the Republic of Ireland during the 2000s. In 2004, the party engaged directly with the Irish government at a meeting in Dublin attended by the then Taoiseach, Bertie Ahern, and the former DUP leader, the Revd Dr Ian Paisley. The meeting was of immense symbolic importance and provided a graphic illustration of the extent to which relations on the island had undergone a transformative change.

In 2007, following the restoration of devolution in Northern Ireland, a further symbolic visit took place when the same two individuals visited the site of the Battle of the Boyne. The 1690 battle saw William of Orange's Protestant army claim victory over the Catholic Jacobite force led by James II. This victory underpinned British and Protestant rule in Ireland and is celebrated by the Orange Order annually on 12 July. The Orange Order marching season in Northern Ireland has, in the past, been marked by violence and heightened tensions between the two communities. The Irish government's decision to develop the Battle of the Boyne site suggests a deepening maturity in relations between North and South and a growing respect for the history and culture of both the Catholic and Protestant traditions on the island.

Not all engagement between North and South, however, has necessarily been harmonious and positive. In 2006, the first loyalist march in Dublin since partition had to be rerouted after Republican protesters rioted in the capital's city centre. The Love Ulster rally involved eight hundred marchers commemorating the victims of Republican violence and was organised by Families Acting for Innocent Relatives (FAIR). Opposition to the march sparked serious violence in the centre of Dublin and resulted in extensive physical damage and a large number of injuries. Animosity towards competing traditions on the island remains apparent and it is clear that public displays of Ulster loyalism in the heart of the Irish capital antagonise the sensibilities of a small (and violent) minority. The reaction of this minority, on this occasion, resulted in heavy costs for businesses in Dublin's city centre. The forced closure of retail premises, damage to property and looting is estimated to have cost millions of euros. The subsequent clean-up cost, borne by Dublin City Council, was in the region of €50,000. Many business leaders also expressed fears about the long-term impact of the riots on Dublin's international reputation (RTÉ News 2006).

Other recent cross-border developments have also sparked controversy, albeit for very different reasons. The fluctuating sterling–euro exchange rate, combined with lower value added tax (VAT) rates and a more competitive trading environment in Northern Ireland, have seen consumers south of the border take advantage of cheaper prices offered by northern retailers. The practice of cross-border shopping has had a serious effect on Irish businesses and on the Irish exchequer. In a report prepared by the Office of the Revenue Commissioners and the Central Statistics Office in Ireland (2009), the impact is estimated to be considerable. The report estimates that the value of cross-border shopping trebled between 2007 and 2009, while the loss to the exchequer more than trebled (see Table 20.2).

Table 20.2 VAT and excise duty revenue lost due to cross-border shopping

Year		Estimate of Value of Cross-border Shopping	Estimate of VAT Revenue Lost	Estimate of Excise Duty Lost	Total Tax Loss
2007	lower estimate	€210m	€21m	€12m	€34m
	higher estimate	€340m	€34m	€19m	€54m
2008	lower estimate	€350m	€36m	€22m	€58m
	higher estimate	€550m	€56m	€34m	€90m
2009	lower forecast	€450m	€46m	€26m	€72m
	higher forecast	€700m	€72m	€40m	€112m

Source: Office of the Revenue Commissioners and CSO (2009). (*Note:* due to rounding, total figures may not match sum of the VAT and excise figures.)

The impact of cross-border shopping prompted Irish Finance Minister Brian Lenihan to appeal to shoppers to do their 'patriotic duty' by spending their euros in the Republic of Ireland (Slattery 2008:18). The call was condemned by political figures of all hues in Northern Ireland, and, indeed, Irish shoppers appear to have taken little heed of the minister's appeal.

The explosion in cross-border shopping has exposed an intriguing dimension to cross-border relations. Traditional Unionist opposition to an all-island economy has waned, as Northern Ireland has been able to take advantage of southern buying power. Simultaneously, however, the Irish government's response to the phenomenon is rooted in a form of protectionism, which is contrary to their traditional support for a united Ireland. Economic self-interest is clearly guiding perspectives on the merits or otherwise of cross-border shopping. As one newspaper columnist has noted, '[i]t's a sign of the times when the DUP and Sinn Féin are both championing an all-Ireland economy, while the Irish government is railing against cross-border shopping' (Clarke 2008). Political principle becomes less strident when confronted with economic reality and provides further evidence of the functional and practical logic that increasingly guides cross-border relations.

Cross-border co-operation has also expanded in other areas. A growth in policy and sectoral co-operation has been more pronounced since the 1990s and has involved not just political and administrative actors, but also civil society groups. Formal co-operation between Northern Ireland and the Republic of Ireland in a range of areas (including those governed by new institutional arrangements) has, on occasion, prompted a cross-border public reaction. An interesting environmental example is provided by 'the proposed all-Ireland incineration plant for toxic waste [which] was blocked by cross-border and cross-community opposition' (Leonard *et al.* 2009:900). In the educational sphere, it is estimated that almost 20 per cent of all schools on the island of Ireland were involved in some kind of cross-border contact in 2000 (see Pollack 2005). Research by the North South Exchange Consortium (2005:1) found that, between 2000 and 2004, 3,000 school and youth groups, involving in excess of 55,000 participants, were involved in cross-border exchange and co-operation activities. It is also important to note that outside the political realm, many civil society groups and professional associations have long been involved in cross-border co-operation (see Whyte 1983b). A range of different organisations, including trade unions, the Churches and sporting associations, have maintained and nurtured cross-border relations. The sensitivity of North–South relations has been overcome with respect to certain activities. Implicitly, this may suggest that political ideologies are flexible.

CONCLUSION

Traditionally, political relations between the administrations North and South were limited and often negative. Some cross-border networks and activities were pursued, but these tended to be in areas where co-operation was practically necessary. Attempts during the 1960s to promote more constructive relations between North and South fell victim to the worsening security and political situation in Northern Ireland after 1969. Sporadic and unsuccessful initiatives to resolve the conflict during the 1970s and early 1980s included consideration of the

North–South dimension. It was only after the signing of the 1985 AIA, however, that North–South relations began to improve.

The 1990s marked an important moment in the consolidation of North–South relations. Significant political development, coupled with improved public amenability on both sides of the border, created a new context within which cross-border relations could be pursued. Of specific note is the 1998 Belfast Agreement, which provides institutional expression (through the NSMC and North–South Implementation Bodies) for the pursuit of cross-border co-operation in a wide range of areas. The EU has also been an important factor in nurturing and encouraging cross-border contact and co-operation. Where once the predominant focus of North–South relations was acutely political, highly sensitive and focused almost exclusively on the constitutional issue, today, political, economic, social, cultural and sectoral cross-border relations exist and encompass a diverse and multi-faceted range of networks and activities.

The development of the peace process in Northern Ireland, and the North–South dynamic it has spawned, has not been completely devoid of controversy or idiosyncrasy. Economic realities and the sensitivities that surround identity have, for different reasons, exposed the limits of North–South relations and co-operation. This inherently points to possible difficulties in further developing cross-border relations.

That being said, North–South cross-border co-operation maintains a largely pragmatic character. Significantly, it has not provided a spur towards the achievement of a united Ireland. Unionist fears that cross-border co-operation would diminish Northern Ireland's link with the UK have proved groundless. The increasingly porous nature of the border between Northern Ireland and the Republic of Ireland has not fundamentally challenged the integrity of Northern Ireland's position as a constituent part of the United Kingdom. Of all the achievements of the Northern Ireland peace process over the course of almost two decades, the development of North–South relations has been especially challenging. It is to the credit of those involved that it has been a largely positive and beneficial experience.

References

Adshead, M. and Tonge, J. (2009) *Politics in Ireland: Convergence and Divergence in a Two-polity Island*. Basingstoke: Palgrave.

Alcock, A. (2001) 'From Conflict to Agreement in Northern Ireland: Lessons from Europe', in J. McGarry (ed.) *Northern Ireland and the Divided World: Post-Agreement Northern Ireland in Comparative Perspective*, pp. 159–80. Oxford: Oxford University Press.

Birnie, E. and Hitchens, D. (2001) 'Chasing the Wind? Half a Century of Economic Strategy Documents in Northern Ireland', *Irish Political Studies* 16(1): 1–27.

Clarke, L. (2008) 'Don't Sell Out High Street Patriotism', *Sunday Times*, 30 November [online]. Available: http://www.timesonline.co.uk/tol/news/world/ireland/article5257853.ece (last accessed 3 December 2009).

Coakley, J. (2005) 'The North–South Relationship: Implementing the Agreement', in J. Coakley, B. Laffan and J. Todd (eds) *Renovation or Revolution? New Territorial Politics in Ireland and the United Kingdom*, pp. 110–31. Dublin: University College Dublin Press.

— (2009) 'Northern Ireland and the British Dimension', in J. Coakley and M. Gallagher (eds) *Politics in the Republic of Ireland*, pp. 383–406. London: Routledge.

Coakley, J. and O'Dowd, L. (2007) 'The Transformation of the Irish Border', *Political Geography* 26(8): 877–85.

Cowen, B. (2007) *Speech by the Tánaiste at the Launch of the Peace III and Interreg IVA Programmes*, Stormont Hotel, Belfast, 14 April [online]. Available: http://www.finance.gov.ie/viewdoc.asp?DocID=5250&CatID=54&StartDate= 01+January+2008&m= (last accessed 30 December 2009).

Dixon, P. (2008) *Northern Ireland: The Politics of War and Peace*. Basingstoke: Palgrave.

English, R. (2002) 'The Growth of New Unionism', in J. Coakley (ed.) *Changing Shades of Orange and Green: Redefining the Union and Nation in Contemporary Ireland*, pp. 95–105. Dublin: University College Dublin Press.

Girvin, B. (1999) 'Northern Ireland and the Republic', in P. Mitchell and R. Wilford (eds) *Politics in Northern Ireland*, pp. 220–41. Oxford: Westview Press.

Government of Ireland (2007) *National Development Plan (2007–2013): Transforming Ireland – A Better Quality of Life for All*. Dublin: Stationery Office.

Hayward, K. (2007) 'Mediating the European Ideal: Cross-Border Programmes and Conflict Resolution on the Island of Ireland', *Journal of Common Market Studies* 45(3): 675–93.

Hennessey, T. (2005) *Northern Ireland: The Origins of the Troubles*. Dublin: Gill & Macmillan.

InterTradeIreland (2006) *Comprehensive Study on the All-island Economy*. Newry: InterTradeIreland.

— (2009) *Annual Charts: All-Island Trade 1995–2008 (Cash Value)* [online]. Available: http://tradestatistics.intertradeireland.com/annual_graphs_.php?id=5 (last accessed 4 December 2009).

Ireland (1998) *Agreement Reached in the Multi-party Negotiations*. Dublin: Stationery Office.

Kennedy, D. (2000) 'Europe and the Northern Ireland Problem', in D. Kennedy (ed.) *Living with the European Union: The Northern Ireland Experience*, pp. 148–68. London: Macmillan.

Kennedy, M. (2000) *Division and Consensus: The Politics of Cross-border Relations in Ireland, 1926–1969*. Dublin: Institute of Public Administration.

Laffan, B. and O'Mahony, J. (2008) *Ireland and the European Union*. Basingstoke: Palgrave.

Laffan, B. and Payne, D. (2001) *Creating Living Institutions: Cross-border Co-operation after the Good Friday Agreement*. Dublin: Institute for British–Irish Studies, University College Dublin.

Leonard, L., Doran, P. and Fagan, H. (2009) 'A Burning Issue? Governance and Anti-incinerator Campaigns in Ireland, North and South', *Environmental Politics* 18(6): 896–916.

McCartney, R. (2000) 'The Union and the Economic Future of Northern Ireland', in R. English and J. Morrison Skelley (eds) *Ideas Matter: Essays in Honour of Conor Cruise O'Brien*, pp. 148–56. Lanham, MD: University Press of America.

Michie, J. and Sheehan, M. (1998) 'The Political Economy of a Divided Ireland', *Cambridge Journal of Economics* 22(2): 243–59.

Murphy, M.C. (2007) 'Europeanization and the Sub-national Level: Changing Patterns of Governance in Northern Ireland', *Regional and Federal Studies* 17(3): 293–315.

Murphy, R.J. and Totten, K. (2000) 'Irish Political Data 2000', *Irish Political Studies* 15(1): 249–335.

North South Exchange Consortium (2005) *Research on the Current Provision of North South School and Youth Exchange and Cooperative Activity 2000–2004* [online]. Available: http://www.nsec.info/downloads/nsec_research_1.pdf (last accessed 2 December 2009).

North South Ministerial Council (2006) *North South Implementation Bodies* [online]. Available: http://www.northsouthministerialcouncil.org/index/north-south-implementation-bodies.htm (last accessed 8 March 2010).

O'Dowd, L., McCall, C. and Damkat, I. (2006) 'Sustaining Cross-border Co-operation: A Cross-sectoral Case-study Approach', *IBIS Working Paper* No. 61, Institute for British–Irish Studies, University College Dublin [online]. Available: http://www.ucd.ie/ibis/filestore/wp2006/61/61_odmcd.pdf (last accessed 24 November 2009).

Office of the Revenue Commissioners and CSO (Central Statistics Office) (2009) *The Implications of Cross-border Shopping for the Irish Exchequer* [online]. Available: http://www.finance.gov.ie/documents/publications/reports/2009/crossborderefb09.pdf (last accessed 24 November 2009).

Pollack, A. (2005) 'Educational Co-operation on the Island of Ireland: A Thousand Flowers and a Hundred Heartaches', discussion paper for Mapping Frontiers, Plotting Pathways workshop, Dundalk Institute of Technology, 21 June [online]. Available: http://www.crossborder.ie/pubs/mfpaper4.pdf (last accessed 24 November 2009).

Roper, S. (2007) 'Cross-border and Local Co-operation on the Island of Ireland: An Economic Perspective', *Political Geography* 26(5): 554–74.

Rowthorn, B. and Wayne, N. (1988) *Northern Ireland: The Political Economy of Conflict*. Oxford: Polity Press.

RTÉ News (2006) 'Gardaí to Submit Report on Dublin Riots', 25 February [online]. Available: http://www.rte.ie/news/2006/0226/loyalist.html (last accessed 3 December 2009).

Ruane, J. and Todd, J. (1996) *The Dynamics of Conflict in Northern Ireland: Power, Conflict and Emancipation*. Cambridge: Cambridge University Press.

Slattery, L. (2008) 'No Relief in Sight as Jobless Rise is Highest Since 1975', *Irish Times*, 4 December, p.18.

Tannam, E. (1999) *Cross-border Co-operation in the Republic of Ireland and Northern Ireland*. Basingstoke: Palgrave.

— (2006) 'Cross-border Co-operation between Northern Ireland and the Republic of Ireland: Neo-functionalism Revisited', *British Journal of Politics and International Relations* 8(2): 256–76.

Teague, P. (1996) 'The European Union and the Irish Peace Process', *Journal of Common Market Studies* 43(4): 549–70.

Tonge, J. (2002) *Northern Ireland: Conflict and Change*. Essex: Longman.

— (2005) *The New Northern Irish Politics?* Basingstoke: Palgrave.

Whyte, J. (1983a) 'The Permeability of the United Kingdom–Irish Border: A Preliminary Reconnaissance', *Administration* 31(3): 300–15.

— (1983b) 'How Much Discrimination Was There Under the Unionist Regime 1921–1968?', in T. Gallagher and J. O'Connell (eds) *Contemporary Irish Studies*, pp. 1–35. Manchester: Manchester University Press.

Chapter 21

Cultural Tourism Development in Irish Villages and Towns: The Role of Authenticity, Social, Cultural and Tourist Capital

Breda McCarthy

INTRODUCTION – THE CULTURAL ECONOMY AND CULTURAL TOURISM

The term 'cultural economy' (and cultural tourism) signifies the transformation of a production-oriented economy to a consumption-oriented one and the greater importance of 'invisibles' in capitalist society (du Gay 1997; Leadbeater and Oakley 1999; Scott and Urry 1994). The cultural economy, as a concept, is supported by policy makers around Europe and appears in many policy statements and strategy documents. Cato *et al.* (2007) highlight that creative industries have the potential to enrich and stabilise disadvantaged areas, as well as generating direct economic benefits. Products and services, such as music, fashion, design, dance, theatre, art and crafts, are generally categorised as 'cultural goods', which are defined by Hirsch (1972:641) as 'non-material goods directed at a public of consumers for whom they generally serve an aesthetic or expressive, rather than a clearly utilitarian function'.

Academics and policy makers now recognise that cultural tourism is a 'living' (not simply representations of the past), socio-cultural construction. In other words, its social connotation is not given, but negotiated, and different people may conceive it in different ways (Cohen 1988). For instance, the appeal of a city often comes from its physical assets and experiences built around those assets, which generally extend to the 'living culture' and the atmosphere of the place (Wilson 2002). Tourists are often attracted to destinations that are linked to art history or contemporary performance (Gibson and Connell 2003; Hughes 2000; Hughes and

This chapter forms part of a study exploring the drivers and barriers to cultural tourism in the south-west of Ireland, which was funded by Fáilte Ireland under its Research Fellowship scheme 2006/7.

Allen 2005). As cultural tourism is increasingly utilised as a means of economic development, the need for creative tourism projects is greater than ever. Increasingly, experiences, such as learning how to dance in situ, in the original traditional setting, are being marketed to cultural tourists (Richards and Wilson 2006).

According to Fáilte Ireland (2009), cultural tourism embraces the full range of experiences visitors can undertake to learn what makes a destination distinctive – its lifestyle, its heritage, its arts, its people. Cultural tourism in Ireland consists of three key sectors: traditional culture, living culture and the built heritage. Heritage tourism has been conceptualised as 'gazing on the past' (Urry 1990). In the 1980s, the availability of European Union (EU) funding for capital projects led to a flood of heritage and museum projects in Ireland (McGettigan and Burns 2001; Stocks 2000). In the 1990s, the marketability of culture and the shift to 'invisibles' came to the fore in Irish tourism. Marketing campaigns sought to capitalise on Ireland's fashionable image and success in music, literature, theatre, film and dance. According to Nicholls (2000), myths and stereotypes help shape tourists' expectations. In the case of Ireland, the success of *Riverdance*, Guinness and the Irish pub, along with rock artists on an international stage (Ó Cinnéide 2005; Strachan and Leonard 2004), have all helped build a brand and re-enforce the conception of Ireland as a musical nation. Developed from a five-minute dance routine commissioned for the interval of the Eurovision Song Contest in 1994, *Riverdance* epitomised the revival and contemporisation of Irish culture. In the 1990s, marketing campaigns developed the themes of activity, authenticity, culture, friendliness and memorable personal experiences, summarised as 'emotional experience positioning' (Prentice and Anderson 2000). Irish Tourism attempted to present Ireland not so much as a place to see, but as a place to experience, combining its historical features with more contemporary ones (Johnson 1999).

Cultural tourism is estimated to be worth €5.1bn annually to the Irish economy (Fáilte Ireland 2009). Policy makers are committed to cultural tourism, seeing it as a means to achieve key goals, notably the greater spatial distribution of visitors, greater seasonal distribution of visitors and achievement of higher spend per visitor (Fáilte Ireland 2007; Údarás na Gaeltachta 2005).

CONCEPTUAL FRAMEWORK: UNDERSTANDING THE DEVELOPMENT OF CULTURAL TOURISM

This chapter seeks to explain the factors driving cultural tourism development. Figure 21.1 displays a model of cultural tourism development that is drawn from the literature (e.g. Lounsbury and Glynn 2001). The figure depicts relationships between stocks of social and cultural capital, stocks of tourism capital, entrepreneurial opportunity, authenticity and wealth creation. While the model is linear in nature, it is recognised that the process of cultural tourism development is a dynamic one, and over time, the created wealth flows back and leads to additional capital stocks. The following sections explore the key components of this model. The theoretical discussion is then supplemented with case study data and anecdotes from the field.

Figure 21.1 Model of cultural tourism development

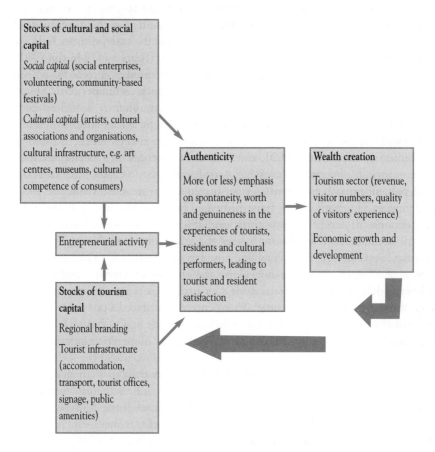

Stocks of Social Capital

The concept of social capital has been heavily emphasised in the sociology literature (e.g. Bourdieu and Wacquant 1992; Burt 1992; Coleman 1990; Portes 1998; Putnam 1993). It has been defined by Adler and Kwon (2002:23) as 'the goodwill available to individuals or groups. Its source lies in the structure and content of the actor's social relations. Its effects flow from the information, influence, and solidarity it makes available to the actor'. Social capital can be distinguished from human capital in two ways: first, it is a more of a collective good, whereas human capital is a quality of individuals, such as intelligence, education and seniority. Second, investment in social capital helps people identify opportunities and it complements human capital (Burt 1997).

One measure of social capital is the number of social enterprises in an area. As they gain economic strength, research to understand the phenomenon has burgeoned (Dorado 2006). The Organisation for Economic Co-operation and Development (OECD) (1999:10) defines social enterprise as 'any private activity conducted in the public interest, organized with an entrepreneurial strategy, but whose main purpose is not the maximization of profit, but the attainment of certain economic and social goals'. Examples of social enterprises include co-operatives, charities and voluntary community groups (Seanor and Meaton 2007). Social entrepreneurs are driven by social needs, which rest on some vision of a better world and are grounded in personal values, such as the desire to address hunger and poverty, unemployment, child abuse, crime, illiteracy, homelessness or pollution or to foster a deeper appreciation of the arts. Social enterprise is also associated with rural regeneration (Zografos 2007). Social enterprise is based on principles of voluntarism, ethical behaviour and a mission with a social cause, such as combating poverty or tackling social exclusion (Chell 2007). Social entrepreneurship is exercised when a person aims to create social value, recognises and pursues opportunities to create this value, employs innovation, tolerates risk and declines to accept limitations in available resources (Peredo and McLean 2006). Social entrepreneurs need to survive without grant aid (Haugh 2005) and the sector is becoming more commercialised as social enterprises begin to charge fees, produce goods for sale and develop new enterprises (Weisbrod 1998).

Research has shown that Ireland has a long tradition of social entrepreneurship (Ní Bhrádaigh 2007). Community-based enterprises played a pivotal role in the socio-economic development of the Gaeltacht (Keane and Ó Cinnéide 1986; Ó Cinnéide and Conghaile 1990). The Gaeltacht co-operative sector, which emerged out of the Irish speakers' civil rights movement, sowed the seeds for the establishment of Irish-language radio and television stations (Coleman 2003). Today there are thirty co-operatives in the Gaeltacht and their aims are to create employment, upgrade services and generally improve the socio-economic conditions of the Gaeltacht. Summer schools, the *Coláiste Samhraigh*, have been in existence since the 1960s. Structured visitor programmes have been developed to help students practise their Irish in a social setting, although the declining number of fluent Irish speakers is a limitation (Convery and Flanagan 1996). With the provision of grant aid, improvements have been made to accommodation facilities, classrooms and halls. These schools attracted 25,000 young people in 2006 (Department of Rural, Community and Gaeltacht Affairs 2007).

In the arts, social enterprise refers to the use of art to revive or sustain rural and depopulated communities. Myerscough (1988:78) argues that the arts can be a potent tool for environmental improvement and for regional and urban development; furthermore, the arts play a social role in the community, 'as a social node around which new social life can cohere'.

Social capital is also manifested in the number of community-based festivals in an area. One rationale for supporting festivals is that they improve the quality of life in a community, and provide a local community with a sense of identity, commonality and spirit that few other goods are capable of producing (Quinn 2005). Quinn (2006), in a study of two major Irish festivals (the Galway Arts Festival and Wexford Festival Opera) concluded that festival tourism intensifies appreciation for a particular art form, and often leads to increased arts activity on a year-round basis, as well as an improvement in standards and venue infrastructure.

Stocks of Cultural Capital

The term 'cultural capital' is associated with Bourdieu (1984), who argued that cultural knowledge confers power and status and is possessed by people from elite or dominant social classes. Researchers (e.g. De Graaf *et al.* 2000) tend to define cultural capital quite narrowly, in terms of participation in, and understanding of, high culture, such as theatre, classical music, museums and art. Cultural capital is also associated with the marketing of non-profit museums, galleries and other related institutions (Rentschler 2007). In this chapter, the term 'cultural capital' is interpreted as an all-embracing term to cover not only cultural competence, but also stocks of cultural resources, creative people and cultural associations and organisations that provide training, education, information, research and technical support.

Social Capital, Entrepreneurial Opportunity and Stocks of Tourist Capital

According to Burt (1997), social capital stimulates entrepreneurial opportunity. Scholars propose that external ties to others give actors the opportunity to leverage their contacts' resources (Adler and Kwon 2002). All acts of entrepreneurship start with the vision of an attractive opportunity (Gibb and Scott 1985; Stevenson and Gumpert 1985). The rise of the cultural tourist, which is attributed to greater affluence, more leisure time, greater mobility, increased access to the arts and higher levels of education (Holcomb 1999; Weiler and Hall 1992), gives rise to new ways of conceiving and creating value. The commercialisation of culture is manifested in various ways: music workshops, the sale of local arts and crafts and souvenirs, packaged holidays, language instruction courses, opening restaurants and cafes in museums, etc.

Baron and Hannan (1994) complain about the indiscriminate use of the term 'social capital' and refer disparagingly to the recent emergence of a 'plethora of capitals' in the sociological literature. Mindful of this fact, I seek to justify the use of yet another capital, 'tourist capital'. To qualify as capital, an entity must possess certain characteristics: it must have an opportunity cost (Baron and Hannan 1994), give rise to benefits that can be measured, have a rate of depreciation, and be a substitute for, or a complement to, other resources (Adler and Kwon 2002). Tourist infrastructure, such as stocks of accommodation and transport, is included in the conceptual framework as capital, since it meets these criteria.

Social capital tends to be seen as a resource with only positive outcomes, but scholars argue that this position is too one-sided (Adler and Kwon 2002). In tightly knit ethnic communities, social capital often leads to business start-up opportunities; however, groups may hinder individual economic advancement by placing heavy personal obligations on their members (Portes 1998). Entrepreneurship can be seen as legitimate in one context, but opportunistic and self-seeking in another (Adler and Kwon 2002; Burt 1997). In a cultural tourism context, if actors are seen as free-riders, or if their entrepreneurial ventures lack authenticity, they may encounter resistance; therefore, social capital becomes a liability or constraint on action. The next section will introduce the notion of authenticity and I will attempt to show how social capital can be both an asset and a liability.

Authenticity

The concept of authenticity has been heavily emphasised in the tourism and sociological literatures (Cohen 1979; Heidegger 1962; MacCannell 1976; Pearce and Moscardo 1986). According to MacCannell (1976), authenticity can be defined as the genuine, worthwhile and spontaneous experience of travel. The work of Goffman (1959) on the front- and back-stage dichotomy, the true and the false, is also central to our understanding of authenticity. In a tourism context, front-stage people are conscious that they are creating a display for tourists, while back-stage individuals are not in the tourist spotlight (Pearce and Moscardo 1986). Pearce and Moscardo (1986:122), in a review of the literature, highlight that authenticity involves being true to oneself and can be interpreted as a 'fusion of self and the external world'.

Arguments have been made that the commodification of culture (i.e. transforming some aspects of culture into saleable products) places 'authenticity' in jeopardy (Taylor 2001). Philosophers such as de Botton (2002) have started to outline the futility of the act of travel. The popular phrase 'been there, done that' suggests that travel is superficial and has been devalued by today's society. Due to the short-term, circumscribed nature of touristic encounters, international tourists never go anywhere real and exist in a tourist 'bubble' (Cohen 1972). Boorstin (1961) argues that tourists seek out 'pseudo events' (Disneyland being a current example) in order to shield themselves from the unpredictable or unpleasant.

MacCannell (1973) diverges from Boorstin's work by proposing that the primary motivation for travel lies in a quest for authenticity, but this quest is always doomed to fail. Authenticity is difficult to find since the tourist industry distorts the product and 'staged authenticity' emerges. He argues that even when tourists are allowed to get a peek backstage, they, the onlookers, are confronted with a false backstage, 'a superlie, the kind that drips with sincerity' (MacCannell 1973: 599). Pearce and Moscardo (1986), however, reject the notion that tourist experiences are inherently contrived or artificial; instead, they propose that authentic encounters do occur and they have a 'gift-like quality'. They argue that authenticity can be achieved either through environmental experiences, people-based experiences or a joint interaction of these elements.

In the literature on cultural tourism, the integrity of artistic expression and the impact of tourism on culture are themes that are well rehearsed by scholars (Copley and Robson 1996; Quinn 2006; Rolfe 1992). Critics of cultural policy sometimes argue that what is primary – the production of culture – becomes secondary when utilitarian motives intervene, such as the need to make profit, entertain an audience, or, in Campbell's (1989:60) words, 'produce pleasure'. It is argued that creativity in the performing arts and the emergence of experimental works may be inhibited if tourist appeal is lacking (Hughes and Allen 2005). In the festival management literature, writers conclude that if changes are made to an event to better suit the needs of tourists, that can become a source of tension between residents and event organisers (Hughes 1998; Mules 2004; Xiao and Smith 2004). In a study of music events in the West of Ireland, Kneafsey (2002) found evidence of the front stage and backstage. At times, musicians feel the need to be shielded from the tourist gaze and retreat backstage to play music that is meaningful to them. In other words, when musicians are paid to play music, they lose interest in it and tourists get a 'staged performance', an inferior representation of reality.

The issue of authenticity is also relevant to practitioners and others involved in the delivery of cultural performances. Through performances, individuals can express themselves and keep their cultural traditions alive. Furthermore, they may be in a better position than tourists to determine what is authentic and not authentic. Scholars note that the whole notion of authenticity 'comes to us constructed by hegemonic voices' (Spivak and Gunew 1993:195). What is and what is not authentic is largely the result of interpretations (albeit contested) by professionals, such as curators and anthropologists (McIntosh and Prentice 1999).

In the context of the traditional arts movement in Ireland, the notion of authenticity has led to heated debates and schisms. Comhaltas Ceoltóirí Éireann (CCE) has played an important role in popularising Irish music. Founded in 1951, it established numerous branches for music education in Ireland and overseas and placed an emphasis on competition and standardisation of playing techniques (Fleming 2004). However, this alienated many musicians who had fears about the loss of musical diversity, local style and repertoire (Kearns and Taylor 2003). These conflicts led to the growth of festivals, which provided musicians with an alternative to competition-based performances. With folk music, the distinctive nature of the music comes directly from the instruments – familiar examples to Irish people being the bodhrán, the uilleann pipes, fiddle and harp. Gibson and Connell (2003:176) note the rise of master classes and workshops, and remark:

'tourist numbers remain relatively small – a handful of individuals in search of a means of learning and contextualising distinctive musical styles'. The growth in the Irish diaspora, the increasing pace of life and commercialisation of societies are used to explain the growing interest in traditional music festivals as people search for 'true meaning' and 'authenticity' (Kearns and Taylor 2003; Kneafsey 2002; Smith 2001). Writers in the field of tourism note that the creation of authenticity is important to tourism 'as a distancing device which prompts desire and the production of value' (Taylor 2001:7).

With the above in mind, I argue that the development of cultural tourism depends on perceptions of authenticity. Authenticity can be analysed from the perspective of tourists, as well as local actors and others involved in the cultural sector. It is proposed that this quality aids, or impedes, the mobilisation of resources and wealth creation. There is some support for this thesis in the tourism literature, and indirectly, in writings on the cultural economy.

CULTURAL TOURISM IN ACTION – CASE STUDIES

In the following case studies, examples are given of cultural tourism initiatives drawn from parts of Co. Clare and Co. Kerry. While the case studies serve as models for other destinations, they also illustrate some of the limitations to the development of cultural tourism and the challenges that local actors face. The research involved thirty-five interviews with policy makers, practitioners, festival organisers and managers of tourist ventures.

South and west Kerry is a prime tourist destination and visitors are attracted by the combination of natural beauty and cultural heritage, such as country houses, castles, museums and monastic remains. Dingle town is reputed to be a haven of traditional music and 'trad sessions' in public houses are an important source of night-time entertainment. A regional airport (Kerry International Airport) has facilitated growth in tourism. The area has a history of in-migration and many well-known visual artists, craftspeople, writers and film-makers live in the area and they evoke the landscape in their work. Co. Kerry contains a Gaeltacht, which is overseen by the development body, Údarás na Gaeltachta.

Co. Clare places an emphasis on the traditional arts: Irish music, song, dance and story-telling. The tourism authority has consistently deployed music in order to attract backpackers, domestic travellers and international tourists. The region's natural attractions include the Burren (a Special Area of Conservation) and the Cliffs of Moher, an iconic attraction, which draws about a million visitors each year. Table 21.1 details the stocks of social and cultural capital in these areas.

Table 21.1 A comparison of capital stocks across two case study regions

South and West Kerry	Clare
Stocks of Cultural and Social Capital	
• 20 community-run festivals • summer schools • *An Díseart*, Dingle (Institute of Education and Celtic Culture) • *Coláiste Íde* (boarding school for girls) • CCE branches • four arts centres • art galleries • state-owned heritage sites and national park • Blasket Island Interpretative Centre • Tech Amergin, Waterville (vocational/adult education centre)	• 30 community-run festivals • Oidhreacht an Chláir, a community group that runs specialised courses in cultural studies in Milltown Malbay • Cruinniú, a traditional arts conference • CCE branches • free weekly concerts in Ennis • 'Trad for Teens' night • Clare Traditional Arts Forum • workshops organised for festival and event organisers • five music schools and seven multi-purpose performing arts venues • state-owned heritage sites and national park • Burren Interpretative Centre
Entrepreneurial Opportunities	
• 'Iveragh Arts': guide to local arts and crafts • a co-operative art gallery • Open Art Trail • packaged tours: Gaeilge Beo (Irish cultural activity holidays); Hidden Ireland Tours; Sciuird Archaeological Tours; Dingle Music School; Celtic Nature	• specialist recording studio (Malbay Studios) • specialist retailing: Ward's Craft and Music Shop, Miltown Malbay; Custy's Traditional Music Shop, Ennis. • packaged tours (Irish Cycling Safaris)

Source: McCarthy (2008a).

Stocks of Social and Cultural Capital

Festivals are endemic in the case study regions and they occur all year round. They rely heavily on social capital. The people who run the events are doing so in an unpaid capacity, often juggling full-time jobs and relying on volunteer labour. The festivals are not professionally staffed and are often under-resourced, yet they deliver a vibrant cultural experience to locals and tourists. Respondents stressed that festival management involves a great deal of commitment, knowledge and skill. According to one respondent:

> A great deal of knowledge and skills are required to run local, provincial events. There are two components – the concept, the creativity, the ideas people – and the need to put the idea into practice. We put together a 100 page safety statement for the County Council . . . Meetings were held with the Gardaí – car parking, traffic management . . . meetings were held with the Environmental Health Officer – important when there are chip vans and hotdog stands. We employ full-time security staff for the weekend. Knowledge of legislation is required – what happens if a volunteer is injured during the festival? An emergency plan is required by the County Council, for instance, access routes for an ambulance, emergency landing for a helicopter . . . Many festivals are put off by concerns over insurance . . . There is a gap and demand for more training and advice in that area. (Personal communication with the founder of the Willie Clancy Summer School, 2007)

Festival managers have to deal with all sorts of challenges, such as lack of finance, red tape and over-dependence on the founder. There is a risk of the festival organiser getting 'burnt out' after a few years, so respondents stressed the need for a good working committee. The following comment illustrates the difficulties involved in making a transition from a small festival to a larger, more commercially orientated festival:

> I really feel that the amount of bureaucracy involved in getting, what is a relatively small amount of funding, is off-putting to festival organizers. I stress that you are not talking about people with professional experience or staff . . . it's a huge issue for anyone thinking about setting up a festival, or running a small festival . . . there is a tension between staying small versus getting bigger – a lot of it has to do with form-filling . . . for a voluntary committee, the level of detail required is a problem. (Personal communication with County Arts Officer, Clare County Council, 2007)

There are other examples of social capital. The Great Blasket Island Forum is an example of a community-driven initiative designed to protect authentic culture. The Great Blasket Island, located off the coast of Co. Kerry, is a National Historic Park, as it once sustained a vibrant Irish-speaking culture and inspired an impressive vernacular literature (Beiner 2005:55). Today, the community is seeking World Heritage Site Status for the Blasket Islands. Respondents talked about the role that the summer schools (Coláiste Samhraigh) played in the local economy. The summer schools have a narrow target market; school leavers in search of language instruction. One respondent, from Údarás na Gaeltachta, remarked that there was potential to broaden the target market, increase visitor length of stay and quality of spend. For instance, the schools could target former Coláiste Samhraigh participants, and parents who visit their children for the day, which could lead to further economic gains (Personal communication with Regional Manager (South), Údarás na Gaeltachta, 2007).

Cultural capital is illustrated by the wide range of cultural associations and organisations providing training, education, information, research and technical support. Some examples are Oidhreach an Chláir (a college for traditional studies), which grew out of the success of a music school/festival in Co. Clare. Diseart, an educational institute in Dingle, is an important resource for a small community: it offers classes in Irish culture to American students and hosts local exhibitions and festivals. Cultural capital is also being built via investment in arts infrastructure. There are four arts centres in Kerry and a purpose-built music centre in Clare. These centres are designed to meet local and tourist demand. Residents no longer need to travel long distances to access performances in major towns. The centres act as multi-purpose venues and are used for festivals, plays, craft fairs and art exhibitions, as well as meetings and workshops.

Entrepreneurial Opportunities

Tourism is an industry that is strongly rooted in the local economies and, over time, local actors began to recognise the potential to offer high-quality products and services based on living culture. The responsiveness of local industry to tourist demand can be seen in the growth of packaged tours, the promotion of local arts and crafts and the hosting of music workshops and traditional music nights in the local pubs.

One example is an Open Arts Trail in west Kerry, which was designed to give the visitor a chance to meet arts and crafts people in their natural setting. It gives tourists the opportunity to understand the hard work and intricate process that goes into making an artistic product. Other examples are the establishment of a co-operative art gallery (the artist essentially cuts out the middle man) and production of local arts and crafts guides for the tourist market in the Iveragh peninsula, south Kerry (personal communication with artist, Iveragh Arts Group, 2007).

An example of public–private partnership is Cill Rialaig, which is the name given to an artists' retreat, art gallery and conservation project in Ballinskelligs, Co. Kerry. A pre-famine village was restored and is today used as an artists' retreat (McCarthy 2008b). The Kerry GeoPark is an example of a regional branding initiative and it emerged out of the belief that arts and culture have the potential to attract the independent traveller, increase bed nights and counteract economic leakage. Outputs include a website, a promotional DVD, and hill-walking and accommodation packages for visitors. The Kerry GeoPark is an example of a multi-stakeholder, community-driven network that has the potential to contribute to cultural tourism development, spread concepts of self-help and co-operation in the community and broaden knowledge of heritage, geology and the environment.

Stocks of Tourism Capital

Regional branding is strong in the case study regions. According to the regional development manager of Shannon Development (personal communication, 2007), the ultimate aim is 'to make Clare the leading county for quality, all-year-round cultural events and festivals'. In south and west Kerry, the potential of the language to assist in differentiating the Gaeltacht led to a new branding campaign, Gael-Saoire (Holidays in the Gaeltacht) in 1997. Stocks of tourism capital are built up in various ways by the local county council and the Department of Arts, Heritage and Tourism. State support includes market research, the creation of a database of musicians in Co. Clare, visitor satisfaction surveys, conferences and workshops and attempts to facilitate transfer of knowledge on best practices and provision of funds. Although tourist infrastructure is clearly evident in the region (accommodation, transport, tourist offices, signage, public amenities, etc.), respondents were critical of some aspects of infrastructure, citing that the roads, signage and public amenities in rural areas all required improvement.

Risks and Benefits of Cultural Tourism Development: Authenticity (or Lack of Authenticity)

Authenticity is a quality valued by musicians, local residents and tourists. The following anecdotes show the concern for spontaneity, worth and genuineness. From the perspective of musicians, their desire to play and learn from one another leads to their participation in festivals, and they willingly pay for their own food, lodging and transportation:

> They just want to be here . . . it's a wonderful thing . . . you can go into a session in a pub, be a very young musician and meet someone older, someone you have looked up to for years, never dreaming you'd be in a position to play with them. It happens in a very natural and unforced way . . . people go for the music, that's their agenda, to have a celebration of music. (Personal communication with Shannon Area Regional Arts Co-ordinator (traditional arts specialist), Co. Clare, 2007)

Discussions with the arts officer in Co. Clare reveal a kind of ambivalence about tourism and concern about repositioning music as a tourist object or spectacle. She remarked that traditional music sessions have an informal and spontaneous nature, which could be eroded by tourism. There was concern about the distortion of music in order to attract tourists:

Music is really based on a tradition; it is based in and amongst the community – the people. I think that the very notion of having music trails – the notion of having set venues where people can go to and see traditional music is almost abhorrent to some people, because that is not what traditional music is about. It's about what is happening in a community, being out and about, that is the disparity between tourism and the actual music itself. It's almost like taking the essence of the community and trying to standardise it and brand it for commercial gain. Most people aren't interested in that at all. (Personal communication with County Arts Officer, Co. Clare, 2007)

The concern about free-riding, in other words extracting value from others without making any contribution to the group, or to productivity, is captured in the following comment:

Musicians often feel that they are the ones who are most neglected in relation to music, it's almost like making money off the backs of musicians and you can be sure that musicians aren't making the money. (Personal communication with County Arts Officer, Co. Clare, 2007)

Authenticity helped festival organisers retain the support of local residents. One respondent remarked that festivals have to be 'for the people and by the people', proposing that the audience for festivals is first and foremost for the local community and not the tourist market (personal communication with the founder of Gaeilge Beo (Irish Cultural Activity Holidays), 2007). It was noted that local residents supported festivals because they were run for altruistic reasons. If festival organisers were seen to benefit economically from the festival, local support would fall away.

From a tourist perspective, tourists sought to attend authentic musical performances and rejected staged performances. One anecdote concerned Glór, a purpose-built music venue, which opened in Co. Clare in 1997 (personal communication with Regional Development Manager, Co. Clare, 2007). The arts programme was designed to attract tourists. However, performances on a stage failed to attract a tourist audience, since they preferred to listen to music in the local pubs, as the locals did.

The concern for authenticity was also found in the community of visual artists. For some, the exploitation of art for tourist gain ultimately degrades artistic quality:

The marriage of art and commerce is an uneasy one . . . it leads to absurdities, distortions of value and outright scandals . . . in living as an artist, there always lurks the danger of shaping one's art in an attempt to second guess an audience or a market. This may be one of the greatest dangers to artistic practice . . . The term art tourism makes me a bit nervous . . . I think of all the tourist spots . . . where artists devise a shtick based on a superficial reference to the local scene and peddle it on the streets and in the galleries. It degrades the whole meaning of art and hinders its ability to reveal the poetry, beauty and sadness of life. (Personal communication with former Artist in Residence, Cill Rialaig Retreat, 2007)

One practitioner stressed that artists have a mission that is not explicitly commercial; they work in isolation and are often eccentric characters. Adhering to a production schedule is not always conducive to creativity:

You must fit into their rules and their structures . . . We don't fit into the system, we are not institutionalised. Yet, the attitude is, produce more – make more money – the economy has to grow and grow – build more houses, produce more. Yet the opposite is the case in the art world. I am not interested in mass production; art does take place in a factory . . . that is not my purpose. Enterprise takes the uniqueness out of my work. I want to improve and sell my work, not reproduce it. (Personal communication with the founder of Sculpture in Stone and Wood, 2007)

It was noted that participation in business often demands a change in the artist's style of working. Artists face new challenges: getting insurance; purchasing new supplies and materials, where previously they used second-hand materials; and planning a product line. One respondent suggested that arts and craftspeople lacked business know-how:

Everything has to come up to a certain standard . . . artists are told they need to have bar-coding before their products can be displayed. They are not told how they can make it happen . . . the attitude is not – how can we make it happen? (Personal communication with the Manager of South Kerry Development Partnership, 2007)

The above comments show that the arts is not simply another industry or tourist resource and that those who deal with musicians, artists and festival organisers, or who seek to gain economic benefit from the arts, must engage with locals in a sensitive and sympathetic manner.

Wealth Creation

The research raises the question: Is cultural tourism conducive to the wealth of regional areas? Data show that tourism revenue in the south-west has increased by 10.6 per cent since 2001. Outside the capital city, Kerry (along with Cork) has the largest inventory of tourist infrastructure in the country and 15 per cent of its workforce is employed in the tourism industry (Kerry County Council 2009).

In Clare, musicians came from all over the world to a small village that hosts the Willie Clancy Festival, one of the largest summer schools worldwide for traditional Irish music, song and dance. The economic value of the festival is not in dispute. According to the Arts Officer for Co. Clare:

It literally supplies Milltown Malbay with a lifeline all year round. Talk to any publican . . . the accommodation providers . . . if they don't make it in this week, they will struggle for the rest of the year. It's literally what keeps the town alive . . . it is of huge benefit, not just to Milltown Malbay, but to the county as a whole. (Personal communication, 2007)

The views of this research respondent correspond with other policy makers. In a study of the Irish music industry (Music Board of Ireland 2002:4), the links between music and the economy are firmly acknowledged: 'Ireland's image abroad is largely associated with music and Irish music has a significant, positive impact on the development of tourism.' Market research revealed that visitors to Kerry are most interested in hearing traditional Irish music (Kerry County Development Board 2004).

Discussions with research respondents reveal that visitors get an opportunity to experience good quality of contact with the locals. Thus, the benefits of cultural tourism are sometimes covert and intangible. In many tourist destinations, economic 'leakage' is a problem: in other words, economic gains accrue to outsiders, such as owners of holiday homes, large hotels and coach tour operators. In this research, respondents emphasised that cultural tourism has the potential to counteract leakage and benefit the local business community.

CONCLUSION

This chapter explored the role and rationale for cultural tourism development in non-urban areas. Ireland, with its scenic landscape, built heritage and the performing arts, has a long history of targeting the cultural tourism market. It has never been in the mass market for sun, sea and sand holidays. Small villages, towns and their hinterland are positioned as having a distinct cultural identity. Traditional Irish music, in particular, helps shape the image of rural and regional parts of Ireland.

There seems to be little doubt that links between tourism, culture and the arts can give rise to economic opportunity in small communities. However, those who seek to profit from culture must ensure that their ventures resonate with broader societal norms about what is authentic and appropriate. It is argued that adherence to authenticity is important to cultural tourism and the emphasis on spontaneity, worth and genuineness leads to the support and satisfaction of local residents, tourists, musicians and other cultural actors. It is critical for the relevant public sector funding bodies to use their influence and ensure that artists and musicians have a say in cultural tourism strategy.

The views of research respondents match those in the literature, such as Hughes (1998). Entrepreneurship can be seen as opportunistic and self-seeking in the context of music tourism. If actors are seen as free-riders, or if their entrepreneurial ventures lack authenticity, they may encounter resistance from locals. Therefore, stocks of social capital can become a liability as individuals seek economic advancement. This conclusion matches the views of scholars such as Portes (1998). Along with social ties, finance, bureaucracy and red tape add to the constraints faced by individuals as they seek to grow their cultural tourism ventures. Those on the ground, the artists and organisers of cultural events, require a good deal of knowledge and business skills in order to take advantage of opportunities in the tourist industry. A lesson learned from this research is that business people need to think carefully about the interaction between commercial and cultural activity.

References

Adler, P. and Kwon, S.W. (2002) 'Social Capital: Prospects for a New Concept', *Academy of Management Review* 27(1): 17–40.

Baron, J. and Hannan, M. (1994) 'The Impact of Economics on Contemporary Sociology', *Journal of Economic Literature* 32(3): 1111–46.

Beiner, G. (2005) 'Commemorative Heritage and the Dialectics of Memory' in M. McCarthy (ed.), *Ireland's Heritages: Critical Perspectives on Memory and Identity*, pp. 55–70. Aldershot: Ashgate Publishing.

Boorstin, D.J. (1961) *The Image: A Guide to Pseudo-Events in America*. New York, NY: Harper and Row.

Bourdieu, P. (1984) *Distinction: A Social Critique of the Judgment of Taste*. Cambridge, MA: Harvard University Press.

Bourdieu, P. and Wacquant, L. (1992) *An Invitation to Reflexive Sociology*. Chicago, IL: University of Chicago Press

Burt, R. (1992) *Structural Holes: The Social Structure of Competition*. Cambridge, MA: Harvard University Press.

— (1997) 'The Contingent Value of Social Capital', *Administrative Science Quarterly* 42(2): 339–65.

Campbell, C. (1989) *The Romantic Ethic and the Spirit of Modern Consumerism*. London: Blackwell.

Cato, M., Arthur, L., Smith, R. and Keenoy, T. (2007) 'So You Like to Play Guitar? Music-based Social Enterprise as a Response to Economic Inactivity', *Social Enterprise Journal* 3(1): 101–24.

Chell, E. (2007) 'Social Enterprise and Entrepreneurship: Towards a Convergent Theory of the Entrepreneurial Process', *International Small Business Journal* 25(1): 5–26.

Cohen, E. (1972). 'Towards a Sociology of International Tourism', *Social Research* 39(1): 164–82.

— (1979) 'Rethinking the Sociology of Tourism', *Annals of Tourism Research* 6(1): 18–35.

— (1988), 'Authenticity and Commoditization in Tourism', *Annals of Tourism Research* 15(3): 371–86.

Coleman, J.S. (1990) *Foundations of Social Theory*. Cambridge, MA: Harvard University Press.

Coleman, S. (2003) 'Community, Language and Culture', in C. Coulter and S. Coleman (eds) *The End of Irish History*, pp. 175–91. Manchester: Manchester University Press.

Convery, F. and Flanagan, S. (1996) *From the Bottom Up: A Tourism Strategy for the Gaeltacht*. An Daingean: An Sagart.

Copley, P. and Robson, I. (1996) 'Tourism, Arts Marketing and the Modernist Paradox', in M. Robinson, N. Evans and P. Callaghan (eds) *Culture as the Tourist Product, Tourism and Culture Towards the 21st Century*, pp. 15–34. Newcastle: University of Northumbria.

de Botton, A. (2002) *The Art of Travel*. Harmondsworth: Penguin.

De Graaf, N., De Graaf, P. and Kraaykamp, G. (2000) 'Parental Cultural Capital and Educational Attainment in the Netherlands: A Refinement of the Cultural Capital Perspective', *Sociology of Education* 73(2): 92–111.

Department of Rural, Community and Gaeltacht Affairs (2007) *Agreed Programme for Government Progress Report* [online]. Available: http://www.taoiseach.gov.ie/attached_files/RTF%20files/CommunityRuraland GaeltachtAffairsProgress07(1).rtf (last accessed 12 August 2009).

Dorado, S. (2006) 'Social Entrepreneurial Ventures: Different Values So Different Process of Creation, No?', *Journal of Developmental Entrepreneurship*, 11(4): 319–43.

du Gay, P. (1997) *Production of Culture/Cultures of Production*. London: Routledge.

Fáilte Ireland (2005) *Annual Report*. Dublin: Fáilte Ireland.

— (2007) *Cultural Tourism: Making it Work for You – A New Strategy for Cultural Tourism in Ireland* [online]. Available: http://www.failteireland.ie/Developing-Markets/Product-Marketing/Cultural-Tourism (last accessed 12 August 2009).

— (2009) *Cultural Tourism* [online]. Available: http://www.failteireland.ie/Developing-Markets/Product-Marketing/Cultural-Tourism (last accessed 12 August 2009).

Fleming, R. (2004) 'Resisting Cultural Standardization: Comhaltas Ceoltóirí Éireann and the Revitalization of Traditional Music in Ireland', *Journal of Folklore Research* 41(2/3): 227–57.

Gibb, A. and Scott, M. (1985) 'Strategic Awareness, Personal Commitment and the Process of Planning in the Small Firm', *Journal of Management Studies* 22(6): 597–631.

Gibson, C. and Connell, J. (2003) *On the Road Again: Music and Tourism*. Clevedon: Channel View Press.

Goffman, E. (1959) *The Presentation of Self in Everyday Life*. Harmondsworth: Penguin.

Haugh, H. (2005), 'A Research Agenda for Social Entrepreneurship', *Social Enterprise Journal* 1(1): 1–12.

Heidegger, M. (1962) *Being and Time* (trans. J. Macquarrie and E. Robinson). Oxford: Blackwell.

Hirsch, P. (1972) 'Processing Fads and Fashions: An Organisation-Set Analysis of Cultural Industry System', *American Journal of Sociology* 77(4): 639–59.

Holcomb, B. (1999) 'Marketing Cities for Tourism', in D. Judd and S. Finstein (eds) *The Tourist City*, pp. 54–70. New Haven, CT: Yale University Press.

Hughes, H. (1998) 'Theatre in London and the Inter-relationship with Tourism', *Tourism Management* 19(5): 445–52.

— (2000) *Arts, Entertainment and Tourism*. Oxford: Butterworth-Heinemann.

Hughes, H. and Allen, D. (2005) 'Cultural Tourism in Central and Eastern Europe: The Views of Induced Image Formation Agents', *Tourism Management* 26(2): 173–83.

Johnson, N. (1999) 'Framing the Past: Time, Space and the Politics of Heritage Tourism in Ireland', *Political Geography* 18(2): 187–207.

Keane, M. and Ó Cinnéide, M. (1986) 'Promoting Economic Development Amongst Rural Communities', *Journal of Rural Studies* 2(4): 281–9.

Kearns, T. and Taylor, B. (2003) *A Touchstone for the Tradition: The Willie Clancy Summer School*. Dingle: Brandon Publications.

Kerry County Council (2009) *Kerry County Development Plan 2009 to 2015* [online]. Available: http://www.kerrycoco.ie/en/allservices/planning/planspolicies/countydevelopmentplan2009-2015/thefile,2473,en.pdf (last accessed 12 August 2009).

Kerry County Development Board (2004) *County Kerry Tourism Research* [online]. Available: http://www.kerrycdb.ie/tourism.pdf (last accessed 12 August 2009).

Kneafsey, M. (2002) 'Cultural Geographies in Practice: Sessions and Gigs: Tourism and Traditional Music in North Mayo, Ireland', *Cultural Geographics* 9(3): 354–8.

Leadbeater, C. and Oakley, K. (1990) *The Independents: Britain's New Cultural Entrepreneurs*. London: Demos.

Lounsbury, M. and Glynn, M. (2001) 'Cultural Entrepreneurship: Stories, Legitimacy and the Acquisition of Resources', *Strategic Management Journal* 22(6/7): 545–64.

MacCannell, D. (1973) 'Authenticity: Arrangements of Social Space in Tourist Settings', *American Journal of Sociology* 79(3): 589–603.

— (1976) *The Tourist: A New Theory of the Leisure Class*. New York, NY: Schocken Books.

McCarthy, B. (2008a) 'Cultural Tourism Clusters: Experiences from Ireland', in Centre for Research into Regional Development (CRRED), conference presentation: 6th Rural Entrepreneurship and Rural Regional Development Conference 22–23 May 2008, University of Glasgow, Crichton Campus, Dumfries, Scotland.

— (2008b) 'Case Study of an Artists' Retreat in Ireland: An Exploration of its Business Model', *Social Enterprise Journal* 4(2): 136–48.

McGettigan, F. and Burns, K. (2001) 'Clonmacnoise: A Monastic Site, Burial Ground and Tourist Attraction', in G. Richards (ed.) *Cultural Attractions and European Tourism*, pp. 135–58. The Netherlands: CABI Publishing.

McIntosh, A. and Prentice, R. (1999) 'Affirming Authenticity: Consuming Cultural Heritage', *Annals of Tourism Research* 26(3): 589–612.

Mules, T. (2004) 'Case Study Evolution in Event Management: The Gold Coast's Wintersun Festival', *Event Management* 9(1/2): 95–101.

Music Board of Ireland (2002) *Shaping the Future: A Strategic Plan for the Development of the Music Industry in Ireland*. Dublin: Department of Arts, Sports and Tourism.

Myerscough, J. (1988) *The Economic Importance of the Arts in Britain*. London: Policy Studies Institute.

Ní Bhrádaigh, E. (2007) 'Sure Weren't We Always Self-sufficient, Didn't We Have to Be! Entrepreneurship in the Gaeltacht of Ireland', in L.P Dana and R.B. Anderson (eds) *International Handbook of Research on Indigenous Entrepreneurship*, pp. 211–31. Cheltenham: Edward Elgar.

Nicholls, J. (2000) 'Introduction', in J. Nicholls and S.J. Owens (eds) *A Babel of Bottles: Drink, Drinkers and Drinking Places in Literature*, pp. 9–20. Sheffield: Sheffield Academic Press.

Ó Cinnéide, B. (2005) 'Creative Entrepreneurship in the Arts', *Entrepreneurship and Innovation* 6(3): 151–8.

Ó Cinnéide, M. and Conghaile, M. (1990) 'Promoting Local Initiative through a Community Development Competition', *Journal of Rural Studies* 6(3): 325–9.

OECD (Organisation for Economic Co-operation and Development) (1999) *Social Enterprises*. Paris: OECD.

Pearce, P. and Moscardo, G. (1986) 'The Concept of Authenticity in Tourist Experiences', *Journal of Sociology* 22(1): 121–32.

Peredo, A. and McLean, M. (2006) 'Social Entrepreneurship: A Critical Review of the Concept', *Journal of World Business* 41(1): 56–65.

Portes, A. (1998) 'Social Capital: Its Origins and Applications in Modern Sociology', *Annual Review of Sociology* 24(1): 1–24.

Prentice, R. and Anderson, V. (2000), 'Evoking Ireland: Modelling Tourism Propensity', *Annals of Tourism Research* 27(2): 490–516.

Putnam, R.D. (1993) *Making Democracy Work: Civic Traditions in Modern Italy*. Princeton, NJ: Princeton University Press.

Quinn, B. (2005) 'Arts Festivals and the City', *Urban Studies* 42(5–6): 927–43.

— (2006) 'Problematising "Festival Tourism": Arts Festivals and Sustainable Development in Ireland', *Journal of Sustainable Tourism* 14(3): 288–306.

Rentschler, R. (2007) 'Painting Equality: Female Artists as Cultural Entrepreneurial Marketers', *Equal Opportunities International* 26(7): 665–77.

Richards, G. and Wilson, J. (2006) 'Developing Creativity in Tourist Experiences: A Solution to the Serial Reproduction of Culture?', *Tourism Management* 27(6): 1209–23.

Rolfe, H. J. (1992) *Arts Festivals in the UK*. London: Policy Studies Institute.

Scott, L. and Urry, J. (1994) *Economies of Signs and Space*. London: Routledge.

Seanor, P. and Meaton, J. (2007) 'Making Sense of Social Enterprise', *Social Enterprise Journal* 3(1): 90–100.

Smith, S. (2001) 'Irish Traditional Music in a Modern World', *New Hibernia Review* 5(2): 111–25.

Spivak, G.C. and Gunew, S. (1993) 'Questions of Multiculturalism' in S. Durning (ed.) *The Cultural Studies Reader*, pp. 193–202. London: Routledge.

Stevenson, H. and Gumpert, D. (1985) 'The Heart of Entrepreneurship', *Harvard Business Review* 63(2): 85–94.

Stocks, J. (2000) 'Cultural Tourism and the Community in Rural Ireland', in D. Hall and G. Richards (eds) *Tourism and Sustainable Community Development*, pp. 233–42. Routledge: Advances in Tourism Research.

Strachan, R. and Leonard, M. (2004) 'A Musical Nation: Protection, Investment and Branding in the Irish Music Industry', *Irish Studies Review* 12(1): 39–49.

Taylor, J. (2001) 'Authenticity and Sincerity in Tourism', *Annals of Tourism Research* 28(1): 7–26.

Urry, J. (1990) *The Tourist Gaze*. London: Sage.

Weiler, B. and Hall, C.M. (1992) *Special Interest Tourism*. Halstead Press: New York.

Weisbrod, B. (1998). *To Profit or Not to Profit: The Commercial Transformation of the Nonprofit Sector*. Cambridge: Cambridge University Press.

Wilson, J. (2002) 'An Holistic Approach to Tourist Place Image and Spatial Behaviour', unpublished PhD dissertation, School of Geography and Environmental Management, University of the West of England, Bristol.

Xiao, H. and Smith, S.L.J. (2004) 'Residents' Perceptions of Kitchener-Waterloo Oktoberfest: An Inductive Analysis', *Event Management* 8(3): 161–75.

Zografos, C. (2007) 'Rurality Discourses and the Role of Social Enterprise in Regenerating Rural Scotland', *Journal of Rural Studies* 23(1): 38–57.

Chapter 22

Twenty-First-Century International Careers: From Economic to Lifestyle Migration

Marian Crowley-Henry

INTRODUCTION

While many chapters in this book examine Ireland-specific research, reports and literature pertaining to contemporary Irish business and society, this chapter takes a different approach. It explores the contemporary career influences and preferences of highly educated knowledge professionals in Europe (Crowley-Henry 2008a), and considers the implications for present and future Irish business and society in the post-Celtic Tiger era. The concept of international careers in modern-day society is studied from a critical and individual, rather than a managerialist or policy, perspective. It investigates what 'career' means to people in the twenty-first century and suggests the ramifications of this for human resource practitioners.

While large proportions of Ireland's and other countries' populations have emigrated for economic, employment or pure survival reasons (Scally 1995; Schrier 1958; Thomas and Znaniecki 1996), findings from the study shared in this chapter consider a trend towards *lifestyle migration* (Crowley-Henry 2008a; Heffernan 2008; Schein 1990). There has been a noticeable shift from the *mass* emigration evident in the Europe of the past, to which Ireland was a very large contributor, to today's situation, in which highly qualified specialists are increasingly proactive in seeking out new markets for their *individual* professional and personal development (Heffernan 2008; Vandamme 2000; Yan *et al.* 2002). The research shared here explores an elite category of international assignees termed 'bounded transnationals' (Crowley-Henry 2009a), whose primary concern is the quality of life/lifestyle on offer in a particular host country environment, rather than a focus on objective career success.

Based on primary, qualitative, exploratory research, concerning a sample of bounded transnationals in the south of France (2002–2005), a career framework is presented that was induced from the findings, and delineates the relational, individual and economic influences on career preference and choice. While the study concerns a geographical case study in the south of France, the findings are discussed in light of the Irish situation: from the perspective of immigrants to Ireland and the modern-day emigrants from Ireland. The findings emphasise the requirement for organisations' human resource practitioners to develop human resource management strategies that open up and elaborate career management and planning beyond extrinsic elements.

The initial sections present the relevant literature from international human resource management and career theory. Next, the research methodology of the study is outlined briefly (for a more detailed discussion see Crowley-Henry 2009b). Then core findings are considered in light of the Irish situation. Finally, recommendations and suggestions for further research are expounded.

GLOBALISATION, LABOUR MOBILITY AND THE MIGRANT WORKER

Globalisation has brought about many changes, one being the growing number of multinational organisations in different host countries (Tregaskis 1998). It is accepted that business globalisation, and the increase in global competition, could have a direct impact on the staffing of expatriate managers (Harvey and Novicevic 2002). According to Patel (2002:18), the so-called 'brain drain', where highly skilled professionals emigrate to another country, has 'long been a byproduct of increased labour mobility and globalization'. Yan, Zhu and Hall (2002:385) postulate that 'as the overall level of globalization increases, the international experience of the average employee accumulates'. A global relocation survey predicts that the number of international assignments/assignees is a trend that will continue to increase (Windham International 2000). Labour mobility within the European Union (EU) is one of the founding pillars of the Maastricht Treaty, and labour mobility is encouraged in many Community policies (Vandamme 2000:446). Vandamme (2000:441) found there to be 5.5 million EU nationals living and/or working in another member state of the EU. These labour mobility developments confirm the need to examine migration in more detail. This chapter focuses on individual perspectives in order to throw light on the practice.

My study focuses on highly educated and skilled workers, as research has found that highly qualified professionals and specialists have become more positively disposed to migration (Vandamme 2000:441). Werner (1996) suggests that, within the EU, the demand for higher-skilled workers, graduates and professionals is rising, while the demand for lower-skilled workers is decreasing. Boswell (2005:5) confirms that European workers are 'more highly qualified than they were a decade ago'.

Saxenian's (1999, 2002) research focus has been centred on Silicon Valley immigrants, specifically highly skilled individuals who move to the west coast of the United States to undertake employment opportunities, primarily in the information technology (IT) profession. It is in this globalisation context that my investigation is set. Despite the boom and wealth from Ireland's Celtic Tiger, and net migration into Ireland over this period, a grouping in the population persists in leaving the country in search of a better life elsewhere. Indeed, given the demise of the Celtic Tiger, increasing numbers of Irish nationals are seeking opportunities internationally (Heffernan 2008). The geographical mobility of knowledge professionals that my study explores is thus most relevant to contemporary Ireland.

INTERNATIONAL HUMAN RESOURCE MANAGEMENT

Much has been written and published about the expatriation process and experience in international human resource management literature (e.g. Borg and Harzing 1995; Brewster and Scullion 1997; Dowling and Welch 2004; Dowling *et al.* 2008; Mendenhall *et al.* 1987; Scullion and Collings 2006; Tung 1998). There have been calls to widen the research on expatriates to incorporate different types of international assignees (Brewster and Suutari 2005; Scullion and Paauwe 2004; Scullion *et al.* 2007). My study responds to the call, at least in part, by focusing on a category of international assignee: the bounded transnationals.

Cultural issues, such as the international assignee's acculturation process (Berry and Sam 1997; Black and Mendenhall 1991), are not developed here as they have been explored elsewhere (see Crowley-Henry 2008b). Rather, the focus is on career drivers; that is, what influences an individual to remain in a host country and work under local, host country terms and conditions of employment. The literature (which has favoured the organisation-assigned expatriate who embarks on a temporary international assignment and is then relocated, still as an employee of the organisation, to the home country on completion of the assignment) stresses the relationship and social aspects that impact upon expatriate success or failure. Trailing spouses (Black and Stephens 1989; De Cieri *et al.* 1991; Harvey 1998; Stone 1991), children in education, dual careers (Harvey 1995, 1996, 1997, 1998) and family responsibilities are all considered as factors influencing the expatriate's assignment success. Such relationships are also assessed with specific regard to the bounded transnational's career preferences and choices.

While the organisation-assigned expatriate's temporary international assignment and its implications for his/her career have been examined to various degrees in international human resource management literature (Dowling and Welch 2004; Yan *et al.* 2002), there is a shortcoming in international career research with regard to the bounded transnational type, which is the focus of my research shared here.

Career Theory

Career has been defined as:

> the overall pattern of a continuous development process, by which an
> individual, via an interactive and interdependent relationship with an
> organizational environment, experiences and makes sense out of a sequence
> of critical events, activities and situations, through which competence is
> acquired, meaning is created, and projections for the future are made. The
> gradually unfolding career contains changes visible to others (the objective
> career) and changes in the individual's perception of her/his activities and
> identity (the subjective career). The two aspects form a duality, becoming
> inseparable. (Larsen and Ellehave 2000:104)

This section gives an overview of the literature on career theory and career
research in an international context. It outlines the range in career theory from
the organisational career to the boundaryless career, including the external (or
objective) and the subjective (more protean) career elements.

Traditional or orthodox career theory concerns the organisational career of
employees as they move vertically up the hierarchy of the organisation (Fletcher
1996). It has generally been applied to those employees currently in managerial
positions or with management potential (Fletcher 1996:109; Larsen and Ellehave
2000:90). The implication is that careers are linear (career ladder) and age/service-
related, unfolding in unchanging organisational settings (Fletcher 1996:109).
Whereas Whyte's (1956) 'organisational man' fits this theory, it is argued that
today's workforce is more distrusting of its employing organisations and leaders
(Keyton and Smith 2009; Rosenbaum and Miller 1996) as a result of initiatives
such as downsizing and mass redundancies (Larsen and Ellehave 2000:99).
Changes in the psychological contract (Gratton and Hope-Hailey 1999; Rousseau
1995), from more relational to transactional contracts, have prompted the
contemporary developments in career theory.

Contemporary literature argues that an elaboration and evolution of the
orthodox career model is required in order to take stock of the present-day realities
(Arthur and Rousseau 1996:7; Larsen and Ellehave 2000:89). While traditional
career theory has 'discounted the role of the person' and stressed 'the presumption
of employee dependence on the employer firm' (Arthur and Rousseau 1996:7), it
is contended that there is 'a move towards a more individualistic notion of careers'
(Gratton and Hope-Hailey 1999:79). Hall argues that organisations cannot be
responsible for an individual's career; that it is up to the person him/herself to
shape his/her career path (Hall and Associates 1996:318). This move towards
individualism on the employee's side is matched with a move toward flexibility
(and away from lifelong employment) on the organisational side (Gratton and
Hope-Hailey 1999:79). The move away from careers being organisationally

managed (Kahn 1996), to employees managing their own careers, has been critiqued (Hesketh 2003).

Sparrow and Hiltrop (1994:429) separate the internal and external career frames of reference into 'individual aspirations and occupational realities', where the 'internal career is generally described in terms of career orientations, career anchors, decisions between personal and professional life, dual-career marriages, and progress through psychological life stages'. The internal career, then, is the individual's subjective view about work life and his/her role in it (Van Maanen and Schein 1977). In comparison, the external or objective career is 'what can be seen and measured about an individual's working life' (Mallon 1995:12). Weick (1996:40) argues that future careers will be more concerned with the internal career dimension.

Rosenbaum and Miller (1996) consider the new environment in which careers are unfolding, in which company loyalty is in question, and in which employees move increasingly inter-organisationally. They see a movement toward the 'mobile worker' who is following a 'boundaryless career'. They explain this further, as follows:

> While the old company man moved up the company ladder, mobile workers move up any ladder onto which they can get a foot. They rise in their careers by hopping from firm to firm, with an eye toward ever-better positions, and the firms which employ them often benefit by gaining ambitious employees who bring new ideas, creativity, and the enthusiasm of new blood. (Rosenbaum and Miller 1996:350)

Arthur and Rousseau (1996:5) concur. To them, boundaryless careers refer aptly to those careers that do not evolve within a single organisation. It has been suggested that international assignees (including bounded transnationals and Irish migrants) are ripe for boundaryless careers (Inkson *et al.* 1997) given the international experience they amass while on international assignment. That international experience is valued by organisations other than their employing organisation, thus prompting their potential inter-organisational career moves.

A further development of career theory is the concept of the protean career (Hall and Harrington, 2004). The protean career is more concerned with the subjective or internal career dimensions, taking contemporary realities in the employment market into consideration, whereas it can be argued that the boundaryless career is influenced by objective career dimensions. With its focus on the individual and his/her role in transforming his/her own career path, Hall (1976: 201) describes the protean career as follows:

> The protean career is a process which the person, not the organization, is managing. It consists of all the person's varied experiences in education, training, work in several organizations, changes in occupational field, etc. . .

The protean person's own personal career choices and search for self-fulfilment are the unifying or integrative elements in his or her life. The criterion of success is internal (psychological success), not external. In short, the protean career is shaped more by the individual than by the organization and may be redirected from time to time to meet the needs of the person.

The emphasis is on internal or subjective success, rather than objective success (position, salary).

Where orthodox career theory has ignored the relevance of non-work related incidents in an individual's life that may shape his/her career ambitions (Hall and Harrington 2004; Larsen and Ellehave 2000:93), the significance of this area is becoming more recognised in career theory, particularly as traditional organisation career paths and/or opportunities are less typical (Parker 1996).

Schein (1978) formulated the concept of career anchors from his longitudinal study of alumni members of the Sloan School. He recognised that an 'occupational self-concept' developed as individuals acquired more and more self-knowledge in their early working lives. The career anchor has three parts: first, the self-perceived talents and abilities an individual has, which are based on real successes in different work settings; second, self-perceived motives and needs, which are based on opportunities for self-tests or self-diagnosis in actual situations and on feedback from others; and third, self-perceived attitudes and values, which are based on the actual relationship between the self and the norms/values of the organisation and work setting (Schein 1978:125). Schein (1978, 1990) empirically investigated whether different individuals have different career anchors and identified the following anchors under which individuals could be categorised:

- technical/functional competence
- general managerial competence
- security/stability
- entrepreneurial creativity
- autonomy/independence
- service/dedication to a cause
- pure challenge
- lifestyle.

Schein's (1978:126) research found that people's views of their careers differed, despite the sample being an arguably homogeneous group of graduates from a management school. The individual nature of careers is underlined. This finding is corroborated in the research I conducted among bounded transnationals. The complexity of factors, structural and agential, impacting upon an individual's career preferences is emphasised.

THE 'BOUNDED TRANSNATIONAL'

While international human resource management has focused on the traditional expatriate assignment as central to its field, my research on bounded transnationals develops the international career subject by focusing on non-host country nationals living and working of their own choice on a potentially permanent basis in another country. A qualitative exploratory research study of the international careers of a sample of international members of the workforce working and living on a potentially permanent basis in the south of France (around the Sophia Antipolis science and technology park) was undertaken over a three-year period (2002–2005). During this period, I was a member of the international community, which enabled the collection of contextual information from participant observation.

Taking international human resource management and career theory as the foundation literature disciplines, my research considers international careers inductively. My research findings, which are based on interviews with over fifty individuals, explore the motivations for embarking on and maintaining an international career in a host country for an indefinite period of time.

Core Findings

Given the depth of the study, the intention and focus here is simply to draw out findings relating to international careers as experienced by the sample in question. To provide a deeper description of the bounded transnational sample in this study, Table 22.1 (page 446) sub-divides the core sample of bounded transnationals based on the various explanations for residing in the south of France, as derived from the interview narratives. It should be noted that these sub-categories are depicted here in their ideal states. However, in practice (and evidenced in the empirical study), there is overlap between states, with some individuals potentially positioned in a number of sub-categories. In addition, it should be noted that individuals may re-position their rationale from sub-category to sub-category. Parallels between these findings and the motivations for migrants to remain resident in Ireland may be drawn. Equally, the table is relevant to Irish migrants, in potentially explaining the complexity involved in determining to stay in a host country.

Table 22.1 shows the various considerations that enter the decision-making process of individuals when assessing the option of remaining in France or returning to the home country, or indeed moving to a third country. As stated, these levels of analysis, which have been elicited from the researcher's interpretation of the interviews and labelled accordingly, overlap and are not exhaustive. However, they do demonstrate and deepen understanding regarding the complexity of concerns that impact upon the individual choice that is made. Of importance is that the work/job or objective career elements are just one component in the overall decision to remain resident in a host country environment. This underlines the necessity for human resource practitioners and organisations to reconsider career management programmes and widen their remit so that they include more extra-work elements.

In relation to Schein's (1978, 1990) career anchors, a key finding from the study conducted by the author found that the bounded transnational sample prioritise the lifestyle anchor over objective career success variables in the decision to remain resident in France. In particular, for the sample researched, the lifestyle on offer in the south of France, with the weather and environment, and the benefits of France's social policies (such as free schooling from the age of three and extended parental leave), came before any objective career ambitions. This was evident from members in the sample sharing that they had turned down offers of employment that would objectively enhance their careers in favour of remaining resident in the area. The host country lifestyle on offer to the individual and to his/her significant others (family, spouse, children) is considered a primary factor in the decision to remain in a host country potentially permanently. This is relevant for Irish business and society, where an increasingly knowledgeable workforce seeks to maximise the lifestyle anchor in collaboration with other objective and subjective career factors in determining the career path to follow. In an era that is witnessing the increasing international interdependence of nations, opportunities exist for Irish nationals to embark on international careers of a potentially permanent duration. Such a move may be for a myriad of reasons, not least of which are those of lifestyle. Similarly, Ireland, which has become home to thousands of migrants during the Celtic Tiger period, retains many of these migrants in the present days of recession, suggesting lifestyle as a rationale for their continued residency. In contemporary times, the economic situation (unemployment once again rearing its head), coupled with the increasingly free movement of workers cross-nationally, would suggest a growing propensity to migration for Irish and other nationals. The pull of the lifestyle on offer elsewhere is as relevant as the push of unemployment in the home country (Ireland).

While Table 22.1 presents the perceived justification for remaining resident in a host country environment, with the lifestyle anchor an underlying trend, it became clear from the narratives that a number of career influencers impact upon decision making (Crowley-Henry and Weir 2009). These influencers (career framework) include:

- the individual (unique characteristics of the person);
- the individual's stakeholders (e.g. family);
- the job in question (tasks, rewards) and the work environment (colleagues, policies);
- host country elements (amenities on offer, weather, environment); and
- the wider society (socio-cultural factors, such as the extent of the multicultural community, labour laws, minimum wage, maternity benefit, etc.).

Table 22.1 Sub-categorisation of bounded transnationals based on the rationale for residing in France

Label	Description	Informed by literature	Sample respondent
Cosmopolitan lifestyle	Craving the admiring glances of contemporaries; wanting to be perceived well by others in having a exotic lifestyle or image.	Schein (1990)	Tracy: 'I love that I am living where other people want to go on holidays', Lisa, Inge, Rick, Katharina, Donal, Vincent, Tim, John
Redemption lifestyle	Wanting to escape the commute, the media, the drinking culture in the home country. Difference is that they choose not to engage with negative aspects in the host environment. There is an element of rebirth, the 'phoenix', a new beginning in avoiding a self-destructive lifestyle; anti-'rat race'.	Schein's (1990) lifestyle anchor	Kate, Philip (commute); Steve (anti-media); Pat (anti-drinking culture)
Proving self	Wanting to be perceived by others as having made the right initial choice; not wanting to take a step back, looking-glass self. Pride.	Cooley's 'looking-glass self' (2003 [1902])	Sarah, Tracy, Natalie
Fear of return	The home country that they left has changed and moved on; a feeling that they would no longer fit in there without the need for readjustment.		Angie, Geraldine

Label	Description	Informed by literature	Sample respondent
Relational (home) / Relational (host)	This relates to the relationships in the home and/or host country between the individual and their significant other (parent, child, spouse), where the duty of care and an empathy with the significant other's desires is taken into consideration, such as offspring, a spouse – immediate family who don't want to move, who feel at home – that bind you to the place, whereas you may like to move yourself.		Tim, Billy, Sarah, Ronald (relational host – children); Catherine, Barry, Fiona, Philip, Milly, Shaun, Steve, Vincent, Gordon, Mark (relational host – spouse/partner), Susan, David (relational home – parents)
Life quality	Wanting to remain in order to enjoy the quality of life on offer.	Schein's (1990) lifestyle anchor	Kate, Donal, Lisa, Alice, Deirdre, Shaun, Natalie, Rick, Francis, Katharina, Tracy, Pat, Ronald, Diane, Hilda, Susan, Catherine, Tim
Home, integration	Feeling more at home in France than in home country.	Berry and Sam's (1997) assimilation	Sarah, Angie, Deirdre, Clare, Joe, Geraldine, Diane, Billy, Hilda
Tough adjustment	Not wanting to go through readjustment phase again.		Mary, Milly, Deirdre, Barry, Catherine
Job	Having a job in the area, equivalent of which one might not get in home country.		Elaine, Mark

Source: developed by author.

The factors impacting on career preference and choice are complex, and they overlap and impact upon each other. However, the findings show that many elements – of structural and agential control – impact upon career decisions. While the literature suggests a more individual approach to careers, in reality this is bounded by external relations and conditions in the wider environment, as well as by individual agential desires and ambitions. This calls for human resource practitioners, career planners and, ultimately, organisations to approach an individual's career from a more comprehensive and holistic perspective over his/her working career, as career preferences can alter. There is much scope for opportunity given the move toward proteanism, or adapting to work roles that better suit the other components of an individual's life at different periods of time. Organisations should continuously look within their own structures when deliberating on staffing, as individuals' career ambitions evolve in line with life and circumstance changes.

CONCLUSIONS

The objective career dimension (job title, financial reward, hierarchical ranking) has traditionally been the focus of practical human resource management initiatives concerning recruitment and retention of personnel. However, my research suggests that factors beyond the objective career dimension come into play in the decision-making process. A focus on a more comprehensive systems approach to careers is emphasised, an approach that involves encompassing subjective and objective career dimensions, as well as structural forces (such as the economic situation, labour market policies, childcare provision, etc.) and life stage elements.

The implications of my research findings for international human resource management and career management insist that a 'one size fits all' approach to careers is not sufficient. Career influencers have different weightings at different periods of time during an individual's career and life stage. A comprehensive approach to addressing the implications is required, where organisations offer flexibility throughout an employee's career so that the individual employee can choose which option is most suitable to her/his particular life circumstances at that period of time. Options should not be closed off should a particular path be chosen; rather they should persist, as changes in an individual's life or personal situation have been shown to be highly influential in career preferences (Hakim 2000) chosen at different points in time (Crowley-Henry 2007; Crowley-Henry and Weir 2007).

My study has examined the individual perspectives of a sample of bounded transnationals. This individual and sociological focus rather than the traditional managerial approach in international human resource management (IHRM) seeks to add to and widen the IHRM field. In exploring issues from an individual perspective, the complex nature of the field of international careers can be analysed in more detail. Career narratives present the myriad of issues that individuals consider and encounter in their career orientation. In addition, my study on bounded transnationals explores an under-researched category of the internationally mobile workforce, which is of relevance to human resource practitioners, employing organisations and society in general.

My findings have implications for further research opportunities, particularly with regard to comparing the sample residing in France to foreign residents wishing to remain long term in Ireland. It also has implications for educated Irish people who voluntarily choose to embark on an international life and career experience as lifestyle migrants, unlike their predecessors, who had to move internationally for economic or work reasons due purely to the poor economic situation in Ireland. Relational and structural influencers need to be considered in order to ascertain a more complete picture and assessment of individual career paths within (or outside) organisations.

Irish knowledge professionals were included in my research, which thus has resonance for Ireland's knowledge base, where highly educated professionals increasingly seek to better their quality of life by engaging in agential action and embarking on an international move of a potentially permanent duration. This has implications for the Irish economy, also, as it suggests the new 'brain drain' is from the more highly skilled categories of employees who leave Ireland for work and lifestyle reasons.

In addition, this research is valuable for foreign residents in Ireland – the skilled and highly educated migrants who have moved here. While many may initially have moved for economic or employment reasons, they may decide to remain in Ireland indefinitely. Factors including quality of life, global political and economic structures that impact on where the individual may find fair and quality employment and payment, the stakeholders (partner, children), who may not wish to be uprooted from where they now consider their home, need to be considered by organisations and policy makers in order to retain quality, skilled talent in Ireland.

References

Arthur, M.B. and Rousseau, D.M. (1996) *Boundaryless Careers*. Oxford: Oxford University Press.

Berry, J.W. and Sam, D.L. (1997) 'Acculturation and Adaptation', in J.W. Berry, M.H. Segal and C. Kagitçibasi (eds) *Handbook of Cross-Cultural Psychology: Vol. 3. Social Behavior and Applications*, 2nd edn, pp. 291–326. Boston, MA: Allyn and Bacon.

Black, J.S. and Mendenhall, M. (1991) 'The U-curve Adjustment Hypothesis Revisited: A Review and Theoretical Framework', *Journal of International Business Studies* 22(2): 225–47.

Black, J.S. and Stephens, G.K. (1989) 'The Influence of the Spouse on American Expatriate Adjustment in Overseas Assignments', *Journal of Management* 15(4): 529–44.

Borg, M. and Harzing, A.W. (1995) 'Composing an International Staff', in A.W. Harzing and J. Van Ruysseveldt (eds) *International Human Resource Management*, pp. 179–204. London: Sage.

Boswell, C. (2005) *Migration in Europe* [online]. Available: http://www.gcim.org/attachements/RS4.pdf (last accessed 4 September 2009).

Brewster, C. and Scullion, H. (1997) 'A Review and Agenda for Expatriate HRM', *Human Resource Management Journal* 7(3): 32–41.

Brewster, C. and Suutari, V. (2005) 'Global HRM: Aspects of a Research Agenda', *Personnel Review* 34(1): 5–21.

Cooley, C. H. (2003 [1902]) *Human Nature and Social Order*. New York, NY: Scribner's.

Crowley-Henry, M. (2007) 'The Protean Career: Exemplified by First World Foreign Residents in Western Europe?', *International Studies of Management and Organization* 37(3): 44–64.

— (2008a) 'International Knowledge Professionals. Contemporary Career Concerns and Implications', in E. Conway (ed.) *Proceedings, Irish Academy of Management 11th Annual Conference* [CD-ROM]. Dublin: Dublin City University.

— (2008b) 'A Narratives' Exploration of Non-traditional International Assignees Locally Resident and Employed in the South of France', paper presented at 4th Workshop on Expatriation, Las Palmas, Gran Canaria, 23–24 October.

— (2009a) 'Constructing Careers: An Interpretive Study of the Bounded Transnational Career', paper presented at Academy of Management Annual Meeting, Chicago, IL, 7–11 August.

— (2009b) 'Ethnography: Visions and Versions', in J. Hogan, P. Dolan, and P. Donnelly (eds) *Approaches to Qualitative Research: Theory and its Practical Application*, pp. 37–63. Cork: Oak Tree Press.

Crowley-Henry, M. and Weir, D. (2007) 'The International Protean Career: Four Women's Narratives', *Journal of Organizational Change Management* 20(2): 245–58.

— (2009) 'Control and the Protean Career: A Critical Perspective from the Multinational's International Assignees', in M. Voronov, J. Wolfram Cox, T. LeTrent-Jones and D. Weir (eds) *Critical Management Studies at Work: Multidisciplinary Approaches to Negotiating Tensions between Theory and Practice*, pp. 299–315. Cheltenham: Edward Elgar.

De Cieri, H., Dowling, P.J. and Taylor, K.F. (1991) 'The Psychological Impact of Expatriate Relocation on Partners', *International Journal of Human Resource Management* 2(3): 377–414.

Dowling, P.J., Festing, M. and Engle, A.D., Sr (2008) *International Human Resource Management*, 5th edn. London: Thomson.

Dowling, P.J. and Welch, D.E. (2004) *International Human Resource Management. Managing People in a Multinational Context*, 4th edn. London: Thomson Learning.

Fletcher, J.K. (1996) 'A Relational Approach to the Protean Worker', in D.T. Hall & Associates (eds) *The Career is Dead – Long Live the Career*, pp. 105–31. San Francisco, CA: Jossey-Bass.

Gratton, L. and Hope-Hailey, V. (1999) 'The Rhetoric and Reality of "New Careers"', in L. Gratton, V. Hope-Hailey, P. Stiles and C. Truss (eds) *Strategic Human Resource Management: Corporate Rhetoric and Human Reality*, pp. 79–100. London: Oxford University Press.

Hakim, C. (2000) *Work-Lifestyle Choices in the 21st Century. Preference Theory*. Oxford: Oxford University Press.

Hall, D.T. (1976) *Careers in Organizations*. Glenview, IL: Scott, Foresman.

Hall, D.T. and Associates (eds) (1996) *The Career is Dead – Long Live the Career: A Relational Approach to Careers*. San Francisco, CA: Jossey-Bass.

Hall, D.T. and Harrington, B. (2004) 'The Protean Career', in *A Sloan Work and Family Encyclopedia Entry* [online]. Available: http://wfnetwork.bc.edu/encyclopedia_template.php?id=249 (last accessed 4 September 2009).

Harvey, M. (1995) 'The Impact of Dual-career Families on International Relocations', *Human Resources Management Review* 5(3): 223–44.

— (1996) 'Addressing the Dual-Career Expatriation Dilemma in International Relocation', *Human Resource Planning* 19(4): 18–39.

— (1997) 'Dual-Career Expatriates: Expectations, Adjustment and Satisfaction with International Relocation', *Journal of International Business Studies* 28(3): 627–57.

— (1998) 'Dual-Career Couples during International Relocation: The Trailing Spouse', *International Journal of Human Resource Management* 9(2): 309–22.

Harvey, M. and Novicevic, M.M. (2002) 'The Hypercompetitive Global Marketplace: The Importance of Intuition and Creativity in Expatriate Managers', *Journal of World Business* 37(2): 127–38.

Heffernan, B. (2008) 'Young Families Emigrate as Brain Drain Grips Economy', *Irish Independent*, 8 September [online]. Available: http://www.independent.ie/business/irish/young-families-emigrate-as-brain-drain-grips-economy-1471409.html (last accessed 4 September 2009).

Hesketh, A. (2003) 'Employability in the Knowledge Economy: Living the Fulfilled Life or Policy Chimera?', Lancaster University Management School working paper [online]. Available: http://www.lums.lancs.ac.uk/publications/viewpdf/000191/ (last accessed 4 September 2009).

Inkson, K., Arthur, M.B., Pringle, J.K. and Barry, S. (1997) 'Expatriate Assignment Versus Overseas Experience: Contrasting Models of International Human Resource Development', *Journal of World Business* 32(4): 351–68.

Kahn, W.A. (1996) 'Secure Base Relationships at Work', in D.T. Hall and Associates (eds) *The Career is Dead – Long Live the Career*, pp. 158–79. San Francisco, CA: Jossey-Bass.

Keyton, J. and Smith, F.L. (2009) 'Distrust in Leaders. Dimensions, Patterns and Emotional Intensity', *Journal of Leadership and Organizational Studies* 16(1): 6–18.

Larsen, H.H. and Ellehave, C.F. (2000) 'Careers in Organizations', in C. Brewster and H.H. Larsen (eds) *Human Resource Management in Northern Europe: Trends, Dilemmas and Strategy*, pp. 89–124. Oxford: Blackwell.

Mallon, M. (1995) 'Careers and the Portfolio Worker', paper presented at the Strategic Direction of Human Resource Management Conference, Nottingham Trent University, Nottingham.

Mendenhall, M.E., Dunbar, E. and Oddou, G.R. (1987) 'Expatriate Selection, Training and Career Pathing: A Review and Critique', *Human Resource Management* 26(3): 331–45.

Parker, M. (1996) 'Review of Boje, D.M., Gephart, R.P. Jr. and Thatchenkery, T.J. (eds), Postmodern Management and Organization Theory', *Management Learning* 27(4): 490–4.

Patel, D. (2002) 'The Round-Trip "Brain Drain"', *HR Magazine* 47(7): 128.

Rosenbaum, J.E. and Miller, S.R. (1996) 'Moving In, Up, or Out: Tournaments and other Institutional Signals of Career Attainments', in M.B. Arthur and D.M. Rousseau (eds) *Boundaryless Careers*, pp. 350–69. Oxford: Oxford University Press.

Rousseau, D.M. (1995) *Psychological Contracts in Organizations. Understanding Written and Unwritten Agreements*. Thousand Oaks, CA: Sage.

Saxenian, A.L. (1999) *Silicon Valley's New Immigrant Entrepreneurs* [online]. Available: http://www.ppic.org/content/pubs/report/R_699ASR.pdf (last accessed 4 September 2009).

— (2002) *Local and Global Networks of Immigrant Professionals in Silicon Valley* [online]. Available: http://www.ppic.org/content/pubs/report/R_502ASR.pdf (last accessed 4 September 2009).

Scally, R.J. (1995) *The End of Hidden Ireland: Rebellion, Famine, and Emigration*. Oxford: Oxford University Press.

Schein, E.H. (1978) *Career Dynamics: Matching Individual and Organizational Needs*. Reading, MA: Addison-Wesley.

— (1990) *Career Anchors: Discovering Your Real Values*. San Francisco, CA: Pfeiffer and Co.

Schrier, A. (1958) *Ireland and the American Emigration, 1850–1900*. Minnesota: University of Minnesota Press.

Scullion, H. and Collings, D.G. (eds) (2006) *Global Staffing*. London: Routledge.

Scullion, H., Collings, D.G. and Gunnigle, P. (2007) 'International Human Resource Management in the 21st Century: Emerging Themes and Contemporary Debates', *Human Resource Management Journal* 17(4): 309–19.

Scullion, H. and Paauwe, J. (2004) 'International Human Resource
Management: Recent Developments in Theory and Empirical Research', in
A.-W. Harzing and J. Van Ruysseveldt (eds) *International Human Resource
Management*, 2nd edn, pp. 65–88. London: Sage.

Sparrow, P. and Hiltrop, J.-M. (1994) *European Human Resource Management in
Transition*. Hertfordshire: Prentice Hall.

Stone, R.J. (1991) 'Expatriate Selection and Failure', *Human Resource Planning*
14(1): 9–18.

Thomas, W.I. and Znaniecki, F. (1996) *The Polish Peasant in Europe and America:
A Classic Work in Immigration History*. Urbana, IL: University of Illinois Press.

Tregaskis, O. (1998) 'HRD in Foreign MNEs: Assessing the Impact of Parent
Origin versus Host Country Context', *International Studies of Management and
Organisation* 28(1): 136–63.

Tung, R.L. (1998) 'American Expatriates Abroad: From Neophytes to
Cosmopolitans', *Journal of World Business* 33(2): 125–44.

Vandamme, F. (2000) 'Labour Mobility within the European Union: Findings,
Stakes and Prospects', *International Labour Review* 139(4): 437–55.

Van Maanen, J. and Schein, E.H. (1977) 'Career Development', in J.R.
Hackman and J.L. Suttle (eds) *Improving Life at Work*, pp. 30–95. Santa
Monica, CA: Goodyear.

Weick, K.E. (1996) 'Enactment and the Boundaryless Career: Organizing as We
Work', in M. Arthur and D.M. Rousseau (eds) *Boundaryless Careers*, pp. 40–
57. Oxford: Oxford University Press.

Werner, H. (1996) 'Economic Integration and Migration: The European Case',
in J. van den Broeck (ed.) *The Economics of Labour Migration*, pp. 159–61.
Cheltenham: Edward Elgar.

Whyte, W. (1956) *The Organization Man*. New York, NY: Simon and Schuster.

Windham International (2000) *Global Relocation Trends: 2000 Survey Report*.
New York, NY: Windham International.

Yan, A., Zhu, G. and Hall, D.T. (2002) 'International Assignments for Career
Building: A Model of Agency Relationships and Psychological Contracts',
Academy of Management Review 27(3): 373–91.

Chapter 23

Achieving Growth in a Regional Economy: Lessons from Irish Economic History

John McHale

INTRODUCTION

In the year to April 2009, Ireland experienced net emigration of just under eight thousand people. While Ireland has a long history of population loss, 2009 was the first year with a net outflow since 1995. It also followed years of strong net immigration that had changed the face of Irish society. The return to net emigration was driven by both a large fall in immigration and a large rise in emigration, with much of the latter accounted for by earlier immigrants returning home – not all were construction workers. For young would-be Irish emigrants, opportunities were restricted by the global nature of the recession and difficulties in gaining legal access to some of the more preferred employment destinations. But, with signs that Ireland will lag behind the global economic recovery, there is concern that the very high unemployment levels for young Irish people – the number of under-25s on the live register rose from 33,300 in December 2007 to 84,400 in December 2009 – could feed a new emigrant flow.

Would a sustained return to net emigration matter? The relationship between migration and development is one of the great unsettled debates in Irish economic history, pitting optimists against pessimists (Williamson 1994). The optimists have pointed to the impressive catch-up of Irish to British wages in the decades following the Great Famine (e.g. O'Rourke and Williamson 2000). The pessimists have instead tended to focus on the poor post-independence performance of the Irish economy (e.g. Kennedy et al. 1988). The debate has been given new impetus by a related debate in development economics spurred by the dramatic increase in labour flows from poor to rich countries in recent decades. This new literature tends to a more optimistic portrait of today's more circulatory migration flows, emphasising such dimensions as the economic value of the diaspora, the spur from migration opportunities to human capital investments, and the sometimes transformative effects of returnees (Kapur and McHale 2005a).

For most countries, a recession-induced turn to limited net emigration should scarcely matter. One of the defining characteristics of the Irish economy, since at least the Great Famine, is that it functions more like a regional than a typical national economy. The distinction between a regional and a national economy turns on the degree of labour mobility across their borders. Irish people have shown themselves especially willing to move, though are hardly unique in this regard.[1] In their pioneering study of Irish economic growth, Frank Barry and his collaborators have highlighted how the combination of labour mobility and increasing returns in key internationally traded sectors can set off a process of cumulative causation where depopulation begets deindustrialisation, divergence and further depopulation (Barry 1999; see also Ó Gráda 1994, Chapter 13; and Whelan 1999). Such unfavourable dynamics appear to have been dominant until the 1950s. The turnaround came with the opening up of the economy, and in particular the adoption of a successful strategy for competing in a growing market for foreign direct investment (FDI). Ireland has now lost its cost advantage in the market for such investment. The government's 'smart economy' strategy aims to revive both foreign- and indigenous-sector growth by creating an effective national innovation system. While it might be thought that location is not critical for knowledge-intensive activities, recent evidence on knowledge industry agglomerations suggests that cities, once critical for reducing the costs of moving goods, are now most important for reducing the 'costs of moving people and ideas' (Glaeser 2008:8). Innovation-supporting regional economies provide the scale, diversity and connections that ensure access to knowledge (Agrawal et al. 2008). There is a danger that Ireland's fledgling 'smart economy' might never properly get off the ground if too many leave and others fail to come.

The rest of this chapter explores this risk from different angles. In the first section, I provide a very brief overview of Ireland's post-Famine demographic history. While the main story is one of dramatic depopulation, we see quite distinct phases of demographic development together with their correlations to economic performance. The next section revisits the debate between the optimists and the pessimists on the effects of Ireland's depopulation. The basic conclusion is that the effects of emigration can vary depending on the circumstances, but it is likely to be damaging to the development of industries where economies of scale are important. Then, in the following section, I take a brief detour to take account of recent international literature on the links between skilled migration and development. The new literature leans to more optimistic conclusions than the earlier work on the 'brain drain', highlighting the dynamic benefits of 'brain circulation'. The final section concludes with some speculations on policy implications.

A WHIRLWIND TOUR OF POST-FAMINE DEMOGRAPHIC HISTORY

Figure 23.1 shows the remarkable path Ireland's population (26 counties) has followed since the eve of the Great Famine. While Irish people exhibited distinctive patterns of high marital fertility, late marriages and high rates of permanent celibacy, migration developments have been the driving force behind the population's path. Of course, the Great Famine itself had a major direct impact, with an estimated one million people (32 counties) perishing from starvation and disease. The population was reduced by an estimated further million, however, through emigration and fewer births (Guinnane 1997). The resulting diaspora in turn helped integrate Ireland into global labour markets by reducing the costs of later emigration – what Hatton and Williamson (2005) call the 'friends and family' effect. Moreover, by raising the land–labour ratio, and thereby the incomes of those remaining behind, these immigrant flows helped to relieve a poverty constraint that had prevented the poorest from emigrating (Ó Gráda and O'Rourke 1997). The opportunities stemming from this integration appear also to have changed household institutions, underpinning a post-Famine shift to unitary inheritance and targeted dowries combined with significant emigration for the non-favoured siblings (Guinnane 1997). The result was sustained outflows over the second half of the nineteenth century. By 1901, the population (26 counties) had fallen to 3.22 million – a 51 per cent fall since 1841. At that time, those living in Ireland aged between 45 and 54 represented less than half of those born in Ireland between 1845 and 1851. While a significant number of the 'missing' had died, most had simply emigrated (Guinnane 1997).

Figure 23.1 Population of Republic of Ireland/26 counties, 1841–2006

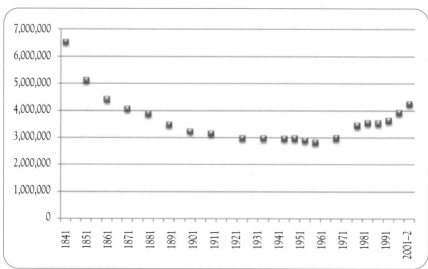

Sources: CSO; Daly (2006)

Net emigration continued as a central feature of the Irish economy through the first half of the last century, with the census-recorded population reaching its nadir in 1961 at 2.82 million (26 counties). In contrast to the decades following the Famine, no further progress was made in closing the income gap with the United Kingdom (UK), and substantial ground was lost to the fast-growing European economies (Kennedy *et al.* 1988). With net emigration peaking at an average of 42,000 between 1956 and 1961, the perception that the new Irish state was failing led to a change in economic strategy (Garvin 2004; Lee 1989). The new strategy had a number of elements – a shift towards 'productive' as against 'social-overhead' investment, a greater willingness to engage in deficit spending, and a (later) bolstering of human capital – but the biggest change was the shift from an inward-looking industrial strategy based on import substitution to one based on export promotion and the encouragement of FDI.

Figure 23.1 also shows the improved population performance in the 1960s and 1970s, as fewer Irish people found their best option in emigration, and many previous emigrants returned. Unfortunately, another economic crisis in the 1980s led to renewed emigration, this time caused by a combination of structural decline in labour-intensive indigenous industries and macroeconomic mistakes following the oil price shocks of the 1970s. Unlike the previous emigration episodes, the 1980s emigrants were highly educated, with the emigration rate for new graduates running at more than 20 per cent in the latter part of the decade.

Figure 23.2 Annual migration flows, April to April, 1987–2009

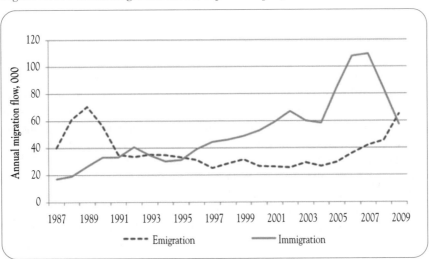

Source: CSO

Fortunes shifted again with the emergence of the Celtic Tiger economy of the 1990s. Figure 23.2 shows the fall in the number of emigrants. The figure also shows the emergence of a new phenomenon – substantial immigration. The inflow was initially dominated by returning Irish, but later broadened to include substantial flows from the new European Union (EU) states and from non-EU developing countries. At its peak in 2007, the immigrant inflow reached 110,000, leading to a significantly more diverse Irish society.

Figure 23.3 Contributions to population growth, April to April, 1987–2009

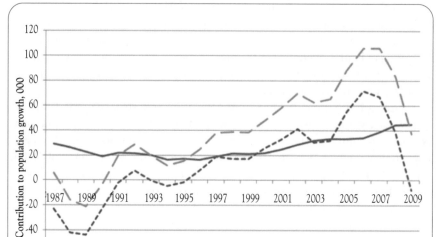

Source: CSO

It is too soon to tell whether the very recent return to net emigration is just a temporary fillip or the beginnings of another significant turn in Ireland's demographic story. Figure 23.3 shows that the net inflow came to an abrupt stop in the year to April 2009. The change reflects both a sharp fall in the immigrant inflow and a sharp rise in the emigrant outflow (thus far mostly returning immigrants). Despite the sharpness of the turnaround, the net outflow has been constrained by the global nature of the recession; employment opportunities may be poor in Ireland, but they are little better elsewhere. The UK, traditionally the most common destination for Irish emigrants, and, indeed, the main competing destination for immigrants, is also mired in recession. Where economic growth has held up better, notably in Australia and Canada, preliminary data shows substantial percentage increases in visas being granted to Irish nationals, though from a relatively low base. For now, the bigger concern relates to the probable large rise in the population 'at risk' for emigration. The Central Statistics Office's (CSO) Quarterly National Household Survey from Quarter 3, 2009, revealed that the number of young adults aged 20 to 24 in employment fell from 253,300 in July–September 2007 to 166,700 in the same period in 2009. There is little doubt that net emigration will increase if competing jurisdictions continue to lead

Ireland in economic recovery. The question I grapple with in the rest of the paper is how much it matters.

OPTIMISTS AND PESSIMISTS: MIGRATION AND IRELAND'S ECONOMIC DEVELOPMENT

Emigration and Post-Famine 'Catch-up'

An estimated four million people emigrated from Ireland (32 counties) between 1850 and 1914 (Ó Gráda 1994). While this might suggest a damaging loss of scale, it was in fact a period of impressive catch-up towards living standards in the leading economies of the day. Irish income per capita rose from two-fifths to three-fifths of the British level over the period (Ó Gráda 1994). Using a computable general equilibrium model, Hatton and Williamson (1998) have estimated that without emigration, income per capita would have been only 75–87 per cent of its actual level.[2] The impact on real urban wages is even more impressive: without emigration they estimate this wage would have been 66–81 per cent of its actual level. Surveying the literature on impacts of the Irish Famine on living standards, O'Rourke (1995:208) concludes that post-Famine emigration played a central role in raising living standards, which 'is at odds with traditional complaints that emigration was a hemorrhage which left the country weaker, draining it of youth and talent, and reducing the home market'.

This impressive catch-up is puzzling when viewed through the lens of increasing returns based growth theory, although it is consistent with models featuring decreasing returns. The real wage will decline in a model with decreasing returns as more labour is added to a fixed factor such as land. This process should also work in reverse, with the real wages of those remaining rising as the numbers working on the land are reduced.[3] According to Hatton and Williamson (2005:178) this is just the working of Smithian economics: '[w]hile the movers may have been able to escape to higher wages abroad, the now scarcer stayers found conditions improving at home'. The expert on Irish emigration to the United States, Arnold Schrier, reached a similar conclusion: 'there can be little doubt that the over-all impact of emigration on the Irish economy was generally favourable' and that 'it appreciably retarded the development of Irish industry is doubtful' (Schrier 1958:85). Kennedy, Giblin and McHugh (1988) agree that emigration raised living standards in the post-Famine period, but see in it the seeds of later failure. They compare the income advances to what happened in medieval Europe following the Black Death. The result was to raise the land to labour ratio, so that there was a substantial improvement in the standard of living of those survivors, but 'no real development or technical advances' (Kennedy et al. 1988:21).

While the evidence on convergence over this period is strong, the absolute and relative performance of the Irish economy was far from impressive over most of the following half century, raising the inevitable pessimist's question about the longer-term effect of the shrunken population. Between 1913 and 1960, Ireland's gross domestic product (GDP) per capita grew at an average compound rate of just 1.06 per cent, which compares to 1.16 per cent for Britain and 1.64 per cent for the United States (calculated from data in Maddison 1995), so that living standards diverged rather than converged.

Better Here Than There? Longer-term Implications of a Shrunken Population

With Ireland's poor economic performance through much of the last century as a background, it is worthwhile to consider possible channels through which emigration might have acted as a drag on longer-term development. I consider three: the short-circuiting of Irish urbanisation; the loss of the most enterprising; and a weakening of pressures for institutional reform.

From Irish Farm to Foreign City

The productivity improvements that come with moves from rural farms to urban factories have been everywhere central to modern industrialisation and growth. The urban growth literature has also emphasised the importance of 'agglomeration economies' to explain the productive pull of urban economies. These agglomeration economies include localised knowledge spillovers, the advantages of being able to spread fixed costs for specialised inputs and outputs (especially non-traded goods) and economies of scale in matching buyers and sellers (including employers and employees). Drawing on the work of Jane Jacobs (1984), Robert Lucas points to the existence of cities as prima facie evidence of the importance of human capital spillovers – without which we would expect 'cities to fly apart' (Lucas 2002:59).

Irish people did urbanise after the Famine. However, much of this urbanisation was from Irish farms to foreign cities. Timothy Guinnane (1997:121–5) sums up the post-Famine urbanisation experience:

The severity of Ireland's overall depopulation reflected two distinct forces. First, rural depopulation was especially pronounced. Second, the growth of Ireland's cities was so slow that they did not offset population losses in the countryside. . . . But the lack of urbanization does not mean that the Irish as a people did not become urban. Most Irish emigrants (at least in the post-Famine period) ended up as city dwellers in Britain or overseas. The difference between rural–urban migration in Ireland and in Germany during the late nineteenth century was that to become urban most Irish left their country. . . . If we include the Irish-born in urban centers in the United States, Canada and Australia, we would see that the Irish countryman or countrywoman moved to a city, but not an Irish city.

On the related process of industrialisation, Roy Foster (1988:371–72) puts it more sharply when he says that:

> Ireland's failure to industrialize is certainly connected with the removal of exactly the sector of the population that would otherwise have constituted an ex-rural workforce looking for relocation. It *was* relocated: but in the textile factories of Scotland and England; and the mines and railroads of North America.[4]

The weak contribution of domestic urbanisation to economic growth continued after independence. Paradoxically, part of the reason stems from an attempt to counter emigration through a rural bias in economic and social policy. Mary Daly (2006:73) has argued that the most effective way to secure a growing population would have been to provide opportunities in Irish rather than foreign cities, 'but this option was rejected as almost an equal evil to emigration'. The efforts to sustain rural life through such policies as transfer payments and decentralisation of industry were ultimately self-defeating. They followed a misplaced objective to stem the decline in the rural population: 'The objective should have been to reverse the decline in the overall population, yet by concentrating on rural Ireland and seeing rural and urban Ireland as opposites, government policies probably contributed to the overall decline in population' (Daly 2006:74).

Losing Innovators

It is not surprising that the relative characteristics of emigrants is controversial. It is often claimed that emigrants tend to be the ones with disproportionate talent and initiative – claims made to the understandable chagrin of the stayers. Although there is little direct evidence on the 'selectivity' of post-Famine Irish emigrants, Ó Gráda (1994:230) argues that 'common-sense intuition suggests some selection bias towards the more talented'. This view is consistent with international evidence that finds recent emigration flows from poorer to richer countries are strongly positively selected (Grogger and Hanson 2008).[5] Guinnane (1997:23) offers a more subtle evaluation of whether Ireland lost its most likely innovators. While noting that those remaining in Ireland were a 'residual population', he does not agree with those who argue 'that emigration took from Ireland the best and most adventuresome, leaving behind people less able and fit to develop the country'. Instead, he argues that those who wanted to live a different type of life are the ones who left: 'Irish people interested in innovative behaviour, in flouting conventional norms, were more likely to live in Irish-*America* or Irish-*Britain* than in Ireland itself.'

Even if it were not the case that it is the especially talented who are most likely to leave, emigration is concentrated among the young. The young, in turn, are likely to be drivers of change. Writing in 1988, at the time of high emigration of

Irish graduates, Kennedy, Gilbin, and McHugh (1988:147) also lament the likely impact of the absence of the young on innovation:

> The heavy loss among persons in their late teens and early twenties tended to make the society conservative and conformist. Debate and dissent, so vital to the life of any community, were dulled by the departure of persons at the very time when their ideas were liveliest and they might be expected to make their biggest contribution to renewal and regeneration.

It is noteworthy that graduate emigration had reached 25 per cent for men and 20 per cent for women at the time the above was written. For recent graduates, we only have anecdotal evidence on emigration rates. In areas such as nursing, it is clear that large numbers of recent graduates have emigrated given the significant demand for their skills, especially in the UK. More generally, the poor state of the jobs market internationally – and tough visa regimes for destinations outside the EU – have attenuated the post-graduation outflow. However, with signs that the world economy is significantly leading the Irish economy in the return to economic growth, the relative attractiveness of the emigration option is bound to increase.

Retaining the most innovative takes on added significance given the government's stated intention to pursue an innovation-focused growth strategy. The recent 'Smart Economy' strategy document states that central to the approach 'is building the innovation or "ideas" component of the economy through the utilisation of human capital—the knowledge, skills and creativity of people—and its ability and effectiveness in translating ideas into valuable processes, products and services' (DoT 2008:7). Improving the skill base of the economy is central to the strategy, with an emphasis on such areas as improving entrepreneurship, mathematical, science and language skills, expanding summer schools in science and engineering with an emphasis on innovation and commercialisation, and also fast-tracking visa arrangements for key researchers and highly skilled staff and their spouses. With employment prospects so poor for today's Irish graduates and skilled immigrants, there is a risk that many of the talented individuals who are envisioned as the foundation for the innovation economy could make their careers elsewhere.

Reforming Institutions

Recent work on the links between migration and development has emphasised causal channels working through institutional reform (e.g. Spilimbergo 2009). Emigration can affect both the demand for better institutions and also the supply of institution builders. On the demand side, the most productive may have the strongest interest in productivity-enhancing institutions, but also the best opportunities for leaving. On the supply side, emigration can strip an economy of specialised skills and leadership capacity. Hirschman (1970) has fruitfully applied his 'exit versus voice' framework to explore how potential and actual emigration can impact state-level institutional reform. The impacts are varied, with the balance itself varying by time and place. Perhaps most obviously, emigration can deprive the entity being left of its 'more activist residents, including potential leaders, reformers, or revolutionaries' (Hirschman 1986:90). On the other hand, emigration can also increase the bargaining power of the potentially footloose, or serve as a 'safety valve' against potentially damaging instability. Emigration can also be the signal of deep institutional malaise that spurs reform. All these effects have been visible at one time or another in Ireland's post-Famine institutional development.[6]

The Great Famine brought significant change to Ireland's rural economy. Most visibly, the emigration option was critical to changes in post-Famine household institutions, such as adoption of practices of unitary inheritance, late marriages, and high marital fertility (Guinnane 1997).[7] Being able to send young adults overseas allowed Irish parents to have larger families, while keeping farms intact and still providing reasonably equal opportunities for all their children. Lee (1989) sees such institutional developments as part of a broader effort by a shocked society to achieve economic security following the Famine. In facilitating such land-based security, however, the emigration option underpinned the dominance of what Lee calls the possessor over the performance ethos in Irish society, which he sees hampering the emergence of a non-agricultural-based enterprise culture well into the last century.

While these institutional adaptations might have been functional in the post-Famine decades, at least at the individual rural household level, there is reason to believe they did damage by short-circuiting urbanisation and reinforcing a culture of rural conservatism. Daly (2006) has also documented how the rural-dominated institutions inherited by the new Irish state led to a conservative policy bias that impeded industrialisation, and paradoxically contributed to the very depopulation – including rural depopulation – that policy makers said they were trying to reverse.

Other historians see evidence of the 'safety valve' function of emigration in the post-Famine decades. Fitzpatrick (1989:174) sees Ireland's 'apparent stability' as 'dangerously dependent on population drainage through emigration'. Any stoppage of this safety valve would, he argues, have led to 'frustrated young people competing for survival in Ireland's congested marriage and employment markets' (Fitzpatrick 1989:175). Interestingly, the weakening of the emigration option during the American recession of the 1870s and during the First World War was coincident with the unrest of the land wars and the rising. Lee (1973:68) concurs, noting the American slump of the 1870s creating in the countryside a 'pool of potential activists' left with time on their hands. While the emigration safety valve might allow a society to blow off steam, it might also relieve pressure and thus democratic reform. Hirschman (1978:103) also raises the possibility that emigration might create space for a more peaceful democratic transition, pointing as possible beneficiaries to Greece, Portugal and Spain in the 1960s and 1970s. Each experienced large-scale emigration, which may have made it easier to negotiate the difficult passage to democracy.

Finally, emigration, particularly when perceived as engendering a population sustainability crisis, can be a spur to reform. As already noted, the emigration crisis of the 1950s is a clear example, indeed one focused on by Hirschman (1981) himself. The increasing concerns that

> Ireland was a dying country . . . led to calls for new economic policies, the adoption of various plans by the different political parties, the appearance of emigration as an issue in a parliamentary election for the first time, and finally the unopposed acceptance (in 1958) of a national economic plan designed to develop Ireland and prevent emigration. (Hirschman 1981:261)

How would a return to sustained emigration, especially of the young and well educated, affect institutional development today? In the wake of a property bubble-induced economic crisis, there are already voices calling for radical reforms of Irish institutions that are perceived as failing Irish society (e.g. O'Toole 2009). As the demographic group that has suffered most from the crisis and as 'outsiders' when it comes to many existing institutional privileges, young adults should be a strong voice for institutional reform if they stay. They also have the skills and energy to modernise public- and private-sector organisations. At least in the short run, it is less obvious that their leaving would put substantial pressure on government for reform. By lowering the unemployment rate, the old 'safety valve' effect is more likely to dominate.

BRAIN CIRCULATION: A NEW VIEW ON MIGRATION AND DEVELOPMENT

Post-Famine emigration tended to be a permanent affair. With greatly lowered transportation and communication costs, today's internationally mobile workers are more likely to be 'circulating pools' than the 'stagnant emigrant pools' of old, and so better connected to both host and home societies. Indeed, the recent international migration literature tends to a more optimistic stance than the earlier 'brain drain' literature. The new view, which can sometimes go too far in ignoring the costs of absence (e.g. Kapur and McHale 2005a), stresses the advantages of gross flows – with people coming and going – and sustained connections, rather than the net losses that were the dominant concern in the older literature.

The new view recognises that both domestic and diaspora human capital are valuable to the domestic economy in a world where people retain connections to their former homes. First, the diaspora can be a source of capital, enterprise and ideas. Members of the diaspora can also serve as 'reputational intermediaries', facilitating transactions in the face of difficulties contracting across borders and helping to improve the 'profile' of the home economy abroad (Kapur and McHale 2005b).[8] Second, adopting a dynamic view of emigration, the 'brain gain' literature emphasises how the prospect of emigration can increase the expected return on human capital. If a sufficiently large number of those making these investments choose not to leave, the net result can actually be an increase in the stock of domestic human capital.[9] Third, given that people circulate, a fraction of the domestic stock will have spent time abroad. To the extent that they return with enhanced skills, savings, connections, and ideas, this enhances economy's human and social capital.

Looking back to Ireland's last bout of large-scale emigration in the 1980s, it is now easier to see it as a relatively more benign economic phenomenon than it seemed at the time. Given the willingness to return once opportunities opened up at home, the emigrant stock could be tapped as a ready source of skilled labour supply that helped sustain the Celtic Tiger economy.[10] But can we be confident the same will happen this time round? While there is little doubt that emigration brings benefits, it is unlikely that the benefits outweigh the direct costs of absence unless there is significant return. Such return is only likely if there is a significant economic turnaround. While we have good reason to expect a return to strong growth, the evidence from regional growth studies points to the link between initial human capital and subsequent growth (e.g. Glaeser 2008). The concern is that thinning human capital through emigration makes a virtuous growth cycle less likely. Growth turned around *despite* high emigration in the 1980s. A key reason was the under-utilisation of Irish human capital-created opportunities for multinational businesses to combine their organisational and technological know-how with competitively priced Irish skilled workers. This competitiveness has been substantially eroded in recent years due to strong wage gains and growing competition for FDI from the new EU states. While we can hope that a growth turnaround would bring young Irish people back before they put down roots elsewhere, this is not guaranteed.

CONCLUSION

When there are advantages to scale, regional economies are susceptible to both vicious and virtuous cycles. These cycles might go some way to explaining the instability of Irish growth over the last 150 years. The economy is now adjusting to the ending of a period of rapid economic growth, the latter stage of which was propelled by a property price and a related construction bubble. This chapter has argued that one risk the economy faces is that a loss of scale through recession-induced net emigration will make it harder to achieve competitive advantage in the innovation-intensive sectors the government is targeting in its new growth strategy.

Even accepting this risk, it is not obvious that there are substantial implications for policy in the short term. As already noted, the sudden shift to net emigration reflects the recession, which the government is compelled to counter regardless of the longer-term risk of falling into a another vicious cycle of population loss and slower growth. This longer-term risk, however, might alter the balance of costs and benefits of certain policy responses. I conclude by briefly considering possible implications for three policy areas: fiscal, labour market activation, and immigration.

The recession has caused a very rapid and pronounced deterioration in the public finances. With government debt rising rapidly as a share of the economy and sovereign bond spreads rising, the government began a large fiscal adjustment in mid-2008. Taking together the measures taken up to December 2009, the discretionary adjustment equals 7.5 per cent of GDP. While the move to stabilise the public finances has reduced fears of a catastrophic loss of national creditworthiness, most economic commentators believed it reduced demand and thus deepened the recession. However, many believe this is also a price worth paying to stabilise the public finances. Could the government have retained the confidence of the sovereign debt markets without such a large fiscal adjustment? There is considerable international evidence that adjustments based on cutting current expenditure tend to be better sustained and less contractionary than adjustments based on cutting capital expenditure and raising taxes. This suggests the government was right to focus on cuts to the public sector pay and social welfare bills in its December 2009 budget. But, with such cuts in place, there should have been more scope to limit cuts to capital spending and even to pursue some targeted tax-based stimulus. To the extent that a less contractionary overall policy would limit the increase in unemployment, this in turn would limit the increase in the population at risk for emigration.

One role of active labour market and education policies is to provide young people with opportunities to wait out the recession, building useful skills at home rather than as emigrants. While the record of active labour market policies is mixed, even modest effects could make these policies worthwhile if they limit what could become permanent losses through emigration. With a large cohort sitting for their leaving certificate and jobs scarce, it is predicted that the demand (and points) for higher education places will be high in 2010. It is challenging in the short run to expand places in colleges and universities. But such expansion is necessary to provide reasonable alternatives to emigration for young people who find their labour market entry now blocked.

Finally, the government should resist the understandable temptation to sharply restrict immigration opportunities for non-EU citizens. Given the large wage gaps that exist between Ireland and developing countries, there will continue to be an excess supply of willing immigrants despite the recession. There is some risk that a larger stock of non-EU immigrants will be partially offset by emigration of other groups. But, over the longer term, their presence should enhance the scale, diversity and international connectedness of the Irish labour force.

Notes

1 Other small countries close to large high-income labour markets also show high degrees of labour mobility. Jamaica provides one of the more dramatic examples. More than 80 per cent of Jamaican-born people with higher education live in an OECD country (Docquier and Marfouk 2005).

2 This estimate is based on the assumption of internationally immobile capital. The impact of emigration is smaller when capital is allowed to move towards labour, with income per capita equal to 91–95 per cent of its actual level.

3 The impact on income per capita is more subtle in the standard decreasing returns to labour model. Once fixed factors are included, emigration will typically reduce income per capita while raising the real wage. Income per capita in the economy could still rise if the other factors are not resident in the economy (e.g. absentee landlords).

4 Interestingly, Jane Jacobs was sceptical that moves from the countryside to the city would improve the lot of those remaining in the latter:

> What I am concerned with here is not the destinations of migrants, but rather the regions they abandon and how these regions are affected by people leaving. The most striking fact is that abandonment has no effect upon stagnant economies – other than to shrink them. (Jacobs 1984:73)

One of the examples she offers is that of Wales, which lost one-third of its population between 1921 and the mid-1980s. Rural emigrants bypassed the 'inert little city of Cardiff . . . and so, most people seeking city work or better incomes left Wales entirely' (Jacobs 1984:72).

5 Grogger and Hanson (2008) start from the observation that bilateral emigrant stocks are pervasively positively selected. To explain this fact, they develop a linear utility version of the classic Roy model. A key result from the model is that the nature of selection depends on the sign of the absolute difference between the skilled wage and unskilled wage gaps between the receiving and sending countries. Since the skilled wage gap tends to be larger, bilateral migration flows are overwhelmingly positively selected.

6 Based on cross-national evidence, Li and McHale (2009) provide evidence that higher emigration rates are associated with greater political stability (suggesting the importance of the safety valve function) but negative related to various measures of the quality of economic institutions, probably reflecting both demand- and supply-side effects.

7 'Emigration reflects the pull of a better life abroad, and this better life made it easier for parents and children to agree that farms in Ireland would not be divided' (Guinnane 1997:22–3).

8 The literature contains suggestive case studies on the role of diasporas in jumpstarting technology industries. However, relatively little work has focused on the key trade-off: are a poor country's scarce skilled workers more valuable at home or abroad? Or, put in terms of our stock flow model, is a member of the

diaspora stock more or less valuable than a member of the domestic stock? In Agrawal, Kapur and McHale (2008), we develop a model in which innovation depends on knowledge access and knowledge access partly depends on membership in networks. We allow for both co-location and diaspora networks. A necessary condition for the movement of an innovator to the diaspora to increase knowledge access of domestic innovators is that the diaspora knowledge access effect is stronger than the co-location effect. This could happen if emigration is associated with positive productivity effects combined with continued strong ties with those remaining at home. We find, however, that the diaspora effect is actually considerably weaker than the co-location effect. This suggests that emigration harms knowledge access, i.e. the diaspora effect does not make up for the effect of thinning local knowledge access.

9 The possibility of such an investment-induced brain gain has been a major focus in the recent theoretical literature on migration and development (Beine et al. 2001). More recently, the possibility of an overall positive effect on domestic human capital has received qualified empirical support. Beine, Docquier and Rapoport (2008) find that countries with low levels of human capital and low emigration rates experience a 'beneficial brain drain', but that more countries are net losers than are net gainers. Chand and Clemens (2008) examine a quasi-natural experiment from Fiji. Post-1987, political instability in Fiji caused the Indian population to be 40 per cent below its pre-1987 trend. Indians were driven to emigrate by political events they saw as adverse to their interests. The political instability thus affected the prospect of emigration for Indians, leading to quasi-natural experiment. Although careful to emphasise that this is a single case study, Chand and Clemens find the high emigration rate for Indians was associated with increases in the stock of Indian human capital in Fiji. Schiff (2005) provides a more sceptical view on the possibility of an overall 'brain gain'.

10 Barrett and O'Connell (2001) provide evidence of a wage premium for returning emigrants compared to observationally identical domestic workers. This suggests that time abroad helped enhance the human capital of returnees.

References

Agrawal, A., Kapur, D. and McHale, J. (2008) 'Brain Drain or Brain Bank: The Impact of Skilled Emigration on Poor-Country Innovation', Working Paper No. 14592, National Bureau of Economic Research, Cambridge, MA.

Barrett, A. and O'Connell, P. (2001) 'Is There a Wage Premium for Returning Irish Migrants?', Economic and Social Review 32(1): 1–21.

Barry, F. (1999) Understanding Ireland's Economic Growth. London: Macmillan.

Beine, M., Docquier, F. and Rapoport, H. (2001) 'Brain Drain and Economic Growth: Theory and Evidence', Journal of Development Economics 64(1): 275–89.

— (2008) 'Brain Drain and Human Capital Formation in Developing Countries: Winners and Losers', *Economic Journal* 118(528): 631–52.

Chand, S. and Clemens, M. (2008) 'Skilled Emigration and Skill Creation: A Quasi-Experiment', Working Paper No. 152, Center for Global Development, Washington, DC [online]. Available: http://www.cgdev.org/content/ publications/detail/123641 (last accessed 2 February 2010).

CSO (Central Statistics Office) (2009) *Quarterly National Household Survey* (3). Dublin: Central Statistics Office.

Daly, M. (2006) *The Slow Failure: Population Decline and Independent Ireland, 1920–1973*. Madison, WI: University of Wisconsin Press.

Docquier, F. and Marfouk, A. (2005) 'Measuring the International Mobility of Skilled Workers (1990–2000) – Release 1.0', Working Paper No. 3381, World Bank, Washington, DC [online]. Available: http://www-wds.worldbank.org/ external/default/WDSContentServer/IW3P/IB/2004/09/22/000160016_20040 922150619/Rendered/PDF/wps3381.pdf (last accessed 2 February 2010).

DoT (Department of the Taoiseach) (2008) *Building Ireland's Smart Economy: A Framework for Sustainable Economic Renewal*. Dublin: Stationery Office.

Fitzpatrick, D. (1989) 'Ireland Since 1870', in R. Foster (ed.) *The Oxford History of Ireland*, pp. 174–229. Oxford: Oxford University Press.

Foster, R. (1988) *Modern Ireland: 1600–1972*. London: Penguin.

Garvin, T. (2004) *Preventing the Future: Why Was Ireland So Poor for So Long?* Dublin: Gill & Macmillan.

Glaeser, E. (2008) *Cities, Agglomeration, and Spatial Equilibrium*. Oxford: Oxford University Press.

Grogger, J. and Hanson, G. (2008) 'Income Maximisation and the Selection and Sorting of International Migrants', Working Paper No. 13821, National Bureau of Economic Research, Cambridge, MA.

Guinnane, T. (1997) *The Vanishing Irish: Households, Migration, and the Rural Economy in Ireland, 1850–1914*. Princeton, NJ: Princeton University Press.

Hatton, T. and Williamson, J. (1998) *The Age of Mass Migration: Causes and Economic Impact*. Oxford: Oxford University Press.

— (2005) *Global Migration and the World Economy: Two Centuries of Policy and Performance*. Cambridge, MA: MIT Press.

Hirschman, A. (1970) *Exit, Voice, and Loyalty*. Cambridge, MA: Harvard University Press.

— (1978) 'Exit, Voice and the State', *World Politics* 31(1): 90–107.

— (1981) *Essays in Trespassing: Economics to Politics and Beyond*. Cambridge: Cambridge University Press.

— (1986) *Rival Views of Market Society and Other Recent Essays*. Cambridge, MA: Harvard University Press.

Jacobs, J. (1984) *Cities and the Wealth of Nations: Principles of Economic Life*. New York, NY: Vintage Books.

Kapur, D. and McHale, J. (2005a) *Give Us Your Best and Brightest: The Global Hunt for Talent and its Impact on the Developing World*. Washington, DC: The Brookings Institution Press/Center for Global Development.

— (2005b) 'Sojourns and Software: Internationally Mobile Human Capital and High Tech Industry Development in India, Ireland and Israel', in A. Arora and A. Gambardella (eds) *From Underdogs to Tigers: The Rise and Growth of the Software Industry in Some Emerging Economies*, pp. 236–74. Oxford: Oxford University Press.

Kennedy, K., Giblin, T. and McHugh, D. (1988) *The Economic Development of Ireland in the Twentieth Century*. London: Routledge.

Lee, J. (1973) *The Modernisation of Irish Society: 1848–1918*. Dublin: Gill & Macmillan.

— (1989) *Ireland 1912–1985: Politics and Society*. Cambridge: Cambridge University Press.

Li, X. and McHale, J. (2009) 'Emigrants and Institutions', paper presented at the Second World Bank Conference on Migration and Development, Washington DC, September.

Lucas, R. (2002) *Lectures on Economic Growth*. Cambridge, MA: Harvard University Press.

Maddison, A. (1995) *Monitoring the World Economy: 1820–1992*. Paris: OECD.

Ó Gráda, C. (1994) *Ireland: A New Economic History, 1780–1939*. Oxford: Clarendon Press.

Ó Gráda, C. and O'Rourke, K. (1997) 'Migration as Disaster Relief: Lessons from the Great Irish Famine', *European Review of Economic History* 1:3–25.

O'Rourke, K. (1995) 'Emigration and Living Standards in Ireland Since the Famine', *Journal of Population Economics* 8(4): 407–21.

O'Rourke, K. and Williamson, J. (2000) *Globalisation and History: The Evolution of a Nineteenth-Century Atlantic Economy*. Cambridge, MA: MIT Press.

O'Toole, F. (2009) *Ship of Fools: How Stupidity and Corruption Sank the Celtic Tiger*. London: Faber and Faber.

Schiff, M. (2005) 'Brain Gain: Claims about its Size and Impact on Welfare are Greatly Exaggerated', in C. Özden and M. Schiff (eds) *International Migration, Remittances, and the Brain Drain*, pp. 201–26. Washington, DC: World Bank and Palgrave Macmillan.

Schrier, A. (1997 [1958]) *Ireland and the American Emigration, 1850–1900*. Chester Spring, PA: Dufour Editions.

Spilimbergo, A. (2009) 'Democracy and Foreign Education', *American Economic Review* 99(1): 528–43.

Whelan, K. (1999) 'Economic Geography and the Long-Run Effects of the Great Irish Famine', *Economic and Social Review* 30(1): 1–20.

Williamson, J. (1994) 'Economic Convergence: Placing Post-Famine Ireland in Comparative Perspective', *Irish Economic and Social History* XXI: 1–27.

Chapter 24

The Europeanisation of Irish Public Policy: Theoretical and Comparative Perspectives

Kate Nicholls

INTRODUCTION

On my first research trip to Ireland as a foreign doctoral student in 2003, I spoke to a taxi driver about my central research question as it was then framed: How had Ireland seemingly taken better advantage of European Union (EU) membership than many other similar countries? Understanding this as a question simply about how Ireland had been able to attract such a high level of support in terms of the EU's Structural Funds, my driver had an immediate answer to my question: 'Ah, well that's because *our* people know how to talk to the people in Brussels.' While there may be something in this, as a social scientist who is primarily concerned with political institutions, processes and decision making at the national level, I was and remain convinced that fully embracing EU membership through gradual, but significant, policy adjustment hinges on underlying and often pre-existing domestic factors, such as the relationship between interest groups and the state, and the institutions and processes that shape this relationship. While such features of national politics may be affected by European integration, many basic characteristics of this state–society relationship were established in Ireland well before the country joined the EU. This chapter elaborates on some of these themes by drawing on the broader theoretical and comparative literature on the Europeanisation of public policy in EU member states in order to identify some of the factors that have facilitated domestic adjustment in the Irish case.

The following discussion is broken into four main sections. The first considers the concept of 'Europeanisation', a term increasingly employed by social scientists to both describe and theorise about the impact of regional integration on EU member states. It draws especially on recent developments in the discipline of political science, highlighting the multiple ways in which individual countries adjust to Europe and pointing out, in particular, the differences between 'top-down' and 'bottom-up' processes of Europeanisation. The second section gives an overview of what political scientists think we know so far about the factors that either facilitate or hinder national-level policy Europeanisation, identifying which of these variables seem particularly pertinent to the Irish case. In sections three and four, I discuss a set of possible facilitating factors that is often neglected by the general literature on policy Europeanisation, as well as the literature on Ireland more specifically: the way in which the state consults with and incorporates societal interest groups. Part of my explanation for the relatively successful Europeanisation of Irish public policy rests on the prior existence of a policy-making tradition that effectively balances both consultative and incorporative elements. I explain why this balance between consultation and incorporation is important, and how Ireland's consensus-oriented political culture has provided a good foundation on which to build such a policy-making tradition. These features of the Irish Europeanisation experience become especially apparent when Irish outcomes are contrasted with other, similarly small and politically centralised, EU member states. Throughout the following analysis, I attempt to pinpoint exactly what political science as a discipline, and the sub-field of comparative politics specifically, brings to this debate.

DIMENSIONS OF PUBLIC POLICY EUROPEANISATION

Until the mid-1990s, most students of the EU focused on explaining the scope and pace of regional integration and describing the new supra-national institutions that evolved as a result of this process. According to this research agenda, the politics of individual member nations were primarily of interest as factors impacting on outcomes at the European level. In other words, domestic politics was of main importance only to the extent that it determined decisions and developments at the supra-national level, so that the process of integration was often viewed as a power game played out between the interests of larger member states, such as France, Germany, and the United Kingdom. More recent work in the field, however, turns this 'causal arrow' around, so that the focus is on the ways in which decisions made at the European level or, more generally, the dynamics of integration influence the political, economic and cultural shifts experienced by and within individual member states. This burgeoning literature is built around the concept of 'Europeanisation', and much effort has gone into identifying the factors that facilitate or hinder the Europeanisation of countries that are subject to this process.

What exactly do we mean by Europeanisation? Presenting a concise answer to this question is not an easy task, not only because the concept usually means something quite different to those working *across* different academic disciplines, but also since the interpretation of the concept is widely contested *within* particular disciplines. Among the different interpretations drawn from anthropology, sociology and cultural studies include: the exportation of European values and institutions to non-European countries; the extent to which 'Europe' is becoming a more unified and stronger cultural and political entity; or shifting cultural attitudes within EU member states (Borneman and Fowler 1997; Olsen 2002). Within the discipline of political science, however, there is an increasing consensus on what we mean by the concept. Generally speaking, Europeanisation refers to the degree to which being party to the process of regional integration and interacting with European-level institutions changes the *politics* or *policy decisions* of individual member states. There are thus two major strands of research here. The first focuses on the Europeanisation of national political institutions and norms, including bureaucratic structures and cultures, patterns of political party competition and interest group behaviour. The second strand concentrates on the impact that interacting with EU institutions, and being subject to EU laws, directives and regulations in particular, has on changes in national public policy decisions and outcomes. Yet, because a general conclusion drawn by political scientists is that public policies have been 'Europeanised' much more extensively than national political institutions as a result of regional integration, it is not surprising that most have concentrated on the latter, nor is it surprising that this is the most developed field in the discipline as a whole. It is for this reason that this chapter centres its analysis on the Europeanisation of public policy in Ireland from a theoretical and comparative perspective.

While limiting this analysis to policy Europeanisation only, and excluding any other meanings of the term, there remains a myriad of ways in which EU membership influences national-level policy outcomes. One helpful way to distinguish between some of these is to highlight the differences between 'top-down' and 'bottom-up' Europeanisation processes (Dyson 2000). Direct, negative or top-down Europeanisation refers to the extent to which more or less compulsory European laws, directives and other decisions are implemented at the local level. Variation in the extent to which such compulsory laws, regulations and directives are implemented (which outside observers might incorrectly presume to lead directly to policy harmonisation across the member states) can be caused by foot-dragging on the part of the bureaucracy, misinterpretation of the law or regulation in question, or outright violation of it where national interests run in conflict with EU-level policies. Top-down Europeanisation, especially the breaking of EU laws and regulations, may lead to national cases being taken to the European Court, or other sanctions. An example of the latter pertaining to the Irish case would be the reprimand issued by the European Council of Ministers in 2001, when the Irish government's budget was viewed to have violated the rules of European Monetary Union (EMU) (FitzGerald 2001; Hancké 2003).

Furthermore, even in the case of some apparently compulsory EU policies, there is often a great deal of choice about how far and how fast to implement a particular framework at the national level. This is especially the case with so-called 'soft laws', often framed as EU directives. An example here would be the 1996 Parental Leave Directive, which led to significant changes in Irish industrial relations legislation, since Ireland was one of the few member states without any parental leave guarantees up to that point. While the compulsory component of the Parental Leave Directive was fairly narrow in scope, and criticised by family policy activists across Europe as being too minimalist, the directive also contained a series of voluntary provisions, or preferred policy options, which were taken up in some member states (Faulkner *et al.* 2005:155–77). This 'room to move' afforded by many European-level policy decisions often provides a good opportunity for national-level actors to mobilise around their preferred policy options. This variation in the extent to which the soft or voluntary components of EU policy frameworks are complied with has led to a focus on the bottom-up, indirect or positive elements of the Europeanisation process. While the top-down variant of Europeanisation concentrates especially on the national impact of EU laws, directives and regulations, its bottom-up counterpart focuses on the much more voluntary process of adapting to Europe involved in knowledge sharing, policy learning, and adjustment to European norms through gradual cultural and political change (Busch 2004; Radaelli 1997; Schmidt 2001).

Concentrating on bottom-up processes tends to point especially toward the role of ideas, discourse and shifting bureaucratic and national political cultures as a result of European integration. Such an approach also allows us to view policy Europeanisation as not just the adoption of formal laws and directives, but also as the reorientation of national ways of thinking about policy problems around Europeanised norms and values. This also allows us to fully appreciate the extent to which there really are substantial differences between member states in terms of their willingness to rethink public policy goals and outcomes in Europeanised terms. One good example of bottom-up policy Europeanisation is the shift in the framing of social policy from 'anti-poverty' to 'social inclusion', a shift that is especially relevant to Irish and UK experiences. Whereas continental Europe has always tended toward framing social policy in terms of social solidarity or equality, Ireland and the UK have traditionally framed social policy in terms of combating poverty through charity (Esping-Andersen 1990). Since the continental, and especially Scandinavian, conception of social policy has been especially influential in the EU, at least at the level of ideas (Wincott 2003), a bottom-up Europeanisation of Irish social policy framing can be observed to have taken place: Ireland's Combat Poverty Agency (CPA), established in 1986, has recently been integrated into the Office for Social Inclusion (OSI).

EXPLAINING THE EUROPEANISATION OF IRISH PUBLIC POLICY: THEORETICAL PERSPECTIVES

Distinguishing between top-down and bottom-up Europeanisation processes points to the multiplicity of ways in which European integration can lead to policy change within EU member states. However, most political scientists seek not only to uncover many possible mechanisms of change, but also to be specific about which mechanisms are the most important on which to focus. This generally leads to the testing of particular theories against specific national cases and policy case studies, which in turn has led to efforts to forge general theories about how policy Europeanisation really works. While there is now a very extensive and varied literature on the Europeanisation of public policy, some contributions have received much more attention than others. One of the most influential theoretical frameworks in the field centres on the twin concepts of 'goodness of fit' or 'misfit' between European-level and national-level policy traditions and preferences. The basic understanding here is that decisions made at the European level are implemented, or carried through, to varying degrees at the national level, and the main reason for this variation is that policy change within a member state will only take place if there is a divergence or misfit between a European-level directive, policy or initiative, and the pre-existing policy framework in that member state. Conversely, change will not take place if there is already a goodness of fit between regional and local policies (Börzel and Risse, 2003; Cowles *et al.* 2001). When it comes to the misfit between EU prescriptions and pre-existing local policy frameworks governing specific policy areas, Ireland and the UK, along with the southern European countries, often make up a team of 'usual suspects' (Faulkner *et al.* 2005). This is especially true when it comes to labour relations and social policy, over which the EU has increasingly expanded its purview. The depth of policy change, as a result of Europeanisation, might thus be expected to be deeper in these cases and across these policy areas than is experienced in others.

While somewhat useful as a starting point for explaining policy change in member states, this analytical framework has been critiqued on empirical grounds: researchers acknowledge that a misfit between EU and national-level policy preferences does not automatically lead to domestic policy change (Radaelli 2003:45–6). Furthermore, change might occur on some level as a response to European developments even where a goodness of fit already exists, given the fact that, as highlighted above, national-level actors might use an opening in the political opportunity structure provided by a review of a particular policy area to pursue a desired policy shift. Even if policy change is 'required', because there is a mismatch between European directives and local policy frameworks, the supposed national policy shift does not always happen. There are numerous instances where continued member state resistance, or simply bureaucratic ineptitude, results in failure to implement European-level policy decisions. To this end, most authors also acknowledge that a misfit between pre-existing local policy and European-level developments is a necessary, but not always sufficient, condition for change. Much of the more difficult theoretical and empirical work in the field, then, is in specifying these additional conditions; researchers must identify the *mediating* factors that determine whether or not EU laws, directives and policy prescriptions are adopted at the national level. Such factors are multiple and multi-faceted, but some specific examples have stood out to researchers in the field.

Above all, this research agenda draws on the concept of 'veto points' in order to explain variation in the Europeanisation process (Cowles *et al.* 2001). This mirrors the focus on the role of political institutions, and especially the way rational actors deal with and have their behaviour shaped by institutions, that has dominated political science in recent years. For political scientists, veto points are decisional sites in which veto 'players' can resist policy proposals, and the number of veto points in a political system is determined by the constitutional and institutional framework governing it (Tsebelis 2002). The more veto points in a political system, the more hurdles there are for a policy proposal to leap over, meaning that policy Europeanisation in EU member states with increased numbers of veto points is more difficult. Examples of institutional features that increase the number of veto points include federalism or (strong) bicameralism. As a comparatively small and politically centralised state, Ireland might thus be expected to be more inclined toward policy Europeanisation than countries such as Italy, Spain or Germany (see Chapter 5). In addition, while veto player theory predicts that multi-party systems with coalition governments provide more opportunities for minor parties, in particular, to exercise veto power than is the case in two-party systems that generate one-party majority governments, small parties that have been part of coalition governments in Ireland in recent decades have generally chosen not to exercise such veto power. This has been attributed to the absence of ideological polarisation in the country (Conley and Bekafigo 2010). This analysis could be extended to highlight the generally consensus-oriented style of politics generally found in Ireland, a factor that will be returned to below.

While the rational-actor model associated with the analysis of veto points and veto players is a widely respected one, factors other than the number of veto points and veto players in a political system surely mediate between EU policy prescriptions and member state compliance or adaptation. Obvious ones that spring to mind include the fact that policy shifts require the support of key political actors, whether these actors are situated inside or outside the state. Even in national contexts where there is a misfit between European-level and national-level policy frameworks, along with relatively few veto points in the political system, policy changes are much less likely to take place if they run against either the interests or ideological preferences of major political players, including the current government, organised interest groups and the public administration. In the Irish context, it is often mentioned that the country has a favourable EU orientation that works in favour of policy Europeanisation, at least at a general level. Not only are Irish political elites generally predisposed to European integration, with both major political parties supportive of initial and continued efforts at regional integration, but these views have also generally been shared by the Irish public (Adshead 2005). While this pro-EU stance has clearly waned in recent years, with a more sceptical public viewpoint coming to light after 2001 surrounding the Treaty of Nice and intensifying more recently with the anti-Lisbon Treaty campaign (see Chapter 19), there has generally been less Euro-scepticism than has been experienced in other European countries (McGowan and Murphy 2003: 189; Murphy and Puirséil 2008). This arguably provided a comparatively good foundation for policy Europeanisation up to this point, even if it remains to be seen how the new wave of Irish anti-EU sentiment affects policy Europeanisation in the future.

While a generally positive view of European integration might provide a general basis for the Europeanisation of Irish public policy, it does not tell us very much about how specific policies are made or implemented. Mirroring the 'public administration turn' in European integration studies (Laffan 2006; Trondal 2007), Irish analysts have pointed to the role of state actors in pursuing a particular national policy framework. In particular, if bottom-up Europeanisation, in which national policies somehow go beyond what the EU legally requires, is to take place, specific bureaucratic actors located in positions of authority over the specific policy area in question must have an interest in pressing ahead with significant change in that policy area (Bugdahn 2005). Overall, however, and while this is no doubt a necessary factor in the facilitation of public policy Europeanisation, there has been too much of an emphasis on bureaucratic and other state actors in the process. What about the role of *non-state* actors? Arguably, there is a general neglect of societal actors, such as interest groups and policy stakeholders, in the Europeanisation process. The remainder of this chapter looks at this issue from just one perspective: assuming that societal actors are somehow important to Europeanisation, how do states establish policy-making institutions and processes so that their participation is channelled in order to facilitate this process?

THE IMPORTANCE OF CONSULTATIVE AND INCORPORATIVE POLICY MAKING

Some analysts might argue that the process of adjusting to Europe is not one that necessarily involves societal interest groups. In fact, the cynical, but common, view of European integration is that it lacks democracy, is driven by faceless bureaucrats, and is resistant to the participation of ordinary people. While this may or may not be the actual case, my argument is that in order for *successful* policy Europeanisation to take place, interest groups pertinent to the specific arena of state activity undergoing this process should have some involvement in policy making (see Chapter 25). By 'successful' I mean the adaptation of EU rules and policies to local circumstances or, in other words, applying laws and directives in such a way that they 'make sense' in the local context. If new rules and regulations do not make sense, they may have negative unintended consequences or may fail to be implemented altogether. The involvement of interest groups is important for two different, but complementary, reasons: both *consultation* and *incorporation* matter to policy Europeanisation, since these two attributes are generally reflected in policy-making institutions and processes that tend to facilitate interest group involvement in policy Europeanisation across a variety of national contexts. The remainder of this chapter explains the importance of both the consultative and the incorporative aspects of policy making, shows how Ireland has a reasonably strong consultative and incorporative policy-making tradition, and, finally, offers some explanation as to why this tradition is stronger in Ireland than in some other comparable national cases.

Genuine consultation over the broad aims of policy in a particular area, as well as the details, is necessary because it can lead to better-informed policy decisions. Policy Europeanisation, whether of a top-down or bottom-up variety, often involves a fundamental overhaul of the national framework governing a particular policy area. Fundamentally reorienting policy perspectives, under democratic conditions at least, requires the co-operation and input of what the policy-making literature sometimes refers to as 'street-level bureaucrats' (Lipsky 1980), such as teachers or social workers who work for the state, as well as key players in the economy, to include unions, workers, employer organisations and individual firms, among others. The state needs to take into account the interests and concerns of core interest groups involved in a specific policy area because stakeholders are often the best experts in the field, even if they sometimes lack the bird's eye view important for linking action in one policy arena to action in related arenas, or to the overall shift in development strategies required in a particular historical moment. In the absence of input from key societal stakeholders and interest groups, policies may have unintended consequences or fail to achieve their goals. While this is true of any major policy shift, genuine consultation is especially crucial for policy Europeanisation in a country such as Ireland since, as noted above, there has often been a greater misfit between EU policy goals and pre-existing frameworks in this case.

While the genuinely consultative aspects of public policy making are extremely important, in most cases of consultation between the citizenry and the state, the state inevitably retains a high degree of control over who is permitted into the discussion and under what conditions, something that is generally required for a major reorientation of national economic and social development strategy. The incorporative aspects of public policy-making institutions and processes are important because implementing strategies in a particular area often requires acting against the interests of key societal or interest groups. For example, adopting guaranteed parental leave legislation might threaten the bottom line of small businesses; trade unions may resist increasingly liberal immigration policy; the promotion and privileging of technical training might threaten the traditionally favoured status of universities. This means that consultative institutions or processes are highly structured spaces, since states in the process of reorienting their development strategies around a specific set of goals and values, which policy Europeanisation often entails, need to incorporate societal groups as much as they need to genuinely take account of their interests and ideas through consultation.

Institutions and processes designed to channel the participation of interest groups in policy making thus need to strike a good balance between genuine consultation and effective incorporation. If a policy-making tradition encourages consultation and negotiation, compromise is more likely to be reached over the details of policy, without undermining its overall direction. The overall direction, in these cases hopefully toward Europeanised policy goals and values, can still be guided by the state. However, where consensus or compromise cannot be reached, the subtle and not so subtle coercive side of incorporative policy making comes into play. Incorporative policy-making institutions are designed not only to induce co-operation, but are also often accompanied by measures to force co-operation or to constrain interests (Collier and Collier 1979). At the very least, states can refuse to allow particular groups into the policy-making circle as a form of punishment for lack of moderation or co-operation on their part. This allows the state to control, at the very least, the terms of the discussion, and allows it to pursue, and in fact gain, legitimacy and a measure of consent for its developmental goals. Controlling interests and preventing resistance to them spilling over into open political conflict is not always possible, but the more robust a state's consultative and incorporative tradition, the more likely it is to make good use of such strategies.

In the absence of effective incorporative institutions and processes, through which trading over policy decisions between players can occur over the long term, states can find the implementation of policy goals against the interests of key interest groups extremely difficult. Without a culture of compromise, the response of such interest groups to required policy shifts may be, in the case of labour or popular groups, to take to the streets, or, on the part of elites, to withdraw investment or political support. A good contrast to Ireland here is Greece. Like Ireland, Greece was relatively economically underdeveloped at the time it joined the then European Economic Community (EEC) in 1981. However, in contrast to Ireland, Greece has arguably failed to take full advantage of its EU membership, and has certainly failed to Europeanise and modernise across many different policy areas (Featherstone and Papadimitriou 2008). One reason for this is Greece's lack of a consultative and incorporative policy-making tradition. While there are close relationships between the union movement and the centre-left PASOK party, and the Orthodox Church and the centre-right New Democracy party, conflicts over policy generally spill into open political conflict, rather than becoming subject to carefully negotiated compromise between key interest groups and the state. Recent examples include the failure to reform the Greek pension system, which is heavily skewed toward the protection of male, full-time, higher-paid and especially public sector workers (Matsaganis 2006; O'Donnell and Tinios 2003; Petmesidou 1991), and the stalemate over higher education reforms that occurred between 2006 and 2008, resulting in violent conflicts between students and police, and the periodic cancellation of classes at some Greek universities during this time.

The argument here is thus that one element of successful policy Europeanisation is the presence of policy-making institutions and processes that have a good mix of two quite different aspects associated with their operation. Yet, what might an institution or policy-making process that effectively balances consultation against incorporation look like? Even though there is no one model, certain institutional forms seem more capable of achieving that balance than others. Two specific categories of state–society interaction are of main interest here: (a) short-term or 'one-off' consultative processes; and (b) neo-corporatist pact-making, social partnership, or other similar, more permanent forms of interest group participation. While short-term or one-off processes are frequently important first steps toward consultation with either broad-based society, or the incorporation of society-based policy 'experts' in certain fields, they are often limited in the sense that they generally do not have self-enforcing or self-reproducing mechanisms built into them. They are frequently undertaken to give a good public face to a particular government action, but do not provide a check on government activity, nor in any way obligate the government to adopt certain recommended measures. Such short-term or one-off processes may include public forums on proposed pieces of legislation, or even the more formal establishment of working groups, commissions of enquiry and other similar bodies in which representatives from government and state agencies work closely with interest group representatives, but especially policy experts in particular fields.

By contrast, longer-term or ongoing processes and institutions provide opportunities for what public policy analysts refer to as 'feedback loops' to be institutionalised. State and non-state actors negotiate over policy detail, the policy framework is implemented, and, crucially, all actors consult over the impact of the policy shift and reformulate it, if necessary. This process becomes institutionalised, or self-reproducing, when the role of interest groups in this cycle is self-consciously established and agreed on. This is one of the major advantages of (usually tripartite) neo-corporatist type policy-making institutions, which, if effective and capable of reproducing themselves, explicitly outline a timetable for the implementation of the agreement and conditions under which it may be renegotiated. Neo-corporatist or neo-corporatist-like institutions and processes constitute one very specific type of ongoing, peak-level, ideally permanent, form of interaction between interest groups and the state (see Chapter 13). Formal social pact-making is self-reproducing and binding in part because it: (a) commits 'social partners' to the implementation of very specific policy targets and action; and (b) tends to induce self-limiting behaviour on the part of the actors involved because the reproduction of the institution relies on compromise, renegotiation and the co-operation of all actors (Nicholls 2006).

THE IRISH POLICY-MAKING TRADITION IN COMPARATIVE PERSPECTIVE

In comparison to Southern Europe and the new Central and Eastern European EU accession countries, in particular, Ireland has an especially strong consultative and incorporative policy-making tradition, which has put the country at an advantage when it comes to the Europeanisation of public policy. Specifically, more recent initiatives, such as the country's social partnership process, overlie a long-standing consultative and incorporative tradition. On one hand, Ireland's inheritance of political institutions from the British meant that the bureaucracy took on the form of what is usually termed the Whitehall model of public administration (Marsh *et al.* 2001). It was, and is, a career public service, and the workings of inter-departmental or select committees and commissions of inquiry mark the policy-making process. Such a tradition allows policy makers to consult with and incorporate the interests and opinions of policy stakeholders, such as presidents of universities in the field of education, or doctors' associations in the health policy arena, along with academics or other outside experts. Although such a tradition provides a strong basis for consultative and incorporative policy making, it has its limits. Principally, it is a particularly elitist model and, in some circumstances, consultation (and incorporation) is not broad enough. The elitism or 'insider' basis of this form of consultation has been reinforced in the Irish case by the near state corporatist form of interest group mediation administered by the Fianna Fáil party machine (see Chapter 11). Second, consultation under this system is most often short-term or one-off in nature, and decisions within it tend not to be binding on political actors.

Policy-making in Ireland through much of the twentieth century was thus consultative, especially in areas in which technical expertise was particularly important. Yet policy-making institutions and processes were also in a significant sense closed. Ordinary citizens might have been able to gain some local influence through local party networks, but at the national level, some interests were clearly favoured over others. Fianna Fáil's populist coalition included agricultural interests, some local manufacturing participation, key trade unions and the Catholic Church (Dunphy 1995). Other societal interest groups might have been excluded from the system. This system came under pressure as early as the 1970s, but more significantly from the mid-1980s, when the severe economic crisis, combined with a series of political crises and scandals, undermined the stability of the system. In other Western democracies at approximately the same time, this turn of events led to the growth of new social movements and, in some cases, new political parties reflecting newly formed social cleavages.

The relatively closed policy-making system changed markedly from the late 1980s, so much so, I argue, that these changes constitute a transformation within Irish democracy itself, because they represented a fundamental change in the way that democracy operated. This transformation is reflected not in the rise of new political parties, nor any formal institutional changes, but in the field of interest group consultation and incorporation. More open forms of interest group intermediation developed underneath, or in parallel to, the old party and parliamentary system (Ó Riain 2004). Although the post-1987 'social partnership' agreements, and the processes that built up around them, were not the only alternative forms of ensuring greater accountability and government responsiveness to shifting societal interests, social partnership is indeed one of those most widely recognised and researched. What made the social partnership agreements different was the fact that they were long-term in nature and self-reproducing because they provide mechanisms for their own review and renegotiation. They are also conducted at the peak level and are relatively formal in the sense that interest groups and the state sign off on the commitments made as a result of negotiations, after which agreements are published and widely available to the public. This limits the extent to which governments can ignore or backtrack on commitments made in the agreements.

Taken together, older and newer forms of interest group participation in policy making provide a good basis for reorienting specific policy areas around Europeanised goals and values. Take, for example, the Europeanisation of family policy since the early 1990s, especially measures for reconciling family and working life. Apart from legal requirements, such as the EU's Parental Leave Directive discussed above, Europeanisation in this arena of state activity has been largely a bottom-up process, in which attention to the policy area at the European level has provided a major opportunity for Irish national actors to press for policy change. Family policy was of significant EU interest during the 1990s, with the European Union Observatory on Family Policies gathering and reporting on individual member states during the course of the decade. Initially, there was an overwhelming misfit between European prescriptions and pre-existing Irish policy in this field. In fact, most pre-existing Irish policy was hostile to the reconciliation of family and working life, and changes to that framework barely made it on to the political agenda. By the end of the 1990s, the topic was one of national debate, and piecemeal changes had been negotiated through a series of consultative and incorporative policy-making institutions. First, the Second Commission on the Status of Women, which reported in 1993, and the Commission on the Family, which reported in 1998, incorporated interests from the charitable and social activist sector in particular (Carroll 1999), while second, the social partnership process played a role in establishing such initiatives as the National Framework for Family-Friendly Policies and the Family-Friendly Workplace Day.

Several features of Ireland's political history and culture explain the success the country had in establishing consultative and incorporative policy-making institutions. First of all, much is made of Ireland's consensus-building political tradition (Mair 1992), and rightly so. Institutions and processes that effectively balance functions of consultation and incorporation work to manufacture consent around a specific policy initiative. In turn, this builds on a relatively robust democratic tradition. Countries without that tradition often have to deal with 'authoritarian legacies' that act as barriers to the creation of consultative and incorporative policy making (Cesarini and Hite 2004). Among these include the fact that polities that have recently emerged from an authoritarian past are much more likely to be 'dual societies', meaning that there is a huge gulf in status, education and, consequently, access to politics and policy-making, between a small elite and society at large. In such societies, while there might be peak-level discussions between the state and organised labour and business in particular, policy consultation is generally minimalist, or occurs after the policy has in fact been written. An example is Portugal, where despite the fact that it is over thirty years since the demise of authoritarian rule, and the fact that the 1974 Revolution of the Carnations was supposed to sweep away the old elite, the country still maintains many of those dual characteristics. Policy making is generally highly legalistic, top-down, and confined to a specific educated class. Furthermore, countries that are arguably still going through the process of democratic consolidation, or that have a debased quality of democracy, in which formal political institutions are democratic but societal attitudes might not be, are more prone to authoritarian behaviour on the part of both state and non-state actors. This, in part, explains the Greek problem noted above: very few consultative and incorporative policy-making institutions exist, and, where they do, they are often undermined by a political culture that is resistant to compromise and consensus making.

CONCLUSION

Selecting Ireland as an exemplar of public policy Europeanisation seems natural, since Ireland is one country that has apparently taken full advantage of regional integration – thus far, at least. However, the preceding discussion has also illustrated how the factors that facilitate policy Europeanisation are best uncovered through the adoption of both a theoretical and comparative perspective. The development of policy-making institutions and processes that effectively balance functions of consultation and incorporation are important, and the Irish democratic tradition, which has traditionally emphasised centrism and centralisation, rather than mass political participation and mobilisation, has provided an excellent foundation upon which such policy-making institutions and processes can be constructed. These observations, arrived at through the adoption of an explicitly comparative approach, generate lessons both for future Irish responses to EU membership, as well as states formerly on the Eastern European 'periphery' that are newcomers to the process of European integration.

First, the Greek experience, in particular, should caution Ireland about the difficulty of forging reasonable and comprehensive policy responses to regional integration when consensus does not exist, or has seriously broken down. For Ireland, maintaining political consensus in the future will be increasingly difficult to achieve in the face of increased social inequality, due to a pattern of rapid economic development that has tended to concentrate wealth; the erosion of the moral authority of the Catholic Church, due not only to general societal modernisation and diversification, but also to a recent series of scandals and missteps; and increased ethnic diversity, due to post-1990 immigration, among other factors. The increasing fragility of the Irish consensus-building tradition is reflected not only in the 2008 anti-Lisbon Treaty campaign, but also policy-making processes and institutions themselves: forging a 'social partnership' agreement in 2006 was arguably a much more fraught process than was the case between 1987 and 2003.

Second, and furthermore, the lessons drawn from a comparison between Irish and Southern European experiences give rise to a cautionary note about the Europeanisation of public policy as European integration heads east. Many new and potential EU member states have democratised much more recently than even Portugal or Greece, raising specific questions about the construction of institutions and processes capable of bridging the gap between societal groups and the state in these countries. In the case of many of the new Central and Eastern European member states, recent histories of communism have left distinctive marks on the organisation of the state bureaucracy, the formation of interest groups, and the way the two interact. Recent literature that looks at the Europeanisation of Central and Eastern Europe has thus, so far, noted a distinct lack of societal participation in the Europeanisation project (Schimmelfennig and Sedelmeier 2005; Sissenich 2006). The point emphasised above is that major reorientations of national development strategies require policy-making processes and institutions that can effectively balance functions of genuine consultation and effective incorporation of key societal groups. Since most Central and Eastern European countries have some tradition of state-dominated incorporation, but very little experience of genuine policy consultation, it is the latter that will need to be developed most extensively.

References

Adshead, M. (2005) 'Europeanization and Changing Patterns of Governance in Ireland', *Public Administration* 83(1): 159–78.

Borneman, J. and Fowler, N. (1997) 'Europeanization', *Annual Review of Anthropology* 26: 487–514.

Börzel, T.A. and Risse, T. (2003), 'Conceptualizing the Domestic Impact of Europe', in K. Featherstone and C.M. Radaelli (eds) *The Politics of Europeanization*, pp. 57–82. Oxford: Oxford University Press.

Bugdahn, S. (2005) 'Of Europeanization and Domestication: The Implementation of the Environmental Information Directive in Ireland, Great Britain and Germany', *Journal of European Public Policy* 12(1): 177–99.

Busch, A. (2004) 'National Filters: Europeanisation, Institutions, and Discourse in the Case of Banking Regulation', *West European Politics* 27(2): 310–33.

Carroll, D. (1999) 'Cross-Cutting Initiatives in Public Policy: Some Irish Examples', in G. Kiely, A. O'Donnell, P. Kennedy and S. Quin (eds) *Irish Social Policy in Context*, pp. 311–15. Dublin: University College Dublin Press.

Cesarini, P. and Hite, K. (eds) (2004) *Authoritarian Legacies and Democracies in Latin America and Southern Europe*. Notre Dame, IN: University of Notre Dame Press.

Collier, R.B. and Collier, D. (1979) 'Inducements versus Constraints: Disaggregating "Corporatism"', *American Political Science Review* 43(4): 967–86.

Conley, R.S. and Bekafigo, M. (2010) '"No Irish Need Apply"? Veto Players and Legislative Productivity in the Republic of Ireland, 1949–2000', *Comparative Political Studies* 43(1): 91–118.

Cowles, M.G., Caporaso, J. and Risse, T. (eds) (2001) *Transforming Europe: Europeanization and Domestic Change*. Ithaca, NY: Cornell University Press.

Dunphy, R. (1995) *The Making of Fianna Fáil Power in Ireland 1923–1948*. Oxford: Clarendon Press.

Dyson, K. (2000) 'EMU as Europeanization: Convergence, Diversity, and Contingency', *Journal of Common Market Studies* 34(4): 645–66.

Esping-Andersen, G. (1990) *Three Worlds of Welfare Capitalism*. Princeton, NJ: Princeton University Press.

Faulkner, G., Treib, O., Hartlapp, M. and Leiber, S. (2005) *Complying with Europe: EU Harmonisation and Soft Law in the Member States*. Cambridge: Cambridge University Press.

Featherstone, K. and Papadimitriou, D. (2008) *The Limits of Europeanization: Reform Capacity and Policy Conflict in Greece*. Basingstoke: Palgrave.

FitzGerald, J. (2001) 'Managing an Economy Under EMU: The Case of Ireland', *World Economy* 24(10): 1353–71.

Hancké, B. (2003) 'The Political Economy of Fiscal Policy in EMU', *European Political Economy Review* 1(1): 5–14.

Laffan, B. (2006) 'Managing Europe from Home in Dublin, Athens, and Helsinki: A Comparative Analysis', *West European Politics* 29(4): 687–708.

Lipsky, M. (1980) *Street-level Bureaucracy: Dilemmas of the Individual in Public Services*. New York, NY: Russell Sage Foundation.

Mair, P. (1992) 'Explaining the Absence of Class Politics in Ireland', *Proceedings of the British Academy* 79: 383–410.

Marsh, D., Richards, D. and Smith, M.J. (2001) *Changing Patterns of Governance in the United Kingdom: Reinventing Whitehall?* New York, NY: Palgrave.

Matsaganis, M. (2006) 'Muddling Through – The Trials and Tribulations of Social Security Policy', in M. Petmesidou and E. Mossialos (eds) *Social Policy Developments in Greece*, pp. 147–73. Aldershot: Ashgate.

McGowan, L. and Murphy, M. (2003) 'Europeanisation and the Irish Experience', in M. Adshead and M. Millar (eds) *Public Administration and Public Policy in Ireland*, pp. 182–200. London: Routledge.

Murphy, G. and Puirséil, N. (2008) '"Is it a New Allowance?" Irish Entry to the EEC and Popular Opinion', *Irish Political Studies* 23(4): 533–53.

Nicholls, K. (2006) 'Why Social Partnership Matters: Irish Policies for Work–Life Balance', *West European Politics* 29(3): 513–39.

O'Donnell, O. and Tinios, P. (2003) 'The Politics of Pension Reform: Lessons from Public Attitudes in Greece', *Political Studies* 51: 262–81.

Olsen, J.P. (2002) 'The Many Faces of Europeanization', *Journal of Common Market Studies* 40(5): 923–4.

Ó Riain, S. (2004) *The Politics of High-Tech Growth*. Cambridge: Cambridge University Press.

Petmesidou, M. (1991) 'Statism, Social Policy and the Middle Class in Greece', *Journal of European Social Policy* 1(1): 31–48.

Radaelli, C.M. (1997) 'How Does Europeanization Produce Domestic Policy Change? Corporate Tax Policy in Italy and the United Kingdom', *Comparative Political Studies* 30(5): 553–76.

— (2003) 'The Europeanization of Public Policy', in K. Featherstone and C.M. Radaelli (eds) *The Politics of Europeanization*, pp. 27–56. Oxford: Oxford University Press.

Schimmelfenning, F. and Sedelmeier, U. (eds) (2005) *The Europeanization of Central and Eastern Europe*. Ithaca, NY: Cornell University Press.

Schmidt, V.A. (2001) 'The Politics of Economic Adjustment in France and Britain: When Does Discourse Matter?', *Journal of European Public Policy* 8(2): 247–64.

Sissenich, B. (2006) *Building States Without Society: European Union Enlargement and the Transfer of EU Social Policy to Poland and Hungary*. Lanham, MD: Rowman and Littlefield.

Trondal, J. (2007) 'The Public Administration Turn in Integration Research', *Journal of European Public Policy* 14(6): 960–72.

Tsebelis, G. (2002) *Veto Players: How Political Institutions Work*. Princeton, NJ: Princeton University Press.

Wincott, D. (2003) 'The Idea of the European Social Model: Limits and Paradoxes of Europeanization', in K. Featherstone and C.M. Radaelli (eds) *The Politics of Europeanization*, pp. 279–302. Oxford: Oxford University Press.

Section V

Interests and Concerns in Contemporary Ireland

The chapters in this section look at some contemporary issues of concern to Irish business and society and so, inevitably, highlight interests that are in tension concerning these issues. In broad terms, the chapters cover: interest groups and their role in society; the development of, and challenges faced by, the civil society sector; feminism, activism and social change; the issues surrounding alcohol advertising; the practice of advertising to children; the challenges for society posed by digital information and communication technologies; and spirituality in the workplace.

Gary Murphy opens the section by examining, in Chapter 25, the issues surrounding interest groups and their political activities. Theoretically, interest groups can play a simple but central role in a democratic society by acting as a conduit between citizens and their government. By analysing interest groups' activities in several central debates in Ireland, this chapter shows that the access and expectations such groups have to, and of, Irish policy makers can be of great significance for policy outcomes.

Another set of groups that stand in the space between citizens and government are civil society groups. In Chapter 26, Geoff Weller first considers Irish civil society's antecedents and its contemporary identity, before identifying the Irish civil society sector's development and its present qualities. The challenges for the sector, particularly those related to its relationship with the state and the question of whether there is a crisis of participation in Irish civil society, are considered.

A vitally important social movement throughout the last hundred years has been the women's movement. In Chapter 27, Jennifer DeWan examines how the women's movement in Ireland has experienced a generational shift. Feminist activism, within a cohesive and autonomous social movement, no longer fully defines the practices and subjectivities activists employ to transform their lives. All this has taken place in the context of dramatic social changes in Ireland that are characteristic of the effects of late capitalism in a European, post-colonial nation-state. These changes have potentially opened up many new opportunities to transform political engagement in general.

Next, in Chapter 28, a major concern in contemporary Ireland is examined in detail: Patrick Kenny and Gerard Hastings explore the controversial issue of alcohol advertising. The alcohol industry maintains that its marketing campaigns operate at the level of brand preferences. Others argue that alcohol advertising contributes to higher overall levels of alcohol consumption. The chapter reviews the empirical evidence on both sides of the debate and presents an overview of current regulations governing alcohol advertising practice in Ireland, drawing some conclusions regarding research into the advertising of this rather special product.

A rather special advertising audience concerns Margaret-Anne Lawlor in Chapter 29. In Ireland, the practice of advertising to children continues to attract strong practitioner, regulatory and public interest. The attractiveness of the children's market to business is examined and ethical issues concerning child-targeted advertising are introduced. In examining the large body of literature in this area, it is suggested that child consumers may be more knowledgeable and evaluative of television advertising than previously recognised.

Chapter 30 considers the impact of a young technology on the privacy of consumers and citizens. Karlin Lillington explores how the ubiquity of digital information and communication technologies has brought about an unprecedented ability to create, sift and analyse information. The temptation to store and/or have access to such information has proved enormously attractive to businesses, as well as to law enforcement agencies. Business and society, in general, face challenges from the shifting data landscape and changing perceptions of privacy in the new age of information technology.

John Cullen, in Chapter 31, addresses some recent changes in the technology of the self. He explores how faith experiences have undergone a broad change away from established religious frameworks, such as churches, towards a more New Age, 'inner-self spirituality', where individuals attempt to come to terms with the meaning of their lives. Personal effectiveness and spiritual management development means management of faith experiences in the workplace.

From interest groups to our spirituality, business's interactions with society are increasingly important. As the authors in this section show, profound changes challenge us to think deeply about these issues and how to manage the balance between society's concerns and those of diverse interests.

Chapter 25

Access and Expectation: Interest Groups in Ireland

Gary Murphy

INTRODUCTION

'What is an interest group?' is a question that has been asked for many years, but it is also a question to which there is rarely a simple answer. It is commonly accepted that interest groups are a central part of the policy-making process in democracies, but one of the difficulties that surrounds the study of such groups is the abundance of neologisms that the field produces. One recent study noted that the following terms to describe what is in essence interest group activity are all in use: 'interest groups, political interest groups, interest associations, interest organisations, organised interests, pressure groups, specific interests, special interest groups, citizen groups, public interest groups, non-governmental organisations, social movement organisations, and civil society organisations' (Beyers et al. 2008:1106). Moreover, a number of what we would perceive as interest groups have also, to some extent, moved beyond interest group politics by actually placing themselves before the electorate at local, European and general elections in an attempt to give their specific issues a higher profile. These groups have thus moved beyond the traditional norm of interest groups not normally seeking public office or competing in elections, and actually pursuing their goals through frequent informal interactions with politicians and bureaucrats (Beyers et al. 2008:1106–7).

No matter which term is used, one of the fundamental tenets of interest group study is that such groups do not seek public office, and obviously groups seeking public office present a significant conceptual difficulty for scholars of interest groups. In the purest sense, a satisfactory definition of an interest group will stipulate two criteria: that the organisation has some autonomy from government and that it tries to influence policy outcomes (Wilson 1991:8). Interest groups play an important role in Irish society, acting as a conduit between citizens and the government. In that context, the question of access to decision makers is crucial for all interest groups.

However, it is not simply governments that interest groups lobby to affect decision making, as they can also pursue their aims and exercise their influence on policy through public or private channels, both directly and indirectly. Beyond access to policy makers and others who may influence decision making, the other key element to take into account when studying interest group behaviour is the expectation such groups have for the lobbying they engage in. Gaining access to decision makers is one thing; the expectation that a group has, once it has been received inside the inner sanctum of power, is quite another in representative democracies where power lies with governments. But interest groups, as we shall see, often have significant input into how public policy is directed in the state. This chapter will set out the theoretical strengths and weaknesses of interest groups in Ireland and examine whether they have had a positive or detrimental effect on Irish democracy.

CONCEPTIONS OF INTEREST GROUP BEHAVIOUR

Interest group activity in Ireland spans numerous strands. It is identified at one level with the process of social partnership, where sectional groups, such as trade unions, employers and farmers' interests, have had central roles since 1987. Self-regulating professional groups, such as accountants, doctors and lawyers, also come under this category of sectional groups, as they represent and articulate the interests of certain sections of society. At a second level, interest group activity spans what we call 'cause-centred groups', who attempt to influence policy outcomes in specific areas. Cause-centred groups advocate for a particular outcome and articulate the interests of people who promote a particular cause. Moral issue groups and environmental issue groups are two good examples of such causes that have seen significant activity in the interest group sphere in modern Ireland.

Academic recognition of interest group behaviour dates to the early twentieth century and Bentley's *The Process of Government* (1908), but widespread interest in such groups can be traced to Truman's post-war classic study *The Governmental Process* (1951). The study of groups is now fully incorporated into wider analyses of the distribution of political power and the nature of the state, to the extent that interaction of groups with the state is crucial to any understanding of the nature of modern governance. There are two distinct models of interest group activity: corporatism and pluralism. The *corporatist* model suggests that interest groups are closely associated with the formal political process and play a critical role in both the formulation and the implementation of major political decisions. Thus, large and powerful interest groups monopolise the representation of the interests of a particular functional section of the population. This usually encapsulates organised labour, farmers and employers, with these interest groups being organised in a hierarchical manner, typically with a powerful major or peak organisation at the top (Murphy 2009a:330–1). Fundamentally, agreements made within a true corporatist system should entail a comprehensive role for interest groups in the implementation of policy and they should be applicable in wider policy domains, not simply the economy (Cawson 1986:37).

The *pluralist* model, by comparison, maintains that individual interest groups apply pressure on political elites in a competitive manner and attributes power in policy making to individual groups operating in particular areas at particular times. In its modern form, the most influential modern exponent of pluralism is the American political scientist Robert Dahl, who argued that although the politically privileged and economically powerful exert greater power than ordinary citizens, no ruling or political elite is able to dominate the political process (Dahl 1961:311). The key feature for Dahl was that the competition between parties at election time, and the ability of interest groups to articulate their views freely, establish a reliable link between the government and the governed and create an effective channel of communication between the two. Thus, a sufficient level of accountability and popular responsiveness is in place for the political system to be regarded as democratic. However, pluralist conceptions of interest group behaviour show that individual interest groups apply pressure on political elites in a competitive manner. Power in policy making is attributed to individual groups operating in particular areas at particular times. This competition is usually disorganised and its main essence is to exclude other interest groups from the policy process. Pluralism also offers no formal institutional role to interest groups in decision making or implementation of policy.

In theory, although not all groups have equal levels of power or resources, the fact that it is relatively easy to form a group should ensure at least some access to the levers of political power (Smith 1990:309). In a pluralist democracy, new groups can emerge and be accommodated within the system by other groups adapting and by the very nature of such a democracy allowing differing groups to form. The key question to be answered, however, is what influence can such groups have? Most pluralists accept that the market in political influence is imperfect and contains actors with differing capacities to alter public policies. Economically, for instance, many pluralists accept that business interests have held a dominant interest in influencing government in the past two decades in most Western European states and that the state is most definitely not neutral. The effect of this is that on some grand economic issues, the state and business interests combine to remove the issue from public debate, with the result that pluralistic politics resides in secondary, non-economic issues (Lindblom 1977:142). To that extent, it has been argued that the single most distinctive feature of the pluralist account of decision making is that it is characterised by conflict rather than consensus (Gallagher *et al.* 2006:450). Despite such conflict, the optimistic nature of pluralism accepts that the outcome of political activity in a pluralist system is a product of the balance of forces between the various forces involved. However, because of its disorganised nature, pluralism has been heavily criticised for being a vague and incomplete theory of political activity (Jordan 1990). Other critics of pluralist theory point out that pluralist explanations of power relationships between groups and the state are based on the admittance of safe political issues into the political arena to the exclusion of conflict-laden issues. Moreover, there is evidence that groups that share in the ideological bias of a government are more likely to be admitted into the policy-making process and those groups that do not conform to the dominant set of values are likely to be excluded from the policy domain. Classic examples here would be the exclusion of trade unions and groups arguing for state intervention in the economy during the dominant new right economic thinking of the 1980s in a number of western European democracies, most notably Britain and the United States of America.

Taking into account the two models of interest group behaviour and the ability of groups to form easily in democratic societies, we can also divide up interest group activity into certain advantages and disadvantages. Heywood (2007:301) posits the following positives and negatives in relation to the activities of interest groups. On the plus side, interest groups can:

- broaden the scope of political participation by providing an alternative to conventional party politics and offering opportunities for grassroots activism
- strengthen representation by articulating interests and advancing views that are ignored by political parties and provide a means of influencing government between elections
- promote debate and discussion by creating a better informed and more educated electorate
- provide some kind of check on government power and in the process defend liberty by ensuring that the state is balanced by a vigorous and healthy civil society
- maintain political stability by providing a channel of communication between government and the people.

On the negative side, interest groups can:

- entrench political inequality by strengthening the voice of the wealthy and privileged in particular
- be divisive, in that they are concerned with the particular, not the general, and advance minority interests against those of society as a whole
- exercise non-legitimate power, in that their leaders, unlike politicians, are not publicly accountable and their influence bypasses the representative process
- make the policy process closed and secretive by exerting influence through negotiation and deals that are not subject to public scrutiny
- create an array of vested interests that are able to block government initiatives and make policy unworkable.

Given that we have now established the theoretical nature of interest groups, the aim of this chapter is to examine some of these positives and negatives, apply them to modern Ireland and try to ascertain whether interest group activity is beneficial or detrimental to modern Irish democracy. Moreover, given the countless examples of interest group influence in modern Ireland, we will limit our inquiries to three areas that have had a significant impact in shaping modern Ireland, and all of which have seen considerable interest group involvement: social partnership; abortion; and referendums on European treaties.

SOCIAL PARTNERSHIP AND THE QUESTIONS OF ACCESS, INFLUENCE AND SECRECY

One of the key theoretical advantages of interest group politics is that interest groups broaden the scope of political participation by providing an alternative to conventional party politics and offering opportunities for grassroots activism. In that context, it is well to reflect that party loyalty in Ireland remains a significant political phenomenon, with those who 'feel close' to a particular party hovering at about 25 per cent since the 1980s (McGraw 2008:631). This loyalty, however, is not reflected in party membership. Weeks (2009:155), using figures supplied by individual party headquarters, notes that overall cross-party membership stands at a total of 118,500. This figure includes 65,000 for Fianna Fáil, which seems excessively high and apparently includes lapsed members whom the party would apparently like to entice back into the fold, though it is very difficult to see how this would actually occur. Marsh (2005:170) suggested that about 80,000 people, under three per cent of the population, were members of political parties, while Mair and van Biezen (2001:9) gave a slightly higher figure of 86,000 or 3.14 per cent at the end of the 1990s.

Given these low political party participation figures, is it possible that interest groups have, to an extent, filled the gap and provided an alternative outlet to conventional party politics for individuals, thus broadening the scope of political participation? In 2008, membership of the Irish Farmers' Association (IFA) stood at about 85,000, while membership of the Irish Congress of Trade Unions (ICTU) was over 600,000 (Murphy 2009a:340–1). While the figure for the trade union movement is large, it should be noted that trade union density (the number of members of trade unions in the overall workforce) stood at only 36 per cent. More graphically again, a recent government report suggested that, in 2006, almost two-thirds of people aged sixteen and over participated in at least one group activity, while participation in political groups was as low as one per cent across all age groups (CSO 2009:5–9). This would tend to suggest that even though membership of political parties is somewhere in the region of three per cent, in reality those members who are active is even lower than this. While much of this group activity could better be described as leisurely pursuits, the important point remains that political participation is low and group membership is becoming more popular. Moving beyond Ireland, the decline of party membership has seen a significant rise in both interest group numbers and numbers in interest groups across Europe (Beyers et al. 2008:1111–12; Jordan and Maloney 2007). Yet it would certainly be a stretch to suggest that trade union membership broadens the scope of political participation and provides an alternative outlet for people, as interest group activity is increasing while trade union membership is actually decreasing.

A central element of western European democracy has been the so-called 'co-opting' of interest groups into the policy process, in which the inter-relationship between governments and interest groups, depending on the specific policy area, can often be of greater significance than general elections for policy outcomes (Richardson 1993:12). This is, in essence, what happened in Ireland in terms of the social partnership agreements through which Ireland was, to all intents and purposes, effectively governed between 1987 and 2009.

It was during a period of deep depression in the mid-1980s that the social partners, unions, employers and farmers, agreed a strategy with government to attempt to overcome Ireland's economic difficulties. This has been followed by six other agreements. Facing a grave fiscal crisis in 1987, the new Fianna Fáil government, acting in conjunction with the social partners, agreed a plan to overcome Ireland's economic problems based on the premise of partnership, whereby interested actors, such as farmers' organisations, trade unions and business groups, would negotiate with the government in what might be called the process of economic governance (Hardiman 2002). This approach has since evolved into a system that aims to keep all the major interests reasonably happy by giving them a role in the broad economic approach of the state, which in turn will perpetuate a national economic and social coalition of sorts. This social partnership cements these economic interests, now known as 'social partners', to a coherent and consistent policy framework. That system continued until the dramatic events of late 2009, when, in the midst of trying to overcome yet another grave fiscal crisis, the Fianna Fáil–Green coalition government refused to accept an offer from the trade union movement that public service workers would, in essence, take twelve days' extra unpaid leave in order to avoid pay cuts. The government rejected the offer and instead unilaterally cut the pay of all public service workers in the 2010 budget.

With the development of the Partnership 2000 agreement, published in 1996, a watershed was reached as, for the first time, agencies from the voluntary sector, including charities and self-help groups, were included in consultation and ultimately negotiations. This new initiative resulted from complaints that the government and the economic partners were missing an opportunity to tackle social exclusion in an integrated fashion by ignoring the voices of other interest groups. The most graphic illustration of this widening of the social partnership parameters was the inclusion of the Irish National Organisation of the Unemployed (INOU) in the negotiations – the first time the unemployed had been seen by the government as an actor with something to offer to social partnership negotiation.

Given the inclusion of this so-called third pillar, could we say that this satisfies the test of groups broadening the scope of political participation by providing an alternative to conventional party politics? For Allen (2000) the answer must be no, as he claims that the whole concept of social partnership is a myth that has functioned mainly as a means of sustaining inequalities in growth and incomes. While this is a particularly left-wing view of social partnership, it is noteworthy that the voluntary organisations felt very much that they were ranked below business and trade union interests by the government, both in the original Partnership 2000 deal and in other subsequent agreements. Yet, notwithstanding vocal protests from this sector about their perceived secondary status, they decided that staying inside the tent was far more preferable to opting out of it. The end result was that this sector was convinced that by being a part of the social partnership process they could realise a second theoretical advantage of interest group behaviour, that of strengthening representation by articulating interests and advancing views ignored by political parties, and provide a means of influencing government between elections.

The economic crisis of 2008 and 2009, which saw the collapse of the property sector and the banks suffer colossal losses, also led to the slow strangulation of the social partnership process. While the Taoiseach, Brian Cowen, was insisting up to early 2009 that social partnership was alive and well, despite the trade union movement refusing to sign up to an economic recovery plan, the final death knell for the process came with the government's refusal to agree to the trade unions' proposal for public sector reform in return for no pay cuts for public sector workers in November 2009. With this act, the government had actually overcome one of the criticisms of interest group activity, namely that it is an exercise in non-legitimate power, whereby the leaders of such groups are not publicly accountable and their influence bypasses the representative process. If the government had accepted this deal, it would, in effect, have indeed bypassed any representative process, and it is interesting that the main opposition to this deal came from backbench Fianna Fáil TDs who, at least some of them claimed, were merely reiterating the views of their private sector constituents. Moreover, this deal, if it had gone through, would also have confirmed the idea of interest groups and governments being engaged in a closed and secretive policy process, where the groups exerted influence through negotiation and made a deal that was not subject to any public scrutiny. Ultimately, however, the failure of the deal led to one of the severest budgets in the history of the state, with pay cuts of up to nine per cent for some public sector workers, and cuts to a whole plethora of social welfare payments.

ABORTION AND THE POLITICS OF DIVISION

One of the crucial negative influences of interest groups is their capacity to be divisive in that they are primarily concerned with the particular nature of their own interests and advance these interests against those that work for society as a whole. In that context, the divisiveness of political debate in Ireland in the 1980s and 1990s offers a good prism through which to examine interest groups as political operatives. Since 1983, there have been five referendums on abortion and two on divorce and, in essence, the campaigns were conducted primarily through the medium of the interest group. While it is beyond the scope of this chapter to go into all these referendums in detail, the original 1983 abortion referendum offers a good case study of the impact of pressure politics on political parties.

The sequence of constitutional amendments dealing with moral issues began with the abortion referendum of 1983 and continued up to and including the abortion referendum of March 2002. It was those groups who wished to impose a distinctly Catholic view of morality on the Irish state who would become the acknowledged leaders in the field of pressure group politics. Indeed, the Society for the Protection of the Unborn Child (SPUC) sprang up completely unannounced in 1981 and within two years had, along with other like-minded groups, under the umbrella of the Pro-Life Amendment Campaign (PLAC), successfully persuaded the government of the day to call a referendum with the purpose of introducing an amendment that would, in effect, guarantee the rights of the unborn child and constitutionally outlaw abortion (Girvin 1986). The Fine Gael–Labour coalition government of the day appeared to be ill-equipped to deal with such a highly organised pressure group – indeed the same could be said for the opposition Fianna Fáil party – and the result was significant social division, the effects of which still linger, as evidenced by the refusal of abortion to disappear as a political issue. For instance, during the 2008 Lisbon Treaty referendum campaign, the pressure group Cóir, who were vigorous opponents of the Treaty, argued that its acceptance through the adoption of the Charter of Fundamental Rights would change Irish law in the areas of abortion and euthanasia (Quinlan 2009:109–12). In fact, the 'Yes' campaign's failure to convince the electorate that issues surrounding abortion, among others, such as conscription and corporate taxation, were not part of the Treaty played a significant part in the defeat of the 'Yes' campaign in the first Treaty referendum in June 2008 (Sinnott *et al.* 2009:27, 39).

The Abortion Referendum of 1983

Interest groups targeted the Constitution as their particular *modus operandi* in attempting to influence public policy on questions of morality. In Ireland, restrictive abortion legislation had remained intact and virtually unchallenged since 1861 under Section 58 of the Offences against the Person Act. Section 59 of the same act also provided that anyone helping a woman have an abortion would be liable to considerable penalties (Hesketh 1990:1–2). Why, if such a situation existed, did the government of the day put a deeply divisive referendum to the people in 1983, when up to just a number of years previously there had been virtually no calls for any repeal of the existing legislation?

In essence, the so-called pro-life campaign was pre-emptive in that its aim was to prevent the future legislation of abortion in Ireland. It anticipated that abortion might become legal through either parliamentary action or court activity, or both.

It seemed to fear that a simple amendment of the existing act could legalise abortion, notwithstanding that the idea of replacing the existing Act with a more permissive or liberal Act was simply not an option that any government would be willing to sign up to or even want to do. Second, the pro-life campaign feared that if abortion was not constitutionally prohibited, there would be a danger that an action could be taken in the Irish courts to challenge the then existing legislative prohibition of abortion in an attempt to have it declared unconstitutional.

In the hectic political atmosphere of 1981–1982, which saw three general elections in the space of eighteen months, the question of an anti-abortion amendment to the Constitution forced its way on to the political agenda. In April 1981, the leader of Fine Gael (then in opposition), Dr Garret FitzGerald, was approached by a group of people who said that they were concerned about the possibility that the Irish Supreme Court might copy its American counterpart's decision in the case of *Roe v. Wade*, which a decade earlier had declared state legislation against abortion to be unconstitutional in the USA. The Fianna Fáil government of Charles Haughey had also been approached by the same group. Dr FitzGerald has since written that it seemed highly improbable to him that the Irish Supreme Court would ever challenge the existing abortion legislation. Nevertheless, such was his personal antipathy to abortion, and conscious as he was of the opposition of the vast majority of the people of Ireland, he was willing to support a constitutional amendment that would limit the court's functions in this matter (FitzGerald 1991:416).

FitzGerald, as Taoiseach, had met PLAC in late 1981 to tell them that a constitutional change in relation to abortion would be incorporated into a general constitutional review that he had proposed. They were dissatisfied with his response (FitzGerald 1991:416). PLAC also met with Fianna Fáil, who were more receptive to the idea of a single referendum on abortion. Haughey wrote to PLAC, stating:

> I am glad to be able to confirm to your executive committee that when elected to office the new Fianna Fáil Government will arrange to have the necessary legislation for a proposed constitutional amendment to guarantee the right of the life of the foetus initiated in Dáil Éireann during the course of this year, 1982, without reference to any other aspect of constitutional change. (O'Reilly 1992:75)

The singularity of this proposal was in direct contrast to the FitzGerald view on the amendment as part of a constitutional package. PLAC continued to keep up the pressure on Fine Gael and the result was that by the time of the November 1982 general election, both Fianna Fáil and Fine Gael had declared they would, if elected, introduce a pro-life abortion amendment into the Irish Constitution. Nowhere in FitzGerald's memoirs (1991) does he state what sorts of pressure tactics were brought to bear on him from such groups. Yet the reality is that his government, and indeed that of Haughey in the same period, was hopelessly ill-equipped to deal with such a highly organised pressure group as PLAC.

In essence, the original referendum on abortion came about quite simply due to the incessant lobbying of a number of highly vocal interest groups who argued that the legal ban on abortion could be overturned in the courts and that a constitutional ban on abortion was imperative. Eventually, the wording that Fianna Fáil put forward, which was acceptable to PLAC, was forced through by the Fine Gael–Labour government against the advice of its own attorney-general, Peter Sutherland. FitzGerald has subsequently written that he should never have accepted

> the original referendum proposal put to me, however harmless it may have appeared at the time, for that commitment to introduce a constitutional amendment on the issue led me into a position that, while intellectually defensible, was much too complicated to secure public understanding or acceptance. (FitzGerald 1991:446)

Then why did he do it? His reaction to his first meeting with the PLAC has been described as 'grovelling' by one PLAC member present (O'Reilly 1992:68).

The perceived electoral power of influence that such groups might well pose is the most plausible explanation behind such acquiescence to PLAC's demands. While such groups have had a negligible effect when they have presented themselves to the electorate in national elections, the fear in the early 1980s of being perceived as 'soft on abortion', as FitzGerald himself said, alluding to a rumour then doing the rounds about him (FitzGerald 1991:416), would have been enough to have been electorally suicidal in the fluid political situation then in existence and in which Fine Gael would come historically close to overtaking Fianna Fáil as the leading party in the state. The PLAC was an umbrella group that formed with the intention of getting a single piece of legislation enacted and did everything in its power to ensure such an outcome.

Subsequent Abortion Referendums

In 1991, the then Taoiseach, Charles Haughey, and Minister for Foreign Affairs, Gerard Collins, were also convinced by anti-abortion activists that Ireland needed a special protocol on abortion in the Maastricht Treaty on European Union (EU), which was due for ratification the following year. The argument presented to the then Fianna Fáil–Progressive Democrat coalition government was that without such a protocol there was a fear that opponents of abortion in Ireland would oppose the Maastricht Treaty.

Given the recorded mobilising power of these groups in previous referendums, this was not a threat to be taken lightly by the government. In December 1991, Collins persuaded his European colleagues to take the protocol on board. It was a decision that had come about through the efforts of the pro-life lobby (O'Reilly 1992:139; Murphy 2003a:34). However, once the Supreme Court famously adjudicated in 1992 that abortion was in fact permissible in Ireland under the eighth amendment to the Constitution, if a mother's life was at risk through suicide, pressure from groups lobbying to overturn this decision became intense. Inevitably, the Supreme Court decision led to yet another round of referendums on this issue in 1992.

However, the three abortion referendums of 1992 on the so-called substantive issue, on the right to travel and the right to information were very different from the 1983 referendum in that the Fianna Fáil caretaker government took a much more hard-line position in relation to the pressure exerted on it by the pro-life groups, withstood the wording offered by such groups and pushed forward with their own wording. Indeed, the government of Albert Reynolds adopted a significantly tougher stance than Haughey's government of only a few months earlier when it came to dealing with such lobbying. This can be put down to Reynolds's personal belief that it was the duty of government, and indeed all political parties, rather than of interest groups, to offer leadership in such sensitive social areas. The whole abortion saga does, however, clearly reiterate the point that in this extremely complex area the capacity of interest groups to be divisive was overwhelmingly seen to be true. Moreover, this issue also emphasises the point that interest groups can make the policy process closed and secretive by exerting influence through negotiation and deals that are not subject to public scrutiny, as was clearly the case with the referendum on the eighth amendment to the Constitution.

In March 2002, the Irish people faced yet another referendum on abortion designed, in essence, to limit the capacity of the Oireachtas to legislate for a complex issue. Why the government went down this road when experience would seem to have shown that the complexities of abortion were not capable of being definitively settled by constitutional action is unclear, but it seems in the final analysis that the Taoiseach, Bertie Ahern, decided that a constitutional amendment was the only way to solve the issue. On this occasion, in an attempt to avoid the division of 1983 and 1992, the proposal followed an extensive governmental consultation process with a whole variety of lobby groups, including the medical profession, the Catholic Church and, indeed, both pro-life and pro-choice groups.

The main pro-life groups, the Pro-Life Campaign and the Pro-Life Movement, gave the amendment their enthusiastic support, but there is no evidence, as there was in the 1983 referendum in particular, of pressure being successfully brought to bear on the government of the day. Indeed, the government itself was somewhat split on the issue, with the Progressive Democrats showing no great enthusiasm for the amendment. Once again, however, the pro-life ranks split, with extreme groups such as Youth Defence and its ally the Mother and Child Campaign opposing the amendment on the grounds of its failure to protect the unborn from the moment of conception. In a clear sign of voter disenchantment with the politics of morality being fought out via referendum, the 2002 turnout at 42.89 per cent was significantly lower than in 1992 (68.16 per cent) and 1983 (53.67 per cent), and the proposal narrowly defeated, with 50.4 per cent voting against it (Murphy 2003b:16). Nevertheless, abortion, as an issue, is never far from the political horizon and cropped up in a significant way, as we have seen, in the Lisbon referendum debates.

CAMPAIGNING IN THE LISBON TREATY: THE CHECKING OF GOVERNMENTAL POWER

A critical positive feature of interest groups is their ability to provide a check on government power and, in the process, to defend liberty by ensuring that the state is balanced by a vigorous and healthy civil society. This can be seen vividly in the campaigns on the Lisbon Treaty. A new dynamic emerged in interest group politics during the 2008 Lisbon Treaty referendum, when a previously unheard-of organisation called Libertas became a key driver in the 'No' campaign. Describing itself as a movement dedicated to campaigning for greater democratic accountability and transparency in the institutions of the EU, Libertas, under its leader, businessman Declan Ganley, brought a completely new dynamic to opposing EU referendums in Ireland.

Up to the Lisbon Treaty, such opposition mostly came from groups on the left of the political spectrum, but for Lisbon, Libertas, arriving unannounced on the political scene early in 2008, actively campaigned on the idea that the Treaty was bad for Irish business. The Lisbon Treaty campaign became a melting pot of sorts for lobby groups from across the political divide, with those on the 'No' side ranging from Cóir (an offshoot of Youth Defence) and other anti-abortion elements, to the Peace and Neutrality Alliance, to People Before Profit, to Libertas.

After the referendum was successfully defeated, Libertas announced that it was considering running candidates in the 2009 elections to the European parliament and reckoned it could win up to seventy seats (Staunton 2008). In December 2008, Libertas reconstituted itself as a pan-European political party, rather than simply an interest group, dedicated to defeating the Lisbon Treaty, as was its original raison d'être, by declaring its intention to run candidates in all the states of the EU.

Libertas eventually contested elections in fourteen European states, running over six hundred candidates, but performed spectacularly badly, winning only one seat in France. Ganley himself ended up losing, albeit narrowly, in the Ireland North West constituency and rather dramatically announced that the electorate had spoken and that he was retiring from politics. He returned, however, to the Irish political scene just three months later, this time to campaign against the second Lisbon Treaty referendum. But, in a completely changed economic environment, the electorate decided to ignore his warnings about their lives being dominated by a European super-state and endorsed the Lisbon Treaty, with 67 per cent voting yes.

The Irish state, of course, has seen parties emerge spectacularly to take a significant share of the electorate's vote at various times. Clann na Poblachta, campaigning mainly on the national question, but also having a radical edge in social policies that Éamon de Valera's Fianna Fáil had lost during its long tenure in power, emerged spectacularly in the mid-1940s and became associated with ending Fianna Fáil hegemony (Murphy 2009b:29–30). Clann na Poblachta's lifespan, though, was to be remarkably short. A generation later both Democratic Left and, more significantly, the Progressive Democrats, at different ends of the political spectrum, emerged to play significant roles in coalition government. Both again, however, like Clann na Poblachta, failed to live up to their promise and faded away. Democratic Left was subsumed into the larger Labour Party but without any concomitant increase in the Labour vote at subsequent general elections. For their part the Progressive Democrats ended up being decimated after the 2007 general election, having gone in a short twenty years from a party who were going to change the face of Irish politics to one that wound up with a leader who had never even been elected to national office.

Rafter (2009) argued that with the disbandment of the Progressive Democrats there was room for a niche party promoting value for public money and acting as an advocate for private enterprise in Irish society. Yet the residual strength of Fianna Fáil, Fine Gael and indeed the Labour Party, combined with the history of parties such as Clann na Talmhan, Clann na Poblachta, Democratic Left and the Progressive Democrats, would suggest that any gains to be made by such a party would dissipate sooner rather than later, but the evidence is that dissipate they will. Even if such a party were to enter a coalition government with either Fianna Fáil or Fine Gael, the historical evidence is again that it would not flourish long term. The Irish electorate, while occasionally happy to vote promiscuously, seems always to ultimately reject the newcomer, forcing it to either disband or join with one of the larger parties. Nevertheless, the fundamental point remains that, by providing a fulcrum for opposition to the government's position on the European question, all opponents of the Lisbon Treaty, not just Libertas, fulfil one of the primary positive functions of interest groups in a liberal democracy: that of providing a check on government power and, in the process, defending liberty by ensuring that the state is balanced by a vigorous and healthy civil society. This can best be judged in action, rather than theory, and opposition to government in European referendums, from both the right and the left, is a healthy sign of liberal democracy in Ireland.

CONCLUSION

Earlier in the chapter, we made reference to the fact that the co-opting of interest groups into the policy process was often of greater significance for policy outcomes than general elections, given the relationship between governments and such groups. As we have seen, modern Ireland has indeed been governed by such a method in two critical areas: the economy, through social partnership: and morally, through various abortion referendums.

Prior to its demise in late 2009, the process of social partnership had, in effect, mediated the way the Irish economy was run. One critical result of this was that the public was effectively excluded from the main nature of economic governance in the state. While trade unionists got to vote on whether their unions should participate in these agreements, and while one could also plausibly argue that the electorate got to have a say on such issues at subsequent general elections, it nevertheless remains the case that these agreements were negotiated in secret. They were not open to any real public scrutiny, with opposition parties, for instance, having no idea of what was going on with regard to these deals, notwithstanding the fact that on conclusion they would be legally binding beyond the outcome of general elections. Yet, within social partnership, despite the criticisms regarding the secrecy of these deals, sectional interests play an important role as a conduit to government for their members, who would not otherwise have any ready access to the decision-making process.

In relation to abortion, certain interest groups managed to persuade governments of various hues to have amendments put to the people and it was these interest groups who campaigned hardest to get these referendums passed or defeated. Ultimately, what Irish society got out of the original eighth amendment to the Constitution on abortion and the so-called right to life was a period of social division, the after-effects of which still linger in Irish society, judging by the reappearance of abortion as an issue in the Lisbon Treaty referendum of 2008. While the Treaty has nothing whatsoever to do with abortion, the fact that the 'Yes' campaign could not properly deal with it and overcome various rumours about the Charter of Fundamental Rights is indicative of the power of the abortion question to mobilise certain elements of Irish society.

Recent referendums on European treaties have also seen interest groups come to the fore. This was most noticeable during the Lisbon Treaty debates of 2008 and 2009. Here, the influence of interest groups could be characterised in a more positive light as they have offered, from both right and left of the political and social spectrum, an alternative voice to the hegemonic governmental position that all European treaties in and of themselves are good for Ireland and its citizens. While this may well be the case, it is important that this view be rigorously investigated, and European referendums are an important focus in that regard. Through their efforts in consciousness raising, thereby creating a better-informed electorate, both 'Yes' and 'No' advocates created the conditions where we saw interest group behaviour benefiting society generally, as questions on Ireland's future in the European project were more systematically examined than in any other referendum since Ireland's original entry to the then European Economic Community in 1973.

Ultimately, one cannot reach a definitive conclusion as to whether interest group activity in Ireland is beneficial or detrimental to Irish society. As we have seen, there have been both significantly positive and negative effects from the lobbying activities of such groups. Irish society is well served by interest groups being able to get access to the levers of governmental power. It is, however, on much more shaky ground when the results of that access favours one section of society over another to the extent that governments do not, in effect, govern for the whole of society, but only for parts of it. While groups may have such an expectation, it is the job of governments to allow them access, but to temper their expectations.

References

Allen, K. (2000) *The Celtic Tiger: The Myth of Social Partnership in Ireland.* Manchester: Manchester University Press.

Bentley, A. (1967) *The Process of Government.* Chicago, IL: University of Chicago Press.

Beyers, J., Eising, R. and Maloney, W. (2008) 'Researching Interest Group Politics in Europe and Elsewhere: Much We Study, Little We Know?', *West European Politics* 31(6): 1103–28.

Cawson, A. (1986) *Corporatism and Political Theory.* Oxford: Basil Blackwell.

CSO (Central Statistics Office) (2009) 'Community Involvement and Social Networks 2006' [online]. Available: http://www.cso.ie/releasespublications/documents/labour_market/2006/comsoc06.pdf (last accessed 21 December 2009).

Dahl, R.A. (1961) *Who Governs? Democracy and Power in an American City.* New Haven, CT: Yale University Press.

FitzGerald, G. (1991) *All in a Life.* Dublin: Gill & Macmillan.

Gallagher, M., Laver, M. and Mair, P. (2006) *Representative Government in Modern Europe: Institutions, Parties and Governments*, 4th edn. New York, NY: McGraw-Hill.

Girvin, B. (1986) 'Social Change and Moral Politics: The Irish Constitutional Referendum 1983', *Political Studies* 34(1): 61–81.

Hardiman, N. (2002) 'From Conflict to Co-ordination: Economic Governance and Political Innovation in Ireland', *West European Politics* 25(4): 1–24.

Hesketh, T. (1990) *The Second Partitioning of Ireland: The Abortion Referendum of 1983.* Dublin: Brandsma Books.

Heywood, A. (2007) *Politics*, 3rd edn. Basingstoke: Palgrave.

Jordan, A.G. (1990) 'The Pluralism of Pluralism: An Anti-theory', *Political Studies* 38(2): 286–301.

Jordan, G. and Maloney, W.A. (2007) *Democracy and Interest Groups.* Basingstoke: Palgrave.

Lindblom, C.E. (1977) *Politics and Markets.* New York, NY: Basic Books.

Mair, P. and van Biezen, I. (2001) 'Party Membership in Twenty European Democracies, 1980–2000', *Party Politics* 7(1): 5–21.

Marsh, M. (2005) 'Parties and Society', in J. Coakley and M. Gallagher (eds) *Politics in the Republic of Ireland*, 4th edn, pp. 160–80. Abingdon: Routledge.

McGraw, S. (2008) 'Managing Changes: Party Competition in the New Ireland', *Irish Political Studies* 23(4): 627–48.

Murphy, G. (2003a) 'Pluralism and the Politics of Morality', in M. Adshead and M. Millar (eds) *Public Administration and Public Policy in Ireland: Theory and Methods*, pp. 20–36. London: Routledge.

— (2003b) 'The Background to the Election', in M. Gallagher, M. Marsh and P. Mitchell (eds) *How Ireland Voted 2002*, pp 1–20. Basingstoke: Palgrave.

— (2009a) 'Interest Groups in the Policy Making Process', in J. Coakley and M. Gallagher (eds) *Politics in the Republic of Ireland*, 5th edn, pp. 327–58. Abingdon: Routledge.

— (2009b) *In Search of the Promised Land: The Politics of Post-War Ireland*. Cork: Mercier Press.

O'Reilly, E. (1992) *Masterminds of the Right*. Dublin: Attic Press.

Quinlan, S. (2009) 'The Lisbon Treaty Referendum 2008', *Irish Political Studies* 24(1): 107–21.

Rafter, K. (2009) 'Wanted: A Champion of Public-Sector Cuts', *Sunday Times*, 19 April, p. 14.

Richardson, J.J. (ed.) (1993) *Pressure Groups*. Oxford: Oxford University Press.

Sinnott, R., Elkink, J.A., O'Rourke, K. and McBride, J. (2009) 'Attitudes and Behaviour in the Referendum on the Treaty of Lisbon', report prepared for the Department of Foreign Affairs [online]. Available: http://www.dfa.ie/uploads/documents/ucd%20geary%20institute%20report.pdf (last accessed 21 December 2009).

Smith, M.J. (1990) 'Pluralism, Reformed Pluralism and Neopluralism: The Role of Pressure Groups in Policy-Making', *Political Studies* 38(2): 302–22.

Staunton, D. (2008) 'Libertas may Contest European Elections', *Irish Times*, 17 July [online]. Available: http://www.irishtimes.com/newspaper/ireland/2008/0716/1216073118337.html (last accessed 2 July 2010).

Truman, D. (1951) *The Governmental Process: Political Interests and Public Opinion*. New York, NY: Knopf Press.

Weeks, L. (2009) 'Parties and the Party System', in J. Coakley and M. Gallagher (eds) *Politics in the Republic of Ireland*, 5th edn, pp. 137–67. Abingdon: Routledge.

Wilson, G.K. (1991) *Interest Groups*. Oxford: Basil Blackwell.

Chapter 26

Civil Society in Ireland: Antecedents, Identity and Challenges

Geoff Weller

INTRODUCTION

The civil society debate is ongoing and full of conflict, reflecting the fact that civil society, as a concept, is contested, with no single shared definition or single theoretical model. Civil society continues to mean many things to many people. The concept of civil society comes perilously close to being the 'play dough' of the social sciences, capable of being formed into almost any shape the theorist chooses (Van Til and Ross 2001:122). At its most basic, civil society is 'that space of organised activity not undertaken by Government or for-profit business' (Daly and Howell 2006:6). This not-for-profit sector of society may be understood, according to Frumkin (2002:9), as:

> a sometimes confusing conglomeration of strongly held private values, as well as a complex set of public purposes. The sector can thus be conceived as a tent covering public-serving charities, member-serving organisations, and a range of informal organisations, including voluntary and grassroots associations.

Civil society organisations are responsible for ensuring pluralism in political systems, exercising restraint on governments, generating policy ideas, and also working to implement government policy (Connolly 2007:4). The idea of civil society has taken root in America and elsewhere because of its articulation by those who led the recent liberation of such Central European nations as the former Czechoslovakia, Hungary and Poland from four decades of Soviet dominion (Van Til and Ross 2001:122). The academic debate, as a result of research on the recent democratisation of Eastern Europe, has framed civil society as essential to democracy (Connolly 2007:4).

The present interest in civil society in Ireland and elsewhere is, according to Salamon *et al.* (1999:3), the result of a 'global associational revolution', evident as:

a massive upsurge of organised private, voluntary activity in virtually every corner of the globe. The product of new communications technologies, significant popular demands for greater opportunity, dissatisfaction with the operations of both the market and the state in coping with the inter-related social and economic challenges of our day, the availability of external assistance, and a variety of other factors, this associational revolution has focused new attention, and new energy, on the broad range of social institutions that occupy the social space between the market and the state.

The authors categorise the 'social space' to which the 'broad range of social institutions' belong as being variously described as: the 'non-profit' sector, the 'voluntary' sector, the 'third' sector, the 'social economy', the 'NGO' (non-governmental organisation) sector, the 'charitable' sector and the 'civil society' sector. In Ireland, as in the rest of Europe and America, all of these terms are in use.

TRACING THE CIVIL SOCIETY SECTOR

Describing the Irish civil society sector is difficult due to the lack of a complete database from which a definition and delineations may be gleaned. The lack of a single comprehensive source, indicating, for example, the activities and size and number of organisations, has been an ongoing issue that has irked researchers engaged in the field (Acheson *et al.* 2004; Department of Social, Community and Family Affairs 2000; Donnelly-Cox *et al.* 2001; Donoghue *et al.* 2006; O'Sullivan 2005). An effort to address this concern, *The Hidden Landscape: First Forays into Mapping Nonprofit Organisations in Ireland* (Donoghue *et al.* 2006) is the most comprehensive mapping project to date. It offers a good deal of information on the Irish civil society sector, plugging gaps in the knowledge of the 'non-profit', or civil society, sector in Ireland. Further, the Taskforce on Active Citizenship, commissioned by the former Taoiseach Bertie Ahern in 2006, has sought to provide statistical evidence of citizen participation in such areas as civic, community, cultural, occupational and recreational life in Ireland.

The roots of the Irish civil society sector are in a variety of traditions. Religious organisations were fundamental in the nineteenth and twentieth centuries to the development of welfare, health and educational services on a not-for-profit basis whilst rural and urban communities drew on less formal traditions of mutual aid to establish co-operative and associational organisations (O'Regan *et al.* 2005:4). Social concerns and movements in Ireland have been reflected in the growth of civil society organisations since the 1960s, particularly in the areas of community development, women's rights, environmental issues and the representation of marginalised groups from a rights-based perspective (Donoghue 1998). Keenan (2008:18) has identified that the sector has had to meet a number of challenges, in a society that has undergone significant changes in the past two decades, which have included: the need to respond appropriately to the changing face of poverty and disadvantage in a growing economy; the growth of new family forms and the introduction of divorce; the impact of immigration and the needs of migrants; the growth of drug use and drug-related crime; and an ageing population. The period has also presented significant opportunities for civil society, including: a much more benign public and private funding environment; increased emphasis on professionalism, innovation and entrepreneurship; the benefits of more affordable and accessible information and communications technology; and an increased focus on evidence- and rights-based initiatives (Keenan 2008:18).

Ireland has been positioned within the broader debates about civil society in the various 'processes of change' occurring locally, nationally and globally (see Callanan 2005; Collins 2002; Deakin 2001; Meade 2005), with academic focus being on work into voluntary and community organisations and community development. Research has examined the economic significance of the Irish civil society sector (Donoghue et al. 2006), the modelling of Irish civil society organisations (Donnelly-Cox and O'Regan 1999), the relationships between the state and Irish language civil society organisations (Donoghue 2004a), foundations in Ireland (Donoghue 2004b) and volunteering amongst young Irish adults (Weller 2008; Weller and O'Rourke 2006).

The most comprehensive recent research on the civil society sector in Ireland (i.e. Donoghue et al. 2006) estimated that it is made up of around 24,000 organisations of varying sizes and capabilities and representing a wide range of interests. The authors suggest that the environment in which the civil society sector operates is undergoing a 'great change [that is] social, economic, demographic, cultural and, if the proposed regulation of charities comes into force, legal' (Donoghue et al. 2006:79; note that the legal change identified by Donoghue has occurred with the introduction of the Charities Act 2009). The authors rightly conclude that the civil society sector has reached a stage in its history where such a survey may offer answers to organisations' 'questions about their futures' (Donoghue et al. 2006:79). The main findings of the report are as follows.

- Half of all responding civil society organisations are 'young', having been established only in the past twenty years.
- The organisations are engaged in a wide range of activities for a large number of beneficiaries, both individuals and organisations, particularly in the fields of development and housing, education and research, sports and recreation, culture and arts, and social services.
- The total income for the sector was estimated at €2.564bn and total expenditure €2.556bn in 2003.
- Most organisations (90 per cent) earned less than the mean income of €738,205, with half of all organisations earning an income of less than €40,000 and expending €39,000 or less.

- The economic contribution of the responding sample came to 2.17 per cent of gross national product (GNP), which when grossed up to include the full sampling frame equals 3.84 per cent.
- Those organisations that reported resource vulnerability (deficits between reported income and expenditure) were in the fields of the environment, culture and the arts, international development and religion.
- Those that were the most resource secure were involved in philanthropy, trade unions, sports and recreation, advocacy, law and politics, and development and housing.
- The number of volunteers in Ireland is 1.5 million, with male volunteers outnumbering female volunteers by a ratio of three to one.
- The organisations report that the most important relationships for generating financial resources were with the state, and the local community or wider society.
- The most important relationships for generating human resources (including volunteers) were found to be the local community and wider society, and to a lesser extent other voluntary and community groups.
- The role played by Irish civil society organisations in communities is important.
- Religious values are declining in significance among civil society organisations in Ireland, as is the importance of religious organisations as providers of financial and human resources, service delivery and for developing public policy. (Donoghue *et al.* 2006:79–83).

The Irish state has been a key actor in the development of the Irish civil society sector. This has been achieved through an active policy of supporting social, educational and health services, particularly through religious organisations, and through its financial support of particular organisations (Acheson *et al.* 2004). The traditional voluntary organisation has given way, in recent decades, to professional or social service voluntary organisations (Donnelly-Cox and Jaffro 1998). These exist alongside community development organisations, with a strong emphasis on community participation and empowerment.

There is no single organisation that represents the whole of the civil society sector in Ireland. Instead, collaborative groups have developed, for example in the areas of disability (Disability Federation of Ireland, currently with seven full member organisations and forty-two associates) and development aid (Dóchas, currently with thirty-seven member organisations), while pressure groups working to affect specific policy have also emerged, such as the Irish Senior Citizens' Parliament (currently with 410 affiliated member organisations) and the Children's Rights Alliance (currently with eighty-eight affiliated member organisations) (Keenan 2008). A number of organisations work to promote the interests of the sector as a whole: these include the Irish Charities Tax Reform Group (currently with 140 member organisations) and The Wheel (currently with 800 member organisations).

The social partnership model in Ireland (see Teague 2006; also Chapters 13 and 14) has provided a template for civil society's relationship with the state and local government (Daly 2007; Donnelly-Cox and Jaffro 1998). Specific policies on the relationship between the state and civil society organisations date from 2000, with the publication of the White Paper *Supporting Voluntary Activity*. Donoghue *et al.* (2006:16) identify that it sets out the core principles that continue to shape the relationship between the state and civil society, recognising:

1   that the non-profit sector is a fundamental component of a vibrant civil society
2   the necessity to consult non-profit service providers and other groups in receipt of state funding about service design and development
3   the sector's diversity and autonomy
4   the sector's role in contributing to policy and relevant legislation
5   the state's legal obligation to deliver services.

The Towards 2016 partnership agreement restates the government's recognition (previously outlined in the White Paper noted above) of the role of community and voluntary organisations in the creation of a vibrant, participative democracy and civil society, and it commits government to significantly increase the role of the sector by deepening the partnership between it and civil society organisations (Government of Ireland 2006). The issues of definition and delineation of the sector have only recently been clearly set out in the legislative framework governing statutory civil society relationships. The issue of a lack of development in this area has been addressed in the Charities Act 2009 (Oireachtas 2009). Despite these recent important government initiatives there is little coherence or consistency in either its view of the sector or what its relationship with it should be. Keenan (2008:18) describes the effect of this as:

> Specific actions sometimes appear to have conflicting goals, while senior politicians and officials seem to act more out of personal conviction than a well-developed philosophy or considered medium-to-long-term strategy. Fundamentally, there appears to be no worked-through perspective on the sector's role and its contribution to society.

This lack of a shared vision for the future of civil society in Ireland is a significant omission in the relationship between the state and civil society. Among other issues, a recent workshop of civil society leaders identified that in order to counter this lack, the sector needs to take the lead by:

• developing a structure for collective advocacy in order to achieve positive social change in Irish society;
• showing leadership, new thinking, a new vision and to work to build a movement;

- achieving a clear vision of how civil society fits with representational politics in a healthy society and to demand that space; and
- leading the debate on the nature of democracy that is right for Irish society (Chapman 2008:4–5).

THE ISSUE OF THE HEALTH OF IRISH CIVIL SOCIETY

Concern has recently grown as to the extent to which Irish citizens are prepared to be involved in civil society; time, work, commuting and patterns of changing values and lifestyles have brought into focus questions about whether there is a 'crisis' of volunteering and community (Taskforce on Active Citizenship 2007; Weller 2008). The issue of the health of Ireland's civil society is increasing in prominence in governmental, academic and media discourse, with concerns regarding deficits in civic engagement leading conversation, comment and policy. The renewed interest in civil society and volunteering may be understood as part of a broader worldwide trend to engage with 'perceived' deficits in civil society (Seligman 2002:28) and to encourage individuals to play a more active role in different aspects of economic, political and social development (Taylor 2003:43). More directly, Daly (2007:2) notes that there is a resurgence in interest in Irish civil society because of a number of factors:

- the inequality of access to the benefits of the successful economy
- the decline in the influence of the Catholic church
- corruption scandals which have undermined trust in political leaders and political institutions
- critiques of Ireland as a nation of consumers, where individual interests predominate over those of the broader society.

Political action on the question of a crisis in civil society may also be attributed directly to the effect of Robert Putnam's meetings with, and suggested 'guru' status for, former Taoiseach Bertie Ahern. Such a high-level interest in civil society has concentrated government efforts to investigate ways of reinvigorating Irish civil society (O'Connor 2005). Prior to announcing the members of his Taskforce on Active Citizenship, the former Taoiseach said in a *Sunday Business Post* article: 'I believe in the intrinsic value of our democratic society and the freedom it confers on all of us to participate. Ironically, for democracy to work, participation is not really optional; it is critical to ensure we have ongoing healthy development' (O'Connor 2005). This belief has clearly shaped recent political efforts and discourse. The effort to reinvigorate and understand Irish civil society has manifested itself via: the government's reassessment of the role of civil society organisations, particularly the role of the voluntary and community sector in meeting the needs of communities (Daly 2007:1); its seeking out of new ways of increasing citizen engagement, through the Taskforce on Active Citizenship

(2007); and an audit of Irish democracy (Harris 2005). The special legal nature of civil society organisations was also, at last, set down in law in the Charities Act 2009 (Oireachtas 2009), which gives legal charitable status to civil society organisations that wish to present themselves to the public as charities, or fundraise directly from the public for charitable purposes. The new-found concern over the health of Irish civil society and its ramifications for democracy was also reflected in a more populist form in RTÉ's *Time of Our Lives Survey* (Daly 2007:1).

A 'CRISIS' IN IRISH CIVIL SOCIETY?

The state-sponsored Taskforce on Active Citizenship's recent reports have sought to answer the question of whether there is a 'crisis' in Irish civil society, particularly in relation to volunteering and the community, and also a loss of trust in institutions, politics and the capacity of communities for collective action. The report outlines its raison d'être as being the result of 'Huge progress [resulting in] social, economic and cultural changes', some of which 'have eroded aspects of community spirit and human well-being' (Taskforce on Active Citizenship 2007:11). The aim of the taskforce was (and continues to be) to instigate an investigation and a discussion on active citizenship in Ireland, a form of citizenship that it defines as requiring active engagement in the civil society:

> In our view, being an active citizen means being aware of, and caring about, the welfare of fellow citizens, recognising that we live as members of communities and therefore depend on others in our daily lives. Active citizens support and become involved in different types of voluntary and community activities; respect and listen to others with different views from their own; play their part in making decisions on issues that affect themselves and others, in particular by participating in the democratic process; respect ethnic and cultural diversity and are open to change; welcome new people who come to live in Ireland. (Taskforce on Active Citizenship 2007:12)

The fact that this Taskforce was established by the former Taoiseach to lead a 'national conversation . . . to establish what Active Citizenship means to people in the changed country that is Ireland today' (Taskforce on Active Citizenship 2007:14) is itself suggestive of a concern, at the very least among the political elites, the patrician and chattering classes, that something may not be quite right in the state of Irish civil society, or at least its perceived potential.

The Taskforce on Active Citizenship's report to government (Taskforce on Active Citizenship 2007), was undertaken in 2006 and is based on findings from a survey of civic engagement undertaken by the Economic and Social Research Institute (ESRI) and a parish-based survey undertaken by the Council for Research and Development, a Commission of the Irish Bishops' Conference (Taskforce on Active Citizenship 2007:16). Prior to that research there had been a number of other reports on civil society in Ireland, upon which the Taskforce sought to build (Joint Committee on Arts, Sport, Tourism, Community, Rural and Gaeltacht Affairs 2005).

The Taskforce on Active Citizenship (2007:17) found an increase in the number of adults who say that they do unpaid and regular volunteering outside the home or were actively involved in the community in the previous twelve months, and an overall stability in the pattern of active engagement. These findings are quite different from other studies that have identified poor levels of volunteering and/or patterns of decline in volunteering (Donoghue 2001; Guinness UDV Ireland 2002; NESF 2003). The taskforce's survey estimates that two million adults (two-thirds of the adult population) are not actively involved in their community, in any form of 'civic activity' (i.e. attending a public meeting, joining an action group, contacting an organisation or public representative over an issue, contacting the media, etc.) (Taskforce on Active Citizenship 2007:17). The census of 2006 suggests that this figure was actually higher, at over 2.8 million in 2006 (CSO 2006).

Census 2006 offers an interesting insight into the state of civil society volunteering in Ireland (Table 26.1). It suggests that the younger the individual is, the less likely it is that s/he will be a volunteer (CSO 2006). The census found that 553,255 persons, representing 16.4 per cent of the population aged 15 and over (3,375,399), were 'involved in one or more voluntary activity'. The 20–24 age group had the lowest participation rate in civil society, with 35,730 individuals recorded as involved in one or more voluntary activity. Of that age group, taken as a whole (342,475 individuals), the census shows that just over 10.4 per cent were engaged in voluntary activity. The individuals volunteering in that group make up just under 6.46 per cent of the whole volunteer population.

Of the 25–34 age group, 83,369 individuals were recorded as involved in one or more voluntary activity. Of that group, taken as a whole (722,439 individuals), the census shows that 11.5 per cent were engaged in voluntary activity. The individuals volunteering from that group make up 15 per cent of the whole volunteer population. Of the 35–44 age group (623,434), 19.5 per cent (121,647) engaged in voluntary activities. The group made up 22 per cent of all volunteers in Ireland.

The 45–54 age group (521,813) had the highest participation rate with 22.7 per cent involved in voluntary activities (118,589 individuals) and accounting for 21.4 per cent of the total volunteers in Ireland. The 55–64 age group (407,055 individuals) had a 21 per cent participation rate in voluntary activities (85,961) and accounted for 15.5 per cent of all volunteers in Ireland. The 65 and over age group (467,926) had a 15 per cent participation rate in voluntary activities (69,940), with volunteers in this group making up 12.6 per cent of those volunteering in Ireland. The figures suggest that civil society in Ireland is engaged with by all age groups, with those aged between 35 and 54 making up the vanguard of volunteers in 2006.

Table 26.1 Civil society volunteering in Ireland in 2006

Age group	Total persons	Total persons involved in one or more voluntary activities	Percentage of age group volunteering	Percentage of whole volunteer population
15–19 years	290,257	38,019	13%	6.9%
20–24 years	342,475	35,730	10.4%	6.46%
25–34 years	722,439	83,369	11.5%	15%
35–44 years	623,434	121,647	19.5%	22%
45–54 years	521,813	118,589	22.7%	21.4%
55–64 years	407,055	85,961	21%	15.5%
65 years & over	467,926	69,940	15%	12.6%

Source: CSO (2006).

A CIVIL SOCIETY IN FLUX

The nature of volunteering is considered by those who took part in the Taskforce's research as essentially changing in very significant ways, with a greater emphasis on responsibilities and skills. However, there is an apparent sense of unease about how wider changes in Irish society and the economy will impact on volunteering and the sense of community in the future (Taskforce on Active Citizenship 2007:19). According to the Taskforce on Active Citizenship, there is a strong interest in the concept of active citizenship and civic participation in Irish society allied with a willingness to participate in measures to achieve these. There is a perception held by half of those questioned, who were at the time working in the civil society sector, that volunteering is declining. Those individuals noted that it is harder to recruit new volunteers (Taskforce on Active Citizenship 2007:16). The authors outline a consensus among the respondents as to the barriers to active citizenship and civic participation: time, new patterns of work and leisure, changing values and choices; and in practical terms, insurance, bureaucratic burdens and lack of facilities (Taskforce on Active Citizenship 2007:16). Many of the respondents felt cut off from decision making, feeling that getting involved did not make the difference it could or should make, in their opinion (Taskforce on Active Citizenship 2007:16). The report suggests that Ireland is average to slightly below average in terms of reported group membership and volunteering compared with other Organisation for Economic Co-operation and Development (OECD) countries, but is rich in informal social networks compared to other economically developed countries.

The Taskforce report concludes that active citizenship is changing and not necessarily declining, with no clear evidence that people are less involved than before. The Survey of Civic Engagement found an increase in both volunteering and community involvement in the four years since the last similar survey in 2002 (Taskforce on Active Citizenship 2007:17). In terms of political involvement, the researchers found: 38 per cent of those who took part in the survey are interested in politics (either 'definitely' or 'somewhat'); 54 per cent said that they thought they could influence decisions at the local level; and there was 76 per cent voter registration in the 20–29 age group (Taskforce on Active Citizenship 2007:17). The authors also conclude that there is a need to acknowledge and support the unique contribution of voluntary and community organisations, viewing them as the 'backbone' of active citizenship (Taskforce on Active Citizenship 2007:19).

The 2007 report by the Institute of Public Administration, *Best of Times? The Social Impact of the Celtic Tiger* (Corcoran et al. 2007), took a different tack from that of the Taskforce on Active Citizenship, considering instead the propensity of Ireland's growing population of suburbanites to engage in voluntary activity/membership in voluntary organisations. The emphasis of this particular study was on local involvement in suburban locations – the focus being on the social fabric of those suburbs. The research found that there is a danger now, and as Ireland's suburbs grow, of the erosion of 'the many ties that bind in suburbia' (Corcoran et al. 2007:197). The study focused on four locations: Lucan, Ratoath, Mullingar and Leixlip (Corcoran et al. 2007:192). The research found that: 31 per cent of the Lucan respondents claim membership of local voluntary organisations; for Ratoath the figure was 34 per cent; for Mullingar 40 per cent; and for Leixlip 48 per cent (Corcoran et al. 2007:192). To understand further local participation, the proportion of respondents engaged at any time in 'a form of action relating to local issues' was surveyed, with results that vary considerably: only 18 per cent of individuals in Mullingar were so involved; in Leixlip, 25 per cent; in Lucan, 47 per cent; and in Ratoath, 51 per cent (Corcoran et al. 2007:195).

Table 26.2 Suburban membership of/activity in voluntary organisations

Location	Membership of local voluntary organizations	Proportion of respondents engaged at any time in 'a form of action relating to local issues'
Leixlip	48%	25%
Lucan	31%	47%
Mullingar	40%	18%
Ratoath	34%	51%

Source: Corcoran et al. (2007).

The report shows that suburbanites found it difficult to deal collectively with the problems they faced as a 'community', this being the result of a lack of institutions at neighbourhood level, which left them 'struggling in their efforts at managing their own local affairs' (Corcoran *et al.* 2007:196–7). The finding of an 'institutional void' that confounded their best efforts to participate collectively in social action is echoed in the Taskforce on Active Citizenship's report to government (Taskforce on Active Citizenship 2007) in relation to the lack of facilities for new housing developments. The report suggests that 'it is difficult for people to feel respected or included or to inculcate a sense of community or citizenship' when government does not take account of their needs (Taskforce on Active Citizenship 2007:19). As more of Ireland becomes suburban every day, this void may only increase without affirmative political will and action.

CONCLUSION

The Taskforce on Active Citizenship suggests that actions should be considered that are capable of drawing together the disparate strands of civil society. This need for more collective action is echoed in the feeling among some leaders of civil society organisations in Ireland that the sector must 'step up' to show leadership, new thinking, a new vision and build an effective movement (Chapman 2008). However, this potential solidarity has yet to result in a coherent political voice, as no single established body represents civil society actors in Ireland. Instead there are many organisations that represent particular groupings and interests. There is an effective voice within the community and voluntary pillar of the social partnership process, most notably in terms of social exclusion. However, the informal nature of the process, which requires an invitation from the taoiseach to engage in dialogue with government, means that it is exclusive and unrepresentative of the sector as a whole.

The effectiveness of any government policy to reinvigorate civil society is questionable as the growth of the Irish economy has 'heightened tension' between the state and civil society organisations, splitting the sector into two camps (Daly 2007:10). The resulting tensions have forced a wedge between an organised state-influenced voluntary or civil society sector and an autonomous civil society that is creatively identifying and responding to concrete needs (O'Sullivan 2005:43, cited in Daly 2007:10). This has led to the concern that the 'illusion of consensus' (Murphy 2002) – of the social partnership between the state and civil society – is not meeting the demands and expectations of citizens (Daly 2007:10). The government's agenda on active citizenship may not have the legitimacy required to engage individuals whose needs might be more effectively met through 'autonomous' means, including forms of direct action, legal action, alternative social and political forums and campaigning and advocacy (Daly 2007:10). The question is whether these activities can fit into the social partnership framework and the government's future vision for civil society and the civil society sector, a vision that some argue (see Collins 2002) is an encroachment too far into the public sphere.

Though the civil society sector has yet to emerge as a united social movement in Ireland, with the same level of political power and will as that demonstrated by other members of the social partnership framework, it is useful to note that new forms of participation have emerged. The emergence of new forms of volunteering, such as employee volunteer programmes, virtual volunteering and episodic volunteering, open up new avenues of involvement in civil society in Ireland. Individuals can serve their community through the workplace if there is the will within the employer organisation to put in place formal and informal policies and practices to encourage and help employees to volunteer in community service activities (Tschirhart 2005:13). Virtual volunteering – the application of online technologies to permit some part of the volunteering process to be carried out at a distance from the civil society organisation (Murray and Harrison 2005:31) – has the potential to engage individuals who otherwise might never be able to take an active part in Irish civil society. Finally, the notion of engaging in a transitory way in civil society has become increasingly popular. Episodic volunteering (Handy *et al.* 2006; Macduff 2005; Weller 2008), though not new, is recognised as growing in popularity to such a degree that it has the potential to become the future of volunteering in Ireland and many other Western countries (Handy *et al.* 2006:32). These new emerging areas of volunteering exist in conjunction with more traditional forms of long-term volunteering. Alongside a new initiative to strengthen and make louder the voice of a united civil society lobby and also a growing use of 'autonomous' means of civil action, these new forms of volunteering hold the potential, should they be harnessed correctly, to invigorate the future of civil engagement in Ireland, to involve more people in their communities and beyond in new and interesting ways, and to open the debate to a wider, more involved audience as to how civil society might reshape itself and Irish society in the twenty-first century.

References

Acheson, N., Harvey, B., Kearney, J. and Williamson, A. (2004) *Two Paths, One Purpose: Voluntary Action in Ireland, North and South.* Dublin: Institute of Public Administration.

Callanan, M. (2005) 'Institutionalising Participation and Governance? New Participative Structures in Local Government in Ireland', *Public Administration* 83(4): 909–29.

Chapman, C. (2008) *Advocacy and the Nonprofit or Civil Society Sector* [online]. Available: http://www.cnm.tcd.ie/dialogue/summer-schools/Cafe%20 Workshop%2016%20Oct%202008%20report.pdf (last accessed 9 September 2009).

Collins, T. (2002) 'Community Development and State Building: A Shared Project', *Community Development Journal* 37(1): 91–100.

Connolly, E. (2007) 'The Role of Civil Society in Poverty Alleviation and Development', working paper, research project on Engagement with Civil Society for Poverty Reduction, Dublin City University.

Corcoran, M., Gray, J. and Peillon, M. (2007) 'Ties That Bind? The Social Fabric of Daily Life in New Suburbs', in T. Fahey, H. Russell and C.T. Whelan (eds) *Best of Times? The Social Impact of the Celtic Tiger*, pp. 175–97. Dublin: Institute of Public Administration.

CSO (Central Statistics Office) (2006) *Census 2006* [online]. Available: http://beyond2020.cso.ie/Census/TableViewer/tableView.aspx?ReportId=7575 8 (last accessed 9 September 2009).

Daly, S. (2007) 'Mapping Civil Society in the Republic of Ireland', *Community Development Journal* 43(2): 157–76.

Daly, S. and Howell, J. (2006) *For the Common Good? The Changing Role of Civil Society in the UK and Ireland*. London: Carnegie UK Trust.

Deakin, N. (2001) *In Search of Civil Society*. Basingstoke: Palgrave.

Department of Social, Community and Family Affairs (2000) *Supporting Voluntary Activity. A White Paper on a Framework for Supporting Voluntary Activity and for Developing the Relationship between the State and the Community and Voluntary Sector*. Dublin: Stationery Office.

Donnelly-Cox, G., Donoghue, F. and Hayes, T. (2001) 'Conceptualising the Third Sector in Ireland, North and South', *Voluntas* 12(3): 195–204.

Donnelly-Cox, G. and Jaffro, G. (1998) *The Voluntary Sector in the Republic of Ireland: Into the Twenty-First Century*. Coleraine: Centre for Voluntary Action Studies.

Donnelly-Cox, G. and O'Regan, A. (1999) 'Resourcing Organisational Growth and Development: A Typology of Third Sector Service Delivery Organisations', working paper, International Research Society for Public Management III.

Donoghue, F. (1998) 'Defining the Nonprofit Sector: Ireland', working paper, Johns Hopkins Comparative Nonprofit Sector Project 28, Johns Hopkins Institute for Policy Studies.

— (2001) *Volunteering in Ireland: The 1990s and Beyond*. Dublin: National College of Ireland.

— (2004a) *Comhsheasmhacht agus Dianseashmhacht: Rólanna, Comhchaidrimh agus Acmhainní na nEagraíochtaí Deonacha Gaeilge/Consistence and Persistence: Roles, Relationships and Resources of Irish Language Voluntary Organisations*. Dublin: Comhdháil Náisiúnta na Gaeilge/Centre for Nonprofit Management, Trinity College Dublin.

— (2004b) *Foundations in Ireland*. Dublin: Centre for Nonprofit Management, Trinity College Dublin.

Donoghue, F., Prizeman, G., O'Regan, A. and Noel, V. (2006) *The Hidden Landscape: First Forays into Mapping Nonprofit Organisations in Ireland*. Dublin: Centre for Nonprofit Management, Trinity College Dublin.

Frumkin, P. (2002) *On Being Nonprofit: A Conceptual and Policy Primer*. Cambridge, MA: Harvard University Press.

Government of Ireland (2006) *Towards 2016: Ten-Year Framework Social Partnership Agreement 2006-2016*. Dublin: Stationery Office.

Guinness UDV Ireland (2002) *Quality of Life in Ireland*. Dublin: Amárach Consulting.

Handy, F., Brodeur, N. and Cnaan, R. A. (2006) 'Summer on the Island: Episodic Volunteering', *Voluntary Action* 7(3): 31–46.

Harris, C. (2005) *The Report of the Democracy Commission. Engaging Citizens: The Case for Democratic Renewal*. Dublin: TASC at New Island.

Joint Committee on Arts, Sport, Tourism, Community, Rural and Gaeltacht Affairs (2005) *Volunteers and Volunteering in Ireland* [online]. Available: http://www.oireachtas.ie/documents/committees29thdail/jcastrag/reports/Volunteers.pdf (last accessed 9 September 2009).

Keenan, O. (2008) *Relationships and Representation, Challenges and Opportunities for the Voluntary and Community Sector in Ireland* [online]. Available: http://www.cnm.tcd.ie/dialogue/summer-schools/CNM%20Context%20Rport.pdf (last accessed 9 September 2009).

Macduff, N. (2005) 'Societal Changes and the Rise of the Episodic Volunteer', in J. Brudney (ed.) *Emerging Areas of Volunteering*, ARNOVA Occasional Paper Series, Vol.1, No.2, pp. 49–61. Indianapolis, IN: Association for Research on Nonprofit Organizations and Voluntary Associations.

Meade, R. (2005) 'We Hate it Here, Please Let us Stay! Irish Social Partnership and the Community/Voluntary Sector's Conflicted Experiences of Recognition', *Critical Social Policy* 25(3): 349–73.

Murphy, M. (2002) 'Social Partnership – Is it "The Only Game in Town"?', *Community Development Journal* 37(1): 80–90.

Murray, V. and Harrison, Y. (2005) 'Virtual Volunteering', in J. Brudney (ed.) *Emerging Areas of Volunteering*, ARNOVA Occasional Paper Series, Vol.1, No.2, pp. 31–47. Indianapolis, IN: Association for Research on Nonprofit Organizations and Voluntary Associations.

NESF (National Economic and Social Forum) (2003) *The Policy Implications of Social Capital*, Report No.28. Dublin: Government Publications.

O'Connor, A. (2005) 'Taoiseach Anxious About "Death of the Community"', *Sunday Business Post*, 13 November [online]. Available: http://archives.tcm.ie/businesspost/2005/11/13/story9640.asp (last accessed 9 September 2009).

Oireachtas (2009) *Charities Act 2009* [online]. Available: http://www.oireachtas.ie/viewdoc.asp?DocID=11424&CatID=87 (last accessed 9 September 2009).

O'Regan, A., Donnelly-Cox, G. and Hughes, E. (2005) 'Model Development for Nonprofit Management: A Case Study of Emergent Issues of Theoretical Sufficiency, Managerial Utility and Pedagogic Capacity', working paper, European Institute for Advanced Studies in Management, Queens University.

O'Sullivan, T. (2005) 'Arguments for Voluntary Action', *Administration* 53(1): 38–53.

Salamon, L.M., Anheier, H.K., List, R., Toepler, S., Sokolowski, S.W. and Associates (1999) *Global Civil Society: Dimensions of the Nonprofit Sector*. Baltimore, MD: Johns Hopkins Center for Civil Society Studies.

Seligman, A. (2002) 'Civil Society as Idea and Ideal', in S. Chambers and W. Kymlicka (eds) *Alternative Conceptions of Civil Society*, pp. 13–33. Princeton, NJ: Princeton University Press.

Taskforce on Active Citizenship (2007) *Report of the Taskforce on Active Citizenship* [online]. Available: http://www.activecitizen.ie/UPLOADEDFILES/Mar07/Taskforce%20Report%20to%20Government%20(Mar%2007).pdf (last accessed 9 September 2009).

Taylor, M. (2003) *Public Policy in the Community*. Basingstoke: Palgrave.

Teague, P. (2006) 'Social Partnership and Local Development in Ireland: The Limits to Deliberation', *British Journal of Industrial Relations* 44(3): 421–43.

Tschirhart, M. (2005) 'Employee Volunteer Programs', in J. Brudney (ed.) *Emerging Areas of Volunteering*, ARNOVA Occasional Paper Series, Vol.1, No.2, pp. 13–29. Indianapolis, IN: Association for Research on Nonprofit Organizations and Voluntary Associations.

Van Til, J. and Ross, S.W. (2001) 'Looking Backward: Twentieth-Century Themes in Charity, Voluntarism, and the Third Sector,' *Nonprofit and Voluntary Sector Quarterly* 30(1): 112–29.

Weller, G.R. (2008) 'Young Irish Adults in Civil Society: Volunteering, Reflexive Identity Work, and Social Capital', unpublished PhD dissertation, Dublin Institute of Technology.

Weller, G.R. and O'Rourke B.K. (2006) 'Confessing Egoism, Professing Altruism, Constructing Volunteer Identity: An Empirical Analysis of A Group of Volunteers' Confessions of Ambition and their Function in the Construction of Volunteer Identity', in A. Beverungun, N. Ellis, T. Keenoy, C. Oswick, I. Sabelis and S. Ybema (eds) *Organisational Discourse: Identity, Ideology and Idiosyncrasy: The Proceedings of the 7th Biennial Conference*, pp. 339–41. Leicester: KMCP.

Chapter 27

The Practice of Politics: Feminism, Activism and Social Change in Ireland

Jennifer K. DeWan

INTRODUCTION

Women in Ireland have been politically active in transforming their lives and the lives of their communities and nation throughout the twentieth century. Indeed, the Irish women's movement in all its historical and political variations has been one of the most successful social movements in Irish history (Connolly 2002; DeWan 2008). The subjectivities and practices of women's activisms to make their lives better, both explicitly feminist and otherwise, have undergone several shifts in relation to larger structural and discursive change. Most recently, the women's movement has experienced a generational shift where feminist activism in a cohesive and autonomous 'women's movement' no longer fully defines the practices and subjectivities activists employ to transform their lives. This generational shift is situated in the context of dramatic social changes in Ireland over the past few decades that are characteristic of the effects of late capitalism in a European post-colonial nation state.

The end of British colonial rule and the establishment of the twenty-six-county Irish state in 1922, the modernisation, industrialisation and secularisation of Irish society from the 1960s onwards, the escalation of sectarian violence and the slow progress towards peaceful power-sharing in Northern Ireland, and the impact of

This chapter is a brief overview of some of the main points covered in my doctoral thesis (DeWan 2008). The ethnographic and historical research for that thesis was conducted in Cork, Ireland over the course of several years and was funded by Columbia University's Scheps Summer Travel Grants and a National Science Foundation Dissertation Enhancement Grant (USA). The write-up was funded by a Woodrow Wilson Grant for Women's Studies and Columbia University. I am grateful to all the individuals and groups that participated in my research. Special thanks must go to the editors and anonymous reviewers for their comments, as well as Sherry Ortner, Sandra McAvoy and Shahzeb Lari for all their help and support.

social movements, especially the women's movement, have contributed to produce profound social, cultural, political and economic changes in contemporary Ireland. In recent decades, the country has experienced marked neo-liberal economic restructuring triggered by the shift from earlier isolationist policies toward more open, market-driven economic and social policies in the 1960s and membership of the European Economic Community (EEC), now the European Union (EU), in 1973. This economic restructuring brought rapid industrialisation, a significant increase in foreign investment by multinational (mostly American) corporations that resulted in unprecedented levels of economic growth, a huge boost in employment (especially for women), and an influx of immigration (both returning Irish emigrants and 'new' immigrants from poor and developing countries), all of which signalled the emergence of the so-called Celtic Tiger in the 1990s. These factors, indicative of late capitalist modernity, are related to the development of a significantly different relationship between the state and its citizens.

In recent years, many social theorists and commentators have lamented a perceived de-radicalisation of politics and a de-politicisation of people in relation to the effects of late capitalism, principally the forces of neo-liberalism and globalisation (Boggs 1999). These terms – late capitalism, neo-liberalism, globalisation – encompass a diverse range of political, social, economic and technological processes that are seen to describe the contemporary 'condition', what some commentators have called 'postmodernity' (Harvey 1989; Jameson 1991; Lyotard 1984). Globalisation and the neo-liberal restructuring of state economies to compete in a 'free market' has resulted in accelerated flows of capital, goods, people and information, precipitating the redistribution of wealth and power and the re-organisation of class structures (Lash and Urry 1987), as well as a profound contraction of social welfare provision in states and the transmission of many social responsibilities on to citizens (Rose 1999). In this way, late capitalism has heralded a new form of governmentality (Foucault 1991), where the state – as well as supra-state forms such as the EU – infiltrate and integrate into the spaces of civil society and the 'private' sphere, while constituting a subjectivity based in what Foucault (1988) termed the 'care of the self' (see Chapters 4 and 31). Neo-liberal states depend on these self-reliant and self-governing subjects to provide for themselves, creating what Paley (2001) has termed the 'paradox of participation', where citizens are encouraged to participate in civil society while being governed 'at a distance' (Rose 1999).

However, these are social processes that require particularities and specificities to make real sense of their effects. They are, to quote Jessop's (2003:2) critique of globalisation, 'polyvalent, promiscuous, controversial' terms that can work to obscure rather than reveal important issues in relation to the contemporary moment. If the effects of late capitalism have altered the relationship of the state to its citizens, these processes have also potentially opened up many new opportunities for actors and practices to emerge and transform the traditional fields of political engagement (Gregory 2007; Harvey 2000; Ong 1999). Political agency cannot be read entirely as the effects of subjectification as a result of large structural changes; people continue to 'practise politics' in a complex relationship with the conditions that construct, enable and constrain those actions, making their subjectivity as much as it is being made. Today, feminist political practices exceed not only the term 'social movement' but also 'feminism', occurring in both familiar and unfamiliar arenas, traditionally 'political' and not, by actors that theories of the contemporary condition cannot fully account for without the benefits of ethnographic 'thickness' (Geertz 1973) to provide some of the particularities and specificities.

This chapter explores some of the complexities of these shifts, including their relationship to social, political and economic change, their ties to the emergence of new forms of power and governmentality, and the effects of these conditions on the practices and subjectivities of feminist activisms. An examination of one way in which people 'practise politics' can function as a means to study more closely the effects of these processes on the relationship of civil society to the late capitalist state. In this sense, feminist political activism becomes a lens through which to explore questions regarding subjectivity, political agency, civil society and state power in the context of late capitalism.

SOCIAL MOVEMENTS AND LATE CAPITALISM

Social movements, as collective practices organised by polictical actors to challenge the status quo (Tarrow 2008), are an integral part of the modern world and reflect modern forms of power. They are, as Crossley (2003: 8) has noted, 'important because they are key agents for bringing about change in societies'. The study of social movements, particularly those social movements commonly referred to as 'new social movements', has become particularly relevant because they provide an ideal way to study the effects of late capitalism on the changing relationship between the state and civil society (Alvarez et al. 1998a; Edelman 1999; Paley 2001). New social movements (e.g. women's movements, environmental movements, civil rights movements, democratic movements) are seen to have emerged in the context of contemporary conditions, and are distinguishable from earlier class-based social movements in their focus on issues relating to identity, culture and quality of life, what Giddens (1991) has termed 'life politics'. According to new social movement theorists, these social movements do not only or explicitly resist political institutions, but focus on 'civil society', the domain of collective action, voluntary and community organisations, and educational and cultural institutions (Aronowitz 1992; Buechler 2000; Cohen 1985; Melucci 1996; Offe 1987). Civil society is, according to Gramsci (1973), the realm of consent (as opposed to coercion), based in the hegemonic (i.e. ideological) control of the ruling class over the 'subaltern' ruled classes, where the micro-physics of modern power constitutes and governmentalises the subject, the power that Foucault (1983:212) believed both 'subjugates and makes subject to'.

By focusing on issues within civil society, new social movements are seen to privilege cultural forms of resistance, working to challenge political institutions by redefining the boundaries of 'the political' (Laclau and Mouffe 1985).

Feminism, as an ideology and a set of practices, provides an important entry into the study of political activism, collective action and social movements, and late capitalist modernity more generally, because it occupies an anomalous space among the new social movements. Often, studies of new social movements underestimate the impact material concerns such as class or economic disadvantage continue to have on identity, cultural or 'life' politics. Because feminism concerns itself with material, economic issues (for instance in relation to equal rights in the workplace), as well as issues of identity, culture and quality of life (for example in relation to long-standing patriarchal structures of power based in gender), Habermas (1987) considers it the only remaining emancipatory liberation movement of the socialist tradition, while all other new social movements are defensive movements, characterised by 'resistance and withdrawal'. Although I agree with Habermas's assertion that feminism is anomalous among the new social movements, its anomaly comes not from its fusion of materialist and cultural concerns, but from its disruption of reductive differentiations between the cultural and the material (Butler 1997). In this sense, a nuanced analysis of feminist political practices and subjectivities can point towards new avenues of thinking about the cultural politics of social movements and collective action, complicating the 'new social movement' paradigm and challenging reductive dichotomies of 'old' and 'new', or 'political' and 'cultural', practices and subjectivities.

FEMINISM AND FRAGMENTATION

Dahlerup (1986:2) defined the women's movement as 'a conscious, collective activity to promote social change, representing a protest against the established power structures and against the dominant norms and values'. While this definition can serve as a very basic marker of what constitutes women's movements globally, what makes an understanding of any particular 'women's movement' complicated is its grounding in feminism, which is itself a problematic and incoherent category, definable only by its insistent lack of boundaries (Ahmed et al. 2000). I see feminism as a constantly changing set of interconnected and often conflicting ideologies and discursive practices aimed at the social transformation of oppressive power relations and social structures based on gender. However, Third World women, women of colour, working-class women, lesbian, bisexual and transsexual women have all shown time and again the many ways in which feminism as ideology and practice has functioned to exclude women, their histories and their avenues of struggle (Abu-Lughod 1998; Anzaldua 1990; hooks 1984; Lorde 1984; Mohanty et al. 1991; Rich 1983; Spivak 1988). Working at the margins of mainstream feminism, these feminist theorists have illustrated the importance of studying women's movements not as monolithic structures, but as dynamic sets of *practices* made up of differently positioned actors who are *practising politics* in a complex relationship with the structural conditions that work to construct, enable and constrain those actions (Ortner 1996). The variable conditions augured by late capitalist modernity serve to highlight that not only is there no monolithic subject of feminism, there is no longer even a monolithic space in which feminist politics are articulated.

Political activism in relation to the transformation of oppressive structures of power based in gender (i.e. those practices that could be identified as 'the women's movement' in Ireland) has played a key role in transforming Irish society over the last century. Despite its importance as an instigator of social change in Ireland, the women's movement is, like other non-nationalist social movements, often excluded from studies of Irish history and politics. When scholars, feminists and commentators do discuss the women's movement, most describe an evolutionary narrative of an autonomous and continuous movement beginning with a 'first wave' of suffragist activity at the turn of the twentieth century that ended with women getting the vote, first from the British in 1918 and then from the newly independent Irish Free State in 1922. The movement then goes into a period of 'abeyance' in mid-century only to emerge as the radicalised 'second wave' with the establishment of the National Commission on the Status of Women in 1970 and the founding of the Irish Women's Liberation Movement (IWLM) in 1971 (see Connolly 2002; Connolly and O'Toole 2005).

For many commentators, both feminist and non-feminist, the 1970s are nostalgically seen as the glory days of contemporary feminist radicalism and political activity that heightened public awareness, resulting in significant social transformation and legal reforms, including high-profile issues such as access to contraception, equal pay in the workplace and the removal of the marriage bar in the civil service. This period also saw a diversification of the movement into a wide variety of single-issue and service provision groups, many of which still exist today, including the Rape Crisis Centres, Women's Aid, AIM, and the Well Woman Centre. What followed was a period of conservative backlash represented most profoundly by the passing of a constitutional amendment in 1983 that equated the right to life of the unborn with a woman's right to life. This backlash resulted in the retrenchment of radical feminist politics, the emergence of a 'cultural' turn, and the decentralisation and fragmentation of the women's movement in the 1990s into networks of localised community and voluntary groups. Today the women's movement is generally characterised as professionalised and 'mainstream', integrated into and reliant on the workings of the state in the form of 'state feminism'.

While the content of this narrative is, in most respects, historically accurate, the form of the narrative and its emphasis on autonomy and continuity excludes many narratives and actors that were, and continue to be, engaged in bringing about social change in relation to women's status in Irish society. In this representation, the women's movement becomes one more link in the narrative of historical development, the story of Ireland's transition from tradition to modernity, or even 'postmodernity'. The evolutionary focus of the narrative, that the women's movement was once unified and is now fragmented, echoes idealised lamentations about the postmodern fragmentation of society that misunderstand that, for many people, the experience of instability and fragmentation is far from new (Massey 1994; Roulston 1997).

Instead of looking at the women's movement and contemporary feminist practices from the perspective of this evolutionary narrative, I argue that fragmentation has *always* defined and constituted activism around women's issues. The history of the women's movement has been more characterised by loose networks of organisations focused on a wide variety of social inequalities and reforms under particular historical and political conditions rather than one monolithic or cohesive entity that encompasses all women's issues under one broad movement. As in many other social movements, the desire to establish and represent a collective identity and a unified movement has been strong among some Irish feminists (Stein 1997). However, conflicts over differences, for example concerning ideological positionings and between 'reform' and 'radical' tactics, disallowed the formation of any long-term cohesiveness. Representing the women's movement as once unified and now fragmented clouds the fact that feminist political practices in Ireland have consistently been characterised by high levels of fragmentation and divisiveness, and only mere moments of unity.

What occurs now under the name 'women's movement' has a long and diffuse genealogy of historical and ideological trajectories that have ebbed and flowed over time, based on the conditions of possibility in that discursive moment. The fight for women's suffrage, women's activities in the labour movement, and the contestations between pacifist and nationalist feminists at the turn of the twentieth century are all related to the work of women's groups during and after the Second World War. These groups formed the *ad hoc* committee which brought about the Commission on the Status of Women in 1970, and these activists and their forms of political practice fed into the development of a radicalised 'liberation movement' in the 1970s. All of these factors have resulted in the conglomeration of the 'women's movement' as it is today, which includes both its professionalised aspects and its grassroots aspects.

When I use the term 'women's movement', I use it very loosely to refer to the wide range of practices conducted by actors who are explicitly and/or implicitly motivated by feminist discourses to change their world. This includes practices that make women's lives better through the development of feminist consciousness, the improvement of conditions, the reformation of legislation, the articulation of rights, the critique and transformation of discourse, the production of cultural meaning, and/or the provision of aid and services. What distinguishes the contemporary women's movement from earlier manifestations are new political and social conditions that have created new contexts in which political subjects relate to the state, establishing new subjectivities and new practices that are not simply reacting to, but constitutive of, new forms of state power.

THE WOMEN'S MOVEMENT NOW

Ireland is a drastically different place than it was when an ad hoc committee representing women's groups from all over the country called in 1968 for the establishment of a National Commission on the Status of Women. Once termed the 'outpost of Western Europe' (Arensberg 1968:33), Ireland is a member state in the EU and at the height of the Celtic Tiger was considered one of the most successful economies in Europe (Peet 2004). The economic restructuring and boom have had a profound impact on Irish society at multiple levels, heightening the structural impacts of social change wrought by modernisation. Women have been particularly affected by these economic and social changes (Kennedy 2003). For instance, women, particularly married women and women with children, account for most of the increase in labour force participation, primarily in the low- and semi-skilled service industry (Cournéde 2006; Kennedy 2003; O'Connor 1998). The success of the Irish economy, as well as the success of the women's movement, led to the restructuring of social relations indicative of late capitalism, and this, in turn, has altered the conditions of possibility for feminist activisms now.

The women's movement has also changed dramatically since the 1970s. Influenced by the radical politics of the European Left and the rapid growth of social movements throughout the West, as well as the Catholic civil rights movement and the outbreak of nationalist and unionist violence in Northern Ireland, feminists in Ireland radicalised in the early 1970s. The desire to establish a collective identity and a unified movement was strong among some Irish feminists in the 1970s, resulting not only in the exclusion of the heterogeneity of women's experiences and women's needs, but also in the exclusion of the diversity of feminist subjects and histories. Conflicts over differences including opinions about nationalism, class, religion and European integration, and the issues that should be addressed by feminist activism, for instance abortion, led to serious divisions and diversification within the movement (Roulston 1999). The continued salience of these divisive issues prevented the formation of any long-term cohesiveness, and the history of the women's movement is marked more by fragmentation than cohesiveness.

STATE FEMINISM AND COMMUNITY ACTIVISM

By the mid-1980s, feminist activists working in variety of different organisations and from a variety of ideological perspectives had successfully publicised many previously stigmatised issues, ranging from divorce to abortion. In addition, feminist activists strategically lobbied the government for equality and contraception legislation, and secured state and/or private funding for a variety of women's services, including women's health clinics, rape crisis counselling, domestic violence refuges, resource centres, and the Council for the Status of Women (now the National Women's Council of Ireland). The tactical shift to a 'divide and conquer' approach of single-issue and service-provision groups meant that these groups quickly and effectively professionalised and institutionalised women's issues in the public discourse. The diversification and professionalisation of the women's movement allowed some aspects of feminist activism to become 'mainstream' (Galligan 1998), integrated into the workings of the state in the form of 'state feminism' (Mahon and Morgan 1999). Although state feminism is a somewhat ambiguous term that has been used in many contexts throughout the world (McBride et al. 1995; Outshoorn and Kantola 2004), I use the term state feminism in the Irish context to refer to the growth of semi-state and supra-state organisations that have emerged with the professionalisation of political activism in Ireland. The majority of these organisations are at least partially, if not almost entirely, funded by national and regional state bodies, including the Department of Community, Equality and Gaeltacht Affairs, the Health Service Executive, and local city and county councils. They function as lobbying and policy-making entities, funding sources, networking and umbrella organisations, resource providers, and bridges to the relevant statutory agencies for the large number of community, voluntary, and grassroots groups that have come to be known as the 'community and voluntary sector'. This is the 'public face' of contemporary feminism that exists today.

Networked to but existing beyond this mainstream, public feminism is another realm of political practices that at times functions as only implicitly feminist (O'Donovan and Ward 1999). On the ground, feminist practices are fragmented and decentralised, existing in a diverse array of local and community groups ranging from local service provision in relation to women's issues such as domestic violence, rape and family planning, to highly 'politicised' groups focused on homelessness, immigrant rights and abortion, to groups organised around and through such seemingly apolitical subject matters as arts and crafts, literature, the Irish language and spirituality. Many groups and/or activists work within and through myriad 'social movement' ideologies (i.e. feminism, socialism/anarchism, labour, anti-war, anti-globalisation/anti-capitalism, community development, environmentalism); others are focused primarily on relieving everyday issues relating to poverty and disadvantage at a local, community level, what Rowbotham and Linkogle (2001) have termed the 'politics of livelihood'. Some groups are funded by the state, city or town councils, or through community development initiatives; others are purely voluntary and rely on cash fundraising, and a very few are funded by private donors or foundations (Donoghue et al. 2006). Although the impact of the recent economic downturn is yet to be fully realised, it will obviously greatly affect the community and voluntary sector and the capacity of organisations to continue to provide support for, and services to, their communities.

While the majority of feminists see the 'mainstreaming' and diversification of the women's movement as the successful integration of feminist politics and the expansion of feminist principles into political institutions and civil society, it has signalled for some feminist activists victory for reform-based, 'liberal' feminism and the end of the 'radical' era of feminist politics. Accustomed to the centralised – and publicised – collective mobilisation they remember from the 1970s, Irish feminists of that generation have expressed concern over the seemingly non-active state of the contemporary women's movement (Smyth 1995). According to Connolly and O'Toole (2005:17), 'for many commentators, the 1990s signalled the onset of a post-feminist era, or at best, a third wave of feminism more characterised by political fragmentation and identity politics than feminist solidarity'.

Yet, this period saw the diversification of feminist practices and subjectivities, the development of a feminist counter-culture, the professionalisation of the women's movement and the emergence of 'state feminism', the establishment of women's studies at Irish universities, and the recognition of the 'community and voluntary sector' in the social partnership process (see Chapters 14 and 26). This period also saw several important legislative reforms on women's rights including divorce, better access to contraception, the right to information about abortion available legally in other countries, the right to travel for abortion, and equality legislation. It is clear both from the activities of mainstream organisations associated with state feminism and from the proliferation of local and community groups focused on bettering women's lives in ever more different ways, as well as the networks formed between and among these strands, that activists continue to practise politics around women's issues even if the conditions that underlie those practices have altered in response to larger economic, political and social changes in Irish society characteristic of late capitalist modernity.

MOVEMENT ACTIVISM

In addition to the varieties of feminist and feminist-like practices in which people are engaged in the context of state feminism and community activism, I observed several moments of activism, which I discuss in more detail elsewhere (DeWan 2008), that strained at the boundaries of both of these strands of political practices. In these moments, activists did not attempt to create a unified social movement in a traditional sense, but practised 'movement activism' where groups and individuals coalesced into campaigns at particular moments for important issues. I call them 'moments' not because they are paradigmatic of current feminist political practices, but because they coalesced into a campaign at a particular moment and then dissolved when that moment was finished. They included activists and workers from the community and feminist activists and service providers involved in state feminism. Indeed, these moments could not have occurred except as the result of practices occurring in both of these arenas, but neither were they limited by them.

Examples of these 'moments' include movement activism that developed in relation to the arrival of the Dutch abortion boat, *Women on Waves*, in Cork Harbour, and the subsequent abortion referendum in 2002, and movement activism related to the drafting of a *Cork Women's Manifesto* to lobby on women's issues leading up to the European and local elections in 2004. Neither of these examples is 'new' in the sense that both were organised around issues that feminist activists have been engaged in for decades, if not longer. However, these moments functioned differently from earlier forms of feminist political practices in that they were fluid, dynamic, unattached to any particular group or ideology, and unhindered by constraints relating to funding and bureaucracy. In addition to the ways in which both state feminism and community activism seek social change despite the structural constraints produced through the processes of late capitalism, these examples of movement activism suggest other ways in which differently positioned political subjects are successfully challenging oppressive structures of power.

'Movement activism' is a term that was used by a feminist activist I spoke with to describe her own style of activist practice:

> I don't think I have an agenda particularly, I don't think I have to be part of an organisation. I've always found it much easier to sort of move in and out of campaigns and so on, or move into campaigns and they sort of finish and you start something else. And I think that's what movement activism is about. (Interview, 12 February 2004; for more details see DeWan 2008)

The way she describes her own relationship with activism emphasises the *movement* of activist practices and subjectivities within and throughout a larger 'women's movement' entity. Activists today seem less concerned with differences or oppositions and more concerned with practices that are pragmatic, flexible and fluid. Another activist described what she thought contemporary activism is:

> Work[ing] on the basis of what's necessary, what's needed here and now at this particular moment in time . . . It's very pragmatic, it's site-specific, it's momentary, therefore it's always whatever kind of format you have, whatever kind of structure you have needs to be really flexible, really adaptable, really open, really able to pick up its bags and osmose into something else, another kind of bag tomorrow or this evening. (Interview, 12 February 2004; for more details see DeWan 2008)

'Movement activism' does not deny that there is a larger social movement structure to which and through which feminist practices are associated, merely that it does not entirely constrain or bound those practices and subjectivities.

In recent years, social movement theorists have offered several compelling theoretical alternatives to the traditional social movement model. Melucci

(1985:798–9) introduced the concept of 'movement networks' or 'movement areas' as:

> The network of groups and individuals sharing a conflictual culture and a collective identity . . . [which] includes not only 'formal' organisations but also the network of 'informal' relationships connecting core individuals and groups to a broader area of participants and users of services and cultural goods produced by the movement.

Alvarez, Dagnino and Escobar (1998b:15–16) have alternatively offered the concept of 'social movement webs' to capture the 'intricacy and precariousness of the manifold imbrications and ties established among movement organisations, individual participants and other actors in civil and political society and the state'. 'Webs' could therefore encompass more than just social movement organisations and their active members, also including more occasional participants, as well as 'sympathisers and collaborators' in statutory agencies, non-governmental organisations (NGOs), universities and other political and cultural institutions. 'Movement activism' allows activists to shift flexibly from one campaign to another, to build 'networks' or 'webs' with differently positioned feminists and other activists and organisations, to achieve objectives without having to worry about social movement ideologies that are seen as exclusive. Roulston (1999:12) suggests that the coalitions that build up between these 'fluid, overlapping, shifting groups' suggest the 'possibility for continuing politics in an era of respect for differences'.

BEYOND RADICALISM AND REFORM

Recently, activists have become more persuaded by participatory and inclusive forms of political practice that function on the social partnership model of consensus. One activist described contemporary forms of activism to me as the ability to find some middle ground between working within the system and working outside it:

> There would be people who think you can be much more effective within and people who think you can be more effective without. Whereas I think at the moment, it's almost the happy situation where there's one foot in each camp. Integrated enough to be able to negotiate and dialogue with the system, and yet outside enough to be recognised as perhaps a voice that might have something different to say. (Interview, 15 April 2004; for more details see DeWan 2008)

Striking a balance between 'reform' and 'radical' tactics seems to many activists to be the best option. Another feminist activist suggested that the best way to strike a balance is through a pragmatic combination of incremental change and what she called 'crisis moments':

> I've always felt that reform was important and I do genuinely believe that, but . . . again it's about balance. And if you completely silence those who are going to say more extreme things, those who have a more imaginative vision, who have a more incisive analysis of why we need reform, your reforms are never going to get far . . . I don't entirely subscribe to the notion that change happens, you know, most solidly if it's incremental. I think that you do sometimes need crisis moments where a lot changes really quickly, and the way you bring about crisis moments is through revolutionary gestures . . . And the question you have to ask is, what are the conditions which would be most likely to enable people to take action? (Interview, 12 February 2004; for more details see DeWan 2008)

Activists' attempts to find some balance between radical and reform styles of activism reveal a different sentiment than would have been expressed by feminist activists working for suffrage and national sovereignty at the turn of the twentieth century, or civil rights and equality in the 1970s, where radical action and shock tactics were seen by many activists as the most effective styles of activism (Stopper, 2006; Ward 1995). Part of this is certainly a tempering due to the professionalisation and institutionalisation of feminism, as I discussed above. However, it is also linked to types of political practice and subjectivities that correspond to the ways in which power relations are organised in late capitalist modernity; activists must be more flexible and diffuse to correspond to and counteract the flexibility of global capital and the diffusion of new forms of governing.

Much of the criticism of state feminism and the reliance of local women's and community groups on state funding circulates around concerns that these two strands of political engagement now define the entirety of the field of feminist political practice, i.e. that there are no 'radical' politics working 'outside' the state. Despite concerns that both state feminism and state funding in the community have limited people's options for effecting social change, in fact these forays into integration with the political institutions of governing provide some of the tools and spaces for more 'radical' or counter-hegemonic practices to occur, for instance the moments of 'movement activism' described above. Expanding on Gramsci's (1973) ideas on civil society, Buttigieg (1995:14) contends that 'autonomous' organisations and activities in civil society 'require the creation of, and help to extend, new spaces of civil society beyond the reach of the governmental, administrative, and juridical apparatuses of the state'. That is, some level of integration and interaction with political society is necessary for these 'other' practices to occur in civil society.

The trend towards movement activism as moments (potentially 'crisis moments') where groups and individuals coalesce into campaigns around important issues is one area where feminists and other activists continue to 'practise politics' in a multitude of ways. Movement activism functioning both within and beyond the 'women's movement', encompassing reform and radical styles of politics by disrupting their opposition, highlights the need for feminists to come to terms with fundamental changes in the nature of governing, the relationship of the state to its citizens, and the role of feminism in making change. Even if that implies coming to terms with conditions that may exceed the concept of 'feminism' itself. As one feminist activist eloquently explained:

> I always think that feminist organisations, we're the only ones who are on a kind of self-destruct mission, because we actually want at some point in time to arrive at the point where we're not necessary any longer, so we always have to think within us, to carry within us the seeds of our own disintegration. Because if we can't see a future where we are not, we can't actually see the kind of future which needs to be our vision. (Interview, 12 February 2004; for more details see DeWan 2008)

'Movement activism' certainly has benefits for activists, in the sense that it is a pragmatic solution to concerns about exclusion, fragmentation and difference in the context of social movements. It is solidarity built through a momentary sense of shared goals as opposed to a shared collective identity. It also provides creative alternatives for activists and organisations suddenly struck by cuts in their state funding and forced to find new ways to make their voices and issues heard. In combination with other forms of political practice, for instance in the form of state feminism and in the context of the community, movement activism provides new and different spaces for activists to effect social change and imagine a better world.

CONCLUSION

Contrary to perceptions that feminist political activism has faded away, or that it has been entirely integrated into and controlled by the state, feminist political activists continue to challenge the structures of power that oppress women beyond the purview of the political institutions of governing. State feminism, community activism, and moments of movement activism all show how feminist political practices have shifted to correspond to changes in forms of power and governing characteristic of late capitalist modernity, and to changes in political subjectivity, in how activists define themselves, their agendas and the types of practices necessary to achieve those agendas. As one activist pointed out to me, it is too easy for people to say that no one is fighting any more, it is more that the fight is on a different level; there may not be a broad-based movement, but activism is happening in other ways.

Using the study of feminist political practices and subjectivities as a lens through which to examine the state and its effects offers the opportunity to analyse changes in the relationship between the state and civil society that acknowledges the dynamic interactions between structures and agency. If, despite the changes in national sovereignty brought through membership of the EU, the Irish state as a concept is still very much a real experience for Irish people, then understanding how the Irish state has changed and will continue to change must be done with a view to how Irish people interact with, are formed by, reproduce, and attempt to alter its effects. Social movements, in all their complicated manifestations (i.e. collective action, cultural politics, movement activism) are one set of ways in which people continue to interact with the state and attempt to bring about social change. They are therefore an extremely valuable arena for understanding how the effects of often obscure concepts and social processes like late capitalism, globalisation, or postmodernity are lived and experienced by people in everyday ways on the ground. My analysis of the subjectivities and practices of feminist political activism and the women's movement in Ireland suggests that instead of reading the current 'moment' as de-radicalised, post-political or 'post-feminist', the structural conditions indicative of late capitalism and the changes it has wrought on civil society and the state have in fact created new spaces for political practices to occur. Feminist and community activists continue to 'practise politics' to improve their lives and the lives of their families, communities and state, and to transform oppressive structures of power based in gender, even as they challenge the very boundaries of 'feminism', 'activism' and 'politics'.

References

Abu-Lughod, L. (ed.) (1998) *Remaking Women: Feminism and Modernity in the Middle East*. Princeton, NJ: Princeton University Press.

Ahmed, S., Kilby, J., Lury, C., McNeil, M. and Skeggs, B. (2000) 'Introduction', in S. Ahmed, J. Kilby, C. Lury, M. McNeil and B. Skeggs (eds) *Transformations: Thinking Through Feminism*, pp. 1–24. London: Routledge.

Alvarez, S., Dagnino, E. and Escobar, A. (eds) (1998a) *Cultures of Politics, Politics of Cultures: Re-visioning Latin American Social Movements*. Boulder, CO: Westview Press.

— (1998b) 'Introduction: The Cultural and the Political in Latin American Social Movements', in S.E. Alvarez, E. Dagnino and A. Escobar (eds) *Cultures of Politics, Politics of Cultures: Re-visioning Latin American Social Movements*, pp. 1–29. Boulder, CO: Westview Press.

Anzaldua, G. (1990) *Haciendo Caras: Making Face/Making Soul*. San Francisco, CA: Aunt Lute Books.

Arensberg, C. (1968) *The Irish Countryman: An Anthropological Study*. Garden City, NY: Natural History Press.

Aronowitz, S. (1992) *The Politics of Identity: Class, Culture, Social Movements*. New York, NY: Routledge.

Boggs, C. (1999) *The End of Politics: Corporate Power and the Decline of the Public Sphere*. New York, NY: Guilford Press.

Buechler, S.M. (2000) *Social Movements in Advanced Capitalism: The Political Economy and Cultural Construction of Social Activism*. New York, NY: Oxford University Press.

Butler, J. (1997) 'Merely Cultural', *Social Text* 15: 265–77.

Buttigieg, J.A. (1995) 'Gramsci on Civil Society', *Boundary 2* 22: 1–32.

Cohen, J.L. (1985) 'Strategy or Identity: New Theoretical Paradigms and Contemporary Social Movements', *Social Research* 52: 663–716.

Connolly, L. (2002) *The Irish Women's Movement: From Revolution to Devolution*. Dublin: Lilliput Press.

Connolly, L. and O'Toole, T. (2005) *Documenting Irish Feminisms: The Second Wave*. Dublin: Woodfield Press.

Cournéde, B. (2006) *Removing Obstacles to Employment for Women in Ireland*, OECD Economics Department Working Papers, 511 [online]. Available: http://www.olis.oecd.org/olis/2006doc.nsf/linkto/ECO-WKP(2006)39 (last accessed 4 August 2009).

Crossley, N. (2003) *Making Sense of Social Movements*. Manchester: Open University Press.

Dahlerup, D. (1986) *The New Women's Movement: Feminism and Political Power in Europe and the USA*. London: Sage Publications.

DeWan, J. (2008) 'The Practice of Politics: Feminism, Activism and Social Change in Ireland', unpublished PhD thesis, Columbia University.

Donoghue, F., Prizeman , G., O'Regan, A. and Noël, V. (2006) *The Hidden Landscape: First Forays into Mapping Nonprofit Organisations in Ireland*. Dublin: Centre for Nonprofit Management, School of Business, Trinity College Dublin.

Edelman, M. (1999) *Peasants Against Globalization: Rural Social Movements in Costa Rica*. Stanford, CA: Stanford University Press.

Foucault, M. (1983) 'Afterword: The Subject and Power', in H. L. Dreyfus and P. Rabinow (eds) *Michel Foucault: Beyond Structuralism and Hermeneutics*, pp. 208–28. Chicago, IL: University of Chicago Press.

— (1988) 'The Ethic of Care for the Self as a Practice of Freedom: An Interview with Michel Foucault', in J. Bernauer and D. Rasmussen (eds) *The Final Foucault*, pp. 1–20. Cambridge, MA: MIT Press.

— (1991) 'Governmentality', in G. Burchell, C. Gordon and P. Miller (eds) *The Foucault Effect: Studies in Governmentality*, pp. 87–104. London: Harvester Wheatsheaf.

Galligan, Y. (1998) *Women and Politics in Contemporary Ireland: From the Margins to the Mainstream*. London: Pinter.

Geertz, C. (1973) *The Interpretation of Cultures*. New York, NY: Basic Books.

Giddens, A. (1991) *Modernity and Self-Identity: Self and Society in the Late Modern Age*. Cambridge: Polity Press.

Gramsci, A. (1973) *Selections From the Prison Notebooks*. New York, NY: Harper and Row.

Gregory, S. (2007) *The Devil Behind the Mirror: Globalization and Politics in the Dominican Republic*. Berkeley, CA: University of California Press.

Habermas, J. (1987) *The Philosophical Discourse of Modernity: Twelve Lectures*. Cambridge, MA: MIT Press.

Harvey, D. (1989) *The Condition of Postmodernity: An Enquiry Into the Origins of Cultural Change*. Oxford: Blackwell Publishing.

— (2000) *Spaces of Hope*. Berkeley, CA: University of California Press.

hooks, b. (1984) *Feminist Theory from Margin to Center*. Boston, MA: South End Press.

Jameson, F. (1991) *Postmodernism, or the Cultural Logic of Late Capitalism*. Durham, NC: Duke University Press.

Jessop, B. (2003) *The Spatiotemporal Dynamics of Capital and its Globalization – and how they Challenge State Power and Democracy*, Department of Sociology, Lancaster University [online]. Available: http://www.lancs.ac.uk/fass/sociology/research/resalph.htm#ik (last accessed 1 September 2009).

Kennedy, S. (2003) 'Irish Women and the Celtic Tiger Economy', in C. Coulter and S. Coleman (eds) *The End of Irish History? Critical Reflections on the Celtic Tiger*, pp. 95–109. Manchester: Manchester University Press.

Laclau, E. and Mouffe, C. (1985) *Hegemony and Socialist Strategy: Towards a Radical Democratic Politics*. London: Verso.

Lash, S. and Urry, J. (1987) *The End of Organized Capitalism*. Cambridge: Polity Press.

Lorde, A. (1984) 'Age, Race, Class and Sex: Women Redefining Difference', *Sister Outsider: Essays and Speeches*, pp. 114–23. Freedom, CA: Crossing Press.

Lyotard, F. (1984) *The Postmodern Condition*. Minneapolis, MN: University of Minnesota Press.

Mahon, E. and Morgan, V. (1999) 'State Feminism in Ireland', in Y. Galligan, E. Ward and R. Wilford (eds) *Contesting Politics: Women in Ireland, North and South*, pp. 55–73. Boulder, CO: Westview Press.

Massey, D. (1994) *Space, Place and Gender*. Minneapolis, MN: University of Minnesota Press.

McBride Stetson, D. and Mazur, A. (1995) *Comparative State Feminism*. London: Sage.

Melucci, A. (1985) 'The Symbolic Challenge of Contemporary Movements', *Social Research* 52: 789–816.

— (1996) *Challenging Codes: Collective Action in the Information Age*. Cambridge: Cambridge University Press.

Mohanty, C., Russo, A. and Torres, L. (eds) (1991) *Third World Women and the Politics of Feminism*. Bloomington, IN: Indiana University Press.

O'Connor, P. (1998) *Emerging Voices: Women in Contemporary Irish Society*. Dublin: Smurfit Print.

O'Donovan, O. and Ward, E. (1999) 'Networks of Women's Groups in the Republic of Ireland', in Y. Galligan, E. Ward and R. Wilford (eds) *Contesting*

Politics: Women in Ireland, North and South, pp. 90–108. Boulder, CO: Westview Press.

Offe, C. (1987) 'Challenging the Boundaries of Institutional Politics: Social Movements Since the 1960s', in C.S. Maier (ed.) *Changing Boundaries of the Political*, pp. 63–105. Cambridge: Cambridge University Press.

Ong, A. (1999) *Flexible Citizenship: The Cultural Logics of Transnationality*. Durham, NC: Duke University Press.

Ortner, S.B. (1996) *Making Gender: The Politics and Erotics of Culture*. Boston, MA: Beacon Press.

Outshoorn, J. and Kantola, J. (eds) (2004) *Changing State Feminism*. Basingstoke: Palgrave MacMillan.

Paley, J. (2001) *Marketing Democracy: Power and Social Movements in Post-Dictatorship Chile*. Berkeley, CA: University of California Press.

Peet, J. (2004) 'Survey: The Luck of the Irish', *The Economist*, 16 October, p. 4.

Rich, A. (1983) 'Compulsory Heterosexuality and Lesbian Existence', in A. Snitow, C. Stansell and S. Thompson (eds) *Powers of Desire: The Politics of Sexuality*, pp. 177–205. New York, NY: Monthly Review Press.

Rose, N.S. (1999) *Powers of Freedom: Reframing Political Thought*. Cambridge: Cambridge University Press.

Roulston, C. (1997) 'Women on the Margin: The Women's Movement in Northern Ireland, 1973–1995', in L. West (ed.) *Feminist Nationalism*, pp. 41–58. New York, NY: Routledge.

— (1999) 'Feminism, Politics and Postmodernism', in Y. Galligan, E. Ward and R. Wilford (eds) *Contesting Politics: Women in Ireland, North and South*, pp. 1–17. Boulder, CO: Westview Press.

Rowbotham, S. and Linkogle, S. (2001) 'Introduction', in S. Rowbotham and S. Linkogle (eds) *Women Resist Globalization: Mobilizing for Livelihood and Rights*, pp. 1–12. London: Zed Books.

Smyth, A. (1995) 'Haystacks in My Mind, or How to be SAFe (Sane, Angry, Feminist) in the 1990s', in G. Giffin (ed.) *Feminist Activism in the 1990s*, pp. 182–91. London: Taylor and Francis.

Spivak, G.C. (1988) 'Can the Subaltern Speak?' in C. Nelson and L. Grossberg (eds) *Marxism and the Interpretation of Culture*, pp. 213–313. Urbana, IL: University of Illinois Press.

Stein, A. (1997) 'Sisters and Queers: The Decentering of Lesbian Feminism', in R.N. Lancaster and M. Dileonardo (eds) *The Gender/Sexuality Reader*, pp. 378–91. New York, NY: Routledge.

Stopper, A. (2006) *Monday's at Gaj's: The Story of the Irish Women's Liberation Movement*. Dublin: Liffey Press.

Tarrow, S. (2008) *Power in Movement: Social Movements and Contentious Politics*. Cambridge: Cambridge University Press.

Ward, M. (1995) *In Their Own Voice: Women and Irish Nationalism*. Dublin: Attic Press.

Chapter 28

Alcohol Advertising in Ireland: The Challenge of Responsibility and Regulation

Patrick Kenny and Gerard Hastings

INTRODUCTION: ALCOHOL IN IRISH LIFE

That alcohol consumption plays a central role in Irish culture is not a new phenomenon. Historical accounts reveal that drunkenness and its attendant social problems were commonplace in Ireland even as early as the fifteenth century (MacManus 1939; Plunkett 1904), while the stereotypical image of the brawling, drunken Irishman was prevalent in the emigrant Irish communities of the nineteenth and twentieth centuries (Stivers 1976). However, it was during the affluent decade of the so-called Celtic Tiger, starting in the mid-1990s, that Irish alcohol consumption grew fastest, with per capita consumption increasing by more than 40 per cent in the late 1990s (Strategic Task Force on Alcohol 2002). The most recent reliable data show that the Irish are among the heaviest alcohol drinkers in the European Union (EU), consuming 10.6 litres of pure alcohol per capita per annum compared with an EU average of 9.1 litres (WHO 2009). Given that serious experimentation with alcohol tends to commence at around fifteen years of age (Hope *et al.* 2005), it seems reasonable to exclude those under fifteen years from the consideration of per capita consumption. Thus, per 'adult' consumption in Ireland stands at 13.35 litres per annum (Mongan *et al.* 2007).

But even these figures disguise the reality of the nation's drinking patterns. Because 23 per cent of Irish adults aged between eighteen and sixty-four years abstain from alcohol completely (Ramstedt and Hope 2005), compared with an average across Europe of approximately 15 per cent (Anderson and Baumberg 2006), an even smaller pool of Irish people account for the nation's disproportionately heavy drinking levels.

More recently, consumption levels have declined as the economy entered recession. Based on taxes received by the Revenue Commissioners, the Drinks Industry Group of Ireland estimates that per capita consumption fell in 2008 to 9.91 litres and per adult consumption decreased to 12.49 litres (Foley 2009).

However, these figures are likely to slightly underestimate actual consumption levels because of higher than usual cross-border shopping levels due largely to improved exchange rates and lower value added tax (VAT) rates in Northern Ireland.

The typical Irish drinking pattern may be as significant, from a public health perspective, as the quantities involved. While Ireland has one of the lowest levels of daily adult drinkers in Europe, it has one of the highest incidences of binge drinking (defined as five or more standard drinks (one standard drink being approximately equivalent to one can of beer, one glass of wine or one shot of spirits) per drinking occasion for men and four or more drinks for women (National Institute on Alcohol Abuse and Alcoholism 2004)), with 48 per cent of men and 16 per cent of women reporting binge drinking once per week. The corresponding figures for the UK are 38 per cent and 12 per cent respectively (Ramstedt and Hope 2005). Similarly, 34 per cent of Irish adults engage in binge drinking every time they consume alcohol, more than three times the average incidence across twenty-nine other European countries and seventeen times higher than Italy (TNS Opinion and Social 2007). On all measures, and at each end of the spectrum, the Irish drinking pattern is more extreme than the moderate continental European approach.

Alcohol-related Harm in Ireland

This typical Irish pattern of heavy episodic drinking is far from risk free. Alcohol is the third largest cause of death in the developed world, after tobacco and hypertension (WHO 2002). It accounts for 28 per cent of all attendances to the accident and emergency departments of acute Irish hospitals, and alcohol-related discharges were responsible for 874,395 bed days between 1995 and 2004 (Mongan et al. 2007). Alcohol consumption is causally related to cancers of the liver, head and neck, oesophagus, colon, rectum and the female breast (Baan et al. 2007). It is estimated that the rate of new alcohol-related cancers in Ireland will double for women and increase by 81 per cent for men up to 2020 (National Cancer Registry 2006).

Young people are not immune to the consequences of heavy drinking patterns. Alcohol consumption during adolescence can lead to structural and developmental changes in the brain (De Bellis et al. 2000; Spear 2002). Despite widespread safer sex campaigns, rates of sexually transmitted infections have escalated by more than 200 per cent since the mid-1990s (Health Protection Surveillance Centre 2006), perhaps a symptom of the significantly higher rate of unintended sexual intercourse on the part of heavy drinkers (Hope et al. 2005).

The side effects of heavy drinking are not limited solely to the medical sphere. Alcohol is a contributory factor in 97 per cent of public order offences, the prevalence of which has increased more than threefold from 1996 to 2002, precisely at the time when Irish drinking levels were themselves rising rapidly

(National Crime Council 2003). Despite a perceived shift in general social norms surrounding drink driving, alcohol plays a role in more than one-third of all fatal road crashes (Bradford *et al.* 2006).

These significant personal and social consequences of unhealthy drinking patterns have inevitably led to controversy about the root causes of Ireland's high consumption levels. Central to this debate are the commercial activities of the alcohol industry, and in particular the influence of the approximately €70m that it spends annually on advertising (Irish College of Psychiatrists 2008). Indeed, the question of how society balances the freedom of commercial practice with the protection of public health is a key issue in the relationship between business and society.

ALCOHOL ADVERTISING AND CONSUMPTION

The precise relationship between alcohol marketing and drinking behaviour is a deeply controversial one. The drinks industry defends the legitimacy of its communications practices by arguing that the market for alcoholic beverages is a mature one and that the effect of advertising in mature markets is to encourage brand switching rather than changing overall consumption amounts (Ambler 1996; Patten 2007). On the other hand, critics of the alcohol industry, especially those in the public health field, argue that alcohol advertising glamorises drinking and fosters a culture supportive of excessive consumption (Dring and Hope 2001). Teasing out this relationship presents significant methodological challenges and each camp can marshal empirical evidence that seems to support its case.

There are two major approaches in the scientific literature. The first analyses actual market data using econometric techniques in order to determine the impact of alcohol advertising on aggregate consumption levels. The second approach, instead of using actual market data, focuses on consumers themselves, attempting to examine the impact of exposure to advertising on their attitudes towards alcohol and on their drinking behaviour.

Advertising and Consumption at the Market Level – Econometric Analysis

Econometric studies of advertising and consumption seek to model the relationship between total expenditure on advertising and total consumer spending on alcohol products. In theory, if advertising influences consumption, variations in aggregate expenditure on advertising should result in corresponding variations in total consumption levels.

Econometric studies have been conducted in the UK (Dorsett and Dickerson 2004; Duffy 1982, 1983, 1990, 1991; Godfrey 1988; Hagan and Waterson 1983; McGuinness 1980, 1983; Walsh 1982), Europe (Calfee and Scheraga 1994), the

United States (Franke and Wilcox 1987; Tegene 1990) and Canada (Bourgeois and Barnes 1979). Econometric studies have also been conducted in regions where alcohol advertising has been banned (Makowsky and Whitehead 1991; Ogborne and Smart 1980; Saffer 1991, 2000; Smart and Cutler 1976; Young 1993). The imposition or lifting of such bans theoretically presents an interesting quasi-experimental context in which a relationship between advertising and consumption can be modelled econometrically.

With very rare exceptions (e.g. Saffer 1991, 2000), these econometric studies indicate that there is no, or at most a very minor, relationship between advertising and consumption. The alcohol industry substantially relies on this research in its defence of the legitimacy of its marketing activities. The industry is further supported in this stance by the evidence from fast-moving consumer goods markets, where advertising in mature industries generally leads to brand switching rather than renewed market growth (Luik and Waterson 1996; McDonald 1992). Ambler (1996), defending the practices of the drinks industry, argues that advertisers are rarely concerned with overall category effects. Rather, it is the advertised brand itself, and its battle for market share, that is the focus of the brand manager's attention. Indeed, according to this school of thought, advertising may actually reduce overall drinking levels, as consumers trade up from larger quantities of cheaper products to smaller quantities of more heavily advertised expensive brands.

The reality, however, is not so simple. Econometric studies have numerous inherent weaknesses that significantly undermine their ability to accurately assess the advertising–consumption relationship. This body of research, by its very nature, is methodologically incapable of supporting the arguments of the alcohol industry.

In the first instance, econometric studies generally have to rely on estimated, as opposed to actual, expenditure figures. Second, and more fundamentally, these estimates only account for media spend and ignore expenditure on advertising creativity. Clearly, a well-conceived and executed advertising campaign based on sophisticated consumer research will have a greater influence than one produced in an amateur fashion. Econometric studies completely ignore this dimension of advertising. Similarly, media vehicle effects (Aaker and Myers 1987) are not considered in the econometric approach.

These studies also fail to control for the influence of advertising spillover from other jurisdictions or media markets. Similarly, with some rare exceptions (for instance Hagan and Waterson 1983), econometric studies do not control for the lagged effects of advertising across time. Nor do they account for the likelihood that, in the context of the thousands of alcohol ads that consumers have been exposed to over many years, the marginal effects of a few euros of extra advertising are likely to be very small.

These weaknesses are compounded by the fact that practically all econometric studies focus only on advertising and ignore the wider marketing communications mix and the inherent integration and mutual reinforcement of messages across different marketing platforms. This is a significant weakness in the evidence base. Given the importance of integrated marketing communications, any analysis that examines only advertising and excludes other forms of marketing is inherently limited. By definition, such econometric studies also fail to capture many of the newest and most innovative marketing approaches that are specifically targeted at younger drinkers. Indeed, as traditional advertising comes under increased scrutiny and restriction, the broadly unregulated areas of ambient and online marketing are likely to attract enhanced budgets and thus assume ever greater importance in commercial practice.

Finally, aggregate econometric studies fail to consider the role of market segmentation and any targeting (deliberate or otherwise) of young consumers by the alcohol industry. Because of their limited experience with alcohol and their ongoing cognitive development, it is these consumers who are most prone to the influence of advertising and more susceptible to dangerous levels of binge drinking (Collins *et al.* 2007). It is possible that the weak population-level impact of advertising evidenced in econometric studies simply reflects the averaging of a very small impact on older, more established drinkers and a more significant impact on younger, less experienced drinkers (Aitken and Hastings 1992).

With such a variety of fundamental limitations, econometric studies can only provide a very anaemic insight into advertising's real world impact.

Advertising and Consumption at the Individual Level – Consumer Studies

The industry's reliance on econometric studies to support its position is somewhat ironic given that businesses do not determine the effectiveness of their own advertising campaigns by using this approach. Instead, marketing effectiveness is normally assessed at the level of individual consumers and their engagement with the brand in question (Hall 2002; Hansen 1995). Taken as a whole, such consumer-based studies paint a very different picture of advertising's impact on behaviour.

There are three broad categories of consumer studies of relevance to the advertising–consumption relationship: cross-sectional surveys, experiments and longitudinal studies. Of these three, both cross-sectional surveys and experiments suffer from a variety of methodological limitations and so provide a limited picture of the relationship between advertising and the consumption of alcohol.

Cross-sectional studies tend to correlate advertising exposure and subsequent attitudes and behaviour, often controlling for other likely confounding factors. By and large, these studies indicate that greater awareness of, and exposure to, alcohol advertising tends to lead towards more favourable attitudes towards alcohol brands and a greater propensity to drink in the future (Adlaf and Kohn 1989; Aitken 1989; Aitken *et al.* 1988; Atkin *et al.* 1984; Austin and Knaus 2000; Grube and

Wallack 1994; Strickland 1984; Wyllie *et al.* 1998a, 1998b). However, the usefulness of cross-sectional studies is undermined by their inability to determine the direction of causality and thus caution must be exercised when interpreting their results. It may be the case that heavy drinkers like advertising because of their consumption, rather than that liking advertising causes their consumption.

In theory, **experiments** should overcome some of the limitations of cross-sectional surveys, as they allow for the manipulation of both control and experimental groups, thus permitting researchers to draw firmer conclusions about cause and effect relationships (Patzer 1996). A number of experiments have either been inconclusive or have shown no discernible effect of advertising on consumption (Kohn and Smart 1984, 1987; Kohn *et al.* 1984; Lipsitz *et al.* 1993), although, more recently, one experimental study has indicated a significant effect of alcohol portrayals in movies and advertisements on consumption by young males (Engels *et al.* 2009). These mixed findings are likely a result of the inherent difficulty of capturing the complexity of the real-life media consumption experience in an experimental setting (Smith and Foxcroft 2007). Indeed, experiments by their nature seek to assess the marginal impact of one or two extra advertisements without controlling for prior exposure to advertising and previous experience with alcohol. Further, as Anderson *et al.* (2009) emphasise, the ethical issues surrounding experiments in this field make them unsuitable for use with young people.

Longitudinal research, on the other hand, avoids the limitations of both experimental and cross-sectional studies. When confounding factors are properly controlled for, longitudinal studies are capable of indicating a causal relationship because they show the influence of changes in advertising exposure on behaviour over time (Anderson *et al.* 2009). In general, this body of research strongly confirms the public health community's position that alcohol advertising contributes to higher levels of consumption (Casswell *et al.* 2002; Casswell and Zhang 1998; Collins *et al.* 2007; Connolly *et al.* 1994; Ellickson *et al.* 2005; Fisher *et al.* 2007; Henriksen *et al.* 2008; Pasch *et al.* 2007; Snyder *et al.* 2006; Stacy *et al.* 2004). Longitudinal studies have also uncovered a significant relationship between media exposure in general – including TV viewing, video music watching and game playing – and subsequent alcohol consumption in a number of different countries and across several different age groups (Hanewinkel *et al.* 2008; Robinson *et al.* 1998; Sargent *et al.* 2006; van den Bulck and Buellens 2005).

More recently, there have been four major systematic reviews of longitudinal studies published in the area of advertising and alcohol consumption (Anderson *et al.* 2009; Meier 2008; Science Group of the European Alcohol and Health Forum 2009; Smith and Foxcroft 2009). These systematic reviews are of one voice in their conclusions on the evidence about the advertising–consumption relationship. As Anderson *et al.* (2009:229) express it:

Longitudinal studies consistently suggest that exposure to media and commercial communications on alcohol is associated with the likelihood that adolescents will start to drink alcohol, and with increased drinking amongst baseline drinkers. Based on the strength of this association . . . we conclude that alcohol advertising and promotion increases the likelihood that adolescents will start to use alcohol, and to drink more if they are already using alcohol.

In summary, then, the alcohol industry argues that alcohol advertising does not influence individual or aggregate consumption levels. It bases its position on a variety of econometric studies that assess the relationship between overall advertising expenditure and aggregate alcohol consumption. However, for a variety of reasons, this econometric research is largely unreliable and certainly useless in assessing the influence of consumption on more vulnerable underage consumers. On the other hand, consumer studies, and especially longitudinal research that tracks the dose–response relationship over time, increasingly shows that advertising is a powerful driver of consumption-related behaviour, especially among the young. In particular, advertising seems to be an even more powerful influence on those underage teenagers who are inexperienced with alcohol and who are still undergoing cognitive development (Casswell et al. 2002; Collins et al. 2007; Ellickson et al. 2005).

The Wider Marketing Mix

Of course, advertising is just one component of a marketing communications mix that is increasingly integrated and self-reinforcing (Kliatchko 2005). While they are beyond the scope of the present discussion, it is worth noting that there is evidence that other marketing approaches, including ownership of alcohol-branded clothing and promotional items (Fisher et al. 2007; McClure et al. 2006), sponsorship (Wyllie et al. 1989), pricing (Coate and Grossman 1988), new product development (Goldberg et al. 1994; Jackson et al. 2000) and online marketing (Casswell 2004) can all contribute to increased alcohol consumption. There is an urgent need for more research in order to understand how the integrated nature of these marketing communications tools influence consumption.

LEARNING FROM BIG TOBACCO

The protagonists in the debate about alcohol advertising are not confined to mere academic argument, but instead seek to shape national policies to support their positions. In this policy contest, the drinks companies have learned very valuable lessons from the mistakes of the global tobacco industry.

Despite the glamour of cigarette smoking in the early twentieth century, itself largely fostered by the growing popularity of Hollywood movies and increasingly sophisticated marketing, concerns started to emerge in the 1950s about the addictive nature of nicotine and its impact on health, as well as the role of advertising in glamorising smoking and attracting young smokers (Brandt 2007). The major tobacco companies rejected these concerns in the face of growing counter-evidence and defended their position largely by reliance on econometric studies, much like the alcohol industry today.

The chief executives of the major tobacco companies ultimately lost political credibility when they each swore before a US congressional committee in 1994 that they did not believe that nicotine was addictive. Unable to withstand the mounting scientific evidence marshalled against them, in 1998 the major US cigarette manufacturers were forced to pay almost $250bn to compensate the individual states for the costs they incurred in tobacco-related health expenses (Brandt 2007).

Given the sheer weight of scientific evidence amassed against them, and their consequent loss of political credibility, cigarette manufacturers were unable to prevent major restrictions on tobacco marketing in countries across the developed world. To be sure, tobacco marketers have remained active, doubling their promotional spend in the USA within a few years of the 1998 Master Settlement (Federal Trade Commission 2009). But the experience of the tobacco companies in the policy and regulatory debates in the developed West presents some instructive lessons for the drinks industry, the most significant of which is the need to be seen to engage seriously with the process of self-regulation as a strategy to forestall tighter legislative restrictions. The alcohol industry in Ireland has shown that it has taken this lesson to heart.

ADVERTISING REGULATION IN IRELAND

The Advertising Standards Authority of Ireland and Central Copy Clearance

All advertising in Ireland is governed by the Code of Standards for Advertising, Promotional and Direct Marketing in Ireland, which is published by the Advertising Standards Authority for Ireland (ASAI). A specific section of this code contains restrictions on alcohol advertising and specifies, among other things, that alcohol advertising should not promote alcohol as a way of improving physical performance or personal qualities, or imply that alcohol will lead to greater personal, business or social success or make the drinker more attractive to the opposite sex. The code also stipulates that alcohol advertising should not be aimed at children nor feature anyone who is, or looks as if they are, under the age of twenty-five, and that alcohol advertising should not be placed in media with a predominantly underage audience (ASAI 2007).

Prior to 2003, the ASAI code only operated retrospectively. In other words, the onus was on the public to make a formal complaint to the ASAI if they felt a breach of the code had occurred. After soliciting a defence from the advertiser, the advertisement would be removed if the ASAI Complaints Committee upheld the complaint.

There are obvious deficiencies with such a system, foremost among which is that it relied on the public being sufficiently well informed and motivated to initiate a complaint. Even in the event of such a complaint being successfully upheld, there was no real sanction for the guilty advertiser. The only effect of a finding against the advertiser was that the offending advertisement had to be withdrawn. Given that this withdrawal would occur some considerable time after the debut of the advertisement, or even after the end of the campaign itself, and that press coverage following a ban could generate even higher profile for the brand involved, the system often resulted in little or no inconvenience for the advertiser and, correspondingly, in little protection for the public.

By 2003, however, the inability of this system to cope with abuse was increasingly evident. Alcohol advertisements were one of the product categories that received most complaints for alleged breaches of the ASAI Code. Furthermore, the rapid change in drinking patterns over the previous decade was generating increasing public concern about the problem of binge drinking, with significant critical media attention being focused on the promotional practices of the drinks industry. This heightened public concern subsequently culminated in the government's Strategic Task Force on Alcohol calling for significant restrictions on alcohol advertising (Strategic Task Force on Alcohol 2004).

As a response to these heightened public concerns, the drinks and advertising industries collaborated in the establishment of Central Copy Clearance Ireland. The aim of this body is to pre-vet all alcohol advertisements to ensure compliance with the ASAI Code. All drinks advertisers are now obliged to present a certificate of compliance from Central Copy Clearance before any media outlet will accept their campaign. This strategy has proved to be an extremely successful one for alcohol companies. Since the establishment of Central Copy Clearance, complaints against alcohol advertisements have all but disappeared and the industry can now boast about the effectiveness of industry self-regulation. Indeed, the elimination of some of the more flagrant breaches of the advertising code has removed a powerful rhetorical weapon from the hands of critics of the industry.

Of course, the decline in the number of complaints about alcohol advertising may not in fact be a result of advertisements adhering more strictly to the codes, but, instead, may instead be due to a lack of motivation to complain on the part of the public. Further, mere compliance with the terms of the ASAI Code does not guarantee that advertising will not influence consumption, especially by those younger consumers who are most vulnerable. Nonetheless, the logical step of pre-vetting advertising campaigns does represent an improvement over the previous system and shows that the alcohol industry in Ireland is willing to move proactively to create a perception of social responsibility.

Industry-funded Social Aspect Organisations

The launch of Mature Enjoyment of Alcohol in Society (MEAS (meas is also the Irish word for 'respect')) in 2003 further bolstered the image of the industry as a responsible stakeholder. MEAS is a 'social aspect' organisation, which, while funded by the drinks industry, operates independently of it to promote the message of responsible drinking primarily through regular seminars and conferences, the website www.drinkaware.ie and a variety of responsible drinking advertisements.

MEAS has also published its own code of practice on alcohol promotions (MEAS 2004). In general, this code is very similar to the ASAI Code, but it goes further by controlling the packaging and merchandising of alcoholic drinks, as well as the promotion of alcohol-related events. The MEAS Code restricts alcohol brands from being placed in close proximity to soft drinks on shop shelves and prohibits promotions if more than 25 per cent of the audience at the event is expected to be under eighteen years old. As with the ASAI Code, members of the public may make a complaint in the event of a perceived breach. If the complaint is upheld, the advertising campaign must be amended; if the advertiser refuses to do this the company faces the possibility of expulsion from MEAS, as well as having the fact of their refusal highlighted in the media.

However, just as in the case of the ASAI Code prior to the establishment of Central Copy Clearance, there are significant weaknesses with this approach. In practically every case, promotional events will have long since ended by the time a complaint is initiated, investigated and adjudicated upon. Neither is there a process in place to prevent repeat offences using the same promotional campaign. Furthermore, the effectiveness of the MEAS system depends on the awareness and motivation of members of the public to make a complaint. The inherent weakness of this is evidenced by the fact that only fourteen complaints were received in all of 2008, with eight of these being upheld. It seems to stretch credibility that such an approach provides systematic protection from irresponsible alcohol promotions.

By establishing the Central Copy Clearance pre-vetting system and funding MEAS, the alcohol industry has sought to position itself as a responsible stakeholder with legitimate concerns about dangerous drinking. It is true that there have been improvements in advertising practices since 2003, but these improvements operate to reduce the prevalence of only the most flagrant breaches of codes of practice and extend only to the more visible forms of above-the-line advertising. The increasingly significant areas of online and viral marketing, which are specifically targeted at younger consumers and are largely beyond regulation, have yet to come under any serious scrutiny.

It is noteworthy that none of the scientific data illustrating a relationship between exposure to advertising and subsequent drinking has been predicated upon advertising being in breach of regulatory codes. It is exposure to advertising itself, irrespective of its adherence to the regulations, that has been shown to influence consumption patterns. The initiatives volunteered by the industry do nothing to actually reduce exposure to alcohol advertising per se.

Government Regulations

The ability to position itself as a responsible stakeholder has served the alcohol industry well. In early 2005, the government indicated that a Bill was being prepared to place substantial legal restrictions on alcohol marketing practices. But in December of that year, the Department of Health and Children announced that, rather than introduce legislation, it had instead entered into a voluntary agreement with the drinks industry to control exposure to alcohol marketing.

This switch from a legislative to a voluntary solution is undoubtedly the result of very effective lobbying on the part of the industry. Parts of the text of the voluntary code were cut and pasted directly from lobbying letters written to the Minister for Health, complete with serious grammatical errors contained in the original (O'Toole 2005). That said, the government's Alcohol, Marketing, Communications and Sponsorship Codes of Practice of 2005 introduced some worthwhile guidelines to control exposure to alcohol marketing.

The Codes reduce exposure to outdoor alcohol advertising by preventing alcohol advertisement being placed within a hundred metres of school entrances, while no more than 25 per cent of advertising space on buses and trains can be booked for alcohol advertising. A maximum of 25 per cent of TV or radio advertisements per day may be for alcoholic beverages and no more than two alcohol ads may appear per commercial break. Interestingly, in its original iteration in 2005, the Codes stipulated that alcohol advertisements could only be placed around programmes with an adult (over eighteen years) audience profile of 67 per cent or greater; the same threshold restrictions were established for cinema and radio advertising, as well as attendance at events sponsored by alcohol brands. In 2008, the Codes were amended to further restrict these audience threshold figures for all media and for alcohol sponsorship of sporting and other events, stipulating that at least 75 per cent of the viewing audience had to be over eighteen years old. It is interesting to note that, according to documents uncovered by the National Youth Federation, the Department of Health and Children had originally argued for the 25 per cent level when the codes were first negotiated in 2005, but the drinks industry had succeeded in getting the government to agree to the much less restrictive 33 per cent level (Downes 2005). Apparently, being perceived as a responsible and proactive stakeholder has its benefits.

However, problems still remain even at the higher threshold level of 75 per cent. Those aged between ten and seventeen (the group which is at most risk of underage drinking) account for just under 14 per cent of the population (CSO 2006). Unless the 75 per cent threshold is significantly raised, there remains a risk that underage adolescents will be disproportionately exposed to television alcohol advertising.

Compliance with these voluntary codes is assessed by the independent Alcohol Communications Monitoring Body, which has access to viewership data for all the relevant media channels. There has been a substantial degree of compliance in the years since they were introduced (Alcohol Marketing Communications Monitoring Body 2007, 2008, 2009). Where breaches have occurred, they have been rare and appear to have been a result of isolated errors, rather than attempts to circumvent the restrictions.

More recently, the Intoxicating Liquor Act 2008 gave the Minister for Justice the power to introduce regulations to limit the sale of alcohol in supermarkets to an area that is separated from the rest of the store by a wall or a gate and also empowers the minister to prevent alcohol being sold below cost. However, the government has to date declined to enact the provisions restricting below-cost selling. It has also decided not to introduce regulations to control the placing of alcohol in supermarkets, opting instead to enter into another voluntary agreement with another newly formed organisation called Responsible Retailing of Alcohol in Ireland. Instead of placing alcoholic beverages behind a wall or gate as outlined in the legislation, the agreement simply ensures that, as far as possible, customers do not have to pass through an area selling alcoholic beverages in order to reach other products in the supermarket. Once again, a voluntary agreement has been preferred over more restrictive legal measures.

CONCLUSION

Alcohol is not an ordinary consumer product – its potentially addictive nature and damaging side effects necessitate careful regulation in the interests of public health and welfare. Central to these regulations is the issue of how alcohol is promoted and, in particular, how these promotions affect young people who are most susceptible to them.

Drinks companies defend their marketing practices by relying on econometric studies, which almost always show that advertising does not increase consumption. For a variety of methodological reasons, this type of research is utterly ineffective in understanding how marketing influences young people. Longitudinal research, which follows teenagers over time, is a more suitable way of assessing advertising's influence. This approach provides very strong evidence of advertising's influence on consumption.

While the influence of advertising has been the subject of extensive investigation, the same cannot be said about other dimensions of the marketing mix. Research is needed to help understand the indirect influence of marketing, particularly via its influence on normative perceptions. Research is also needed on new, online and viral marketing approaches, which, by their very nature, are likely to pass under the policy radar. These below-the-line promotional techniques will become increasingly important for the drinks industry if tighter restrictions continue to be placed on traditional advertising. Both the influence of governmental initiatives to reduce underage exposure to alcohol advertising, and the impact of the drinks industry's efforts at self-regulation, require investigation.

References

Aaker, D.A. and Myers, J.G. (1987) *Advertising Management*, 3rd edn. Englewood Cliffs, NJ: Prentice-Hall International.

Adlaf, E.M. and Kohn, P.M. (1989) 'Alcohol, Advertising, Consumption and Abuse: A Covariance Structural Modelling look at Strickland's Data', *British Journal of Addiction* 84(7): 749–57.

Aitken, P.P. (1989) 'Television Alcohol Commercials and Under-age Drinking', *International Journal of Advertising* 8(2): 133–50.

Aitken, P.P. and Hastings, G.B. (1992) 'Advertising and Youthful Drinking', in M. Plant, B. Ritson and R. Robinson (eds) *Alcohol and Drugs: The Scottish Experience*, pp. 82–9. Edinburgh: Edinburgh University Press.

Aitken, P.P., Leathar, D.S. and Scott, A.C. (1988) 'Ten-to-Sixteen Year Olds' Perceptions of Advertisements for Alcoholic Drinks', *Alcohol and Alcoholism* 23(6): 491–500.

Alcohol Marketing Communications Monitoring Body (2007) *Limiting the Exposure of Young People to Alcohol Advertising: First Annual Report 2006*. Dublin: Alcohol Marketing Monitoring Communications Body.

— (2008) *Limiting the Exposure of Young People to Alcohol Advertising. Second Annual Report 2007*. Dublin: Alcohol Marketing Communications Monitoring Body.

— (2009) *Limiting the Exposure of Young People to Alcohol Advertising. Third Annual Report 2008*. Dublin: Alcohol Marketing Communications Monitoring Body.

Ambler, T. (1996) 'Can Alcohol Misuse be Reduced by Banning Advertising?', *International Journal of Advertising* 15(2): 167–74.

Anderson, P. and Baumberg, B. (2006) *Alcohol in Europe: A Public Health Perspective. A Report for the European Commission*. London: Institute of Alcohol Studies.

Anderson, P., de Bruijn, A., Angus, K., Gordon, R. and Hastings, G. (2009) 'Impact of Alcohol Advertising and Media Exposure on Adolescent Alcohol Use: A Systematic Review of Longitudinal Studies', *Alcohol and Alcoholism* 44(3): 229–43.

ASAI (Advertising Standards Authority for Ireland) (2007) *Manual of Advertising Self Regulation*. Dublin: ASAI.

Atkin, C., Hocking, J. and Block, M. (1984) 'Teenage Drinking: Does Advertising Make a Difference?', *Journal of Communication* 34(2): 157–67.

Austin, E.W. and Knaus, C. (2000) 'Predicting the Potential for Risky Behaviour for Those "Too Young" to Drink as the Result of Appealing Advertising', *Journal of Health Communications* 5(11): 13–27.

Baan, R., Straif, K., Grosse, Y., Secretan, B., Ghissani, B.V., Altieri, A. and Cogliano, V. (2007) 'Carcinogenity of Alcoholic Beverages', *Lancet Oncology* 8(4): 292–3.

Bourgeois, J.C. and Barnes, J.G. (1979) 'Does Advertising Increase Alcohol Consumption?', *Journal of Advertising Research* 19(4): 19–29.

Bradford, D., O'Farrell, A. and Howell, F. (2006) *Alcohol in Fatal Road Crashes in Ireland in 2003*. Naas: Population Health Directorate, HSE.

Brandt, A.M. (2007) *The Cigarette Century: The Rise, Fall and Deadly Persistence of the Product that Defined America*. New York, NY: Basic Books.

Calfee, J.E. and Scherga, C. (1994) 'The Influence of Advertising on Alcohol Consumption: A Literature Review and an Econometric Analysis of Four European Nations', *International Journal of Advertising* 13(4): 287–310.

Casswell, S. (2004) 'Alcohol Brands in Young People's Everyday Lives: New Developments in Marketing', *Alcohol and Alcoholism* 39(6): 471–6.

Casswell, S., Pledger, M. and Pratap, S. (2002) 'Trajectories of Drinking from 18 to 26 Years: Identification and Prediction', *Addiction* 97(11): 1427–37.

Casswell, S. and Zhang, J.F. (1998) 'Impact of Liking for Advertising and Brand Allegiance on Drinking and Alcohol-related Aggression: A Longitudinal Study', *Addiction* 93(8): 1209–17.

Coate, D. and Grossman, M. (1988) 'Effects of Alcoholic Beverage Prices and Legal Drinking Ages on Youth Alcohol Use', *Journal of Law and Economics* 31(1): 145–71.

Collins, R., Ellickson, P., McCaffrey, D. and Hambarsoomians, K. (2007) 'Early Adolescent Exposure to Alcohol Advertising and its Relationship to Underage Drinking', *Journal of Adolescent Health* 40(6): 527–34.

Connolly, G.M., Casswell, S., Zhang, J. and Silva, P.A. (1994) 'Alcohol in the Mass Media and Drinking by Adolescents: A Longitudinal Study', *Addiction* 89: 1255–63.

CSO (Central Statistics Office) (2006) *Census of Ireland Preliminary Report*. Dublin: Stationery Office.

De Bellis, M.D., Clark, D.B., Beers, S.R., Soloff, P.H., Boring, A.M., Hall, J., Kersh, A. and Keshavan, M.S. (2000) 'Hippocampal Volume in Adolescent-onset Alcohol Use Disorders', *American Journal of Psychiatry* 157(5): 737–44.

Dorsett, J. and Dickerson, S. (2004) 'Advertising and Alcohol Consumption in the UK', *International Journal of Advertising* 23(2): 149–71.

Downes, J. (2005) 'Documents Reveal Extent of Lobbying on Drink Law', *Irish Times*, 3 December, p. 9.

Dring, C. and Hope, A. (2001) *The Impact of Alcohol Advertising on Teenagers in Ireland*. Dublin: Health Promotion Unit, Department of Health and Children.

Duffy, M. (1982) 'The Effect of Advertising on the Total Consumption of Alcoholic Drinks in the United Kingdom: Some Econometric Estimates', *International Journal of Advertising* 1(2): 105–17.

— (1983) 'The Demand for Alcoholic Drink in the UK, 1963–1978', *Applied Economics* 15(1): 125–40.

— (1990) 'Advertising and Alcoholic Drink in the UK: Some Further Rotterdam Model Estimates', *International Journal of Advertising* 9(3): 247–57.

— (1991) 'Advertising and the Consumption of Tobacco and Alcoholic Drink: A System-wide Analysis', *Scottish Journal of Political Economy* 38(4): 369–85.

Ellickson, P.L., Collins, R.L., Hambarsoomians, K. and McCaffrey, D.F. (2005) 'Does Alcohol Advertising Promote Adolescent Drinking? Results from a Longitudinal Assessment', *Addiction* 100(2): 235–46.

Engels, R.C.M.E., Hermans, R., van Baaren, R.B., Hollenstein, T. and Bot, S.M. (2009) 'Alcohol Portrayal on Television Affects Actual Drinking Behaviour', *Alcohol and Alcoholism* 44(3): 244–9.

Federal Trade Commission (2009) *Cigarette Report for 2006* [online]. Available: http://www.ftc.gov/os/2009/08/090812cigarettereport.pdf (last accessed 30 December 2009).

Fisher, L.B., Miles, I.W., Austin, S.B., Camargo, C.A. and Colditz, G.A. (2007) 'Predictors of Initiation of Alcohol Use Among US Adolescents: Findings from a Prospective Cohort Study', *Archives of Pediatrics and Adolescent Medicine* 161(10): 959–66.

Foley, A. (2009) *The Drinks Market Performance in 2008. A Report Prepared for the Drinks Industry Group of Ireland* [online]. Available: http://www.drinks industry.ie/easyedit/files/Document%20Final.rtf (last accessed 30 December 2009).

Franke, G. and Wilcox, G. (1987) 'Alcoholic Beverage Advertising and Consumption in the United States', *Journal of Advertising* 16(3): 22–30.

Godfrey, C. (1988) 'Licencing and the Demand for Alcohol', *Applied Economics* 20(11): 1541–58.

Goldberg, M.E., Gorn, G.J. and Lavack, A.M. (1994) 'Product Innovation and Teenage Alcohol Consumption: The Case of Wine Coolers', *Journal of Public Policy and Marketing* 13(2): 218–27.

Grube, J.W. and Wallack, L. (1994) 'Television Beer Advertising and Drinking Knowledge, Beliefs and Intentions Among Schoolchildren', *American Journal of Public Health* 84(2): 254–9.

Hagan, L.W. and Waterson, M.J. (1983) *The Impact of Advertising on the United Kingdom Alcoholic Drink Market.* London: Advertising Association.

Hall, B. (2002) 'A New Model for Measuring Advertising Effectiveness', *Journal of Advertising Research* 42(2): 23–32.

Hanewinkel, R., Morgenstern, M. and Tanski, S.E. (2008) 'Longitudinal Study of Parental Movie Restrictions on Teen Smoking and Drinking in Germany', *Addiction* 103(10): 1722–30.

Hansen, F. (1995) 'Recent Developments in the Measurement of Advertising Effectiveness: The Third Generation', *Marketing and Research Today* 23(November): 259–69.

Health Protection Surveillance Centre. (2006) *Sexually Transmitted Infections 2005: Annual Summary Report.* Dublin: Health Service Executive.

Henriksen, L., Feighery, E.C. and Schleicher, N.C. (2008). 'Receptivity to Alcohol Marketing Predicts Initiation of Alcohol Use', *Journal of Adolescent*

Health 42(1): 28–35.

Hope, A., Dring, C. and Dring, J. (2005) *The Health of Irish Students: College Lifestyle and Attitudinal (CLAN) Survey.* Dublin: Department of Health and Children.

Irish College of Psychiatrists (2008) *Calling Time on Alcohol Advertising and Sponsorship in Ireland: Supporting a Ban on Alcohol Advertising in Ireland, Protecting Children and Adolescents* [online]. Available: http://www.irishpsychiatry.ie/PDF/ALCOHOL%20ADVERTISING%20IN%20ROI%20REPORT%20(3).pdf (last accessed 30 December 2009).

Jackson, M.C., Hastings, G., Wheeler, C., Eadie, D. and MacKintosh, A.M. (2000) 'Marketing Alcohol to Young People: Implications for Industry Regulation and Research Policy', *Addiction* 95 (Supplement 4): S597–608.

Kliatchko, J. (2005) 'Towards a New Definition of Integrated Marketing Communications', *International Journal of Advertising* 24(1): 7–34.

Kohn, P.M and Smart, R.G. (1984) 'The Impact of Television Advertising on Alcohol Consumption: An Experiment', *Journal of Studies on Alcohol* 45(4): 295–301.

— (1987) 'Wine, Women, Suspiciousness and Advertising', *Journal of Studies on Alcohol* 48(2): 161–6.

Kohn, P.M., Smart, R.G. and Ogborne, A.C. (1984) 'Effects of Two Kinds of Alcohol Advertising on Subsequent Consumption', *Journal of Advertising* 13(1): 34–48.

Lipsitz, A., Brake, G., Vincent, E.J. and Winters, M. (1993) 'Another Round for the Brewers: Television Ads and Children's Alcohol Expectancies', *Journal of Applied Social Psychology* 23(6): 439–50.

Luik, J. and Waterson, M.J. (eds) (1996) *Advertising and Markets.* Henley-on-Thames: NTC Publications.

MacManus, M. (1939) *Irish Cavalcade 1550–1850.* London: Macmillan.

Makowsky, C.R. and Whitehead, P.C. (1991) 'Advertising and Alcohol Sales: A Legal Impact Study', *Journal of Studies on Alcohol* 52(6): 555–67.

McClure, A.C., Dal Cin, S., Gibson, J. and Sargent, J.D. (2006) 'Ownership of Alcohol-branded Merchandise and Initiation of Teen Drinking', *American Journal of Preventive Medicine* 30(4): 277–83.

McDonald, C. (1992) *How Advertising Works.* Henley-on-Thames: NTC Publications.

McGuinness, T. (1980) 'An Econometric Analysis of Total Demand for Alcoholic Beverages in the UK, 1956–1975', *Journal of Industrial Economics* 29(1): 85–109.

— (1983) 'The Demand for Beer, Spirits and Wine in the UK, 1956–1979', in M. Grant, M. Plant and A. Williams (eds) *Economics and Alcohol*, pp. 238–42. New York, NY: Gardner Press.

MEAS (Mature Enjoyment of Alcohol in Society) (2004) *Code of Practice on the Naming, Packaging and Promotion of Alcoholic Drinks.* Dublin: MEAS.

Meier, P. (2008) *Independent Review of the Effects of Alcohol Pricing and Promotion. Part A: Systematic Reviews* [online]. Available: http://www.dh.gov.uk/en/Publichealth/Healthimprovement/Alcoholmisuse/DH_4001740 (last accessed 30 December 2009).

Mongan, D., Reynolds, S., Fanagan, S. and Long, J. (2007) *Health-related Consequences of Problem Alcohol Use: Overview* 6. Dublin: Health Research Board.

National Cancer Registry (2006) *Trends in Irish Cancer Incidence 1994–2002 with Projections to 2020* [online]. Available: http://www.ncri.ie/pubs/pubfiles/proj_2020.pdf (last accessed 30 December 2009).

National Crime Council (2003) *Public Order Offences in Ireland* [online]. Available: http://www.crimecouncil.gov.ie/downloads/Public_Order.pdf (last accessed 30 December 2009).

National Institute on Alcohol Abuse and Alcoholism (2004) *NIAAA Newsletter. Number 3* [online]. Available: http://pubs.niaaa.nih.gov/publications/Newsletter/winter2004/Newsletter_Number3.pdf (last accessed 30 December 2009).

Ogborne, A.C. and Smart, R.G. (1980) 'Will Restrictions on Alcohol Advertising Reduce Alcohol Consumption?', *British Journal of Addiction* 75(3): 293–6.

O'Toole, F. (2005) 'Caving in to Drinks Industry', *Irish Times*, 20 December, p. 14.

Pasch, K.E., Komro, K.A. and Perry, C.L. (2007) 'Outdoor Alcohol Advertising Near Schools: What does it Advertise and How is it Related to Intentions and Use of Alcohol Among Young Adolescents?', *Journal of Studies of Alcohol and Drugs* 68(4): 587–96.

Patten, M. (2007) 'Banning Drink Ads Will Not Achieve Anything', *Irish Times*, 10 October, p. 16.

Patzer, G.L. (1996) *Experimental-research Methodology in Marketing: Types and Applications*. Westport, CT: Quorum Books.

Plunkett, H. (1904) *Ireland in the New Century*. London: John Murray.

Ramstedt, M. and Hope, A. (2005) 'The Irish Drinking Habits of 2002: Drinking and Drinking-related Harm in a European Comparative Perspective', *Journal of Substance Use* 10(5): 273–83.

Robinson, T.N., Chen, H.L. and Killen, J.D. (1998) 'Television and Music Video Exposure and Risk of Adolescent Alcohol Use', *Pediatrics* 102(5): E54.

Saffer, H. (1991) 'Alcohol Advertising Bans and Alcohol Abuse: An International Perspective', *Journal of Health Economics* 10(1): 65–79.

— (2000) 'Alcohol Consumption and Alcohol Advertising Bans', NBER Working Paper Series, Working Paper No. 7758 [online]. Available: http://www.nber.org/papers/w7758 (last accessed 30 December 2009).

Sargent, J.D., Willis, T.A., Stoolmiller, M., Gibson, J. and Gibbons, F.X. (2006) 'Alcohol Use in Motion Pictures and Its Relation with Early-onset Teen Drinking', *Journal of Studies on Alcohol* 67(1): 54–65.

Science Group of the European Alcohol and Health Forum (2009). *Does Marketing Communication Impact on the Volume and Patterns of Consumption of Alcoholic Beverages, Especially by Young People? A Review of Longitudinal Studies* [online]. Available: http://ec.europa.eu/health/ph_determinants/life_style/alcohol/Forum/docs/science_o01_en.pdf (last accessed 30 December 2009).

Smart, R.G. and Cutler, E.E. (1976) 'The Alcohol Advertising Ban in British Columbia: Problems and Effects of Beverage Consumption', *British Journal of Addiction* 71: 13–21.

Smith, L.A. and Foxcroft, D.R. (2007) *The Effect of Alcohol Advertising and Marketing on Drinking Behaviour in Young People: A Systematic Review.* London: Alcohol, Education and Research Council [online]. Available: http://www.aerc.org.uk/documents/pdfs/finalReports/AERC_FinalReport_0040.pdf (last accessed 30 December 2009).

— (2009) 'The Effect of Alcohol Advertising, Marketing and Portrayal on Drinking Behaviour in Young People: Systematic Review of Prospective Cohort Studies', *BMC Public Health* 9: 51.

Snyder, L.B., Milici, F.F., Slater, M., Sun, H. and Strizahakova, Y. (2006) 'Effects of Alcohol Advertising Exposure on Drinking Among Youth', *Archives of Pediatrics and Adolescent Medicine* 160(1): 18–24.

Spear, L. (2002) 'Adolescent Brain and the College Drinker: Biological Basis of Propensity to Use and Misuse Alcohol', *Journal of Studies on Alcohol (Supplement)* 14: 71–81.

Stacy, A.W., Zogg, J.B., Unger, J.B. and Dent, C.W. (2004) 'Exposure to Televised Alcohol Ads and Subsequent Adolescent Alcohol Use', *American Journal of Health Behaviour* 28(6): 498–509.

Stivers, R. (1976) *Hair of the Dog: Irish Drinking and the American Stereotype.* University Park, PA: University of Pennsylvania Press.

Strategic Task Force on Alcohol (2002) *Interim Report* [online]. Available: http://www.dohc.ie/publications/pdf/stfa.pdf?direct=1 (last accessed 30 December 2009).

— (2004) *Second Report* [online]. Available: http://www.dohc.ie/publications/pdf/stfa_second.pdf?direct=1 (last accessed 30 December 2009).

Strickland, D.E. (1984) 'The Advertising Regulation Issue: Some Empirical Evidence on Alcohol Advertising and Teenage Consumption Patterns', in H.D. Holder and J.B. Hallan (eds) *Control Issues in Alcohol Abuse Prevention: National, State and Local Designs for the 80s,* pp. 109–24. Chapel Hill, NC: Human Ecology Institute.

Tegene, A. (1990) 'The Kalman Filter Approach for Testing Structural Change in the Demand for Alcoholic Beverages in the United States', *Applied Economics* 22(10): 1407–16.

TNS Opinion and Social (2007) *Attitudes Towards Alcohol: Special Eurobarometer 272.* Brussels: European Commission [online]. Available: http://ec.europa.eu/health/ph_determinants/life_style/alcohol/documents/ebs272_en.pdf (last accessed 30 December 2009).

van den Bulck, J. and Buellens, K. (2005) 'Television and Music Video Exposure and Adolescent Alcohol Use While Going Out', *Alcohol and Alcoholism* 40(3): 249–53.

Walsh, B. (1982) 'The Demand for Alcohol in the UK: A Comment', *Journal of Industrial Economics* 30(4): 439–46.

WHO (World Health Organisation) (2002) *World Health Report 2002: Reducing Risks, Promoting Healthy Life* [online]. Available: http://www.who.int/whr/2002/en/whr02_en.pdf (last accessed 30 December 2009).

— (2009) *Health For All Database* [online]. Available: http://www.euro.who.int/HFADB (last accessed 30 December 2009).

Wyllie, A., Casswell, S. and Stewart, J. (1989) 'The Response of New Zealand Boys to Corporate and Sponsorship Alcohol Advertising on Television', *British Journal of Addiction* 84(6): 639–46.

Wyllie, A., Zhang, J.F. and Casswell, S. (1998a) 'Responses to Televised Alcohol Advertisements Associated with Drinking Behaviour of 10–17 Year Olds', *Addiction* 93(3): 361–71.

— (1998b) 'Positive Responses to Televised Beer Advertisements Associated with Drinking and Problems Reported by 18 to 29 Year Olds', *Addiction* 93(5): 749–60.

Young, D. (1993) 'Alcohol Advertising Bans and Alcohol Abuse: Comment', *Journal of Health Economics* 12(2): 213–28.

Chapter 29

Children's Interaction with Television Advertising

Margaret-Anne Lawlor

INTRODUCTION

Children's personal purchasing power and their influence on household purchasing decisions, such as choice of car, holiday and food items, have long been recognised in the marketplace. Since the 1960s, advertisers and their agencies have recognised the importance of, and courted, the lucrative child market. In Ireland, there is currently a strong practitioner, regulatory and public interest in the field of advertising to children. However, a polarisation of positions prevails, whereby on the one hand, critics of advertising would contend that children's relative youth and ongoing cognitive development militates against their ability to understand the commercial remit of television advertising. On the other hand, a school of thought has emerged in recent years, positing that children may have a larger and more sophisticated understanding of advertising than previously assumed.

This chapter considers the debate in the literature and also at a wider societal level regarding the practice of advertising to children. It commences by offering a contextual overview of the child market in terms of the lucrative nature of the child market and the role of the age variable in describing this market. Ethical concerns regarding the targeting of the child consumer are then introduced. The chapter then proceeds to offer an examination of the literature regarding children's ability to discern between television advertising and programming, and concludes with an exploration of children's overall understanding of advertising intent.

THE CHILD MARKET IN CONTEXT

McNeal (1998) draws attention to the fact that child consumers do not actually constitute one market, but rather comprise three markets simultaneously. First, McNeal suggests that children are part of a primary market in which they spend their own money. For example, a 2009 Bank of Ireland study of the child-related expenses incurred by parents reported that primary school children received approximately €4 pocket money per week, whilst secondary school children received approximately €13 pocket money per week (Bank of Ireland 2009). Elsewhere, Hibernian Life (now Hibernian Aviva) published figures in 2007 indicating that primary school children in their Irish study received on average €10 pocket money per week, whilst secondary school children were given €20 per week by their parents (Hibernian Life 2007). Second, children are also a market of influencers in terms of the family purchasing decisions to which they contribute. Third, they constitute what McNeal (1998) terms a future market – tomorrow's adult generation of consumers. From an Irish demographic perspective, approximately one-fifth of the population in 2006 was aged under fifteen years (CSO 2009), thus constituting a sizeable cohort in the Irish marketplace.

In particular, food and drink manufacturers have long viewed child consumers as a very attractive market. In 2008, a report was published by the Federal Trade Commission in the United States, giving insights into forty-four food and beverage companies that had been compelled to release information on their 2006 marketing budgets. The report indicated that $1.6bn (just over €1.1bn) was spent by these companies on advertising activities targeting children.

With regard to the child–family relationship, the changing nature of Irish society reflects the changes experienced elsewhere in Europe and, indeed, in the United States. The increasing trend towards single-parent families, as well as an increase in the number of dual-career couples, has resulted in reduced family time and parent–child interaction. Friend (2000) posits that one outcome of these social changes is the phenomenon of developmental compression, whereby children are assuming adult tasks and responsibilities at an earlier age. For example, children are being given autonomy by their parents in household chores, such as shopping and meal preparation. In this respect, Kurnit (2000) has observed that children's assumption of traditional adult tasks has led to the 'KGOY' phenomenon – 'kids growing older younger'. Stoltman (1999:295) refers to the same phenomenon as 'age compression'. Both authors voice their concern that societal pressures on parents are forcing children to acquire adult knowledge and experiences at an earlier age than may be suited to their development.

Another interesting societal development lies in the increasing constraints on parental time referred to above, which may result in a parental guilt factor. McDermott et al. (2006) highlight the fact that the constraints of modern life mean that many children and parents have less time for conversation and recreation together. Adults who are unable to spend as much time as they would like with their children may seek to overcompensate for this by increasing their expenditure on children (Geuens et al. 2003). In this manner, parents may be more prone to accede to children's purchasing requests as compensation for their frequent absence from the child's everyday lifestyle.

Finally, the literature has traditionally viewed parents as exerting the most influence on children, as opposed to other socialisation agents, such as peers, media and schoolteachers (Moschis and Churchill 1978; Moschis and Moore

1979, 1980). However, in view of the social trends highlighted above regarding some parents' reduced presence in children's day-to-day lives, it has been suggested that children are increasingly spending more time with their peers, with the result that the peer 'voice' is exerting more visible influence on children's consumption in areas such as celebrity endorsement and 'socially conspicuous' brand choices (Dotson and Hyatt 2005:37).

DEFINING A CHILD BY AGE

An important underlying dimension of the discussion on child consumers is the way in which we define the concept of a child. We can accept that childhood is the precursor stage to adolescence and adulthood, but the problem lies in arriving at a widely agreed-upon age definition of a child. For example, the European Society for Opinion and Market Research (ESOMAR) defines a child as being fourteen years and under, whilst the Broadcasting Commission of Ireland (BCI) regards a child as being aged up to eighteen years.

Wright-Isak (1999) offers an interesting perspective on the difficulty in defining a child. She suggests that implicit in the advertising/children debate is a perceived need to protect the innocence of children. She contrasts this vision of youthful naivety with the example of how Victorian children aged as young as six years were often sent to work in factories or as chimney sweeps. Indeed, we can further contrast the perception of childhood innocence with the current example of how some clothing outlets in Ireland and the United Kingdom are targeting girls aged as young as eight years with clothing more suited to female adults. As such, it has been suggested that the child is a socially constructed concept (Young 2003) and therefore our idea of what or who a child is, is based on the culture, time and place in which we live.

For example, Kurnit (2000) observes how, over the last forty years, marketers have moved from regarding the child market in the 1960s as being one homogeneous group, aged up to, and including thirteen years, to regarding it as constituting five distinct market segments in today's marketplace. According to Kurnit (2000), these five segments are toddlers (aged up to two years), pre-schoolers (three to five years), kids (six to eight years), tweens (nine to twelve years) and teens (thirteen years plus).

Many practitioners and academics continue to use age as a primary means of defining a child. In an advertising context, the role of age as a causal variable in children's understanding of advertising has been noted (Martin 1997; Young 2003). Therefore, the question must be asked as to why age is so widely used to define and segment the child market. After all, it could be argued that other segmentation variables, such as education level, income, social class and purchase-related behaviour, are equally relevant. The response to this argument is that various age groups of children differ substantially in terms of their cognitive development, communication abilities and physical development, and therefore children of different age groups will differ in their understanding and perception of the world (Kurnit 2000; Stipp 1993). For example, the developmental psychology and marketing literature has consistently suggested that children aged up to five years possess more limited learning faculties than children aged six years and over (Macklin 1994; Peracchio 1992). It follows that different marketing strategies are required for each segment or age group of children.

Therefore, it is widely acknowledged in the literature that age is critical in explaining children's ability to process information about the world around them. In an advertising context, Barenblatt (1981) documents the use of either children's age or school level as a defining variable in the research exploring the child/advertising relationship. The next section considers the ethical concerns that prevail with regard to the practice of advertising to children.

TARGETING THE CHILD MARKET – RESERVATIONS AND UNEASE

There can be no doubt that the phenomenon of television advertising to children is one of the most emotion-laden and controversial areas in marketing. For many years, a large number of researchers, policy-makers, regulatory bodies, parent groups and consumers have criticised advertising to children on the grounds that it is unethical and takes advantage of a vulnerable group in society (e.g. Banks 1975; Burr and Burr 1976; Moore and Lutz 2000; Ward 1974). More specifically, Ellis (2000) enumerates some of the ethical arguments that prevail in this debate:

- Children are misled by advertising and cannot distinguish between programme content and advertisements.
- Advertising food to children encourages them to eat in an unhealthy way and thus increases the possibility of child obesity and dental problems.
- Advertising directed at children exploits, manipulates and causes negative behaviour.
- Advertising to children creates pester power, which, in turn, divides families and undermines parental authority.

The extent to which advertising to children is an unfair practice has been consistently debated in the literature and by various groups in society since the 1960s (e.g. Gunter and Furnham 1998). Cook (2007) draws attention to the gulf that lies between critics of marketing, who view the child consumer as a victim of corporate exploitation, and another school of thought, which contends that exposure to the consumption landscape facilitates the child in exercising his/her individual autonomy. Rubin (1974) suggests that the development of public policy on advertising should be considered in the context of the research evidence addressing the child's use of advertising. The problem, or indeed the challenge, for researchers in this field is that, in many aspects of the literature, there is confusion and disagreement concerning children's ability to discern between television advertising and programming, as well as their facility for explaining this difference.

The debate on the ethical implications of advertising to children has equally powerful arguments on both sides. An instant resolution is difficult to find because, as with all things ethical, there are problems in identifying what exactly is ethical behaviour. Drumwright and Murphy (2004) suggest that the ethical concerns in advertising comprise the objections and moral issues that arise in this area. They cite examples such as advertisements targeting children and advertisements for dangerous products. However, the inherent challenge in identifying and arriving at ethical standards is that everyone tends to have their own interpretation as to what constitutes such aspirations (Schlegelmilch 1998).

In an Irish context, the practice of advertising to children continues to generate substantial practitioner, regulatory and public debate. In 2003–2004, the debate concerning advertising and children intensified in Ireland when the BCI, a statutory body in charge of the licensing and monitoring of television and radio services in Ireland, engaged in a series of stages of public consultation. The objective of this exercise was to draft a Children's Advertising Code to govern broadcast advertising to children in Ireland. This code was duly published in October 2004 and came into force in January 2005.

Following a statutory review in 2008, the BCI presented details of a report indicating that a number of aspects of the Children's Advertising Code required further consideration and possible revision (BCI 2009). These areas include children's relative inexperience and credulity regarding advertising, product prohibitions in advertising, and ongoing concerns regarding the advertising of certain types of food, including those with high fat, sugar and salt content.

Having introduced ethical concerns regarding the practice of advertising to children, in the next section we explore children's ability to distinguish between television programmes and advertising.

CAN CHILDREN DISTINGUISH BETWEEN TELEVISION PROGRAMMES AND ADVERTISING?

Whilst there is a large body of literature pertaining to children and advertising, it does not always offer clear answers to the questions that have been introduced above. For example, disagreement prevails regarding what exactly children know and understand about advertising's raison d'être, and the age at which this knowledge develops (Mallalieu et al. 2005). Furthermore, the vast bulk of this research was conducted in the 1970s and 1980s, with an overwhelming emphasis on American children's consumption of advertising (Friestad and Wright 2005; Lawlor and Prothero 2003).

A starting point in the discussion on children's interaction with television advertising is to consider children's exposure to television as a medium. The central role of television in children's lives has been reaffirmed by the publication in 2009 of the results of a major Irish study, *Growing Up in Ireland*. Funded by the Department of Health and Children, in association with the Department of Social and Family Affairs and the Central Statistics Office, the study surveyed 8,500 nine-year-old children in Ireland. Findings indicate that nearly 50 per cent of all nine-year-olds in Ireland have a television in their bedroom. Furthermore, two-thirds of these children watch between one and three hours a day of television, whilst another nine per cent spend between three and five hours watching television per day (Growing Up in Ireland 2009). As a point of comparison, children in the United Kingdom watch an average of five hours of television a day whilst over three-quarters of children aged between five and sixteen years have a television in their bedroom (ChildWise 2007/8).

Gunter and Furnham (1998) sound a note of caution when interpreting children's television viewing and their apparent exposure to television advertisements. They sensibly contend that the fact that one is exposed to a commercial break does not automatically mean that one attends to that communication. For example, technological facilities such as the remote control allow children to edit their own viewing. Another factor to consider is whether children actually pay attention to the advertisements, in that television viewing may be one of many activities they are undertaking simultaneously.

Having addressed children's exposure to television, it is important to ascertain whether children recognise that television advertising and television programming constitute two different forms of communication. A child's ability to discern between a programme and an advertisement is an area that has attracted much disagreement, specifically with regard to whether children aged under five years can make this distinction. For example, Preston (2000) suggests that the age of five years is an essential watershed in this discussion, because it is from this age onward that many researchers agree that children can distinguish between programming and advertising (Blosser and Roberts 1985; Butter *et al*. 1981; Gaines and Esserman 1981; Preston 2000; Roedder 1999). However, it must be emphasised that there is an equal number of authors who would disagree with the contention that children aged five years can differentiate between advertising and television programmes (Brucks *et al*. 1988; Kunkel and Roberts 1991; Rubin 1974; Stephens and Stutts 1982; Young 1990).

The extent to which the various studies differ in their views on this issue is highlighted as follows. Wartella and Ettema's (1974) study of children aged under three years indicated that the children were able to distinguish between an advertisement and a programme. Elsewhere, Levin, Petros and Petrella (1982) supported this argument, suggesting that the under-fives in their study were advertising-aware and that the cues they used to make the distinction were the visual and aural aspects of the advertisement.

In a different study, children aged four and five years were asked to watch a television programme called *Captain Kangaroo* (Butter *et al*. 1981). Four thirty-second advertisements were interspersed throughout the programme, and the children were asked to indicate when a commercial appeared on screen. A separator was used in the viewing whereby a voice announced that 'The Captain will return after this message', and this separator was used for each of the four advertisements. Seventy per cent of the four-year-old children and 90 per cent of the five-year-old children were able to identify all four advertisements. Interestingly, when asked 'what is the difference between a commercial and the Captain Kangaroo show?', 90 per cent of the four-year-old children were unable to explain the difference.

This is a key finding because it highlights that while younger children are able to differentiate between a programme and an advertisement, they are often unable to explain the difference. As Butter et al. (1981:56) pointed out, 'young children may know they are watching something different than a program but do not know that the intent of what they are watching is to invite purchase of a product or service'. Thus, children's ability to distinguish an advertisement does not always equate with understanding the difference between advertising and programming.

Contrasting findings were offered a year later in a study by Stephens and Stutts (1982). They inserted a segment of another programme into the middle of a cartoon where an advertisement break would normally appear. Their sample of five-year-olds incorrectly identified this programme segment as being an advertisement. Similarly, Young (1990) contended that the five- to seven-year-old children in his study were unable to make the distinction. They identified advertisements correctly 53 per cent of the time, as opposed to being able to identify programmes some 70 per cent of the time. So, too, Kunkel and Roberts (1991) argued that the under-fives in their study were not able to distinguish an advertisement from a programme.

A related question arises from the increasing blurring between television programmes and advertisements that feature the same characters. Buckingham et al. (1999:6) draw attention to this phenomenon, referring to it as 'trans-media intertextuality', whereby the same characters appear in programmes, advertising, computer games and merchandising. Kunkel (1988) contends that in many cases it is becoming more difficult for the child to make the programme/advertising distinction, because the same characters often appear both in the programme and in advertisements during the commercial break. More recently, a study involving two groups of children aged five to seven years and eleven to twelve years indicated that both groups of children were able to discern between programmes and advertisements by virtue of cues, such as content, length and timing of advertisements (Mallalieu et al. 2005). However, this study also indicated that some confusion arose among five- to seven-year-olds when an advertisement appeared in the middle of a programme.

Bandyopadhyay, Kindra and Sharp (2001) suggest that children may differentiate between the two forms of communication by using clues such as the difference in sound, content and length, attention-arousing devices, levels of repetition and the overall difference in genre between an advertisement and a programme. Another means by which children make the programme/advertisement distinction appears to be the position of the advertisement relative to the programme. For example, a commercial break that appears at the end of one programme may be easier for children to discern than a break in the middle of a programme (Hoy *et al.* 1986). It is therefore critical to emphasise, in light of the above studies, that children may use simple perceptual cues to help them recognise an advertisement, but this still does not address their deeper understanding of advertising.

In view of the above, some authors contend that it is difficult to conclude that children aged up to six years age can effectively differentiate between a programme and an advertisement (Roedder 1981; Roedder *et al.* 1983). Having discussed children's ability to differentiate between the two genres, the section that follows explores the phenomenon of children's understanding of advertising's raison d'être.

CHILDREN'S UNDERSTANDING OF ADVERTISING INTENT

There is a substantial body of literature pertaining to the child's understanding of advertising intent, and a common theme in these studies is that intent is assumed to mean a selling or commercial purpose. Again, it becomes clear that the key studies examining children's understanding of advertising have all been age-related (see Bandyopadhyay *et al.* 2001). The importance of examining children's understanding of advertising intent lies in the argument that, if children do not understand that advertising has a commercial objective, then advertising to such children may be unethical, on the basis that it takes advantage of their innocence and credulity (Gunter and Furnham 1998; Martin 1997).

Young (2000) suggests that, for children to understand advertising, they must appreciate that (a) a particular source (i.e. advertiser) is responsible for the advertisement and (b) the source is seeking to encourage the message recipients (i.e. advertising audience) to purchase the advertised good. In earlier studies (e.g. Rossiter and Robertson 1974), the suggestion was that children under eight years had limited understanding, if any, of the purpose of advertising. With a view to investigating this level of comprehension, researchers in the 1970s and 1980s began to consider the merits of using both verbal and non-verbal research methods to ascertain children's understanding. Macklin (1985) posits that Rossiter (1976) was the first advertising researcher to draw attention to the tendency, in most research relating to children and advertising, to rely on verbal recall. He contended that children (aged eight years and under) might not be able to respond to open-ended questions, which require them to contextualise and articulate their ideas. Rossiter (1976) correspondingly administered a study in which children were required to use non-verbal measures, such as pictures and drawings, to represent their memory of a favourite cereal.

The use of non-verbal measures in child research was later echoed in a key study by Donohue, Henke and Donohue (1980), who argued that young children's understanding of advertising might be greater than researchers had previously speculated. The reason for this was that children's grasp of language and their verbal abilities might not allow them to articulate a level of understanding. Again, this reflected Rossiter's (1976) earlier thinking. Donohue, Henke and Donohue (1980) suggested that children's understanding might be explored using a different method, namely non-verbal measures such as pictorial images. In their study, children aged between two and six years were shown an advertisement for a cereal featuring an animated character named Toucan Sam. The children were asked what Toucan Sam wanted them to do, as a result of watching the advertisement. To assist in answering the question, the children were shown two pictures, one showing an in-store scene, the other depicting an image of a child watching television. The study reported how children tended to select the first image, namely the shop scene, thus suggesting an understanding of advertising as having a commercial objective. However, one could speculate that, given two images from which to choose, the children had a one in two chance of selecting each image and the results should accordingly be considered in this light.

From a conceptual perspective, Donohue, Henke and Donohue's (1980) research generated a number of rich findings. They contended that young children, namely those aged two to six years, were aware of the selling intent of the advertisements to which they had been exposed. A second outcome was the children's ability to recognise the concept of audience segmentation, in that they were able to suggest which programmes, and correspondingly which advertisements, were likely to be watched by individual members of their family. Another finding was the child's facility for empathising with the characters in the advertisement. In other words, they had a strong feeling and understanding for how a particular character would like them to behave, for example to purchase the product being advertised.

Interestingly, Macklin (1985) replicated this study and confirmed the above findings, namely that the children sampled (aged three to five years) tended to select the picture illustrating a shopping scene, rather than the television scene. In an extension of the study, however, Macklin added two other pictures to the two above and found that, when asked again about the purpose of an advertisement, young children did not select the correct picture, i.e. the shopping scene. She argued therefore that her study would appear to refute the notion that young children understand the selling purpose of advertising. Macklin (1985) also posed a methodological question in which she posited that the original study by Donohue, Henke and Donohue (1980) may have been too simple (by using two pictures), or indeed her own study may have been too difficult by using four pictures.

Even so, the use of non-verbal assessment amongst younger children has been encouraged in the literature (e.g. Martin 1997). In essence, the suggestion is that some form of non-verbal communication (e.g. the use of pictorial images) may be more suitable to children aged five years and under, as such respondents may be able to express themselves more clearly in this way instead of relying solely on the written or spoken word.

In their 1974 study, Robertson and Rossiter sought to broaden the debate by expanding on the concept of intent. The two authors posed a number of questions: Can children distinguish between programmes and commercials? Do children understand the purpose of advertising? How does the child develop resistance to commercial persuasion? And, if a child understands advertising's purpose, is he/she less persuadable? (Robertson and Rossiter 1974:13).

In the study, an open-ended interviewing technique indicated that the children sampled (boys aged between six and eleven years) attributed two types of intent to advertising – assistive and persuasive. Assistive intent refers to those advertisements that assist the recipient by offering information, whereas persuasive intent refers to those advertisements that seek to encourage the recipient to purchase.

Robertson and Rossiter (1974) stated their findings as a number of propositions, which would, in turn, suggest that they required further testing, as the authors themselves recognised. The first proposition was that the older the child, the more likely he/she is to recognise the persuasive intent of an advertisement. For example, approximately 53 per cent of the first grade pupils (aged six to seven years) attributed a persuasive intent compared to 99 per cent of fifth grade pupils (aged ten to eleven years). Robertson and Rossiter (1974) therefore contended that an ability to recognise advertising's persuasive intent is very much age-dependent and, furthermore, that younger children are more open to persuasion. Indeed, it is interesting to note that Robertson and Rossiter (1974) allude to an ethical issue as to whether such children have an increased requirement for protection from advertising.

A multiple method approach was undertaken by Oates, Blades and Gunter (2002) and Oates et al. (2003). In the first study, Oates, Blades and Gunter (2002) sought to assess understanding of advertising intent by adopting an experimental approach. A sample of six-, eight- and ten-year-olds were shown a cartoon into which unfamiliar advertisements were inserted. Following this, the children were asked a number of questions, including a question about the purpose of advertisements. The authors found that none of the six-year-olds and only one-quarter of the eight-year-olds referred to advertising's persuasive intent. Approximately one-third of the ten-year-olds referred to this dimension of intent. Therefore, the authors referred to the children as having an overall limited understanding of advertising intent, and they also contended that their findings contradicted those of Donohue, Henke and Donohue's (1980) study of two- to six-year-olds.

In a follow-up study by Oates et al. (2003), a focus group study of six- to ten-year-olds was undertaken. The children were asked about the role and source of television advertisements. The findings indicated that these children had a limited understanding of advertising in that none of the six-year-olds referred to the persuasive nature of advertising. A small number of the eight-year-olds and some of the ten-year-olds did so (Oates *et al.* (2003) did not quantify these numbers). For the purposes of comparing the above studies, Table 29.1 below illustrates, in each case, the age of the child respondents, the method of measurement (verbal versus non-verbal) and the response received from the children regarding advertising intent.

Table 29.1 Studies of children's understanding of advertising intent

Authors	Children's Age	Measure Used	Perceived Intent
Ward (1972)	5–12 years	Verbal	Persuasive/selling
Robertson and Rossiter (1974)	First grade pupils	Verbal	Informational/ assistive
Ward, Wackman and Wartella (1977)	Kindergarten	Verbal	Persuasive/selling
Donohue, Henke and Donohue (1980)	2–6 years	Non-verbal	Persuasive/selling
Butter *et al.* (1981)	4–5 years	Verbal	Persuasive/selling
Gaines and Esserman (1981)	4 years	Verbal	Persuasive/selling
Blosser and Roberts (1985)	4–11 years	Verbal	Informational/ teaching/selling/ entertaining/ persuasive
Macklin (1985)	3–5 years	Non-verbal	Persuasive/selling
Macklin (1987)	Pre-school	Non-verbal	Informational/assistive
Chan (2000)	5–12 years	Verbal	Selling
Oates, Blades and Gunter (2002)	6–10 years	Experimental/ Verbal	Persuasive
Oates *et al.* (2003)	6–10 years	Verbal	Persuasive/assistive

Sources: Lawlor and Prothero (2008); Martin (1997).

In terms of synthesising the literature on children's understanding of advertising intent, a number of observations arise. First, Table 29.1 identifies how the majority of researchers in this area have placed overwhelming emphasis on the persuasive/selling intent of advertising. In other words, these studies sought to establish whether the children sampled could understand that advertising exists to persuade and/or sell. Indeed, in this very respect, Blosser and Roberts (1985) are in a minority in terms of broadening the concept of intent to include information, teaching and entertainment in addition to selling and persuasion.

More recently, Lawlor and Prothero (2008) considered the extant studies regarding children's understanding of advertising intent and contended that an overwhelming emphasis had consistently been placed on whether children were able to understand advertising intent in terms of its information, persuasion and selling objectives. As such, children were being required to consider the advertiser's perspective. Lawlor and Prothero's (2008) study sought to broaden the debate about intent by questioning whether children view advertising as being richer or more complex than the advertiser's perspective, which had traditionally been the focus of extant research. In their study, children aged between seven and nine years were asked to discuss the raison d'être of advertising. Three different perspectives emerged in children's discussions on advertising intent. Essentially, the children viewed advertising as serving three masters. First, they understood the presence of a commercial source, namely the advertiser, who used advertising to persuade and to encourage purchase. Second, from the viewer's perspective, advertising was seen to exist to offer information, entertainment and viewer convenience, an example of the latter being the planning of one's activities around the advertisement break in a programme. Finally, from the television channel's perspective, advertising was seen to constitute a source of programme funding and to facilitate the television channels and their programme schedules.

Having considered the extant studies relating to children's understanding of advertising, I contend that a key question therein was whether children could understand advertising intent. As raised, this question suggests a 'yes' or 'no' answer. In contrast, Lawlor and Prothero's (2008) study proposes a classification that highlights the degrees or nuances of a child's understanding of advertising. Four levels of understanding are proposed. The first level relates to an unsophisticated understanding, which prevails where a child is unable to recognise the persuasive intent of advertising or to decode the advertiser's intended message. A second level relates to a basic understanding of advertising, where the child is able to discern between advertising and programming by way of peripheral cues, such as programme credits and duration of an advertisement. A third level relates to a semi-sophisticated understanding of advertising, whereby a child can exhibit an understanding of advertising's persuasive intent. Finally, a fourth level relates to a highly sophisticated level of understanding, where a child can demonstrate an understanding that advertising may serve interests including, but not limited to, the advertiser. These other interests include the viewer and host television station. This classification, therefore, seeks to develop the debate concerning children's understanding of advertising by proposing that there can be different degrees of such understanding.

CONCLUSION

This chapter considered the lucrative nature of the child market and ethical arguments regarding the practice of advertising to children, with specific reference to the question as to whether children understand advertising's persuasive intent. A child's ability to discern between a television advertisement and a programme was explored and the lack of an overall consensus in the literature was demonstrated with regard to whether children can make this distinction, and the age at which they can make this distinction. Even more importantly, a note of caution was sounded by some researchers that, even where children can discern between the two genres of communication, using cues such as the relative length of an advertisement vis-à-vis a programme, and the presence of a continuity announcer, this discernment does not equate with an understanding as to *why* there is a difference between the two genres.

Also explored was the large body of literature considering the child's understanding of advertising intent. Martin (1997) has argued that where children cannot discern such intent, the practice of advertising to children is open to ethical scrutiny on the basis that it is exploitative of their relative innocence and credulity. The BCI's introduction of a Children's Advertising Code in Ireland in 2005, and its subsequent review of this code in 2008, is indicative of the primary position that the practice of advertising to children occupies on the social policy agenda. Yet I would argue that rather than solely viewing advertising as doing something *to* children, we need to equally consider what it is that children do *with* advertising. For example, as illustrated in Table 29.1 above, researchers have tended to place strong emphasis on whether children recognise and understand the commercial intent of advertising. Yet it is important to reiterate that such objectives constitute the advertiser's perspective and that both the academic and practitioner communities have to date largely refrained from exploring the child's perspective on advertising over and above that of the advertiser's agenda. Oates *et al.* (2003:60) have contended that 'no definitive study of children's understanding of advertising intent exists'. Perhaps this is because many of the extant studies have tended to focus rather narrowly on certain aspects of the child/advertising interface, rather than approaching the relationship as being larger, more complex and deeper than previously thought.

With regard to the latter approach, Blosser and Roberts's (1985) study was one in a minority in seeking to broaden the concept of advertising intent by suggesting that advertising could exist, not just for selling and persuasion purposes, but could also serve to inform, teach and entertain the child viewer. Similarly this chapter discussed Lawlor and Prothero's (2008) study, which indicated that their child participants viewed advertising as serving not just the advertiser, but two other interests, namely those of the viewer, in terms of offering information, entertainment and convenience; and of the television channel, in terms of generating programme funding and facilitating programme schedules. Therefore, to return to the question posed above – what do children do with advertising? – this study indicated that the children viewed advertising as being a resource that could be used to perform a number of functions for advertisers, viewers and television channels. As such, Lawlor and Prothero (2008) concluded that, rather than viewing advertising as being something that affects children, in the manner of the stimulus-organism-response (SOR) mechanism, the children in their study presented themselves as being more appraising and knowledgeable about advertising than the interpretation offered by many previous researchers in their own studies. Furthermore, by empathising with the different masters that advertising may serve, the children in Lawlor and Prothero's (2008) study presented themselves as having a nuanced understanding of advertising intent. I would therefore suggest that future research should develop this line of inquiry regarding children's interaction with advertising by exploring how children across all age groups view advertising in general, and more specifically advertising intent. It is useful to return to Martin's (1997) ethical concern that where children cannot discern advertising's commercial remit, advertising that targets them may be unethical and exploitative. Studies such as those conducted by Blosser and Roberts (1985) and Lawlor and Prothero (2008) illustrate the potentially fertile ground for researchers and marketers to explore, namely children's knowledge of, and appreciation of, the various interests that advertising can serve.

However, this is not to suggest that all children will exhibit the same level of cognisance towards advertising, and the presence of the ongoing social policy debate about the practice of advertising to children is to be welcomed. Marketers need to be fully au fait with the premise that children are not mini-adults, as they are often presented in the media and popular culture, and that certain levels of delicacy and care must be exhibited when targeting this cohort.

Finally, many of the key studies focusing on the child–advertising interface were conducted in the 1970s and 1980s, and much of this research has been concentrated in the United States. Hopefully an outcome of the ongoing policy debate about child-targeted advertising will be to augment academic, practitioner and societal interest in the principles and procedures that underpin this area of marketing. This should, in turn, encourage further researchers to enter this field. As such, the role of television and television advertising in children's lives today must be critically viewed in the context of the vastly different media landscape of the twenty-first century, as well as the current socio-cultural trends in Ireland, and further afield, concerning the prevalence of 'time-poor' parents and families. For example, the presence of the parent as gatekeeper of the child's television viewing cannot always be guaranteed due to changes in family types and in parental work commitments. It is important, therefore, that the debate about the practice of advertising to children, and the procedures underpinning this practice, should continue to be aired, but equally it should be informed by contemporary research that reflects our evolving social and technological environment.

References

Bandyopadhyay, S., Kindra, G. and Sharp, L. (2001) 'Is Television Advertising Good for Children? Areas of Concern and Policy Implications', *International Journal of Advertising* 20(1): 89–116.

Bank of Ireland (2009) *Parents Should Plan Ahead to Ease the Financial Headache of a Child's Education Expenses* [online]. Available: http://www.bankofirelandlife.ie/News/Parents-should-plan-ahead-to-ease-the-financial-he.aspx (last accessed 19 August 2009).

Banks, S. (1975) 'Public Policy on Ads to Children', *Journal of Advertising Research* 15(4): 7–12.

Barenblatt, L. (1981) 'A Critical Review of Recent Research on the Effects of Television Advertising on Children', in J.F. Esserman (ed.) *Television Advertising and Children – Issues, Research and Findings*, pp. 17–42. New York, NY: Child Research Service.

BCI (Broadcasting Commission of Ireland) (2005) *Children's Advertising Code* [online]. Available: http://www.bci.ie/codes/childrens_code.html (last accessed 19 August 2009).

— (2009) *BCI Publishes Statutory Review of Children's Advertising Code* [online]. Available: http://www.bci.ie/news_information/press227.html (last accessed 19 August 2009).

Blosser, B.J. and Roberts, D.F. (1985) 'Age Differences in Children's Perceptions of Message Intent', *Communication Research* 12(4): 455–84.

Brucks, M., Armstrong, G.M. and Goldberg, M.E. (1988) 'Children's Use of Cognitive Defences Against Television Advertising: A Cognitive Response Approach', *Journal of Consumer Research* 14(4): 471–82.

Buckingham, D., Davies, H., Jones, K. and Kelley, P. (1999) *Children's Television in Britain*. London: British Film Institute.

Burr, P.L. and Burr, R.M. (1976) 'Television Advertising to Children: What Parents are Saying About Government Control', *Journal of Advertising* 5(4): 37–41.

Butter, E.J., Popovich, P.M., Stackhouse, R.H. and Garner, R.K. (1981) 'Discrimination of Television Programs and Commercials by Preschool Children', *Journal of Advertising Research* 21(2): 53–6.

Chan, K. (2000) 'Hong Kong Children's Understanding of Television Advertising', *Journal of Marketing Communications* 6(1): 37–52.

ChildWise (2007/8) *The Monitor Report: Children's Media Use and Purchasing (2007/8) SMRC*. Norwich: ChildWise.

Cook, D.T. (2007) 'The Disempowering Empowerment of Children's Consumer "Choice" – Cultural Discourses of the Child Consumer in North America', *Society and Business Review* 2(1): 37–52.

CSO (Central Statistics Office) (2009) *Population Statistics 2006* [online]. Available: http://www.cso.ie/statistics/popnbyage2006.html (last accessed 31 July 2009).

Donohue, T.R., Henke, L.H. and Donohue, W.A. (1980) 'Do Kids Know what TV Commercials Intend?', *Journal of Advertising Research* 20(5): 51–7.

Dotson, M.J. and Hyatt, E.M. (2005) 'Major Influence Factors in Children's Consumer Socialization', *Journal of Consumer Marketing* 22(1): 35–42.

Drumwright, M.E. and Murphy, P.E. (2004) 'How Advertising Practitioners View Ethics', *Journal of Advertising* 33(2): 7–24.

Ellis, B. (2000) 'Advertising to Children in Europe', paper presented at the National Marketing Conference, Dublin, October.

Friend, B. (2000) 'How and Why Kids Benefit from a Responsible Commercial TV Environment', paper presented at the Global Kid Power Conference, Lisbon, October.

Friestad, M. and Wright, P. (2005) 'The Next Generation: Research for Twenty-First Century Public Policy on Children and Advertising', *Journal of Public Policy and Marketing* 24(2): 183–85.

Gaines, L. and Esserman, J. (1981) 'A Quantitative Study of Young Children's Comprehension of Television Programs and Commercials', in J.F. Esserman, (ed.) *Television Advertising and Children – Issues, Research and Findings*, pp. 95–106. New York, NY: Child Research Service.

Geuens, M., De Pelsmacker, P. and Mast, G. (2003) 'How Family Structure Affects Parent–Child Communication about Consumption', *Advertising and Marketing to Children* 4(2): 57–62.

Growing Up in Ireland (2009) *Growing Up in Ireland – National Longitudinal Study of Children* [online]. Available: http://www.growingup.ie/fileadmin/user_upload/documents/No1_Being_9_Years_Old.pdf (last accessed 19 August 2009).

Gunter, B. and Furnham, A. (1998) *Children as Consumers – A Psychological Analysis of the Young People's Market*. London: Routledge.

Hibernian Life (2007) *The Bank of Mum and Dad – Savers or Spenders* [online]. Available: http://www.hibernian.ie/group/mediacentre/latestnews/saversorspenders/ (last accessed 19 May 2009).

Hoy, M.G., Young, C.E. and Mowen, J.C. (1986) 'Animated Host Selling Advertisements: Their Impact on Young Children's Recognition, Attitudes and Behaviour', *Journal of Public Policy and Marketing* 5(1): 171–84.

Kunkel, D. (1988) 'From a Raised Eyebrow to a Turned Back: The FCC and Children's Product-Related Programming', *Journal of Communications* 38(4): 90–108.

Kunkel, D. and Roberts, D. (1991) 'Young Minds and Marketplace Values: Issues in Children's Television Advertising', *Journal of Social Issues* 47(1): 57–72.

Kurnit, P. (2000) *Kids Getting Older Younger* [online]. Available: http://www.kidshopbiz.com/pdf/kids_older_younger.pdf (last accessed 19 August 2009).

Lawlor, M.-A. and Prothero, A. (2003) 'Children's Understanding of Television Advertising Intent', *Journal of Marketing Management* 19(3-4): 411–31.

— (2008) 'Exploring Children's Understanding of Television – Beyond the Advertiser's Perspective', *European Journal of Marketing* 42(11/12): 1203–23.

Levin, S., Petros, T. and Petrella, F. (1982) 'Pre-Schoolers' Awareness of Television Advertising', *Child Development* 53(4): 933–7.

Macklin, M.C. (1985) 'Do Young Children Understand the Selling Intent of Commercials?', *Journal of Consumer Affairs* 19(2): 293–304.

— (1987) 'Preschoolers' Understanding of the Information Function of Advertising', *Journal of Consumer Research* 14(2): 229–39.

— (1994) 'The Impact of Audiovisual Information on Children's Product-Related Recall', *Journal of Consumer Research* 21(1): 154–64.

Mallalieu, L., Palan, K.M. and Laczniak, R.N. (2005) 'Understanding Children's Knowledge and Beliefs about Advertising: A Global Issue that Spans Generations', *Journal of Current Issues and Research in Advertising* 27(1): 53–64.

Martin, M.C. (1997) 'Children's Understanding of the Intent of Advertising: A Meta-analysis', *Journal of Public Policy and Marketing* 16(2): 205–16.

McDermott, L., O'Sullivan, T., Stead, M. and Hastings, G. (2006) 'International Food Advertising, Pester Power and its Effects', *International Journal of Advertising* 25(4): 513–40.

McNeal, J. (1998) 'Tapping the Three Kids' Markets', *American Demographics* April: 37–41.

Moore, E.S. and Lutz, R.J. (2000) 'Children, Advertising, and Product Experiences: A Multimethod Inquiry', *Journal of Consumer Research* 27(1): 31–48.

Moschis, G.P. and Churchill, G.A. (1978) 'Consumer Socialisation: A Theoretical and Empirical Analysis', *Journal of Marketing Research* 15(4): 599–609.

Moschis, G.P. and Moore, R.L. (1979) 'Decision Making Among the Young: A Socialisation Perspective', *Journal of Consumer Research* 6(2): 101–12.

— (1980) 'Purchasing Behaviour of Adolescent Consumers', in R.P. Bagozzi, K.L. Berhardt, P.S. Busch, D.W. Cravens, J.F. Hair and C.A. Scott (eds) *Proceedings of the American Marketing Association*, pp. 89–92. Chicago: American Marketing Association.

Oates, C., Blades, M. and Gunter, B. (2002) 'Children and Television Advertising: When do They Understand Persuasive Intent?', *Journal of Consumer Behaviour* 1(3): 238–45.

Oates, C., Blades, M., Gunter, B. and Don, J. (2003) 'Children's Understanding of Television Advertising: A Qualitative Approach', *Journal of Marketing Communications* 9(2): 59–71.

Peracchio, L.A. (1992) 'How Do Young Children Learn to Be Consumers? A Script-Processing Approach', *Journal of Consumer Research* 18(4): 425–40.

Preston, C. (2000) 'Are Children Seeing through ITC Advertising Regulations?', *International Journal of Advertising* 19(1): 117–36.

Robertson, T.S. and Rossiter, J.R. (1974) 'Children and Commercial Persuasion: An Attribution Theory Analysis', *Journal of Consumer Research* 1(1): 13–20.

Roedder, D.L. (1981) 'Age Differences in Children's Responses to Television Advertising: An Information-Processing Approach', *Journal of Consumer Research* 8(2): 144–53.

Roedder, D.L., Sternthal, B. and Calder, B.J. (1983) 'Attitude–Behaviour Consistency in Children's Responses to Television Advertising', *Journal of Marketing Research* 20(4): 337–49.

Roedder John, D. (1999) 'Through the Eyes of a Child: Children's Knowledge and Understanding of Advertising', in C. Macklin and L. Carlson (eds) *Advertising to Children: Concepts and Controversies*, pp. 3–26. Thousand Oaks, CA: Sage.

Rossiter, J.R. (1976) 'Visual and Verbal Memory in Children's Product Information Utilisation', *Advances in Consumer Research* 3(1): 523–8.

Rossiter, J.R. and Robertson, T.S. (1974) 'Children's TV Commercials: Testing the Defences', *Journal of Communication* 24 (Autumn): 137–44.

Rubin, R.S. (1974) 'The Effects of Cognitive Development on Children's Responses to Television Advertising', *Journal of Business Research* 2(4): 409–19.

Schlegelmilch, B. (1998) *Marketing Ethics: An International Perspective*. London: International Thomson Business.

Stephens, N. and Stutts, M.A. (1982) 'Preschoolers' Ability to Distinguish between Television Programming and Commercials', *Journal of Advertising* 11(2): 16–26.

Stipp, H. (1993) 'New Ways to Reach Children', *American Demographics* 15(8): 50–6.

Stoltman, J. (1999) 'The Context of Advertising and Children: Future Research Directions', in M.C. Macklin and L. Carlson (eds) *Advertising to Children: Concepts and Controversies*, pp. 291–8. Thousand Oaks, CA: Sage.

Ward, S. (1972) 'Children's Reactions to Commercials', *Journal of Advertising Research* 12(2): 37–45.

—— (1974) 'Consumer Socialisation', *Journal of Consumer Research* 1(2): 1–14.

Ward, S., Wackman, D.B. and Wartella, E. (1977) *How Children Learn to Buy*. Beverley Hills, CA: Sage.

Wartella, E. and Ettema, J. (1974) 'A Cognitive Developmental Study of Children's Attention to Television Commercials', *Communication Research* 1 (January): 44–69.

Wright-Isak, C. (1999) 'Advertising to Children in the Twenty-First Century: New Questions Within Familiar Themes', in M.C. Macklin and L. Carlson (eds) *Advertising to Children: Concepts and Controversies*, pp. 275–80. Thousand Oaks, CA: Sage.

Young, B. (1990) *Television Advertising and Children*. Oxford: Oxford University Press.

— (2000) 'The Child's Understanding of Promotional Communication', *International Journal of Advertising and Marketing to Children* 2(3): 191–203.
— (2003) 'Does Food Advertising Influence Children's Food Choices? A Critical Review of Some of the Recent Literature', *International Journal of Advertising* 22(4): 441–59.

Chapter 30
Do Modern Business Communications Technologies Mean a Surveillance Society?

Karlin Lillington

INTRODUCTION

In the space of a few decades, businesses have been transformed by communications technologies that generate, store, sift and analyse information (Agar 2003; Aspray and Campbell-Kelly 1996; Cortada 2007; Shurkin 1996). The transition has been so smooth and subtle that most do not even notice it taking place, but, over time, companies have moved from an era in which only the largest organisations might have had a single mainframe computer processing a limited range of data, to the current situation where even the smallest firm has individual desktop PCs and laptops storing, processing, receiving and sending massive amounts of information, from the trivial to potentially commercially sensitive data. In an even shorter space of time, companies have witnessed the arrival of the Internet as a mass communication medium and the migration from landlines with answering machines to digital, Internet Protocol (IP)-based phone systems and a mobile phone-equipped workforce. In communications, the business letter gave way to the fax, which has given way to email. Most recently, organisations have been inundated with the chattering business classes' lusty embrace of instant messaging, text messages, Blackberries, iPhones, blogs, Facebook, LinkedIn, Twitter and a whole, increasingly interwoven, online universe of social media and networking technologies.

That transition may seem benign – simply a matter of easier, faster, better. But going from analogue to electronic and digital has major, and often hidden, implications and consequences. It has been, in effect, a changeover from clumsy, hard to search and expensive to store paper and vague landline call records, to a landslide of easily stored, searched and mined electronic data produced as a by-product of new information and communications technologies attached to virtually every action taken in the office and home of today. This chapter addresses some of the complex data privacy and data management issues that arise from the arrival and widespread use of such electronic and digital technologies. It looks at how and why a wide range of data are generated, and who might be interested in gaining access to retained data. The data retention and storage environment in Ireland is outlined, along with some of the implications for Irish businesses and citizens. Finally, shifting perceptions of public and private are examined in the context of the growth of social networking activities, with a cautionary look forward.

DIGITAL DATA STREAMS

Commonplace technologies, many of which are now central to some of the most basic operations of an organisation, also generate numerous streams of digital data. When a person makes a mobile phone call, a chain of events is initiated, with each link in the chain minutely recorded. The number, but also the location, of the caller is pinpointed, because surrounding mobile masts know where the handset is and several 'triangulate' the location in order to try to ensure a call is not dropped. For a global system for mobile communications (GSM) handset, the caller's location may be tracked to within thirty metres in a city setting, but with a third-generation (3G) handset, or a handset with global positioning system (GPS) functionality turned on, the caller can be placed within a few metres of her location. The recipient number is also recorded, as is the receiver's location. The call's duration is noted and stored. Under Irish law, enacted under the Criminal Justice (Terrorist Offences) Act 2005, these call traffic details were held for three years, but Ireland will lower this retention period to two years for phone call data and a year for Internet traffic data under the options mandated by the data retention Directive 2006/24/EC of the European Parliament. While call traffic data information is needed by telecommunications service providers in order to bill customers, such information can also be very useful – sometimes pivotal – evidence in criminal trials. For this reason, law enforcement agencies have a legitimate interest in obtaining access to such data. Internationally, courts have recognised a counterbalancing right to privacy, and the public debate over data retention has therefore focused on finding an acceptable compromise – a proportionality – between providing lawful access to, and appropriate protection of, call data.

Internet usage, now a ubiquitous activity in practically every business, also generates digital footprints. While it is true that an individual computer user can hide his identity fairly easily from other individual computer users by adopting a persona or using anonymising software (a reality reflected in the famous 1993 *New Yorker* magazine cartoon of a net-surfing dog explaining, 'On the Internet, nobody knows you're a dog' (Steiner 1993)), there is a digital trail, nonetheless, which can reveal to informed observers a plethora of information about the individual, including personal identity and a virtual curriculum vitae of activity. Individual computers connected to the Net are given a unique IP address, which may be permanent, or may change if randomly assigned to facilitate each individual online session. That IP address is tracked through any number of the Internet's labyrinthine networks of millions of computers as the user sends email, downloads files or browses the web. Meanwhile, the individual computer, or a company's network, is also hanging on to every fragment of data that streams in as the computer user types at the keyboard, receives and sends email, or roams online. Every bit and byte of data relating to online activity, including content of emails, remains on the servers of the Internet Service Provider (ISP) until deleted by the ISP. Companies providing online services – search engines like Google or Bing, online merchants and markets like Amazon or eBay, resources like Wikipedia or Dictionary.com, news sites – they all know that you, or more precisely your IP address, have been there. Some sites plant small bits of tracking code, called cookies, onto the visitor's computer and thus know when people make a repeat visit and may record what they view while on the site.

Internet browsers – such as Microsoft's Internet Explorer (IE), Apple's Safari, Google's Chrome and Mozilla's Firefox – are enthusiastic hoarders of information, for example, storing (caching) the unique addresses (or URLs – uniform resource locators) of every web page visited. Even when the user believes such data have been deleted, this is generally not the case. Setting aside the likelihood that such data will be retained for some time in the company network's servers or at the ISP, it is also very difficult to eradicate data from an individual computer. Simply deleting the data only makes it invisible to the user and gives the computer permission to write over the memory space with new data. But the data is still there in fragments and generally can be retrieved with special programs (Norton Utilities, for example, is a well-known consumer retrieval program for rescuing accidentally deleted data on home or business computers, but there are highly specialised industrial-strength retrieval tools used by computer forensics experts). Even wiping the entire hard drive is no guarantee that data are gone. In response to these dangers, organisations that handle sensitive information, such as the Pentagon in the United States, often require that hard drives containing classified information be physically destroyed when no longer needed (Seifried 2001).

All these data streams can be highly revealing about an individual's every activity and movement. Mobile phone use can place an individual in a particular place at a particular time; one's Internet use and, especially, one's daily searches in the age of ubiquitous Googling can be a window into one's nature. That the nature revealed may be unrepresentative of the individual's general character is likely to be lost in the singular fact of its recording. Occasional embarrassing or compromising search requests made in the privacy of one's home become solidified in retained data that may not be quite a true reflection of normal interests and concerns.

Glancing at a typical day's Internet viewing history on a single computer, a basic retention function built into any web browser, reveals how detailed a picture of activities and interests emerges from stored data of this sort. Indeed, this is why viewing cached web pages is a key investigative tool for the computer forensics expert examining computers seized as evidence in an investigation of wrong-doing. As a specific subset of web user activity, search engine searches are highly revealing and keywords alone can lead to the unveiling of the individual behind the search, as was demonstrated by reporters looking at anonymous search datasets from 650,000 people released for research by AOL in 2006:

> Though each user's logs were only associated with a random ID number, several users' identities were readily discovered based on their search queries. For instance, the *New York Times* connected the logs of user No. 4417749 with 62-year-old Thelma Arnold. These records exposed, as she put it, her 'whole personal life'. (Eckersley *et al.* 2006)

The source of all this data is eloquently described by Schneier (2008:65):

> More and more, we leave a trail of electronic footprints as we go through our daily lives. We used to walk into a bookstore, browse, and buy a book with cash. Now we visit Amazon, and all our browsing and purchases are recorded. We used to throw a quarter in a toll booth; now E-ZPass records the date and time our car passed through the booth. Data about us are collected when we make a phone call, send an e-mail message, make a purchase with our credit card, visit a website . . .

Schneier (2008:66) notes that the common thread in all these cases is computers, and adds that 'this tidal wave of data is the pollution problem of the information age'.

When an individual technology user is an employee, and when data are generated in the course of business operations, such information can also provide an alarmingly intimate view of business operations, such as strategic planning, recent client and supplier contacts, internal network and building plans, financial transactions, project pitches or employee records: all information that could be of enormous interest to competitors, hackers or fraudsters. Such information is the type frequently copied and taken by disgruntled employees before leaving their jobs (Krebs 2009). Most people, and the organisations they work for, only hazily take note of their data flow, primarily because they are unaware of what they generate. As noted earlier, though, in most cases, such data are the unperceived result of other activities, for example, an Internet search, a mobile call or an email.

DATA RETENTION: ITS USE AND ABUSE

All of this activity creates virtual data mountains of material that is stored for a variety of reasons – for government interactions with citizens, for business purposes, or at the behest of governments for law enforcement agencies. Holding data for any of these purposes is generally termed 'data retention'. However, the term has taken on two meanings. On the one hand, data retention is a benign designation for data generated and held by all sorts of entities that, in most nations, have some formal obligations for protecting and managing them – in other words, data protection and data privacy imperatives. However, within this category falls data linked to an individual that is of commercial interest or that is connected to personal services, such as healthcare or governmental social services. Many would not see this type of data retention and management as entirely 'benign' (Raab and Bellamy 2005; Solove 2004:6), and the intrinsic value of such data is underlined by the fact that in the USA, which lacks the type of data protection laws that exist in the European Union (EU) and restrict the usage of commercial data, some personal data of this sort can be managed and sold on by large 'data broker' companies such as ChoicePoint. ChoicePoint provides a case in point regarding the serious problems that can arise when such databases are poorly secured: a 2008 data breach compromised 13,750 consumer's records, leaving them open to identity theft, while a 2006 breach exposed 163,000 consumer records and led to at least 800 cases of identity theft (EPIC 2009).

On the other hand, the term 'data retention' is also used to indicate the more overtly controversial mandatory retention and storage of a variety of data for defined periods of time for potential law enforcement use. Persistent and long-lived, archived and easily searched by increasingly powerful algorithms, these data become an electronic trail of scattered, discrete pieces of information, often – especially when retrieved via search technologies – stripped of the context that tells the story of why a person was here or there, doing this or that, at a particular time. This is data without an alibi, contributing to the fraught problem of privacy in what critics see as a de facto surveillance society in which gathering data is justified simply because 'we can' and because it could potentially be of use for some as yet unknown reason at an undefined future point.

Hence, traditionally, there have been two eager consumers for retained data: governments, particularly their law enforcement arms; and corporations. Law enforcement was not slow to realise it could be most interesting to have access to large swathes of potentially revealing electronic data, while businesses wanted the personal Internet usage information that lets them target customers more precisely and lucratively. Some argue that individuals should be more concerned about business than government interest in data, such as that generated by Internet activity:

Everything you do on the Net produces data. That data is, in aggregate, extremely valuable, more valuable to commerce than it is to the government. The government (in normal times) really cares only that you obey some select set of laws. But commerce is keen to figure out how you want to spend your money, and data does that. With massive amounts of data about what you do and what you say, it becomes increasingly possible to market to you in a direct and effective way. (Lessig 2006:216)

Since the advent of widely used information and communications technologies – especially the Internet – there has been a continuous battle between those who would like to see electronic data reaped and potentially harvested – governments, law enforcement agencies and businesses – and privacy advocates arguing for the protection of personal and business privacy. The former seek tools for fighting crime or increasing revenue; the latter argue that just because technology offers the tools for ongoing widespread surveillance does not mean it should be used for such purposes.

Ironically, given that they are also anxious to gain access to and mine customer and client data, businesses have been particularly sensitive about the gathering, storing and potential sifting, misuse or leakage of commercial information. As a result, large businesses, conservative and libertarian politicians protective of enterprise, and privacy advocates have ended up as rather odd bedfellows who, prior to the terrorist attacks of 11 September 2001 in the USA, more or less successfully kept at bay repeated government and law enforcement attempts to gain widespread access to digital data and filter or store it. But post-9/11, 'the fight against terrorism' has been used as an argument for pushing through data retention legislation, giving governments and law enforcement agencies the right to require that electronic communications data be stored and made searchable upon request, for varying periods of time (O'Harrow 2005).

DATA RETENTION IN IRELAND

While a complete historical overview of data retention and the resulting issues is beyond the scope of this chapter, and can be found elsewhere (McIntyre 2008), a brief overview is apposite here. In 2001, it was revealed that Irish telecommunications companies were holding customer call data for six years and handing over data upon request to police investigators, an untenable situation in the view of the Irish Data Protection Commissioner. Much discussion followed between the Data Protection Commissioner's office, the Irish government and industry, but without resolution (McIntyre 2007). However, the Irish government introduced a secret Cabinet direction in 2002 that mandated retention of call data. This was eventually revealed in 2003, because the government had to give an outline of current practice in order to propose formal, publicly debated data retention legislation (Lillington 2003a). Eventually, after several threats from the then Data Protection Commissioner, Joe Meade, to take the government to the High Court on the grounds that the existing Cabinet direction was unconstitutional (because it affected the population as a whole, but was not brought in as mandated with oversight by the Houses of the Oireachtas), legislation was introduced and passed as a last-minute amendment to another Bill, in the Criminal Justice (Terrorist Offences) Act 2005 (Lillington 2006). By this time, the EU had controversially brought in a directive that mandated some degree of data retention in all member states (Article 29 Data Protection Working

Party 2006; Vaas 2005), starting with the retention of call traffic data for up to two years and to be expanded in 2008 to include email traffic data. Ireland's approach to bringing in data retention in each instance was roundly condemned by international privacy advocacy groups, including the Washington DC-based Electronic Privacy Information Centre (EPIC) and London-based Privacy International and Statewatch (Lillington 2003a). Part of the criticism was founded on concern that Ireland's initial data retention laws, which required the storage of traffic information (but not content) of phone and mobile calls and faxes, had one of the longest storage periods in Europe and internationally, initially at three years, then moving to the EU maximum of two (McIntyre 2007:14–16).

The privacy advocacy group Digital Rights Ireland (DRI) took a High Court challenge to Ireland's data retention law, arguing that it was a violation of the Irish Constitution and of Irish, EU and international human rights and rights to privacy. It is interesting to note that in March 2009 a German court set a precedent in the area when it ruled that German data retention legislation was an invalid invasion of privacy, and not proportionate as required by the European Court of Human Rights, a view reiterated a year later at a higher level by the German Constitutional Court, which accepted the principle but not the implementation of data retention in Germany. The Romanian court meanwhile declared that nation's data retention laws invalid as well. In Ireland in May 2010, the Irish High Court accepted the basic points of DRI's constitutional challenge to data retention, including its request to refer the case to the European Court of Justice, where it remains at present undecided. DRI's suit is, in effect, if not in law, a class action case taken on behalf of the Irish public (Ireland does not at this time have provisions for class action suits), with DRI arguing that the average citizen would not understand the implications of what technology is able to reveal, and needed an informed advocate.

Many privacy advocates argue that the topic of data retention is complex, abstract and technical, and poorly understood by the general public. For this reason, they often face public indifference on an issue and decisions that will have long-lasting implications. At the heart of the concerns of privacy advocates is what they see as a lack of proportionality in retaining years of data for no specific reason, except that it might in future be useful. As DRI Chairman T.J. McIntyre puts it:

> This is a complete reversal of the assumption that people are innocent until proven guilty. This legislation is the first time we have seen any state impose mass surveillance on its population on the basis that at some point in the future, someone might commit a crime. (Lillington 2008a:74)

IRISH BUSINESS CONCERNS ABOUT DATA RETENTION

Businesses, especially in the technology sector, have expressed concern about the potential risks and costs of data retention and the possible effect on the overall

Irish business climate. A wake-up call of sorts about the potential liability of stored information was without doubt issued to businesses in the wake of the long US Department of Justice versus Microsoft case, formally initiated in 1998 after preliminary hearings and which reached an approved settlement in 2004, in which stored emails played a major role in an ultimate finding against Microsoft (US Department of Justice 2009). All businesses are more aware of their data retention obligations and risks following the introduction of stringent business operations legislation, such as the Sarbanes-Oxley Act of 2002 in the USA and similar EU requirements. And businesses have always been sensitive about information management and leaks.

Over recent years, the issue of data retention has split government departments in Ireland, with the Department of Justice pursuing lengthy retention periods, and the Department of Communications attempting to rein in proposals, partly on the grounds that longer retention periods would damage Ireland's business environment and lessen the country's attractiveness to foreign multinationals. The Department of Communications has expressed concern that retention would particularly alarm the information technology and telecommunications sectors the state has striven hard to attract, because these are industry sectors that work in areas that depend upon and manage data, and that generally also have greater awareness of the broader issues surrounding data retention. A document obtained under the Freedom of Information (FOI) Act revealed that the then Department of Communications, Marine and Natural Resources wrote to the Department of Justice in 2003 to suggest that 'businesses may . . . have concerns regarding confidentiality of sensitive business communications' (Lillington 2003b). The Department of Communications also expressed concern that a proposed Bill mandating data retention was 'likely to impose significant costs on [telecoms] operators and service providers. This is a matter of considerable concern to the Department in light of the global downturn in the information and communications technologies sector' (Lillington 2003b).

When legislation for data retention was passed in the Dáil, several leading companies were alarmed enough to speak publicly on the issue. Microsoft Ireland, Iona Technologies (now part of Progress Software) and Oracle Ireland were all worried by the scope of legislation, as well as by the lack of independent oversight of such legislation. The managing director of Microsoft Ireland at the time warned that

> Irish legislation is going beyond what is required from an EU perspective and is going to put significant additional costs on businesses from an administrative and a capital investment perspective. While we respect and understand the needs and concerns of the law enforcement agencies, there is also a need to take personal privacy concerns and the broader needs of business into consideration . . . I feel that the legislation as it currently stands has not been considered in the context of the potential impact that it will have on business in general and the ICT industry specifically. (Lillington 2006)

The co-founder of Iona Technologies, while acknowledging that law enforcement had legitimate concerns about tackling crime and protecting citizens, added:

> Our society also has a right to protect itself from unwarranted personal intrusion by agencies of this State and those of other states. In addition, businesses have a right in particular to protect themselves against accidental disclosure of commercially sensitive information and industrial espionage . . . Given the context of poorly managed IT projects by the State, what confidence can the Irish public and businesses have that agencies of this State, and companies by law acting on their behalf, can adequately gather and in particular protect highly sensitive information? (Lillington 2006)

Industry lobby groups, including ICT Ireland and the Irish Business and Employers' Confederation (IBEC), also expressed formal concern about the issue (Lillington 2006). And telecommunications companies and lobby groups have also indicated their worries about the costs of implementing the directive, especially as the Irish government, unlike those of several other EU states, has made no provision to cover the substantial costs to phone providers and ISPs of storing and managing data. They have warned that extra costs associated with storage and making data accessible to law enforcement are costs that will be passed on to customers. The director of the Internet Service Providers Association of Ireland (ISPAI) told a conference on data retention: 'We will see companies leaving the Republic and the EU because they're concerned about the confidentiality of their business information' (Lillington 2006). A few years later, the ISPAI director also observed:

> This could definitely affect our economy because we are so reliant on the technology industry, the shared services sector and so on. If companies start saying 'Hey, the regime in Ireland is onerous', that could tip the balance for those companies locating elsewhere. (Lillington 2008b)

Such concerns about international perception do have some legitimate grounds. Ireland's approach to data retention has led to the state being given a privacy red card for 'systemic failure to uphold safeguards' (Privacy International 2007). Privacy International, the organisation that provided this evaluation of Ireland's approach to data retention, has for a decade produced an annual privacy league table of nations by looking at international reports and speaking to experts in the area of privacy: officials in charge of protecting privacy, academics, activists, journalists and researchers. On a scale of one to five, Ireland scored a 2.5 in 2007, due almost entirely to its poor record on data retention and what Privacy International deemed flimsy government leadership in the area. It was the second year in a row that Ireland retained such a dismal score, only half a mark above being classified as an 'extensive surveillance society' (Privacy International 2007). While Ireland scored well in some areas – such as already having a comprehensive privacy law, some protections against exposing suspected Internet file-sharers, and having an implicit, if not explicit, constitutional right to privacy – data retention policy dragged the score down towards the bottom internationally.

PRIVACY 2.0: NEW NORMS FOR A NEW AGE?

Alongside the formal issue of data gathering and retention by commerce and by government and law enforcement, a complicating factor has emerged in recent years that some might argue is proof that Sun Microsystems co-founder and former CEO Scott McNealy was right when he famously quipped in 1999: 'You have zero privacy anyway. Get over it' (as quoted in Sprenger 1999). That factor is the emergence of the online social networking universe, in which information is willingly divulged by users of an explosion of social media services (discussion forums, Twitter, blogs, Facebook, Bebo, MySpace, peer-to-peer file sharing networks, etc.) for a perceived benefit – networking, information exchange, casual socialising, setting up meetings, discussing projects, sharing pirated content (music, film, books). Such use has generated an altered view of privacy and, for many users, blurred (or, critics might argue, eroded) the division between public and private aspects of one's life and work.

That shift is termed 'Privacy 2.0' by Zittrain (2008:200–34), who argues that such use creates fresh challenges as people willingly, and perhaps unthinkingly, divulge information themselves and make it available to others. These others may then use the information in ways not intended by the provider of that information, including making deliberately malicious use of such data. Zittrain (2008:200–1) observes that:

> the Net enables individuals in many cases to compromise privacy more thoroughly than the government and commercial institutions traditionally targeted for scrutiny and regulation. The standard approaches that have been developed to analyze and limit institutional actors do not work well for this new breed of problem, which goes far beyond the compromise of sensitive information.

Zittrain (2008:202) goes on to argue that perhaps a casual attitude about disseminating information is not a recent development – he notes that the general public has always been willing to part with personal data for any number of reasons, and even though polls have repeatedly indicated a public concern about privacy, 'the public's actions frequently belie these claims', to the confusion of researchers and lawmakers. Web users, with their voluntary proliferation and propagation of data, are perhaps only a logical extension of that ambiguity and, to some extent, steer a 'third way' through privacy issues, particularly in their use of social media. That third way is grounded to some degree in one's age:

> The values animating our concern for privacy are themselves in transition. Many have noted an age-driven gap in attitudes about privacy perhaps rivalled only by the 1960s generation gap on rock and roll . . . [and yet] . . . while young people appear eager to share information online, they are more worried than older people about government surveillance. (Zittrain 2008:231)

Younger people seem happy enough to put personal information online, tag it so that it can be easily found, and reveal details that other generations would have kept within a small circle of friends and family. Zittrain (2008:234) shrugs off the argument that images of drunken exploits posted to Facebook pages will lose students future jobs when viewed by prospective bosses, for 'soon those making hiring decisions will themselves have had Facebook pages'. Such developments make for an emergent, highly complex privacy landscape, different from anything that has come before, in which various stakeholders – governments, businesses, individuals – simultaneously desire access to others' data, while wishing to control access to their own, fail to adequately protect stored data against malicious access or casual loss, or willingly share data without much thought about the potential for its long-term endurance and availability as archived, easily mined, digital bytes.

Society is definitely in transition towards some new way of viewing privacy and stored data. However, that does not remove 'the burden of . . . monitored facts' (Lessig 2006:218), the pooled random detritus of our monitored digital footprints:

> The burden is on you, the monitored, first to establish your innocence, and second to assure all who might see these ambiguous facts that you are innocent. Both processes, however, are imperfect; say what you want, doubts will remain. There are always some who will not believe your plea of innocence. Modern monitoring only exacerbates the problem. Your life becomes an ever-increasing record; your actions are forever held in storage, open to being revealed at any time, and therefore at any time demanding a justification. (Lessig 2006:218)

CONCLUSIONS

In the search for an acceptable balance between data generation, data protection and data retention, no easy answer presents itself for societies or for businesses. Given the yearly proliferation of new technologies that generate an ever larger and longer digital data shadow, it seems highly unlikely that the challenge will become more containable or manageable. With technologies generally racing ahead of our ability to fully understand their implications, and with even their creators finding it difficult to know exactly how they will be used, often the horse has long bolted from the stable before anyone realises the door was open in the first place.

In addition, different societies take different views of where the line stands between a right to data protection and privacy and acceptable – even welcomed – use of personal data. The growing importance of global e-commerce, and the enthusiasm internationally for outsourcing many of the 'back office' tasks that involve personal data processing, means states can struggle to find an acceptable middle ground – witness the long negotiations between the EU and the USA to settle on the Safe Harbor agreement for exchanging the personal data of their citizens (Thompson and van Wagonen Magee 2003).

And one of the greatest obstacles to managing the 'data pollution' problem is that most people fail to realise it exists. Digital data is not concrete and obvious, like files of paper or recorded tape. It is invisible to almost all, moves silently through the globe's fibre optic networks and copper cables, and sits quietly within massive servers and small desktop computers. Media coverage of hacked corporate computers, Internet fraudsters, missing laptops and stolen storage drives has at least helped more citizens and businesses to understand how worryingly easy it can be to lose digital data, or have it taken. But the broader issues of data retention and data protection get little public airing or engagement and businesses continue to remain largely ignorant of the ways in which their daily business practices may inadvertently be helping to construct a surveillance society.

References

Agar, J. (2003) *The Government Machine: A Revolutionary History of the Computer*. Cambridge, MA: MIT Press.

Article 29 Data Protection Working Party (2006) 'Opinion 3/2006 on the Directive 2006/24/EC of the European Parliament and of the Council on the Retention of Data Generated or Processed in Connection with the Provision of Publicly Available Electronic Communications Services or of Public Communications Networks and Amending Directive 2002/58/EC' [online]. Available: http://ec.europa.eu/justice_home/fsj/privacy/docs/wpdocs/2006/wp119_en.pdf (last accessed 9 September 2009).

Aspray, W. and Campbell-Kelly, M. (1996) *Computer: A History of the Information Machine*. New York, NY: Basic Books.

Cortada, J. (2007) *The Digital Hand*, Vols 1, 2 and 3. New York, NY: Oxford University Press.

Eckersley, P., Schoen, S., Bankston, K. and Slater, D. (2006) 'Six Tips to Protect Your Search Privacy', Electronic Frontier Foundation, San Francisco, CA [online]. Available: http://www.eff.org/wp/six-tips-protect-your-search-privacy (last accessed 5 November 2009).

EPIC (Electronic Privacy Information Center) (2009) 'Choicepoint' [online]. Available: http://epic.org/privacy/choicepoint (last accessed 18 December 2009).

Krebs, B. (2009) 'Data Theft Common by Departing Employees', *Washington Post*, 26 February [online]. Available: http://www.washingtonpost.com/wp-dyn/content/article/2009/02/26/AR2009022601821.html (last accessed 5 November 2009).

Lessig, L. (2006) *Code: Version 2.0*. New York, NY: Basic Books.

Lillington, K. (2003a) 'Don't Believe State on Data Retention', *Irish Times*, 14 March, p.39.

— (2003b) 'Data Retention Plans Cause Considerable Unease', *Irish Times*, 23 June, p. 14.

— (2006) 'Data Retention Policies May Poison Business Environment', *Irish Times*, 24 March, p. 36.

— (2008a) 'License to Pry?', *Irish Times*, 11 February, pp. 74–6.

— (2008b) 'Fears of Economic Fallout from Internet Data Retention Plans', *Irish Times*, 25 April, p. 41.

McIntyre, T.J. (2007) 'Data Retention: History and Current Developments', *Data Protection Law and Policy* 14 February: 16.

— (2008) 'Data Retention in Ireland: Privacy, Policy and Proportionality', *Computer Law and Security Report* 24(4): 326–34.

O'Harrow, R. (2005) *No Place to Hide: Behind the Scenes of Our Emerging Surveillance Society*. New York, NY: Free Press.

Privacy International (2007) *The 2007 International Privacy Ranking* [online]. Available: http://www.privacyinternational.org/article.shtml?cmd[347]=x-347-559597&als[theme]=Data%20Protection%20and%20Privacy%20Laws (last accessed 2 November 2009).

Raab, C. and Bellamy, C. (2005) 'Joined-up Government and Privacy in the United Kingdom: Managing Tensions Between Data Protection and Social Policy (Part I)', *Public Administration* (83)1: 111–33.

Schneier, B. (2008) *Schneier on Security*. Indianopolis, IN: Wiley.

Seifried, K. (2001) 'Protecting Information from Exposure' [online]. Available: http://www.seifried.org/security/articles/20010910-protecting-information-from-exposure.html (last accessed 12 November 2009).

Shurkin, J. (1996) *Engines of the Mind: The Evolution of the Computer from Mainframes to Microprocessors*. New York, NY: Norton.

Solove, D. (2004) *The Digital Person: Technology and Privacy in the Information Age*. New York, NY: New York University Press.

Sprenger, P. (1999) 'Sun on Privacy: Get Over It', *Wired News*, 26 January [online]. Available: http://www.wired.com/news/politics/0,1283,17538,00.html (last accessed 9 September 2009).

Steiner, P. (1993) 'On the Internet, Nobody Knows You're a Dog' [cartoon], *New Yorker* 69(20): 61.

Thompson, M. and van Wagonen Magee, P. (2003) 'US/EU Safe Harbor Agreement: What It Is and What It Says About the Future of Cross Border Data Protection', Federal Trade Commission, Washington, DC [online].

Available: http://www.ftc.gov/speeches/thompson/thompsonsafeharbor.pdf (last accessed 2 November 2009).

US Department of Justice (2009) 'United States v. Microsoft: Current Case' [online]. Available: http://www.justice.gov/atr/cases/ms_index.htm (last accessed 5 November 2009).

Vaas, L. (2005) 'EU Passes Contentious Data Retention Law', *eWeek*, 12 December [online]. Available: http://www.eweek.com/c/a/Database/EU-Passes-Contentious-DataRetention-Law/ (last accessed 9 September 2009).

Zittrain, J. (2008) *The Future of the Internet and How to Stop it*. New Haven, CT: Yale University Press [online]. Available: http://futureoftheinternet.org/static/ZittrainTheFutureoftheInternet.pdf (last accessed 9 September 2009).

Chapter 31

Spirituality, Work and Irish Society
John Cullen

INTRODUCTION

Religion continues to demonstrate a capacity to both influence and infiltrate social, political and economic affairs and impact on the lives of many people outside the boundaries of specific congregations. Although it has long been recognised that religion can assert a tangible influence on work, productivity and economic growth, it is important to bear in mind that the ways in which it does this are not static. As our societies transform, the means by which religion influences workplaces and practices also changes. This chapter is specifically concerned with the ethics of the spiritualisation of work and organisations. The first section explores why theories of self-oriented spirituality (as opposed to faith based on religious dogma) continue to exist at a 'macro', societal level, and the subsequent section looks at how this significant force has manifested in contemporary workplaces. The third section examines practices that attempt to introduce specific forms of spiritual behaviours in the workplace and how these may impact on workers who are subjected to them. The penultimate section explores how changes in the Irish socio-economic context have impacted the spiritualisation of work and workers. The chapter ends by highlighting some of the issues arising from the discussion and identifies some research questions surfacing from them.

SPIRITUALITY, SELF AND SOCIETY

Sociological thought varies on the reasons for the rise of spirituality and it is curious to note that an interest in spirituality from organisational and management perspectives thrived during the emergence of the late-capitalist consumer society, particularly during the years of the global economic recovery from the mid-1990s (Ackers and Preston 1997; Korac-Kakabadse 2002). Marx (1974 [1844]) viewed the continuing practice of religion and faith in modernity to be a response to the alienation produced by bourgeois activity and excessive division of labour. Scientific discoveries about the origins of the universe, life and the nature of the human psyche problematised accepted understandings of the divine (Armstrong 2000). However, in a large number of cases, religion, rather than disappearing completely, appears to have undergone a transformation in how individuals themselves engage with it. Religion has been replaced with spirituality (Heelas and Woodhead 2005).

This means that individuals in spiritualised societies have a tendency to look less to established religious frameworks, such as churches, for guidance on how to behave, cosmological information on how they will be judged or rewarded for appropriate behaviour in this life or the next, forgiveness for listed transgressions, or solace during times of distress. Rather, more energy is placed on attempting to understand the meaning of one's existence in the context of life experiences, leveraging one's personal learning and investigation, and adopting a syncretic approach to acquiring spiritual wisdom from a number of diverse, and often unrelated, sources (Heelas 1996). This is not to say that all individuals actively seek to dissociate themselves from the faith traditions they may have been born into or enculturated in, but even those who continue to identify with specific religious frameworks are less likely to follow the dogma laid down by members of a professional clergy, or the discourse of a given theological framework (Heelas and Woodhead 2005). In modernity, one's religion as a personal life narrative may have been largely exploded, but its residues have seeped into other areas of life, including work (the subject of the next section of this chapter).

Religion has also been perceived as a dynamic force that undergoes constant change and renewal (Stark and Bainbridge 1985). When mainstream religion loses its influence, the result is not that faith traditions go into abeyance, but that they change form instead. The result is that

> the central importance of self-development to Western industrialized cultures that depend so heavily on consumption has left traditional religious doctrines open to the choice of each individual hence creating a type of 'spiritual supermarket' from which each individual can choose. (Rindfleish 2005:345)

Giddens (1991) has remarked how the growth in the turn to the self in modernised societies has resulted in the commodification of self-actualisation, which Rindfleish (2005:357) describes as 'the consumption of the self'.

A key figure in the development of the study of the sociology of spirituality is Paul Heelas, who discussed the shift away from traditional forms of organised religion, which instructed individuals on how to behave, think and feel in order to achieve salvation, towards a more reflexive sense of inner spirituality; the 'New Age' movement which began in the nineteenth century and flourished in Western democratic states during the heyday of the counter-culture movement in the 1960s. This expressive shift has been described by Taylor (1989) as an imperative for each individual to find a unique, personal path by which to live our lives.

New Age spirituality involves a range of facets, but essentially involves believing in: the sacredness of self; one's own inner goodness; a sense that modernity and the pressures of life distract people from unearthing their true potential; the primacy of individual self-determination; and the interconnectedness of all faith traditions. It is not surprising, perhaps, to see how spirituality has the potential to be a resource to individuals experiencing feelings of suffocation within an oppressive, and alienating, modern order. Since many of those who participated in the counter-culture movement at the high point of the New Age movement subsequently went on to become key figures in the 'new' or 'knowledge' economy of the 1990s, many of their beliefs and practices travelled with them into workspaces and organisations, which themselves were hugely influenced by the principles and ideologies of the New Age and 'inner self-spirituality' (Heelas 2008 *passim*). The 'massive subjective turn of modern culture' (Heelas and Woodhead 2005:2) has meant that meaning is sought in all areas of the individual's experience, and a key site for this project to achieve 'authentic' selfhood is the workplace.

SPIRITUALITY AND WORK

The emergence of a strong interest in spirituality in organisational and management contexts, from the perspectives of practising managers, consultants and researching academics, which appears to have emerged since the mid-1980s (Calás and Smircich 2003), continues to grow (Benefiel 2003). Cavanagh (1999), Howard (2002) and Nash (1999), among others, have noted that the number of spiritually related organisational and management publications appears to be increasing. Spiritually related topics have more recently appeared in influential business journals such as *Harvard Business Review* and *MIT Sloan Management Review*, rendering the spirituality of managers and employees a valid area of study for management research, comment and investigation. Mitroff and Denton (1999) reported that senior executives in a number of American organisations ranked spiritual aspects of their appointments, such as the ability to realise their potential, or being associated with ethical organisations, as being stronger sources of personal motivation than making money.

There is no clear definition of what organisational spirituality actually is, but one overview attempts to synthesise existing efforts to refine the concept. This suggests that spirituality:

> in the context of organizations attempts to (1) clarify and integrate selves, social communities and the transcendent, and (2) interconnect these in ways which serve and enrich them, and (3) make meaningful, the individual, the communities in which they work and serve, the broader global community and the Divine. (Cullen 2008:267–8)

As sociologists of religion have argued (e.g., Heelas 1996; Heelas and Woodhead 2005), rather than indicating a lack of interest in spiritual matters, increased modernisation and secularisation appear to lead instead to an increased need for spiritual practices. The emergence of the spirituality and management discourse can be seen as 'a means to counteract self-interest at a time when all other messages seem to point in the opposite direction' (Calás and Smircich 2003:327), with Ackers and Preston (1997:679) seeing the 'desperate business search for new forms of social cohesion' as indicative that the employee–employer relationship has been thinned to the extent that it involves only economic interchanges.

These points focus on the rise of religion/faith/spirituality as a salve for the enervating frustrations of modernity, particularly rationalised workplace practices. More famous, however, have been explorations of how workplace productivity is influenced by the spiritual cultures of its workforces. Chief among these is Weber's (2002 [1930]) proposal of a Protestant work ethic, in which hard work, success and productivity were deemed by certain sects indicative of salvation, and which, in turn, leads to particular forms of capitalism succeeding in specific locales. Similarly, the Islamic work ethic 'has its origin in the Quran, the sayings and practice of Prophet Mohammed, who preached that hard work caused sins to be absolved . . . and views dedication to work as a virtue' (Yousef 2000:515).

The process by which spirituality and work began to be considered outside the context of the sociology of religion is provided by Bell and Taylor (2004), who outline how humanist philosophers and psychologists such as Eric Fromm (1978) and Abraham Maslow (1971) saw Fordist organisations as constraining the development of a self that could achieve authenticity. The rationalisation of work meant that 'managers and other employees were expected to complete their allotted task without involving their essential self, apparently reflecting the global triumph of scientific consciousness' (Ackers and Preston 1997:678).

Bell and Taylor's (2004) examination of the development of the human potential movement in the 1970s offers some clarity as to how spirituality is understood in contemporary organisational or work contexts. Worried about the alienating effects of industrialisation and the growth of the consumer society, which effected a rejection of the spiritual, Maslow and Fromm became concerned with the constraints that organisations place on 'the development of an authentic self' (Bell and Taylor 2004:447). With a greater emphasis on collaborative working and a need for self-actualisation through work, Whyte (1956) proposed a new form of work ethic better suited to the emergence of large, bureaucratic organisational forms in the second half of the twentieth century. This 'social ethic', according to Bell and Taylor (2003:345), allows 'managers to exercise pastoral power over the subjects through disciplinary technologies that focus on the scientific governing of the soul using primarily psychological techniques'. Both Maslow and Fromm advocated a greater concentration on internal life and the pursuit of self-knowledge, as opposed to the pursuit of material advancement, as a mechanism for reducing greater societal ills. Fromm and Maslow, according to Bell and Taylor (2004), had differing views on how the relationship between work and organisations, on the one hand, and spiritual life, on the other, would need to be reconfigured for this to happen. Fromm (1978) urged organisations to change so that individuals working for them would have the freedom to pursue self-actualisation. Maslow (1971), on the other hand, viewed involvement in work as being key to reaching self-actualisation, which is similar to Weber's (2002 [1930]) concept of the 'calling'.

It might be suggested that both have happened to various degrees. The section that follows examines how individual managers/employees have increasingly been encouraged to seek meaning in their work through training and development programmes that attempt to spiritualise the individual manager/employee. On the other hand, there is evidence to suggest that workplaces have themselves become increasingly spiritualised. Willmott's (1993) introduction of the concept of 'corporate culturism' discusses how the notion of developing 'strong' corporate cultures was advocated by the 'excellence' gurus of the 1980s and 1990s as part of the global restructuring of how capital and labour was used. With a greater stress on concepts such as employee flexibility and commitment to the organisation, Willmott (1993) outlines how managers and employees were increasingly compelled to internalise these values and make them their own.

Employees' subjective perceptions of their work, their personal work ethic, and their capacity to learn and innovate became a central economic resource for the organisation. The quality of the relationship between employees and their employing organisation was now the responsibility of the individual worker, and their capacity to self-actualise was transformed from a personal to an organisational resource. Casey (1999) subsequently wrote of how the introduction of (apparently) people-centred concepts, such as the idea of 'family' atmospheres, into organisational cultures could produce strict forms of self-regulation among employees, where individuals are tacitly constrained from voicing opinions or expressing emotions that run counter to the established grain of the corporate culture. Rather than being environments where individuals could flourish and find personal routes to meaning and self-actualisation, spiritualised (or even quasi-spiritualised) work environments have the potential to deny workers paths to genuine self-exploration and intellectual emancipation.

THE SPIRITUALISATION OF THE WORKER

Contemporary human resource strategies have moved away from attempting to control the behaviours of employees and focus increasingly on managing the '"insides" – the hopes, fears and aspirations – of workers' (Deetz 1995, cited in Alvesson and Willmott 2002:620), mimicking somewhat the eighteenth-century switch in the focus of punishment from the body to the soul, as described by Foucault (1977). It should come as no surprise that the societal impetus for each individual to determine her/his own inner originality, which had been emerging since the eighteenth century (Taylor 1989), should become manifest in our contemporary organisational configurations.

Concerns about the ethics of 'soul work', or encouraging spirituality in organisational contexts, however, have been raised. Benefiel (2003:385), for example, points out the possible inappropriateness of an organisation encouraging spirituality with a view to increasing greater financial yield: 'The two discourses [management and spirituality] stand as foreign languages to one another . . . If we are to do scholarly work that understands spirituality in organisations, we face a mammoth task. We face nothing short of creating a new language'. Ackers and Preston (1997:677) express the concern differently: 'we question both whether a largely involuntary business organization has an ethical right to claim the "souls" of its managers and whether this is likely to be a realizable goal, in any case'. They note the introduction of a spiritual tone into management development programmes since the early 1980s, which was due partly to the 'revival of the charismatic form of authority' (Ackers and Preston 1997:677) in the work of corporate culture 'gurus' who attempted to convert individual executives and corporate culture, and which transcended rationalist understandings of what management development is for and what it does.

The 'new gurus' of the 1980s attempted to induce catharsis, personal change and the dissolution of inherited ways of thinking in favour of finding new 'promised lands' of organisational perfection, often presented as 'excellence' (Peters and Waterman 1982) or effectiveness (Covey 1989). Using the support of texts designed to induce a sharp sense of disappointment in current organisational realities, the excellence and effectiveness gurus sought to elicit epiphanies and conversions amongst managers and executives that demanded journeys of deep introspection and change (Cullen 2009). Researchers, however, have pointed out that these 'epiphanogenic technologies' do not align with the New Age project of searching for one's own sense of authentic selfhood, but are instead normative tools that are productive of docile subjects who are only effective within conservative orders (Jackson 1999, 2001; McGee 2005). Although these personal change programmes promise greater levels of productivity, satisfaction and happiness, more recent research has focused on how adherence to these prescriptive programmes might impact on those who participate in them (Ackers and Preston 1997; Bell and Taylor 2004; Carlone 2006; Cullen 2009; McGee 2005).

In short, programmes that attempt to fundamentally reconfigure one's sense of selfhood through the adoption of new practices or perspectives often do so without reference to the ways in which one's cultural identity has been developed over time. While often presented as transparently helpful to personal development, the promoters of these programmes demonstrate little concern for how they might impact on the lives of the individuals who consume them. Laing (1990) writes that lack of clarity about identity can lead to heightened levels of anxiety that are sometimes pathological. An ontologically insecure person lacks a sense of 'personal consistency or cohesiveness' (Laing 1990: 42), which is then manifested in various forms of anxiety.

Of course, this is not to suggest that individuals who consume a self-help text, engage in a personal development programme or attend a seminar by a management guru automatically lose all sense of identity and run off to join a corporate cult! Lichtermann (1992) wrote that, while there has been much research on the content of 'self-help' books and the ideologies about the subject and its relation to broader social frameworks that they communicate, very few studies of how such texts are consumed, understood and applied by readers have been undertaken. His study found that educated, middle-class readers

> read and impute authority to the [self-help] books in a complex way that can not simply be deduced from content-based criticism of the genre. They read the books ambivalently, and in ongoing relation to other frameworks for situating personal selfhood in a social context. (Lichtermann 1992:432)

Lichtermann (1992) describes the process of reading self-help texts ambivalently as an example of 'thin culture' (a conscious inversion of Geertz's (1973) 'thick description'), which does not support a deep commitment from readers. Instead, they function as quasi-entertainments that readers might find helpful with a particular issue at hand. Watson (1994) found a similar level of ambivalence among a group of managers towards management fads and fashions: on the one hand, managers often held them in disdain, seeing them as quick-fix panaceas, while, on the other, they often enjoyed new ideas and concepts. This, of course, is probably fine where learning and development initiatives are deployed among experienced managers in a context where they have established personal capital and a supporting network of fellow managers equipped to resist any attempts to alter their identity in line with corporate needs. It is, however, more sinister in the context of the socialisation of organisational newcomers and where there are attempts to bring about a culturalist (Willmott 1993) programme in an organisational setting.

SPIRITUALITY, WORK AND IRISH SOCIETY

Although the influence of the Roman Catholic Church has rapidly waned in Ireland (Inglis 1998), the vast majority of adults in the Republic of Ireland, 92 per cent, identified as Roman Catholic in the most recent census in 2006. It comes as little surprise, then, that the Catholic Church continues to influence spiritual identity in a country where it has long held a dominant political and social position of influence. It is not, however, the only social force that has impacted on how workers in Ireland have determined their identities.

The United States of America has played an enormous role in Irish social and economic history. The decision by several large American manufacturers to locate their operations in Ireland played a crucial role in alleviating decades of Irish domestic economic underperformance during the second half of the 1990s (MacSharry and White 2000). A remark in 2000 by a former Tánaiste – 'geographically we are closer to Berlin than Boston. Spiritually we are probably a lot closer to Boston than Berlin' (Harney 2000: para. 4) – was frequently quoted in the Irish media during the years of the economic boom, and incidents which might be interpreted as potentially damaging to the Irish–American relationship were treated as potential diplomatic crises (Cullen 2006). The Irish government was the first in the world to declare an official national day of mourning following the 11 September attacks in 2001 (which included the destruction of one of the most powerful symbols of capitalism, the World Trade Center), but did not do the same following the death on 2 April 2005 of Pope John Paul II, the leader of the faith tradition with which most Irish people identify.

Roman Catholicism is a particularly important factor in how Irish culture has developed, and, in turn, has had a hugely significant role in determining how Irish selves are configured. Inglis (1998:12) outlines how (although there is more than one experience of Irish Catholic religiosity), since the start of the twentieth century, the 'moral power of the [Roman Catholic] Church was created and maintained through the rational, bureaucratic, hierarchical organization of the Church with its considerable physical and human resources, and the dominant position it held in Irish education, health and social welfare'. This was embedded through a system of legitimisation, which allowed individuals to attain and maintain social, cultural and symbolic capital. Inglis (1998) noted that, by the late 1980s, the power of the Church had begun to decline and Irish society began to enter a period of full modernisation, but that Catholicism remained a defining feature of Irish social life.

In the words of Thomas Luckmann (1967:89), 'we find a situation in which everybody is still socialized into the "official" model of religion, but the model is not taken at face value by anybody'. There have been several attempts outside the formal institutional framework of the Roman Catholic Church to explore a more 'new-agey' Irish Catholic spirituality and unearth authentic selfhood, ranging from the Jesuit-sponsored Sacred Space website and Pray-As-You-Go podcasts to the late John O'Donohue's *Anam Cara* (1999) and other writings that attempt to syncretise neo-paganism with Catholic spirituality. The forms in which Catholicism is practised and experienced may be undergoing significant processes of change, yet Catholicism itself remains the dominant cultural discourse in Irish society.

With Roman Catholicism still a significant 'source of the self' (Taylor 1989), it is important to remember that the philosophical roots of many human resource development (HRD) or organisational development (OD) programmes deployed in Irish organisations have their sources in other faith traditions. This is important, as Inglis's (1998) examination of how Roman Catholicism influenced Irish 'habitus' emphasises its incompatibility with other faith traditions. Deploying a spiritual management and personal development programme, which has its philosophical roots in a specific faith tradition, in organisations operating within a broader national cultural framework shared by most of its members, managers and employees, could very reasonably be seen as tantamount to an attempt to 'convert' employees to another sense of selfhood.

Neville (2008:218–9) writes: 'Historically, the search for the self was actively denied or repressed under Roman Catholicism, with the result that little interpretative space and social tolerance has been accorded to the project of self analysis.' Whereas Catholic thinking lionises poverty and postulates that the poor are the riches of the Church, this is certainly not the case with other established and emerging Christian denominations (Wolfe 1998). When such spiritually oriented programmes are deployed in Irish organisations, little thought is given to the difficulties that might arise when one cultural understanding of the self is offered to individuals who have inherited another cultural form of self-understanding.

If Irish Catholicism is becoming more reflexive and driven by inner spirituality, it is following practices that have long been manifest in the professional cultures of the knowledge and service industries, which emerged first in North America, and then in the UK (Huczynski 1993), before being dispersed across Western secular societies. Bell and Taylor (2003:345) suggest that this itself has led to a fundamental reconfiguration of the European Protestant work ethic:

> At the turn of this century the discourse of workplace spirituality provides us with a new work ethic, one that attempts to resolve the ambivalent relationship between self and organization by drawing upon the Protestant ethic and re-visioning it according to New Age values. The New Age work ethic is different from the social ethic in that it reflects the current loss of faith in scientific progress as well as a disillusion with mainstream religion. It attempts to re-enchant disciplinary technologies through the management of individual metaphysics as a source of inner power and organizational success. (Bell and Taylor 2003:345)

PROBLEMS, QUESTIONS AND AVENUES FOR FURTHER RESEARCH

Spiritually inspired change programmes are often deployed in organisations to help workers become happier, more productive employees, who get greater satisfaction from their work, without any consideration for their existing beliefs, mental health or life expectations. Imagine if managers were advocated to prescribe pharmaceuticals to achieve the same goals!

Harvey (2005) has pointed out that neo-liberal economies require a high degree of employee flexibility for organisations to remain competitive in rapidly changing, globalised marketplaces. A spiritualised employment environment, where individuals are encouraged to determine their own value, changes the responsibility for personal change and engagement with an organisation's market away from the institution to the individual employee. It is not just that workers must be flexible, though; they must also take responsibility for their own flexibility. Indeed, part of organisational success, following what Boltanski and Chiapello (2006) name 'the new spirit of capitalism' that emerged in the wake of the 1960s counter-culture movement, is dependent on the mobility of its staff. If the organisation is forced to alter how it does business as a result of market change, employees are held responsible for ensuring that their skills and aptitudes change according to the new circumstances facing the organisation. An additional burden is placed on employees to ensure their own relevance, and, even during times of stability, this means that new projects and developmental opportunities must be sought out and participated in.

The effect of this constant need to fundamentally redesign and develop one's identity in the spiritualised workplace is the production of what McGee (2005) refers to as a 'belaboured' sense of self. Managerial self-improvement texts, part of 'the increasingly intensive cultural appropriation of subjectivity as a modality of ordering relationships at work' (Costea *et al.* 2008:664), might possibly be construed as tools of organisational domination in how they encourage individuals to maintain a malleable sense of selfhood, which can be recombined and reconfigured to meet the needs of rapidly changing economic circumstances.

Finally, the introduction of spiritual development programmes and the fostering of expressive organisational cultures are often conducted without reference to what happens when organisations are forced to downsize. What happens to the well-being and self-esteem of employees, who have been working in organisations that have been attempting to develop a sense of expressive individualist selfhood amongst their staff, and encouraging them to commit their 'whole selves' to organisational goals, when these same organisations make them redundant?

CONCLUSION

Attempts to provide frameworks for individuals to find inner peace, a sense of purpose or a meaningful existence have long existed in societies around the world. Foucault (1994 [1982]: 225) discusses 'technologies of the self'

> which permit individuals to effect by their own means, or with the help of others, a certain number of operations on their own bodies and souls, thoughts, conduct, and way of being, so as to transfer themselves in order to attain a certain state of happiness, purity, wisdom, perfection, or immortality.

Foucault (1994 [1982]:228) goes on to assert that the precept of 'care of the self' is as important as the principle 'know thyself', but that this has been obscured by Christian moral philosophy, making 'self-renunciation the condition for salvation' and by legal systems primarily concerned with the governance of relationships with others. Care of the self was a society-wide phenomenon replaced in the early Christian era with a new self ethic, which in turn resulted in the experience of new genres of selfhood.

Foucault (1978) writes how interdictions on certain sexual practices served to 'increase the desire to speak about sexuality and increase the pleasure gained from violating these taboos' (Mills 2003:84). In a not entirely unrelated way, the interest in self-improvement is fed by a general understanding that most people are not happy with their lives. Heelas (1996:146) states that '[t]he population is fed a constant diet of advice on how to change for the better. There is little doubt that this generates a climate of discontent.' Because there is a vast range of self-help books and personal improvement initiatives available inside and outside organisational life, a consciousness of imperfections that individuals may not heretofore have been aware of is brought to light. The availability of self-help texts and personal improvement products creates a market for pain.

The implications of this have proved significant for management development and organisational practice. Dunne, Harney and Parker (2008:272) identify a 'sober call to self-management' amidst the growing centrality of management knowledge and business practices in everyday life. The process of workplace spiritualisation through learning initiatives or cultural practices has absorbed the dictates of a market, paradoxically promising that happy, fulfilled selfhood is possible, whilst simultaneously demonstrating that it is practically impossible to achieve.

Any move to create a work environment where the path to such selfhood is assured must be considered an example of an attempt to create what Rose (1989:107) calls 'a managerial technology for promoting worker commitment and contentment'. Regardless of the overtly stated paternalism of spiritualising a workplace, more critical approaches to the study of organisational spirituality suggest that its introduction masks covert attempts to produce docile workforces (Jackson 2001), busily immersed in an exhausting continuum of personal improvement (McGee 2005), in environments where conflict and confrontation are tacitly deplored (Forray and Stork 2002).

Stating that work should be a fulfilling, meaningful experience for employees and managers is perhaps beyond critique; many have had experiences that have not been like this, and perhaps we may know of individuals who were destroyed by their engagement with particular organisations. However, attempts by an organisation to create the means by which we become happy or fulfilled are not far removed from forcing individuals to alter their political affiliations, religious/spiritual beliefs or sexual orientation to fit in with the needs of an existing social or organisational order. As such, attempts to create spiritualised, expressivist workplaces, either through spiritual learning initiatives or spiritualised culture change projects, should be considered opportunities to conduct a critical analysis of exactly why such initiatives are being deployed.

Although 'current interest in spirituality in the workplace may be understood by critical scholars as an ideological attempt to capture the power of religion for the purposes of supporting capitalist interests' (Bell 2008:293), it is important to remember that religion/spirituality/faith, like all significant cultural practices, is not always necessarily a dehumanising concept. Many of us have met people who have found great personal solace in their beliefs and manage not to judge or dehumanise others as a result of their convictions. Faith can inspire campaigns for social justice, charitable activity, or function as support during times of crisis or bereavement (Rowe 2008; Seale 1998).

Although studies of management and organisation, coming from critical perspectives, are suspicious of religion and its role in maintaining certain orders in society, Bell (2008) highlights that theorists have more recently begun to explore how, at an individual level, employees are using their own spiritual identities as a means of resisting attempts to manage employee subjectivity. Future research on the spiritualisation of workplaces and organisations must unearth underlying rationales for these activities, but must also take into consideration the managers and employees who are expected to engage with such initiatives.

References

Ackers, P. and Preston, D. (1997) 'Born Again?: The Ethics and Efficacy of the Conversion Experience in Contemporary Management Development', *Journal of Management Studies* 34(5): 677–701.

Alvesson, M. and Willmott, H. (2002) 'Identity Regulation as Organizational Control: Producing the Appropriate Individual', *Journal of Management Studies* 39(5): 619–44.

Armstrong, K. (2000) *The Battle for God: Fundamentalism in Judaism, Christianity and Islam*. London: HarperCollins.

Bell, E. (2008) 'Towards a Critical Spirituality of Organization', *Culture and Organization* 14(3): 293–307.

Bell, E. and Taylor, S. (2003) 'The Elevation of Work: Pastoral Power and the New Age Work Ethic', *Organization* 10(2): 329–49.

— (2004) 'From Outward Bound to Inward Bound: The Prophetic Voices and Discursive Practices of Spiritual Management Development', *Human Relations* 57(4): 439–66.

Benefiel, M. (2003) 'Irreconcilable Foes? The Discourse of Spirituality and the Discourse of Organizational Science', *Organization* 10(2): 383–91.

Boltanski, L. and Chiapello, E. (2006) *The New Spirit of Capitalism*. London: Verso.

Calás, M. and Smircich, L. (2003) 'Introduction: Spirituality, Management and Organization', *Organization* 10(2): 327–28.

Carlone, D. (2006) 'The Ambiguous Nature of a Management Guru Lecture: Providing Answers while Deepening Uncertainty', *Journal of Business Communication* 43(2): 89–112.

Casey, C. (1999) '"Come Join Our Family": Discipline and Integration in Corporate Organizational Culture', *Human Relations* 52(2): 155–78.

Cavanagh, G.F. (1999) 'Spirituality for Managers: Context and Critique', *Journal of Organizational Change* 12(3): 186–99.

Costea, B., Crump, N. and Amiridis, K. (2008) 'Managerialism, the Therapeutic Habitus and the Self in Contemporary Organizing', *Human Relations* 61(5): 661–85.

Covey, S.R. (1989) *The Seven Habits of Highly Effective People: Powerful Lessons in Personal Change*. London: Simon and Schuster.

Cullen, J. (2006) '"They Don't Understand Our Country": Carole Coleman interviews President George W. Bush', in M.P. Corcoran and M. Peillon (eds) *Uncertain Ireland: A Sociological Chronicle, 2003–2004*, pp. 209–21. Dublin: Institute of Public Administration.

— (2008) 'Self, Soul and Management Learning', *Journal of Management Spirituality and Religion* 5(3): 264–92.

— (2009) 'How to Sell Your Soul and Still Get into Heaven: Stephen Covey's Epiphany-Inducing Technology of Effective Selfhood' *Human Relations* 62(8): 1231–54.

Dunne, S., Harney, S. and Parker, M. (2008) 'Speaking Out: The Responsibilities of Management Intellectuals: A Survey', *Organization* 15(2): 271–82.

Forray, J.M. and Stork, D. (2002) 'All for One: A Parable of Spirituality and Organization', *Organization* 9(3): 497–509.

Foucault, M. (1977) *Discipline and Punish: The Birth of the Prison*. Middlesex: Penguin.

— (1978) *The History of Sexuality: Volume 1, An Introduction: The Will to Knowledge* (trans. R. Hurley). London: Penguin.

— (1982) 'The Subject and Power', in H. Dreyfus and P. Rabinow (eds) *Michel Foucault: Beyond Structuralism and Hermeneutics*, pp. 208–26. Brighton: Harvester.

— (1994 [1982]) 'Ethics, Subjectivity and Truth', in P. Rabinow (ed.) *The Essential Works of Michel Foucault 1954–1984*. New York, NY: New York Press.

Fromm, E. (1978) *To Have or to Be?* London: Cape.

Geertz, C. (1973) *The Interpretation of Cultures*. New York, NY: Basic Books.

Giddens, A. (1991) *Modernity and Self-Identity*. Cambridge: Polity Press.

Harney, M. (2000) *Remarks by Tánaiste, Mary Harney, at a Meeting of the American Bar Association in the Law Society of Ireland, Blackhall Place, Dublin on Friday 21st July 2000* [online]. Available: http://www.entemp.ie/press/2000/210700.htm (last accessed 27 July 2009).

Harvey, D. (2005) *A Brief History of Neoliberalism*. Oxford: Oxford University Press.

Heelas, P. (1996) *The New Age Movement: The Celebration of the Self and the Sacralization of Modernity*. Oxford: Blackwell.

— (2008) *Spiritualities of Life: New Age Romanticism and Consumptive Capitalism*. Oxford: Blackwell.

Heelas, P. and Woodhead, L. (2005) *The Spiritual Revolution: Why Religion is Giving Way to Spirituality*. Oxford: Blackwell.

Howard, S. (2002) 'A Spiritual Perspective on Learning in the Workplace', *Journal of Managerial Psychology* 17(3): 230–42.

Huczynski, A. (1993) *Management Gurus: What Makes Them and How to Become One*. London: Routledge.

Inglis, T. (1998) *Moral Monopoly: The Rise and Fall of the Catholic Church in Modern Ireland*. Dublin: University College Dublin Press.

Jackson, B.G. (1999) 'Re-engineering the Sense of Self: The Manager and the Management Guru', *Journal of Management Studies* 33(5): 571–90.

— (2001) *Management Gurus and Management Fashions: A Dramatistic Inquiry*. London: Routledge.

Korac-Kakabadse, N. (2002) 'Guest Editorial', *Journal of Managerial Psychology* 17(3): 150–2.

Laing, R.D. (1990) *The Divided Self: An Existential Study in Sanity and Madness*. London: Penguin.

Lichterman, P. (1992) 'Self-Help Reading as a Thin Culture', *Media, Culture and Society* 14(3): 421–47.

Luckmann, T. (1967) *The Invisible Religion*. New York, NY: Macmillan.

MacSharry, R. and White, P. (2000) *The Making of the Celtic Tiger: The Inside Story of Ireland's Boom Economy*. Dublin: Mercier Press.

Marx, K. (1974 [1844]) 'On the Jewish Question', in *Karl Marx: Early Writings* (trans. R. Livingstone and G. Benton), pp. 211–41. London: Penguin.

Maslow, A. (1971) *The Farther Reaches of Human Nature*. Harmondsworth: Penguin.

McGee, M. (2005) *Self-Help, Inc: Makeover Culture in American Life*. New York, NY: Oxford University Press.

Mills, S. (2003) *Michel Foucault*. London: Routledge.

Mitroff, I.I. and Denton, E.A. (1999) 'A Study of Spirituality in the Workplace', *Sloan Management Review* 40(4): 83–92.

Nash, L. (1999) 'What Policy Should GenCorp Adopt Toward Religious Network Groups?' *Harvard Business Review* 77(5): 34–35.

Neville, P. (2008) 'Reading Self-Help Books', in M.P. Corcoran and P. Share (eds) *Belongings: Shaping Identity in Modern Ireland*, pp. 217–30. Dublin: Institute of Public Administration.

O'Donohue, J. (1999) *Anam Cara: Spiritual Wisdom from the Celtic World*. London: Bantam Books.

Peters, T. and Waterman, P. (1982) *In Search of Excellence: Lessons from America's 7 Best Run Companies*. London: Harper Collins Business.

Rindfleish, J. (2005) 'Consuming the Self: New Age Spirituality as "Social Product" in Consumer Society', *Consumption, Markets and Culture* 8(4): 343–60.

Rose, N. (1989) *Governing the Soul: The Shaping of the Private Self*. London: Free Association Books.

Rowe, D. (2008) *What Should I Believe? Why Our Beliefs about the Nature of Death and the Purpose of Life Dominate Our Lives*. London: Routledge.

Seale, C. (1998) 'Theories in Health Care and Research: Theories and Studying the Care of Dying People', *British Medical Journal* 317, 1518–20.

Stark, R. and Bainbridge, W. (1985) *The Future of Religion: Secularisation, Revival and Cult Formation*. Berkeley, CA: University of California Press.

Taylor, C. (1989) *Sources of the Self: The Making of Modern Identity*. Cambridge: Cambridge University Press.

Watson, T.J. (1994) '"Management Flavours of the Month": Their Role in Managers' Lives', *International Journal of Human Resource Management* 5(4): 893–909.

Weber, M. (2002 [1930]) *The Protestant Work Ethic and the Spirit of Capitalism* (trans. T. Parsons). New York, NY: Routledge.

Whyte, W.H. (1956) *The Organization Man*. New York, NY: Simon and Schuster.

Willmott, H. (1993) 'Strength is Ignorance; Slavery is Freedom: Managing Culture in Modern Organizations', *Journal of Management Studies* 30(4): 515–52.

Wolfe, A. (1998) 'White Magic in America: Capitalism, Mormonism, and the Doctrines of Stephen Covey', *New Republic* 218(8): 26–34.

Yousef, D.A. (2000) 'Organizational Commitment as a Mediator of the Relationship Between Islamic Work Ethic and Attitudes Toward Organizational Change', *Human Relations* 53(4): 513–37.

Index